Modal Logic as Metaphysics

Modal Logic as Metaphysics

Timothy Williamson

OXFORD
UNIVERSITY PRESS

OXFORD

UNIVERSITY PRESS

Great Clarendon Street, Oxford, OX2 6DP,
United Kingdom

Oxford University Press is a department of the University of Oxford.
It furthers the University's objective of excellence in research, scholarship,
and education by publishing worldwide. Oxford is a registered trade mark of
Oxford University Press in the UK and in certain other countries

First published 2013
First published in paperback 2015

Published in the United States of America by Oxford University Press
198 Madison Avenue, New York, NY 10016, United States of America

British Library Cataloguing in Publication Data
Data available

Library of Congress Cataloging in Publication Data
Data available

ISBN 978–0–19–955207–8 (Hbk.)
ISBN 978–0–19–870943–5 (Pbk.)

To Ana

Contents

Preface

The title of this book may sound to some readers like *Good as Evil*, or perhaps *Cabbages as Kings*. If logic and metaphysics appear disjoint, the reason is not just the lingering spell of a logical positivist conception of metaphysics as cognitively meaningless and logic as cognitively meaningful but analytic. Many contemporary philosophers who acknowledge metaphysics as continuous with the rest of science are still inclined to assign logic a more special status. They see it as a neutral referee of disputes between scientific theories, including metaphysical theories, blowing the whistle when the rules are broken, not as a disputing party in its own right. If so, logic says nothing over which there could be such a dispute, on pain of non-neutrality; thus logical theories are quite different in status from scientific theories. This book is written in the contrary conviction that, just as metaphysics is much more like the rest of science than was once thought, so too is logic. Indeed, one role for logic is to supply a central structural core to scientific theories, including metaphysical theories, in essence no more above dispute than any other part of those theories.

For quantified modal logic in particular, one of its many roles is to supply a central structural core to theories of modal metaphysics. That such a core should be highly contentious is especially unsurprising, given the history of quantified modal logic. Its very legitimacy as a branch of logic was once widely disputed. Even when its legitimacy is granted, some of its most salient principles remain in dispute. A central cluster of such issues forms the focus of this book. They concern what are known as the Barcan formula and its converse, whose meaning and early history Chapter 2 explains. The debate about them has always involved complex interactions of mathematical and philosophical considerations, and rightly so. Chapter 1 explains the underlying metaphysical issues in non-technical terms. The main question is whether it is necessary or contingent which things there are. The opposed theories are called 'necessitism' and 'contingentism'. Once we properly understand each side's viewpoint, we can appreciate why the issue is hard to resolve. There is a similar division in the philosophy of time between views called 'permanentism' and 'temporaryism'; parallels with it form a subsidiary thread running through the book. Chapter 3 connects the metaphysical issues to the 'possible worlds' model theory of modal logic, a branch of mathematics applied to formal semantics and the main technical achievement of modal logic. More generally, the chapter explains how to read systems of modal logic as metaphysical theories, and so enable the model theory of modal logic to be applied to metaphysics. Chapter 4 is a critical examination of one of the best developed forms of contingentism. Chapter 5 introduces higher-order modal logic and its various interpretations, in the hope of encouraging philosophers to make more use of such a powerful instrument so well adapted to their purposes. Chapters 6 and 7 make the intended application for present purposes, arguing that necessitism betters contingentism in providing an adequate theory of higher-order modal logic. Chapter 8 discusses modal metaphysics and the status of possible worlds semantics from a necessitist perspective. In the course of the book broader methodological themes emerge in relation to more specific issues; they are surveyed in the Afterword.

Readers may find less than they expected in the book on some traditional philosophical issues about modal logic, such as the legitimacy of quantified modal logic and the nature of possible worlds. Although the present view of logic and metaphysics as related parts of total science has similarities with Quine's holism in 'Two Dogmas of Empiricism', those views do nothing to justify his scepticism about the intelligibility of modal logic, especially quantified modal logic. That scepticism has not stood the test of time. By any normal scientific standard, it is intelligible to say that there are things that would have dissolved if they had been put in water, and correspondingly intelligible to say that there are things that could have dissolved in water. To condemn such statements as unintelligible by some special philosophical standard is bad science and bad philosophy. Books on modality have no more obligation to spend their readers' time on defences of the intelligibility of modal discourse than books on the mind have to spend it on defences of the intelligibility of mentalistic discourse. Chapter 2 briefly explains why Quine's critique fails even against its original target, Carnap's quantified modal logic.

Contemporary philosophers are more likely to expect a book on the metaphysics of modal logic to concentrate on the nature of possible worlds, and in particular to engage at length with David Lewis's modal realism. Although Lewis's attitude to modality is sometimes viewed as the opposite of Quine's, he is more accurately understood as reducing modal language to Quineanly acceptable language, by postulating a non-standard cosmological theory with many mutually isolated spatiotemporal systems and identifying them with possible worlds. Since cosmological theories in physics are naturally understood as embodying no restriction of their purview to exclude Lewis's multiple spatiotemporal systems, many of which are supposed to violate their laws, his cosmology is inconsistent with physicists', and so in competition with them as a theory of total spatiotemporal reality. On such matters, physicists may be felt to speak with more authority than metaphysicians. The effect of Lewis's influential and ingenious system-building was to keep centre stage a view that imposed Quine's puritan standards on modality long after Quine's own eliminativist application of those standards had been marginalized. Chapter 1 briefly explains why modal realism is best understood as a deviant form of necessitism.

By far the clearest success of possible worlds is their role in the tradition of formal semantics for modal languages initiated by Carnap. Understanding that role properly requires far more attention to the structure of the semantics, and less to the metaphysics of the worlds themselves, than is often realized. That partly accounts for the distribution of emphasis in this book. Above all, however, I have pursued those issues in the intersection of quantified modal logic with metaphysics that interest me most.

The main questions in this book are not primarily technical ones. Nevertheless, the more I have worked on them, the more I have become convinced that the best way to resolve them is by developing rival answers to them into systematic metaphysical theories, each with its own structural core of higher-order modal logic, and comparing the results by the normal standards for theory comparison in science, as discussed in the Methodological Afterword. That process can only be adequately carried out with some degree of technicality. The formulas in this book reflect that. We never had any reason to expect metaphysics to be easy. We should be grateful to have the technical power of modern logic at our command, to give us some grounds for hope that we can do better than our illustrious predecessors.

When I first planned to write a book on metaphysical issues in quantified modal logic, I envisaged it as drawing together material in my previous papers on the subject but presenting it in a less technical, more accessible way. My ambitions in that respect were limited by the realization that higher-order modal logic provides the best setting in which to resolve the issue between contingentism and necessitism. However, I have kept technicalities out of Chapter 1 and the Methodological Afterword, and taken only a minimal acquaintance with formal logic for granted in explaining matters elsewhere.

I first encountered work on metaphysical issues in quantified modal logic as a first-year undergraduate, poring over the readings in an anthology (Linsky 1971), in particular Saul Kripke's 'Semantic Considerations on Modal Logic' (Kripke 1963). I did no research in the area myself for many years, because the ground seemed too well trodden. However, I became interested in questions about being and predication (Williamson 1987/1988 and 1989), some of which surface in this book, for example in section 4.1. Extending my line of thought into the modal dimension, I developed an argument in favour of necessitism—one related only very distantly to the arguments in this book—which I presented as 'Necessary Identity and Necessary Existence' at the 14th International Wittgenstein Symposium in Kirchberg am Wechsel in 1989 (Williamson 1990b). After a few years preoccupied with vagueness, I began to write papers and talks on the subject from time to time, starting with a review essay on a festschrift for Ruth Barcan Marcus (Williamson 1996b) and a talk on possibilia to the Portuguese Philosophical Society in Lisbon. I presented 'Bare Possibilia' to a conference on analytic ontology at the University of Innsbruck in 1997; Winfried Löffler replied (Williamson 1998, Löffler 1998). 'Existence and Contingency' (Williamson 2000a) was my half of a symposium with Ian Rumfitt at the Joint Session of the Aristotelian Society and the Mind Association at Nottingham in 1999, having previously been given as the Weatherhead Lecture on Philosophy of Language at Tulane University and as a talk at the Graduate Center of City University New York in 1998. 'Necessary Existents' (Williamson 2002a) was first given as a lecture to the Royal Institute of Philosophy in London.

This book has been written over four yours of research leave from most of my duties in the Faculty of Philosophy at the University of Oxford, comprising two terms of sabbatical leave (2008–9), a Research Leave Award from the Arts and Humanities Research Council for one term (2009), and a Leverhulme Trust Major Research Fellowship for three years (2009–12). I am very grateful to all three institutions for this opportunity. It has permitted me to spend far more time thinking and writing, often in long uninterrupted periods, than would otherwise have been feasible. I hope that the book is much better as a result; it is certainly much prompter. Such opportunities are an unsung benefit of British academic life. New College Oxford has formed a beautiful environment in which to write the book: when I was stuck, a walk in its gardens would often do the trick.

Most of the book has been written from scratch. However, much of Chapter 4 is based on 'Stalnaker on the Interaction of Modality with Quantification and Identity' (Williamson 2006), first presented as a talk to the Belgian Society for Logic and Philosophy of Science in Brussels. Chapter 7 is largely based on 'Necessitism, Contingentism and Plural Quantification' (Williamson 2010). Section 8.3 draws extensively on 'Truthmakers and the Converse Barcan Formula' (Williamson 1999a), as do sections 1.3 and 8.2 on 'The Necessary Framework of Objects' (Williamson 2000b). Even in these cases, few paragraphs have survived unchanged. Elsewhere, although ideas from the earlier papers are used, the presentation and much of the content is quite new. Chapters 2, 3, and 5, most of Chapter 6, sections 1.8 and 8.4, and the Methodological Afterword are not based on my previous publications.

A Graduate Workshop organized by Nicholas Jones and Lee Walters on 'Philosophical Implications of Second-Order Modal Logic' at the Centre for Logic and Language in the Institute of Philosophy, London, in 2010 was based on what I had written up to then; Øystein Linnebo, Ian Rumfitt, and Gabriel Uzquiano were the commentators; the graduate speakers were Paal Antonsen, Brian Ball, Timothy Chan, Salvatore Florio, Peter Fritz, Simon Hewitt, Frederique Janssen-Lauret, Calista Lam, Julien Murzi, Jonathan Payne, Rafal Urbaniak, and Alastair Wilson. Also at the Institute, I gave a masterclass in 2012 for the British Postgraduate Philosophy Association, organized by Simona Aimar and Grant Reaber, at which Jeremy Goodman, Grant Reaber, and Sam Roberts were the commentators on draft chapters of the book. The LOGOS project at the University of Barcelona organized an all-day interrogation on a draft of the book in 2012. I also presented material for the book in two talks at the Munich Center for Mathematical Philosophy at the Ludwig-Maximilian University Munich, several lectures at the Arché Centre in St Andrews, and a week-long seminar at the University of Hamburg, where Stephan Krämer presented a response to Chapter 5. Other occasions on which I presented or discussed material for the book include: the 2008 International Lauener Symposium on Analytical Philosophy in honour of Ruth Barcan Marcus in Berne; a workshop on philosophical logic at Oxford University; a workshop on metaphysics at Nottingham University; a graduate conference on the philosophy of logic and mathematics at Cambridge University; a workshop on the philosophy of language and semantics at All Souls College Oxford, where the commentator was Dilip Ninan; a workshop on metaphysics at Oxford University, where the commentator was Jeff Russell; a graduate conference on modality at Toronto University, where the commentators were Dominic Alford-Duguid and James Davies; a conference on modal epistemology organized by the Emmy Noether research group at Cologne University; the Mesthene Lecture at Rutgers; one of my Petrus Hispanus lectures at the University of Lisbon; a mind and language seminar at New York University, where the commentator was Paul Horwich; a discussion group on a draft of the book at Oxford University. I also gave lectures based on material for the book at the following universities: Edinburgh; Glasgow; Belgrade; Barcelona; Peking; Carnegie Mellon; Cornell; Notre Dame; Rice; Texas A&M; Yale. The book has benefited enormously from the questions, objections, and suggestions I have received from commentators and audiences on those occasions.

I was very fortunate to have as referees for Oxford University Press Philip Bricker, Kit Fine, and Ted Sider. All three provided extensive, detailed, thoughtful, and constructive comments. I hope that they will feel that the result justifies their efforts.

The Leverhulme Trust paid for two research assistants for 2011–12, Peter Fritz and Daniel Deasy. Both went through the manuscript with a fine toothcomb, to bracing effect, and helped in many other ways too. They refuted my previous scepticism about the value of research assistants in philosophy.

I owe a huge debt of gratitude to many people who have given me written comments or the like on material that went into this book, in addition to that mentioned already. As well as those previously named, they include: Miroslava Andjelković; Tom Baldwin; Roderick Batchelor; Alexander Bird; Sarah Broadie; John P. Burgess; Paolo Crivelli; Harry Deutsch; John Divers;

Cian Dorr; Delia Graff Fara; Graeme Forbes; Jeremy Goodman; John Hawthorne; Eli Hirsch; Lloyd Humberstone; Dominik Kauss; Marcus Kracht; Hannes Leitgeb; Stefano Manfredi; Genoveva Martí; Alex Oliver; Alex Orenstein; Manuel Pérez Otero; Philip Percival; Agustín Rayo; Nathan Salmon; Daniele Sgaravatti; Stewart Shapiro; Robert Stalnaker; Jason Stanley; Yannis Stephanou; Marius Thomann; Giuliano Torrengo; Alberto Voltolini; Stephen Williams; Crispin Wright; Byeong-uk Yi; Elia Zardini; others who would have been listed had my memory been better. Education is a two-way process; I have learned much about metaphysical issues in modal and higher-order logic as the supervisor or co-supervisor for the Oxford D.Phil. of extraordinarily able past and present students: Andrew Bacon, Corine Besson, David Efird, Peter Fritz, Ofra Magidor, Andrew McCarthy, and Barbara Vetter. At Oxford University Press, Peter Momtchiloff has been an unfailingly supportive editor. Another ex-student, Javier Kalhat, was the efficient copy-editor.

This book is dedicated with love to my wife Ana, who has kept the show on the road while I devoted myself to higher-order modal logic. One day, perhaps, she and my children Alice, Conrad, and Arno will forgive me for writing a book with such a dull title.

1

Contingentism and Necessitism

1.1 The question

Things could have been otherwise. It is contingent how they are. Although the coin came up heads, it could have come up tails. Is it also contingent *what* things there are? 'Yes' seems the obvious answer. The universe could have evolved differently, so that there was never any money, or even any non-pecuniary physical object shaped like this coin. In those circumstances, not only would this coin not have been a coin, it would not have been anything at all; it simply would not have been. Thus there is actually something that could have been nothing. Conversely, there could have been something that is actually nothing, such as a coin of a design never actually produced. There could have been fewer things than there actually are; perhaps there could have been nothing whatsoever.[1] Equally, there could have been more things than there actually are. Even keeping fixed how many things there are, the number could have been made up by different things. Not only is it contingent what general kinds of thing have instances, it is contingent what particular things there are to be instances of any kind at all. Or so it seems.

Some philosophers have taken a different view. On theoretical grounds, they have denied that it is contingent what there is, holding that it is necessary what things there are, while allowing that it is contingent *how* those things are. The pieces in the puzzle are given, however they are rearranged. Wittgenstein in *Tractatus Logico-Philosophicus* seems to say so. He tells us:

It is obvious that an imagined world, however different it may be from the real one, must have *something*—a form—in common with it. (2.022)

---

[1] But the debate sparked by the subtraction argument in Baldwin 1996 for the conclusion that 'there might be nothing' is explicitly about whether there might be nothing *concrete*. If there are sets or numbers, there is not nothing at all.

Objects are just what constitute this unalterable form. (2.023)

Objects are what is unalterable and subsistent; their configuration is what is changing and unstable. (2.0271)

Of course, the interpretation of such passages is highly controversial. For example, it is contentious exactly what Wittgenstein meant by 'object'. Since our main aim is not Wittgenstein exegesis, we will read it interchangeably with 'thing' on the liberal reading already used (see also *Tractatus* 2.01). Then the passages convey the claim that it is necessary what there is, contingent how it is. As usual, Wittgenstein does not straightforwardly endorse the claim. On the Tractarian account of language, such metaphysical passages are nonsense of a more or less sophisticated sort; whatever they may *show*, they do not really *say* anything at all. However, we can disagree with Wittgenstein about that, and deny that we are the victims of an illusion of understanding when we read the passages as conveying intelligible theoretical claims, true or false, whatever their author's intentions. Frank Ramsey did just that. Abandoning the mysticism of the *Tractatus*, he endorsed the claim that it is necessary what there is, and did more than Wittgenstein to defend it by explicit argument.[2]

Call the proposition that it is necessary what there is *necessitism*, and its negation *contingentism*. In slightly less compressed form, necessitism says that necessarily everything is necessarily something; still more long-windedly: it is necessary that everything is such that it is necessary that something is identical with it.[3] In a slogan: ontology is necessary. Contingentism denies that necessarily everything is necessarily something. In a slogan: ontology is contingent.

Necessitists need not deny that it is contingent which *kinds* of thing are instantiated, at least for some kinds. Thus they can happily accept that it is contingent that there are animals. Since there could have been no animals, by their lights an animal is only contingently an animal. But it does not follow that an animal is only contingently something. For the necessitist, it could have been something without being an animal. Similarly, the kind

---

[2] See Ramsey 1925, pp. 210–12, and 1927, pp. 56–7, and for critical discussion Prior 1967, pp. 147–53, Hazen 1986, and Almog 1989, pp. 209–12, 218–19.

[3] For convenience, 'There is an F' and 'Something is an F' will be treated as interchangeable; nothing important depends on this. If the necessary is not always necessarily necessary, necessitism should be understood as also committed to the corresponding claims for each iteration of necessity. For simplicity, such glosses will normally be left tacit.

animal, if there is such a thing, would have been something without being instantiated, if there had been no animals.

Contingentists deny the universal claim of necessitism but of course need not deny all its instances. They may agree with platonist necessitists that the number 7 is non-contingently something.

Given the austerity of the opposing general claims, neither necessitism nor contingentism by itself entails a unique specific account of a particular example. Neither of them entails that there are animals, or that there are not, or that it is contingent what animals there are, or that it is contingent whether there are animals. Contingentism does not even entail that an animal is only contingently something: the general doctrine says that there are or could be counterexamples to necessitism, not what they are. Nevertheless, for purposes of illustration, it is often convenient to discuss a contingentist or necessitist who describes an example in ways that follow not from the general doctrine by itself but only from its conjunction with independently plausible auxiliary assumptions neutral between the two views.

Necessitism and contingentism are not doctrines about what can or cannot be known or thought or said of what there is. The necessity at issue here is metaphysical. What is metaphysically necessary is what could not have been otherwise, what would have obtained whatever had obtained; not even the laws of physics can be assumed to be metaphysically necessary in this sense.[4] But whether anyone could have known or thought or said that the circumstance at issue obtained is irrelevant. Necessitism and contingentism are the views just outlined, irrespective of what any other philosopher meant. Nevertheless, many philosophers have cast light on the issue.

This book compares necessitism and contingentism. Which is true? Of course, the question has a false presupposition if the definitions of 'necessitism' and 'contingentism' lack meaning or content. But if every enquiry must

---

[4] For a characterization of metaphysical possibility in terms of counterfactual conditionals see Williamson 2007, pp. 155–61. Most arguments in the present book are robust in respect of how far, if at all, metaphysical possibility outruns physical possibility; they tend to appeal to mundane physical possibilities rather than wildly science fictional merely metaphysical possibilities. Metaphysical possibility will not be assumed to be metaphysically basic, or fundamental, or irreducible, or perfectly natural, or anything like that, although its role in true metaphysical generalizations provides evidence that it is at least somewhat natural (section 3.3), and semantic arguments for its reducibility to quantification over worlds or situations are flawed (section 8.4).

first establish its own meaningfulness we are on an infinite regress, since the enquiry into the meaningfulness of the previous enquiry must first enquire into its own meaningfulness, and so on. Better to act on the assumption of intelligibility: readers can decide for themselves whether they understand the book as they go along, and recycle it if not.

Wittgenstein's talk of unalterability suggests a temporal as well as a modal dimension of stability. He seems to claim constancy in what there is across times as well as possibilities. Parallel to necessitism, *permanentism* says that always everything is always something. Parallel to contingentism, *temporaryism* denies that always everything is always something. Necessitists are not automatically permanentists, nor are temporaryists automatically contingentists. For a fatalist might be a necessitist by denying all contingency whatsoever, yet still hold that what there is changes on a necessary schedule. In practice, however, most necessitists will be permanentists too. For the same reason, most temporaryists will be contingentists. There is no *good* reason to hold that what is necessarily something may become, or once have been, nothing. Contingentism and permanentism are easier to combine. If time is more like a dimension of space than we ordinarily imagine, 'everything' and 'something' can range unrestrictedly over the entire contents of spacetime, so their range is constant over time. Even in that case, perhaps the entire contents of spacetime could have been other than they actually are. Although this book focuses on the modal dispute between necessitism and contingentism, many of its considerations have parallels for the temporal dispute between permanentism and temporaryism. The links are sometimes mentioned for illustration or interest.[5]

The rest of this chapter is an informal metaphysical and logical exploration of the dispute between necessitism and contingentism. The aim is not yet to come down on one side or the other, but provisionally to explain and clarify what is at stake.

---

[5] Strictly speaking, we should also consider the combined modal-temporal principle that necessarily always everything is necessarily always something, which entails the conjunction of necessitism and permanentism but is not obviously entailed by it: if something is constant along the time dimension for the actual value on the modal dimension and constant along the modal dimension for the present value on the temporal value, it does not follow that it is constant across all values on the modal and temporal dimensions. Nevertheless, any reason to accept both necessitism and permanentism is likely to be a reason to accept the combined modal-temporal principle too, and any reason to reject either necessitism or permanentism is automatically a reason to reject the combined principle. See Deasy 2013 for discussion of the space of options.

1.2 Forms of necessitism

Why take necessitism seriously? Isn't it just obvious that many things, such as the coin, could have not been? A temporaryist may add: isn't it just obvious that most or all of those things once were not and sooner or later will again not be? If a philosopher produces a clever theoretical argument for necessitism (or permanentism), we may learn much from diagnosing the fallacies in it, just as we may learn much from diagnosing the fallacies in a clever argument for radical scepticism, but in each case are we not entitled to confidence in advance that the argument will indeed be fallacious?

A generic reply on behalf of necessitism (and permanentism) is that much of what once seemed obvious has turned out to be false. Perhaps we should treat radical scepticism as a serious option too. Such a reply is uninteresting, for it can be made on behalf of any hypothesis at all, however silly. If all propositions are treated as serious options, enquiry is deadlocked. Any blogger can multiply hypotheses faster than serious enquirers can evaluate them; any attempt to eliminate a hypothesis by argument can be met by the demand to treat the negations of the argument's premises as serious options. For enquiry to progress, it must take only a limited range of options seriously.

Are there more specific grounds for taking necessitism (and permanentism) seriously? One consideration is that a physical object such as the coin is composed of microscopic particles. We may call them 'atoms', even if they count as subatomic in the terminology of physics. Suppose, for definiteness, that atoms are essentially concrete. Such atomism can be deployed on behalf of necessitism (and permanentism) in either of two mutually incompatible ways, one *eliminativist*, the other *reductionist*.

According to eliminativism, there are only the atoms. Really there is no coin: appearances to the contrary are illusions, and 'coin' talk is at best a fancy abbreviation of complicated talk about atoms. So there is no coin to be a counterexample to necessitism (or permanentism). Since atoms are not objects of common sense, it is not obvious whether necessitism (or permanentism) holds for them. Only theoretical enquiry can properly address the question.

According to reductionism, by contrast, there are not only the atoms. There really is a coin too: it is no atom, but rather the sum of many atoms. Necessarily always, they are exactly its atomic parts and it is something if and only if each of them is something. In particular, necessitism (or permanentism) holds for the coin if and only if it holds for the atoms. Of course, the sum was once a non-coin, sooner or later it will again be a non-coin, and it could have been a non-coin now, but that is merely change and contingency in how it is, not in whether it is, given necessitism. For the same reason as before, it is not obvious whether necessitism (or permanentism) holds for atoms. Thus it is not obvious whether it holds for macroscopic objects either. As before, the question of necessitism (or permanentism) should be investigated by theoretical enquiry.

Neither defence of necessitism is attractive. Both face the charge of obvious falsehood. The eliminativist denies that there are macroscopic objects. The reductionist makes every atom of a macroscopic object essential to it. Since the atoms that constitute a coin at a given time are never exactly the atoms that constitute a coin a minute later, the sum with which the reductionist identifies the coin is never strictly a coin a minute later, so the coin in your pocket is never strictly a coin in your pocket a minute later. By contrast, the sum of those atoms presumably is strictly the sum of those atoms a minute later. Even if we can live with such departures from full-blooded common sense, they are not enough to make necessitism plausible. Even if physics can show that what atoms there are is unchanging, how could it show that it is non-contingent? Why could there not have been more or fewer atoms than there actually are, perhaps in a universe with different physical laws from our own? If atoms in the relevant sense have no basis in physical theory, why postulate them? Mereological considerations do not explain away an illusion of contingency in what atoms there are. They leave us still without good grounds for taking necessitism seriously.

Given, contrary to eliminativism, that there is this coin, necessitism implies that it is necessarily something; it does not imply that this coin is necessarily a coin. Reductionism lets one reject the conditional that if this coin is necessarily something it is necessarily a coin, but still forces one to accept the conditional that if this coin is necessarily something it is necessarily a sum of atoms, and so concrete.[6] But presumably just as there could have been no such concrete things as these atoms, so there could have been no such concrete thing as this coin. Therefore it is not necessary that this

---

[6] The term 'concrete' is used informally throughout this book. For present purposes, we need not decide between various ways of making it precise (being material, being in space, being in time, having causes, having effects, . . .).

coin is concrete. Given necessitism, that implies that this concrete coin could have been non-concrete. Conversely, if this coin had been non-concrete, presumably it would still have been possibly a coin, and so possibly concrete.[7] Indeed, given that there could have been more concrete things than there actually are, necessitism implies that something actually non-concrete could have been concrete.[8] Thus, on plausible auxiliary assumptions, necessitism requires the barrier between the concrete and non-concrete to be modally (and temporally) permeated in both directions.

It is tempting to paraphrase that conclusion thus: given necessitism, something concrete could have been abstract and something abstract could have been concrete. However, that is to treat 'non-concrete' and 'abstract' as synonyms. They are not. 'Abstract' is not purely negative in meaning; it has its own positive paradigms, such as numbers and directions. Nor are 'concrete' and 'non-abstract' synonyms. 'Concrete' is not purely negative in meaning either; it has its own positive paradigms, such as sticks and stones. It is a fallacy to treat 'abstract' and 'concrete' as contradictories, although they may be contraries.[9] Perhaps some things are neither, even if nothing can be both. In particular, the counterfactual supposition about this coin that it is something non-concrete in no way entails that it is abstract. Abstract objects such as numbers and directions play specific theoretically defined roles. The counterfactual supposition about this coin does not entail that it plays any similar role. Had this coin not been concrete, it would still not have been abstract. The temporal analogy helps here. When an iceberg melts, it does not become an abstract object; it merely ceases to be concrete.

---

[7] One could make the argument formal by appealing to the B principle of modal logic that if something obtains, it is necessarily possible for it to obtain. This principle is valid in the modal system S5 discussed in the next chapter. Alternatively, one could simply rely on the particular independently plausible instance of B at issue.

[8] Here it is assumed on behalf of the necessitist that matters of identity and distinctness are non-contingent. This assumption is discussed in section 1.7.

[9] See Williamson 1998, p. 266, and Linsky and Zalta 1996, p. 293 (contrast Linsky and Zalta 1994, p. 446). Sider 2001, p. 127, in effect defines 'concrete' as 'non-abstract' too. When arguing for the mereological axiom of unrestricted composition, and in particular for his premise that it is never vague whether composition occurs, Sider claims that 'if it were vague whether a certain class had a fusion then it would be vague how many concrete objects exist'. However, this neglects a necessitist option, on which the class has a fusion just when a certain object o is concrete in the informal positive sense, but o is non-abstract whether or not the class has a fusion, and the number of non-abstract objects remains constant. Even if the number of concrete objects in the informal positive sense varies, 'concrete' in that sense may well be vague and so not serve Sider's argument. See also Hawthorne 2006, p. 106. Incidentally, if sets count as abstract and sets of concrete things as concrete, the latter count as both concrete and abstract.

For example, it is no longer spatially located, not even where the atoms that once composed it are. A permanentist willing to postulate an intermediate category between the concrete and the abstract can agree that nothing concrete at one time is abstract at another. Likewise, a necessitist willing to postulate the intermediate category can agree that nothing concrete in some possible circumstances is abstract in others.

Nevertheless, necessitists and permanentists typically deny some popular essentialist theses. A property P is essential to an object o only if necessarily whenever o is something, o has P (it is controversial whether that condition is also sufficient for the property to be essential). Many philosophers regard membership of a natural kind as essential to its members.[10] Thus a tiger is essentially a tiger, and gold is essentially gold. Hence a tiger is always necessarily if anything a tiger, and gold is always necessarily if anything gold. Given those claims, necessitism implies that tigers are necessarily tigers, and gold necessarily gold; permanentism implies that tigers are eternally tigers, and gold eternally gold. But presumably there could have been no tigers and no gold; once there were no tigers and no gold. Consequently, necessitists and permanentists should reject the essentialist theses as stated.[11] However, they can still maintain slightly modified versions of them. Thus a tiger is essentially if concrete a tiger, and gold is essentially if concrete gold. Whether essentialist theses should be so modified cannot be decided straight off, without theoretical enquiry.

Another controversial by-product of necessitism is its multiplication of entities. Necessitists who defend their view by appeal to contingently non-concrete things rather than recombinations of necessary atoms are likely to be forced into postulating very large numbers of possibly concrete things. If there could have been at least n concrete things then, given necessitism, there actually are at least n possibly concrete things. Moreover, if there could have been at least n concrete things in many different ways, then the upshot may be that there actually are many more than n possibly concrete things. The necessitist may have to accept that there actually is at least some very

---

[10] See Kripke 1980 and Fine 1994.

[11] See also Parsons 1994, p. 11, and Linsky and Zalta 1996, pp. 291-2. Alternatively, some necessitists and permanentists might keep the unrestricted essentialist theses but deny that there could have been no tigers or no gold, asserting instead that there could have been no *concrete* tigers and no *concrete* gold. However, that requires implausibly watering down standard theories of tigers and gold to allow for non-concrete tigers and non-concrete gold. The biology of tigers constrains them to be in space and time; the chemistry of gold constrains it likewise.

large infinite cardinal number of possibly concrete things.[12] That is a cost
of necessitism. Whether it is worth paying is unclear prior to theoretical
investigation. Some compensating benefits of necessitism will emerge in the
course of this book.

Similar issues arise for pure set theory, which postulates large infinities of
sets even without postulating any concrete objects, or non-sets of any kind.
A standard first-order set theory such as Zermelo-Fraenkel set theory has
models with only countably many sets, the smallest infinite cardinality.[13]
However, despite their mathematical interest, such models are not serious
candidates for the real universe of pure sets. They are riddled with unnatural
gaps, cramped by ad hoc ceilings. Orthodoxy postulates unimaginably more
pure sets, inaccessibly many, because a theoretically compelling principle
of plenitude for sets requires them.[14] Multiplying entities is sometimes a
necessity for the sake of theoretical plausibility, because the alternative is
massive loss of simplicity, elegance, and economy in principles.[15] Whether
that is so in the case of necessitism remains to be seen. Its theoretical virtues
will become clearer in Chapter 6.

On these clarifications of what necessitism and permanentism imply, and
what they do not, neither is obviously false. Even if we know pre-theoretically
that this coin could have not been something concrete, that does not enable
us to know pre-theoretically that it could not have been something non-
concrete. Granted, we cannot know pre-theoretically that there can be contingently non-concrete things, but our inability to know pre-theoretically
that there can be things of a kind does not imply an ability to know pre-
theoretically that there cannot be things of that kind. It is not common
sense that all objects are common-sense objects. However strange the consequences of necessitism and permanentism, common sense has limited authority
over such claims. We can properly evaluate them only by theoretical enquiry.

Of course, none of that constitutes positive evidence for necessitism or
permanentism. It merely leaves us with a metaphysically interesting open
question. Later chapters will explore the theoretical attractions of necessitism.

---

[12] This concern is emphasized by Löffler 1998 and Sider 2009. If the necessary is not always necessarily
necessary, then the possibly possible is not always possible, so we must also consider merely possibly
possibly concrete things, and so on. This only slightly changes the overall metaphysical picture.

[13] This famously follows from the downward Löwenheim-Skolem theorem.

[14] Such a conception was developed in Zermelo 1930 (with a second-order system) and has since
become widespread amongst set theorists.

[15] The legitimacy of such trade-offs is not denied by those who defend quantitative ontological parsimony as a theoretical virtue; see Nolan 1997 and Baker 2003.

1.3 Possible Fs

Suppose that this stick of oak wood had not been concrete, perhaps because no oak tree ever grew. For a necessitist, it would still have been something, yet neither abstract nor concrete. *What*, then, would it have been, specifically? It would still have been something that *could have been* a stick. The necessitist may therefore answer that it would have been a *possible stick*.

Someone might object that it is absurd to postulate a non-concrete possible stick, because being concrete is necessary for being a stick. But that is to mistake the intended sense of 'possible stick'. The objector reads 'x is a possible stick' as equivalent to something like 'x is a stick and x could have existed'. Call that the *predicative reading* of 'possible stick'. On this reading, it is trivially necessary that all possible sticks are sticks. Assume, with the objector, that it is necessary that all sticks are concrete. Therefore, on the predicative reading, it is necessary that all possible sticks are concrete. But necessitists are not committed to the claim that if the stick had not been concrete, it would still have been a possible stick on the predicative reading, for they are not committed to the silly claim that if the stick had not been concrete, it would still have been a stick. The predicative reading is irrelevant to necessitism.

On the relevant alternative reading, 'x is a possible stick' is simply equivalent to 'x could have been a stick'. Call that the *attributive reading* of 'possible stick'. If the stick had not been concrete, even though it would not still have been a stick it would still have been a possible stick, on this alternative reading, because it necessarily could have been a stick.[16] It is not necessary that all possible sticks are sticks on the attributive reading. The necessitist's talk of non-concrete possible sticks has no absurd consequences of the sort the objector imagines.

The distinction generalizes, of course. The concatenation 'possible F' is structurally ambiguous. On the predicative reading, 'x is a possible F' is equivalent to 'x is an F and x could have existed'. On the attributive reading, 'x is a possible F' is equivalent to 'x could have been an F'. The predicative reading arises when the function of 'possible' in 'possible F' is analogized to something like the function of 'South African' in 'South African diamond'. Just as 'South African diamond' can be paraphrased as 'diamond that is South

---

[16] This is another instance of the B principle in modal logic.

African', making 'x is a South African diamond' equivalent to 'x is a diamond and x is South African', so 'possible F' is paraphrased as 'F that is possible', making 'x is a possible F' equivalent to 'x is an F and x is possible'; 'x is possible' is then in turn paraphrased as 'it is possible that x exists' and so as 'x could have existed', which yields the predicative reading.[17] But not all combinations of adjectives and nouns conform to the predicative pattern. We cannot paraphrase 'alleged diamond' as 'diamond that is alleged'; the latter looks ill formed, and in any case not all alleged diamonds are diamonds. Rather, 'x is an alleged diamond' is equivalent to 'it is alleged that x is a diamond' (by contrast, 'it is South African that x is a diamond' looks ill formed and corresponds to no reading of 'x is a South African diamond'). The attributive reading of 'possible F' arises when the function of 'possible' in it is analogized to something like the function of 'alleged' in 'alleged diamond'. Then 'x is a possible F' is equivalent to 'it is possible that x is an F', which is paraphrased as 'x could have been an F'.

The attributive reading of 'possible F' is often more natural than the predicative one. For instance, the remark 'We are all possible murderers' is more naturally interpreted as 'Each of us could have been a murderer' than as 'Each of us is a murderer and could have existed'. Similarly, if I say 'You are a possible president', I am in effect saying 'You could be president', not 'You are president and could exist'.

The two readings of 'possible F' usually overlap in extension, by the principle that whatever holds could have held. For example, all sticks are possible sticks on both readings. On the predicative reading, 'x is a stick' entails 'x is a possible stick', in other words 'x is a stick and x could have existed', because it entails 'x is a stick and x exists' on any reasonable understanding of 'exists' and the modal principle does the rest (more will be said about 'exists' in section 1.5). On the attributive reading, 'x is a stick' entails 'x is a possible stick', in other words 'x could have been a stick', by the modal principle alone. To reach deeper water, we must consider the *merely* possible.

It is merely possible for something to hold if and only if it is possible for it to hold, but it does not hold. On the predicative reading of 'possible F', 'possible' operates on a tacit 'exists', not on 'F' itself, so 'x is a merely possible F' is equivalent to 'x is an F and it is possible that x exists, but x does not exist'. Presumably, there are no merely possible sticks on that reading; as

---

[17] As usual, we are not interested in epistemic readings of 'it is possible that'.

already noted, on any reasonable understanding of 'exists' 'x is a stick' entails 'x exists'. By contrast, on the attributive reading of 'possible F', 'possible' operates on 'F' itself, so 'x is a merely possible F' is equivalent to 'x could have been an F, but x is not an F'. Necessitism requires merely possible sticks on that reading, not on the predicative reading. If the stick had not been concrete, it would have been a merely possible stick, and a merely possible concrete thing, only on the attributive reading.

With predicative readings throughout, it is trivial that all merely possible Fs are possible Fs, and uncontroversial that the converse can fail: an ordinary stick is a possible stick without being a merely possible stick. 'Possible F' is equivalent to 'existing F or merely possible F'. On Quine's view, 'exist' is equivalent to 'is something' and has trivially universal application; thus there are no merely possible Fs, and the possible Fs are simply the Fs.[18] Equally, with attributive readings throughout, it is trivial that all merely possible Fs are possible Fs, and uncontroversial that the converse can fail: any F is a possible F without being a merely possible F. 'Possible F' is equivalent to 'F or merely possible F'. Unlike the two readings of 'possible F', the two readings of 'merely possible F' are always disjoint in extension. For a merely possible F on the predicative reading is an F, while a merely possible F on the attributive reading is no F. For a similar reason, the predicative reading of 'possible F' is always disjoint in extension from the attributive reading of 'merely possible F'.[19]

Similar distinctions apply to temporal modifiers. For example, on the attributive readings, 'x is a past president' is equivalent to 'x was a president' and 'x is a future president' to 'x will be a president'. On the predicative readings, 'x is a past president' is equivalent to 'x is a president and x once existed' and 'x is a future president' to 'x is a president and x will exist'. The attributive readings are more natural. If one said to Bill Clinton in 1984 'You are a future president' and in 2004 'You are a past president', one spoke truly on the attributive readings but falsely on the predicative ones, since he was not yet president in 1984 and no longer president in 2004.

For a permanentist, the coin was already something, a future coin, before it was made, and will still be something, a past coin, after it is destroyed, on

---

[18] See Quine 1948/1949.

[19] Schnieder 2007 gives detailed arguments for attributing a similar account of possibilia employing an attributive reading of phrases like 'possible F' to Bolzano. Schnieder contrasts Bolzano's theory with one employing the predicative reading, such as Meinong's. For Quine's view see his 1948/1949.

the attributive but not on the predicative readings. Of course, on this view, being made is not being caused to become something (rather than nothing), and being destroyed is not being caused to cease to be something (rather than nothing). It is more like this: being made is being caused to be concrete, and being destroyed is being caused to cease to be concrete. Similarly, an event is something before and after it occurs, but perhaps it is concrete only while it is occurring.

For the permanentist, the no longer or not yet concrete is typically characterized in terms of what it was or will be. For example: it is a past or future coin, or a coin in 1900 or 2100. Socrates is dead, because he was alive and is so no longer. Similarly, for the necessitist, the merely possibly concrete is typically characterized in terms of what it merely could have been. For example: it is a merely possible coin. Some further properties follow rather trivially. Thus the temporarily or contingently non-concrete is both non-heavy and non-metal, since whatever is heavy or metal is concrete. It is self-identical, because everything is. It is identical with that particular thing, which nothing else is, although anything else has an analogously unique property. Past objects also have properties that depend on what happens later. My father is remembered, and has grandchildren, although he did not have them when he was alive. Such logical or extrinsic additions do not greatly change the overall metaphysical picture.

A temporaryist may ask a permanentist: but what is the past or future coin *now*? Similarly, a contingentist may ask a necessitist: but what is the merely possible coin *actually*? Such questions are in effect a challenge to give more 'concrete' properties of the alleged temporarily or contingently non-concrete thing. However, it is contentious to presuppose that everything non-abstract has such more 'concrete' properties. Permanentists and necessitists will naturally reject the challenge, since they deny that the abstract and the concrete are jointly exhaustive. Whether they are right to do so is a theoretical question, to which we cannot expect the answer to be obvious.

Where is the past or future coin now? Where is the merely possible coin actually? Nowhere.

The challenger may argue that an object needs non-modal properties to ground its modal properties. For instance, a lump of clay is malleable (a modal property) because it has a certain microphysical structure (a non-modal property). The analogous principle in the temporal case is obviously false: what I was yesterday is not grounded in what I am today, in any useful sense. Even in the modal case, the principle is not obviously true. Indeed, its very meaning is unclear. What is the supposed distinction between 'modal' and 'non-modal' properties? Malleability is easy to put on the 'modal' side, because the word has the modal suffix '-ability'. But we cannot assume the mere absence of explicit modal indicators in the phrase 'microphysical structure' sufficient for the corresponding properties to be 'non-modal'. Presumably, the microphysical structure has consequences for what the object can or cannot do or have done to it, otherwise it would not ground malleability. So why exactly does microphysical structure count as 'non-modal'? Perhaps the question has a good answer, but that too is to be found by theoretical enquiry.[20] We cannot rely on untutored common sense alone.

1.4 Unrestricted generality

Necessitism is the claim that necessarily everything is necessarily something. The quantifiers 'everything' and 'something' here should be understood as absolutely universal, with no tacit contextual restriction whatsoever. Nobody accepts the corresponding arbitrarily restricted schema 'Necessarily every F is necessarily some F' as valid for all substitutions for 'F', since it excludes the possibility of being contingently an F. A baker is contingently a baker. Of course, some special restrictions may validate the schema: necessarily every number is necessarily some number. Necessitism is simply the limit case where 'F' is read as 'thing', understood as an automatically universally applicable term.

Both necessitists and contingentists can also use quantifiers with various restrictions, and may even regard such uses as typical of everyday discourse. In particular, necessitists can simulate contingentist discourse by tacitly restricting their quantifiers to the concrete. Then they sound like contingentists, saying 'Concrete things are only contingently something'. But they just mean that concrete things are only contingently something *concrete*. The restriction makes the words express different claims from those they express

---

[20] For further discussion of the distinction between modal and non-modal properties see section 8.2. The idea that modal properties must be based on non-modal properties is obviously similar to the controversial idea that dispositions must be based on categorical (non-dispositional) properties, although they may not be equivalent (being possibly concrete may be insufficient for having a disposition to be concrete). For a recent defence of the view that fundamental natural properties have dispositional essences see Bird 2007.

when used unrestrictedly. The disagreement is made explicit only when both sides use their quantifiers unrestrictedly. In what follows, our interest is in the unrestricted uses.

Some philosophers deny that unrestricted uses of quantifiers are intelligible. The most serious concern about such uses is their close association with the paradoxes of set theory. In standard contemporary set theory, there is no absolutely universal set, for otherwise it has a subset of just the non-self-membered sets. Is that set a member of itself? It is if it isn't and it isn't if it is (Russell's paradox). However, one cannot generate a contradiction just by using unrestricted quantifiers. The contradiction always depends on auxiliary assumptions; for instance that the things over which we are quantifying form a set. We can reject those assumptions without rejecting unrestricted quantification. It can be given a robust defence; that is work for elsewhere.[21] This book simply treats the unrestricted quantifiers as intelligible. If so, the purposes of a conversation sometimes require unrestricted readings of the quantifiers, in either a natural or a formal language. This book contributes to a conversation with just such purposes.

Even if the paradoxes did somehow force quantifiers to be restricted, the relevant restrictions would primarily concern quantification over abstract objects, such as sets. They would not rule out quantification over absolutely all non-abstract objects. Since the point of the necessitism–contingentism and permanentism–temporaryism disputes primarily involves non-abstract objects, versions of them would survive, concerning the theses that necessarily every non-abstract thing is necessarily some non-abstract thing and that always every non-abstract thing is always some non-abstract thing. However, we continue to discuss the theses in their unrestricted forms.

Earlier, we considered the charge that there is no live issue because necessitism is too obviously false. Now we must consider the charge that there is no live issue for the opposite reason, because necessitism is too obviously true. The idea is that if 'something' covers merely possible coins as well as coins, then trivially this coin is necessarily something, and so on. The idea is fallacious. That 'something' is unrestricted implies that the things it ranges over include whatever merely possible coins there are, if any. It does not imply that there are or could be any merely possible coins for 'something' to range over.

---

[21] Cartwright 1994 and Williamson 2003a defend the legitimacy of the unrestricted readings of the quantifiers. For recent arguments for and against see the essays in Rayo and Uzquiano 2006 and for more on the first-order (non-modal) logic of unrestricted quantification Rayo and Williamson 2003.

However widely 'something' ranges, it does not range over an assassin of Kant, for he was not assassinated. Unrestricted quantification is only a device for talking about what was already there. It does not trivialize necessitism.

A qualification is needed. David Lewis and other modal realists interpret the modal operators 'necessarily' and 'possibly' as quantifiers over something like maximal concrete spatiotemporal systems such as our own, which they call 'possible worlds'. They regard the explicit use of such quantifiers as metaphysically more perspicuous than the use of modal operators, because the former way of speaking articulates more of the relevant structure. In ordinary contexts, modal realists hold, the implicit quantifiers over worlds tacitly restrict explicit individual quantifiers in their scope to inhabitants of the spatiotemporal system at issue. On their view, 'There could have been no donkeys' is true because some such spatiotemporal system contains no donkeys. However, modal realists also allowed unrestricted quantification; they use it when doing metaphysics. Speaking unrestrictedly, they say that some things are not worldmates (do not belong to the same spatiotemporal system). We understand the application of modal operators to sentences with unrestricted quantifiers. Thus by elementary modal logic 'Some things are not worldmates' entails 'Possibly some things are not worldmates'. The argument would be invalid if the quantifier were tacitly restricted in the conclusion but not in the premise. So, although usual, it is not mandatory for the implicit quantifiers over worlds to restrict explicit individual quanti-fiers in their scope to inhabitants of the world at issue.[22] A similar point applies to the concomitant modal realist idea that in ordinary contexts the implicit quantifiers over worlds tacitly make free variables in their scope denote (if anything) inhabitants of the spatiotemporal system at issue, coun-terparts of their original denotations. Speaking unrestrictedly, modal realists say that something is a mereological fusion of disjoint spatiotemporal systems. But by elementary modal logic 'Something is a fusion of disjoint spatiotem-poral systems' entails 'Something is possibly a fusion of disjoint spatiotemporal systems'. The conclusion would be trivially false if the implicit free variable in the scope of 'possibly' bound from outside by 'something' were interpreted by counterpart theory, since no inhabitant of a world is a fusion of disjoint

---

[22] Lewis explicitly allows that modifiers such as 'at world W' need not induce restrictions on all quanti-fiers in their scope in his 1986, p. 6. For examples of his use of unrestricted quantifiers in stating consequences of modal realism see 1986, p. 133. Incidentally, Lewis endorses a formula that says 'Everything actual necessarily exists' as a theorem of counterpart theory, where quantifiers are world-restricted (Lewis 1968, pp. 31–2).

spatiotemporal systems. So, although usual, it is not mandatory for the implicit quantifiers over worlds to trigger a counterpart-theoretic treatment of free variables in their scope. Thus modal realism should permit a reading of the modal statement of necessitism, 'Necessarily everything is necessarily something', with no explicit quantifier restricted and no counterpart-theoretic treatment of implicit free variables. That unrestricted reading is more faithful to the spirit of necessitism than any other the modal realist framework permits. So interpreted, the generalizations over worlds implicit in the two occurrences of 'necessarily' are redundant; they make no difference. The sentence becomes equivalent to the trivial logical truth 'Everything is something'. Thus modal realism trivializes necessitism. Although modal realists deny that everything in one world has a counterpart in every other world, and a fortiori deny that everything in one world is in every other world, the generalizations thereby denied have world-restricted quantifiers and do not express necessitism.

However, few philosophers and fewer non-philosophers are modal realists. It is possible for there to be (unrestrictedly) no donkeys. The best modal realism can do is that it is possible for there to be (restrictedly) no donkeys, because some maximal spatiotemporal system contains no donkeys. It is not enough. Similarly, it is possible for (unrestrictedly) no spatiotemporal system to contain donkeys. The best modal realism can do is that it is possible for (restrictedly) no spatiotemporal system to contains donkeys, because some maximal spatiotemporal systems contain no donkeys. That too is not enough. Modal realists may deny the modal premises, that it is possible for there to be (unrestrictedly) no donkeys and for (unrestrictedly) no spatiotemporal system to contain donkeys. That hardly improves their position. But present purposes require no full-scale critique of modal realism.[23] Modal realism trivializes key conclusions of this book; it makes them true, not false. This book defends them under assumptions, such as the falsity of modal realism, that make them non-trivial.

Many philosophers use a framework of possible worlds without being modal realists. They treat possible worlds as devices for somehow representing

---

[23] For one line of criticism of standard versions of counterpart theory, a crucial component of modal realism, see Fara and Williamson 2005. Another objection to Lewis's modal realism is that it implies that laws of nature vary across worlds, and therefore across spatiotemporal systems. Since proposed fundamental laws of nature are normally intended to hold unrestrictedly, his modal realism is incompatible with fundamental physical theories on their intended interpretation. Although it may be replied that we really only have evidence about the physics of our own spatiotemporal system, the evidence for fundamental physical theories is considerably stronger than the evidence for modal realism as a basis for theorizing about the physics of other spatiotemporal systems.

possibilities. If one such device represents this thing as a coin, it does not follow that every other such device represents it as a possible coin, that is, represents it as represented by some such device as a coin. Compare: if I say that it is a coin, it does not follow that everyone else says that someone says that it is a coin. Within such alternative frameworks of possible worlds, necessitism is not trivial, even on the unrestricted reading of the quantifiers. Compare: if I say that it is (unrestrictedly) something, it does not follow that everyone else says that it is (unrestrictedly) something.

Similar issues arise for permanentism. However, the analogue of modal realism for time, a four-dimensional conception of spacetime, is a far less eccentric view than modal realism. It *seems* to command scientific support from the theory of Special Relativity.[24] On the four-dimensional view, unrestricted quantifiers automatically range over the entire contents of spacetime. Thus permanentism is in more danger than necessitism of trivial-ization.[25] But if the difference between space and time goes deeper than the four-dimensional conception suggests, then it is not trivially guaranteed that there was never something which is no longer (unrestrictedly) something, or that there will never be something which is not yet (unrestrictedly) something. Although four-dimensionalists may deny that everything at one time has a counterpart at every other time, and a fortiori deny that every-thing at one time is at every other time, the generalizations thereby denied have time-restricted quantifiers and do not express permanentism.

1.5 Necessitism and Meinongianism

If we read 'exists' as 'is (unrestrictedly) something', we can restate necessitism as 'Necessarily everything necessarily exists' and permanentism as 'Always everything always exists'. This is the reading of 'exists' of most logical interest, since no particular restriction of the quantifiers is logically privileged. How-ever, the word 'exists' tends to be philosophically misleading, for it also has restricted uses. The noise they generate can make the intended unrestricted reading hard to hear. For example, one might naturally say 'Events do not

---

[24] Putnam 1967 is a classic statement of the point, but it remains controversial. For a more recent discus-sion see Zimmerman 2011.

[25] By pursuing the structural similarity of the pairs 'here' and 'everywhere' and 'I' and 'everyone' to the pairs 'actually' and 'necessarily', and 'now' and 'always', one might also define analogues of necessitism and permanentism for places and people. Presumably, they would be trivially true.

exist; they occur'. In saying so, one does not imply that there are no events, as one would on an unrestricted use of 'exist'. Again, some of the pre-theoretic resistance to claims such as 'Numbers exist' and 'Sets exist' may come from a tendency to hear 'exist' as restricted to something like concrete substances: on such a reading, the claims are clearly false. It also makes 'Necessarily everything necessarily exists' and 'Always everything always exists' express obvious falsehoods. Concrete substances could have not been concrete substances, and once were not concrete substances. In none of these cases does the unrestricted reading of 'exist' yield an *obviously* true thesis. Rather, it produces a metaphysical thesis whose truth value is unclear and cannot be settled without serious theoretical enquiry.

The distinction between restricted and unrestricted readings is less obvious for 'exists' than for the quantifiers 'something' and 'everything'. It is therefore more likely to cause philosophical confusion. Consequently, it is best not to use 'exists' as a key term when formulating philosophical theses. In this book the word occurs only in explicit or implicit quotation marks, mentioned rather than used.

A necessitist who restricts 'exist' to concrete substances or things in space or time will typically endorse the claim 'Some things do not exist'. This might suggest a similarity between necessitism and notorious views associated with Alexius Meinong, who used a restricted 'existence' predicate. However, although I have often heard the two theories conflated in discussion, they have little in common. One of Meinong's most distinctive principles is the notorious characterization schema 'The F is an F' (except for a few tricky substitutions for 'F'). Necessitism is committed to no such principle. The most blatant case is Meinong's instantiation of his principle even with impossible descriptions: he held that the round square is a round square. Obviously, necessitism has no such consequence. Nor, given that there is not but could have been a golden mountain, does necessitism entail that the golden mountain is a golden mountain. To see this, we may combine necessitism with any standard theory of definite descriptions, on which 'The F is an F' entails 'There is an F'.[26] Even with these auxiliary assumptions, necessitism does not imply that there is a golden mountain. Therefore, with or without them, it does not imply that the golden mountain is a golden mountain. It does imply that there is a *merely possible* golden mountain, but

---

[26] It is irrelevant whether Meinong would accept such a theory of descriptions, since its role here is only in showing what is consistent with necessitism.

only on the attributive reading: something could have been a golden mountain, but is not a golden mountain. A predicative reading would yield the more Meinongian result 'Some golden mountain is merely possible' in the sense 'Some golden mountain could have existed but does not exist'; again, necessitism has no such consequence. Finally, although necessitism implies 'There is a merely possible golden mountain' on the attributive reading, it does not imply the corresponding modal instance of Meinong's principle, 'The merely possible golden mountain is a merely possible golden mountain'. For on most standard theories of definite descriptions, 'The F is an F' entails 'There is exactly one F'. Thus 'The merely possible golden mountain is a merely possible golden mountain' entails 'There is exactly one merely possible golden mountain'. Even granted the auxiliary assumptions, necessitism does not imply 'There is exactly one merely possible golden mountain' (on any reading). Presumably, there could have been *many* golden mountains, so on the necessitist view there are many merely possible golden mountains.[27] Qualifying 'golden mountain' with 'unique' makes little difference. There could have been two golden mountains, each of which could have been a golden mountain even if neither the other nor any third thing had been a golden mountain; thus each of them is actually a merely possible unique golden mountain. Hence, for necessitists, there are many merely possible unique golden mountains. Thus necessitism does not even imply 'The merely possible unique golden mountain is a merely possible unique golden mountain'. Necessitism is nothing like Meinongianism.[28]

---

[27] For the same reason, the definite descriptions 'the possible fat man in that doorway' and 'the possible bald man in that doorway' in Quine 1948/1949 are improper.

[28] Sophisticated reconstructions of Meinongianism, as in Parsons 1980, Zalta 1988, and Priest 2005, reinterpret the characterization schema so as to avoid its worst consequences. Such views may be logically consistent with necessitism, but are in no way consequences of, or made plausible by, necessitism. Indeed, Priest endorses a form of necessitism, with a constant domain of objects (2005, p. 21) and an 'existence' predicate restricted to concrete objects (2005, p. 106). But on his noneism, following Routley 1980, 'non-existent objects . . . have no mode of being whatsoever' (2005, p. 14), whereas a necessitist can insist that, trivially, every object has the plainest of all modes of being, being something. As Quine points out, following John Bacon, just as eating is eating something, so being is being something (1969, p. 94). Priest's noneism effectively equates the logical distinction between being and non-being with the vague distinction of no special logical interest between being concrete and being non-concrete. Furthermore, whereas Priest describes his noneism as 'naturally committed to the idea that every term denotes something' (2005, p. ix), necessitism gives no encouragement to that idea. In storytelling, one can pretend that a term denotes something even though it does not (for more on fictional names see section 4.1). A non-denoting term is semantically defective, but still a term. Similarly, a necessitist may hold, contrary to Priest's noneist account of intentionality, that in bad cases independently motivated conditions on reference sometimes preclude any object, concrete or not, from being the object of one's thought.

Although 'merely possible unique golden mountain' is no uniquely identifying description, the necessitist should not assume that we can never uniquely identify a merely possible inhabitant of space and time. Imagine a factory where knives are assembled by a machine which fits together a blade from one belt and a handle from another. The blades are uniform in shape; so are the handles. The machine actually fitted blade B to handle H to form a knife K and blade B* to handle H* to form a knife K*. However, if the blade belt had been delayed by one second, the machine would have fitted blade B to handle H*, to form a knife distinct from K, K* and anything else actually in space and time. Perhaps there is only one merely possible knife that could have been formed from B and H* in just such circumstances. If so, our description 'possible knife that would have been assembled from blade B and handle H* had the blade belt been delayed by one second' uniquely identifies a merely possible inhabitant of space and time.

Permanentism is harder than necessitism to confuse with Meinongianism. We obviously cannot assume that the past or future contains a golden mountain, let alone a round square. Uniquely identifying a past concrete object is typically much easier than uniquely identifying a possible concrete object. For example, we can now specify the unique object that at a specified past time was at a specified place and of a specified kind. Similar methods often work for uniquely identifying a future concrete object, for example as the unique object that at a specified future time will be at a specified place and of a specified kind, although of course it is usually harder to *know* that such a description is satisfied than in the case of the past. We have no way of knowing the future comparable to networks of perception, memory and testimony as ways of knowing the past. The epistemological asymmetries may explain why we have no practice of referring to future concrete objects by name comparable to our practice of referring to past concrete objects by name. They do not constitute metaphysical or logical asymmetries.[29]

---

[29] On some views, the future is open in ways that make future-directed operators more like modal operators than like past-directed ones. The comments in the text are not intended to pre-empt such views. The point is just that they are not needed to explain epistemological asymmetries; any motivation for them must lie elsewhere.

1.6 Actualism and possibilism

Necessitism and contingentism may remind some readers of views associated with the terms 'possibilism' and 'actualism' respectively. However, the use of the latter two terms has become badly confused. There is a widespread feeling of dissatisfaction with the possibilism–actualism distinction.

One may be given this explanation: the actualist holds that everything is actual, while the possibilist holds that not everything is actual, although everything is possible. If so, what is it for something to be actual, or to be possible? 'To be actual is to be in the actual world' is no better than a pseudo-explanation, for 'in the actual world' is more obscure than 'actual'.

Modal realists such as David Lewis posit or claim to hear a reading on which 'the actual world' refers just to our spatiotemporal system, even though there are other spatiotemporal systems spatiotemporally unrelated to ours. However, most participants in the actualism–possibilism debate reject modal realism, and hold that if there are such other spatiotemporal systems, they are just as actual as our own. The debate is not supposed to be about whether there are other spatiotemporal systems. One might believe that there are many other such systems and still count as an actualist, regarding their inhabitants as no less straightforwardly real and actual than the inhabitants of our own system, just as the inhabitants of other countries are no less straightforwardly real and actual than the inhabitants of our own country. If we presuppose modal realism, we cannot explain what is at stake in the actualism–possibilism debate.[30]

On a less loaded account, what is actual is simply what there actually (unrestrictedly) is. The reference to a world was a digression. Analogously, what is possible is what there could (unrestrictedly) be. But, on standard accounts of the logic of 'actually', it is a modal operator whose insertion makes a difference to truth value only when in the scope of another modal operator such as 'possibly' or 'necessarily'. If there is a talking donkey then there actually is a talking donkey, even though there *could have been* a talking

---

[30] Lewis calls the thesis that everything is actual 'terminological actualism', and its conjunction with the thesis that actuality consists of our spatiotemporal system (give or take some abstract entities) 'metaphysical actualism' (1986, pp. 99–100). Metaphysical actualism is an interesting thesis in its own right, but it is not at stake here.

donkey without there actually being a talking donkey.[31] Therefore, since whatever is is, whatever is actually is: if there is something, then there actually is such a thing. So on this understanding, actualism is trivially true and possibilism trivially false. Thus the actualist needs another reading of 'actual' than the one well understood in modal logic. On the supposed alternative reading, being actual had better be actually doing something harder than just being, otherwise the supposed dispute is silly. But what is that harder thing, if a dispute about whether everything does it is as fundamental to modal metaphysics as the dispute between actualism and possibilism is supposed to be? And why should the alternative to the view that everything actually does the harder thing be a view on which everything *could* do the harder thing? Why cannot something be impossible, in the sense that it could not do the harder thing? Although we might complicate the definitions of 'actualism' and 'possibilism' in attempts to construct a more sensible dispute, it is better to make a fresh start with fresh terminology and clearer distinctions.[32] Thus the proposal is to abandon that debate as hopelessly

---

[31] Technically, 'Actually P' as uttered in a context *c* and evaluated with respect to a world *w* is standardly assigned the truth value of 'P' as uttered in *c* and evaluated with respect to the world of *c*. Hence 'Actually P' as uttered in a context *c* and evaluated with respect to a world other than the world of *c* may differ in truth value from 'P' as uttered in the same context and evaluated with respect to the same world. Thus not every instance of 'P if and only if actually P' is a theorem of a logic such as the system S5A (Crossley and Humberstone 1977) which in effect axiomatizes those formulas true as uttered in any context and evaluated with respect to any world in any model (the generally valid formulas, in the terminology of Davies and Humberstone 1980). However, every instance of that schema is a theorem of any logic that axiomatizes those formulas true as uttered in any context and evaluated with respect to the world of that context in any model (Davies and Humberstone's real world valid formulas). 'P if and only if actually P' is trivially real world valid. Although the English word 'actually' is capable of readings other than this rigid one, they do not make 'actualism' express an interesting claim. In particular, treating 'actually' as non-rigid or as a mere scope-indicating device does not make 'P if and only if actually P' non-trivial in unembedded occurrences. For a modal realist, 'actual' typically restricts quantifiers in its scope to the spatiotemporal system in which it is uttered, but, as already noted, the debate is not supposed to be about whether there are other such systems.

[32] For example, Forbes 1989 takes the question to be: whose sense of 'exist' is more basic? But a question about the relative basicness of senses looks to be a confusingly indirect proxy for a fundamentally metaphysical question. Bennett 2005 is a more recent example of an attempt to clarify the issues (see also Bennett 2006). Despite the relevance of the wide range of philosophical considerations that paper deploys, it fails to assign clear contents to the opposing 'views'. One source of the trouble in much of the recent literature is a tendency even on the part of those who officially reject Lewis's modal realism to use its language to characterize both actualism and possibilism, with unmodalized talk of 'domains' of worlds and their 'inclusion' relations, even though such a way of speaking is far from neutral; it relies on a picture of possible worlds and their inhabitants all simultaneously laid out together. One cannot restore neutrality afterwards by adding that one is, of course, not assuming modal realism. The damage has already been done, through reliance on modal realist metaphors when making judgements of plausibility. The non-neutrality of formulations in terms of possible worlds is discussed in more detail in section 3.6.

muddled, and to get on with the clearer necessitism–contingentism debate, and other clearer debates too, instead. For example, there is a legitimate debate for and against modal realism. But to roll that debate together with the one for and against necessitism is utterly to confuse both issues. Although modal realists are in effect necessitists, the necessitism–contingentism debate becomes most interesting when both sides reject modal realism, and take contingency more seriously than modal realists do.[33]

Similarly, permanentism and temporaryism may remind some readers of views associated with the terms 'eternalism' and 'presentism' respectively. However, the use of the latter two words is also unclear. There is a widespread feeling of dissatisfaction with the eternalism–presentism distinction. One may be given this explanation: the presentist holds that everything is present, while the eternalist holds that not everything is present. If so, what is it for something to be present?[34]

One proposal is that something is present when and only when it is spatially located. But then presentism entails that everything is spatially located, and so is incompatible with the platonist thesis that there are spatially unlocated abstract objects such as numbers. But presentism was not supposed to have such ramifications for the philosophy of mathematics. Even on the more restricted proposal that if something is in time, it is present when and only when it is spatially located, presentism is then incompatible with the anti-physicalist speculation that spatially unlocated mental events are occurring. But presentism was not supposed to have such ramifications for the philosophy of mind. Conversely, a four-dimensionalist about spacetime who holds that there are only atoms spatially located at all times is counted a presentist, which is again not how the presentism–eternalism distinction was supposed to work.

On a less loaded account, what is present is simply what there presently (unrestrictedly) is. But, on standard accounts of the logic of 'presently', its insertion makes no difference in truth value, at least when not in the scope of a temporal operator. If there is a Roman emperor then there presently is a Roman emperor. Therefore, since whatever is is, whatever is presently is: if there is something, then there presently is such a thing. So on this understanding, presentism is trivially true and eternalism trivially false. Thus being

---

[33] For more on what it is to take contingency seriously see sections 7.4 and 8.4.

[34] See, for example, Crisp 2003, p. 211 (the slight refinements he later introduces are not important here) and Markosian 2004, p. 47.

present had better be presently doing something harder than just being, otherwise the supposed dispute is silly. But what is that harder thing, if a dispute about whether everything does it is as fundamental to temporal metaphysics as the dispute between presentism and eternalism is supposed to be? Although we might complicate the definitions of 'presentism' and 'eternalism' in attempts to construct a more sensible dispute, it is better to make a fresh start with fresh terminology and clearer distinctions. Thus the proposal is to abandon that debate as hopelessly muddled, and to get on with the clearer permanentism–temporaryism debate, and other clearer debates too, instead. For example, there is a legitimate debate for and against various four-dimensionalist views. But to roll that debate together with the one for and against permanentism is utterly to confuse both issues. Although four-dimensionalists are in effect permanentists, the permanentism–temporaryism debate becomes most interesting when both sides reject four-dimensionalism, and take change more seriously than four-dimensionalists do.

This book shows primarily how to reorient debate in the metaphysics of quantified modal logic around the necessitism–contingentism dispute, and secondarily how to reorient debate in the metaphysics of quantified temporal logic around the permanentism–temporaryism dispute. Of course, many other issues in those areas are also worth debating, but misconceptions about the necessitism–contingentism and permanentism–temporaryism distinctions tend to confuse discussion of other issues too.

1.7 Identity and distinctness

In developing some putative counterexamples to necessitism, we treated it as committed to a classical modal logic of identity, on which identicals are necessarily identical and distinct things are necessarily distinct. For example, in discussing the idea that there could have been more things than there actually are, we did not contemplate the necessitist trying to avoid onto-logical inflation by responding that one actual thing could have been each of many things. Similarly, on the version of permanentism sketched earlier, identicals are always identical and distinct things are always distinct. The issue deserves further explanation.

The logical arguments for the necessity and permanentness of identity are straightforward, and widely accepted in at least some form. Suppose that

x is identical with y. Therefore, by the indiscernibility of identicals, x is whatever y is. But y is necessarily identical with y. Therefore x is necessarily identical with y.[35] By analogous reasoning, x is always identical with y. More strongly: necessarily always, if x is identical with y then necessarily always x is identical with y. Of course, we understand 'x' and 'y' here as variables whose values are simply things, not as standing for definite descriptions such as 'the winning number' that denote different things with respect to different circumstances.

The logical arguments for the necessity and permanentness of distinctness are slightly less straightforward, but in the same spirit. Suppose that x is distinct from y. If tomorrow x will be identical with y, then by the permanentness of identity tomorrow x will always be identical with y, so tomorrow x will be identical with y today, so x is identical with y (the 'today' makes the 'tomorrow' redundant), which is a contradiction. Therefore tomorrow x will still be distinct from y. The argument generalizes, so x is always distinct from y. The modal argument is similar. If, in counterfactual circumstances C, x were identical with y, then by a version of the necessity of identity in C x would be identical with y in all circumstances other than C too, so in C x would be identical with y in the actual circumstances, so x is identical with y ('in the actual circumstances' makes 'in C' redundant), which is a contradiction. Therefore in C x is distinct from y. The argument generalizes, so x is necessarily distinct from y. To sum up: necessarily always, if x is distinct from y then necessarily always x is distinct from y.

If we test the arguments by formalizing them and evaluating the steps in models of the simplest and most natural kinds, they come out valid. Although we can always rig up ad hoc modellings that count them invalid, by not interpreting the identity sign directly in terms of identity, such tricks can be performed for any argument whatsoever. Chapter 4 discusses such questions in detail.[36]

For the necessitist or permantentist to mess with the modal or temporal logic of identity in order to avoid ontological inflation would be a lapse of methodological good taste, or good sense, for it means giving more weight to ontology than to the vastly better developed and more successful discipline

---

[35] The argument goes back to Barcan 1947; see section 5.3 for discussion. Ramsey 1927, p. 57, already proposes without proof that 'numerical identity and difference are necessary relations'.
[36] See Gibbard 1975 and Gallois 1998 for defences of contingent and temporary identity respectively. For some critical discussion of such views see Hawthorne 2003.

of logic. More specifically, the classical modal or temporal logic is a strong, simple, and elegant theory. To weaken, complicate, and uglify it without overwhelming reason to do so merely in order to block the derivation of the necessity or permanence of identity would be as retrograde and wrong-headed a step in logic and metaphysics as natural scientists would consider a comparable sacrifice of those virtues in a physical theory. We will be guided throughout this book by a conception of theories in logic and meta-physics as scientific theories, to be assessed by the same overall standards as theories in other branches of science.[37]

Messing with the modal or temporal logic of identity in order to avoid ontological inflation would also be ineffective, for not all the putative coun-terexamples depend on the modal or temporal logic of identity: the merely possible golden mountain does not. The best necessitist and permanentist strategy is to accept the ontological inflation and argue that it is theoret-ically harmless. Indeed, the necessity and permanentness of identity and distinctness nicely fit the necessitist and permanentist picture, on which the fundamental structure of things is modally and temporally fixed.

Some marginal versions of necessitism and permanentism employ deviant modal and temporal logics of identity. They permit contingent and temporary identity.[38] But our evaluation of the doctrines will focus on the central forms, with a classical modal and temporal logic of identity. The logic of identity is not the main topic of this book.

The contingentist has more qualms than the necessitist about the argu-ments for the necessity and permanentness of identity. For they assume that y is necessarily and always y: but how can it be if y is not necessarily and always something? How can y be self-identical when there is nothing to be self-identical? Thus the best versions of contingentism and temporaryism may involve some restriction on the necessity and permanentness of iden-tity. However, the restriction is minimal. Necessarily always, if x is identical with y, then necessarily whenever x is something x is identical with y. Correspondingly with the necessity and permanentness of distinctness: necessarily always, if x is something not identical with y, then necessarily

---

[37] For more on this theme see Chapters 3 and 6 and the Afterword. Obviously 'science' is not restricted to natural science; it includes mathematics too. Note that although one may try to mitigate such complications of modal or temporal logic by claiming modality or time not to be fundamental, those complications become significant theoretical costs of that claim itself.

[38] The main examples invoke counterpart theory; see Lewis 1968, p. 36.

x is never identical with *y*. Although contingentism and temporaryism could also be combined with more deviant modal and temporal logics of identity, that is not the concern of this book.

By comparing contingentism and temporaryism with necessitism and permanentism against a background modal and temporal logic that treats identity as classically as is consistent with both sides, we avoid the distractions, complications, and artefacts of logical deviance and achieve a fairer and more perspicuous view of the dispute.

1.8 Dying and never being born

On first hearing, necessitism and permanentism seem to promise us divine attributes: necessity and permanentness of being. Once we realize that we are being offered no more possibility or duration of concreteness, power, consciousness, or life than we already knew ourselves to have, we may conclude that the questions are of no practical significance. But that is too quick. For the abstract metaphysical difference may nevertheless constrain and clarify our thinking about matters of moral and emotional concern: for instance, in fearing death or feeling glad that one was born, or in considering the lives and deaths of others.

Epicurus makes a notorious case that death is no misfortune: 'death, the most frightening of bad things, is nothing to us; since when we exist, death is not yet present, and when death is present, then we do not exist'.[39] Of the various ways of filling in the ellipses in the argument, some involve the thought that after death one is nothing, and therefore not something that can bear properties such as being unfortunate. Even if that thought were correct, it would not be conclusive, for the misfortune of death might consist in properties mortals have while still alive. Nevertheless, it provides room for logical manoeuvre in trying to persuade oneself that death is less bad than it appears, room that permanentism eliminates. Even if one becomes something non-concrete after death, from a purely logical point of view one remains a bearer of properties. That point too is not conclusive, since a non-concrete bearer of properties may still be incapable of bearing a given property, such as being unfortunate. For instance, some hold that what is

---

[39] Epicurus 1997, p. 29. See Hershenov 2007 for a recent version of Epicureanism on this point.

good or bad for one consists in one's having experiences of relevant kinds.[40] However, that requires a narrowly reductive conception of goodness and badness. It is good for me too that my loved ones flourish, even if I am unaware of their flourishing. Only a gross egotist thinks that it is more important whether his children appear to him to be happy than whether they really are happy. Why should it not be good for me even after my death, if I am still something then, that those whom I loved when I lived continue to flourish?[41] Thus it may also be bad for me after my death that I am dead, even though I cannot experience my being dead. Given permanentism, what is then bad is not the loss of being, since I still have it, but the loss of life, or something closely related.[42] Although we cannot expect to resolve such complex issues without coordinating a variety of considerations of different types, the dispute between permanentism and temporaryism constitutes one dimension of the problem.[43]

The dispute between necessitism and contingentism impinges on matters of moral and emotional concern in partly analogous ways. Suppose that you are wondering whether to have children, in this world full of evils, and fear that it might turn out better for them never to have been born. A contingentist may suggest that the comparison is meaningless, because if they had never been born (or conceived) there would have been nothing to have any level of well-being at all. In the absence of an input to the welfare function, no output is defined. Necessitists have no such easy way out of the comparison. If they reject it, they cannot do so on general logical or metaphysical grounds; they will have to find much more specific considerations.[44] Although deciding between necessitism and contingentism will not by itself force the answer to the question of value, it is a step towards answering that question.

This book focuses on questions of logic and metaphysics. The next chapter traces how logical issues of necessitism versus contingentism and of permanentism versus temporaryism emerged in the twentieth century, through the development of modal and temporal logic.

---

[40] Epicurus suggests such a view in the same passage, a few sentences earlier.

[41] Aristotle gives a classic expression of this idea in the *Nicomachean Ethics* 1100a (book 1, chapter 10). For discussion see Solomon 1976. For a contrary view and further references see Taylor 2005.

[42] Nagel 1970, p. 3, argues that it is the loss of life rather than the non-being ('nonexistence') to which we object in death.

[43] For more on the logical aspects of the problem see Yourgrau 1987 and Ruben 1988. For a recent general discussion of the relation between well-being and death see Bradley 2009.

[44] For some relevant discussion see Parfit 1984, pp. 487–90, Broome 2004, pp. 63–8, and Bradley 2009, pp. 98–111.

2

The Barcan Formula and its Converse: Early Developments

2.1 The Barcan Formula

The metaphysical dispute discussed in Chapter 1 between contingentism and necessitism turns out to be intimately connected with some technical issues in quantified modal logic, over two principles usually known as the Barcan formula and its converse. When those principles are interpreted in the relevant way, they are typically accepted by necessitists, rejected by contingentists. Indeed, in some natural logical settings, each of them is equivalent to the central necessitist claim that necessarily everything is necessarily something. From a technical perspective, whether the Barcan formula and its converse are theorems of a quantified modal system has major ramifications for how it works. The business of this chapter is to introduce the formulas, and to explain how they emerged in twentieth-century logic, how they gradually came to seem metaphysically problematic, how early contingentist attempts to avoid them came to grief, and why later contingentist attempts were forced into significant restrictions in their logic. To understand this development, we must follow changes in the interpretation of modal logic. The story continues through later chapters. It constitutes, amongst other things, a case study in the history of relations between logic and metaphysics. To put it crudely, the Barcan formula and its converse appeared in the context of logical positivism, where logic and metaphysics were considered disjoint. For if all logic is good and all metaphysics is bad, then no logic is metaphysics. On a less pejorative version of the argument, if all metaphysics makes claims about how things are and no logic does, then the same conclusion follows. For a mixture of technical and philosophical reasons, any such separation of logic and metaphysics became increasingly hard to maintain, especially for principles like the Barcan formula and its converse.

Quantified modal logic is a combination of quantified logic and modal logic. Quantified logic studies logical consequence for a language with quantifiers such as 'some' ($\exists$) and 'every' ($\forall$), individual variables and perhaps variables of other types too, as well as the standard truth-functional connectives such as negation ($\neg$), conjunction (&), disjunction ($\vee$), the conditional ($\rightarrow$), and the biconditional ($\leftrightarrow$). Modal logic studies logical consequence for a language with modal operators such as 'possibly' ($\Diamond$) and 'necessarily' ($\Box$), as well as the truth-functional connectives. Thus quantified modal logic studies logical consequence for a language with both quantifiers and modal operators, and of course the truth-functional connectives.[1] It therefore inherits any philosophical problems raised by the logic of a quantified language and also any philosophical problems raised by the logic of a modal language. But it also raises some new philosophical problems of its own, concerning the interaction between the quantifiers and the modal operators. The Barcan formula and its converse are principles about that interaction. Let us start with the emergence of the Barcan formula in twentieth-century logic.

The history of quantified modal logic in some form goes back to Aristotle's modal syllogistic, if not before. However, the first publication of a fully formal system of quantified modal logic came only in March 1946, with the article 'A Functional Calculus of First Order Based on Strict Implication' in *The Journal of Symbolic Logic*, by Ruth Barcan (later Mrs J.A. Marcus and Ruth Barcan Marcus).[2] She takes the preferred axiomatic system S2 of unquantified modal logic from the seminal text *Symbolic Logic* by C.I. Lewis and C.H. Langford (1932), expands the language by adding individual and predicate variables and a quantifier $\exists$ binding only the former, and extends

---

[1] Most of the relevant technical background for this book can be found in Hughes and Cresswell 1996.

[2] Lewis and Langford 1932, pp. 178–98, presents a more or less formal system of modal logic with quantification on propositional but not individual variables; see section 5.2 for discussion. Hochberg claims that it 'is fashionable, but more myth than fact, to date quantified modal logic from Barcan's March 1946 paper' (2002, p. 288). His reason for rejecting the date is that although Carnap published his article and book on quantified modal logic later (1946 and 1947 respectively), he had been working on the book since 1942, and completed a draft of it in 1943. Carnap develops an axiomatic system of first-order modal logic in the article (1946, pp. 54–64) but not in the book. Hochberg does not discuss how long Barcan had been working on the Ph.D. dissertation from which she extracted her article, but she completed it in draft in early 1945 (Marcus 1993, p. x). In any case, it is usual to reckon priority in science by date of publication, and not just for reasons of verifiability: science is a communal enterprise, so it matters when an idea enters the public domain.

Lewis and Langford's axiomatization by adding axiom schemata and rules of inference for the quantifier. The rest of the article is occupied with deriving further theorems and rules from her axiomatic basis. The methodology is austerely syntactic. No semantics is proposed for the formal language, not even an informal reading of the formulas in ordinary English. Of course, it is clear from the reference to Lewis and Langford that the symbol ◊ is intended as some sort of possibility operator and from the logical background that ∃ is intended as some sort of 'existential' quantifier. Since the variables it binds are described as 'individual' and the system as 'first order', we expect to be able to read a formula like ∃x Fx as 'Some individual is F' or 'Something is F'.[3]

Unlike contemporary modal logicians, who normally take □ or ◊ as their primitive modal operator, Barcan Marcus follows Lewis and Langford in taking as primitive a symbol for strict implication, contrasted with the truth-functional material implication. In contemporary symbols, it is the difference between $A \to B$ and $\Box(A \to B)$. Informally: whereas every falsehood materially implies everything, no contingent falsehood strictly implies everything (although every necessary falsehood does); whereas every truth is materially implied by everything, no contingent truth is strictly implied by everything (although every necessary truth is). The aim of the 1946 paper is to develop axiomatically a logic of first-order quantification based on strict implication as far as possible along the same lines as a standard logic of first-order quantification based on material implication.

Since Barcan Marcus formulates her axiom schemata with strict implication as the main connective, all their instances make necessitated claims. There is one distinctive schema for the interaction of modal operators and quantifiers:

(1) $\Box(\Diamond \exists v\, A \to \exists v\, \Diamond A)$

The instances of (1) comprise those formulas of the object language obtained by substituting an individual variable for v and an open or closed formula for A. In the non-vacuous case, the variable v occurs free in A. We may think of A as stating a condition on the value of v. Thus an instance of (1) says that necessarily, if there could have been an individual that satisfied the condition, then there is an individual that could have satisfied the condition. As with the other axiom schemas and rules of inference, no attempt is made in the article to justify (1) or explain its significance.

---

[3] Formulas are always given in the notation of this book, instead of the original.

Its main role in the paper is to permit the derivation of the result of putting strict implication for material implication in the standard non–modal principle $\forall v\,(A \rightarrow B) \rightarrow (\forall v\, A \rightarrow \forall v\, B).$[4]

The phrase 'the Barcan formula' has come to be used not for (1) but for its unnecessitated variant:

BF $\Diamond \exists v\, A \rightarrow \exists v \,\Diamond A$

Of course, BF is not really a single formula of the object language, but rather a schema with infinitely many formulas as its instances. We can derive a logical equivalent of BF by contraposing it and using the duality of 'possibly' with 'necessarily' and of 'some' with 'every':

BF′ $\forall v \,\Box A \rightarrow \Box\, \forall v\, A$

In English: if everything necessarily satisfies a condition, then necessarily everything satisfies the condition. BF′ is sometimes called 'the Barcan formula' too. On standard assumptions, if BF is a valid schema, in the sense that all its instances are true, then BF′ is a valid schema in the same sense, for if BF′ is invalid, it has a false instance for some formula A, so that instance has a true antecedent and a false consequent, so everything is necessarily such that A holds, although possibly something is such that A fails; thus possibly something is such that $\neg A$ holds, although nothing is possibly such that $\neg A$ holds, so the corresponding instance of BF for $\neg A$ has a true antecedent and a false consequent, and is therefore false, so BF is invalid too. Conversely, if BF′ is a valid schema, then so is BF, by similar reasoning. Since BF is easier to engage with imaginatively than BF′, it will be taken as the canonical form.

In most contemporary systems of quantified modal logic, any *modal closure* of a theorem is itself a theorem, where a modal closure of a formula B is any formula that results from prefixing B with a finite string (which may be the null string) of universal quantifiers and necessity operators in any order.[5] For example, any instance of (1) is a modal closure of the corresponding

---

[4] See Barcan 1946a, p. 5 (theorem schema 19). The modalized principle is $\Box(\forall v\, \Box(A \rightarrow B) \rightarrow \Box(\forall v\, A \rightarrow \forall v\, B))$. Conversely, one can derive (1) from schema 19 and the other axiom schemas, since the result of substituting a tautology for A reduces to $\Box(\forall v\, \Box B \rightarrow \Box\, \forall v\, B)$, which is equivalent to (1) (compare BF′).

[5] For reasons explained in Chapter 1, n. 31, systems of 'real world' validities have $P \leftrightarrow @P$ but not $\Box(P \leftrightarrow @P)$ as a theorem, where @ is a rigidifying 'actually' operator. Such cases are irrelevant to (1) and BF, which are supposed to be generally valid if valid at all, and so in either case not merely real world valid. The use of modal closures is inspired by the use of 'closures' in Kripke 1963, p. 69, although he makes A a closure of B only when A is closed and B open.

instance of BF. In such a system of modal logic, every instance of BF is a
theorem only if every instance of (1) is a theorem. Some hold that although
a formula may be true even though its universal generalization or necessitation is not true, it should count as *logically* true only if its universal generalization and its necessitation also count as logically true. Conversely, BF is
derivable from (1) in the system of the 1946 paper by the principle that
what is necessarily the case is the case.

Let *full BF* be the schema whose instances are all modal closures of instances of BF. Thus all instances of (1) are instances of full BF. However, not
all instances of full BF are theorems of the 1946 Barcan system, which lacks
the necessitation rule that whenever B is a theorem so is $\Box B$. Indeed, the
system inherits from S2 the feature of having no theorems of the form $\Box\Box B$.
In particular, therefore, necessitations of instances of (1) are not derivable,
despite being instances of full BF. This feature is generally considered an
incidental defect of the system; surely $\Box\Box(P \rightarrow P)$ deserves to be a theorem.
The limitations of S2 play no role in the later metaphysical discussion.[6] In
more promising candidates for a quantified logic of metaphysical modality,
all instances of BF are derivable only if all instances of full BF are derivable.
However, we still distinguish BF from full BF, since in principle a special
characteristic of the actual world might make all instances of BF true without making all instances of full BF true, if our world but not others satisfied
a principle of plenitude for possibilia (ontological maximality). In practice,
the actual world shows no sign of being special in any such way.

Formally, contingentism as defined in Chapter 1 is consistent even with
full BF. Without auxiliary assumptions, one cannot deduce from full BF the
formalization of the defining necessitist claim that necessarily everything is
necessarily something, whose negation is the defining contingentist claim.
In practice, however, almost all contingentists reject BF, and a fortiori (1)
and full BF, when $\exists$ is read as an unrestricted individual quantifier and $\Diamond$ as
an operator for metaphysical possibility. According to them, there could

---

[6] To check that the quantified system inherits the property of having no theorems of the form $\Box\Box A$ from
the corresponding unquantified system, one can easily verify by induction on the length of proofs that
whenever a formula B is a theorem of the former, the result of deleting all quantifiers and variables in B
is a theorem of the latter (where predicate letters become sentence letters). Although the preferred system
in Lewis and Langford 1932, S2 is seldom considered in contemporary logic. Since the necessitation
rule fails, it is not a normal system in the technical sense. Moreover, since contradictions are possibly
possible in S2, it cannot be interpreted in terms of possible world models of the usual kind, although
Kripke 1965 interpreted it in terms of models with some non-normal worlds in which everything is
possible. For extensive information on S2 see Hughes and Cresswell 1968, pp. 230–3, 249–52, 272–80.

have been something that is actually nothing—because, for example, there could have been more things than there actually are. But, everyone agrees, there is not something that could have been actually nothing, where 'actually' (@) is a rigidifying operator that always returns the semantic evaluation to the world of utterance. For even if something there actually is could have failed to be something, the failure could only be counterfactual, since by hypothesis it is not actual. In symbols, BF has this instance:

(2) $\Diamond \exists x \ @ \neg \exists y \ x = y \rightarrow \exists x \ \Diamond @ \neg \exists y \ x = y$

But since the rigidifying effect of @ makes $\Diamond$ redundant in $\Diamond @$, the consequent is equivalent to $\exists x \ @ \neg \exists y \ x = y$, which in turn has the same truth value as $\exists x \ \neg \exists y \ x = y$ because @ makes no difference when not in the scope of another modal operator; but $\exists x \ \neg \exists y \ x = y$ is inconsistent in first-order logic with identity. Thus the consequent of (2) is clearly false, whereas its antecedent is by normal contingentist lights obviously true.

Strictly speaking, (2) is not an instance of BF in the language of Barcan Marcus's original system, which does not contain the @ operator. But that does not matter, because we can achieve the same effect simply by using $@ \neg \exists y \ x = y$ informally to interpret the atomic 1-place predicate F ('is such that it is actually nothing') in this instance of BF:[7]

(3) $\Diamond \exists x \ Fx \rightarrow \exists x \ \Diamond Fx$

For a more colourful interpretation of (3), read F as 'is a child of John F. Kennedy and Marilyn Monroe', assuming that they did not actually have a child. On this reading, the antecedent is clearly true; they could have had a child. But who or what is there to verify the consequent, by being something that is not, but could have been, their child? Contingentists can appeal to the plausible doctrine of the essentiality of origins to argue that anyone who is not actually their child could not have been their child.[8] Although some actual atoms could have *constituted* their child, the mereological sum of those atoms—assuming that there is such a thing—could not have been *identical* with a child of theirs. People but not mereological sums of atoms continually change their atomic composition. Contingentists need not be impressed by the efforts of some metaphysicians to insist that composition is identity. Thus they can insist that this reading falsifies the consequent of (3).

---

[7] Assuming that Fx entails $\exists y \ x = y$ does not harm the example.
[8] See Kripke 1980, pp. 110–15.

Contingentists can use simpler examples against Barcan Marcus's original axiom schema (1), and therefore against full BF. For instance, they can substitute the open formula $x=y$ for A:

(4) $\Box(\Diamond\exists x\, x=y \rightarrow \exists x\, \Diamond\, x=y)$

As value of the variable y, assign any ordinary material object: say, the mountain K2. Then (4) in effect says that, necessarily, if there could have been K2 then there is something that could have been K2. Contingentists will respond that this scenario is possible: nothing is K2, so nothing even could have been K2, but still there could have been K2. More formally, from the obvious truth $\exists x\, x=y$, they argue to $\Box\Diamond\exists x\, x=y$ by the principle that the actual is necessarily possible, and from there to $\Box\exists x\, \Diamond x=y$ by (4) and standard modal reasoning; but $\Box\exists x\, \Diamond x=y$ is obviously false by normal contingentist lights: it is not necessary for there to be something that could have been K2; for, necessarily, whatever could have been K2 *is* K2, and it is not necessary for there to be K2. Thus (4) is false. One cannot argue directly against instances of simple BF in this specific way.

We know from Chapter 1 how necessitists react to such alleged counter-examples. Take (3) first. When F is read as 'is actually nothing', they reject the antecedent, on the grounds that there could not have been something that is actually nothing. When F is read as 'is a child of John F. Kennedy and Marilyn Monroe', they accept both the antecedent and the consequent, arguing that the latter is verified by a merely possible child, something that is not, but could have been, concrete. In the case of (4), they accept $\Box\exists x\, x=y$ and therefore $\Box\exists x\, \Diamond x=y$ for any value of y. More generally, necessitists accept every instance of BF, on the grounds that if a condition could have been satisfied, it would have been satisfied by something that was necessarily something, and so is actually something; thus there actually is something that satisfies the condition. Indeed, since necessitists attribute universal and necessary force to such reasoning, they accept every instance of full BF, and so every instance of Barcan Marcus's axiom schema (1).

Thus necessitists and contingentists divide over 'the Barcan formula'. However, her original 1946 article contains no hint of this metaphysical dispute. Indeed, it leaves the interpretation of the modal operators unspecified. In that sense, it is obviously anachronistic to discuss the import of Barcan Marcus's 1946 article in such metaphysical terms. But innovators are not always best placed to assess the significance of their innovations.

2.2 The Converse Barcan Formula

Barcan Marcus proves the converse of her special axiom schema (1) in her system, without appeal to (1) itself:[9]

(5) $\Box(\exists v \Diamond A \to \Diamond \exists v\, A)$

In English, an instance of (5) says that necessarily, if there is something that could have satisfied a condition, then there could have been something that satisfied the condition. The main idea of the proof is simple. By her quantifier rules (formulated in terms of strict implication) it is provable that A strictly implies $\exists v\, A$. Hence, by the rule that if it is provable that A strictly implies B then it is provable $\Diamond A$ strictly implies $\Diamond B$, it is provable that $\Diamond A$ strictly implies $\Diamond \exists v\, A$. Thence one obtains (5) by the rule that if it is provable that C strictly implies D and the variable v is not free in D then it is provable that $\exists v\, C$ strictly implies D (any witness for C will do for D, which does not depend on v).

As with (1), Barcan Marcus's theorem entails its unnecessitated variant. The latter has come to be called 'the converse Barcan formula':

CBF $\exists v \Diamond A \to \Diamond \exists v\, A$

Like BF, CBF is not really a single formula of the object language, but rather a schema with infinitely many formulas as its instances. Of course we can derive a logical equivalent of CBF by contraposing it and using the duality of 'possibly' with 'necessarily' and of 'some' with 'every':

CBF' $\Box \forall v\, A \to \forall v\, \Box A$

In English: if necessarily everything satisfies a condition, then everything necessarily satisfies the condition. On standard assumptions, CBF is a valid schema if and only if CBF' is a valid schema.

Let *full CBF* be the schema whose instances are all modal closures of instances of CBF. Thus all instances of (5) are instances of full CBF. As before, not all instances of the full schema are theorems of the 1946 system. In particular, necessitations of instances of (5) are underivable. As before, this is generally considered an incidental defect of the system. In more promising candidates for a quantified logic of metaphysical modality, all instances of

---

[9] Barcan 1946a, p. 7.

CBF are derivable only if all instances of full CBF are derivable. However, we still distinguish CBF from full CBF, since in principle a special characteristic of the actual world might make all instances of CBF true without making all instances of full CBF true, if our world but not others contained nothing but necessary beings (ontological minimality). In practice, the actual world shows no sign of being special in that way, just as it shows no sign of being special with respect to BF.

Contingentists reject CBF, and a fortiori (5) and full CBF, if $\exists$ is read as an unrestricted individual quantifier and $\lozenge$ as an operator for metaphysical possibility. Their most straightforward argument is by substituting $\neg\exists y\ x=y$ ('x is nothing') for A:

$$(6) \qquad \exists x\ \lozenge\neg\exists y\ x=y \rightarrow \lozenge\exists x\ \neg\exists y\ x=y$$

For typical contingentists, any ordinary material object verifies the antecedent: it is something that could have been nothing. But the consequent of (6) is uncontroversially false. For $\exists x\ \neg\exists y\ x=y$ ('Something is nothing') is inconsistent in standard non-modal first-order logic with identity, and therefore impossible. Indeed, by denying its consequent and applying modus tollens one can derive from (6) the necessity of being:

$$(7) \qquad \forall x\ \square\exists y\ x=y$$

This is just the necessitist claim that everything is necessarily something. Furthermore, by working with full CBF or (5) in place of CBF, and the necessary impossibility of $\exists x\ \neg\exists y\ x=y$ in place of its simple impossibility, one derives the stronger necessitist claim that necessarily everything is necessarily something, the necessary necessity of being:

$$\text{NNE} \qquad \square\forall x\ \square\exists y\ x=y$$

Thus, even independently of her special axiom schema (1), Barcan Marcus's 1946 system is necessitist in spirit, if anachronistically interpreted in metaphysical terms. Strictly speaking, NNE is not a formula of her language, which lacks a dedicated identity predicate, but of course we can still interpret one of her 2-place predicate variables as meaning identity.

The challenge to contingentists is to identify a fallacy in Barcan Marcus's proof of the relevant instance of (5). They have a natural line. Her proof involves the claim that $\neg\exists y\ x=y$ strictly implies $\exists x\ \neg\exists y\ x=y$, in other words:

$$(8) \qquad \square(\neg\exists y\ x=y \rightarrow \exists x\ \neg\exists y\ x=y)$$

The assertion of this open formula is presumably to be understood as the implicit assertion of a universal generalization:

(9) $\forall x\ \Box(\neg\exists y\ x{=}y \to \exists x\ \neg\exists y\ x{=}y)$

But contingentists will reject (9), and therefore (8), on the grounds that if Kanchenjunga had been nothing, there would still not have been something that was nothing. They can unproblematically accept the similar formula in which the universal quantifier and the necessity operator are reversed:

(10) $\Box\forall x\ (\neg\exists y\ x{=}y \to \exists x\ \neg\exists y\ x{=}y)$

For (10) is simply the necessitation of a truth of standard non-modal first-order logic (it does not even depend on the logic of identity). But to obtain (9) from (10) one needs an instance of CBF′, which is tantamount to what one was supposed to be proving.[10]

As we have seen, contingentists cannot accept (8) as a theorem, where (8) is the necessitation of (11): they can accept the rule of necessitation only by rejecting as a theorem the formula (8) necessitates:

(11) $\neg\exists y\ x{=}y \to \exists x\ \neg\exists y\ x{=}y$

Thus a contingentist must either reject (11) as a theorem, or reject the rule of necessitation, which leads from the theoremhood of (11) to the theoremhood of (8). Let us consider each option in turn.

First, suppose that the contingentist rejects (11) as a theorem. But (11) is a theorem of standard non-modal first-order logic. It is simply an instance of the principle of 'existential generalization', $A \to \exists v\ A$. Thus the contingentist is under pressure to adopt some form of 'free logic', in which that principle is not unrestrictedly valid. The contingentist is under the same pressure to reject the principle of 'universal instantiation', $\forall v\ A \to A$, for the duality of the quantifiers makes the two principles equivalent. Instead, the contingentist may accept restricted (but 'free'!) variants on the classical rules, such as these for the universal quantifier:

FUI $\vdash \forall v\ A \to (Et \to A[t/v])$

FUG   If $\vdash A \to (Ev \to C)$ and v is not free in A then $\vdash A \to \forall v\ C$

---

[10] This contingentist line is taken from Kripke 1963, although he discusses a slightly different form of the proof. The invalid axiom of Barcan Marcus's system on this view is one according to which $\forall v\ A$ strictly implies A.

Here ⊢ stands for theoremhood, v is any variable, t is any term free for v in A, $A[t/v]$ is the result of substituting t for all free occurrences of v in A and Et is equivalent to $\exists x\ t=x$ (where t and x are distinct terms). FUI and FUG are the restrictions of classical 'unfree' rules by the 'existence' predicate E.[11]

Alternatively, suppose that the contingentist accepts (11) as a theorem, but not (8), and so rejects the rule of necessitation.[12] Since $\exists x\ \neg\exists y\ x=y$ is uncontroversially inconsistent even in free logic, we can simplify the example. On this suggestion, the contingentist accepts (12) but not (13) as a theorem:

(12) $\exists y\ x=y$

(13) $\Box\exists y\ x=y$

Once necessitation is restricted, a contingentist can endorse all non-modal theorems of classical 'unfree' first-order logic.

Since those putative failures of necessitation all involve open formulas such as (11) and (12), a contingentist might take them lightly, on the grounds that open formulas lack fixed interpretations and so serve a merely instrumental role in the proof theory and semantics. Indeed, Kripke axiomatized quantified modal logic with only closed formulas as theorems, to avoid failures of necessitation.[13] In his system, only (10) is asserted; (8), (9), (11), (12), and (13) are not.

However, a similar problem arises for formulas with proper names in place of free variables. Consider (14) and (15) instead of (12) and (13) respectively:

(14) $\exists y\ k=y$

(15) $\Box\exists y\ k=y$

If k names K2, (14) says that K2 is something, (15) that it is necessarily something. Contingentists will regard (15) as false on this interpretation, and

---

[11] For systems of modal free logic see Garson 1984/2001; early work in the area includes Thomason 1970. The non-modal principles of first-order logic to which appeal was made on behalf of the contingentist earlier in the chapter are derivable even in free logics. In practice, the axiomatizations of such 'free' modal logics are often quite complicated; see for example Hughes and Cresswell 1996, p. 293.

[12] The proposal to restrict the rule of necessitation in view of such cases goes back to Prior 1957, p. 50; see Adams 1981, Deutsch 1990, Menzel 1991, and Wiggins 1994 for more discussion.

[13] See Kripke 1963; his axiomatization is corrected by Fine 1983. For a recent treatment see Hughes and Cresswell 1996, pp. 304–9.

reject it as a theorem. Like (12), (14) is a non-modal theorem of classical unfree first-order logic. Thus contingentists will either reject (14) as a theorem, which is to adopt a free logic even for the non-modal fragment of the language, or accept (14) as a theorem but restrict the rule of necessitation. If they hold the closure of validity under necessitation fixed, they may regard (14) as a counterexample to the validity of unfree logic; if they hold the validity of (14) fixed, they may regard the step from (14) to (15) as a counterexample to the closure of validity under necessitation. Kripke avoids the issue only by excluding proper names and other closed singular terms from his formal language. Since such closed singular terms are perfectly legitimate, even on Kripke's own views in the philosophy of language, their exclusion is wholly artificial.

Once closed singular terms are included in the language, non-modal classical 'unfree' logic and necessitation enable us to prove of any named or demonstrated individual that it has necessary being. That does not quite take us all the way to NNE, the necessary necessity of being, for whatever we name or demonstrate is presumably something, so we cannot directly apply arguments of the (14)–(15) form to show that if there had been something that actually is not, it would have had necessary being. However, that provides no positive support for the bizarre view that (7) is contingently true, that everything has necessary being but it could have been otherwise. After all, if there had been something that actually is not, an argument of the (14)–(15) form could then have been formulated to show that it had necessary being.

Another loophole concerns actual objects that for some reason cannot be named or demonstrated. We cannot directly apply arguments of the (14)–(15) form to show that they have necessary being.[14] Might we fall short even of (7), because although all named or demonstrated objects have necessary being, some unnamed and undemonstrated objects have merely contingent being? That view too seems hopelessly unmotivated. Anything unnamed and undemonstrated in natural languages still has a name in some abstract language, so there is an abstract argument of the (14)–(15) form for its necessary being. The impossibility is only in mastering such a language by getting into a referential relation to the object. But once we know that

---

[14] See Williamson 2007, pp. 16–17, on such essentially elusive objects. If there is exactly one essentially elusive object, we can use the definite description 'the essentially elusive object' to fix reference to it. Presumably, therefore, there is at least one essentially elusive object only if there is more than one.

there always are such abstract arguments, formulating them ourselves becomes unnecessary.

In practice, therefore, non-modal classical logic and necessitation force NNE. Thus contingentists must choose: either adopt free logic even for the non-modal fragment of their language or restrict necessitation (perhaps both).

A contingentist who rejects free logic for the non-modal fragment will deny that all logical truths are necessary truths, on the basis of counter-examples of the form (14). In postulating contingent logical truths, the contingentist may invoke Tarski's classic model-theoretic account of logical truth. Tarski defines logical truth in purely non-modal terms: roughly, a sentence is logically true if and only if it is true under every reinterpretation of its non-logical atomic constituents. For purposes of logical theory, the absence of modal and epistemological entanglements from the definition has great methodological advantages, since it enables metalogical reasoning to be subject to mathematical standards of rigour.[15] It is not ad hoc for contingentists to maintain both that (14) is logically true, because true on each reinterpretation of its only non-logical atomic constituent, the constant k, since every such interpretation of k assigns it a referent over which the unrestricted quantifier $\exists y$ ranges, and that (15) is not logically true, because false on a reinterpretation of k that assigns it a contingent being as referent. If open formulas are allowed, similar remarks apply to them, since the contingentist can require every variable to be assigned a value, which may be a contingent being.

Even if a contingentist rejects necessitation in order to retain classical unfree logic for non-modal formulas, their logic for the whole language will in a sense still be free. For any reasonable system of modal logic will have a central core that is closed under necessitation. The core consists of every formula every finitely iterated necessitation of which is a theorem. Although all the non-modal theorems together form an unfree logic, the core non-modal theorems constitute a free logic, since they exclude formulas such as (12) and (14). Thus, whether or not contingentists retain the rule of necessitation, their system overall has aspects of a free modal logic.[16] This

---

[15] Tarski 1936 is his original account. Etchemendy 1990 criticizes it for its lack of something like a modal element. Williamson 2003a employs a Tarskian account of logical consequence in the context of an unrestricted reading of the quantifiers.

[16] Of course there are many varieties of free logic, some of which will be distinguished later in the book. The present remarks do not depend on exactly which free logic the contingentist selects. For an up-to-date introduction to free logic see Priest 2008, pp. 290–307.

is an early indication that contingentism has costs in logical complexity and weakness. The restrictions on instantiation (for ∀) and generalization (for ∃) complicate quantificational reasoning, at least in modal contexts, and their intended effect is a loss of logical power. Since both simplicity and strength are virtues in a theory, judged by normal scientific standards, these restrictions in contingentist logic should give one pause. Of course, contingentists insist that the price is worth paying.

Necessitists, by contrast, can accept a Barcan-style proof of any instance of full CBF. Of course, given Kripke's analysis, they cannot expect such a proof to be dialectically effective in dispute with contingentists. But a formal system is not primarily intended as a debating tool. Rather, it codifies in precise form some ways of reasoning, so that each application of them, however complex, can in principle be mechanically recognized as such. Whether those ways of reasoning really preserve truth from premises to conclusion on an intended interpretation is another matter. Those who accept both classical unfree logic and a modal logic with the rule of necessitation can genuinely derive any instance of full CBF from them. They may be necessitists, or alternatively people whose first loyalty is neither to necessitism nor to contingentism, but instead to some simple logical principles from which necessitism turns out to be derivable. For them, persuading others to adopt their principles need not be an urgent priority.

BF, unlike CBF, is independent of the other axioms and rules of the 1946 Barcan system. However, this asymmetry turned out to depend on the weakness of the underlying propositional modal logic. In 1956, Prior published a proof that BF is derivable in a quantified modal logic based on S5, the natural propositional modal logic for metaphysical modality on the assumption that modal status is not itself contingent: whatever is possible is necessarily possible, and whatever is necessary is necessarily necessary. Lemmon later extended the proof to the much weaker propositional modal logic KB, whose characteristic axiom just says that whatever is so is necessarily possible.[17] B, unlike S5, lacks even the standard T axiom that whatever is so is possible (or equivalently, that whatever is necessary is so). The B axiom is also derivable in S5, since whatever is so is possible (by the T axiom) and therefore necessarily possible (by the S5 axiom). Very few metaphysicians

---

[17] Prior 1956 gives the proof for S5. The proof of the corresponding result for KB is attributed to E.J. Lemmon in Prior 1967, p. 146; one is also given in Føllesdal's 1961 thesis. See Hughes and Cresswell 1996, p. 247, and Føllesdal 2004, p. 66, for details.

have rejected the B axiom for metaphysical modality. If something is so, how could it have been metaphysically impossible? Indeed, most metaphysicians accept S5 as the propositional modal logic of metaphysical modality, but in any case the most prominent objections to S5 in that role target the principle that whatever is necessary is necessarily necessary rather than the B principle.[18]

Naturally, the proofs of BF in KB and S5 rely on principles of quantified modal logic acceptable to a necessitist but not to a contingentist. They reinforce the moral that the contingentist will use some form of free modal logic, while the necessitist retains a more classical form of quantified modal logic. In the setting of the contingentist's free modal logic, the proofs can be adapted to show just that each of full BF, full CBF, and full NNE is equivalent to each of the others. They simply become alternative formulations of necessitism.[19]

---

[18] See, for example, Salmon 1989. Salmon also argues for scepticism about the logical validity of the B principle, but does not argue that it has false instances (1989, pp. 25–9). The argument against B in Dummett 1983, involving a natural kind term, is convincingly answered by Reimer 1997 and Rumfitt 2010, pp. 60–4. The related argument against B in Stephanou 2000, involving a proper name, is answered by Gregory 2001; see also Hayaki 2005.

[19] Here is a proof sketch, which can be carried out in a standard modal free logic with an 'existence predicate' E, such as the one in Hughes and Cresswell 1996, p. 293. The underlying propositional modal logic has all truth-functional tautologies and formulas of the forms $\Box(A \to B) \to (\Box A \to \Box B)$ and $A \to \Box \Diamond A$ (B) as axioms and modus ponens and necessitation as rules of proof (the latter is legitimate because all the axioms are necessary on a standard contingentist view). The axioms for identity are $\forall v\ v{=}v$ (reflexivity; universally quantified in order not to imply that an object would have been self-identical even if it had lacked being) and all instances of $u{=}v \to (A \to A^*)$, where A^* differs from A only in having free occurrences of u where A has free occurrences of v or vice versa (Leibniz's Law). We establish a circle of implications: (i) from full CBF to full NNE; (ii) from full NNE to full BF; (iii) from full BF to full CBF. We sometimes use the name of a schema to denote a suitable instance of it.

(i) By the rules for the quantifier and E, $\vdash \forall v\ Ev$; by the rule of necessitation, $\vdash \Box \forall v\ Ev$; thus $\vdash$ CBF $\to \forall v\ \Box Ev$, so $\vdash \Box$CBF $\to \Box \forall v\ \Box Ev$. Arbitrary modal closures of instances of NNE are derived likewise from corresponding instances of full CBF (also for (ii) and (iii)).

(ii) By B, $\vdash \forall v\ \Box A \to \Box \Diamond \forall v\ \Box A$, so $\vdash \forall v\ \Box A \to \Box \forall v\ \Diamond \forall v\ \Box A$ (the inserted quantifier is vacuous); but $\vdash \forall v\ \Box A \to (Ev \to \Box A)$, so $\vdash \forall v\ \Box A \to \Box \forall v\ \Diamond(Ev \to \Box A)$; since $\vdash \Box \forall v\ \Diamond(Ev \to \Box A) \to (\text{NNE} \to \Box \forall v\ \Diamond \Box A)$, $\vdash \text{NNE} \to (\forall v\ \Box A \to \Box \forall v\ \Diamond \Box A)$; by B, $\vdash \Diamond \Box A \to A$, so $\vdash \text{NNE} \to (\forall v\ \Box A \to \Box \forall v\ A)$.

(iii) By Leibniz's Law $\vdash u{=}v \to (\Box(u{=}u \to u{=}u) \to \Box(u{=}u \to u{=}v))$, so $\vdash u{=}v \to \Box(u{=}u \to u{=}v)$, so $\vdash \Diamond \exists u\ u{=}v \to \exists u\ \Box(u{=}u \to u{=}v)$, so $\vdash$ BF $\to (\Diamond \exists u\ u{=}v \to \exists u\ \Diamond \Box(u{=}u \to u{=}v))$, so by B $\vdash$ BF $\to (\Diamond \exists u\ u{=}v \to \exists u\ (u{=}u \to u{=}v))$, so by reflexivity $\vdash$ BF $\to (\Diamond \exists u\ u{=}v \to \exists u\ u{=}v)$, or equivalently $\vdash$ BF $\to (\Diamond Ev \to Ev)$, so $\vdash \Box$BF $\to (\Box \Diamond Ev \to \Box Ev)$, so by B $\vdash \forall v\ \Box$BF $\to \forall v\ (Ev \to \Box Ev)$; but $\vdash \forall v\ A \to (Ev \to A)$, so $\vdash \Box \forall v\ A \to (\Box Ev \to \Box A)$, so $\vdash \Box \forall v\ A \to \forall v\ (\Box Ev \to \Box A)$. Hence $\vdash \forall v\ \Box$BF $\to (\Box \forall v\ A \to \forall v\ (Ev \to \Box A))$; but $\vdash \forall v\ Ev$, so $\vdash \forall v\ \Box$BF $\to (\Box \forall v\ A \to \forall v\ \Box A)$.

2.3 Ibn-Sina

Putting (1) and (5) together, Barcan Marcus obtained the necessary equivalence of 'something possibly' and 'possibly something':

(16) $\Box(\Diamond \exists v\, A \leftrightarrow \exists v\, \Diamond A)$

Necessarily, a condition could have been satisfied if and only if there is something that could have satisfied it.

It is not widely known that an equivalence similar to (16) was first proposed more than nine centuries before Barcan Marcus's 1946 paper. It occurs in the work of the great Persian philosopher and polymath Ibn-Sina (Avicenna, 980–1037). In discussing the interaction of quantification and modality, he wrote:[20]

> But to say that *some people possibly are not writers* is modally the same as saying that *possibly some people are not writers*, and although one implies the other the meaning of the one may be opposite to the other.

Thus he acknowledges the difference in meaning made by the difference in order between the two sentences, while nevertheless apparently maintaining their necessary equivalence. The contentious metaphysical implications are not easy to spot in his example. However, his quantification is restricted to people, which causes trouble. Presumably, there could have been no people, in which case *possibly some people are not writers* would still have been true, while *some people possibly are not writers* would have been false. Derestricting the quantifiers removes that blemish. In any case, we may call the unnecessitated biconditional schema 'Ibn-Sina's principle':

ISP $\Diamond \exists v\, A \leftrightarrow \exists v\, \Diamond A$

Similarly, let *full ISP* be the schema whose instances are all modal closures of instances of ISP. Of course, Barcan Marcus came on the principle independently of Ibn-Sina, and in constructing a formal system of first-order quantified modal logic, which Ibn-Sina did not have. Still, we should give credit where it is due. We leave to others the hard work of making sense of this tantalizing glimpse in its historical and systematic context.[21]

[20] I owe both the information and the translation to Zia Movahed (personal communication); see Movahed 2006. The text is from *Kitab al-Ibara*, the third volume of his work *al-Shifa*, known in Latin as *Sufficientia* (Ibn-Sina 1970, p. 116).

[21] Prior (1957, pp. 115–16) identifies an endorsement of ISP in Peirce 1901. Peirce speaks of the range of possibility as a 'range of ignorance'.

2.4 Carnap

When BF and CBF first appeared as formal schemata, they were not linked to the theses of necessitism and contingentism, or to any other metaphysical issue. Barcan Marcus did not discuss their interpretation in her original paper. The semantic question was discussed by Rudolf Carnap in 'Modalities and Quantification' in the next issue of *The Journal of Symbolic Logic*, and in more detail in *Meaning and Necessity*, published the following year; although neither his article nor his book cited Barcan Marcus's work. Carnap provided the first formal semantics for quantified modal logic, well ahead of his time in systematicity and rigour, and applied it to BF and CBF. It will repay our study.

Naturally, Carnap did not interpret his 'necessity' operator in terms of the now current notion of metaphysical necessity. Rather, he spoke of 'logical necessity', which he assimilated to logical truth by the principle that the sentence $\Box A$ is true if and only if the sentence A is L-true.[22] L-truth is Carnap's explication of logical truth as analyticity. For an informal condition on the adequacy of his explication, he stipulated that a sentence should count as L-true in a semantical system S if and only if the sentence 'is true in S in such a way that its truth can be established on the basis of the semantical rules of the system S alone, without any reference to (extra-linguistic) facts'.[23] As Carnap recognized, such a criterion of analyticity is not immediately applicable to an open formula, so special measures are needed to interpret formulas like $\forall x\, \Box Fx$ in which a variable inside the scope of a modal operator is bound by a quantifier outside. The treatment of such formulas is obviously crucial for the status of BF and CBF. Quine had already raised the issue in 1943; reviewing Quine's article soon afterward, Alonzo Church proposed meeting Quine's challenge with an intensional interpretation of quantification related to but distinct from the one Carnap was to adopt.[24] This was the context in which Carnap discussed what are here called BF and CBF, or rather ISP, for he treated it as a single equivalence.

At first sight, Carnap's semantic framework for modal logic looks very similar to contemporary possible worlds semantics. He evaluates sentences

---

[22] Carnap 1947, p. 174; see also Carnap 1946, p. 34. Cocchiarella and Freund 2008, pp. 64–5, interpret Bergmann 1960 as objecting to this as a definition of $\Box$ on the grounds that it is circular when A itself contains occurrences of $\Box$, and respond that the circularity can be removed by an inductive definition.

[23] Carnap 1947, p. 10.

[24] See Quine 1943 and Church 1943, both discussed in Carnap 1947, pp. 137–8.

as holding or not holding in *state-descriptions*, which he likens to Leibniz's possible worlds and Wittgenstein's possible states of affairs. For each atomic sentence A, a state-description contains exactly one of A and $\neg A$, and no other sentences. A sentence is L-true if and only if it holds in all state-descriptions. Carnap's definition of holding proceeds by recursion on the structure of formulas. The clauses for truth-functional operators are as expected: $A \,\&\, B$ holds in S if and only if A holds in S and B holds in S; $\neg A$ holds in S if and only if A does not hold in S, and so on. The modal operators are treated like quantifiers over state-descriptions: $\Box A$ holds in S if and only if A holds in every state-description, and $\Diamond A$ holds in S if and only if A holds in some state-description. Since the modal operators range over the fixed set of state-descriptions, with no restriction to those which are 'accessible' from the current point of evaluation, Carnap's semantics validates the system S5. In particular, all instances of its characteristic principles $\Diamond A \rightarrow \Box \Diamond A$, $\Box A \rightarrow \Box\Box A$ and $\Box A \rightarrow A$ are L-true.

Carnap's treatment of quantification in modal contexts is simpler in the 1946 article than in *Meaning and Necessity*. It is best to start with the former. The 1946 treatment is straightforwardly substitutional. Thus $\forall v\, A$ holds in a state-description S if and only if every substitution instance of A is true in S, and $\exists v\, A$ holds in S if and only if some substitution instance of A holds in S.[25] Here a substitution instance of A is the result of uniformly substituting an individual constant, a closed atomic singular term, for all free occurrences of v in A. The implied response to Quine's challenge to interpret quantification into modal contexts is direct: since open formulas play no role in the semantics, formulas of the forms $\Box A$ and $\Diamond A$ are evaluated only when A is closed, and quantified modal sentences are as fully interpreted as unquantified ones. For example, consider the closed formula $\exists x\, \Box Fx$ ('Something is necessarily F'), with quantification into a modal context, for a monadic atomic predicate F. By Carnap's semantics, it is true in a state-description S if and only if some closed formula $\Box Fa$ is true in S, so Fa is true in every state-description. Since F is atomic, Fa is false in some state-description, so $\exists x\, \Box Fx$ is false in every state-description. The semantic evaluation simply bypasses the open formula $\Box Fx$.

---

[25] The semantics is given at Carnap 1946, p. 50. However, even there it is explicitly treated as a simplification of the semantics to be given in Carnap 1947. See also Carnap 1947, p. 183, n. 3, for a comparison of the two semantic theories.

As Carnap recognized, his semantics validates BF, CBF, and ISP. For if $\Diamond \exists v\, A$ holds in S, then $\exists v\, A$ holds in some state-description S*, so some substitution instance $A*$ of A holds in S*, so $\Diamond A*$ holds in S; but $\Diamond A*$ is a substitution instance of $\Diamond A$, so $\exists v\, \Diamond A$ holds in S; thus every instance of BF is L-true. Conversely, if $\exists v\, \Diamond A$ holds in S, then some substitution instance $\Diamond A*$ of $\Diamond A$ holds in S, so $A*$ holds in some state-description S*; but $A*$ is a substitution instance of A, so $\exists v\, A$ holds in S*, so $\Diamond \exists v\, A$ holds in S; thus every instance of CBF is L-true. Informally, an 'existential' generalization is equated with the infinite disjunction of its instances over a fixed substitution class, and a disjunction of possibilities is equivalent to the possibility of the disjunction. Similarly, a universal generalization is equated with the infinite conjunction of its instances over the same substitution class, and a conjunction of necessities is equivalent to the necessity of the conjunction.[26]

In effect, Carnap's project is to take the semantics of a first-order non-modal language and use its resources to build the semantics of the corresponding first-order modal language, without invoking anything extraneous. This is a natural approach, given his semantic conception of modality. The semantics of the non-modal language determines a unique set of state-descriptions. Unsurprisingly, he lacks the contemporary conception of modality as a metaphysical dimension of how things are, to be described in the language rather than constituted by it.

This difference in underlying outlook has further technical ramifications in Carnap's semantics. His state-descriptions are linguistic constructs, not metaphysical postulates. They are just those sets of sentences containing each closed atomic sentence or its negation (and not both), and no other sentences. No metaphysical criterion of possibility is applied to weed out state-descriptions containing formalizations of sentences like 'Felix is a dog' (where Felix is in fact a cat), for example, which are now widely regarded as stating impossibilities. Carnap's criterion of possibility is purely logical.

Naturally, an atomic sentence A holds in a state-description S if and only if A belongs to S. However, identity sentences are given special treatment. They are not classified as atomic for purposes of the definition of a state-description. Rather, $a=a$ holds in every state-description, while $a=b$ holds in no state-description if a and b are distinct individual constants. Thus identities are settled by the intra-linguistic criterion of the identity of the terms

---

[26] See Carnap 1946, pp. 37 and 54.

themselves, and therefore count as either logically true or logically false, rather than being left open to be stipulated as true by some state-descriptions and as false by others. The background assumption is not just that distinct individual constants do in fact designate distinct individuals, but that the language has been so constructed that the meanings of distinct individual constants semantically guarantee that they designate distinct individuals: as it were, the individual constants designate in a semantically perspicuous way.

The upshot of Carnap's definitions is that whether a sentence is L-true depends purely on intra-linguistic matters. The semantic resources needed to characterize the non-modal language already suffice to characterize the modal language too. In this respect, his account is much more informative than contemporary possible worlds model theories. The latter permit every non-empty set, whatever its members, to play the role of the set of worlds in some models. A world is treated as a mere point of evaluation, whose nature does not constrain which atomic formulas may hold at it in a model. A model may contain any set of such points. A model theory singles out no model as the intended one. It defines what it is for a sentence to be true in a given model, but not what it is for the sentence to be true *simpliciter*. By contrast, Carnap's account determines a unique set of state-descriptions, and specifies which formulas hold in each of them. Given the semantics of the non-modal language, Carnap defines what it is for a sentence of the form $\Diamond A$ or $\Box A$ to be true *simpliciter*, not merely true in a given model.[27]

The most obvious objection to a substitutional account of quantification such as Carnap's is that the substitution class of terms may be too small: some individuals may be denoted by no term in the class. Indeed, that is inevitable if there are uncountably many individuals—as there are uncountably many

---

[27] It is therefore incorrect to speak of 'Carnapian model theory', as John Burgess does in arguing that Carnap provides no semantics 'in the sense of a philosophical account of meaning' for quantified modal logic (Burgess 2008, p. 216). Burgess is right that a mathematical model theory such as Kripke's is no semantics in that sense, but the semantic theories in Carnap 1946 and 1947 are not mere model theories. Of course, the semantics of the non-modal language must do more than define truth in a state-description in order to determine conditions for the simple (i.e. not relative to a state-description) truth of an atomic sentence: in effect, it must specify the condition for a state-description to be simply true. But that condition depends only on the semantics of the non-modal sentences that constitute state-descriptions, and so is no particular problem for the semantics of quantified modal logic (see Carnap 1947, pp. 5–6, for an illustrative recursive definition of simple truth for a non-modal language). One can also show that any sentence in which atomic formulas occur only within the scope of modal operators is either L-true or L-false on both versions of Carnap's theory, and so is (simply) true if and only if L-true; thus determining the L-truth conditions of such sentences suffices for determining their truth conditions.

real numbers—and all expressions of the language are finitely constituted from a finite lexicon, since then the substitution class contains only countably many terms. If some individual is denoted by no individual constant, Carnap's semantic clauses are still well defined, but characterize meanings of little interest. Thus his semantic framework is at best of very limited applicability.

In *Meaning and Necessity*, Carnap develops a more sophisticated treatment of quantification in modal contexts. Unfortunately, it is still vulnerable to the main objection to a substitutional account of quantification, even though it is not itself fully substitutional. The reason is that state-descriptions are defined as the same linguistic constructs as before, in line with Carnap's linguistic conception of logical necessity. In effect, since a state-description provides information only about named individuals, a generalization can be evaluated at it only in terms of the behaviour of those named individuals. Any unnamed object drops out as irrelevant. Carnap explicitly assumes a one-one correspondence between individuals and individual constants, even though the semantics of the language cannot by itself guarantee that there is such a correspondence.[28] Thus what Carnap provides is a semantic treatment of a sort of quantification that is not semantically equivalent— and presumably not even materially equivalent—to the most natural sort of quantification. Nevertheless, despite this major drawback, Carnap's 1947 account merits discussion here in its own right, because he applies a systematic distinction between extension and intension to the semantics of quantification in a seemingly very natural way which has continued to exert influence, despite being marginalized by later developments.

The new account is much closer in overall form than the old to a contemporary treatment of quantification in modal contexts. Carnap relativizes the evaluation of formulas to assignments of values to variables. Thus $\forall v\, A$ holds in a state-description S on an assignment $\underline{a}$ if and only if A holds in S on every v-variant of $\underline{a}$, where a v-variant of $\underline{a}$ is any assignment differing from $\underline{a}$ at most over v. Similarly, $\exists v\, A$ holds in S on $\underline{a}$ if and only if A holds in S on some v-variant of $\underline{a}$. The other clauses remain as before, except that both their right-hand and left-hand sides are relativized to the same assignment.[29]

---

[28] Carnap 1947, p. 181.

[29] The semantics is given at Carnap 1947, pp. 182–4. Carnap later took further steps towards a contemporary model-theoretic perspective on the semantics of modal logic, with non-linguistic entities in place of constants as values of variables and models in place of state-descriptions; see Carnap 1963a, p. 891, n. 10.

The new semantics validates the system S5, for the same reason as before. Moreover, since the explicit quantifiers range over a fixed set of values, it still validates BF, CBF, and ISP, as Carnap shows. For if $\lozenge \exists v\, A$ holds in S on $\underline{a}$, then $\exists v\, A$ holds in some state-description S* on $\underline{a}$, so A holds in S* on some v-variant $\underline{a}*$ of $\underline{a}$, so $\lozenge A$ holds in S on $\underline{a}*$, so $\exists v\, \lozenge A$ holds in S on $\underline{a}$; thus every instance of BF is L-true. Conversely, if $\exists v\, \lozenge A$ holds in S on $\underline{a}$, then $\lozenge A$ holds in S on some v-variant $\underline{a}*$ of $\underline{a}$, so A holds in some state-description S* on $\underline{a}*$, so $\exists v\, A$ holds in S* on $\underline{a}$, so $\lozenge \exists v\, A$ holds in S on $\underline{a}$; thus every instance of CBF is L-true.[30] That is virtually the same argument as before, in a new guise.

The difference between Carnap's new semantics and a contemporary treatment emerges in his account of assignments. The linguistic nature of state-descriptions motivates a linguistic nature for the values of variables too. Given an assignment $\underline{a}$, how do we evaluate an open atomic formula such as Fv in a state-description S, which consists only of closed atomic sentences or their negations? The value $\underline{a}(v)$ of the variable v must in effect deliver some individual constant a in S, so that Fv holds in S on $\underline{a}$ if and only if the closed sentence Fa belongs to S. Carnap's semantic framework embodies the method of extension and intension: the intension of an expression e is a function mapping each state-description S to the extension of e in S. Since an individual constant serves as the extension of an individual variable in a state-description on an assignment—the individual it designates plays no official role in the semantics—the intension of an individual variable on an assignment is a function from state-descriptions to individual constants. Carnap calls such functions *individual concepts*. Although he allows us to think of them informally as functions from states of the world to individuals, he is clear that their official nature is linguistic. The value $\underline{a}(v)$ of a variable v on an assignment $\underline{a}$ maps a state-description S to the individual constant $\underline{a}(v)(S)$. Thus an atomic formula A holds in S on $\underline{a}$ if and only if the result of replacing each variable v in A by $\underline{a}(v)(S)$ is in S. Whether an atomic formula holds in a state-description on an assignment is a purely formal matter. For closed atomic sentences, the new account is equivalent to the old.

The special treatment of identity formulas is generalized in the same way. If t_1 and t_2 are individual variables or constants, $t_1 = t_2$ holds in a state-description S on an assignment $\underline{a}$ if and only if $\underline{a}^+(t_1)(S)$ is the same individual constant as

---

[30] See Carnap 1947, pp. 178–9 and 186.

$\underline{a}^+(t_2)$(S), where $\underline{a}^+(t)$(S) is $\underline{a}(t)$(S) if t is a variable and t itself if t is an individual constant. Thus extensional coincidence (Carnap's 'equivalence') between the variables x and y in S under $\underline{a}$ suffices for $x=y$ to hold in S under $\underline{a}$; intensional coincidence (Carnap's 'L-equivalence') is not necessary. For identity sentences between individual constants, the new account is equivalent to the old; all such sentences are either L-true or L-false.

Since the new semantics reduces the condition for an open atomic or identity formula to hold in a state-description on an assignment to the condition for a corresponding closed sentence to hold in the state-description, it is just as dependent as the old semantics for its interest on the assumption that every individual is designated by some individual constant.

An example will illustrate the difference between the two versions of Carnap's theory:

(17) $\exists x \, (\neg a=x \,\&\, \Diamond a=x)$

Here a is an individual constant. On the 1946 treatment, (17) is L-false. For $\neg a=a \,\&\, \Diamond a=a$ holds in no state-description, because $a=a$ holds in every state-description, while for any individual constant b other than a, $\neg a=b \,\&\, \Diamond a=b$ likewise holds in no state-description, because $a=b$ holds in no state-description. Thus no substitution instance of $\neg a=x \,\&\, \Diamond a=x$ holds in any state-description. On the 1947 treatment, (17) is L-true whenever the language contains at least two individual constants, a and b, and at least one atomic predicate (excluding =), so there are at least two state-descriptions (differing in which atomic formulas they contain). For let S be any state-description. Let S* be any state-description other than S, and $\underline{a}$ any assignment such that $\underline{a}(x)$(S) is b and $\underline{a}(x)$(S*) is a. Then $a=x$ holds in S* but not in S on $\underline{a}$, so $\neg a=x \,\&\, \Diamond a=x$ holds in S on $\underline{a}$, so (17) holds in S on any assignment. The underlying difference is that the substitution of constants for variables is world-independent in 1946 and world-dependent in 1947.

Although two individual concepts can contingently coincide in extension, Carnap's account forbids two individual constants to have two such individual concepts as their intensions. He treats the individual constants but not the variables as *rigid*, in the sense that their intensions deliver the same extension in every state-description. For such terms, coincidence in extension guarantees coincidence in intension, so non-coincidence in intension guarantees non-coincidence in extension. But he does not see this as a necessary condition for terms to be individual constants. Rather, he treats it as a specific feature of the language in question that makes it semantically perspicuous. In Carnap's terminology, the individual constants are assumed to be *L-determinate* designators: informally, a designator is L-determinate in a semantical system S 'if and only if the semantical rules of S alone, without addition of factual knowledge, *give* its extension'. Carnap contrasts *giving* an extension with merely *describing* it by means of a definite description. Giving is supposed to involve a more perspicuous mode of presentation. However, Carnap explicitly rejects the suggestion that genuine proper names are not descriptive, and opts instead for an apparatus of individual expressions of 'standard form', modelled on systems of coordinates. A name of standard form of an object is its canonical name; in a similar spirit, the numerals are sometimes regarded as the canonical names of the natural numbers. Although an individual constant can be introduced by means of a definite description, it will not in general be of standard form.[31] Carnap develops the semantics of a language in which all individual constants are L-determinate because it is a simple case, not because it is the general case. Since the L-determinacy of the individual constants is no general requirement, he does not impose it on the individual variables (relative to an assignment). Their values include both L-determinate and L-indeterminate individual concepts: an individual concept is L-determinate if and only if it has the same extension in every state-description. In explaining the difference between the 1946 and 1947 semantics, he justifies the greater complexity of the latter thus: 'This wider range of values for the individual variables in S_2 seems more adequate'.[32]

Carnap could have formulated a fully substitutional account of quantification with definite descriptions as well as individual constants in the substitution class of closed singular terms.[33] One might thereby hope to simulate by substitutional means the effect of quantification over all individual concepts,

---

[31] See Carnap 1947, pp. 69–81; the quotation is from p. 72. In Carnap's sample language, the individuals are positions; naturally, his reason for selecting positions concerns not their metaphysics but rather the convenience of denoting them by coordinates. Føllesdal, in his 1961 Ph.D. dissertation, argued that Carnap saves his theory of definite descriptions from collapsing modal distinctions only by an ad hoc restriction on the formation rules of the language (reprinted as Føllesdal 1968/1969 and 2004, pp. 67–74). However, Martí 1994 shows that Føllesdal's argument fails even if the restriction is lifted, and Kremer 1997 points out on semantic grounds that no such collapse occurs in Carnap's system. For Quine's similar but more generic argument see n. 35. For a recent technical discussion of Carnap's account of definite descriptions for a modal language see Heylen 2010.

[32] See Carnap 1947, p. 181 for the assumption about L-determinacy and p. 183 for the quotation.

[33] The usual precautions would have to be taken to ensure that quantifiers within the descriptive material did not introduce circularity; see Marcus 1993, p. 84.

whether L-determinate or not. Carnap rejected that alternative because the restriction to individual concepts expressed by some closed term of the language excludes all but a minuscule fraction of the individual concepts. His language contains only countably many terms. But since he envisages it as containing a countable infinity of individual constants and at least one non-logical atomic predicate, it will contain a countable infinity of closed atomic sentences. There will be continuum many state-descriptions, since they are in one-one correspondence with the subsets of the set of closed atomic sentences. There will be an even greater infinity of individual concepts, since for every set of state-descriptions some individual concept maps all and only its members to the individual constant a.[34] The underlying point is that if □ expresses analyticity, then free variables in its scope should be assigned values of a type appropriate for them to be the meanings of closed expressions of the relevant category, but those values need not actually be the meanings of closed expressions in the language.

The effects of what may be described as Carnap's quantification over individual concepts are not limited to validating a sentence like (17), which on a contemporary reading implies the contingency of distinctness.[35] We can explore them by contrasting his view of the relation between pairs of sentences of the form of (18) and (19) with contemporary views:

(18) $\Box \exists x \, A$

(19) $\exists x \, \Box A$

---

[34] Carnap 1947, p. 181. If the language contains only finitely many individual constants and finitely many non-logical atomic predicates, there are only finitely many state-descriptions and individual concepts, so countably many closed descriptive terms may suffice to express all the individual concepts.

[35] The point of the qualification 'what may be described as' is that the phrase 'quantification over individual concepts' does scant justice to Carnap's method of extension and intension. The criticisms of Carnap's account of quantified modal logic in Quine 1961, pp. 152–3, and Quine 1960, pp. 197–8, do not take this aspect of it seriously. They rely on an argument, given in passages from Quine's correspondence quoted in Carnap 1947, pp. 196–7, that expressions in Carnap's quantified modal language can be treated as referring to their intensions in a semantics that no longer bifurcates semantic values into intensions and extensions; thus the quantifiers simply range over individual concepts. Quine correctly points out that this does not solve the problem of interpreting quantified modal logic, because puzzle cases will arise of the form $s=t$ & $\neg \Box s=t$ where s and t refer to the same individual concept. For Carnap, however, the terms s and t must still have distinct intensions in such a case, even if their shared extension is itself an intensional object. On his view, coincidence in intension, not just extension, is always required to support intersubstitutability in modal contexts, irrespective of what sort of entity the extension happens to involve. Thus Quine's objections fail to refute Carnap's claim to have given a workable semantics for quantified modal logic. See also the reply to Quine in Carnap 1947, pp. 197–202, and Martí 1997, Lindström 2001, and Heylen 2010.

On a contemporary reading, an instance of (19) usually makes a much bolder claim than an instance of (18) does, for (18) may be true because different things satisfy the relevant condition in different circumstances, whereas (19) requires that some one thing satisfies the condition in all circumstances. Necessarily, some number is how many planets there are; it does not follow that some number is such that necessarily *it* is how many planets there are. Most contingentists and necessitists agree that (18) does not always entail (19). According to many contingentists, (19) does not always entail (18) either. For example, any human is possibly human, and so by S5 logic is necessarily possibly human. Thus (20) is true:

(20) $\exists x \,\Box\Diamond Hx$

But many contingentists will reject (21):

(21) $\Box\exists x \,\Diamond Hx$

For they argue that since the distinction between humans and non-humans goes to their essences, necessarily whatever could be human *is* human, so (21) falsely implies the impossibility of the total absence of humans. For necessitists, however, the possible total absence of humans does not imply the possible total absence of possible humans. Had you lacked spatial location, you would not have been human, but you would still have been possibly human. More generally, (19) entails (18), according to necessitists. For they endorse classical 'unfree' reasoning even with respect to counterfactual possibilities, so for them $\Box A$ entails (18), hence (19) entails (18) since x is not free in (18).

For Carnap too, (19) entails (18), by a version of the necessitist argument. If $\exists x \,\Box A$ holds in a state-description S on an assignment a, then $\Box A$ holds in S on some v-variant a^* of a, so A holds in every state-description on a^*, so $\exists x A$ holds in every state-description on a, so $\Box\exists x A$ holds in S on a.

Carnap also denies that (18) always entails (19).[36] For example, since (17) is L-true, so is its necessitation:

(22) $\Box\exists x \,(\neg a = x \,\&\, \Diamond a = x)$

But (23) is L-false:

(23) $\exists x \,\Box(\neg a = x \,\&\, \Diamond a = x)$

---

[36] Carnap 1946, p. 56, notes that (19) always entails (18) and that (18) does not always entail (19); see also Carnap 1947, p. 186. The counterexample goes back at least to Stewart Shapiro (Martí 1994, n. 17).

For if (23) holds in a state-description S on an assignment $\underline{a}$, then $\Box(\neg a=x \; \& \; \Diamond a=x)$ holds in S on some ν-variant $\underline{a}^*$ of $\underline{a}$, so $\neg a=x \; \& \; \Diamond a=x$ holds in every state-description on $\underline{a}^*$; consequently, for every state-description S*, a is a distinct constant from $\underline{a}(x)(S^*)$ but, for some state-description S**, a is the same constant as $\underline{a}(x)(S^{**})$, which is a contradiction. However, this example depends on the non-extensionality of $\neg a=x \; \& \; \Diamond a=x$ as a context for the variable x. A formula A is extensional as a context for the variable ν if and only if its truth value depends purely on the extension of ν, not on its intension: more precisely, for every state-description S, assignment $\underline{a}$ and ν-variant $\underline{a}^*$ of $\underline{a}$, if $\underline{a}(\nu)(S)$ is $\underline{a}^*(\nu)(S)$ then A holds in S on $\underline{a}$ if and only if A holds in S on $\underline{a}^*$. In this case, $\neg a=x \; \& \; \Diamond a=x$ is non-extensional as a context for x because if $\underline{a}(x)(S)$ is b, $\underline{a}(x)(S^{**})$ is a and $\underline{a}^*$ is the x-variant of $\underline{a}$ such that $\underline{a}^*(x)(S^*)$ is b for every state-description S*, then although $\underline{a}(x)(S)$ is $\underline{a}^*(x)(S)$, $\neg a=x \; \& \; \Diamond a=x$ holds in S on $\underline{a}$ but not on $\underline{a}^*$.

On Carnap's semantics, (18) entails (19) whenever A is extensional as a context for x. For assume extensionality and suppose that (18) holds in a state-description S on an assignment $\underline{a}$. Then $\exists x \, A$ holds in every state-description on $\underline{a}$, so A holds in every state-description S* on some x-variant $\underline{a}[S^*]$ of $\underline{a}$. Let $\underline{a}^*$ be the x-variant of $\underline{a}$ such that for every state-description S*, $\underline{a}^*(x)(S^*)$ is $\underline{a}[S^*](x)(S^*)$. By extensionality, A holds in every state-description S* on $\underline{a}^*$, so $\Box A$ holds in S on $\underline{a}^*$. But $\underline{a}^*$ is an x-variant of $\underline{a}$, so (19) holds in S on $\underline{a}$, as required.[37] But the informal objections to any entailment from (18) to (19) do not depend on non-extensionality.

Here is an example. Let F be an atomic monadic predicate. When the empty domain is excluded, (24) is a truth of first-order logic:

(24) $\exists x \, (\exists y \, Fy \rightarrow Fx)$

Similarly, (24) is L-true on Carnap's semantics, since his language has at least one individual constant and so at least one assignment of values to variables. For if a state-description S contains a sentence of the form Fa, then $\exists y \, Fy \rightarrow Fx$ holds in S on any assignment $\underline{a}$ for which $\underline{a}(x)(S)$ is $\underline{a}$, so (24) holds in

---

[37] The argument is given in Hughes and Cresswell 1968, p. 196, and 1996, p. 332 (the latter omits the required restriction to extensional contexts). The argument that there is such an assignment $\underline{a}^*$ involves an implicit use of the axiom of choice. Since the language may contain no closed term whose intension is a suitable individual concept, the argument does not go through for the purely substitutional semantics, even if the substitution class contains all closed definite descriptions. For discussion of the move from (18) to (19) in the context of attempts to eliminate *de re* modality see Fine 1978, pp. 296–7. For more on the logic of individual concepts see Kripke 1992.

S on every assignment; if S contains no sentence of the form Fa, then $\exists y \, Fy$ holds in S on no assignment, so $\exists y \, Fy \to Fx$ holds vacuously in S on every assignment, so (24) is again L-true. Thus (25) is also L-true:

(25) $\Box \exists x \, (\exists y \, Fy \to Fx)$

If one grants that necessarily there is something, one should accept (25) on its usual reading, however one interprets F. On a truth-functional reading of 'if', there must be something which is fat if anything is. But the formula $\exists y \, Fy \to Fx$ is extensional as a context for the variable x, since it contains no modal operators, so (25) entails (26) on Carnap's 1947 semantics:

(26) $\exists x \, \Box(\exists y \, Fy \to Fx)$

Thus Carnap must count (26) as L-true too. More specifically: some individual concept i is such that for every state-description S, $i(S)$ is in the extension of F in S if any individual constant is. Since $\Box(\exists y \, Fy \to Fx)$ is true in every state-description on any assignment $\underline{a}$ for which $\underline{a}(x)$ is i, (26) is L-true. But (26) is hopeless on its usual reading, for many interpretations of F. Read F as 'wins the lottery'. Whoever wins the lottery could have lost it while somebody else won.

The difference between the two interpretations over (26) primarily concerns the quantifiers and variables rather than the modal operators. For (26) becomes more puzzling, not less, if we understand $\Box$ in terms of logical rather than metaphysical necessity, while keeping fixed our understanding of the quantifiers and variables in terms of individuals. How could any given individual be *logically* incapable of losing the lottery to someone else? By contrast, if we understand the quantifiers and variables in terms of individual concepts rather than individuals, (26) becomes less puzzling, even if we understand $\Box$ in terms of metaphysical necessity.

Although such examples do not refute Carnap's treatment of quantification in terms of individual concepts, they do bring out how different it is from one in terms of individuals. Indeed, he preferred translating his formulas into natural language with explicit quantification over individual concepts rather than explicit quantification over individuals, because it yielded unproblematic claims of contingent coincidence between individual concepts in place of problematic claims of contingent identity between individuals.[38]

---

[38] Carnap 1947, pp. 186–93.

In effect, Carnap replaces first-order quantification in modal contexts with a restricted form of second-order quantification. An individual concept corresponds to a description that necessarily applies to a unique individual, although there may be no individual to which it necessarily applies. From a technical perspective, modal logics with quantification over all individual concepts exhibit incompleteness phenomena typical of second-order rather than first-order logic.[39] The objection to such a treatment is not that something is wrong with higher-order modal logics. They play a major role later in this book. The point is rather that first-order quantification into modal contexts makes sense as it stands, without reduction to higher-order quantification, by any reasonable standard of intelligibility. The long philosophical tradition to the contrary has produced no convincing arguments. We understand 'Some people can play chess and others can't' like other ordinary quantified sentences, without need of individual concepts. But if we interpret all our quantifiers as higher-order, we lose our first-order quantifiers. Instead, we should start with quantifiers interpreted in a genuinely first-order way, and add overtly higher-quantifiers once they are really needed. In this respect, the simpler semantics in the 1946 article better adumbrated later developments. We will revisit quantification over individual concepts in section 5.3.

In retrospect, the substitutional aspect of Carnap's accounts looks like a distortion of his most promising ideas. Informally, he presents the extension of a singular term as an individual, not as an individual constant, the extension of a monadic predicate as a class of individuals, and so on. He could have preserved that more natural way of thinking by using functions from expressions to their extensions in place of state-descriptions, and interpreting the quantifiers as ranging over all individuals and '=' as identity, thereby obviating the need for the artificial and implausible assumption that every individual is designated by some individual constant. Such functions resemble the models of contemporary model theory, although they supply

---

[39] See Garson 1984, pp. 289–302, and Hughes and Cresswell 1996, pp. 335–42, for the incompleteness of systems with quantification over all individual concepts and an otherwise standard frame-based model theory, although they apply only to systems based on propositional modal logics somewhat weaker than S5. Completeness can be restored by letting the domain of a model be an arbitrary set of individual concepts; see Garson 1984, pp. 268 and 277–80. For some historical comments on the role of Kaplan and Kripke see Bacon 1980, p. 194. Carnap's own logic is incomplete for a different reason: if A is not L-true then $\neg\Box A$ is L-true, and conversely, so recursively enumerating all the L-truths in his language requires in effect recursively enumerating all non-theorems of first-order logic with an infinite domain (preceded by $\neg\Box$), which is impossible; see section 3.1 for more discussion. For a recent attempt to unify a wide range of quantified modal logic in a semantic framework with quantification over individual concepts see Garson 2005.

no set to restrict how widely the quantifiers range. In the latter respect, they are even closer to models as characterized in Tarski's original 1936 paper on the concept of logical consequence.[40] Call such functions *universal interpretations*. On Carnap's semantics, the non-modal sentence E_n, usually read as saying that there are at least n individuals, is L-true if there are at least n individual constants, and L-false otherwise. On the revised non-substitutional semantics, E_n is L-true if there are at least n individuals, and L-false otherwise.[41] Although Carnap might have found the revised semantics uncongenial, as an insufficiently metalinguistic treatment of modality, he was not well placed to make any precise objection to its intelligibility.

Within such an objectual variant of Carnap's framework, semantic constraints become restrictions on the class of universal interpretations. For example, if the extension of an individual constant a is an object o, then the L-determinacy of a corresponds to a restriction to universal interpretations that assign a the extension o. This is made explicit in the object-language sentence $\exists x\, \Box x = a$, rather than being confined to the implicit metalinguistic background. Despite the partial resemblance to contemporary model theory, the framework still delivers a condition for a modal sentence to be true *simpliciter*, not merely one for it to be true in a universal interpretation, given the semantics of the non-modal fragment. For the latter determines which universal interpretation is the intended one. Since the framework at least delivers a condition for a modal sentence to be true in a universal interpretation, we can derive the condition for it to be true in the intended universal interpretation, which is the condition for it to be true *simpliciter*. Since the modal operators are interpreted as mandatorily ranging over all universal interpretations within the semantic constraints, there is no specifically modal parameter in the semantics of the modal language for the semantics of its non-modal fragment to leave unfixed. The modalities remain semantic, not metaphysical.

One may be suspicious of the underlying conception of semantics. For instance, Carnap never adequately clarifies the idea of L-determinacy. Some languages are supposed to contain L-indeterminate individual constants. Thus semantics determines the extensions of some individual constants and

---

[40] Tarski 1936 does not mention domains of quantification in explaining what an interpretation is. Arguably, that is no oversight or expository convenience; rather, it expresses a universalist conception of logic quite different from the model-theoretic perspective, despite Tarski's seminal contribution to model theory. See Mancosu 2006 for more discussion.

[41] See Rayo and Williamson 2003 for a completeness theorem for first-order non-modal languages when the quantifiers receive a mandatory unrestricted reading.

not of others. What is supposed to make the difference? Moreover, the L-indeterminate individual constants force the logic to be free. For $\Box a{=}a$ is L-true on the objectual semantics for every individual constant a; but if a is L-indeterminate then $\exists x\ \Box x{=}a$ is not L-true, so the rule of 'existential' generalization fails. The rule of universal instantiation fails for similar reasons. But neither rule fails for a if it is L-determinate, since then it is intensionally equivalent to a variable under some permissible assignment. Thus the so-called freedom of the logic is really just a symptom of a mismatch in semantic treatment between the individual variables and the individual constants. Some intensions—the 'non-rigid' ones—have been permitted to the individual constants but not to the individual variables (under an assignment), even though individual variables take the place of individual constants. Such an asymmetry is not obviously well motivated. Since treating individual concepts as the values of the lowest-order variables turned out to be a bad option, an attractive way out is to accept the simple thought that the task of the semantics includes determining the extensions of *all* individual constants, so that all count as L-determinate and the classical quantifier rules hold without exception.[42] That option has the additional advantage of validating the classical identity rules too, for if $a{=}b$ holds anywhere and both a and b are L-determinate individual constants then $A \leftrightarrow A*$ holds everywhere, if A and $A*$ differ only in the substitution of a for b or vice versa. Such lines of thought reinforce the impression that although Carnap's semantics did not constitute a stable equilibrium, it was tipping in the direction of later developments.

2.5 Barcan Marcus again

Ruth Barcan Marcus later employed a substitutional reading of quantification in modal contexts similar to Carnap's to defend BF, in papers from 1961 onwards.[43] Conceding that BF looks implausible at first sight, especially when the modalities are read as logical, she proposed to dissolve the problem with a substitutional account, which, she claimed, clarified quantification into modal and temporal contexts in other respects too.

---

[42] Carnap excludes empty singular terms from his language. Following Frege, he artificially handles otherwise non-denoting definite descriptions by fixing a default object for them to denote. He proposes the convention that the default object should be the null thing, 'that thing which is part of every thing' (many would regard the latter phrase as one more non-denoting definite description). See Carnap 1947, pp. 36–8.

[43] Marcus 1961, 1962.

For simplicity, we may assume that the substitution class of closed singular terms to be substituted for the individual variables consists of all individual constants in the language. Thus quantifiers occur in a substitution instance of a formula A only where they already occur in A itself, so the substitutional treatment of quantification raises no problem of circularity.

In a sample treatment, Barcan Marcus considered a language with only finitely many individual constants. Semantically, therefore, $\exists x\, A$ is treated just like the finite disjunction of all substitution instances of A, and $\forall x\, A$ just like the finite conjunction of those substitution instances. In effect, therefore, every formula of the quantified modal language is semantically equated with some formula of the corresponding quantifier-free modal language, which is already closed under finite disjunctions and conjunctions. Thus the problem of interpreting the quantified modal language is reduced to the problem of interpreting the quantifier-free modal language. For that, Barcan Marcus uses a finite domain of individuals, every member of which is named by some individual constant.[44] Both the domain and the naming relation are held constant across models. Formulas are evaluated as true or false in models, which interpret an atomic predicate over the domain. Since the modal operators are read as logical modalities, they are taken to range over all models defined on the given domain. Thus $\Diamond A$ is true in a model M if and only if A is true in some model; $\Box A$ is true in M if and only if A is true in every model. As indicated, $\exists x\, A$ is true in M if and only if some substitution instance of A is true in M; $\forall x\, A$ is true in M if and only if every substitution instance of A is true M. All instances of BF and CBF are true in all models, just as in Carnap's 1946 semantics, with models in place of state-descriptions.[45]

---

[44] But in later work Barcan Marcus says of substitutional semantics 'No domains are assigned to worlds at all; the variables do not range over objects, they are place markers for *syntactically* proper names' (1985/1986, p. 212; her italics).

[45] For the semantics see Marcus 1961, p. 319. Since models as there defined include no denotation relation between constants and members of the domain, the relation must be model-independent. She compares her semantics to that in Carnap 1947 (although really it is closer to the simpler, more natural treatment in Carnap 1946), and credits the method of her construction to McKinsey 1945 (mis-cited as 1946) and 1948/1949. McKinsey supervised her study of logic at New York University, from which she graduated in 1941; after writing her Ph.D. under the supervision of Frederic Fitch at Yale, she was a postdoctoral fellow in 1948–1949 at the University of Chicago, where she joined Carnap's seminar (Marcus 1961, pp. ix–x). If every individual in the domain is named by some constant and every constant names some individual in the domain, her semantics obliterates the two distinctions Evans draws between his 'Fregean' truth theories, in which truth rather than satisfaction is semantically basic, and her substitutional truth theories (1977, pp. 85–6). However, the substitutional nature of her account also plays a role in handling quantification into modal contexts. For more discussion of Fregean truth theories see Davies 1981, pp. 114–23; on substitutional quantification, Kripke 1976 and Davies 1981, pp. 142–8.

Barcan Marcus's semantics, like Carnap's, provides conditions for truth *simpliciter* only once enough is added to determine an intended model. However, since that simply involves interpreting the names and non-logical atomic predicates, Barcan Marcus has already explained how to extend the semantics (including the model theory) of a quantified non-modal language to a semantics for the quantified modal language that results from adding operators for logical modalities, so as to validate BF and CBF. Indeed, the argument for the validity of BF and CBF is robust with respect to many details of the semantics. It does not depend on whether the number of names is finite or infinite, or on whether every member of the domain is named, or on whether the naming relation or the domain is held fixed. It goes through whatever class of names in the language acts as the substitution class for the quantifiers and whatever class of models for the language the modal operators range over (of course, the semantics would need to specify both classes).

BF and CBF cease to be valid if the substitution class is built into the model and allowed to vary freely.[46] For example, since $\exists x \, \neg a{=}x$ is true in a model M whenever $a{=}b$ is false in M for some constant b in the substitution class of M, $\Diamond\exists x \, \neg a{=}x$ is true in every model. But $\exists x \, \Diamond\neg a{=}x$ is false in any model M* whose substitution class is just $\{a\}$, for its truth in M* requires $\Diamond\neg a{=}a$ to be true in M*, contrary to the truth of $a{=}a$ in every model. Thus BF fails. Conversely, since $\exists y \, a{=}y$ is false in any model M whose substitution class contains no constant b such that $a{=}b$ is true in M, $\Diamond\neg\exists y \, a{=}y$ is true in every model, so $\exists x \, \Diamond\neg\exists y \, x{=}y$ is true in any model with a non-empty substitution class; but $\exists x \, \neg\exists y \, x{=}y$ is true in no model, so $\Diamond\exists x \, \neg\exists y \, x{=}y$ is true in no model. Thus CBF fails too. However, if we work with models for a given language, not possible worlds, building in a substitution class may look ad hoc. In any case, Barcan Marcus's aim was not to show that every form of substitutional semantics validates BF and CBF, but rather to provide a simple form of it that does so. In that aim, she succeeded. But what interest have the meanings she thereby gives the formulas? How well do they fit their usual readings?

If $\Box$ is read as an operator for logical necessity, the truth of $\Box A$ should imply the logical truth of A. On the usual model-theoretic conception, the

---

[46] Compare Copeland 1982. His proof is for a version of substitutional semantics similar to Kripke's possible worlds semantics, unlike the purely model-theoretic account in Marcus 1962, in which the modal operators mandatorily range over all models rather than being restricted to an arbitrary set of models or worlds.

logical truth of A implies the truth of A in all models, where every set is the domain of some models. But in Barcan Marcus's semantics, the truth of $\Box A$ in a model depends only on the truth of A in models with the same (finite) domain. This restriction looks inappropriate on the model-theoretic conception of logical truth. Its effects are limited simply because the domain plays no role in the substitutional semantics for the quantifiers. If we merely expand the domain by adding some nameless objects, we can still apply the semantics to determine a condition for $\exists x\, A$ or $\forall x\, A$ to be true in the new model M in terms of the conditions for substitution instances of A to be true in M. The problem is just that the new truth condition is unnatural and uninteresting, because it restricts the generalizations to named members of the domain. For most purposes, no such restriction is desirable. Why should a biologist restrict a generalization about fruit flies to those that have been individually named? If we have a domain, we want the quantifiers to range over all its members.

Can one solve the problem by notionally expanding the language to suit the model? Here is one proposal. A model can have any non-empty set as its domain. Models differ in what non-logical atomic predicates and names they interpret (by assigning extensions over their domain). A model interprets a sentence A if and only if it interprets every non-logical predicate and name in A. An *explicit model* is one in which every member of the domain has a name. Sentences are evaluated only in explicit models that interpret them. For modal operators, $\Box A$ is true in an explicit model M if and only if A is true in every explicit model that interprets A; $\Diamond A$ is true in M if and only if A is true in some explicit model that interprets A. For quantifiers, $\forall x\, A(x)$ is true in M if and only if $A(a)$ is true in M for every name a that M interprets; $\exists x\, A(x)$ is true in M if and only if $A(a)$ is true in M for some name a that M interprets. This proposal removes many of the most awkward effects of substitutional quantification.

The proposal validates BF. For suppose that $\Diamond \exists x\, A(x)$ is true in an explicit model M that interprets it. Then $\exists x\, A(x)$ is true in some explicit model M$*$ that interprets it. Hence $A(a)$ is true in M$*$ for some name a that M$*$ interprets. Thus if M interprets a, $\Diamond A(a)$ is true in M, so $\exists x\, \Diamond A(x)$ is true in M. If M does not interpret a, there is an explicit model M$^+$ just like M except that it interprets a (for the domain of M is non-empty). Hence $\Diamond A(a)$ is true in M$^+$, so $\exists x\, \Diamond A(x)$ is true in M$^+$. But then $\exists x\, \Diamond A(x)$ is true in M too, for it does not contain a (otherwise M would not interpret $\Diamond \exists x\, A(x)$), and the interpretation of a makes no difference to the interpretation of quantifiers because M is already explicit. Either way, the instance of BF in question is true in M. The proposal also validates CBF. For suppose that $\exists x \lozenge A(x)$ is true in an explicit model M that interprets it. Then $\lozenge A(a)$ is true in M for some name a that M interprets. Hence $A(a)$ is true in some explicit model M* that interprets it, so $\exists x A(x)$ is true in M*, so $\lozenge \exists x A(x)$ is true in M.

However, the revised proposal also has some ugly consequences. For example, since the interpretation of names varies freely across models, for any two names a and b, $a{=}b$ is true in some models and false in others, so $\lozenge a{=}b$ & $\lozenge \neg a{=}b$ is always true. Consequently, $\exists x \exists y (\lozenge x{=}y$ & $\lozenge \neg x{=}y)$ is true in any explicit model that interprets at least two names. That makes the contingency of identity very cheap, a result unwelcome to Barcan Marcus. On the other hand, if the interpretation of names is held fixed across models, as in her toy semantics, then either $a{=}b$ counts as logically true or $\neg a{=}b$ does. But on what general conception of logic does it determine the truth value of 'Hesperus = Phosphorus'?

In her subsequent work, Barcan Marcus gave less importance to substitutional quantification. She suggested that although it may still have uses in the treatment of non-objectual discourse, for example involving fictional names such as 'Santa Claus', it is inappropriate for the interpretation of objectual discourse (fictional names will be discussed in section 4.1). The latter involves an identity predicate, which must receive its standard interpretation, which in turn requires names to be associated with objects as their bearers. Once we have a pool of objects, we want to interpret quantifiers over those objects. The substitutional interpretation loses its significance.[47] She also revised her interpretation of the modal operators, away from a purely logical reading towards a more metaphysical one, intended to accommodate the Aristotelian essentialism with which Quine had threatened her.[48]

2.6 Prior

The philosophically contentious nature of BF and CBF was not immediately apparent. The explanation is not just the reading of the modal operators in terms of logical or analytic modalities, which made quantification into modal contexts hard to interpret informally. For BF and CBF were accepted

---

[47] See Marcus 1985/1986, p. 213.
[48] See Marcus 1971; Marcus 1967 is less metaphysically committed.

even on other readings of the modal operators. For example, when Arthur Burks published a system of quantified modal logic with operators for causal necessity and possibility in 1951, he endorsed BF′ and CBF′ (equivalent to BF and CBF) with the terse justification that to say that for every spatiotemporal region the corresponding instance of a universal generalization is true on causal grounds is logically equivalent to saying that the universal generalization over all spatiotemporal regions is itself true on causal grounds.[49] He does not connect the formulas with the metaphysical issues that a contemporary metaphysician would associate with them on his causal reading, such as whether the structure of spacetime is independent of the causal order.

As late as 1962, in their standard history of logic, William and Martha Kneale suggested that, properly interpreted, BF and CBF are logical truths, without mentioning issues about the contingency of being. They acknowledge that pairs of English sentences such as 'There is something which may be on fire' and 'There may be something on fire' are not equivalent: 'For the first can be used to state that something is inflammable, and the second to say that our information does not rule out the existence of a fire'. However, they attribute the differences to contextually understood restrictions on the modal operators in a natural language that are irrelevant to expressions of the formal language. 'In modal logic', they claim, 'the diamond signifies only self-consistency and according to this strict interpretation the two formulae just mentioned [$\exists x\, \Diamond Fx$ and $\Diamond\exists x\, Fx$] seem to be logically equivalent, at least for the non-empty universe which logicians commonly assume'.[50] The conception of possibility as self-consistency suggests a purely logical interpretation of the modal operators, as in Carnap, although elsewhere they tentatively classify 'the proposition that nothing can be both red and green all over at the same time' as a necessary truth that is known a priori but is non-analytic in the sense that it does 'not follow from laws of formal logic even when explicit definitions are admitted as new transformation rules', in which case it is not a logical truth.[51] Although unwilling to rule out a metaphysical conception of possibility and necessity, they were unable to read it clearly into formulas with quantification into modal contexts.

[49] Burks 1951, p. 378.

[50] Kneale and Kneale 1962, p. 615. The point of assuming a non-empty universe is that in a model with an empty domain $\exists x\, \Diamond Fx$ is automatically false, but $\Diamond\exists x\, Fx$ is presumably true because $\exists x\, Fx$ is still self-consistent.

[51] Kneale and Kneale 1962, p. 637. They claim that 'every proposition which can be known a priori is necessary'.

Given the difficulty philosophers had in interpreting quantified modal logic, it is no surprise that the metaphysical implications of BF and CBF first became visible through their analogues in temporal logic. No 'logical' or 'analytic' conception of the past and future confused the issues, and differences in meaning between formulas took more concrete forms. In *Formal Logic* (1955), Arthur Prior had endorsed BF and CBF, claiming an equivalence between 'Necessarily everything φ's' and 'Everything is under a necessity of φ-ing' by analogy with the permutability of two universal quantifiers.[52] In *Time and Modality*, published two years later, he criticized BF when $\Diamond P$ is read as 'It either is or has been or will be the case that P'. As an instance of BF, he gave 'if it either is or has been or will be the case that someone is flying to the moon, then there is someone who either is flying or has flown or will fly to the moon'. Prior explained:

> [I]t is not easy to be quite happy about this. For suppose that in fact someone will fly to the moon some day, but not anyone who now exists. Then it will be true that it either is, has been, or will be the case that someone is flying to the moon; but it will not be true that there is someone who either is flying or has flown or will fly to the moon.[53]

He recognized that some metaphysical theories have the resources to resist this conclusion. For example, a metaphysician may deny that persons are genuine individuals, and analyse discourse apparently about them in terms of discourse really about genuine individuals, assumed to be fundamental and permanent. More plausibly, one may take a four-dimensional view of spacetime, and treat the unrestricted quantifiers as ranging over its entire contents. Nevertheless, Prior argues that such metaphysical theories should not be built into logic, since they can be consistently denied. Thus BF should not count as logically valid in temporal logic.[54] Prior extended his

---

[52] Prior 1955, p. 210 (the preface to the first edition is dated May 1953).

[53] Prior 1957, p. 26 (the book is based on Prior's John Locke lectures, delivered at Oxford in 1955–1956). Events moved faster than Prior was supposing: Neil Armstrong was born in 1930.

[54] Prior 1957, pp. 31–4; he cites W.V. Quine and J.J.C. Smart as defenders of the four-dimensional view. The methodology of clarifying metaphysical issues in quantified modal logic by reference to quantified tense logic remained popular for some time after Prior. Richmond Thomason 1969, p. 127, is explicit: 'I will appeal mostly to the temporal interpretation, since it is the one which seems to be most valuable heuristically where quantification theory is concerned; we have some idea of how to identify individuals across temporal worlds, since we have an idea of what temporal change is like. But "metaphysical change" is more problematic'. For other examples see Cocchiarella 1969a, p. 35, and Montague 1970a, pp. 124 and 126, and in contemporary philosophy Dorr 2011.

critique of BF from temporal to modal logic: 'if tense-logic is haunted by
the myth that whatever exists at any time exists at all times, ordinary modal
logic is haunted by the myth that whatever exists exists necessarily'.[55]

Prior considered a general defence of BF in temporal logic, based on
'a permanent pool of objects, some now existing and some only having
existed or going to exist', and a parallel defence of BF in modal logic, based
on a necessary pool of objects, some actual and some mere possibilia.[56]
Combining the temporal and modal dimensions yields a permanent and
necessary pool of objects to verify BF on both readings. He found such
a view presupposed by the theory of ampliation in medieval semantics,
on which the primary effect of temporal and modal qualifications of the
copula is to modify the application of terms. Thus the difference between
'Some F is a G' and 'Some F will be a G' is that in the former 'F' and 'G'
signify only present Fs and Gs respectively, whereas in the latter they signify
both present and future Fs and Gs. Similarly, the difference between 'Some
F is a G' and 'Some F can be a G' is that in the former 'F' and 'G' signify
only actual Fs and Gs, whereas in the latter they signify both actual and
merely possible Fs and Gs.[57]

The fixed pool idea perplexed Prior. He took it to involve a failure of the
entailment from 'There are facts about x' to 'x exists', and objected 'If there
are facts about x, I cannot see what *further* fact about x would consist in its
existing'.[58] For if x is merely possible or past or future, but still in the pool,
if there is no fact about x that it is (say) blue-eyed, why is there no fact about
x that it is *not* blue-eyed? Again, why is there no fact about x that it could
have been blue-eyed, or that it was blue-eyed, or that it will be blue-eyed?
Prior saw no way of drawing a principled distinction between facts about x
that entail 'x exists' and others that do not, but his deeper objection was to
the idea that even one fact about x might not entail 'x exists'. His argument

---

[55] Prior 1957, p. 48. Myhill 1958 criticizes BF on the grounds that there could have been more things
than there actually are (compare Ramsey 1927). However, Myhill's system was criticized for permitting the derivation of BF, contrary to his intentions; see Lemmon 1960, Føllesdal 2004 (1961), p. 141
(added in 1963), and Prior 1967, pp. 145–7.

[56] Prior 1957, pp. 30 and 49.

[57] See Prior 1957, p. 30, and Knuuttila 1993, pp. 121 and 167. The ampliated reading of the sentences is
de re rather than *de dicto*: in scholastic terminology they are taken *in sensu diviso* rather than *in sensu
composito*. Thus, in the modal case, their overall form is that of a quantified sentence about possible
beings, not the ascription of a modal status (possibility or necessity) to the corresponding non-modal
sentence on its unampliated reading.

[58] Prior 1957, p. 31. He specifies that 'x' stands for a proper name.

relied on no heavy-duty metaphysical conception of facts. Rather, his point is that whatever holds of x, there must be something for it to hold of, so 'x exists' is true. How can 'x is not blue-eyed', 'x was blue-eyed', 'x will be blue-eyed', or 'x could have been blue-eyed' be true if nothing holds of x?

If we read 'x exists' as equivalent to 'x is concrete', Prior's argument is quite implausible. 'There are facts about x' does not entail 'x is concrete'. In particular, 'x is not blue-eyed', 'x was blue-eyed', 'x will be blue-eyed', or 'x could have been blue-eyed' do not entail it. But Prior's argument becomes far more plausible if we read 'x exists' as equivalent to 'x is something', with the quantifier unrestricted. How can it hold of x that it is not blue-eyed, or that it was blue-eyed, or that it will be blue-eyed, or that it could have been blue-eyed, unless it holds of something? We will return to this issue in section 4.1.

On Prior's unrestricted reading of 'x exists', it is inconsistent to describe the permanent pool by saying 'Some objects in it do not exist, although they existed once or will exist', and inconsistent to describe the necessary pool by saying 'Some objects in it do not exist, although they could have existed'. However, the inconsistency of such Meinongian descriptions of the fixed pool does not mean that there is no fixed pool. As seen in section 1.5, necessitism and permanentism do not require Meinongianism. Prior never properly confronted the idea that the use of 'x exists' on which it becomes untrue when x dies is not that on which it is equivalent to 'There are facts about x'.

Prior's neglect of this point emerges in the passage above when he objects to BF in temporal logic. He twice states the consequent in the relevant instance as 'there is someone who either is flying or has flown or will fly to the moon'. His use of 'someone' rather than 'something' imposes a restriction to persons to which a defender of BF for unrestricted quantifiers is not committed. On the permanentist view explained in Chapter 1, merely past or future persons are not persons. Prior can hardly be blamed for not separating permanentism from Meinongianism. He did as much as anyone to identify the metaphysical import of BF; complete clarity is rarely achieved in one step.

Although Prior failed to locate the best defence of BF, his attempt to develop temporal and modal logic without BF has independent interest. We may concentrate on the modal case, and use 'x is something' (with the quantifier unrestricted) in place of 'x exists' to clarify the contrast with necessitism.

Prior's guiding principle is that if x had been nothing, there would have been no truths about x. More precisely, for any proposition p about x, he claims not just that if x had been nothing then p would not have been about x, but that there would have been no such proposition as p at all. Prior puts this by saying that p would have been 'unstatable', but he means that p would have been unstatable because there would have been nothing to state, not that it would have been an unstatable proposition. Moreover, if there had been no such proposition as p, a fortiori there would have been no such true proposition as p, and p would not have been true.

For Prior, a proposition about x is a singular proposition, typically expressed by a simple or complex sentence in which a name or demonstrative for x is used. Thus being about x is inherited under propositional operations: if p is about x, so too is its negation, any conjunction of which it is a conjunct, and so on.

The obvious notions of possibility and necessity for a proposition are possible truth and necessary truth respectively. Thus if the sentence A expresses the proposition p, then $\Diamond A$ expresses the proposition that p is possible, in other words that p is possibly true, and $\Box A$ expresses the proposition that p is necessary, in other words that p is necessarily true. Since truth requires stability, necessary truth requires necessary stability. Thus a sentence of the form $\Box A$ is true only if A contains no name of a contingent being, since otherwise the proposition A expresses is not necessarily stable, and so is not necessarily true. For example, even $\Box(Fa \to Fa)$ is false when 'a' names a contingent being. Prior needs a less draconian standard of necessity too. For that, he uses the operator $\neg\Diamond\neg$, which for him is weaker than $\Box$: $\neg\Diamond\neg A$ is true if and only if the proposition expressed by $\neg A$ could not have been true, and so if and only if the proposition expressed by A is true in all possible circumstances in which it is statable. Thus $\neg\Diamond\neg(Fa \to Fa)$ is true. For Prior, A is logically valid if and only if the logical form of A is such that whenever A expresses a proposition p, p is true in all possible circumstances in which it is statable. Thus $Fa \to Fa$ and $\neg\Diamond\neg(Fa \to Fa)$ are logical laws but $\Box(Fa \to Fa)$ is not. Prior develops a modal system Q on this basis, with a temporal analogue. As this example shows, the rule of necessitation fails in Q for $\Box$: even if A is a theorem, $\Box A$ may not be. Q provides only a weaker version of the rule: if A is a theorem, so too is $\neg\Diamond\neg A$. This restriction leaves BF and CBF underivable in Q, just as Prior wanted.[59]

---

[59] For detailed motivation and exposition of Q see Prior 1957, pp. 29–54; 1967, pp. 137–74; 1968, pp. 257–92; Loptson 1980; Menzel 1991, pp. 331–46.

Although Q is motivated in detail by natural-seeming metaphysical considerations, the result is peculiarly awkward. Weak necessity behaves messily. In particular, it is not closed under tautological consequence. For example, from $\neg\Diamond\neg A$ and $\neg\Diamond\neg(A \to B)$ we cannot conclude $\neg\Diamond\neg B$. For let A mean that David is the father of Solomon, and B that David is a father. Then $\neg\Diamond\neg A$ may be true because, in any possible circumstances in which it is stable that David is the father of Solomon, David *is* the father of Solomon, since having David as his father is an essential property of Solomon, and $\neg\Diamond\neg(A \to B)$ may be true too because, in any possible circumstances in which David is the father of Solomon, David is a father, but $\neg\Diamond\neg B$ may still be false because in circumstances in which David lives childless it is stable but false that he is a father.

Even worse are Q's expressive limitations. Consider (27) and (28), read as 'David is nothing' ('David does not exist') and the contradiction 'David is a king who is not a king' respectively:

(27) $\neg\exists x\ d{=}x$

(28) $Kd\ \&\ \neg Kd$

Informally, given Prior's metaphysical starting point, (27) describes a possibility while (28) does not. But Q cannot distinguish (27) from (28). The reason is this. On Prior's assumptions, the two formulas share the same *modal profile*, in the sense that the propositions they express are true in exactly the same possible circumstances, false in exactly the same possible circumstances, and therefore stable in exactly the same possible circumstances. For in any circumstance in which David is something, both propositions are stable and false; in any circumstance in which David is nothing, both propositions are unstable. But on Prior's account of Q, the semantic contribution of a closed formula to formulas of which it is a constituent is a function of its modal profile: same modal profile, same semantic contribution. All standard forms of possible world semantics follow that principle too.[60] Thus (27) and (28) embed in the same way: formulas that differ only in having (27) in place of (28) or vice versa have the same truth value. Prior wants 'David could have been nothing' (or 'David might not have existed') to be true and 'David could have been a king who was not a king [at the same time]' false, but Q

---

[60] In many-dimensional modal logics, the notion of modal profile must be generalized, but not in ways relevant to the difference between (27) and (28).

does not allow it. For example, we can try formalizing those sentences by (29) and (30):

(29) $\Diamond\neg\exists x\ d{=}x$

(30) $\Diamond(Kd\ \&\ \neg Kd)$

But both (29) and (30) are false in Q, because neither (27) nor (28) expresses a proposition that could have been true. We may therefore try formalizing them by (31) and (32) instead, using the weaker notion of possibility:[61]

(31) $\neg\Box\exists x\ d{=}x$

(32) $\neg\Box\neg(Kd\ \&\ \neg Kd)$

Now the trouble is that both (31) and (32) are true in Q, because (27) and (28) express propositions that could have been unstatable. Either way, no modal distinction between (27) and (28) is captured. That (27) and (28) have the same modal profile shows that no other embedding, however complex, will make the distinction in Q. Further such difficulties arise if we add a counterfactual conditional to the language: Prior does not want to equate what would have been the case if David had been nothing with what would have been the case if he had been a king who was not a king, but putting (28) for (27) as the antecedent of a counterfactual conditional should make no difference to the truth value of the conditional, given their sameness in modal profile.

No principled defender of Q can deny the distinction between (27) and (28). Technically, Q is a mess. A metaphysical justification is its only hope. But without the supposed modal distinction between (27) and (28), and similar pairs, such a justification has no chance.

For such reasons, philosophers and logicians have largely abandoned Q.[62] Nevertheless, its failure constitutes a revealing hint of the difficulties facing any attempt to stabilize the logical metaphysics of contingentism and temporaryism. We will see in later chapters how far subsequent attempts to overcome the difficulties have succeeded.

---

[61] A redundant double negation has been eliminated in (31).

[62] For related criticisms of Q see Fine 1977a, pp. 148–51, and 1985, pp. 171–8; Plantinga 1983, pp. 15–20; Deutsch 1990, pp. 92–3, and 1994, pp. 278–9; Menzel 1991, pp. 346–8. Efird 2010, pp. 105–7, adopts a version of Q, but adds predicate-modifier modal operators, following Wiggins 1976; however, they do not help to make distinctions such as that between (27) and (28).

2.7 Truth-value gaps

We can already generalize the argument in the previous section from sameness in modal profile beyond Q. In technical respects, Q can be assimilated
to theories that postulate truth-value gaps in modal or temporal contexts. If
the proposition a formula A expresses (perhaps on an assignment of values
to variables) is unstatable in some counterfactual circumstance, then neither
A nor $\neg A$ is treated as true in that circumstance: A is treated as a truth-value
gap, neither true nor false.

To generalize the argument, consider any semantic theory that attributes
such a neutral, gappy status to atomic formulas in just those circumstances
in which the actual denotation of some singular term in the formula is
nothing. Suppose that the theory computes the semantic effect of complex
non-modal operators according to any standard three-valued semantics. In
particular, if a complex formula A is built from simpler formulas $B_1, \ldots, B_n$
by any of the usual truth-functional operations, then if $B_1, \ldots, B_n$ are all true
or false in a circumstance C on an assignment $\underline{a}$ of values to variables, A has
the truth value in C on $\underline{a}$ computed by the standard two-valued truth tables,
while if $B_1, \ldots, B_n$ are all neutral in C on $\underline{a}$ then A is also neutral in C on $\underline{a}$
(it does not matter for the argument what policy is followed when some
but not all of $B_1, \ldots, B_n$ are neutral). Similarly, $\exists x \, A$ in C is treated like a
disjunction over everything in C: if A is true in C on some x-variant $\underline{a}*$
of $\underline{a}$ such that $\underline{a}*(x)$ is something in C and not neutral on any x-variant $\underline{a}*$ of
$\underline{a}$ such that $\underline{a}*(x)$ is something in C, then $\exists x \, A$ is true in C on $\underline{a}$; if A is false
in C on every x-variant $\underline{a}*$ of $\underline{a}$ such that $\underline{a}*(x)$ is something in C, then $\exists x$
A is false in C on $\underline{a}$; if A is neutral on any x-variant $\underline{a}*$ of $\underline{a}$ such that $\underline{a}*(x)$
is something in C, then $\exists x \, A$ is neutral in C on $\underline{a}$ (it does not matter for the
argument what policy is followed when A is neutral on some but not all
x-variants $\underline{a}*$ of $\underline{a}$ such that $\underline{a}*(x)$ is something in C). Dually, $\forall x \, A$ in C is
treated like a conjunction over everything in C. For modal operators, we
assume as usual that on any assignment the modal profile of A determines
the modal profiles of $\Diamond A, \Box A$, and so on for any other modal operators in the
language; the details of how it does so are irrelevant for present purposes.[63]

On those assumptions, (27) and (28) have the same modal profile. For let
'd' name an object o. Consider any circumstance C. If o is something in C,

---

[63] To compare the constraints in the text with the motivation for Q see the references in n. 59.

then $\exists x\ d{=}x$ is true in C on any assignment $\underline{a}$ because $d{=}x$ is true in C on the x-variant $\underline{a}*$ of $\underline{a}$ such that $\underline{a}*(x)$ is o, and false in C on any x-variant $\underline{a}*$ of $\underline{a}$ such that $\underline{a}*(x)$ is anything in C other than o, so $\neg\exists x\ d{=}x$ is false in C on $\underline{a}$, and Kd & $\neg Kd$ is false in C on $\underline{a}$ by the two-valued truth tables, since Kd is true or false in C on $\underline{a}$. On the other hand, if o is nothing in C, then the atomic formula $d{=}x$ is neutral in C on every assignment, so $\exists x\ d{=}x$ is also neutral in C on every assignment; similarly, since Kd is neutral in C on every assignment, so is $\neg Kd$ and therefore so too is Kd & $\neg Kd$. Thus (27) and (28) have the same modal profile on any assignment: they are false in the same circumstances, neutral in the same circumstances, and true in no circumstances. Since the modal profile of a formula exhausts its semantic contribution to sentences in which it occurs, (27) and (28) embed in the same way: substituting one for another in a sentence leaves its truth value unchanged. Such a system is therefore unable to distinguish the supposed possibility of (27) from the impossibility of (28).

Instead of formalizing 'exists' with the quantifier and identity, we could use an atomic monadic predicate E true in a circumstance C of o if and only if o is something in C. Then $\neg Ed$ could replace (27) without affecting the overall argument.

At least one semantic treatment of truth value gaps violates the argument's assumption that modal profiles are compositional: supervaluationism.[64] The idea is first to consider all two-valued valuations that evaluate atomic formulas containing a singular term that denotes nothing in a circumstance C (on a given assignment) arbitrarily as true or false in C, and otherwise proceed according to the usual interpretation. Then a formula A is true on the supervaluation if A is true on all the two-valued valuations; A is false on the supervaluation if A is false on all the two-valued valuations; otherwise A is neither true nor false on the supervaluation (all in C on the assignment). For example, if what 'd' names is nothing in C, then Kd is true in C on some of the two-valued valuations and false in C on the others, so $\neg Kd$ is false in C on the former and true in C on the latter. Thus Kd is neither true nor false in C on the supervaluation. However, Kd & $\neg Kd$ is false in C on all of the two-valued valuations, and therefore false in C on the supervaluation: supervaluationism permits a false conjunction without a false conjunct. But both $\neg\exists x\ d{=}x$ and $\neg Ed$ are neither true nor false in C on the

---

[64] See van Fraassen 1966 for the application of supervaluationist semantics to empty singular terms.

supervaluation. Thus supervaluationism permits a difference in modal profile between (27) and (28), and so offers the contingentist the prospect of distinguishing the former, as expressing a possibility, from the latter, as expressing an impossibility.

However, the difference in supervaluationist treatment between (27) and (28) is too specific to the logical structure of (28). Let the monadic atomic predicate F express any property incompatible with David's essence: for instance, being a prime number. Then Fd receives the same modal profile as (27) or $\neg Ed$: if David (the denotation of 'd') is something in C then Fd is false in C; otherwise, Fd is neutral in C. Thus the supervaluationist cannot distinguish modally between Fd and (27) or $\neg Ed$. But contingentists need such a distinction. For example, trivially, if David had been a prime number then David would have been a prime number, but the contingentist cannot allow that if David had not been something then David would have been a prime number. Again, for contingentists, David's not being something is compossible with the sun's shining, but David's being a prime number is not compossible with the sun's shining. Thus supervaluationism fails to deliver what contingentists need.

Could supervaluationists add special constraints on admissible valuations, for example to exclude two-valued valuations that count 'David is a prime number' as true in C irrespective of whether 'David' names anything in C? Thus the supervaluation would always count 'David is a prime number' as false rather than neutral in C. But if such constraints are legitimate, they remove the point of introducing the supervaluationist apparatus in the first place. For it was simply an instrumental device to handle truth-value gaps conveniently when the denotation of a name is absent from a circumstance. But if such absences need not produce truth-value gaps, as by hypothesis for 'David is a prime number', then it is vastly more convenient to avoid them altogether, for example by stipulating that all atomic formulas with empty names are false (section 4.1 develops this policy). A supervaluationist treatment of empty names is well motivated only on the Priorian assumption that they automatically force truth-value gaps in atomic sentences, for deep metaphysical reasons associated with the name rather than the predicate, and on that assumption, we saw, the treatment fails.

A different tactic for gap theorists is to interpret $\neg$ as weak negation, so that $\neg A$ is true rather than neutral when A is neutral, which would also enable them to distinguish modally between Fd and (27) or $\neg Ed$. But this tactic too makes the resort to the complications of truth-value gaps unnecessary. For then $\neg\neg Ed$ and $\neg\neg\exists x\ d{=}x$ are true in all those circumstances in which what 'd' names is something and false in all other circumstances, so we can distinguish bivalently between circumstances in which 'd is something' (or 'd exists') is true and the rest. Similarly, for any atomic formula A, $\neg\neg A$ is false whenever A is false or truth-valueless and true whenever A is true. Consequently, all the required distinctions can be made with bivalent formulas.

Finally, the gap theorist might treat some predicates bivalently, such as $=$ and E, permitting gaps only for other predicates, such as K, thereby distinguishing (27) from (28). However, this asymmetry is ad hoc. Once contingentists and temporaryists have conceded that the absence of a denotation for 'd' from a circumstance does not automatically deprive an atomic sentence of truth or falsity in that circumstance, they gain nothing by refusing to extend the bivalent treatment to all atomic formulas, perhaps by counting them all false in such circumstances.[65] Truth-value gaps complicate rather than help contingentism and temporaryism, and are irrelevant to necessitism and permanentism. We therefore assume bivalence henceforth.

2.8 Logical modalities

Before Kripke, the operators $\Box$ and $\Diamond$ in modal logic were usually read as expressing logical necessity and possibility. This created some general technical difficulties, which deserve discussion in their own right. The best starting point is Carnap's carefully articulated semantics.

As noted in section 2.4, the guiding principle behind Carnap's semantics for modal logic is that the sentence $\Box A$ is true if and only if the sentence A is L-true. L-truth is explicated as truth in all models (state-descriptions). Truth *simpliciter* is equivalent to truth in the intended model, the state-description containing exactly the atomic sentences and negations thereof that are true on their intended readings, whatever they happen to be. Thus $\Box A$ is true in the intended model if and only if A is true in all models. But that equivalence should not depend on which state-description happens to be true, for its role is to define $\Box$. So we can generalize it to any model M: $\Box A$ is true in M if and only if A is true in all models. That is in effect Carnap's semantics

---

[65] Our present concern is only with objections to bivalence from contingentism and temporaryism.

for the necessity operator. In effect, he treats it as a logical constant: for present purposes, we are not interested in models that interpret $\square$ as expressing anything other than logical necessity.

Despite the simplicity and naturalness of Carnap's approach to logical modality, it has some odd effects, even in propositional modal logic. Let P be a non-logical atomic sentence. Thus P is not logically true, so P is false in some models, so $\square P$ is false in any model M, so $\neg\square P$ is true in all models, so $\neg\square P$ is logically true. However, $P \to P$ is true in all models, so $\square(P \to P)$ is true in any model M, so $\neg\square(P \to P)$ is not logically true. Since $\neg\square(P \to P)$ is a substitution instance of $\neg\square P$ (by substitution of $P \to P$ for P), logical truth is not closed under uniform substitution.[66] But closure under uniform substitution is normally considered mandatory for a logical system.[67]

Of course, within Carnap's overall approach one can still define the largest class of logical truths closed under uniform substitution. Call a formula A *logically true under substitution* if and only if every substitution instance of A is logically true. Trivially, if A is logically true under substitution then so is every substitution instance of A, simply because any substitution instance of a substitution instance of A is itself a substitution instance of A. Indeed, Carnap defined just such a notion for propositional modal logic in order to prove S5 sound and complete for it. But the interest of logical truth under substitution remains subordinate to that of logical truth.[68]

The obvious rationale for insisting on the closure of logical truth under uniform substitution in a propositional system is a reading of the non-logical sentence letters as propositional variables. An assignment $\underline{a}$ maps each such variable P to a proposition $\underline{a}(P)$. This induces a mapping $\text{prop}_{\underline{a}}$ of each formula A of the language to a proposition $\text{prop}_{\underline{a}}(A)$ in a natural way. For example, $\text{prop}_{\underline{a}}(\neg A)$ is the negation of $\text{prop}_{\underline{a}}(A)$, and $\text{prop}_{\underline{a}}(A \ \& \ B)$ is the conjunction

---

[66] Here and henceforth we are using 'substitution instance' in a different sense from the one employed in sections 2.4 and 2.5, which concerned the relation between a quantified sentence $Qv\,A$ and the result of uniformly substituting a constant for all free occurrences of the variable v in A. For a propositional modal language L with just the primitive operators $\neg$, $\&$, and $\square$, a uniform substitution as now understood is a total function σ from formulas of L to formulas of L that commutes with all logical operators, in the sense that for all formulas A and B, $\sigma(\neg A) = \neg\sigma(A)$, $\sigma(A \ \& \ B) = \sigma(A) \ \& \ \sigma(B)$, and $\sigma(\square A) = \square\sigma(A)$. The definition extends naturally to more complex languages.

[67] Burgess (1999, p. 176) treats non-closure under uniform substitution as a symptom of philosophical confusion, although he does not attribute it to Carnap. For more on issues of substitution see Burgess 2003 and Schurz 2005.

[68] The notion is called 'L-true by MPL' and defined in Carnap 1946, pp. 40–1, after which he gives the completeness proof (see also Burgess 1999, p. 177). Some evidence that Carnap did not regard the notion as philosophically central is that it does not appear in Carnap 1947.

of $\text{prop}_a(A)$ and $\text{prop}_a(B)$. If we regard logical truth as primarily a feature of propositions, the obvious standard for a formula A to count as logically true in a secondary sense is for $\text{prop}_a(A)$ to be logically true (in the primary sense) for every assignment a. Then logical truth for formulas is automatically closed under uniform substitution. For suppose that A is logically true. Let σ be a uniform substitution. Consider any assignment a. Define an assignment a^* by the rule that for any non-logical sentence letter P, $a^*(P) = \text{prop}_a(\sigma(P))$. One easily shows by induction on the complexity of formulas that for any formula B, $\text{prop}_{a^*}(B) = \text{prop}_a(\sigma(B))$. In particular, therefore, $\text{prop}_{a^*}(A) = \text{prop}_a(\sigma(A))$. Since A is logically true (in the secondary sense), $\text{prop}_{a^*}(A)$ is logically true (in the primary sense); therefore, so is $\text{prop}_a(\sigma(A))$. Since this holds for any assignment a, $\sigma(A)$ is logically true, as required.[69]

In principle, Carnap's framework permits such an approach. His intensions for sentences, functions from state-descriptions to truth values, will serve as propositions. Such a proposition is logically true (in the primary sense) if and only if its value is truth for every state-description. Just as in his semantics for quantified modal logic, the holding of a formula at a state-description can be relativized to an assignment. Under this relativization, Carnap's semantics says that $\square A$ holds at a state-description S on an assignment a if and only if A holds at all state-descriptions on a. A formula is logically true just if it holds at all state-descriptions on all assignments, in other words, just if all assignments give it a logically true intension. On this version of the semantics, logical truth for formulas is closed under uniform substitution. In particular, since some assignments map the propositional variable P to the logically true intension, $\square P$ is true at all state-descriptions on those assignments, so $\neg\square P$ no longer counts as logically true.

But that is not Carnap's approach. He is explicit that the modal systems for which he provides a fully developed semantics do not have propositional variables. He has no objection in principle to adding such variables, but his immediate concern is with a first-order modal language whose only variables are individual ones.[70] Thus he treats the atomic sentences as already

---

[69] Burgess (1999, p. 176, and 2003) explains the justification of closure in terms of the treatment of sentences letters as propositional variables, and attributes the non-closure to a deviant interpretation on which they must be assigned logically independent values.

[70] In Carnap 1946, he denies that his systems contain propositional variables (p. 38). In Carnap 1947, he gives the semantics for the system S_2 constructed by adding an operator for logical necessity to the system S_1 (p. 182), which has only individual variables (p. 3). He contemplates languages with propositional variables at p. 181.

interpreted. We are to imagine them as each having an intension independently of the assignment of values to variables. In general, Carnap distinguishes variables from constants for any grammatical type. Thus adding variables of sentential type would in no way delegitimize constants of sentential type, which is what the atomic sentences are in the language Carnap discusses. The previous failure of logical truth to be closed under uniform substitution occurs with respect to a non-logical atomic sentence constant P in that language. The justification of closure for a sentential language without such constants is irrelevant.

A parallel issue arises for individual constants and variables. Where a and b are distinct individual constants, $a=b$ is not logically true, so it is false at some state-descriptions, so $\Box a=b$ is false at all state-descriptions, so $\neg\Box a=b$ is logically true. But for Carnap $a=a$ is logically true, so $\Box a=a$ is true at all state-descriptions, so $\neg\Box a=a$ is not logically true. Since $\neg\Box a=a$ is a substitution instance of $\neg\Box a=b$, because we can substitute a for both a and b, logical truth fails to be closed under uniform substitution in this case too. It is different for individual variables. Some assignments map the distinct variables x and y to the same individual concept, so $x=y$ is true at all state-descriptions on those assignments, so $\Box x=y$ is also true at all state-descriptions on those assignments, so $\neg\Box x=y$ is not logically true.[71] Nevertheless, closure still fails in the former case. To relativize the intensions of a and b to assignments would expunge a major difference between individual constants and variables. A state-description already determines whether $a=b$ holds, independently of the assignment. It does not so determine whether $x=y$ holds.

That analysis of the reasons for which logical truth is not closed under uniform substitution in Carnap's system does not depend on any extraneous idiosyncrasy of his semantics, for example in its treatment of the non-logical atomic symbols. Instead, the non-closure stems from his guiding principle for the semantics of the necessity operator, which in turn is a simple, natural way of encoding logical truth as a sentential operator in the object-language. This hints that logical modalities may be implicitly metalinguistic.

The technical problems for Carnap's approach get worse in first-order modal logic, even without quantification into modal contexts. Suppose, as

---

[71] In the semantics of Kanger 1957, the operator for logical necessity universally quantifies all free variables in its scope (see Lindström 1998 for discussion), so $\neg\Box x=y$ is logically true too.

before, that for every closed formula A of first-order non-modal logic and model M, $\Box A$ is true in M if and only if A is true in all models. Thus if A is logically true, so true in all models, then $\Box A$ is true in all models, so $\neg\Box A$ is false in all models, so not logically true. On the other hand, if A is not logically true, and so is false in some models, then $\Box A$ is false in all models, so $\neg\Box A$ is true in all models, so logically true. Thus $\neg\Box A$ is logically true if and only if A is not logically true. But then, if some axiomatic system were sound and complete for logical truth on such a semantics for first-order modal logic, so that a Turing machine could enumerate the closed logical truths of that logic, another Turing machine could enumerate the closed non-theorems of first-order non-modal logic simply by listing those closed non-modal formulas A for which the former machine listed $\neg\Box A$. But no Turing machine can enumerate the closed non-theorems of first-order non-modal logic, for a Turing machine *can* enumerate the closed theorems of first-order non-modal logic, since it has a sound and complete recursive axiomatization: if both classes could be so enumerated, that would provide a decision procedure for the theoremhood of closed formulas in first-order non-modal logic, which Church proved impossible. Therefore first-order modal logic on this semantics cannot be soundly and completely axiomatized in a formal system.[72]

In Carnap's framework, the issue is slightly complicated by the requirement that all models have the same domain. If the domain is finite, the resultant set of theorems is decidable after all. However, when the domain is infinite, the set of closed first-order non-modal formulas true in all models over it is undecidable, and the argument goes through as before.[73]

Unaxiomatizability is not a fatal flaw in a semantically presented logic. Second-order logic is unaxiomatizable on its standard interpretation, as are the modal extensions of it discussed in Chapters 5 and 6. The truth itself may be unaxiomatizable, as Gödel showed of arithmetic. Nevertheless, in practice the recognition of unaxiomatizability often stimulates the search for axiomatizable alternatives, even if they involve some change of subject.

---

[72] See Cochiarella 1975 and 1986, pp. 49–51.

[73] Let D be an infinite domain. By the standard upward and downward Löwenheim-Skolem theorems for first-order non-modal logic, any first-order non-modal formula false in some infinite model is false in some model over D. The formulas of first-order non-modal logic false in at least one finite model are recursively enumerable. Thus if the closed formulas of first-order non-modal logic false in at least one model over D were recursively enumerable, so would be the closed formulas of first-order non-modal logic false in at least one model.

The problem of axiomatizability arises for any semantics on which for every closed first-order non-modal formula A, $\neg\Box A$ is logically true if and only if A is not logically true. The left-to-right direction of this biconditional is compelling: if A is logically true in first-order non-modal logic, $\Box A$ should be logically true in first-order modal logic, and in any case $\neg\Box A$ should not be logically true.[74] To break the biconditional, one must therefore break its right-to-left direction. One must sometimes allow $\neg\Box A$ not to be logically true even when A is not logically true. Equivalently, the logical consistency of A should not generally imply the logical truth of $\Diamond A$.[75] Thus if the modal operators act like quantifiers over worlds, their range must be restricted, so that it does not automatically contain a world in which the logically consistent formula A is true. The next chapter concerns Kripke's model-theoretic semantics for modal logic, which turns out to solve both of the technical problems for Carnap's framework considered in this section.

---

[74] For reasons noted in section 2.2, some contingentists accept $\exists y\ x=y$ and $\exists y\ a=y$ as logically true (where a is an individual constant) while denying that $\Box\exists y\ x=y$ and $\Box\exists y\ a=y$ are logically true. This does not solve the problem in the text, for even theoremhood for closed formulas without individual constants is undecidable in first-order non-modal logic.

[75] The logical truth of A may still imply the logical truth of $\Diamond A$, because all instances of the T principle $A \rightarrow \Diamond A$ are logically true, or because $\Box A$ is logically true whenever A is by the rule of necessitation and all instances of the D principle $\Box A \rightarrow \Diamond A$ are logically true.

3

Possible Worlds Model Theory

3.1 Kripke

In his short paper 'Semantical Considerations on Modal Logic' (1963), Saul Kripke decisively advanced the technical understanding of quantified modal logic by providing a clear formal semantic analysis, inspired by the idea of possible worlds but without the problems characteristic of Carnap's approach. In particular, he perspicuously explained the role of the Barcan formula and its converse within this framework. His account is so compelling that it has shaped almost all subsequent discussion of the issues. Ultimately, it turns out to do less than many may have hoped towards resolving the more metaphysical questions. Nevertheless, it still provides the most tractable way to check inferential relations amongst formulas of the relevant languages. In effect, model theory in Kripke's style is the best non-modal guide to modal logic.[1]

Kripke solves the problems for Carnap's approach explained in section 2.8 by distinguishing between models and worlds. The modal operators still act like quantifiers over worlds, but each model has its own set of worlds, which can be the members of any non-empty set whatsoever. The model can exclude some logically permissible assignments of truth values to atomic formulas. The logical consistency of A no longer implies the logical truth of $\Diamond A$, for A may be true at some world in some model without being true at some world in all models.

---

[1] Kripke's early articles were the culmination of multiple interrelated attempts by various logicians to clarify the semantics of modal logic. For a historical survey see Copeland 2002. Work from the 1950s on the semantics of quantified modal logic is represented in Bayart 1958, 1959; Hintikka 1961; Kanger 1957a, 1957b, 1957c; Kripke 1959b; Montague 1960, but something like the contemporary perspective is probably first achieved in Kripke 1963. Lindström 1998 argues that Kanger is closer to Carnap than to Kripke in interpreting the modalities metalinguistically.

A further dimension of Kripke's models is a binary relation of *relative possibility* (accessibility) between worlds. The formula $\Box A$ is true at a world w in a model if and only if A is true at every world w^* accessible from w in the model; similarly, $\Diamond A$ is true at w if and only if A is true at some world w^* accessible from w. The motivating idea is that w^* is possible relative to w if and only if whatever is true in w^* is possible in w, or equivalently, whatever is necessary in w is true in w^*. Such a relation is needed to handle modal logics weaker than S5, so that matters of possibility and necessity may themselves be contingent. For instance, the 4 axiom $\Box P \rightarrow \Box\Box P$ fails in some models in which relative possibility is non-transitive, so P may be contingently necessary. Even the T axiom $\Box P \rightarrow P$ fails in some models in which relative possibility is non-reflexive.

Different classes of Kripke models fit different interpretations of the modal operators. Many systems of first-order modal logic are sound, complete, and closed under uniform substitution with respect to suitable classes of such models. In particular, not all models fit the interpretation of $\Box$ and $\Diamond$ as logical modalities. For example, all formulas of the form $\Box(A \,\&\, \neg A)$ are vacuously true at a dead end, a world from which no world is accessible in the model. Yet $\neg\Box(A \,\&\, \neg A)$ is presumably a logical truth when $\Box$ is treated as a logical constant for logical truth.

The stronger claim is sometimes made that Kripke's model theory is unsuitable for the logical interpretation, because it puts non-logical restrictions on the class of worlds in a model.[2] That claim is too quick. What matters is whether some subclass of Kripke models is appropriate to the logical interpretation. For both the propositional and the first-order case, we can consider the class of models M such that for each model N for the non-modal fragment of the language, some world in M determines the same truth values as N for all non-modal formulas; all worlds in M are to be mutually accessible.[3] If the modal operators act in M like quantifiers over all those worlds, it is arguable that for every formula A, $\Box A$ is true in the model if and only if A is logically true, even if A contains modal operators. Given the conclusions of section 2.8, that is just the equivalence we want when A is fully interpreted and contains no free variables, and $\Box$ is treated as a logical

---

[2] See Hintikka 1980 and Hintikka and Sandu 1995, p. 281. Burgess 2003 criticizes these claims from a different standpoint from the present one.

[3] In the first-order case, we cannot require M to contain a distinct world for each model of the first-order non-modal language, for there are too many models to form a set. Such cardinality restrictions are pervasive in set-theoretic model theory. They are not distinctive of Kripke's approach.

constant for logical truth. Alternatively, if we treat the non-logical sentence or predicate letters as variables, we might consider instead the class of all models M such that for some assignment a of propositions or properties to those variables, for each model N for the non-modal fragment of the language compatible in some appropriate sense with a, some world in M determines the same truth values as N for all non-modal formulas; again, all worlds in M are to be mutually accessible.

Although such an application of Kripke's model theory to logical modalities may be feasible, it hardly fits the spirit of his work. For example, Kripke prefers theoremhood to be closed under uniform substitution.[4] We saw in section 2.8 the obstacles to imposing that constraint on modal logic with a logical interpretation of the modal operators. Again, on the treatment of individual constants suggested by his later work, they are rigid designators, designating the same individual at each world. That treatment validates the necessity of identity in the form $a=b \rightarrow \Box a=b$. But although 'Hesperus = Phosphorus' is a truth, it is hardly a truth of *logic*.[5]

A decisive innovation of Kripke semantics is the distinction between possible worlds and models. Its point is to allow the range of possibility to vary while the logic remains fixed. The set of worlds accessible from a world in a model of a given logic may differ from the set of worlds accessible from another world in the same or another model of the same logic. But fixing the logic should fix the range of *logical* possibility too. The point still applies if one builds specific meaning postulates into the logic of the language, as Carnap did.[6] Thus, even if one could somehow interpret logical modalities by a special case of Kripke semantics, doing so would nullify the distinctive advantages of that approach. It is more naturally applied to a non-logical interpretation of the modal operators, on which the model theory does not determine the range of possibility. That suggests a reading of the operators as metaphysical rather than logical. From this perspective, the structure of Kripke's model theory already makes room for the category of a posteriori necessities he was later to champion.[7]

We saw in section 2.4 how, on Carnap's logical interpretation of the modal operators, the semantics of a quantified modal language supervenes

---

[4] Compare Kripke 1963, p. 66 n. 11.
[5] See Kripke 1980, pp. 97–105.
[6] See Carnap 1952.
[7] Kripke 1980, pp. 100–44.

on the semantics of its non-modal fragment: no distinctively modal para-meter waits for the model to fix its value. Kripke's model theory for modal logic is quite different. The semantics of the non-modal fragment of the language leaves open a wide range of options for the set of worlds and the relation of relative possibility, thereby underdetermining the semantics of the modal language, in ways to be explored. That is no criticism of the model theory. It is simply a reminder that some aspects of the semantics of the modal language remain to be determined by less formal considerations. Kripke never claimed otherwise.

3.2 Kripke models for normal propositional modal logic

In order to be more precise about the formal structure of Kripke's model theory, let us start with the simpler case of a standard propositional modal language, before moving on to the complications of model theory for a quantified modal language. This section explains some technical aspects of the model theory. Section 3.3 will assess what philosophical gains we can expect and what we cannot from such a model theory in the propositional case, for the issues are similar but easier to understand than they become when quantifiers are introduced.

For definiteness, we consider a language with a countable infinity of atomic formulas $P, Q, R, \ldots$, and primitive operators for conjunction (&), negation ($\neg$), and necessity ($\square$). As usual, other symbols are introduced as metalinguistic abbreviations; for example, $\Diamond$ is $\neg\square\neg$.

Kripke defines a *model structure* for such a language as a triple $<W, R, w_0>$, where W is a set, R is a set of ordered pairs of members of W ($R \subseteq W^2$) and $w_0 \in W$. Informally, one can think of W as the set of worlds, R as the relation of relative possibility, w_0 as the actual world, and the whole model structure as a metaphysical theory of the structure of modal reality. However, Kripke's informal motivation is not itself part of the model theory proper. Every non-empty set W, irrespective of the nature of its members, is the first component of various model structures; every subset R of W^2 is the second component of at least one model structure with W as its first component, and every member w_0 of W is the third component of a model structure with W and R as its first and second components respectively. For example, in one model structure W is the set of apples, R is the relation of coming from the same tree, and w_0 is Newton's inspirational apple. Just as a physical phenomenon can inspire and be the intended application of a purely mathematical definition of a type of structure, even though many structures of that type have nothing to do with the original physical phenomenon, so the metaphysical phenomenon of modality inspired and was the intended application of Kripke's purely mathematical definition of a model structure, even though many model structures have nothing to do with metaphysical modality.[8]

We need more than a model structure to evaluate formulas as true or false, because we need something to tell us when to evaluate an atomic formula as true. We use a function V to assign each atomic formula an intension, a function from members of W to 0 or 1. Informally, $V(P)(w) = 1$ just when P is true at the world w. Formally, a *model* on a model structure $<W, R, w_0>$ is an ordered quadruple $<W, R, w_0, V>$, where V is such a function. We can now recursively define the truth of a formula A in a model M = $<W, R, w_0, V>$ at a member w of W ('at a world'), written M, $w \vDash A$:[9]

M, $w \vDash A$ if and only if $V(A)(w) = 1$, for atomic A

M, $w \vDash A$ & B if and only if   M, $w \vDash A$ and M, $w \vDash B$

M, $w \vDash \neg A$ if and only if   not M, $w \vDash A$

M, $w \vDash \Box A$ if and only if   for every $x \in W$ if wRx then M, $x \vDash A$

(Here 'wRx' abbreviates '$<w, x> \in R$'.) Thus the derived semantic clause for $\Diamond$ is the dual:

M, $w \vDash \Diamond A$ if and only if   for some $x \in W$, wRx and M, $x \vDash A$

Informally, we can read the clause for $\Box$ as saying that being necessary at a world is being true at every world possible from its perspective. Dually, being possible at a world is being true at some world possible from its perspective.

---

[8] See also Plantinga 1974, pp. 126–8.

[9] The definition in the text differs trivially from, but is equivalent to, the original one in Kripke 1963. Instead of functions from atomic formulas to intensions he has binary functions from atomic formulas and worlds to truth values. He officially equates a model on a model structure with a function of the latter kind, so his definition of the truth of a formula at a world in a model must be read as making tacit reference to the model structure as well as the model and the world, since the model in his sense need not by itself determine the relation R.

To derelativize truth in a model from the world parameter, we equate it with truth in the model at its actual world: M ⊨ A if and only if M, w_0 ⊨ A. A formula is *valid* on a model structure if and only if it is true in every model on that model structure. Similarly, a system of propositional modal logic is valid on a model structure if and only if every theorem of the system is valid on that model structure. The *logic* of a model structure is the set of all formulas valid on it; the logic of a class of model structures is the set of all formulas valid on all model structures in the class.

For many technical purposes, designating one member of W as actual turned out to be an unnecessary complication. In contemporary modal logic, Kripke's talk of model structures has therefore been largely replaced by talk of *frames*, which are like model structures except for lacking a designated actual world. Thus a frame is any ordered pair <W, R> such that W is a set and R ⊆ W^2. Similarly, a model on a frame <W, R> is a triple <W, R, V>, with no such designated world. Since the choice of actual world plays no role in the definition of 'M, w ⊨ A' for the language in question, in that respect it makes no difference whether M has a designated actual world or not.[10] If M has no such designated world, a formula has no truth value in M *simpliciter*, but may still be true *everywhere* in M (M, w ⊨ A for every $w \in$ W). Henceforth, a model with a designated actual world is *pointed* or 'centred'; when not so qualified, 'model' will mean a model with no designated world. A formula is valid on a frame if and only if it is true everywhere in every model on that frame. Similarly, a system of propositional modal logic is valid on a frame if and only if every theorem of the system is valid on that frame. The *logic* of a frame is the set of all formulas valid on it; the logic of a class of frames is the set of all formulas valid on all frames in the class.

Following Kripke, relations between modal logics and classes of frames have been extensively studied. In contemporary terms, various proposed modal axioms correspond to structural conditions on frames. For example, the 4 axiom $\Box P \rightarrow \Box\Box P$ is valid on a frame <W, R> if and only if R is transitive; the B ('Brouwersche') axiom $P \rightarrow \Box\Diamond P$ is valid on <W, R> if and only if R is symmetric; the T axiom $\Box P \rightarrow P$ is valid on <W, R> if and only if R is reflexive. The K axiom $\Box(P \rightarrow Q) \rightarrow (\Box P \rightarrow \Box Q)$ is valid on every frame, as of course are all truth-functional tautologies.

---

[10] The argument depends on the fact that the language lacks features such as an 'actually' operator @, whose semantic clause is: M, w ⊨ @A if and only if M, w_0 ⊨ A (where M = <W, R, w_0, V>).

Obviously, the rule of modus ponens preserves validity on a frame: whenever $A \to B$ and A are both valid on a frame, so too is B. Likewise, modus ponens preserves validity on a model structure.

The rule of necessitation also preserves validity on a frame: whenever a formula A is valid on a frame, so too is $\Box A$. For if $\Box A$ is not valid on $<W, R>$, then for some model $M = <W, R, V>$ and $w \in W$, not $M, w \vDash \Box A$, so wRw^* but not $M, w^* \vDash A$ for some w^*, so A is not valid on $<W, R>$. By contrast, necessitation does not always preserve validity on a model structure: even if A is valid on $<W, R, w>$, $\Box A$ may not be, since the truth of A in all models on $<W, R, w>$ may depend on the special position of w in the structure of the relation R. For example, let $X = \{0, 1, 2\}$ and S be the reflexive symmetric relation that relates i to j if and only if i differs from j by at most 1. Then (1) is valid on the model structure $<X, S, 0>$, because 0 has S to only two worlds:

(1) $(\Diamond(P \,\&\, Q) \,\&\, \Diamond(P \,\&\, \neg Q)) \to \Box P$

But (1) is false at 1 in some models on $<X, S>$, because 1 has S to all three worlds, so (2) is not valid on $<X, S, 0>$:

(2) $\Box((\Diamond(P \,\&\, Q) \,\&\, \Diamond(P \,\&\, \neg Q)) \to \Box P)$

Necessitation can fail for a model structure but not for a frame because validity on the former, unlike validity on the latter, is specific to the perspective of the designated actual world.

Another difference between frames and model structures concerns the property of *Halldén-completeness*. A logic is Halldén-complete if and only if whenever $A \lor B$ is a theorem and A and B have no non-logical expression in common, either A is a theorem or B is a theorem. The logic of any given model structure is Halldén-complete. For suppose that neither A nor B is valid on the model structure $<W, R, w>$, where A and B have no non-logical expression in common. Then for some model $M_A = <W, R, w, V_A>$ not M_A, $w \vDash A$ and for some model $M_B = <W, R, w, V_B>$ not M_B, $w \vDash B$. Since A and B have no atomic formula in common, some intension V coincides with V_A on the atomic formulas in A and with V_B on the atomic formulas in B. Thus A is evaluated in $M = <W, R, w, V>$ just as in M_A, and B is evaluated in M just as in M_B. Hence not $M, w \vDash A$ and not $M, w \vDash B$, so not $M, w \vDash A \lor B$, so $A \lor B$ is not valid on $<W, R, w>$. By contraposition, if $A \lor B$ is valid on $<W, R, w>$ then either A is or B is. By contrast, the logic of some frames is not

Halldén-complete.[11] A frame can have this sort of disjunctive logic because validity on it is neutral between the perspectives of different worlds, whereas validity on a model structure is specific to the perspective of its actual world.

The formulas valid on any given frame are closed under uniform substitution, in the sense that for any uniform substitution σ, whenever A is valid on the frame, so too is σA.[12] For suppose that σA is not valid on the frame $<W, R>$, so for some model $M = <W, R, V>$ and $w \in W$, not $M, w \vDash \sigma A$. Let $V*$ assign intensions by the rule $V*(B)(x) = 1$ if and only if $M, x \vDash \sigma B$ for $x \in W$, and $M*$ be the model $<W, R, V*>$. One can easily show by induction on the complexity of B that M treats σB like $M*$ treats B, in the sense that for every formula B and $x \in W$: $M*, x \vDash B$ if and only if $M, x \vDash \sigma B$. In particular, therefore, not $M*, w \vDash A$, so A is not valid on $<W, R>$. A similar argument shows that the formulas valid on any given model structure are also closed under uniform substitution.

A system S of propositional modal logic is *normal* if and only if S has all substitution instances of the K axiom and all truth-functional tautologies as theorems and is closed under modus ponens, uniform substitution, and necessitation. The only specifically modal requirements here are the K axiom and necessitation. Given the non-modal background logic, they are jointly equivalent to the condition that $\square$ preserves logical consequence in S: whenever a conclusion C follows in S from a set X of premises, $\square C$ follows

---

[11] A toy example is the frame $<\{0, 1\}, \{<0, 0>\}>$. Since 0 but not 1 is a reflexive point, the formula $\square P \rightarrow P$ is valid on the model structure $<\{0, 1\}, \{<0, 0>\}, 0>$ but not on the model structure $<\{0, 1\}, \{<0, 0>\}, 1>$; thus $\square P \rightarrow P$ is also invalid on the frame. Conversely, since 1 but not 0 is a dead end in the frame, the formula $\square Q$ is valid on the model structure $<\{0, 1\}, \{<0, 0>\}, 1>$ but not on the model structure $<\{0, 1\}, \{<0, 0>\}, 0>$; hence $\square Q$ is also invalid on the frame. Thus the disjunction $(\square P \rightarrow P) \vee \square Q$, whose disjuncts have no non-logical expression in common, is valid on both model structures, and so valid on the two-world frame, even though neither of its disjuncts is. More generally, let $<W_1, R_1>$ and $<W_2, R_2>$ be any two frames such that not every formula valid on $<W_1, R_1>$ is valid on $<W_2, R_2>$, not every formula valid on $<W_2, R_2>$ is valid on $<W_1, R_1>$, and W_1 is disjoint from W_2. Let A be a formula valid on $<W_1, R_1>$ but not on $<W_2, R_2>$. Since validity on a frame is invariant under one-one uniform substitutions of atomic formulas and we have infinitely many such formulas to choose from, we can pick a formula B valid on $<W_2, R_2>$ but not on $<W_1, R_1>$ that has no atomic formulas in common with A. Thus the disjunction $A \vee B$ is valid on both frames even though neither disjunct is. But it is easy to show that the formulas valid on both frames are just those valid on their union $<W_1 \cup W_2, R_1 \cup R_2>$, since the two components do not interfere with each other. Thus $A \vee B$ is valid on the frame $<W_1 \cup W_2, R_1 \cup R_2>$ even though neither A nor B is. The logic of $<W_1 \cup W_2, R_1 \cup R_2>$ is just the intersection of the logic of $<W_1, R_1>$ and the logic of $<W_2, R_2>$, because the components are disjoint. It is characteristic of Halldén-incomplete modal logics to be the intersection of two logics neither of which extends the other (Lemmon 1966c). Humberstone 2005, pp. 575–6, notes an equivalent contrast between validity on a frame and validity at a given point in a frame.

[12] 'Uniform substitution' is defined as in Chapter 2, n. 66.

in S from $\{\square A : A \in X\}$, where to say that C follows in S from X is to say that for some formulas $A_1, \ldots, A_n$ in X, $(A_1 \& \ldots \& A_n) \to C$ is a theorem of S.[13]

The weakest normal modal logic, also called K, is the logic of the class of all frames. It can be axiomatized by taking all substitution instances of the K axiom and all truth-functional tautologies as its axioms and modus ponens and necessitation as its primitive rules of inference. The logic of any class of frames is normal. The logic of the class of all frames $<W, R>$ such that R is an equivalence relation is S5, which can be axiomatized by adding all substitution instances of the T, B, and 4 axioms to the axiomatization of K (for which reason S5 is also known as KTB4), or alternatively by adding all substitution instances of the E axiom $\Diamond P \to \square \Diamond P$ in place of those of the 4 and B axioms (for which reason S5 is also known as KTE). S5 is also the logic of the class of all frames $<W, R>$ such that R is the universal relation, which holds between every world and every world $(R = W^2)$: a normal modal logic can be the logic of many classes of frames, or of none.[14] The logic of the class of all frames $<W, R>$ such that R is transitive and reflexive is S4, which can be axiomatized by adding all substitution instances of the T and 4 axioms to the axiomatization of K (for which reason S4 is also known as KT4), and so on.

It is easy to check that if a system S of propositional modal logic closed under uniform substitution is characterized by a class of models in the sense that the theorems of S are exactly the formulas true everywhere in every model in the class, then S is normal. Conversely, each normal propositional modal logic S has a *canonical model* $M_S = <W_S, R_S, V_S>$ such that the theorems of S are exactly the formulas true everywhere in M_S. The construction of M_S is straightforward. Informally, the idea is to equate worlds with complete descriptions that are consistent in S. Formally, a set of formulas is *S-consistent* if and only if no negation of a conjunction of its members is a theorem of S; it is *maximal S-consistent* if and only if it is S-consistent and not a proper subset of any S-consistent set. Then W_S is defined to be the set of maximal S-consistent sets of formulas. A maximal S-consistent set w is defined to have R_S to a maximal S-consistent set $w*$ if and only if for every formula A,

---

[13] Logical consequence in a system S of propositional modal logic is defined in terms of theoremhood in S because, as usual in modal logic, S is conveniently identified with the set of its theorems.

[14] A normal modal logic that is not the logic of any class of frames is *incomplete*; see Hughes and Cresswell 1984, pp. 52–67, for discussion and examples.

if $\Box A$ is in w then A is in $w*$, or equivalently, whenever A is in $w*$, $\Diamond A$ is in w. Informally, $w*$ is possible relative to w if whatever is necessary in w is true in $w*$, or equivalently, whatever is true in $w*$ is possible in w. For any atomic formula A and maximal S-consistent set $w, V_S(A)(w)$ is defined to be 1 if and only if $A \in w$. One proves by induction on the complexity of the formula A that for any $w \in W_S$, A is true at w in M_S if and only if $A \in w$. If A is a theorem of S, then A belongs to every maximal S-consistent set; therefore A is true everywhere in M_S. If A is not a theorem of S, then $\neg A$ belongs to some maximal S-consistent set; therefore A is false somewhere in M_S.[15] Hence the theorems of S are exactly the formulas true everywhere in M_S, as required. Therefore a system of propositional modal logic is normal if and only if it is closed under uniform substitution and characterized by a model. Thus the normal systems form a natural kind within a Kripkean semantic framework.[16]

Those properties do not fully generalize from the canonical model $<W_S, R_S, V_S>$ to the canonical frame $<W_S, R_S>$ for S. Of course, a formula valid on $<W_S, R_S>$ is true everywhere in every model on $<W_S, R_S>$, so in particular everywhere in $<W_S, R_S, V_S>$, so it is a theorem of S, but the converse fails. A theorem of a normal system S need not be valid on the canonical frame for S, since it may be false somewhere in some other model on that frame. In such cases S is not the logic of any class of frames that includes its canonical frame. It may be the logic of some other class of frames, or of none.[17]

Such results about the model theory of modal logic are simply theorems of mathematics. They are proved by purely mathematical reasoning, with no modal element. Kripke-style model theory can be formalized within

---

[15] On canonical models see Hughes and Cresswell 1984, pp. 22–5.

[16] Even the inconsistent system, of which all formulas are theorems, counts as normal. The frame of its canonical model is simply $<\{\}, \{\}>$; it has no models on non-empty frames because $P \& \neg P$ is never true at a world. In defining a frame, we did not require W to be non-empty. Of course, W is non-empty for any model structure $<W, R, w>$, since $w \in W$. Thus the inconsistent system is not the logic of any model structure. Including the inconsistent system makes the class of normal systems more natural, because closed under more operations. For example, for all normal systems S_1 and S_2 there is a normal system $S_1 \oplus S_2$, the smallest normal system to extend both S_1 and S_2, only if the inconsistent system counts as normal, for the consistent normal systems Ver (see Hughes and Cresswell 1984, pp. 33–6) and S5 have the theorems $\Box(P \& \neg P)$ and $\neg\Box(P \& \neg P)$ respectively, so Ver $\oplus$ S5 is inconsistent.

[17] S is *canonical* if and only if it is the logic of the frame of its canonical model. In normal propositional modal logic, every incomplete system is non-canonical, but not every non-canonical system is incomplete (Hughes and Cresswell 1984, pp. 100–3).

a standard first-order language for set theory with enough vocabulary to describe the syntactic structure of formulas of the propositional modal object language. Modal operators have no place in that metalanguage; nor have special expressions for worlds, relative possibility, or the actual world, in any but the purely mathematical sense already explained. In particular, the semantic clauses for $\square$ and $\lozenge$ use ordinary quantifiers and introduce no modal element. In the metalanguage, $\square$ and $\lozenge$ are mentioned but not used; it cannot express their association with necessity and possibility.[18]

To reinforce the point, let us explicitly prove a simple model-theoretic fact: the formula $P \rightarrow \square P$ is valid on a frame $<W, R>$ if and only if R implies identity ($R \subseteq \{<w, w>: w \in W\}$). For the left-to-right direction, suppose that R does not imply identity. Thus for two distinct elements $w, w* \in W$, $wRw*$. Let V assign intensions by this rule: $V(A)(x) = 1$ if and only if $x = w$. Let M be the model $<W, R, V>$. Then M, $w \vDash P$ but not M, $w* \vDash P$; since $wRw*$, not M, $w \vDash \square P$, so not M, $w \vDash P \rightarrow \square P$, so $P \rightarrow \square P$ is not valid on $<W, R>$. Conversely, for the right-to-left direction, suppose that $P \rightarrow \square P$ is not valid on $<W, R>$. Thus for some model M = $<W, R, V>$ and $w \in W$, not M, $w \vDash P \rightarrow \square P$, so M, $w \vDash P$ but not M, $w \vDash \square P$, so for some $w* \in W$, $wRw*$ and not M, $w* \vDash P$. Since M, $w \vDash P$ but not M, $w* \vDash P$, $w*$ is distinct from w, so R does not imply identity. QED. In particular, therefore, $P \rightarrow \square P$ is invalid on the frame $<W, R>$ where W is $\{0, 1\}$ and R is the universal relation on $\{0, 1\}$, since the universal relation implies identity only on a set with at most one member. Although we might interpret this result by saying that there are contingent truths in the frame $<W, R>$, we proved it by purely non-modal reasoning. The frame we chose consists of purely mathematical objects and is subject to no relevant contingency.

Since the model theory provides only bare formal constraints on systems of modal logic, one may hope to distinguish a restricted class of special models as in some sense the intended ones for a given informal interpretation of the modal operators. In this book, we are primarily interested in interpreting $\square$ and $\lozenge$ as expressing metaphysical necessity and possibility respectively. For that reading, the accessibility relation of an intended model

---

[18] Compare Kripke's comment: 'It is noteworthy that the theorems of this paper can be formalized in a metalanguage (such as Zermelo set theory) which is "extensional," both in the sense of possessing set-theoretic axioms of extensionality *and* in the sense of postulating no sentential connectives other than the truth functions. Thus it is seen that at least a certain non-trivial portion of the semantics of modality is available to an extensionalist logician' (1959a, p. 3).

should fit the account of relative possibility in section 3.1; thus a world $w*$ will be accessible from a world w if and only if whatever is true in $w*$ is possible in w. Since truth entails metaphysical possibility, every world is trivially accessible from itself in an intended model. Thus we want models where accessibility is reflexive. But it is not good enough to proceed ad hoc, merely jotting down constraints as they occur to us: how can we tell when the list is complete? We need a more systematic approach.

3.3 Metaphysical universality in propositional modal logic

We must first articulate the pre-theoretic standard we want theorems of the logic of metaphysical modality to meet. In doing so, we take for granted the understanding of metaphysical modality briefly sketched in section 1.1, as good enough to work with. We are not trying to answer sceptics about metaphysical modality, or to reduce it to something else.

The word 'logic' may suggest all sorts of constraints: for example, that truths of logic should be necessary, or that they should be a priori, or that they should be analytic. The present approach is much simpler. We want a theory of metaphysical modality that consists of all sufficiently general truths about it. Such a truth does not lose its interest for metaphysics by being contingent, or a posteriori, or synthetic, and so should not be excluded from our theory on those grounds. As we shall see, on an appropriate understanding of generality, the set of sufficiently general truths in a modal language has the formal characteristics of a modal logic. The scientific value of insisting on a more restrictive application of the word 'logic' is unclear. However, the aim of this book is not to argue that such alternative understandings are illegitimate, but simply to investigate the logic of metaphysical modality on the present simple understanding of 'logic', and thereby show what logic is like on that conception. Even if it were forced to use a different title, the investigation would still have to be carried out.

'It is metaphysically necessary that all tigers are animals' may express a true generalization about metaphysically necessity. For present purposes, however, it is not general enough. The aim is to prescind from more specific subject matters, such as tigers or even animals, to investigate the more general structure of metaphysical modality. Thus we are not concerned to specify a particular intended interpretation of the language, one that distinguishes 'tiger' from 'robot' in meaning. In the case of propositional modal logic, that would involve assigning particular interpretations to the atomic sentences, for example deciding whether to interpret P as strictly implying Q or as not strictly implying Q. We want to work at a higher level of generality, one that covers both cases. In effect, the intended standard universally generalizes on the atomic sentences, replaced by propositional variables, in order to capture structural principles about metaphysical modality. For the language of propositional modal logic, the only symbols whose intended interpretations are held fixed are the modal and truth-functional operators. For example, the formula $\Box P \to \Box\Box P$ meets the standard if and only if, however P is interpreted, it is necessarily necessary if necessary. We can formulate the idea by quantifying into sentence position. The formula $\Box P \to \Box\Box P$ (in the original language) is a sufficiently general truth if and only if the formula $\forall X\,(\Box X \to \Box\Box X)$ (in an extended language) is true (on its intended interpretation). We call such sufficiently general truths 'metaphysically universal'.

More generally, we form the *universal generalization* of a formula A of the original propositional modal language by uniformly substituting distinct propositional variables for distinct atomic sentences throughout A and prefixing the result with universal quantifiers on each variable (in accordance with given well-orderings of the atomic sentences and variables). Then A is *metaphysically universal* if and only if the universal generalization of A is true on its intended interpretation, which treats the truth-functional operators as usual and makes $\Box$ express metaphysical necessity.[19] Metaphysical universality corresponds to logical truth by the standard of Tarski's seminal 1936 account, if both the truth-functional operators and the modal operators are treated as logical constants. That is a distinguished and fruitful enough precedent for regarding the present investigation as logic. Whether or not we regard $\Box$ and $\Diamond$ with their metaphysical readings as properly logical constants in some other sense, we hold their interpretation constant for present

---

[19] Hartry Field has used Liar-like paradoxes to argue that valid arguments need not preserve truth (2009, pp. 263–8). If a disquotational principle for truth does indeed fail for the relevant universal generalizations, then the intended standard of metaphysical universality should be stated by using the universal generalizations themselves in the object-language itself or an extension thereof, rather than ascriptions of truth to them in the informal metalanguage. At worst, the metalinguistic formulations are more convenient and good enough approximations for present purposes. The question 'What are the true metaphysically universal principles?' is no more metalinguistic than the question 'What are the true chemical principles?'.

purposes because we are interested in what general principles they satisfy. We hold the interpretation of the truth functors constant too because unless we do so we cannot express a wide enough range of such principles. Whatever we think of the terminological issues, scientific curiosity impels us to ask which modal formulas are metaphysically universal. Without the technical resources of modal logic, we have no hope of a systematic answer. They enable us to reason about metaphysical universality over the infinite class of formulas of the modal language, rather than just considering a few formulas piecemeal, one by one as they occur to us, and provide powerful techniques for determining what is derivable from what.

Tarski's account of logical truth is a special case of his account of logical consequence. Logical truths are the logical consequences of the empty set of premises. The formula A is a logical consequence of the set of formulas Γ just in case, on every interpretation that treats the logical constants as intended and the non-logical constants like variables, if every formula in Γ is true then A is true. Therefore when Γ is finite and conjunction and the material conditional are treated as logical constants, A is a logical consequence of Γ if and only if the material conditional with a conjunction of the members of Γ as antecedent and A as consequent is logically true. Thus we can assess arguments as well as statements in the language of modal language by the standard of metaphysical universality, applied to the material conditional from a conjunction of the premises to the conclusion, at least when the premise set is finite. The natural extension of this approach to arguments with infinitely many premises is by extending the metalanguage in which metaphysical universality is defined to permit infinite conjunctions. We could also extend the object-language itself to permit such conjunctions, although the definition does not require that. For simplicity, this chapter concentrates on finitary object-languages and metalanguages. We do not attempt to extend the finitary standard of metaphysical universality to arguments with infinitely many premises by stipulating such an argument to be metaphysically universal just if the material conditional with the conjunction of some finite subset of its premises as antecedent and the conclusion as consequent is metaphysically universal, for the compactness of logical consequence cannot in general be taken for granted: A may be a logical consequence of Γ without being a logical consequence of any finite subset of Γ. For example, if A_∞ formalizes 'There are infinitely many stars' and, for each natural number n, A_n formalizes 'There are at least n stars' in a suitable language with a suitable choice of logical constants, then A_∞ is a logical consequence of the infinite set $\{A_1, A_2, A_3, \ldots\}$ without being a logical consequence of any of its finite subsets. Although standard first-order logic is compact, that is one of its special features, not the general case. For simplicity, we focus on metaphysical universality for single formulas rather than arguments.

The metaphysical universality of a formula of propositional modal logic depends on the truth of a formula with universal quantification into sentence position on the intended interpretation of the metalanguage. But what exactly is the intended interpretation of such quantification? One option is to understand it ontologically, as quantification over objects of a special sort, such as propositions. Alternatively, we might treat it as an irreducible form of quantification in its own right, with no such ontological commitment. Let us postpone such questions until later (Chapter 5), and see how much progress we can make while relying on an informal understanding of such quantification, on which $\forall X\, A$ entails any result $A(X/B)$ of uniformly replacing free occurrences of X in A by an interpreted sentence B, even in an extended language, with the usual proviso that no free occurrence of a variable in B thereby becomes bound.

A system S of propositional modal logic is *sound for metaphysical universality* if and only if every theorem of S is metaphysically universal; S is *complete for metaphysical universality* if and only if every metaphysically universal formula of the language is a theorem of S. Exactly one system, individuated by the set of its theorems, is sound and complete for metaphysical universality. Its theorems are just the metaphysically universal formulas. Call that system MU. In that sense, MU is the uniquely correct logic of metaphysical modality for our propositional modal language. But which system is MU, in axiomatic or model-theoretic terms?

Sometimes, the connection between the intended interpretation and a mathematical model theory for a formal language is made by one intended model or many mutually isomorphic models. As already seen, we cannot expect that here, because the atomic sentences lack intended interpretations. The best we can hope for is a unique intended model structure <W, R, w>, where in some sense to be specified W is the set of genuine worlds, R is the relation of genuine relative possibility, and w is the genuine actual world. The formulas valid on such an intended model structure should be exactly the metaphysically universal ones. In other words, the logic of the intended model structure should be MU.

The hypothesis of an intended model structure vindicates the decision to take the target theorems as the metaphysically universal formulas, rather than just those meeting the more restrictive criterion of metaphysical □-universality. A formula is metaphysically □-universal just if all its modal closures are true, where its modal closures are the results of prefixing it with arbitrary strings of necessity operators as well as the relevant universal quantifiers. For validity on a model structure is truth at its designated world in all models based on that structure, not necessity (and necessary necessity, ...) at that world in all those models. Thus it is the model-theoretic analogue of metaphysical universality, truth under all assignments, not of metaphysical □-universality. Metaphysical □-universality is closer to validity on a frame than to validity on a model structure. In particular, metaphysical □-universality, like validity on a frame and unlike validity on a model structure, is automatically closed under necessitation. But an intended frame is not enough, for unless something determines which world in the frame represents actuality (even if we do not know which it is), the role of the model theory remains too instrumental. If we intend anything model-theoretic, we intend a model structure, not just a frame. The appropriate constraint on the actual world of an intended model structure is that the formulas true at it in all models based on the structure be exactly those true in actuality, that is, simply true, under all assignments. In other words, validity on the model structure should be equivalent to metaphysical universality.

MU may be 'by accident' the logic of an unintended model structure, whose worlds have no other special connection with metaphysical modality. However, it is not clear in advance what further precise desiderata we can reasonably impose on an intended model structure, beyond having MU as its logic. A more cautious strategy is to wait until we have a promising candidate, and then see how closely it is connected to metaphysical modality. In practice, if we can soundly *argue* that the logic of a given model structure is MU, the premises of our argument are likely to make a non-accidental connection of a relevant sort. We therefore concentrate on finding a model structure whose logic can be argued to be MU, although a few comments on further sorts of connection are also apposite.

The assumption that MU is the logic of a model structure yields some further information about MU. A system of propositional modal logic is *quasi-normal* if and only if it extends K and is closed under modus ponens and uniform substitution. In section 3.2 we saw in effect that the logic of any model structure is quasi-normal and Halldén-complete; it is of course consistent. Thus if there is an intended model structure, MU is a consistent Halldén-complete quasi-normal logic. In other words, it meets five conditions. First, MU is consistent, in the sense that it does not contain every formula. Second, MU is Halldén-complete: whenever $A \lor B$ is a theorem and A and B have no non-logical expression in common, either A is a theorem or B is a theorem. Third, MU extends the smallest normal system K: every theorem of K is a theorem of MU. Fourth, MU is closed under modus ponens. Fifth, MU is closed under uniform substitution. Is it independently plausible that MU meets those five conditions?

MU obviously meets the first, fourth, and fifth conditions. It is consistent, for the universal generalization of $P \,\&\, \neg P$ is false on its intended interpretation. It is closed under modus ponens, for if $A \to B$ and A are metaphysically universal, their universal generalizations are true, so the universal generalization of B is true by the standard logic of universal quantification, so B is metaphysically universal. MU is closed under uniform substitution, for if B is a substitution instance of A, any counterexample to the universal generalization of B is a counterexample to the universal generalization of A, so if the latter is true so is the former, so if A is metaphysically universal so is B. MU also meets the second condition, Halldén-completeness. For suppose that neither A nor B is metaphysically universal and they have no non-logical expression in common. Then there is a counterexample to the universal generalization of A and a counterexample to the universal generalization of B. By the disjointness of the non-logical constants of A and B, those counterexamples can be combined into a counterexample to the universal generalization of $A \lor B$ (the counterexamples are actual, not merely possible). Thus $A \lor B$ is also not metaphysically universal.[20]

Arguing that MU extends K is less straightforward. The natural strategy is to take a standard axiomatization of K and argue that its axioms are metaphysically universal and that metaphysical universality is closed under its rules of inference, modus ponens and necessitation. Unfortunately, closure

---

[20] The argument for the Halldén-completeness of MU is similar to Halldén's original argument from the Halldén-incompleteness (as we now say) of a system to its incompleteness with respect to normal interpretations (as he says). See Halldén 1951 and, for further discussion, Schumm 1993. Humberstone 2007 argues that a Halldén-incomplete modal logic is appropriate for agnostics about counterfactual possibility. That is consistent with the Halldén-completeness of MU, since MU captures the true modal generalizations rather than remaining neutral between different hypotheses about them.

under necessitation is not obvious. Perhaps some formula A is metaphysically universal even though $\Box A$ is not, because the universal generalization of A is only contingently true. Admittedly, we have no special reason to doubt that metaphysical universality is closed under necessitation. Within the confines of a standard language of propositional modal logic, no plausible counterexample has ever been offered. Although many truths are contingent, the language is so limited in expressive resources that the only sentences in it with true universal generalizations may be those whose necessitations also have true universal generalizations.[21] Someone might argue: if A but not $\Box A$ is metaphysically universal, that makes the actual world special, because it differs from some possible worlds in validating A; but it is not plausible that the actual world is special. Why should we be so lucky as to live in an A-validating world? However, if some possible worlds validate A and some do not, the actual world must fall into one category or the other. There is no clear reason to count the worlds validating A as more special than those invalidating A. For all we have been told, far more worlds may validate A than invalidate it. Such considerations are a shaky basis for confidence in the closure of MU under necessitation.

Fortunately, without assuming that MU is closed under necessitation we can still argue that it extends K, by an alternative strategy. First, we re-axiomatize K with modus ponens as the only rule of inference. The new axioms are the iterated necessitations of the old axioms, that is, all truth-functional tautologies and instances of $\Box(A \to B) \to (\Box A \to \Box B)$ (an iterated necessitation of a formula is the result of prefixing it by a finite number, possibly zero, of occurrences of $\Box$). Clearly all theorems of the new system are theorems of K, and one can establish the converse by showing necessitation to be a derived rule of the new system (if A is a theorem so is $\Box A$, by induction on the length of the proof of A). Thus the two axiomatizations are equivalent. It is clear enough that the new axioms are metaphysically universal. As already noted, metaphysical universality is closed under modus ponens. Therefore every theorem of K is metaphysically universal, as required. The converse is false, for at least two reasons. The obvious one is that the T axiom $\Box P \to P$ is metaphysically universal but no theorem of K. A less obvious

---

[21] By contrast, if we add the 'actually' operator @, $P \leftrightarrow @P$ is metaphysically universal although $\Box(P \leftrightarrow @P)$ is not. An example will be given in section 3.6 of a metaphysically universal first-order formula whose necessitation some contingentists will regard as not metaphysically universal.

reason is that K is Halldén-incomplete, for although $\Diamond(P \to P) \vee \neg\Diamond(Q \to Q)$ is a theorem of K, neither disjunct is. Therefore MU is not K, and so must be stronger than K. By adding all iterated necessitations of the T axiom to the preceding re-axiomatization of K, we can re-axiomatize KT, the weakest normal modal logic with the T axiom, and plausibly argue that KT too is a subsystem of MU.

Since MU is a consistent Halldén-complete quasi-normal modal logic, it meets five salient necessary conditions for a system to be the logic of some model structure. They are not quite jointly sufficient.[22] Nevertheless, they are promising evidence for the possibility of defining a model structure whose logic is MU.

Can we use the canonical model for MU to define an intended model structure? The definition of the canonical model in section 3.2 is applicable only to normal systems. We have seen that although MU is consistent and quasi-normal, it may not be normal: we cannot take its closure under necessitation for granted. Nevertheless, the idea of a canonical model can be extended to quasi-normal logics. The trick is that every quasi-normal system S has a normal kernel N(S), the strongest normal subsystem of S; it comprises just those formulas every iterated necessitation of which belongs to S.[23] Of course, if S *is* closed under necessitation, and so normal, N(S) is just S itself. Since N(S) is normal, it has a canonical model

---

[22] Proof: There are incomplete but Halldén-complete normal modal logics (see Schumm 1981, p. 198, and 1993, p. 202). Any such system meets the five conditions without being the logic of a model structure. For it is easy to show that if a normal modal system S is the logic of a model structure <W, R, w>, then S is also the logic of the model structure <W*, R*, w>, where <W*, R*> is the sub-frame of <W, R> generated by w (W* consists of the members of W to which w has the reflexive ancestral of R and R* is the restriction of R to W*, so members of W not in W* make no difference to truth at w; see Hughes and Cresswell 1984, pp. 78–81). But then S is the logic of the frame <W*, R*>, for if $x \in$ W* then x is some number n of steps of R* from w, so for any theorem A of S, since $\square^n A$ is also a theorem of S because S is normal, for any model M on <W*, R*>, M, $w \vDash \square^n A$, so M, $x \vDash A$, so A is valid on <W*, R*>; conversely, if A is valid on the frame <W*, R*> then a fortiori A is valid on the model structure <W*, R*, w> and so is a theorem of S. Thus an incomplete normal system, being the logic of no frame, is also the logic of no model structure. Despite appearances, this result is consistent with theorem 15.25 at p. 484 of Chagrov and Zakharyaschev 1997 (deriving from Wroński 1976), for 'frame' there means a *general frame*, which restricts the truth sets of atomic formulas to a distinguished subalgebra of sets of worlds (Chagrov and Zakharyaschev 1997, p. 238).

[23] Formally, N(S) = {A: for all $n \geq 0$, $\square^n A \in$ S}. It is routine to check that N(S) is normal. Furthermore, any normal subsystem S* of S is a subsystem of N(S) too, for if $A \in$ S* then $\square^n A \in$ S*, so $\square^n A \in$ S, so $A \in$ N(S). Thus N(S) is the largest normal subsystem of S. If S extends S4, we can simplify the condition for membership of N(S): $A \in$ N(S) if and only if $\square A \in$ S. See Segerberg 1971, pp. 173–5, for canonical models for quasi-normal systems.

$M_{N(S)} = <W_{N(S)}, R_{N(S)}, V_{N(S)}>$. The formulas true everywhere in $M_{N(S)}$ are the theorems of N(S). As before, W_S is the set of maximal S-consistent sets of formulas. Since N(S) is a subsystem of S, every maximal S-consistent set is a maximal N(S)-consistent set, so $W_S \subseteq W_{N(S)}$. We can therefore define a new sort of canonical model $M^+_S = <W_{N(S)}, W_S, R_{N(S)}, V_{N(S)}>$ for S itself by distinguishing the maximal S-consistent worlds, for the formulas true at every distinguished world in the model are exactly the theorems of S. In particular, for S = MU, a formula is true at every world in W_{MU} in the canonical model $M^+_{MU} = <W_{N(MU)}, W_{MU}, R_{N(MU)}, V_{N(MU)}>$ for MU if and only if it is metaphysically universal.

Despite these advantages, the canonical model of MU also has several disadvantages for present purposes, whether we treat MU as quasi-normal or as normal.

First, the model is unpointed and has no natural candidate for the actual world. Many different members of W_{MU} (maximal MU-consistent sets) under different interpretations constitute the set of true formulas. More specifically, we can interpret every member of any given set Γ of atomic formulas as a tautology and every other atomic formula as a contradiction, so the set w_Γ of all formulas true on that interpretation is a maximal MU-consistent set, and therefore a candidate for the actual world. Whenever Γ and Δ are distinct sets of atomic formulas, w_Γ and w_Δ are incompatible, so there are at least as many candidates for the actual world as there are sets of atomic formulas: an uncountable infinity. We can hardly expect to get an intended model structure in any strong sense from a model with no natural candidate for the actual world, even if we can somehow get a model structure whose logic happens to be MU.

Second, even if we abstract from the specific distribution V_{MU} or $V_{N(MU)}$ of truth values to atomic formulas in the canonical model, what remains may be structurally unsuited to forming the basis of an intended model structure. For simplicity, assume that MU is normal. The canonical frame $<W_{MU}, R_{MU}>$ may not be a suitable intended frame. That all metaphysically universal formulas are so much as valid on that frame is not obvious: how do we know that MU is not one of those normal modal logics that are invalid on their canonical frame? Even if MU is the logic of $<W_{MU}, R_{MU}>$, it will be the logic of many other frames too, not all of which are even isomorphic to each other. For example, one can combine an arbitrarily large infinity of disjoint mutually isomorphic copies of $<W_{MU}, R_{MU}>$ into a single enormous super-frame on which exactly the same formulas are valid as on $<W_{MU}, R_{MU}>$.[24] There are infinitely many such non-isomorphic frames of different sizes. Although their division into disconnected parts may be unattractive, the canonical model of MU has a similar feature. The frame of the canonical model of any consistent quasi-normal system S has pairs of worlds that are maximal S-consistent sets neither of which has the ancestral of the accessibility relation to the other; each world classifies the other as impossible, necessarily impossible, necessarily necessarily impossible, and so on. This follows almost trivially from the definition of a canonical model.[25] Thus there are maximal MU-consistent sets neither of which has the ancestral of the canonical accessibility relation to the other. It should not follow that modal reality itself contains incommensurable worlds in any significant sense.

Third, and more generally, the canonical model and all its components are set-theoretic constructs out of syntactic items. They are not designed to anchor modal language in any reality outside itself. In particular, by construction the number of worlds in the canonical model and its sub-models is at most the number of sets of formulas of the formal language, no matter

---

[24] Frames are isomorphic when there is an isomorphism (a structure preserving function) between them. Formally, f is an isomorphism from a frame $<W, R>$ to a frame $<W\#, R\#>$ if and only if f is a one-one function from W onto $W\#$ such that for all $w, x \in W$, $f(w)R\#f(x)$ if and only if wRx. To adapt the definition to model structures, add the requirement that f is an isomorphism from $<W, R, w_0>$ to $<W\#, R\#, w_{0\#}>$ only if $f(w_0)$ is $w_{0\#}$. To adapt the definition to models, add the requirement that f is an isomorphism from $<W, R, V>$ to $<W\#, R\#, V\#>$ only if $V\#(A)(f(w))$ is always $V(A)(w)$, and so on. For many technical purposes in modal logic, we can generalize isomorphisms to bisimulations, which satisfy weaker constraints; if a world w in a model M is related by a bisimulation to a world $w*$ in a model M* then the same formulas are true at w in M and at $w*$ in M* (see van Benthem 2002, p. 393; Hughes and Cresswell 1984, pp. 70–5, present a similar idea with different terminology). However, this may simply reflect an expressive limitation of the language of propositional modal logic, which cannot capture the structural difference between the two. When it comes to identifying an intended frame, model structure, or model, any structural difference is significant, so it is natural to require at least uniqueness up to isomorphism, if not literal uniqueness.

[25] Let S be a consistent quasi-normal modal system and P an atomic formula. Since every member of $\{\Box^n P: n \geq 0\}$ is mapped to a theorem of K by the substitution of a tautology for P, $\{\Box^n P: n \geq 0\}$ is S-consistent and so a subset of a maximal S-consistent $u \in W_S$. By a similar argument, $\{\Box^n \neg P: n \geq 0\} \subseteq v$ for some $v \in W_S$. As is easily shown, if $wR_{N(S)}x$ then $\{\Box^n P: n \geq 0\} \subseteq w$ only if $\{\Box^n P: n \geq 0\} \subseteq x$ and $\{\Box^n \neg P: n \geq 0\} \subseteq w$ only if $\{\Box^n \neg P: n \geq 0\} \subseteq x$. Since $P \in \{\Box^n P: n \geq 0\}$ and $\neg P \in \{\Box^n \neg P: n \geq 0\}$, no $w \in W_S$ is such that $\{\Box^n P: n \geq 0\} \subseteq w$ and $\{\Box^n \neg P: n \geq 0\} \subseteq w$. Thus neither $uR_{N(S)}{}^n v$ nor $vR_{N(S)}{}^n u$ for any n. Of course, this does not rule out some other $w \in W_S$ such that $wR_{N(S)}{}^n u$ and $wR_{N(S)}{}^n v$; in some but not all cases this possibility is realized (Hughes and Cresswell 1984, pp. 94–7).

how fine-grained extra-linguistic modal reality itself is.[26] To anchor the formal language semantically in any such reality, one must look beyond model theory itself, perhaps to an independent metaphysical theory of the nature of possible worlds.

A natural idea is to construct a non-linguistic analogue of the canonical frame, with sets of propositions rather than of formulas as worlds, and extend it to a model structure by identifying the actual world with the set of true propositions. Many theories of propositions permit such a construction. It avoids the objections to using the canonical frame. But which sets of propositions should we use, and what accessibility relation between them?

The aim, at least in this book, is not to explain metaphysical modality in clearer or more basic terms but merely to identify a natural model structure for us to intend. We may therefore identify it in modal terms without vicious circularity. The obvious suggestion is to replace formulas in the definition of the canonical model for MU by propositions, and MU-consistency by something like possibility itself.

To develop the idea, we need some background theory about propositions. For simplicity, we assume that every proposition p has a negation $\sim p$, and every set of propositions Γ a conjunction $\Pi\Gamma$ and a disjunction $\Sigma\Gamma$, with respect to which all propositions form a complete atomic Boolean algebra, with the usual laws. The laws make the theory of propositions coarse-grained by equating Boolean equivalences. Thus there is just one tautology, 1, and just one contradiction, 0. As usual, we define a partial order $\leq$ on the elements of the algebra by stipulating that $p \leq q$ if and only if $\Pi\{p, q\} = p$. Informally, we treat $\leq$ as entailment. Under this partial order, $\Pi\Gamma$ is the greatest lower bound of Γ, and $\Sigma\Gamma$ its least upper bound. Completeness just means that these bounds are defined for all sets of propositions, infinite as well as finite. The top and bottom elements of the algebra are 1 and 0 respectively. An atom is a proposition q such that $q \neq 0$ and for any proposition $p, p \leq q$ only if $p = 0$ or $p = q$. Atoms are not mutually independent atomic propositions in the usual sense but rather mutually exclusive maximal consistent propositions. By the laws of Boolean algebra, an atom q entails or excludes every proposition p ($q \leq p$ or $q \leq \sim p$). The algebra

---

[26] Bricker 1987 discusses such cardinality questions. He allows languages with infinitely long sentences, but our present concern is with a standard language for propositional modal logic, in which all formulas are finite strings of symbols from a countable lexicon. Thus the set of formulas is only countably infinite, and so has only continuum many subsets, which Bricker plausibly argues to be too small.

is atomic in the sense that any consistent proposition p is entailed by some atom q $(q \leq p)$.[27]

That account of propositions is purely non-modal. In particular, entailment is defined in terms of propositional identity and conjunction, neither of which was characterized in modal terms. All other features of the algebra can be characterized in terms of entailment. That it is a complete atomic Boolean algebra in effect just means that it has the structure of the natural generalization of classical non-modal propositional logic to infinitary conjunction and disjunction. For all that has been said, many of the atoms may entail metaphysical impossibilities, for example that Socrates is a fish.

To handle modality, we assume that every proposition p has a necessitation Lp, true if and only if p is necessary. If p is the proposition that things are so, Lp is the proposition that it is necessary that things are so. To relate L to the Boolean algebra, we assume simply that the necessitation of a conjunction is the conjunction of the necessitations of its conjuncts: for every set of propositions Γ, $L\Pi\Gamma = \Pi\{Lp: p \in \Gamma\}$. This extends the law of every normal modal logic that a finite conjunction is necessary if and only if every conjunct is necessary. The special case when Γ is empty says that $L1 = 1$, since 1 is the greatest lower bound of the empty set; this resembles the rule of necessitation. It also follows that the function L is monotonic in the sense that if p entails q then Lp entails Lq, for if $\Pi\{p, q\} = p$ then $\Pi\{Lp, Lq\} = L\Pi\{p, q\} = Lp$. Entailment preserves necessity, but not as a result of a modal characterization of entailment.[28]

---

[27] Atomicity and completeness are independent constraints: not all atomic Boolean algebras are complete, and not all complete Boolean algebras are atomic. Following Bricker, Stalnaker (2003, p. 34) acknowledges the need for an assumption similar to atomicity in constructing worlds as maximal consistent sets of propositions, in the manner of Adams (1974); see also Stalnaker 2012, pp. 25–6. Henkin-style completeness proofs rely on a syntactic analogue of this assumption: Lindenbaum's Lemma, which says that every consistent theory has a complete (therefore maximal) consistent extension. Canonical models in modal logic were introduced to serve such completeness proofs. However, the proof of Lindenbaum's Lemma relies on the compactness of (syntactic) consistency: if every finite subset of a set of sentences is consistent, so is the set itself. The lemma fails in some non-compact languages. For a toy example, let a language consist only of infinitely many atomic sentences S_0, S_1, S_2, . . . , where S_i means that the number of planets is finite but at least i. The consistent sets of sentences are just the finite ones, so no set is maximal consistent. Such examples pose no threat to the assumption that the algebra of propositions is atomic. The propositions expressed by the sentences in any consistent subset of $\{S_0, S_1, S_2, \ldots\}$ are all entailed by a non-contradictory proposition that specifies an exact number of planets but is inexpressible in this limited language.

[28] The application of Boolean algebra with an additional operator to modal logic goes back to McKinsey 1941 and McKinsey and Tarski 1948, and was generalized in Lemmon 1966a and 1966b. Usually, the algebras are not required to be complete and atomic, and L is only required to commute with finite conjunctions. The present stronger requirements are motivated by the intended interpretation in terms of metaphysical modality, which has typically not been the aim of the algebraic tradition.

On a variant approach, the function L is defined in terms of the Boolean structure: $L_1 = 1$; $Lp = 0$ if $p \neq 1$. This makes L commute with conjunction as required, for if $q \neq 1$ for some $q \in \Gamma$ then $\Pi\Gamma \neq 1$ and $0 = Lq \in \{Lp: p \in \Gamma\}$, so $L\Pi\Gamma = 0 = \Pi\{Lp: p \in \Gamma\}$; otherwise, $\Gamma \subseteq \{1\}$, so $\Pi\Gamma = 1$ and $\{Lp: p \in \Gamma\} \subseteq \{1\}$, so $L\Pi\Gamma = 1 = \Pi\{Lp: p \in \Gamma\}$. Indeed, the definition validates all theorems of S5. It is therefore highly restrictive. It also forces the modal individuation of propositions, for if $L(p \leftrightarrow q)$ is true then $L(p \leftrightarrow q) \neq 0$, so $p \leftrightarrow q = 1$, so $p = q$ by the laws of Boolean algebra; conversely, if $p = q$ then $L(p \leftrightarrow q) = L(p \leftrightarrow p) = L_1 = 1$, so $L(p \leftrightarrow q)$ is true; thus propositions are identical if and only if they are necessarily equivalent. By contrast, the previous approach keeps L primitive and leaves all such questions open, since it can be interpreted over any frame $<W, R>$ with the subsets of W playing the role of propositions and Lp defined as $\{w \in W: x \in p$ for all x such that $wRx\}$. For the sake of generality, we therefore continue to treat L as primitive; the commutativity constraint already implies that $L_1 = 1$, and we still have the special case on which $Lp = 0$ whenever $p \neq 1$.

Our little theory of propositions is not indubitable. For example, one may suspect that there are too many propositions to form a set: as standardly defined, an algebra is a set-theoretic structure. Nevertheless, the theory is at least a good enough approximation to the truth for its consequences to be worth exploring, to test the philosophical potential of possible worlds semantics.

The obvious plan is to take the atoms of the algebra, the maximal consistent propositions, to form the set of worlds $W^\wedge$ of the intended model structure.[29] A proposition p is true at such a world w if and only if w entails p. The actual world $w^\wedge$ is the conjunction of all true propositions, which is

---

[29] In the tradition of algebraic semantics for modal logic, the standard construction of a frame from a modal algebra uses the ultrafilters of the algebra as the worlds of the frame (see for example van Benthem 1979, p. 2). In the present case, an ultrafilter is a set U of propositions such that (for all propositions p, q) (i) $1 \in U$; (ii) if $p \in U$ and $\Sigma\{\sim p, q\} \in U$ then $q \in U$; (iii) either $p \in U$ or $\sim p \in U$, and not both. An ultrafilter V is accessible from an ultrafilter U in the frame if and only if for every proposition p, if $Lp \in U$ then $p \in V$. The idea is for p to be true at U if and only if $p \in U$. The trouble with this construction for present purposes is that it does not guarantee that truth at a world is preserved under infinitary conjunction. For example, suppose that the number of atoms is infinite. Say that p is *almost ubiquitous* just if $q \leq p$ for all but finitely many atoms q. Let T be the set of almost ubiquitous propositions. Then T is a proper filter, in the sense that it meets conditions (i) and (ii) above and $0 \notin T$. By a standard result (using the axiom of choice), it follows that $T \subseteq U$ for some ultrafilter U. For each atom q, $\sim q$ is almost ubiquitous, so $\sim q \in U$, so $\sim q$ is true at U. But $\Pi\{\sim q: q$ is an atom$\} = 0 \notin U$, so that conjunction is false at U. In algebraic terms, the problem is that there are non-principal ultrafilters. See also Chagrov and Zakharyaschev 1997, pp. 212–13.

an atom because it entails or excludes every proposition without being a contradiction. The accessibility relation $R^\wedge$ is defined by analogy with the canonical model construction: given atoms w and x, $wR^\wedge x$ if and only if for every proposition p, if $w \leq Lp$ then $x \leq p$. Thus the intended model structure is $<W^\wedge, R^\wedge, w^\wedge>$. Although $W^\wedge$ may contain many hopelessly impossible worlds, they make no difference to whether MU is the logic of $<W^\wedge, R^\wedge, w^\wedge>$. For if a proposition p is impossible, then $L\sim p$ is true, so $w^\wedge \leq L\sim p$, so if $w^\wedge R^\wedge x$ then $x \leq \sim p$ by definition of $R^\wedge$, so not $x \leq p$ because x is consistent; thus p is true at no world accessible from the actual world in the model structure. Likewise, suppose that p is not only impossible but lacks each finite iteration of possibility. Then $L^n\sim p$ is true for each natural number n ($L^0 q = q$ and $L^{n+1}q = L^n Lq$ for any q), so p is false at any world to which $w^\wedge$ bears the reflexive ancestral of $R^\wedge$. Thus worlds at which p is true play no role in evaluating any formula of the language at the actual world in any model based on this model structure. We could eliminate all such worlds from the intended model structure by restricting its set of worlds to those to which $w^\wedge$ bears the reflexive ancestral of $R^\wedge$, but it is unclear what serious gain doing so would bring. For present purposes, we retain $<W^\wedge, R^\wedge, w^\wedge>$ as already defined. What can we do with this model structure?

When we apply a logic, identifying an intended model perspicuously connects truth in a model, a mathematically defined relation of sentences to models, and simple truth, a semantically defined property of sentences. On its intended interpretation, a sentence is simply true if and only if it is true in the intended model. As a corollary, this yields the required implication from model-theoretic logical truth to simple truth. If a sentence is true in all models, in particular it is true in the intended model. Without an intended model, we need a subtler way of showing that model-theoretic logical truths are true. Since the formal language of propositional modal logic has no intended model, at best only an intended model structure, over which atomic formulas may be interpreted in local contexts, a reasonable desideratum is that the formulas valid on the candidate intended model structure be exactly the metaphysically universal ones. In other words, the logic of the model structure should be MU, sound and complete for metaphysical universality. The proposal is that this condition is necessary for being an intended model structure with respect to metaphysical universality. It may not be sufficient, for any two isomorphic model structures have the same logic, but one of them may be intended while the other is not, for example because one of them consists of worlds in some informally intended sense while the other does not. To determine whether the logic of $<W^\wedge, R^\wedge, w^\wedge>$ is indeed sound and complete for metaphysical universality, we must relate the definition of metaphysical universality to the definition of $<W^\wedge, R^\wedge, w^\wedge>$.

A formula is metaphysically universal if and only if its universal generalization is true. A *faithful interpretation* is any assignment of propositions to formulas that respects the intended meanings of the connectives. Given our little theory of propositions, we may explicate that idea as follows. An assignment I is faithful if and only if for all formulas A and B, $I(\neg A) = {\sim}I(A)$, $I(A \& B) = \Pi\{I(A), I(B)\}$, and $I(\Box A) = LI(A)$. Then the universal generalization of A is true, so A is metaphysically universal, if and only if $I(A)$ is true for every faithful interpretation I.

Each faithful interpretation I determines a model $M_I = <W^\wedge, R^\wedge, w^\wedge, V_I>$ on the intended model structure in the natural way. We need only define the truth value of each atomic formula A at a world w, which we do by stipulating that $V_I(A)(w) = 1$ if and only if $w \leq I(A)$ ($I(A)$ is true at w). We want to show that the truth values of formulas in the model match those of the propositions I assigns them. More precisely, for every formula A: $M_I \vDash A$ if and only $I(A)$ is true. To show that, we must establish something more general, that the truth values of formulas track those of the corresponding propositions across all worlds in the model. More precisely, for every formula A and $w \in W^\wedge$: $M_I, w \vDash A$ if and only if $w \leq I(A)$. That can be established on the basis of the theory of propositions previously outlined, by induction on the complexity of the formula A.[30]

---

[30] Proof: The basis of the induction is trivial: the result holds when A is atomic by definition of V_I. For the induction step for $\neg A$, the crucial point is that $w \leq {\sim}I(A)$ if and only if not $w \leq I(A)$ because w is an atom. For $A \& B$, the point is that $w \leq \Pi\{I(A), I(B)\}$ if and only if $w \leq I(A)$ and $w \leq I(B)$, which holds whether or not w is an atom. The least trivial part of the argument is the induction step for $\Box A$. The induction hypothesis is that for all $x \in W^\wedge$: $M_I, x \vDash A$ if and only $x \leq I(A)$. From that, we must show that for $w \in W$: $M_I, w \vDash \Box A$ if and only if $w \leq I(\Box A)$. One direction is easy. If $w \leq I(\Box A) = LI(A)$ then $x \leq I(A)$ whenever $wR^\wedge x$ by definition of $R^\wedge$, so by induction hypothesis $M_I, x \vDash A$ whenever $wR^\wedge x$, so $M_I, w \vDash \Box A$. For the converse, suppose that $M_I, w \vDash \Box A$. Let $[w] = \{p: w \leq Lp\}$. Suppose that $\Pi([w] \cup \{{\sim}I(A)\}) \neq 0$. So, since the algebra is atomic, $x \leq \Pi([w] \cup \{{\sim}I(A)\})$ for some $x \in W^\wedge$. For every proposition p, if $w \leq Lp$ then $p \in [w]$ so $x \leq p$; thus $wR^\wedge x$. Consequently, since $M_I, w \vDash \Box A$, $M_I, x \vDash A$, so by induction hypothesis $x \leq I(A)$; but $x \leq {\sim}I(A)$, contradicting the atomicity of x. Thus $\Pi([w] \cup \{{\sim}I(A)\}) = 0$ after all. Therefore $\Pi[w] \leq I(A)$ by the laws of a complete Boolean algebra (for if $\Pi(\Gamma \cup \{{\sim}p\}) = 0$ then $\Pi\{\Pi\Gamma, p\} = \Sigma\{\Pi\{\Pi\Gamma, p\}, 0\} = \Sigma\{\Pi\{\Pi\Gamma, p\}, \Pi(\Gamma \cup \{{\sim}p\})\} = \Pi\{\Pi\Gamma, \Sigma\{p, {\sim}p\}\} = \Pi\{\Pi\Gamma, 1\} = \Pi\Gamma$, so $\Pi\Gamma \leq p$). Hence $L\Pi[w] \leq LI(A)$ by the monotonicity of L. But $w \leq \Pi\{Lp: w \leq Lp\} = L\Pi[w]$, so $w \leq LI(A) = I(\Box A)$, as required. Thus for every formula A and $w \in W^\wedge$: $M_I, w \vDash A$ if and only $w \leq I(A)$.

In particular, therefore, the result holds when w is $w^\wedge$, the actual world of the model, which is the conjunction of all truths. Thus $I(A)$ is true if and only if M_I, $w^\wedge \vDash A$. But $w^\wedge$ is the designated world of M_I, since it is based on $<W^\wedge, R^\wedge, w^\wedge>$, so $I(A)$ is true if and only if A is true in M_I. For a formula, that is the appropriate connection between being mapped to a true proposition by a faithful interpretation and being true in the corresponding model on the intended model structure.

As a corollary, we can now argue that $<W^\wedge, R^\wedge, w^\wedge>$ meets the constraint on an intended model structure: the metaphysically universal formulas are exactly those valid on $<W^\wedge, R^\wedge, w^\wedge>$. For if A is valid on $<W^\wedge, R^\wedge, w^\wedge>$, then for every faithful interpretation I, since A is true in M_I, $I(A)$ is true; thus A is metaphysically universal. Conversely, suppose that A is metaphysically universal. Let $M = <W^\wedge, R^\wedge, w^\wedge, V>$ be any model on $<W^\wedge, R^\wedge, w^\wedge>$. Let I be the faithful interpretation such that for every atomic formula B, $I(B) = \Sigma\{x \in W^\wedge : V(B)(x) = 1\}$. Thus $V_I = V$, for $V_I(B)(w) = 1$ if and only if $w \leq I(B)$ if and only if $V(B)(w) = 1$. Hence $M_I = <W^\wedge, R^\wedge, w^\wedge, V_I> = <W^\wedge, R^\wedge, w^\wedge, V> = M$. Since A is metaphysically universal, $I(A)$ is true, so A is true in $M_I = M$. Thus A is valid on $<W^\wedge, R^\wedge, w^\wedge>$. Hence the logic of $<W^\wedge, R^\wedge, w^\wedge>$ is sound and complete for metaphysical universality, as required.[31]

At no point did the argument assume metaphysical universality to be closed under necessitation. Thus even if MU is a non-normal system of modal logic, it is still the logic of $<W^\wedge, R^\wedge, w^\wedge>$.

If one chooses to interpret the atomic formulas of the language fully, thereby mapping each of them to a unique proposition, one determines

[31] The soundness and completeness theorem can be understood from a more abstract algebraic perspective, in terms of standard results. A *complete atomic modal algebra* is a complete atomic Boolean algebra with an additional operation L that commutes with multiplication (conjunction) over all sets of elements. For any complete atomic modal algebra, the *associated frame* is the frame whose worlds are the atoms of the algebra, where w can access x just if for every element p of the algebra, if $w \leq Lp$ then $x \leq p$. For any frame $<W, R>$, let the *full modal algebra* over $<W, R>$ be the Boolean algebra over the power set of W with the usual set-theoretic operations and the additional operation L, where $Lp = \{w \in W : \{x \in W : wRx\} \subseteq p\}$ for $p \subseteq W$. Then for any $w \in W$, any formula A is true at w in some model based on $<W, R>$ if and only if $w \in I(A)$ for some interpretation I over the full modal algebra over $<W, R>$, the constraints on such an interpretation being analogous to those on a faithful interpretation in the text (see Blackburn, de Rijke, and Venema 2001, p. 278). But any complete atomic modal algebra is isomorphic to the full modal algebra over its associated frame (Thomason 1975, p. 439), by an isomorphism that maps each element p of the original algebra to the set of atoms below it. The isomorphism induces a correspondence between interpretations over the two algebras. Thus, for any atom w in a complete atomic modal algebra, any formula A is true at w in some model based on the associated frame if and only if w is below $J(A)$ for some interpretation J over the original algebra. Letting the complete atomic modal algebra be the algebra of propositions and w the conjunction of all truths, one then deduces the soundness and completeness theorem in the text in the usual way.

a unique faithful interpretation *I*, where each formula *A* of the object-language is true on this intended interpretation if and only if the proposition *I*(*A*) is true. But we showed earlier that *I*(*A*) is true if and only if *A* is true in the model M_I. Thus simple truth coincides with truth in M_I. Hence M_I meets a natural constraint on an intended model. For present purposes, however, we continue to treat the atomic formulas like variables.

Historically, Kripke's model-theoretic approach to the formal metalogic of modal logic displaced an earlier algebraic approach.[32] Here, however, we have used the algebraic approach to connect Kripke models with one of their main intended applications, to metaphysical modality.

In principle, we can reason about validity on the model structure $<W^\wedge, R^\wedge, w^\wedge>$ in non-modal set-theoretic terms, then use the identity of its logic with MU to transfer the results to metaphysical universality. The catch is that the accessibility relation $R^\wedge$ for the intended model structure was defined in modal terms: for any atoms *w* and *x*, $wR^\wedge x$ if and only if $x \leq p$ whenever $w \leq Lp$. *Lp* here must be the genuine necessitation of the proposition *p*, not just some formal simulacrum thereof, otherwise the constraint that $I(\Box A) = LI(A)$ lacks its required effect in the account of faithful interpretations. Of course, whatever holds of model structures in general holds of the intended model structure in particular. For any model structure, the formulas valid on it include all theorems of the minimal normal modal logic K and are closed under modus ponens and uniform substitution—even if MU lacks necessitation, it is at least quasi-normal. But when we go beyond those banalities and try to determine whether an axiom such as B or 4 is valid on the intended model structure, we find that doing so just takes us back to the same principle in the metalanguage (try). That is scarcely surprising, for the definition of the intended model structure and the proofs of its desirable properties relied on no principles expressible in the standard language of propositional modal logic beyond those banalities.

One might try to define an intended model structure differently, in non-modal terms, aiming to facilitate the identification of its logic by presenting its structure more perspicuously. However, such a definition would make it far harder to show the logic to be MU. One might simply be shifting the wrinkle in the carpet. Model theory is much less helpful than some may have hoped in determining the correct logic of metaphysical modality.

---

[32] For a contemporary survey of the algebraic approach to modal logic see Lemmon 1966a and 1966b.

This philosophical anti-climax should not obscure the genuine advantages of Kripkean model theory. It provides a much clearer view of inferential relations in modal logic. For example, the best way of showing one modal principle to be underivable from others is usually by producing a model in which the latter are valid while the former is not. Again, once we have a soundness and completeness theorem for an axiomatically presented modal system S, such as one that says that the theorems of S are exactly the formulas valid on a specified class of frames, it is sometimes easier to show a formula to be derivable from the axioms and rules of inference of S by showing it to be valid on that class of frames than by actually deriving it. In other cases, the most natural way of characterizing a modal system is by specifying a suitable class of models or frames; we may not even know how to provide a sound and complete axiomatization. The underlying cognitive point is that it is often much easier for us to reason non-modally about models or frames than to do the corresponding reasoning in modal terms. However, neither the axiomatic nor the model-theoretic method will greatly help us determine which formulas are metaphysically universal until we can identify the intended model structure in non-modal terms. We are not yet in a position to extract much useful information about metaphysical universality by purely mathematical reasoning.[33]

On the other hand, if we try a more direct approach to metaphysical universality, without appeal to model theory, we are back with the problem that if we simply list modal axioms or rules of inference we judge metaphysically universal or metaphysical universality preserving, even if our judgements are correct, the question still arises: can all metaphysically universal modal formulas be derived from those on the list? An omission need not be one of the familiar candidate axioms. It may be complex and hard to assess or even to conceive.

Despite the difficulties, the model theory does facilitate some progress in characterizing the logic of metaphysical modality, MU. Here are two examples.

First, we can argue that MU, if normal, is complete, that is, it is none of those normal modal logics that fail to be the logic of any frame. That MU

---

[33] The same applies to $W_{N(MU)}$ in the canonical model for MU. It was defined in terms implicitly of metaphysical modality, as the set of maximal MU-consistent sets, MU as the set of metaphysically universal formulas, and metaphysical universality as the truth of the universal generalization of a modal formula.

is the logic of the model structure $<W^\wedge, R^\wedge, w^\wedge>$ entails that if MU is normal, it is the logic of a frame, and so complete.[34] Unfortunately, since none of the most plausible or popular candidates for MU is an incomplete normal system, this result makes little difference in practice.

The second result is of more philosophical interest. There is a compelling argument that if possibility and necessity are non-contingent, then MU is exactly the system S5. The non-contingency of possibility and necessity amounts to the metaphysical universality of the 4 and E axioms. Of course, it is controversial whether possibility and necessity are non-contingent.[35] However, it is a widespread and attractive assumption, so let us make it to see where it leads.

We can axiomatize S5 with modus ponens as the only rule of inference and the following axioms: all formulas of the form $\Box A$ where A is a truth-functional tautology and all instances of the K schema, the T schema $\Box A \rightarrow A$, the 4 schema $\Box A \rightarrow \Box\Box A$, and the E schema $\neg\Box A \rightarrow \Box\neg\Box A$.[36] By doing without necessitation as a primitive rule of inference, while securing the same effect by other means, this axiomatization makes the metaphysical universality of theorems of the system easier to assess. All instances of the 4 and E schemas are metaphysically universal by hypothesis; the metaphysical universality of the other axioms is uncontroversial. Since modus ponens preserves metaphysical universality, it follows that every theorem of S5 is metaphysically universal. Thus MU is at least as strong as S5. Might MU be stronger than S5? That is, might some non-theorems of S5 be metaphysically universal?

---

[34] The reasoning follows that in n. 22.

[35] See Chapter 2, n. 18. Since schemas B and 4 are consequences of schema E and the uncontroversial schema T, objections to B and 4 are implicitly objections to E.

[36] Clearly all truth-functional tautologies are derivable by the T schema. The key to establishing the equivalence of the axiomatization to a more standard one with necessitation as a primitive rule is to show that necessitation is here a derived rule, so that $\Box A$ is derivable whenever A is. We can do that by induction on the length of the proof of A. For the basis, A is an axiom. If A is of the form $\Box B$ where B is a truth-functional tautology, derive $\Box A$ by the 4 schema. If A is an instance $\Box B \rightarrow \Box\Box B$ of the 4 schema, derive $\Box(\Box B \rightarrow \Box\Box B)$ from A, the instance $\neg\Box B \rightarrow \Box\neg\Box B$ of the E schema, the instance $\Box\Box B \rightarrow \Box\Box\Box B$ of the 4 schema, the axioms $\Box(\neg\Box B \rightarrow (\Box B \rightarrow \Box\Box B))$ and $\Box(\Box\Box B \rightarrow (\Box B \rightarrow \Box\Box B))$ (which are both necessitated tautologies) and corresponding instances of the K schema. If A is an instance of the K or E schemas, derive $\Box A$ similarly. If A is an instance $\Box B \rightarrow B$ of the T schema, derive $\neg\Box B \rightarrow \Box(\Box B \rightarrow B)$ from the axioms $\neg\Box B \rightarrow \Box\neg\Box B$ and $\Box(\neg\Box B \rightarrow (\Box B \rightarrow B))$ and a corresponding instance of the K schema; derive $\Box B \rightarrow \Box(\Box B \rightarrow B)$ from the axiom $\Box(B \rightarrow (\Box B \rightarrow B))$ and another instance of the K schema and put the two halves together. For the induction step, we need only show that if $\Box(A \rightarrow B)$ and $\Box A$ are derivable then so is $\Box B$, which is immediate by the K schema.

An informal argument shows that MU is no stronger than S5. For, by a theorem of Schiller Joe Scroggs, every proper extension of S5 is the logic of a single finite frame.[37] Let the frame have just n worlds. Then the proper extension of S5 has this theorem:

Alt$_n$ $\Box P_1 \vee \Box(P_1 \to P_2) \vee \ldots \vee \Box((P_1 \& \ldots \& P_n) \to P_{n+1})$

For consider a model with a world w at which Alt$_n$ is false. To falsify the ith disjunct of Alt$_n$, w must have access to a world at which P_j is true for all $j < i$ but P_i is false. Clearly, these worlds must be distinct for distinct i, since they make incompatible truth value assignments. Thus $n + 1$ worlds are needed to falsify the $n + 1$ disjuncts of Alt$_n$. By hypothesis, the frame has only n worlds. Therefore Alt$_n$ is valid on the frame, and so is a theorem of the proper extension of S5. But Alt$_n$ is not metaphysically universal. For let I be a faithful interpretation such that for each i, $I(P_i)$ is the proposition that there are at least i donkeys. Then for each i, I maps the ith disjunct of Alt$_n$ to a falsehood, because it is metaphysically possible for there to be exactly $i - 1$ donkeys. Thus $I(\text{Alt}_n)$ is false, so Alt$_n$ is not metaphysically universal. Hence MU is not a proper extension of S5, so MU is exactly S5. If you can vindicate the 4 and E axioms for metaphysical modality, you thereby exclude all but one candidate for the logic of metaphysical modality in the language.

The argument illustrates how formal and informal considerations interact to yield information about MU. Indeed, if MU is S5, we can go further, and apply the familiar model theory of S5 to MU. S5 is the logic of any infinite frame that is universal in the sense that every world is accessible from every world. S5 is also the logic of the class of all finite universal frames, from which fact its decidability easily follows.[38] On the initial metaphysical assumptions, these simple, purely mathematical characterizations of MU provide a perspicuous view of its formal structure, even if we assign no special metaphysical significance to the constituents of the frames.

A significant limitation of this argument about S5 so far is that it does not extend to logical consequence. Scroggs's theorem does not generalize in the

---

[37] See Scroggs 1951 and Segerberg 1971, pp. 122–8. The 'extensions' are required to be quasi-normal. Requiring them also to be normal, and so closed under necessitation, opens an apparent gap in the argument: what if MU is not closed under necessitation? Fortunately, the gap is merely apparent, for every quasi-normal extension of S5 is normal (Segerberg 1971, pp. 187–90). Burgess 1999, p. 177, makes similar use of Scroggs's theorem, although with respect to a different sort of modality (he also provides another argument for the same conclusion based on one in Carnap 1946).

[38] See Hughes and Cresswell 1984, pp. 145 and 152–3 for a modern exposition of equivalent results, and for historical references Hughes and Cresswell 1996, pp. 156–7.

natural way to consequence relations, for one can define relations for the language that satisfy all the usual structural constraints on a logical consequence relation, and are stronger than the usual consequence relation for S5 (truth preservation in all models on universal model structures) but weak enough for each formula Alt_n to remain invalid: they impose no finite bound on the number of worlds.[39] Since, as already seen, for finite sets of premises logical consequence reduces to logical truth (when, as here, the truth functors are treated as logical constants), the only new arguments such consequence relations validate have infinitely many premises. Nevertheless, even if one accepts the metaphysical universality of every theorem of S5 and the metaphysical non-universality of every formula Alt_n, one still needs a further argument to show that the usual consequence relation for S5 is exactly that for metaphysical modality.

Fortunately, the extra argument can be supplied, using earlier results about the model structure $<W^\wedge, R^\wedge, w^\wedge>$. We will reason about the validity of arguments on frames and model structures, defined as follows. An argument is valid on a model structure if and only if the conclusion is true in every model on the model structure in which every premise is true. An argument is valid on a frame if and only if it is valid on every model structure on that frame. A conclusion A has the usual S5 consequence relation to a set of premises Γ if and only if the argument from Γ to A is valid on all universal frames. We will also speak of the metaphysical universality of arguments. In the framework of faithful interpretations, the argument from Γ to A is metaphysically universal if and only if for every faithful interpretation I for which $I(B)$ is true for every formula B in Γ, $I(A)$ is also true.

---

[39] Proof: Call a model $<W, R, V>$ *mean* just if for every atomic formula P, either $\{w \in W: V(P)(w) = 1\}$ is finite or $\{w \in W: V(P)(w) = 0\}$ is finite. Say that $\Gamma \vDash^+ A$ just if, in every mean model on a universal frame, A is true at every world at which every formula in Γ is true. By induction on the complexity of formulas, in a mean model on a universal frame, every formula is either true at only finitely many worlds or false at only finitely many worlds, so $\vDash^+$ is closed under uniform substitution (by contrast, in an infinitary language the constraint on atomic formulas would not extend to all complex ones). Of course, $\vDash^+$ also satisfies the usual structural rules for a consequence relation (reflexivity, thinning, and cut). Since S5 is sound and complete (for single formulas) for finite universal frames, and every model on a finite frame is mean, $\{\} \vDash^+ A$ just if A is a theorem of S5; hence $\{\} \vDash^+ Alt_n$ for no natural number n. Moreover, if A bears the usual S5 consequence relation to Γ, then a fortiori $\Gamma \vDash^+ A$. But the converse fails. For let $P_0, P_1, P_2, \ldots$ be distinct atomic formulas, and $\Gamma = \{\Diamond(P_0 \mathbin{\&} \neg P_1), \Diamond(P_0 \mathbin{\&} P_1 \mathbin{\&} \neg P_2), \Diamond(P_0 \mathbin{\&} P_1 \mathbin{\&} P_2 \mathbin{\&} \neg P_3), \ldots, \Diamond(\neg P_0 \mathbin{\&} \neg P_1), \Diamond(\neg P_0 \mathbin{\&} P_1 \mathbin{\&} \neg P_2), \Diamond(\neg P_0 \mathbin{\&} P_1 \mathbin{\&} P_2 \mathbin{\&} \neg P_3), \ldots\}$. In no mean model are all members of Γ true, for that would require P_0 to be true at infinitely many worlds and false at infinitely many worlds. Therefore, vacuously, $\Gamma \vDash^+ Q \mathbin{\&} \neg Q$. But in some non-mean models on universal frames all members of Γ are true. Thus $Q \mathbin{\&} \neg Q$ does not bear the usual S5 consequence relation to Γ.

Assume that every theorem of S5 is metaphysically universal, and that no formula Alt_n is metaphysically universal. Then, given the treatment above of the model structure $\langle W^\wedge, R^\wedge, w^\wedge \rangle$ and its connections with faithful interpretations, we can show that metaphysical universality coincides with the usual S5 consequence relation in our language. Since the logic of $\langle W^\wedge, R^\wedge, w^\wedge \rangle$ is complete for metaphysical universality, every metaphysically universal formula is valid on $\langle W^\wedge, R^\wedge, w^\wedge \rangle$, so every theorem of S5 is valid on $\langle W^\wedge, R^\wedge, w^\wedge \rangle$. Consider the sub-frame $\langle W*, R* \rangle$ of $\langle W^\wedge, R^\wedge \rangle$ generated by $w^\wedge$, where W* is the set of points in $W^\wedge$ accessible from $w^\wedge$ in a finite number of steps of $R^\wedge$ and R* is the restriction of $R^\wedge$ to W*. By standard purely model-theoretic reasoning one can show that R* is universal on W* and that the arguments valid on $\langle W*, R* \rangle$ are exactly those valid on $\langle W^\wedge, R^\wedge, w^\wedge \rangle$. Since the logic of that model structure is sound for metaphysical universality, no formula Alt_n is valid on $\langle W^\wedge, R^\wedge, w^\wedge \rangle$, so none is valid on $\langle W*, R* \rangle$, so W* is infinite. We now show that an argument with premise set Γ and conclusion A is metaphysically universal if and only if A bears the usual S5 consequence relation to Γ. First, suppose that the argument is not metaphysically universal. Thus for some faithful interpretation I, $I(B)$ is true for every formula B in Γ but $I(A)$ is false. Consequently, by what was shown earlier, B is true in the model M_I on $\langle W^\wedge, R^\wedge, w^\wedge \rangle$ for every B in Γ, but A is false in M_I. Hence the argument is invalid on $\langle W^\wedge, R^\wedge, w^\wedge \rangle$ and so invalid on the universal frame $\langle W*, R* \rangle$. Thus A does not bear the usual S5 consequence relation to Γ. Conversely, suppose that A does not bear the usual S5 consequence relation to Γ. Thus the argument is invalid on some universal frame $\langle W, R \rangle$. But one can show purely model-theoretically that, since our modal language has only countably many atomic formulas, any argument in it invalid on some universal frame is invalid on every infinite universal frame.[40] Thus

---

[40] Proof: Given a formula C of the propositional modal language, let C^Q be the formula of first-order non-modal monadic logic that results from substituting $\forall x$ for $\Box$, $\exists x$ for $\Diamond$, and Px for each atomic formula P throughout C. The non-modal language is countable because the modal language has only countably many atomic formulas. Then the modal argument from Γ to A is invalid on the universal frame $\langle W, R \rangle$ if and only if $\{C^Q: C \in \Gamma \cup \{\neg A\}\}$ is satisfiable in the domain W. By the upward Löwenheim-Skolem theorem for a first-order non-modal language without identity, any set of formulas satisfiable in a given domain is satisfiable in any larger domain. By the downward Löwenheim-Skolem theorem for a countable first-order non-modal language, any set of formulas satisfiable in a given infinite domain is satisfiable in any countably infinite domain. Consequently, in a countable first-order language without identity, any set of formulas satisfiable in some domain is satisfiable in any infinite domain. Thus if the modal argument from Γ to A is invalid on some universal frame, then $\{C^Q: C \in \Gamma \cup \{\neg A\}\}$ is satisfiable in some domain, so $\{C^Q: C \in \Gamma \cup \{\neg A\}\}$ is satisfiable in any infinite domain W, so the argument from Γ to A is invalid on any infinite universal frame $\langle W, R \rangle$.

the argument is invalid on the infinite universal frame $\langle W*, R*\rangle$, and so on $\langle W^\wedge, R^\wedge, w^\wedge\rangle$. Hence in some model M on $\langle W^\wedge, R^\wedge, w^\wedge\rangle$ every formula in Γ is true but A is false. But we saw earlier that every model M on $\langle W^\wedge, R^\wedge, w^\wedge\rangle$ is a model M_I for some faithful interpretation I. Consequently, by what was shown earlier, $I(B)$ is true for every formula B in Γ but $I(A)$ is false. Thus the argument is not metaphysically universal. The upshot is that metaphysical universality coincides with the usual S5 consequence relation for arguments as well as single formulas in propositional modal language—given that all theorems of S5 are metaphysically universal and the assumptions on which the construction of the model structure $\langle W^\wedge, R^\wedge, w^\wedge\rangle$ was based.

A caveat is needed. The result does not automatically extend to a language with uncountably many atomic formulas. For let the cardinality of $W^\wedge$ be κ, and suppose that the language contains more than 2^κ atomic formulas, so more atomic formulas than $W^\wedge$ has subsets. Then in any model on $\langle W^\wedge, R^\wedge, w^\wedge\rangle$ two atomic formulas P and Q are true at exactly the same worlds; $W^\wedge$ contains too few worlds to differentiate so many atomic formulas from each other. Let Γ consist of $\neg\Box(P \leftrightarrow Q)$ for each pair of distinct atomic formulas P and Q. Thus no model on $\langle W^\wedge, R^\wedge, w^\wedge\rangle$ makes all members of Γ true. Therefore the argument from Γ to a contradiction is vacuously valid on $\langle W^\wedge, R^\wedge, w^\wedge\rangle$, and so metaphysically universal. But Γ does not bear the usual S5 consequence relation to a contradiction, because the argument is invalid on a sufficiently large universal frame. As we increase the expressive resources of the language, we eventually reach a divergence between the usual consequence relation for S5 and validity on a given model structure. The discrepancy may be slight, confined to arguments with a vast infinity of premises, but it is a salutary reminder of the difference between model theory and modal metaphysics.

Of course, we cannot expect to establish a characterization of MU in purely mathematical terms by purely mathematical means. Such a characterization is not itself a purely mathematical statement, since MU was defined in modal terms. Some appeal to informal considerations about metaphysical possibility is essential.

For philosophers who reject some axioms of S5, it is much less clear how to argue even informally for an alternative purely mathematical characterization of MU. Scroggs's theorem has no analogue for natural candidates below S5 to be equated with MU. For example, if you reject the 4, E, and B axioms, and are inclined to identify MU with KT, the weakest normal modal system in which necessity entails truth, how are you to construct a general argument that every metaphysically universal formula is already a theorem of KT?[41]

Of course, you can conjecture that MU is some given system S, axiomatically or model-theoretically presented, and challenge sceptics to find a counterexample, either a metaphysically non-universal theorem of S or a metaphysically universal non-theorem of S. If they present a purportedly false instance of the universal generalization of a theorem of S, you try to argue that the instance is instead true. If they present a non-theorem of S whose universal generalization is purportedly true, you try to find an instance of it that you can argue to be false. Thus you defend the equation MU = S piecemeal, inductively. That is better than nothing, but a systematic, principled argument for the equation would be far more satisfying.

The tentative construction of the intended model structure assumed a set of all propositions. What happens if there are too many propositions to form a set? For example, for each ordinal number α, let p_α be the proposition that α is the smallest ordinal ever to be someone's favourite. Then for any two ordinals α and β, p_α and p_β are jointly incompossible but, it seems, each separately possible. If so, p_α and p_β are distinct propositions. Thus there are at least as many propositions as ordinals. Since there are too many ordinals to form a set, there are too many propositions to form a set. Such examples are not decisive, because an alternative has not been conclusively ruled out: that p_α is genuinely possible for only set-many ordinals α, while, for all other ordinals α, p_α is the same impossible proposition. Nevertheless, they must be taken seriously.

One response is this. Our language for propositional modal logic is finitary, so each formula contains only finitely many atomic formulas; thus, if it is metaphysically non-universal, only finitely many propositions are needed to make a false instance of its universal closure. Since the whole language contains only countably many formulas, only countably many of them are metaphysically non-universal. Thus some countable set of propositions provides

---

[41] Humberstone 1996a sketches a completeness proof for S4 in a framework of homophonic model theory for modal logic in a modal metalanguage. However, he is clear that the proof requires the prior assumption that S4 is indeed the strongest correct logic in the relevant language for the relevant sort of modality. His style of argument does not resolve an open question as to whether all metaphysically universal formulas are derivable in a given system. Thus it offers less than we normally expect of a completeness theorem. For example, without the completeness proof for first-order non-modal logic, it would be a genuinely open question whether we needed to add further axioms to derive some complex quantificational validities.

false instances of the universal closures of all metaphysically non-universal formulas of the language. By closing such a set of propositions under the usual operations (conjunction on sets of propositions, negation, and necessitation) we can construct a suitable set-sized algebra. Under the usual assumption of atomicity, a model structure can be defined from that algebra just as before. By construction, the logic of that model structure will be sound and complete for metaphysical universality. It is not quite an intended model structure, since it distinguishes only set-many possibilities and so by hypothesis leaves many possibilities undistinguished from each other, but at least it validates exactly the right formulas.

That response works if the necessitation operator is defined by the equations $L1 = 1$ and $Lp = 0$ whenever $p \neq 1$. For then closing the initial set of propositions under the Boolean operations trivially subsumes the required values of L, which are just 0 and 1. The closure of a set under the Boolean operations is always set-sized. But that definition of L commits us to the principles of S5. In that case, as already seen, MU is just S5, and any infinite model structure with a universal accessibility relation validates all and only metaphysically universal formulas. That is the easy case.

If the metaphysical universality of S5 is not to be taken for granted, we should not define L by those equations. But then there is no general guarantee that the initial set of propositions has a set-sized closure under L and the Boolean operations, including infinitary conjunction.[42] Although the initial

---

[42] Proof: Model worlds as ordinals. Thus propositions are true or false at ordinals. Naturally, for any proposition p, $\sim p$ is true at an ordinal α just if p is not true at α, and for any set Γ of propositions, $\Pi\Gamma$ is true at α just if every member of Γ is true at α. Similarly, given an accessibility relation between ordinals, there is an operation L such that for any proposition p, Lp is true at an ordinal α just if p is true at every ordinal accessible from α. For example, let β be accessible from α just if $\beta < \alpha$. Put $q_0 = 0$ (a contradiction); $q_{\alpha+1} = Lq_\alpha$ for each ordinal α; $q_\lambda = \Sigma\{q_\alpha : \alpha < \lambda\}$ (an infinite disjunction) for each limit ordinal λ. Then it is easy to show by induction on α that q_α is true at β just if $\beta < \alpha$. Thus for any two ordinals α and β where $\beta < \alpha$, q_α and q_β are distinct propositions, because q_α but not q_β is true at β. Hence, starting from any initial set of propositions, the Boolean operations and L generate more than set-many propositions. This toy model is simple but not very interesting, since the accessibility relation is irreflexive, so Lp does not always entail p; for instance, L0 is true at the ordinal 0 but the proposition 0 is not. Here is a more 'realistic' model with a reflexive accessibility relation R. Let α have R to β just if either $\alpha = \beta$ or $\alpha = \beta + 1$ or both $\beta < \alpha$ and α is a limit ordinal. Let the proposition p be true at 0 and false at every other ordinal. Define an auxiliary proposition $l = \Pi\{\sim L \sim p, \sim L \sim L \sim p\}$. One can easily show that l is true at all limit ordinals and false at all other ordinals. Put $r_0 = \Pi\{p, \sim p\}$; $r_1 = p$; $r_{\alpha+1} = \Sigma\{r_\alpha, \Pi\{\sim l, L \sim L \sim r_\alpha\}\}$ if α is a successor ordinal; $r_{\alpha+1} = L\Sigma\{l, r_\alpha\}$ if α is a limit ordinal; $r_\lambda = \Sigma\{r_\alpha : \alpha < \lambda\}$ if λ is a limit ordinal. One shows by induction on α that r_α is true at β just if $\beta < \alpha$ (there are numerous cases to consider, all routine). Hence for any two ordinals α and β, r_α and r_β are distinct propositions. Thus, starting from any initial set of propositions containing p, the Boolean operations and L generate more than set-many propositions.

set has a set-sized closure under L and all finitary Boolean operations, we need infinitary conjunction to guarantee us a conjunction of all truths, the actual world. Thus, outside the S5 comfort zone, a different strategy is needed.

A natural alternative is to continue working with all propositions, even if they do not form a set, but to replace the set-theoretic definitions of 'Boolean algebra' and 'model structure' by higher-order analogues. Thus 'W' and 'R' become respectively one-place and two-place predicates of propositions, and so on (Chapter 5 explains relevant aspects of higher-order logic in detail). For such a construction to work, any propositions must have a conjunction, even if they are too many for a set. One must take care not to introduce any assumptions that would distinguish enough of those conjunctions from each other to entail a Russellian paradox. Circumspectly applied, that strategy promises to yield a higher-order analogue of an intended model structure for propositional modal logic, whose logic is sound and complete for metaphysical universality; in other words, MU will be the logic of the higher-order analogue of a model structure.

If that strategy works, we may conjecture, MU will also be the logic of some model structure in the standard set-theoretic sense, even if that model structure was not really intended. The question is delicate, because some normal propositional modal logics are characterized only by enormous frames whose size is at least that of an inaccessible cardinal.[43] In a standard set theory such as ZFC, it is unprovable that there are such large sets, so unprovable that those logics are characterized by any frame at all. However, most set theorists treat the assumption that there are inaccessible cardinals as an innocuous truth.

We can deduce that if MU is the logic of a higher-order analogue of a model structure then it is also the logic of a set-based model structure from the principle KP3, formalized by Stewart Shapiro as one articulation of a remark by Georg Kreisel. KP3 concerns sets of formulas of a standard second-order language with identity but no non-logical constants. Informally, KP3 says that any such set simultaneously satisfiable over some things (possibly more than set-many) is simultaneously satisfiable over set-many things. Shapiro shows that KP3 is equivalent to a reflection principle for second-order set theory, and that if there are at least $\aleph_2$ inaccessible cardinals it is consistent

---

[43] See Kracht 1999 for details. The issues for frames and for model structures are intimately related, as explained in n. 22.

for KP3 and second-order set-theory to have a standard model.[44] From a contemporary set-theoretic perspective, KP3 looks quite plausible.[45] It applies to the present problem thus. A standard recursive 'translation' maps each propositional modal formula A to a non-modal first-order formula tA with the second-order variable R and the first-order variable w free, corresponding to the condition for A to be true in a Kripke model. For example, $t(\Box P \to P)$ is $\forall x(Rwx \to Xx) \to Xw$, where the monadic predicate X corresponds to the atomic formula P.[46] Let $\forall tA$ be the non-modal second-order formula obtained by prefixing to tA universal quantifiers on all the predicates in it (treated as second-order variables) corresponding to atomic formulas in A. For example, $\forall t(\Box P \to P)$ is $\forall X \, (\forall x \, (Rwx \to Xx) \to Xw)$. Thus $\forall tA$ corresponds to the condition for A to be valid on a model structure. Let MU* be the set containing $\forall tA$ for each metaphysically universal formula A and $\neg \forall tA$ for each metaphysically non-universal formula A of the propositional modal language. If MU is the logic of a higher-order analogue of a model structure, then MU* is simultaneously satisfiable over some things (the worlds of the higher-order analogue), so by KP3 MU* is simultaneously satisfiable over set-many things, which by construction of MU* means that MU is the logic of some model structure in the set-theoretic sense, as required. Although we may not have always had that model structure in mind, it does at least validate exactly the right formulas.[47]

We have seen some advantages and limitations of the model-theoretic approach in the simple case of propositional modal logic. We now return to the more complicated case of Kripke's models for quantified modal logic, and his semantic analysis of the Barcan formula and its converse. Those are the topics of the next two sections respectively, in which the ideas of metaphysical universality and faithful interpretation are temporarily put aside so that the model theory can be understood on Kripke's terms. The two ideas are extended to first-order modal logic in the final two sections of the chapter.

---

[44] See Shapiro 1987, pp. 321–8, and 1991, pp. 146–7 (where the principle is labelled 'KP2'). 'Satisfiable' here means satisfiable on the standard (not Henkin) semantics for second-order logic.

[45] McGee 1992, pp. 284–92, argues tentatively for a principle inconsistent with KP3. Goméz-Torrente 1999, pp. 399–402, criticizes McGee's argument and concludes that the burden of proof remains on opponents of KP3.

[46] See for example van Benthem 2002, p. 396.

[47] Stalnaker 2012, pp. 31–42, develops a different account, realist in some respects and instrumentalist in others, of the relation between possible worlds models and what they represent. However, he does not discuss whether the logic of any of his model-theoretic structures is sound and complete by some intended standard.

3.4 Kripke models for first-order modal logic

We extend the propositional modal language to a first-order one by adding a universal quantifier $\forall$, a countable infinity of individual variables, a countable infinity of individual constants, a countable infinity of n-place atomic predicates as non-logical constants for each natural number n, and a two-place logical atomic predicate '=' as a logical constant.[48] As usual, $\exists v$ is treated as a metalinguistic abbreviation for $\neg \forall v \neg$. The individual terms of the language are its individual constants and individual variables.

We will first briefly recall models for first-order non-modal logic, before considering the extension to the modal case. Standardly, a model for first-order non-modal logic is an ordered pair <D, V> of a domain D and an extension specification V. D may be any non-empty set. V interprets each individual constant c by giving it a denotation $V(c)$ in D, and each n-place non-logical atomic predicate F by giving it an extension of ordered n-tuples of members of D, so $V(F) \subseteq D^n$.

To give a compositional semantics for quantification, we evaluate both open and closed formulas as true or false relative to an assignment of values to variables. In a model, an assignment $\underline{a}$ assigns each individual variable v a value $\underline{a}(v)$ in the domain. The denotation $\text{den}_{\underline{a}}(t)$ of an individual term t on an assignment $\underline{a}$ is $V(t)$ if t is a constant and $\underline{a}(t)$ if t is a variable. To say that the formula A is true in the model M on the assignment $\underline{a}$, we write M, $\underline{a} \vDash A$.

Here is the clause for the truth of an atomic formula containing the n-place non-logical atomic predicate F in a model $M = <D, V>$, where $t_1, \ldots, t_n$ are individual terms:

$$M, \underline{a} \vDash Ft_1 \ldots t_n \quad \text{if and only if} \quad <\text{den}_{\underline{a}}(t_1), \ldots, \text{den}_{\underline{a}}(t_n)> \in V(F)$$

That clause correctly handles even atomic sentences, which Kripke treats as 0-place predicates, if we stipulatively identify the unique 0-length sequence with the empty set, and 0 (falsity) and 1 (truth) with the empty set and its singleton respectively. The identity predicate '=' is interpreted independently of V:

$$M, \underline{a} \vDash t_1 = t_2 \quad \text{if and only if} \quad \text{den}_{\underline{a}}(t_1) = \text{den}_{\underline{a}}(t_2)$$

---

[48] In Kripke 1963, an identity predicate qua logical constant and individual constants are not treated as part of the formal language. As noted in section 2.2, adding individual constants to the language makes trouble for Kripke's proof theory.

The semantic clauses for truth functors such as ¬ and & are obvious. The model interprets the quantifiers as restricted to its domain. Where $a[v/d]$ is the assignment like a except that it makes d the value of the variable v:

$$M, a \vDash \forall v\, A \quad \text{if and only if} \quad \text{for every } d \in D: M, a[v/d] \vDash A$$

If A is a closed formula, its truth in a model is independent of the assignment, so for any assignment a: $M \vDash A$ if and only if $M, a \vDash A$. We extend this derelativization to open formulas by treating them as if universally generalized on their free variables. Thus for any formula A: $M \vDash A$ if and only if for every assignment a: $M, a \vDash A$.

How to adapt this apparatus to possible worlds semantics? As before, the constituents of a model M include a set W of worlds, a relation $R \subseteq W^2$ of relative possibility, and an actual world $w_0 \in W$. A critical issue is whether to relativize the domain of quantification to the world of evaluation. Kripke does so. Thus D becomes a function mapping each world w to a set $D(w)$, informally understood as 'the set of all individuals existing in' w. He explains that 'of course' $D(w)$ may vary with w, 'just as, intuitively, in worlds other than the real one, some actually existing individuals may be absent, while new individuals, like Pegasus, may appear'.[49] Correspondingly, the interpretation function V now maps each n-place non-logical atomic predicate F to an *intension* $V(F)$, a function mapping each $w \in W$ to the extension $V(F)(w)$ of F at w, a set of n-tuples of individuals in the union of the domains of the various worlds, so $V(F)(w) \subseteq (\cup_{x \in W} D(x))^n$. $V(F)(w)$ may vary with w to permit F to express a property or relation that individuals have contingently.

Although the language of Kripke's 1963 paper omits individual constants, once they are added the most straightforward way for V to treat them is by mapping each constant c to an individual in the union of the domains, so $V(c) \in \cup_{x \in W} D(x)$. In Kripke's terminology, individual constants are rigid designators: they do not denote different individuals at different worlds. This fits his account of proper names in natural languages. It also fits his account of assignments of values to variables: an assignment a maps each variable v to an individual $a(v) \in \cup_{x \in W} D(x)$ independently of the world parameter. By treating variables as rigid designators, Kripke avoids the difficulties noted in

[49] See Kripke 1963, p. 65. The 'Pegasus' example does not fit Kripke's later views on names in fiction. He later withdrew the related remark on the same page that 'Holmes does not exist, but in other states of affairs, he would have existed' on the grounds that 'granted that there is no Sherlock Holmes, one cannot say of any possible person that he *would have been* Sherlock Holmes, had he existed' (1980, p. 158). As Kripke notes in the latter case, the inadequacy of the example does not refute his general claim.

section 2.4 for Carnap's non-rigid treatment. Moreover, such a match in treatment between variables and constants facilitates a smooth logic. In Chapters 4 and 5 we will see some of the problems that mismatches create.[50] Since both variables and constants are rigid, we can define the denotation of an individual term t on an assignment just as in the non-modal case.

Where $<W, R>$ is a frame and D a domain function over W, the ordered triple $<W, R, D>$ is an *inhabited frame*. An unpointed model on $<W, R, D>$ is an ordered quadruple $<W, R, D, V>$, where V is as before. Similarly, a pointed model on $<W, R, D>$ is an ordered quintuple $<W, R, w, D, V>$, where $w \in W$. Equally, $<W, R, w, D, V>$ is a pointed model on the *inhabited model structure* $<W, R, w, D>$.

Kripke evaluates the truth of a formula A in a model M at a world w on an assignment a (M, w, $a \vDash A$). The clause for atomic formulas becomes this:

$$M, w, a \vDash Ft_1 \ldots t_n \quad \text{if and only if} \quad <den_a(t_1), \ldots, den_a(t_n)> \in V(F)(w)$$

This subsumes the clause for atomic sentences in the semantics for propositional modal logic as the special case where $n = 0$. The simplest generalization of the previous semantic clause for '=' is just this:

$$M, w, a \vDash t_1 = t_2 \quad \text{if and only if} \quad den_a(t_1) = den_a(t_2)$$

Although the assignment parameter is inert in the clauses for the truth-functional and modal operators, we write them down too for the record:

$$M, w, a \vDash A \ \& \ B \quad \text{if and only if} \quad M, w, a \vDash A \text{ and } M, w, a \vDash B$$

$$M, w, a \vDash \neg A \quad \text{if and only if} \quad \text{not } M, w, a \vDash A$$

$$M, w, a \vDash \Box A \quad \text{if and only if} \quad \text{whenever } wRw^*: M, w^*, a \vDash A$$

Kripke restricts generality at a world to the domain of that world. In present notation, his clause for the universal quantifier is this:

$$M, w, a \vDash \forall v \, A \quad \text{if and only if} \quad \text{for every } d \in D(w): M, w, a[v/d] \vDash A$$

The derived dual clause for $\exists$ is of course this:

$$M, w, a \vDash \exists v \, A \quad \text{if and only if} \quad \text{for some } d \in D(w): M, w, a[v/d] \vDash A$$

---

[50] Kripke writes 'Let's call something a *rigid designator* if in every possible world it designates the same object' (1980, p. 48) and 'I say that a proper name rigidly designates its referent even when we speak of counterfactual situations where that referent would not have existed', although he notes that doing so involves delicate issues (1980, p. 21 n. 21).

Since the clauses for the modal operators shift the world of evaluation, we cannot restrict the assignment itself to 'the' world of evaluation.

We derelativize truth from the world and assignment parameters as usual. In a model M, truth at a world w is truth at w on all assignments: M, $w \vDash A$ if and only if for all a, M, w, $a \vDash A$. Truth in a pointed model M is truth at the actual world w of M: M $\vDash A$ if and only if M, $w \vDash A$. A formula is valid on an inhabited model structure if and only if it is true in every model on that model structure.

Kripke's choice of variable domains raises further questions about the evaluation of atomic formulas. Suppose, for example, that we wish to determine whether a formula $\exists x \, \Box Hx$ is true at a world w in a model M, where H is an atomic predicate. Unpacking the semantic clauses, we find that M, $w \vDash \exists x \, \Box Hx$ if and only if for some $d \in D(w)$, whenever $wRw*$, $d \in V(H)(w*)$. Suppose that for some $w*$, $wRw*$ but $d \notin D(w*)$: can it still be that $d \in V(H)(w*)$? In other words, can something be in the extension of an atomic predicate at a world even though it does not 'exist' at that world? For instance, if we read Hx as 'x is human', then $\exists x \, \Box Hx$ says that something is necessarily human. If humanity is an essential property of humans, then plausibly any human is necessarily a human. But would one still have been human even if one had never been conceived?

The idea that having a property requires being something suggests the constraint that for any n-place atomic predicate F and $w \in W$, $V(F)(w) \subseteq D(w)^n$. Only what there is satisfies an atomic predicate. By analogous reasoning for the logical constant '=', if M, w, $a \vDash t_1 = t$ then $\text{den}_a(t_1)$ and $\text{den}_a(t_2)$ should belong to $D(w)$. The previous clause for '=' violates that condition; $\text{den}_a(t_1)$ and $\text{den}_a(t_2)$ may be identical without belonging to $D(w)$. To respect the condition, we could add the conjunct that $\text{den}_a(t_1) \in D(w)$ to the right-hand side. The *domain constraint* says that an atomic formula is true at a world on an assignment only if the domain of the world contains the denotation of each individual term in the formula on that assignment.

Kripke refrains from imposing the domain constraint. His reason is that doing so would prevent the set of theorems from being closed under uniform substitution.[51] Consider (3), for instance, where H is atomic:

(3) $\forall x \, \Box(Hx \to \exists x \, Hx)$

---

[51] See Kripke 1963, p. 66 n. 11. Although he gives no example of such a failure of uniform substitution, the context warrants the assumption that he had in mind cases like that described.

The domain constraint validates (3), for at any world w on any assignment $\underline{a}$ in a model if Hx is true then $\underline{a}(x) \in V(H)(w)$, but $V(H)(w) \subseteq D(w)$ by the constraint, so $\exists x\, Hx$ is true; thus $Hx \to \exists x\, Hx$ is always true. Substituting $\neg Hx$ for Hx in (3) yields (4):

(4) $\forall x\, \Box(\neg Hx \to \exists x\, \neg Hx)$

The domain constraint does not validate (4): in models where the extension of Hx at each world is its domain, anything in the domain of w but not that of an accessible world is a counterexample at w.

Kripke's aversion to failures of uniform substitution is well motivated, since variables—here predicate variables—should be capable of taking the same semantic values as complex expressions of the same grammatical category. But it is less clear that examples like (3) and (4) constitute failures of uniform substitution. For Hx is not a variable of any category. It is a formula with internal semantic complexity, even though it has no proper sub-formula: it combines the atomic predicate H with the individual variable x. To treat $\neg Hx$ as itself a substitution instance of Hx is therefore to treat $\neg H$ as a complex predicate, of the same grammatical category as H and so substitutable for it. In effect, that is to parse $\neg Hx$ as $(\neg H)x$ and treat $\neg$ as a predicate modifier. But the semantic clause for $\neg$ above manifestly treats it as operating on open or closed sentences, not on predicates, and so requires parsing $\neg Hx$ as $\neg(Hx)$. For a theorist who allows variable domains, accepts the domain constraint on the basis of the more general principle that only what there is satisfies predicates (simple or complex), and evaluates formulas bivalently, as true or false, $\neg(Hx)$ and $(\neg H)x$ are not logically equivalent. At a world whose domain lacks the value of the variable x, $(\neg H)x$ is false, but since Hx is equally false, $\neg(Hx)$ is true. Stalnaker's later implementation of that view is discussed at more length in Chapter 4. Since Kripke does not address such a view, he is in no position to assume that complex formulas are substitution instances of simple predicative formulas. Thus his objection to the domain constraint fails, because he has not shown it to be incompatible with closure under uniform substitution.

If the domain constraint is rejected, the natural clause for '=' is the one displayed earlier. Thus $x=x$ is true even at a world whose domain lacks the value of x. For the only natural motivation for excluding that combination derives from the domain constraint. Hence $\forall x\, \Box x=x$ comes out true everywhere in every model. In a slogan: 'Everything is necessarily self-identical, but not everything necessarily exists'.

Kripke also considers a non-bivalent version of the domain constraint, found in Hintikka and Prior, on which Hx is a truth-value gap rather than false at worlds whose domain lacks the value of x; thus $\neg Hx$ is equally truth-valueless at such worlds. He presents his preference for bivalence without the domain constraint as a choice of one tenable linguistic convention over others.[52] However, in section 2.7 we saw evidence that gappy treatments are incompatible with general conditions of adequacy for the semantics of a quantified modal language.

3.5 The Barcan and converse Barcan formulas in Kripke's model theory

As Kripke emphasizes, BF and CBF are valid in his model theory only over very restricted classes of models. He points out that BF fails at a world w when something in the domain of a world accessible from w is not in the domain of w, and that CBF fails at w when something in the domain of w is not in the domain of a world accessible from w. He provides simple counter-models to the formulas in each case.[53]

To make the correspondence precise, call an inhabited frame $<W, R, D>$ *non-increasing* if and only if for all w and w^* in W such that wRw^*, $D(w^*) \subseteq D(w)$. Similarly, $<W, R, D>$ is *non-decreasing* if and only if for all w and w^* in W such that wRw^*, $D(w) \subseteq D(w^*)$. Informally, in a non-increasing frame, no new inhabitants appear when one goes to a counterfactual possibility. In a non-decreasing frame, no old inhabitants disappear when one goes to a counterfactual possibility.

We can prove that BF is valid on an inhabited frame if and only if it is non-increasing. For suppose that $<W, R, D>$ is non-increasing. Suppose also that M, w, $a \vDash \Diamond \exists x\, A$ for a model M = $<W, R, w, D, V>$, assignment a and formula A. Then for some $w^* \in W$, wRw^* and M, w^*, $a \vDash \exists x\, A$, so for some $d \in D(w^*)$, M, w^*, $a[x/d] \vDash A$, so M, w, $a[x/d] \vDash \Diamond A$; but $d \in D(w)$ since the frame is non-increasing, so M, w, $a \vDash \exists x\, \Diamond A$. Thus BF is valid on $<W, R, D>$.

---

[52] Citing Hintikka 1961 and Prior 1957, Kripke (1963, p. 66) subsumes the view as an application to modal logic of Frege's and Strawson's treatment of reference failure.

[53] Kanger 1957, p. 36, Hintikka 1961, p. 127, and Føllesdal 2004, p. 55 (original from 1961), discuss related semantic conditions necessary or sufficient for the validity of BF, but the analysis in Kripke 1963 makes the situation much clearer.

Conversely, suppose that <W, R, D> is not non-increasing. Thus in some case $wRw*$, $d \in D(w*)$ but $d \notin D(w)$. For a one-place predicate F let $V(F)(u) = \{e \in D(u) : e \notin D(w)\}$ for all $u \in W$, $M = $<W, R, w, D, V> and $\underline{a}$ be any assignment. Thus M, $w*$, $\underline{a}[x/d] \vDash Fx$, so M, $w*$, $\underline{a} \vDash \exists x \, Fx$ because $d \in D(w*)$, so M, w, $\underline{a} \vDash \Diamond \exists x \, Fx$. But if M, w, $\underline{a} \vDash \exists x \, \Diamond Fx$ then for some $f \in D(w)$ M, w, $\underline{a}[x/f] \vDash \Diamond Fx$, so for some u, wRu and M, u, $\underline{a}[x/f] \vDash Fx$, so $f \in V(F)(u)$, so $f \notin D(w)$ by definition of V, which is a contradiction. Thus BF is not valid on <W, R, D>.

Similarly, we can prove that CBF is valid on an inhabited frame if and only if it is non-decreasing. For suppose that <W, R, D> is non-decreasing. Suppose also that M, w, $\underline{a} \vDash \exists x \, \Diamond A$ for some model M = <W, R, w, D, V>, assignment $\underline{a}$ and formula A. Then for some $d \in D(w)$, M, w, $\underline{a}[x/d] \vDash \Diamond A$, so for some $w* \in W$, $wRw*$ and M, $w*$, $\underline{a}[x/d] \vDash A$; but $d \in D(w*)$ because the frame is non-decreasing, so M, $w*$, $\underline{a} \vDash \exists x \, A$, so M, w, $\underline{a} \vDash \Diamond \exists x \, A$. Thus CBF is valid on <W, R, D>. Conversely, suppose that <W, R, D> is not non-decreasing. Thus in some case $wRw*$, $d \in D(w)$ but $d \notin D(w*)$. Let $V(F)(u) = D(u)$ for all $u \in W$, M = <W, R, w, D, V> and $\underline{a}$ be any assignment. Thus M, $w*$, $\underline{a}[x/d] \vDash \neg Fx$, so M, w, $\underline{a}[x/d] \vDash \Diamond \neg Fx$, so M, w, $\underline{a} \vDash \exists x \, \Diamond \neg Fx$ because $d \in D(w)$. But if M, w, $\underline{a} \vDash \Diamond \exists x \, \neg Fx$ then for some u, wRu and M, u, $\underline{a} \vDash \exists x \, \neg Fx$, so for some $d \in D(u)$, M, u, $\underline{a}[x/d] \vDash \neg Fx$, which contradicts the definition of V. Thus CBF is not valid on <W, R, D>.

Although neither argument assumes the domain constraint, both still go through even if the constraint is imposed, since the chosen intensions already respected it: in each case $V(F)(u) \subseteq D(u)$ for all $u \in W$. The main difference imposing it makes for BF and CBF is to validate CBF on all frames in the special case of atomic formulas A. For if M, w, $\underline{a} \vDash \exists x \, \Diamond Fx$ then for some $d \in D(w)$ and $w* \in W$, $wRw*$ and $d \in V(F)(w*)$, so $d \in D(w*)$ by the domain constraint even if the frame of M is not non-decreasing, so M, $w*$, $\underline{a} \vDash \exists x \, Fx$, so M, w, $\underline{a} \vDash \Diamond \exists x \, Fx$. For related reasons, the proof that CBF is valid only on non-decreasing frames requires $\neg Fx$ to be true, not merely not false, at a world whose domain lacks the object assigned to x. By contrast, the proof that BF is valid on all and only non-increasing frames is not sensitive to that assumption.[54]

The equivalences enable one to build a counter-model to BF and CBF on any uninhabited frame <W, R> in which at least one member of W has R to at least one other member of W. In particular, if W has at least two

---

[54] For the asymmetry see Kripke 1963, pp. 67–8.

members and R is the universal relation on W there are such counter-models. Thus BF and CBF fail even in models of S5 with varying domains.

To state semantic conditions for the validity of BF and CBF on model structures rather than frames, we need local analogues of the global properties of non-increasingness and non-decreasingness. An inhabited frame $<W, R, D>$ is non-increasing at a world w if and only if for all worlds $w*$ such that $wRw*$, $D(w*) \subseteq D(w)$; no new inhabitants appear when one goes to a counterfactual possibility from w. Similarly, $<W, R, D>$ is non-decreasing at w if and only if for all worlds $w*$ such that $wRw*$, $D(w) \subseteq D(w*)$; no old inhabitants disappear when one goes to a counterfactual possibility from w. Then unnecessitated BF is valid on an inhabited model structure $<W, R, w, D>$ if and only if the inhabited frame $<W, R, D>$ is non-increasing at w; unnecessitated CBF is valid on $<W, R, w, D>$ if and only if $<W, R, D>$ is non-decreasing at w. The proofs are virtually identical with those earlier for frames.

If the relation R is symmetric, the inhabited frame $<W, R, D>$ is non-increasing if and only if it is non-decreasing, so BF is valid on $<W, R, D>$ if and only if CBF is. Thus it is no great surprise that, as noted in section 2.2, full BF and full CBF are interderivable given the B axiom, which is valid on all and only symmetric frames. However, the symmetry of R does not imply that $<W, R, D>$ is non-increasing at a world if and only if it is non-decreasing at that world. For example, let $<W, R, D>$ be an inhabited frame in which R is the universal relation on $W = \{w, w*\}$ and $D(w)$ is a proper subset of $D(w*)$. Thus globally the frame is neither non-increasing nor non-decreasing. Locally, however, at w it is non-decreasing but not non-increasing, while at $w*$ it is non-increasing but not non-decreasing. Hence unnecessitated BF is valid on the inhabited model structure $<W, R, w*, D>$ but invalid on the inhabited model structure $<W, R, w, D>$, while unnecessitated CBF is valid on $<W, R, w, D>$ but invalid on $<W, R, w*, D>$. Both full BF and full CBF are invalid on both inhabited model structures. Since R is the universal relation on W here, in both cases not only the B axiom but all theorems of propositional S5 are valid. Thus neither BF nor CBF is derivable from the other even in the setting of S5 if necessitating them is not permitted. If there actually is something that could have been nothing, it does not follow that there could have been something that actually is nothing. Equally, if there could have been something that actually is nothing, it does not follow that there actually is something that could have been nothing.

Obviously, BF and CBF are both valid on any inhabited frame in which the domain function is constant, all worlds having the same domain.[55] The converse is not quite true. For example, BF and CBF are both valid on any inhabited frame in which the worlds are partitioned into equivalence classes, where each world is accessible from every world in its own equivalence class and from no world in any other equivalence class, and domains are constant within an equivalence class but may vary from one equivalence class to another. S5 is valid on any such frame. However, on any inhabited frame <W, R, D> in which R is the universal relation on W, BF and CBF are both valid only if D is constant. Proponents of S5 as the logic of metaphysical necessity standardly treat the intended accessibility relation R as universal, since philosophically we have no good reason to postulate more than one such equivalence class of worlds.

Domain constancy also helps validate principles of counterfactual logic closely related to BF and CBF. Read the binary connective $\square\!\!\rightarrow$ as the subjunctive conditional 'if it were the case that . . . , it would be the case that —'. These two principles are analogous to BF$'$ and CBF$'$, the universal-necessity forms of BF and CBF respectively:

$$\text{BF}_{\square\!\!\rightarrow} \qquad \forall v\,(A \mathrel{\square\!\!\rightarrow} B) \rightarrow (A \mathrel{\square\!\!\rightarrow} \forall v\, B)$$

$$\text{CBF}_{\square\!\!\rightarrow} \qquad (A \mathrel{\square\!\!\rightarrow} \forall v\, B) \rightarrow \forall v\,(A \mathrel{\square\!\!\rightarrow} B)$$

Here the variable v must not occur free in A, although it may in B. In effect, BF$_{\square\!\!\rightarrow}$ and CBF$_{\square\!\!\rightarrow}$ are BF$'$ and CBF$'$ for the complex local necessity operator $A \mathrel{\square\!\!\rightarrow}$. In a constant domain model, a universal generalization is semantically equivalent to the (possibly infinite) conjunction of its instances, once names for all members of the domain and an infinitary conjunction operator are added to the language. Then BF$_{\square\!\!\rightarrow}$ and CBF$_{\square\!\!\rightarrow}$ are semantically equivalent to formulas of the propositional forms (5) and (6) respectively:

---

[55] Constant domains do not imply the validity of BF and CBF on all non-Kripkean semantics. For instance, some versions of counterpart theory falsify BF and CBF in constant domain models, since the counterpart relation can simulate variable domains (see Corsi 2003 for more on BF and CBF in counterpart semantics). More interestingly, in neighbourhood semantics with constant domains, BF corresponds to the closure of necessity under infinite conjunctions, while the principles of normal modal logic imply only its closure under finite conjunctions (see Arló-Costa 2002 for more on BF and CBF in neighbourhood semantics, and Goldblatt and Mares 2006 for another approach to the semantics of quantified modal systems without BF or CBF that does not rely on variable domains).

(5) $\wedge_{i\in I} (A \;\square\!\!\rightarrow B_i) \rightarrow (A \;\square\!\!\rightarrow \wedge_{i\in I} B_i)$

(6) $(A \;\square\!\!\rightarrow \wedge_{i\in I} B_i) \rightarrow \wedge_{i\in I} (A \;\square\!\!\rightarrow B_i)$

Both (5) and (6) are corollaries of the attractive principle of deductive closure for the counterfactual consequences of a given antecedent: if C follows logically from the set of premises Γ, then $A \;\square\!\!\rightarrow C$ follows logically from $\{A \;\square\!\!\rightarrow B: B \in \Gamma\}$.[56]

Only the argument for (5) applies deductive closure to an infinite premise set Γ. Almost all theories of counterfactuals validate deductive closure for finite premise sets. Most, including Stalnaker's, validate it for infinite premise sets too. However, Lewis's preferred theory validates deductive closure only for finite premise sets. For example, he allows that for each natural number n, if this line were longer it would be less than $1/n$ of an inch longer, even though it is not the case that if this line were longer it would be for every n less than $1/n$ of an inch longer. Correspondingly, he rejects the Limit Assumption that of the worlds at which the antecedent is true at least one is as similar as any other to a given world.[57] One might agree with Lewis that the similarity structure of worlds may not satisfy the Limit Assumption, but still find his treatment of such examples unconvincing. Pre-theoretically, deductive closure has the same rationale for infinite premise sets as for finite ones: deduction is legitimate under a counterfactual supposition.[58] On this view, the error is in Lewis's semantics itself, not in the denial of the Limit Assumption.[59] For some natural number n, it is false that if this line were

---

[56] To derive (5), let C be $\wedge_{i\in I} B_i$ and Γ be $\{B_i: i \in I\}$, so the former follows from the latter by infinitary conjunction introduction, so by deductive closure $A \;\square\!\!\rightarrow \wedge_{i\in I} B_i$ follows from $\{A \;\square\!\!\rightarrow B_i: i \in I\}$, each member of which follows from $\wedge_{i\in I} (A \;\square\!\!\rightarrow B_i)$ by conjunction elimination. Conversely, to derive (6), let $j \in I$, C be B_j, and Γ be $\{\wedge_{i\in I} B_i\}$, so the former follows from the latter by conjunction elimination, so by deductive closure $A \;\square\!\!\rightarrow B_j$ follows from $A \;\square\!\!\rightarrow \wedge_{i\in I} B_i$; since j was arbitrary, $\wedge_{i\in I} (A \;\square\!\!\rightarrow B_i)$ follows from $A \;\square\!\!\rightarrow \wedge_{i\in I} B_i$ by infinitary conjunction introduction.

[57] See Lewis 1973, pp. 19–21, for the Limit Assumption, and p. 132 for his rule of Deduction within Conditionals, equivalent to the deductive closure principle for finite premise sets.

[58] In the presence of 'actually'-like operators, deductive closure may need qualification just as necessitation does, even for finite premise sets; see Williamson 2007, pp. 295–6. This has no bearing on the issue at hand.

[59] Deductive closure is validated by any semantics for counterfactuals of the following general form: for some function F taking $w \in W$ and $X \subseteq W$ to $F(X, w) \subseteq W$: M, w, $\underline{a} \vDash A \;\square\!\!\rightarrow B$ if and only if $F(\{x: M, x, \underline{a} \vDash A\}, w) \subseteq \{x: M, x, \underline{a} \vDash B\}$. $F(X, w)$ represents what would obtain from the standpoint of w if what X represents obtained. The selection function F may depend on context and may obey various structural constraints: for example, $F(X, w) \subseteq X$; $F(X, w) = \{\}$ only if $X = \{\}$; if $w \in X$ then $w \in F(X, w)$. The theory in Stalnaker 1968 conforms to this pattern with an extra requirement for $F(X, w)$ to have at most one member. The deviation from it in Lewis 1973 may result from an attempt to do in the semantics what should have been left to the pragmatics. For more discussion see Pollock 1981, pp. 240, 251–4, 259–65.

longer it would be less than $1/n$ of an inch longer. Let us provisionally trust deductive closure for infinite premise sets more than the details of Lewis's semantics of counterfactuals. Thus, given domain constancy, $\mathrm{BF}_{\square\rightarrow}$ and $\mathrm{CBF}_{\square\rightarrow}$ hold.

From $\mathrm{BF}_{\square\rightarrow}$ and $\mathrm{CBF}_{\square\rightarrow}$ we can derive BF and CBF themselves, given the plausible definition of $\square B$ in terms of counterfactuals and propositional quantification as $\forall P (P \square\rightarrow B)$: the necessary is what would hold whatever held.[60] For we can instantiate $\mathrm{BF}_{\square\rightarrow}$ and $\mathrm{CBF}_{\square\rightarrow}$ with the propositional variable P in place of A, universally generalize on it, and then apply standard quantifier manipulations to derive (7) and (8) respectively:

(7) $\qquad \forall v \, \forall P \, (P \square\rightarrow B) \rightarrow \forall P \, (P \square\rightarrow \forall v \, B)$

(8) $\qquad \forall P \, (P \square\rightarrow \forall v \, B) \rightarrow \forall v \, \forall P \, (P \square\rightarrow B)$

Substituting the definiendum for the definiens reduces (7) and (8) to BF′ and CBF′ respectively. Thus necessitists can see BF and CBF in effect as special cases of more general principles about counterfactuals. Correspondingly, contingentists will see their objections to BF and CBF as carrying over to those more general principles. In any case, we must return to the modal principles themselves, and their metaphysical status.

Some philosophers have tried to resolve the dispute over BF and CBF by arguing that it is purely verbal. Kripke's model theory enables us to define a quantifier restricted to the variable domains, which therefore violates BF and CBF, but it also enables us to define a wider-reaching quantifier over the union of those domains, which therefore satisfies both principles.[61] If so, the necessitist wins at once, for the first quantifier is a restriction of the second, and we saw in section 1.4 that the controversy between necessitism and contingentism concerns only the unrestricted quantifier, presumably modelled by that over the union of the domains. But the contingentist may reply that we should not take the models so literally. The apparent tension between contingentism and possible worlds model theory is examined more rigorously in section 3.6.

That BF and CBF are valid on all and only non-increasing and non-decreasing inhabited frames respectively, and the analogous results for inhabited model structures, are simply minor theorems of mathematics,

---

[60] See Williamson 2007, pp. 155−65, 171−7, 293−304. For more on quantification into sentence position see section 5.2.

[61] See Cocchiarella 1969a and Scott 1970.

established like other results of model theory by purely mathematical reasoning, with no modal element. Since what matters is only the structure of the inhabited frames, not the nature of their constituents, some counter-models to BF and CBF have variable domains whose members are all numbers or pure sets.[62] We need not check whether those entities *really* have contingent being, because that question is quite irrelevant to whether the model falsifies BF and CBF. Similarly, some models of BF and CBF have constant domains whose members are sticks and stones. We need not check whether those entities *really* have necessary being, because that question is quite irrelevant to whether the model verifies BF and CBF. Consequently, we should not expect variable domains model theory by itself to explain why BF and CBF fail; nor should we expect constant domain model theory by itself to explain why BF and CBF hold. The model theory does not engage modal reality in any way that would enable it to provide such explanations.

Nevertheless, we may still hope that the model theory will somehow contribute to determining the status of BF and CBF on their intended interpretations. Can we extend the ideas of metaphysical universality and an intended model structure in section 3.3 from propositional to first-order modal logic?

3.6   Metaphysical universality in first-order modal logic

The brief initial characterization in section 3.3 of metaphysical universality generalizes easily to first-order modal logic. Just as a formula of propositional modal logic is metaphysically universal if and only if its universal generalization is true on its intended interpretation, so a first-order modal formula is metaphysically universal if and only if its universal generalization is true on its intended interpretation. The idea is simple, but some clarification will help.

We formed the universal generalization of a propositional modal formula in a second-order extension of the object-language by uniformly substituting distinct propositional variables for distinct atomic sentences throughout

---

[62] This is no place to question whether there really are sets: model theory is permeated with set-theoretic assumptions.

and prefixing the result with universal quantifiers on each of its variables (in accordance with given well-orderings of the atomic sentences and variables). On the intended interpretation, the quantifiers range over propositions, $\Box$ expresses metaphysical necessity, and the truth-functional connectives have their standard readings. Similarly, we form the universal generalization of a first-order modal formula in a second-order extension of the object-language by uniformly substituting distinct new individual variables for distinct individual constants and distinct n-place predicate variables for distinct non-logical n-place atomic predicates throughout and prefixing the result with universal quantifiers on all its free variables (in accordance with given well-orderings of the individual constants, atomic predicates, and variables). For example, the universal generalization of the instance $\Diamond \exists x\, Rxa \rightarrow \exists x\, \Diamond Rxa$ of BF is $\forall X\, \forall y\ (\Diamond \exists x\, Xxy \rightarrow \exists x\, \Diamond Xxy)$. Thus $\Diamond \exists x\, Rxa \rightarrow \exists x\, \Diamond Rxa$ is metaphysically universal if and only if $\forall X\, \forall y\ (\Diamond \exists x\, Xxy \rightarrow \exists x\, \Diamond Xxy)$ is true on its intended interpretation. Metaphysical universality is the minimal modification of truth required to capture the formal validity of logic.

Of course, the metaphysical universality of A entails the truth of A itself on its intended interpretation only if A has a full intended interpretation. For instance, $Fa \rightarrow Fa$ is metaphysically universal, but has no intended interpretation if nothing is the intended denotation of the constant a. In a language well designed for expressing good scientific theories, the denotation of any constant is one of the values over which variables of the same type range, and the value of any variable is a legitimate denotation for a constant of the same type. Therefore, in such a language, a sentence is true if its universal generalization is, so metaphysical universality implies truth. For example, $\exists y\, a=y$ is metaphysically universal because its universal generalization $\forall x\, \exists y\, x=y$ is true, indeed an uncontroversial logical truth, so in such a language $\exists y\, a=y$ is true. Thus the logic of a well-designed language for science is not completely free. For a restriction to completely free logic undermines the application of scientific method by permitting one to hold on to a universal generalization after one of its instances has been refuted: one denies Ga but still asserts $\forall x\, Gx$ by also denying $\exists y\, a=y$, still retaining the constant a in the language. We assume that the formal languages under consideration in this chapter are well designed in the relevant sense, so that metaphysical universality implies truth. For our present aim is neither to model natural languages, for example in their use of fictional and mythological names (discussed in section 4.1), nor to stick to what is knowable a priori in some sense, which might exclude whether some names refer. Rather, our business is to clarify the structure of metaphysical universality in a broadly scientific spirit. Non-referring uses of 'Pegasus' have no more place in such an enquiry than they have in physics or zoology. Of course, the term 'phlogiston' did occur in scientific language, but if it failed to refer (rather than referring to an empty kind) then its presence in any scientific theory was a defect in that theory. Consequently, we should not distort our formal language by allowing for such a term.

The requirement that the language be well designed does not prejudge the issue against contingentism, for it does not tell us that $\Box \exists y\ a{=}y$ is true: its universal generalization is $\forall x\ \Box \exists y\ x{=}y$, which, unlike $\forall x\ \exists y\ x{=}y$, is a principle contingentists can deny.

As a first approximation, we understand the quantifier $\forall X$ on a one-place predicate variable X as quantifying over all properties in a plenitudinous sense in which any well-defined one-place predicate expresses a property. Similarly, we understand the quantifier $\forall X$ on an n-place predicate letter X for $n \geq 2$ as quantifying over all n-place relations in the same plenitudinous sense, in which any well-defined n-place predicate expresses an n-place relation. The propositional quantifiers in section 3.3 are understood as the special case where $n = 0$. This understanding of second-order quantification is refined and modified in Chapter 5, but will do for now.

Since '=' is counted a logical constant, it is not replaced by a predicate variable in the universal generalization, otherwise the intended logical truth $\forall x\ x{=}x$ fails to come out metaphysically universal (not all two-place relations are reflexive). Similarly, if a propositional language contains an atomic sentence $\bot$, treated as a logical constant for falsity, it is not replaced by a propositional variable in the universal generalization, otherwise the intended logical truth $\neg A \leftrightarrow (A \to \bot)$ fails to come out metaphysically universal.

The intended interpretation of the first-order quantifiers is absolutely unrestricted. For otherwise instances of BF might fail to come out metaphysically universal merely as a result of some restriction on those quantifiers, for example to lottery-winners. As seen in section 1.4, such a restricted interpretation prevents us from addressing the central metaphysical issues at stake between contingentism and necessitism.

Notoriously, the lack of restriction means that sentences such as $\exists x\ \exists y\ \neg x{=}y$ count as metaphysically universal, simply because they are true on the unrestricted reading; there actually are at least two things. That does no harm, once we understand what is going on. In particular, it does not automatically mean that $\Box \exists x\, \exists y\, \neg x{=}y$ counts as metaphysically universal: that depends on whether it actually is necessary that there are at least two things. On some versions of contingentism, there could have been just one thing, or nothing at all. Such examples also suggest that contingentists should be especially wary of assuming that metaphysical universality is closed under necessitation. Of course, a contingentist who believes it necessary that there are both the empty set and its singleton set may be happy to accept $\Box \exists x\, \exists y\, \neg x{=}y$.

For propositional modal logic, section 3.3 tentatively connected metaphysical universality to the model theory by an intended model structure $\langle W^\wedge, R^\wedge, w^\wedge \rangle$, defined on the atoms of a complete atomic Boolean algebra of propositions, on the assumption that there is such an algebra. Metaphysical universality was shown to coincide with formal validity on the intended model structure. We thereby gain information about the logic of metaphysical modality through non-modal reasoning about the intended model structure. A natural aim is to extend those arguments to first-order modal logic.

For the same reasons as in the propositional case, we should aim, at least initially, for an intended model structure, rather than an intended model or frame. The metaphysically universal formulas are not those valid on a given model, for any model constrains the interpretation of the atomic predicate incompatibly with our present intention to use them to achieve generality. Nor does an intended frame satisfy our intentions, for it fails to specify an actual world. Moreover, the metaphysically universal formulas are those valid on an intended frame only if metaphysical universality is closed under necessitation; as just noted, contingentists should be especially wary of that assumption.

We may even expect the very same intended model structure as in the propositional case to do for first-order modal logic too. The difference is that an uninhabited model structure no longer suffices. To enforce the intended unrestricted interpretation of the quantifiers at the actual world $w^\wedge$ of the intended model structure, we want its domain $D^\wedge(w^\wedge)$ to be the set of every actual thing. Moreover, as seen in section 1.6, the qualification 'actual' on its intended reading excludes nothing from such occurrences of 'every' and 'thing', for they are not embedded in the scope of a modal operator. Thus $D^\wedge(w^\wedge)$ should contain absolutely everything, without restriction.

That proposal faces an immediate obstacle. $D^{\wedge}(w^{\wedge})$ is a set, since by definition of an inhabited model structure $D^{\wedge}$ is a function from members of $W^{\wedge}$ to sets; but no set contains absolutely everything. For by Cantor's theorem any set has more subsets than members, and so does not contain all its subsets. Of course, this problem is not specific to modal model theory. It arises equally for ordinary first-order non-modal model theory. When the first-order quantifiers are intended to be unrestricted, a first-order language has no intended model in the standard set-theoretic sense. Not even pure set theory has an intended model, for no set contains absolutely every set.[63] The generic nature of this problem warns against drawing morals from it specific to the modal case. Rather than embark on a long digression through the theory of unrestricted quantification, we may therefore tentatively continue for now with the set-theoretic framework of standard model theory, while prescinding from its most restrictive consequences, in the hope that the non-set-theoretic modal conclusions we reach by arguing in those terms will still be reachable by arguing in whatever terms eventually replace them. One promising although controversial proposal is to substitute higher-order logic for set theory in the metalanguage.[64] These issues will be revisited in section 3.7, and in more detail in Chapter 5.

Independently of problems about unrestricted quantification, a specifically modal issue arises simply from the natural constraint, analogous to one in section 3.3, that the logic of an intended inhabited model structure be sound and complete for metaphysical universality. An inhabited model structure satisfies the constraint if and only if, for all formulas A of first-order modal logic: A is valid on that model structure if and only if A is metaphysically universal.

To see the problem, first note the purely technical point that the open formula $\exists y\ x=y$ is valid on an inhabited model structure only if (unnecessitated) BF is also valid on that model structure. For suppose that $\exists y\ x=y$ is valid on $\langle W, R, w, D\rangle$. Let d be something in $D(w^*)$ for some $w^* \in W$, $\underline{a}$ be

---

[63] For some discussion of this well-known problem see McGee 1992.

[64] For such proposals see Boolos 1985, Rayo and Uzquiano 1999, and Williamson 2003a. Many of the essays in Rayo and Uzquiano 2006 bear on the general problem. The higher-order strategy involves reinterpreting the apparently first-order quantification over such things as properties and relations in the definition of metaphysical universality for a first-order language as irreducibly second-order quantification, whose semantics must itself be given in a higher-order language. As explained in section 5.7 and Williamson 2003a, pp. 456–7, the plural reading of second-order quantification proposed in Boolos 1985, followed by Rayo and Uzquiano 1999, is unsuitable for these purposes. A more intensional reading is needed.

an assignment on which $\underline{a}(x)$ is d, and M be a model on $<$W, R, w, D$>$. By hypothesis, M, w, $\underline{a}$ ⊨ $\exists x\ x=y$, so by the semantic clauses $d \in D(w)$. Hence $D(w^*) \subseteq D(w)$ for all $w^* \in$ W, so $<$W, R, w, D$>$ is non-increasing at w. Hence, by the characterization established in section 3.5, (unnecessitated) BF is valid on $<$W, R, w, D$>$.

Now suppose that some inhabited model structure $<$W, R, w, D$>$ is intended. Hence $<$W, R, w, D$>$ satisfies the constraint on intended inhabited model structures: its logic is sound and complete for metaphysical universality. But $\exists y\ x=y$ is metaphysically universal, because its universal generalization $\forall x\ \exists y\ x=y$ is true, indeed provable in first-order logic. Therefore, by completeness, $\exists y\ x=y$ is valid on $<$W, R, w, D$>$. So, by the previous technical point (unnecessitated) BF is also valid on $<$W, R, w, D$>$. Therefore, by soundness, (unnecessitated) BF is metaphysically universal. Thus, by the constraint, there is an intended inhabited model structure only if (unnecessitated) BF is metaphysically universal.[65]

The argument assumes nothing about intended inhabited model structures to differentiate them from other inhabited model structures except that they are sound and complete for metaphysical universality. In particular, it applies equally whether their worlds are treated as primitive, or constructed, for example out of the Boolean algebra of propositions in section 3.3.

The hypothesis that there is an intended inhabited model structure has not been shown to entail the metaphysical universality of full BF. The argument is specific to the actual world of the model structure. For all it shows, BF may have false instances at non-actual worlds in models on an intended inhabited model structure, and corresponding instances of full BF may be false even at the actual world in such models, in which case full BF is invalid on the model structure, and so not metaphysically universal. However, most contingentists regard unnecessitated BF as actually having false instances, not just as being capable of having them: for example, John F. Kennedy and Marilyn Monroe could have had a child, even though there is actually nothing that could have been their child. Most contingentists must therefore deny that quantified modal logic has an intended inhabited model structure in the sense of the constraint. Although very cautious contingentists may be unwilling to commit themselves to there actually being false instances of BF while still convinced that there could have been, even they will not intend

---

[65] For related philosophical discussion see Plantinga 1974, pp. 128–31.

an inhabited model structure that obviously trivially validates BF. For a contingentist to say 'Maybe BF actually has no counterexamples, but it certainly could have done' is as risky as for a common-sense metaphysician to say 'Maybe there are actually no tables and chairs, but there certainly could have been'. Likely explanations of error about actual cases predict error about the merely possible cases too.

Contingentists cannot evade the argument by postulating jointly intended families of inhabited model structures in place of individually intended inhabited model structures, where the constraint on such an intended family is that for all formulas A of first-order modal logic: A is valid on all model structures in the family if and only if A is metaphysically universal. For by just the same reasoning as before, if there is such a family, since $\exists y\ x=y$ is metaphysically universal, by the right-to-left direction of the new constraint $\exists y\ x=y$ is valid on all model structures in the family, so by the technical point (unnecessitated) BF is valid on all model structures in the family, so by the left-to-right direction of the new constraint (unnecessitated) BF is metaphysically universal.

The argument manifests no glitch in the definition of metaphysical universality. It rightly counts $\exists y\ x=y$ as metaphysically universal (as usual, on an unrestricted reading of the quantifier). On the intended reading of the quantifier, it is true whatever object is assigned to the variable x. We can equally well make the argument with the closed formula $\exists y\ a=y$ in place of $\exists y\ x=y$, since they have the same condition for metaphysical universality and the allowed denotations of the name a in the model structure are the same as the allowed values of the variable x. Contingentists might try tinkering with the model theory to avoid the result. For example, to block the argument about $\exists y\ x=y$ they might define validity on a frame as truth in all models at the actual world on all assignments of values in the domain of the actual world. To block the argument about $\exists y\ a=y$ they might require all models to assign denotations in the domain of the actual world to all individual constants. Both restrictions would be needed, since the redefinition of validity does not block the argument for constants and the constraint on the denotations of constants does not block the argument for free variables. From a model-theoretic perspective, both restrictions introduce unmotivated ad hoc complications. The need for them merely emphasizes the point that the model theory sits more comfortably with necessitism than it does with contingentism. The model theory is best kept in its simpler, more standard form.

Although necessitists accept the metaphysical universality of BF, indeed of full BF, the foregoing argument by itself is unlikely to be what persuades them. For it relies purely on non-modal reasoning. As explained in section 1.4, although the object-language quantifiers are unrestricted on their intended readings, that does not trivialize BF. Even necessitists should regard BF as a necessary but highly informative theoretical claim in modal metaphysics, not a triviality. Given necessitism, we may use an inhabited model structure to encode modal facts: but introducing the quantified modal language by reference to that structure leaves the metaphysical significance of BF and other principles hopelessly obscure. The great advantage of possible worlds model theory is to enable us to reason about modal logic in non-modal terms, more specifically, in a language without modal operators. An inevitable cost of that advantage is the inexpressibility in those terms of any question about how much could have been otherwise. Although necessitists may accept such an intended inhabited model structure, they should grant it no primary explanatory or meaning-giving role (see further section 8.4). The interest of the model structure depends on the interest of the modal operators, not the other way round.

Contingentists may still hope for an inhabited model structure related in some less straightforward way to metaphysical universality. As we saw for propositional modal logic, many different model structures may have a logic sound and complete for metaphysical universality, without even being isomorphic to each other. In the first-order case, the domain $D(w)$ of the actual world w of such a model structure would somehow represent or go proxy for everything without containing everything, thereby leaving some objects over to belong to the domains only of other worlds and thereby falsify some instances of BF, if required. However, if an object in the domain $D(w*)$ of another world $w*$ but not in $D(w)$ represents an object that could have been but actually is not, the representing is no relation between the actual thing in $D(w*)$ and something else that could have been but actually is not, for there is no such thing as the latter—contingentists and necessitists should agree on at least that much, as Chapter 1 explained. At best, the object in $D(w*)$ represents an object that could have been but actually is not in something like the sense in which a statue may represent a god who hurls thunderbolts, even though, despite the myths, there is no god who hurls thunderbolts to represent.

We cannot even assume that the representing is some modal analogue of one-one. Many contingentists argue against BF from the premise that there could have been numerically more things than there actually are.[66] Since everything in D(w*) actually is, there are no more things in D(w*) than there actually are, so the inhabited model structure can verify that contingentist premise only by letting the domain of some world represent more things than it actually contains.[67]

Not all versions of contingentism allow that there could have been numerically more (or fewer) things than there actually are. For example, according to Alvin Plantinga, although not everything is necessarily something, necessarily everything has an essence that is necessarily something and could not have been an essence of anything else.[68] Thus necessarily there are as many essences as there could have been things. On his view it is contingent which things there are, but not contingent how many things (including essences) there are. The essence-of relation works like an especially intimate and individualized form of representation. However, few contingentists limit ontological contingency as much as Plantinga does; he is no representative contingentist.

For contingentists, although an inhabited model structure may correctly classify closed formulas of the first-order modal language as valid or invalid, the compositional means by which it does so in the model-theoretic semantics are of scarcely more than instrumental significance. As David Lewis recognized, when we use possible worlds model theory as a device of standard metalogic, 'We are doing mathematics, not metaphysics'.[69]

Contrary to the impression some contingentists may have had, Kripke's model theory does not explain the supposed failure of BF to be metaphysically universal, or justify the belief that it is not metaphysically universal.

---

[66] For more sophisticated cardinality concerns about necessitism see Sider 2009 and Hawthorne and Uzquiano 2011. The most serious of such concerns are associated with the vague idea that the number of sets is unlimited in potentiality rather than in actuality (they form an 'indefinitely extensible totality' or a 'potential absolute infinity'). However, this idea, if it can be made coherent, already applies to the *pure* sets. Since pure sets are independent of the concrete, literal change or contingency in what pure sets there are is quite implausible. Thus the relevant sense of 'potentiality' cannot be explicated in terms of metaphysical possibility (see Fine 2006, pp. 31–2). Fine postulates an irreducible and not easily intelligible notion of 'postulational possibility' instead (Fine 2006, pp. 33–5). The alleged failure of BF for postulational possibility has no direct implications for necessitism (or permanentism). Since the analogues of BF, CBF, and NNE are more or less uncontentious when the modalities are interpreted metaphysically while the quantifiers are restricted to pure sets, yet cardinality concerns already arise, it is unclear why the appropriate treatment, whatever it is, should not generalize to necessitism once the quantifier restriction is lifted.

[67] This is a difficulty for the account of intended* models in Menzel 1990.

[68] See Plantinga 1974 and 1976.

[69] See Lewis 1986, p. 17.

If the model theory is treated in a fully realist way, it trivially validates BF, by yielding an intended inhabited model structure. That does not mean that either the model theory is rubbish or BF is valid on its intended interpretation; a theory may be useful when treated instrumentally. But it emphasizes that any case for contingentism comes from modal metaphysics, not from possible worlds semantics.[70] Indeed, contingentism cannot associate itself with much of the explanatory success of the possible worlds approach. For by far the greatest and clearest achievements of the possible worlds approach have come in the model theory of modal logic. The philosophical gains have been flimsy by comparison, often barely more than presentational (when points are worded in terms of possible worlds but could easily have been put in modal terms) or else hopelessly controversial (when they rely on modal realism). Although contingentists may tell some sort of representational story to connect the model theory with the intended modal interpretation, their story is too indirect to make the model theory much more than a complicated digression. By contrast, necessitists can connect the model theory to the intended interpretation more directly, as we will see in the next section. That asymmetry is not decisive in favour of necessitism, because the model theory has no explanatory priority in semantics. Nevertheless, necessitism has a theoretical advantage over contingentism in giving a clearer, simpler, and more satisfying account for quantified modal languages of the relation between truth in a model and truth.

3.7 Intended inhabited model structures for necessitism

Necessitists face fewer obstacles than contingentists do to defining an intended inhabited model structure for quantified modal logic. The absence of a universal set is a problem for necessitists and contingentists alike. As a temporary measure, we base the technical development on the pretence that the first-order quantifiers of the object-language are intended to range over a

---

[70] The discussion of counter-models to BF at p. 263 of Williamson 1998 was intended in the spirit of these comments. It has sometimes been misinterpreted as an attempt to use Kripke's model theory to prove the rejection of BF incoherent. For detailed discussion of the issues from a contingentist perspective see Pérez Otero 2010.

given set-sized domain, of otherwise unspecified size. Later in the section, we put aside the pretence and assess what is left. Likewise, we temporarily assume that there is a set of all propositions.

Given the background theory in section 3.3 of propositions as forming a complete atomic Boolean algebra, necessitists can take the intended uninhabited model structure $\langle W^\wedge, R^\wedge, w^\wedge \rangle$ for propositional modal logic and inhabit each world by adding a constant domain D (no longer a function). The result is a structure $\langle W^\wedge, R^\wedge, w^\wedge, D \rangle$, which automatically validates full BF and full CBF. We temporarily pretend that D is the intended domain of the first-order quantifiers, and read the universal generalization of a formula accordingly. A system S of first-order modal logic is *sound for metaphysical universality* if and only if every theorem of S is metaphysically universal. S is *complete for metaphysical universality* if and only if every metaphysically universal formula of the first-order modal language is a theorem of S. An inhabited model structure meets the natural constraint on an intended inhabited model structure if and only if its first-order modal logic, the set of formulas of the first-order modal language valid on it, is sound and complete for metaphysical universality. The constraint is proposed as a necessary condition for intendedness, not as a sufficient one.

We argued in section 3.3 that, on reasonable assumptions, the propositional modal logic of $\langle W^\wedge, R^\wedge, w^\wedge \rangle$ is sound and complete for metaphysical universality. The connection was made through the apparatus of faithful interpretations, functions mapping formulas to propositions in ways that respect the meanings of the connectives. The next task is to extend that argument to first-order modal logic, using the same theory of propositions, in order to argue that the first-order modal logic of $\langle W^\wedge, R^\wedge, w^\wedge, D \rangle$ is sound and complete for metaphysical universality, and so meets the earlier constraint on an intended inhabited model structure.

For present purposes, the apparatus of faithful interpretations must be relativized to the domain. Thus a faithful interpretation treats the object-language quantifiers as ranging exactly over D. A faithful interpretation I also maps each individual constant c to an individual $I(c)$ in D. I maps each n-place non-logical atomic predicate F to an n-place function $I(F)$ from members of D^n to propositions. I maps each formula A to a proposition $I_a(A)$ relative to an assignment a of values in D to all first-order variables. For any individual term t, $I_a(t)$ is $I(t)$ if t is a constant and $a(t)$ if t is a variable. I is a faithful interpretation of the first-order language if and only if I meets those conditions and these compositional ones: $I_a(Ft_1 \ldots t_n) = I(F)(<I_a(t_1), \ldots,$ $I_a(t_n)>)$; $I_a(t_1=t_2) = 1$ if $I_a(t_1) = I_a(t_2)$ and 0 otherwise; $I_a(\neg A) = \sim I_a(A)$; $I_a(A \ \& \ B)$ $= \Pi\{I_a(A), I_a(B)\}$; $I_a(\Box A) = LI_a(A)$; $I_a(\forall v A) = \Pi\{I_{a[v/d]}(A): d \in D\}$.[71] Then the universal generalization of A is true, and so A metaphysically universal, if and only if $I_a(A)$ is true for every faithful interpretation I and assignment a.

In the definition of a faithful interpretation, the clause for '=' reflects the Kripkean conception of identity statements with rigid designators as either necessarily true or necessarily false.[72] The clauses for $\neg$, $\&$, and $\Box$ are just as in the propositional case, except for the relativization to an assignment. The clause for $\forall$ exploits the assumption, already used for other purposes in section 3.3, that the Boolean algebra of propositions is complete, so that even an infinite set of propositions has a conjunction, in order to treat a universal generalization as a conjunction over every member of the domain. That would be unacceptable to a contingentist, since it excludes variation in the domain of quantification. More specifically, it verifies every instance of full BF and CBF, for $I_a(\Box \forall v A) = LI_a(\forall v A) = L\Pi\{I_{a[v/d]}(A): d \in D\} =$ $\Pi\{LI_{a[v/d]}(A): d \in D\}$ (since L commutes with conjunction) $= \Pi\{I_{a[v/d]}(\Box A): d \in D\}$ $= I_a(\forall v \ \Box A)$.

Even for a necessitist, the conjunctive proposition assigned to a universally quantified formula does not present its conjuncts *as* covering everything (in the domain). Propositions here are not expected to encode modes of presentation. This point is also manifest in the way in which the proposition assigned to an atomic formula depends on the values of its variables, independently of how those values are presented. Indeed, the proposition assigned to $x=y$ depends on the values of the variables only to the extent that it depends on the truth value of the formula under the assignment.

Each faithful interpretation I determines a model $M_I = <W^\wedge, R^\wedge, w^\wedge, D, V_I>$ on the model structure in the natural way. For each individual constant $c, V_I(c) = I(c)$. For each non-logical n-place atomic predicate F and world w, $V_I(F)(w) = \{<d_1, \ldots, d_n> \in D^n: w \leq I(F)(<d_1, \ldots, d_n>)\}$, the set of n-tuples of members of the domain mapped to a proposition true at w by the function

---

[71] See Rasiowa and Sikorski 1963, pp. 226–8 and 481–8, for a similar treatment of first-order modal logic in terms of complete Boolean algebras with infinitary operations. Gallin 1975, p. 108, also gives such a clause for the universal quantifier in defining Boolean-valued models for higher-order modal logic (for technical purposes), and shows at pp. 121–2 that the assumption of the completeness of the algebra is unavoidable. Gallin applies such models in proofs of set-theoretic independence results.

[72] See section 1.7.

with which I interprets F. We must show that the truth values of formulas in the model match those of the propositions I assigns them. More precisely, for every formula A and assignment $\underline{a}$: M_I, $\underline{a} \vDash A$ if and only $I_{\underline{a}}(A)$ is true. To show that, we must establish something more general, that the truth values of formulas track those of the corresponding propositions across all worlds in the model. More precisely, for every formula A, assignment $\underline{a}$ and $w \in W^{\wedge}$: M_I, w, $\underline{a} \vDash A$ if and only if $w \leq I_{\underline{a}}(A)$. That can be proved by induction on the complexity of A.[73]

In particular, the result holds when w is $w^{\wedge}$, which is both the actual world of the model and the conjunction of all truths. Thus A is true in M_I under $\underline{a}$ if and only if $I_{\underline{a}}(A)$ is true. That is the proper connection for first-order modal logic between a formula's being mapped to a true proposition by a faithful interpretation and its being true in the corresponding model on the intended inhabited model structure.

As a corollary, we can now argue that the first-order modal logic of $<W^{\wedge}, R^{\wedge}, w^{\wedge}, D>$ is sound and complete for metaphysical universality, so $<W^{\wedge}, R^{\wedge}, w^{\wedge}, D>$ meets the earlier constraint on a intended inhabited model structure, the desired analogue for first-order modal logic of the result in section 3.3 for propositional modal logic. For if A is valid on $<W^{\wedge}, R^{\wedge}, w^{\wedge}, D>$, then for every faithful interpretation I and assignment $\underline{a}$, since A is true in M_I on $\underline{a}$, by the above $I_{\underline{a}}(A)$ is true; thus A is metaphysically universal. Conversely, suppose that A is metaphysically universal. For any model $M = <W^{\wedge}, R^{\wedge}, w^{\wedge}, D, V>$, let I be the faithful interpretation such that for any individual constant c, non-logical n-place predicate letter F and $d_1, \ldots, d_n$ in D,

$$I(c) = V(c)$$

$$I(F)(<d_1, \ldots, d_n>) = \Sigma\{x \in W^{\wedge}: <d_1, \ldots, d_n> \in V(F)(x)\}$$

---

[73] As in the propositional case, the natural way to argue for that conclusion is by induction on the complexity of the formula A. The basis of the induction is again trivial for atomic formulas with non-logical predicates, by definition of V_I. For '=': if M_I, w, $\underline{a} \vDash t_1 = t_2$ then in M_I $I_{\underline{a}}(t_1) = \mathrm{den}_{\underline{a}}(t_1) = \mathrm{den}_{\underline{a}}(t_2) = I_{\underline{a}}(t_2)$, so $w \leq 1 = I_{\underline{a}}(t_1 = t_2)$; conversely, if $w \leq I_{\underline{a}}(t_1 = t_2)$ then $I_{\underline{a}}(t_1 = t_2) \neq 0$ since w is an atom, so $I_{\underline{a}}(t_1 = t_2) = 1$, so in M_I $\mathrm{den}_{\underline{a}}(t_1) = I_{\underline{a}}(t_1) = I_{\underline{a}}(t_2) = \mathrm{den}_{\underline{a}}(t_2)$, so M_I, w, $\underline{a} \vDash t_1 = t_2$. The step for atomic formulas with non-logical predicates is even more trivial. The induction steps for ¬, &, and □ are much as in section 3.3, but relativized to an assignment. The main new case is the induction step for ∀. The induction hypothesis is that for every assignment $\underline{a}$: M_I, w, $\underline{a} \vDash A$ if and only $w \leq I_{\underline{a}}(A)$. First, suppose that M_I, w, $\underline{a} \vDash \forall v A$. Then for every $d \in D$: M_I, w, $\underline{a}[v/d] \vDash A$. Hence, by the induction hypothesis, for every $d \in D$, $w \leq I_{\underline{a}[v/d]}(A)$. Therefore $w \leq \Pi\{I_{\underline{a}[v/d]}(A): d \in D\} = I_{\underline{a}}(\forall v A)$. The proof of the converse simply reverses those steps. Thus for every formula A, assignment $\underline{a}$ and $w \in W^{\wedge}$: M_I, w, $\underline{a} \vDash A$ if and only if $w \leq I_{\underline{a}}(A)$.

The latter is a proposition true at exactly those worlds at which $<d_1, \ldots, d_n>$ is in the extension of F according to M. Then $M_I = M$.[74] Since A is metaphysically universal, $I_a(A)$ is true for any assignment a, so A is true in $M_I = M$ on any assignment. Thus A is valid on $<W^\wedge, R^\wedge, w^\wedge, D>$, as required. Therefore, under necessitism, the set of metaphysically universal formulas of the first-order modal language is the logic of the intended inhabited model structure.

If we choose to fully interpret individual and predicate constants of the language too, thereby mapping each atomic formula to a unique proposition on each assignment, we have determined a unique faithful interpretation I, where each formula A of the object-language is true on its intended interpretation if and only if the proposition $I(A)$ is true.[75] But we showed earlier that $I(A)$ is true if and only if A is true in the model M_I on the intended model structure. Since M_I corresponds to the intended faithful interpretation I, it deserves to count as the intended model. Thus we also have an appropriate equivalence between the truth of a formula in the intended model and its simple truth.

The logic of the intended inhabited model structure will be none of the more familiar first-order modal logics. For let n be a natural number and E_n a first-order non-modal sentence saying that there are at least n things (in the domain). If D has at least n members, $\Box E_n$ is valid on $<W^\wedge, R^\wedge, w^\wedge, D>$ and so metaphysically universal. If D has fewer than n members, $\Box \neg E_n$ is valid on $<W^\wedge, R^\wedge, w^\wedge, D>$ and so metaphysically universal. But neither $\Box E_n$ nor $\Box \neg E_n$ is a theorem of any standard modal logic, for $n \geq 2$. The results of logic are no more required to be uncontentious than those of any other

---

[74] Proof: $V_I = V$, since for any $w \in W^\wedge$:

$$V_I(F)(w) = \{<d_1, \ldots, d_n> \in D^{\wedge n}: w \leq I(F)(<d_1, \ldots, d_n>)\}$$
$$= \{<d_1, \ldots, d_n> \in D^{\wedge n}: w \leq \Sigma\{x \in W^\wedge: <d_1, \ldots, d_n> \in V(F)(x)\}\}$$
$$= \{<d_1, \ldots, d_n> \in D^{\wedge n}: <d_1, \ldots, d_n> \in V(F)(w)\}$$
$$= V(F)(w)$$

Hence $M_I = <W^\wedge, R^\wedge, w^\wedge, D, V_I> = <W^\wedge, R^\wedge, w^\wedge, D, V> = M$.

[75] Philosophers of an internalist bent may argue that even fully interpreted expressions sometimes suffer reference failure. Although this applies to predicates as well as singular terms, for the purposes of set-theoretic model theory it makes serious trouble only in the latter case, since in the former an empty extension can be assigned. Such internalists may revise the model theory by allowing for empty terms. However, that generates a troublesome asymmetry in treatment between variables and constants. Alternatively, internalists may regard the phrase 'fully interpreted' in the text as elliptical for 'fully *and successfully* interpreted'. For discussion of related issues see Besson 2009.

science are. When we treat quantifiers (read unrestrictedly) and modal operators (read metaphysically) as logical constants, we must expect metaphysically loaded logical truths.

Lifting our neutrality about the intended domain for a paragraph, we can argue thus. For any n, there could have been at least n donkeys, so $\Diamond E_n$ is true, so $\Box \neg E_n$ is false. Since it is its own universal generalization, it is not metaphysically universal. Therefore D has at least n members, so $\Box E_n$ is metaphysically universal.

If metaphysical possibility and necessity are non-contingent matters, then, by the reasoning at the end of section 3.3, we may treat $R^\wedge$ as the universal relation $W^{\wedge 2}$ on an infinite set $W^\wedge$, for worlds inaccessible from the actual world of a model structure for S5 play no role in determining the truth value of any formula in a model on that structure. We have just seen that in practice D will also be infinite. Since the domain is constant, the mathematical structure of $<W^\wedge, W^{\wedge 2}, w^\wedge, D>$ is completely determined by the cardinalities of $W^\wedge$ and D, both of which are presumably very large. Nevertheless, one might guess that, by some extension of the Löwenheim-Skolem theorem to first-order modal logic in a language with only countably many expressions, differences between different orders of infinity would be inexpressible in the resultant logic. Since the first-order non-modal logic of unrestricted generality is completely axiomatized by adding all sentences E_n as extra axioms to a standard axiomatization of the usual first-order non-modal logic of restricted generality, a prima facie natural conjecture is that the logic of $<W^\wedge, W^{\wedge 2}, w^\wedge, D>$ is completely axiomatized by adding all sentences $\Box E_n$ as extra axioms to a standard axiomatization of first-order S5 with BF, which is complete with respect to the class of constant-domain models on infinite frames with a universal accessibility relation.[76]

Unfortunately, matters are not so simple. The logic of $<W^\wedge, W^{\wedge 2}, w^\wedge, D>$ is sensitive to the relation between the size of $W^\wedge$ and the size of D. For suppose that $W^\wedge$ is at least as large as D. Then the formula $\forall x \Diamond \forall y (Fy \leftrightarrow x=y)$ has a model on $<W^\wedge, W^{\wedge 2}, w^\wedge, D>$ in which for each member d of D there is a world at which the extension of F is exactly $\{d\}$, so $\neg \forall x \Diamond \forall y (Fy \leftrightarrow x=y)$

---

[76] For the completeness of the non-modal first-order logic of unrestricted quantification, see Rayo and Williamson 2003. For completeness results for first-order S5 + BF, see Kripke 1959a, Bayart 1959, and Hughes and Cresswell 1996, pp. 264–5. It is easy to show that requiring the accessibility relation to be universal rather than an equivalence relation and centring such a frame to make it a model structure does not change the logic in these cases.

is not valid on $\langle W^\wedge, W^{\wedge 2}, w^\wedge, D \rangle$, so, by the supposed completeness of the logic of that model structure for metaphysical universality, $\neg\forall x \Diamond\forall y\ (Fy \leftrightarrow x=y)$ is not metaphysically universal. By contrast, if for every subset X of $W^\wedge$ the proposition ΣX true at exactly the members of X belongs to D, then, by Cantor's theorem, D is larger than $W^\wedge$. In that (more plausible?) case, $\forall x \Diamond\forall y\ (Fy \leftrightarrow x=y)$ has no models on $\langle W^\wedge, W^{\wedge 2}, w^\wedge, D \rangle$, because there are too few worlds to go round, so $\neg\forall x \Diamond\forall y\ (Fy \leftrightarrow x=y)$ is valid on $\langle W^\wedge, W^{\wedge 2}, w^\wedge, D \rangle$, so, by the supposed soundness of the logic of that model structure for metaphysical universality, $\neg\forall x \Diamond\forall y\ (Fy \leftrightarrow x=y)$ is metaphysically universal. Even granted that metaphysical universality is equivalent to validity on a particular constant-domain model structure with infinitely many worlds, a universal accessibility relation, and infinitely many individuals, the resultant first-order logic of metaphysical modality cannot be identified without further metaphysical reflection.

The uncertainty is not confined to necessitism. The metaphysical universality or otherwise of $\neg\forall x \Diamond\forall y\ (Fy \leftrightarrow x=y)$ is a metaphysical question for contingentists too. Even if they hope to resolve it negatively by arguing that although the actual individuals do not outnumber the possible worlds, there could have been more individuals (but not more possibilities?) than there actually are, they still face a further metaphysical conundrum as to the metaphysical universality or otherwise of the formula $\neg\Box\forall x \Diamond\forall y\ (Fy \leftrightarrow x=y)$, which is logically weaker than $\neg\forall x \Diamond\forall y\ (Fy \leftrightarrow x=y)$ in S5 for contingentists but not necessitists.

Let us now drop the pretence of a fixed set-sized domain for the object-language quantifiers. If we intend the unrestricted reading of the quantifiers, the set-theoretic apparatus of model theory will need replacing by something second-order, but the upshot will otherwise be much the same for necessitists, in particular with respect to metaphysical universality. The same goes for quantification in the metalanguage over propositions, if they fail to form a set. As in section 3.3, we can use Shapiro's principle KP3 to argue that if the logic of some higher-order analogue of an intended inhabited model structure is sound and complete for metaphysical universality, so too is the logic of some inhabited model structure in the standard set-theoretic sense.

For those sceptical of the unrestricted reading, our intentions may be less specific: we intend to quantify over a large enough domain, but there may be no unique large enough domain over which we intend to quantify. In that case, the closest we can come to metaphysical universality may be validity on an intended family of large enough model structures. The status of the formula $\forall x \Diamond \forall y \, (Fy \leftrightarrow x=y)$ becomes even less clear, since $W^{\wedge}$ may be larger than D in some but not all model structures $<W^{\wedge}, W^{\wedge 2}, w^{\wedge}, D>$ in the intended family. Nevertheless, the necessitist logic of metaphysical universality remains strong: for example, the earlier argument presumably still shows that for all $n \, \Box E_n$ is valid on every model structure in the intended family (just as for set theory the axiom of infinity holds in every intended model), and so metaphysically universal by the soundness of the logic of the intended family for metaphysical universality.

Is this degree of engagement between logic and metaphysics problematic? Some view logic as a neutral arbiter of metaphysical disputes, whose proper function is compromised by any metaphysical commitments of its own.[77] Attempts are sometimes made to fence off purely logical claims as in some sense *analytic*, in a sense that would make them uncontroversial, whereas metaphysical claims are correspondingly *synthetic*, and inherently liable to controversy.[78] The history of logic tells strongly against any such contrast. All major logical principles have been rejected on metaphysical grounds. According to some, future contingencies violate the law of excluded middle; according to others, the set of all non-self-membered sets makes contradictions true. Even the structural principle that chaining together valid arguments yields another valid argument has been rejected in response to sorites paradoxes. In each case, a deviant metaphysics corresponds to the deviant logic. Of course, if one is trying to persuade deviant metaphysicians of the errors of their ways, one will not get far by appealing to logical principles they reject. But that obvious dialectical exigency marks out no stable realm of logic. Any logical principle has persuasive force in some dialectical contexts and not in others. Logic has no metaphysically neutral core. Like

---

[77] Kaplan 1994, p. 42, expresses such an attitude towards modal logic; it is endorsed by Kripke 2011, p. 374. Kaplan's paper concerns the generation of 'unwanted' theorems of modal logic by possible worlds semantics, which may be compared to the present issue, although his main example involves higher-order quantification and does not concern the specific interpretation of the modal operators. However, he insists that $\forall x \Diamond \forall y \, (Fy \leftrightarrow x=y)$ should not be ruled out on logical grounds (p. 43). Another example is Garson 2006, p. 292, who complains that on the standard objectual interpretation of the first-level quantifiers, the semantics cannot 'serve as a neutral device for exploring alternative views about possible objects and substance'. That is true as far as it goes, but in what other science is the uninformativeness of a theory considered a virtue?

[78] For some problems for such attempts, see Williamson 2007, pp. 48–133. Of course, if analytic truths can be controversial, the attempt fails anyway.

any other science, its findings are open to legitimate challenge, even when the challenges are in fact mistaken.

As acknowledged in section 3.3, some readers may prefer to use the word 'logic' differently. They can rephrase the conclusions of this chapter by using another word. But whatever advantages may accrue to their way of using 'logic', they will not include isolating some claims that are in principle metaphysically uncontroversial. There are none.

The controversy is particularly unsurprising in the present case, because we treated metaphysically modal operators and unrestricted quantifiers as logical constants when defining metaphysical universality, in order to keep hold of our subject matter. Indeed, for formulas with no non-logical predicates, such as $\Box E_n$, logical truth simply coincides with truth. In this area as in others, logic and metaphysics overlap. That is a challenge to relish, not a confusion to define away.

4

Predication and Modality

4.1 The being constraint

Kripke's semantics for quantified modal logic permits the extension of an atomic predicate at a possible world to contain objects outside the domain of that world; he does not impose the domain constraint (section 3.4). Thus his semantics invalidates formulas like these:

(1) $\Box \forall x \, \Box (Fx \to \exists z \, x=z)$

        $\Box \forall x \, \Box \forall y \, \Box (Rxy \to (\exists z \, x=z \, \& \, \exists z \, y=z))$

Yet such formulas, on their intended readings, are deeply plausible. For necessitists, of course, they are routine logical truths, since by full BF and CBF they are equivalent to the results of moving all the modal operators to the front, and therefore to iterated necessitations of theorems of first-order non-modal logic with identity, such as (1−) and (2−), in which the antecedents Fx and Rxy are redundant:

(1−) $\forall x \, (Fx \to \exists z \, x=z)$

(2−) $\forall x \, \forall y \, (Rxy \to (\exists z \, x=z \, \& \, \exists z \, y=z))$

For contingentists, those equivalences fail and principles such as (1) and (2) are less trivial; nevertheless, they retain a powerful prima facie attraction. How could a thing be propertied were there no such thing to be propertied? How could one thing be related to another were there no such things to be related?

More specifically, we can ask the unrestricted question 'How many things have the property P?' If x has P, then presumably x should be counted in answer to that question: exactly one thing is x and has P, so at least one thing is x. But if at least one thing is x then x is something. Similar considerations apply to polyadic relations.

Of course, failures of (1) and (2) might be unproblematic if the quantifiers were restricted. For example, if we restrict 'somebody' to the members of a club in the circumstances under consideration, we can truly say 'Somebody could have lived without being somebody': a member of the club could have lived without being a member of that club. But the quantifiers in (1) and (2) are to be read as unrestricted. Denials of (1) and (2) sound like failures to grasp the radical nature of unrestricted quantification. Since such quantification is best not interpreted in terms of a set-like domain, let us call the generalization of (1) and (2) to n-place predicates for all n and all interpretations of those predicates the *being constraint*. It resembles what Alvin Plantinga calls 'serious actualism'.[1]

Admittedly, some instances of the being constraint make hard cases for contingentism. Consider a knife actually made of a blade and a handle. If the blade and the handle had never been joined, it would not have been a knife; according to most contingentists, it would have been nothing at all. Nevertheless, could it not still have had the property (in a liberal sense) of being referred to, for example as the possible knife that would have been made of that blade and that handle? For those contingentists, however, acquiescence in such descriptions risks disaster. On their view, in the envisaged counterfactual circumstances there is no possible knife that would have been made of that blade and that handle; the empty description singles out nothing. In those circumstances, one could still reflect, perhaps truly, 'A knife could have been made of that blade and that handle, and it would have been impossible for any other knife to be made of that blade and that handle', but that would involve no relation of reference to a merely possible knife. The well-attested pattern of reference-fixing by means of a uniquely denoting definite description does not explain how to fix reference by means of a definite description that is not uniquely denoting, whatever its modal properties. *We*, in our actual circumstances, refer to the knife, and thereby characterize various

---

[1] See Plantinga 1983, p. 11. Following the suggestion in Prior 1967, p. 161, Cocchiarella 1968, 1969a, and 1969b develops a temporal and modal logic based on a distinction between 'existence-entailing' attributes like being red and attributes that are not 'existence-entailing' like being thought to be red. At first sight the latter violate the being constraint. However, since Cocchiarella permits quantification over past or merely possible beings that lack 'existence', he seems to be a necessitist who uses 'existence' to mean something like concreteness; if so, his view is compatible with the being constraint. For his theories of predication in a modal setting adapted to various views of universals see Cocchiarella 1986. For a detailed logical study of such constraints ('the Falsehood Principle') see Fine 1981a.

counterfactual circumstances in which there is no such knife, but none of that violates the being constraint.[2]

The being constraint has an analogue with temporal operators in place of modal ones, and a similar rationale. Unsurprisingly, some of its instances make hard cases for temporaryism. Even after the knife has been destroyed, surely it may continue to have effects, to be remembered and referred to, to have been destroyed, and therefore to have properties and relations (in the liberal sense). Indeed, the range of such hard cases is much wider than for the modal being constraint. Queen Anne is dead. My father became a grandfather only after his death. We have no algorithm for re-describing every such case consistently with the temporal being constraint. But that may be less a problem for the constraint than for temporaryism itself. For our pre-theoretic descriptions of the cases appear to involve quantification over past or future objects just as much as they appear to involve attributions of properties and relations to particular past or future objects. For example, 'Many people have become grandparents only after their death' sounds obviously true. The phenomenon may be just that we are often happy to talk as though permanentism were true. Temporaryists then face the challenge of explaining how such talk is useful if permanentism is false. This chapter, like the others, focuses on the modal debate.

The contentiousness of (1) and (2) depends on the modal or temporal operators. When they are deleted, the results (1−) and (2−) are routine theorems of first-order non-modal logic with identity, even if the logic is free. Some *instances* of (1−) and (2−) are contentious:

(1=) $Fa \rightarrow \exists z\ a=z$

(2=) $Rab \rightarrow (\exists z\ a=z\ \&\ \exists z\ b=z)$

Positive free logicians typically reject (1=) and (2=) on the grounds that (for instance) Anna Karenina is pitied and named 'Anna Karenina' even though there is no Anna Karenina, but they can and do accept (1−) and (2−), which do not entail (1=) and (2=) in free logic.

However, (1=) follows in any standard free modal logic from (1), the B principle, and the extra premise that there could have been Anna Karenina (for instance):

(3) $\Diamond \exists x\ a=x$

---

[2] For related challenges to the domain constraint see Salmon 1987.

For (4) follows from (1) and (3) in free modal logic:

(4) $\quad \Diamond\Box(Fa \to \exists z\ a{=}z)$

From (4), (1=) follows by B. Similarly, (2=) follows in any standard free modal logic from (2) given B, (3), and the analogous premise for b. Thus, with the auxiliary premises, the being constraint has controversial non-modal consequences, and the objection to the latter from fiction becomes an objection to the constraint itself, if the relevant name denotes a possible being, or more accurately, if there could have been something that it actually denotes.

Conversely, if there could not have been something that 'Anna Karenina' actually denotes, the alleged counterexamples to (1=) and (2=) involving it are hard to sustain. For how then does 'Anna Karenina' differ, in its contribution to the truth conditions of simple predications where it takes subject position, from a purely and simply non-denoting name? For example, I hereby introduce the name (or pseudo-name) 'Qwerty'. I have done nothing whatsoever to secure it a denotation. In this context, 'Qwerty' is purely and simply non-denoting. Evidently, therefore, neither 'Qwerty is pitied' nor 'Qwerty is named "Qwerty"' is true. Since 'Anna Karenina is pitied' and 'Anna Karenina is named "Anna Karenina"' are true only if what 'Anna Karenina' denotes is pitied and named "Anna Karenina" respectively, they are not true if 'Anna Karenina' is denotationally just like 'Qwerty'. In that case, the antecedent of (1=) or (2=) is not true and the alleged counterexamples to the being constraint fail. On the other hand, if 'Anna Karenina' denotes something, then 'Anna Karenina is something' is true, so the consequent of (1=) and (2=) is true and the alleged counterexamples still fail. Thus the counterexamples work only if 'Anna Karenina' denotes nothing but is not denotationally just like 'Qwerty'. What is the relevant denotational difference between 'Anna Karenina' and 'Qwerty'? It might be replied: 'Anna Karenina' denotes Anna Karenina but 'Qwerty' does not denote Qwerty. That reply is unsatisfying, for at least two reasons. First, it is arguably meaningless, since it uses the meaningless term 'Qwerty' outside quotation marks. Second, it is insufficiently general, because the denotational difference between 'Anna Karenina' and 'Qwerty' is evidently supposed to be an instance of a general denotational difference between fictional names and purely and simply empty names.

What is the relevant *general* denotational defect from which 'Qwerty' suffers but 'Anna Karenina' supposedly does not? It is not the property of denoting nothing, because by hypothesis 'Anna Karenina' also denotes nothing. Nor is it the property of not yielding a true sentence of the form '"N" denotes N' when substituted for 'N', for whether a term yields such a true disquotational sentence is itself to be explained compositionally by the denotational status of the term. The most promising candidate for the relevant general denotational defect is that of being a term t such that there could not have been something that t (as actually used) actually denotes. Following this strategy, the proponent of the alleged counterexamples to (1=) and (2=) holds that there could have been (but is not) something that 'Anna Karenina' (as actually used) actually denotes, while there could not have been something that 'Qwerty' (as actually used) actually denotes.[3]

After Kripke's work, however, the envisaged view of fictional names rests on a discredited descriptivism about names. Although there could have been someone named 'Anna Karenina' with most of the properties described in the novel, there could equally have been someone else named 'Anna Karenina' with those properties. Does the name actually denote both? In any case, such descriptive fit is largely irrelevant to how names denote.[4] Although 'Anna Karenina' could have been used to denote someone, so could 'Qwerty'; such counterfactual uses are irrelevant. They would be independent of its use as a fictional name. As 'Anna Karenina' is actually used (in the present context), there could not have been something that it actually denotes. The strategy of using fictional names to refute (1=) and (2=) relies on too naïve a philosophy of language to carry weight. For the same reason, such a strategy is ineffective against (1) and (2), given premises like (3).

To take a mythological example, suppose that Corin is a devotee of the whole Olympian pantheon. To the questions 'Does Corin worship Athene?' and 'Does Corin worship Hera?', the natural answer is 'Yes'. Thus 'Corin worships Athene' and 'Corin worships Hera' seem true, and are naturally formalized as Wca and Wch. Do such examples undermine the being constraint? To the question 'Does Corin worship at least two Olympian gods?', the equally natural answer is 'Yes', on the grounds that Athene and Hera are distinct Olympian gods whom he worships. Thus 'Corin worships at least two Olympian gods' seems equally true, and it is naturally formalized as

$$\exists x\, \exists y\, (Gx \mathbin{\&} Gy \mathbin{\&} \neg x{=}y \mathbin{\&} Wcx \mathbin{\&} Wcy)$$

[3] Bacon 2011 develops such a view in detail. To handle counterfactual uses of fictional names, 'actually' can be interpreted as rigidly referring back to the counterfactual circumstance at issue.

[4] See Kripke 1980, especially pp. 156–8.

If the latter claim is true, then this case against the being constraint collapses, because generalization with $\exists$ on premises such as *Wca* and *Wch* is sound. On a soberer judgement, the displayed claim is false, because there are no Olympian gods. If so, and 'Corin worships at least two Olympian gods' has been correctly formalized, then we should distrust natural judgements about our relation to mythology, including 'Corin worships Athene' and 'Corin worships Hera', and again the case against the being constraint collapses. Even in such uses, we may go along with the myth further than we realize. Alternatively, 'Corin worships at least two Olympian gods' may have been incorrectly formalized. If so, the fault lies with the treatment of predications involving 'worship' more generally, and we should reject the formalization of 'Corin worships Athene' and 'Corin worships Hera' as *Wca* and *Wch*, so we lose the premises for a counterexample to the being constraint. Such cases appear to threaten the constraint only on a narrowly partial survey of the data from natural language.

In general, we should distrust attempts to use fictional or mythological names to refute metaphysical or logical theses. Such terms have a confusing variety of uses. As the name is used in the novel itself, it is merely part of the story that 'Anna Karenina' denotes. Such a non-denoting use does not verify the antecedent of (1=), and so presents no counterexample. By contrast, in literary criticism, 'Anna Karenina' may be used to denote a fictional character created by Tolstoy, not a woman but a cultural artefact, and therefore something. Such a denoting use verifies the consequent of (1=) and so presents no counterexample. Other cases are possible too. For example, someone may use 'Anna Karenina' under the misapprehension that it really denotes someone. The more carefully such uses are studied, the less they seem to threaten classical theses of logic or metaphysics.[5] In particular, opponents of the being constraint do better to attack it directly, with overtly modal examples, rather than indirectly through half-baked theories of fiction.

A key test of the being constraint concerns identity. Presumably, self-identity is as easy a property as any to have (in the liberal sense of 'property'). Thus if the being constraint fails at all, it fails for self-identity. Conversely, if

---

[5] See van Inwagen 1977, Fine 1982a, and Salmon 1998 and 2002. In my first term as an undergraduate, I listened avidly to Kripke's discussion of fictional names in his 1973 John Locke lectures; see now Kripke 2011, pp. 52–74. For another discussion of fictional ontology see Thomasson 1999. For a well-developed contingentist application of free modal logic to mythological examples see Bacon 2011.

the being constraint holds for self-identity, it holds generally. A critical case is therefore (5):

(5) $\Box \forall x \, \Box(x{=}x \rightarrow \exists z \; x{=}z)$

A defence of (5) amounts to a general defence of the being constraint.

Does self-identity entail being? Rather than relying on dubious assumptions about fictional or mythological names, contingentists may argue against (5) from the tempting premise that necessarily everything is necessarily self-identical:

(6) $\Box \forall x \, \Box x{=}x$

From (5) and (6) one can reason uncontentiously to the necessitist conclusion NNE, that necessarily everything is necessarily something. Thus a contingentist more attached to (6) than to (5) may drop (5) in order to avoid NNE, and so reject an instance of the being constraint. Their attachment to (6) is presumably based on the idea that since logic guarantees self-identity, the object is not needed to make it true. But that is confused. In the non-modal case, although the reflexivity of identity ($\forall x \; x{=}x$) is indeed a logical truth, any instance of it still requires something to be the value of the variable x. Similarly, in the modal case, the general logical principle $x{=}x$ cannot make its own instances out of nothing. Although, obviously, whatever the value of the variable, it is self-identical, that does not mean that it would still have been self-identical if there had been no such thing.

A contingentist might try to defend (6) by appealing to Kit Fine's argument that 'Socrates is self-identical' is true regardless of the circumstances, rather than true however the circumstances turn out, so that its truth does not require Socrates to be something.[6] Despite Fine's best efforts, however, the distinction between truth regardless of the circumstances and truth however the circumstances turn out remains obscure. It is supposed to correspond to the distinction between a true proposition that imposes a condition on circumstances that all possible circumstances meet (truth however the circumstances turn out) and a true proposition that imposes no condition on circumstances at all (truth regardless of the circumstances). If we take Fine's explanation at face value, and let the quantifier $\forall w$ range over possible circumstances, this corresponds to the distinction between the

---

[6] See Fine 2005a, p. 324.

truth of $\forall w\, A$ where A has free occurrences of the circumstantial variable w (truth however the circumstances turn out) and the truth of $\forall w\, A$ where A lacks such free occurrences, so the quantifier is redundant (truth regardless of the circumstances). Since the identity relation has no argument place for the world or circumstance of evaluation, the truth of $\forall w\, s{=}s$ falls under the latter case. Thus 'Socrates is self-identical' comes out true regardless of the circumstances, rather than true however the circumstances turn out, just as Fine claims. Clearly, this way of thinking depends on taking the circumstantial variable very seriously, as corresponding to a constituent of the proposition itself. If it does not, no distinction can be drawn along those lines. But it is very doubtful that contingentists can afford to take the apparatus of quantification over possible circumstances as seriously as that. For quantification over possible circumstances is relevantly like quantification over possible worlds; we saw in section 3.6 that possible worlds semantics is highly problematic for contingentists, when treated as providing an intended model structure for quantified modal discourse rather than as a merely instrumental device. Moreover, further difficulties will emerge for contingentists in Chapter 7 when they try to simulate the use necessitists can make of quantification over worlds, and section 8.4 will give evidence against a reduction of modal operators discourse to such quantifiers. These arguments too apply equally to quantification over possible circumstances. Thus contingentists should not assign circumstantial variables the required role. Indeed, Fine himself rejects the reference to circumstantial variables in drawing his distinction between truth regardless of the circumstances and truth however the circumstances turn out; instead, he takes the distinction as primitive. However, he does try to explain what distinction he has in mind, and his attempts to do so rely heavily on just such overt quantification over circumstances or worlds.[7] In general, it is not a sound methodology to use a theory to draw a distinction, reject the theory, and keep the distinction 'as primitive'. In applying the distinction, one is all too likely to be relying implicitly on the theory one officially rejects. The benefits of a theory cannot so easily be separated from its costs. Thus contingentists are ill advised to defend (6) by appeal to Fine's distinction.

Contingentists do better to drop (6), in which case they lose their objection to (5). Thus they might as well accept the being constraint for self-identity.

---

[7] See Fine 2005a, p. 325.

If self-identity is the hardest case for the being constraint, as suggested earlier, they might as well accept the being constraint generally. They can thereby accommodate the compelling idea that having any property or relation at all, however trivial, requires being something. Indeed, the being constraint makes contingentism more wholehearted. Without it, contingentism looks ambivalent: the supposed counterexamples to the being constraint are pictured as casting enough of a modal shadow on circumstances from which they are absent to bear properties and relations without being present themselves. Although such spatial pictures are easily imaginable in themselves, they betray the contingentist when applied to the being constraint, since they represent the supposed counterexamples to it as merely elsewhere, within range of an unrestricted quantifier and therefore something in the relevant sense, and merely out of range of a quantifier restricted to local things. They give comfort only to those who have failed to grasp how radical is the nothingness required of counterexamples to the being constraint. Hard-line contingentists will accept the constraint.

It may be objected that we get even harder cases for contingentism of the being constraint by substituting for the atomic formula $x=x$ a truth-functional tautology with the same variable, for example $Fx \to Fx$. In place of (5) and (6) we have (5*) and (6*) respectively:

(5*) $\Box \forall x \, \Box((Fx \to Fx) \to \exists z \; x=z)$

(6*) $\Box \forall x \, \Box(Fx \to Fx)$

In this bivalent setting, $Fx \to Fx$ behaves like any other truth-functional tautology. It is false under no circumstances, so true under all, by the truth table for the material conditional. Thus one can apply necessitation, universal generalization, and necessitation again. Hence (6*) is a trivial logical truth, even for contingentists. But one can reason just as uncontentiously from (5*) and (6*) as from (5) and (6) to the necessitist conclusion NNE. Since (6*) is non-negotiable, contingentists must therefore drop (5*) in order to avoid NNE. Therefore, the objection runs, contingentists must reject the being constraint anyway.

The objection assumes that (5*) instantiates the being constraint, more specifically, that (5*) is a substitution instance of (1), which it is if and only if $Fx \to Fx$ is a substitution instance of Fx. But why should $Fx \to Fx$ be a substitution instance of Fx? For Fx already has semantic structure, that of a predication, which should be preserved in any substitution instance, which will be obtained by substituting a monadic predicate for F and an individual term for x. By contrast, $Fx \rightarrow Fx$ has the overall semantic structure of a conditional formula, rather than a predication; that its constituent Fx has the structure of a predication is irrelevant. Thus $Fx \rightarrow Fx$ is no substitution instance of Fx, so (5*) is no substitution instance of (1). Therefore contingentists' rejection of (5*) is not *ipso facto* rejection of the being constraint.

Is asserting (5) as an instance of the being constraint while denying (5*) well motivated for contingentists? The rationale for asserting (5) is that since $x=x$ is a predication, it ascribes a property or relation (in a liberal sense) to the value of x, and having any property or relation (in that sense) requires being something. That rationale extends to (5*) if and only if $Fx \rightarrow Fx$ ascribes a property or relation (in the liberal sense) to the value of x. But since $Fx \rightarrow Fx$ lacks the form of a predication, contingentists have a principled basis for denying that it ascribes a property or relation (even in the liberal sense) to the value of x, even though its constituent Fx does so.

Such a sharp logical division between simple formulas like Fx and complex ones like $Fx \rightarrow Fx$ may seem to force implausibly artificial choices on the analysis of natural language. If we formalize 'John is single' as the simple sentence Fj, we treat it as entailing 'John is something' ($\exists x\ x=j$) by the being constraint (in a contingentist system). If we formalize 'John is unmarried' as the complex sentence $\neg Mj$, the negation of the formalization of 'John is married', we treat it as not entailing 'John is something' by the being constraint (in a contingentist system). But since 'single' and 'unmarried' are equivalent (on the relevant readings), 'John is single' and 'John is unmarried' have the same entailments. Thus either they both entail 'John is something', in which case both 'single' and 'unmarried' are *really* positive in content, despite the misleadingly negative appearance of 'unmarried', or neither 'John is single' nor 'John is unmarried' entails 'John is something', in which case both 'single' and 'unmarried' are *really* negative in content, despite the misleadingly positive appearance of 'single'. We therefore seem to be stuck with a tricky decision of obscure import as to which of 'unmarried' and 'single' has the misleading appearance.

Fortunately, those are not the only options. We can add a variable-binding, predicate-forming operator λ to the formal language. Starting with the simple predicate M for 'is married', we can define the predicate $\lambda x(\neg Mx)$ for 'is unmarried' ('is such that it is not the case that it is married') and formalize

'John is unmarried' as $\lambda x(\neg Mx)j$, so that it entails 'John is something' by a substitution instance of (1) with the complex predicate $\lambda x(\neg Mx)$ in place of F. Given that 'John is unmarried' has the overall form of a predication, the entailment to 'John is something' goes through. It does not matter whether the predicate is simple or complex. Rather, the crucial contrast is between predicate negation and sentence negation: 'John is (not married)' has the form Fa but 'Not (John is married)' does not.

In the case of $Fx \rightarrow Fx$, the relevant substitution instance of the being constraint (1) is not (5*) but (5**), in which the complex predicate $\lambda y(Fy \rightarrow Fy)$ replaces F:

$$(5^{**})\quad \Box\forall x\, \Box(\lambda y(Fy \rightarrow Fy)x \rightarrow \exists z\, x{=}z)$$

Given the being constraint, contingentists should assert (5**) but deny (5*). In order to block the deduction of the anti-contingentist (5*) from (5**), they must also reject (7):

$$(7)\quad \Box\forall x\, \Box((Fx \rightarrow Fx) \rightarrow \lambda y(Fy \rightarrow Fy)x)$$

On this view, that one is a frog if one is a frog does not strictly imply that one is such that one is a frog if one is a frog.

The λ operator may also prove useful to temporaryists. For example, by formalizing 'John is married' and 'John is unmarried' as Mj and $\lambda x(\neg Mx)j$ respectively, and denying the equivalence of the latter with $\neg Mj$, they can classify both sentences as false after John's death. That is not to claim that such a strategy provides easy solutions to all the previous hard cases for temporaryism under the being constraint. For example, it does not explain the apparent truth of statements such as 'Many past wars have present effects'. Nevertheless, without it the problems for temporaryism would be even worse.

The case for the being constraint is watertight for both necessitists and permanentists and highly plausible for both contingentists and temporaryists. In order to provide the latter with the expressive resources they need to articulate their best defence of the constraint, we must permit them a modal or temporal logic with something like the λ operator. Robert Stalnaker has developed just such a contingentist system, and investigated some of the philosophical issues it raises. His work provides a good basis for subsequent discussion. Even necessitists, and contingentists who reject the being constraint, should regard his system as a valuable test of wholehearted contingentism.

4.2   Stalnaker's quantified modal logic with identity: orthodox semantics

Stalnaker approaches quantified modal logic by considering two languages.[8] One is a first-order non-modal language like that in section 3.4, but with an added λ operator and a denumerable infinity of individual constants. He gives it the usual model-theoretic semantics for first-order logic, extended by a natural clause for λ.[9] The other is a propositional modal language like that in section 3.2. He gives it a standard Kripke semantics. Stalnaker then combines the two languages into a language for quantified modal logic with identity. Correspondingly, he combines features of the semantics for the two original languages into what we may call his *orthodox semantics* for the combined language: although it differs slightly from the usual Kripke semantics, in ways noted later for many purposes the differences can be ignored.

Complex expressions in Stalnaker's combined language are built up thus. If F is an n-place predicate ($n \geq 0$) and $t_1, \ldots, t_n$ are singular terms (individual variables or constants), $Ft_1 \ldots t_n$ is a sentence. If A and B are sentences, $\neg A$, $\Box A$, and $A \& B$ are sentences. If F is a one-place predicate, $\forall F$ is a sentence. If A is a sentence and v an individual variable, $\lambda v(A)$ is a one-place predicate. Metalinguistic abbreviations are used freely in obvious ways.

In a standard first-order language with no λ operator, the quantifier combines the roles of variable-binding and generalizing. By contrast, Stalnaker separates those roles: λ binds variables while ∀ generalizes. Informally, we may read λv as 'is such that ...' and ∀ as 'everything'. Thus we may read $\forall \lambda v(A)$, like $\forall v\, A$ in a standard first-order language, as 'Everything is such that A'. One side effect of the reorganization is that, if F is a one-place atomic predicate, $\forall F$ ('Everything Fs') is a well-formed sentence without individual variables.

Stalnaker's orthodox model-theoretic semantics for his combined language uses uncentred models <W, R, D, V> just like those in section 3.4.[10]

---

[8] The exposition of Stalnaker's account of quantified modal logic is based on Stalnaker 1994 as reprinted in revised form in Stalnaker 2003. For his earlier work on abstraction in modal logic see Stalnaker and Thomason 1968a and 1968b and Stalnaker 1977. For detailed further discussion of predicate abstraction in relation to the debate between necessitism and contingentism see Percival 2011.

[9] Instead of λ before the variable, Stalnaker uses a circumflex ˆ over it, in order to minimize the departure from the standard notation for first-order logic. For present purposes, the λ is a useful reminder of his proposed semantic structure. In other trivial ways too Stalnaker's notation has been changed for the sake of uniformity with the rest of this book.

[10] A few very trivial changes have been made to details of the semantics for the sake of uniformity. They do not affect the validity of any formula.

As before, R is a binary relation over the non-empty set W. At this level of generality, Stalnaker is not concerned to impose any constraints such as reflexivity, symmetry, or transitivity on R. In practice that makes little difference, since the crucial models for later arguments have those features anyway. D assigns a set domain $D(w)$ to each member w of W. $D(w)$ may be empty and may vary with w. No world in W is singled out as the actual one. V assigns intensions to what Stalnaker calls the 'descriptive' vocabulary: the non-logical n-place atomic predicates ($n \geq 0$) and the individual constants. As usual, the intension $V(F)$ of an n-place predicate F is a function from members of W to sets of n-tuples (extensions). Stalnaker imposes the domain constraint, so $V(F)(w) \subseteq D(w)^n$. The intension $V(c)$ of an individual constant c is a partial function, so $V(c)(w)$ may be undefined and may vary with w. Stalnaker imposes the analogue of the domain constraint for individual constants, so if defined $V(c)(w) \in D(w)$. This treatment permits individual constants to behave like non-rigid definite descriptions, uniquely satisfied by nothing at some worlds and by different things at different worlds.

An assignment $\underline{a}$ in the model is a partial function from worlds to members of the union of all the domains, $\bigcup_{w \in W} D(w)$. For any assignment $\underline{a}$, individual variable v and $o \in \bigcup_{w \in W} D(w)$, $\underline{a}[v/o]$ is the assignment that maps v to o but otherwise is like $\underline{a}$.

Stalnaker provides orthodox semantic rules by which such a model $<W, R, D, V>$ determines, relative to an assignment $\underline{a}$, a function $V_{\underline{a}}$ that maps each singular term, predicate, and sentence to an intension of an appropriate type. In particular, the intension of a sentence maps each member of W to a truth value, I or o. Here are the rules, where $w \in W$, v is an individual variable, $t_1, \ldots, t_n$ are singular terms, e is an atomic descriptive expression, F is an n-place predicate ($n \geq 0$), G is a one-place predicate, and A and B are sentences:

$V_{\underline{a}}(v) = \underline{a}(v)$

$V_{\underline{a}}(e) = V(e)$

$V_{\underline{a}}(=)(w) = \{<o, o>: o \in D(w)\}$

$V_{\underline{a}}(Ft_1 \ldots t_n)(w) = $ I if $<V_{\underline{a}}(t_1)(w), \ldots, V_{\underline{a}}(t_n)(w)> \in V_{\underline{a}}(F)(w)$ (and so is defined); otherwise $V_{\underline{a}}(Ft_1 \ldots t_n)(w) = $ o

$V_{\underline{a}}(\neg A)(w) = $ I $- V_{\underline{a}}(A)(w)$

$V_a(A \ \& \ B)(w) = \text{minimum}\{V_a(A)(w), V_a(B)(w)\}.$

$V_a(\Box A)(w) = 1$ if whenever $wRw*$, $V_a(A)(w*) = 1$; otherwise $V_a(\Box A)(w) = 0$

$V_a(\forall G)(w) = 1$ if $V_a(G)(w) = D(w)$; otherwise $V_a(\forall G)(w) = 0$

$V_a(\lambda v(A))(w) = \{o \in D(w): V_{a[v/o]}(A)(w) = 1\}$

A formula A is *true everywhere* in a model $<W, R, D, V>$ just if $V_a(A)(w) = 1$ for every $w \in W$ and assignment a. Since these models lack a designated actual world, the semantics provides no standard of truth at the actual world of a model. A formula is *valid* on the orthodox semantics just if it is true everywhere in every model. As usual, a schema is valid just if all its instances are valid.

To recover Stalnaker's orthodox model theory for his first-order non-modal language, delete 'W' and 'R' from the definition of a model, re-interpret 'D' as designating a single domain and 'V' as mapping descriptive expressions to extensions rather than to intensions, omit the clause for $\Box A$, and delete '(w)' throughout the other semantic clauses. Similarly, one can recover Stalnaker's orthodox model theory for his propositional modal language by the obvious deletions.

A notable feature of Stalnaker's orthodox model theory for his first-order modal language is the key role it gives to the domain of w, the world of evaluation. The domain constraint for non-logical atomic predicates and individual constants is built into his definition of a model. The restriction '$o \in D(w)$' in the clauses for '=' (the only atomic predicate treated as a logical constant) and for λ expressions (the only non-atomic predicates) ensures that all other predicates satisfy the domain constraint too. Similarly, the clause for $\forall$ restricts the quantifier to the domain of the world of evaluation. The restriction can be articulated with an 'existence' predicate E, which abbreviates $\lambda x(\exists \lambda y(x=y))$, for $V_a(E)(w)$ is always $D(w)$. Thus any universal closure of $Ft_1 \ldots t_n \to Et_i$ is valid in all models, as is $\forall \lambda x(Ex)$.

Since Stalnaker does not require the domain function D to be constant, his semantics invalidates the Barcan formula and its converse in the usual way. Of course, they must now be formulated with λ:

BF $\forall \lambda x(\Box A) \to \Box \forall \lambda x(A)$

CBF $\Box \forall \lambda x(A) \to \forall \lambda x(\Box A)$

The system is contingentist, at least in avoiding necessitism. However, as Stalnaker notes, a qualified form of CBF is valid:

QCBF $\quad \Box\forall\lambda x(A) \to \forall\lambda x(\Box(Ex \to A))$

QCBF is a weak consequence of CBF. It says that if necessarily everything meets a certain condition, then everything is such that necessarily it is something only if it meets that condition. The qualification Ex in QCBF finesses the usual contingentist objection to CBF, which substitutes Ex for A and thereby makes the antecedent of CBF a triviality and the consequent into an expression of necessitism: the same substitution makes the consequent of QCBF a triviality too. On Stalnaker's semantics, if the antecedent of QCBF is true, then at every accessible world everything in the domain satisfies $\lambda x(A)$, so everything in the domain of the original world is such that in every accessible world if it is in the domain of that world then it satisfies $\lambda x(A)$, so the consequent is true; thus QCBF is valid.

Stalnaker's orthodox semantics validates a strong modal theory of identity, because it always interprets the identity predicate by identity over the domain and treats individual variables as rigid designators: they are assigned values absolutely, not relative to worlds; if they have the same value at any world, they have the same value at every world. As he notes, EI ('the essentiality of identity') is valid:

EI $\quad \forall\lambda x(\forall\lambda y(x{=}y \to \Box(Ex \to x{=}y)))$

If things are identical, then their identity is necessary for either of them to have being. The qualification Ex is needed, given Stalnaker's contingentism, for even the identity predicate obeys the domain constraint: if you are only contingently something, you are only contingently yourself. As he notes, his orthodox semantics also validates a strengthened version of EI:

NEI $\quad \forall\lambda x(\forall\lambda y(\Box(x{=}y \to \Box(Ex \to x{=}y))))$

If things had been identical, then their identity would have been necessary for one of them to have being.

For the analogue of EI for failure of identity, no such qualification as Ex is needed, since $\neg x{=}y$ is true at any world whose domain does not contain values for both variables.

ND $\quad \forall\lambda x(\forall\lambda y(\neg x{=}y \to \Box\neg x{=}y))$

If things are distinct, it is impossible for them to be identical. Stalnaker notes that his orthodox semantics validates ND.

4.3 Stalnaker's quantified modal logic with identity: unorthodox semantics

Stalnaker provides an axiomatic system of propositional modal logic that is sound and complete for his semantics of the propositional modal language. Similarly, he provides an axiomatic system of first-order non-modal logic that is sound and complete for his semantics of his first-order non-modal language. Combining the axioms and rules of the two systems, he provides an axiomatic system of first-order modal logic. One might hope that it is sound and complete for his orthodox semantics of his first-order modal language, since the latter semantics results from combining the former two. However, Stalnaker proves that the hope is vain, by providing unorthodox semantic theories that validate the combined axiomatization but invalidate some formulas that are valid on the orthodox semantics; consequently, those formulas are underivable in that axiomatization. Thus the combined axiomatization, although sound, is not complete for the orthodox semantics of the combined language.

It is less clear what significance Stalnaker attaches to his results. In one case, he says that his unorthodox semantics allows for a 'nonstandard conception of individuals and their modal properties' (a form of counterpart theory); whether or not that conception is defensible, 'the issue is a philosophical one that cannot be settled by logical theory'.[11] That might lead one to interpret Stalnaker as denying that the formulas invalidated by the unorthodox semantics are genuine logical truths. Presumably, the orthodox semantics would be at fault, for employing too narrow a range of models and thereby validating formulas that are in some sense too substantive to deserve the status of logical truth. But Stalnaker later describes the relevant formulas as 'logical principles that are valid'.[12] If he is employing a notion of validity only relative to a semantic theory, then of course any formula of the language is valid relative to some semantic theories and invalid relative to others. In a postscript added in 2002, he describes a formula valid on the

---

[11] Stalnaker 2003, p. 154.
[12] Stalnaker 2003, p. 157.

orthodox but not the unorthodox semantic theory as 'less central' to the logic in question than a formula valid on both semantic theories.[13] In still later comments on the matter, Stalnaker emphasizes the difficulty of disentangling logical and metaphysical issues.[14]

Let us postpone the assessment of philosophical significance, and examine the axiomatization in detail. Let $\vdash$ mean provability in the system, which is restricted to closed formulas. In what follows, x and y can be replaced by any individual variables, $s, t, t_1, \ldots, t_i, \ldots, t_n$ are any singular terms, $1 \leq i \leq n$, and $A^s/_t$ is the result of substituting s for all free occurrences of t in A, re-lettering bound variables in A where necessary to avoid clashes. Here are Stalnaker's axioms and rules:

Propositional Logic	If A is a truth-functional tautology then $\vdash A$
Modus ponens	If $\vdash A \rightarrow B$ and $\vdash A$ then $\vdash B$
K schema	$\vdash \Box(A \rightarrow B) \rightarrow (\Box A \rightarrow \Box B)$
Necessitation	If $\vdash A$ then $\vdash \Box A$
Abstraction	$\vdash \forall \lambda x(\lambda y(A)x \leftrightarrow A^x/_y)$
Quantification	$\vdash \forall \lambda x(A \rightarrow B) \rightarrow (\forall \lambda x(A) \rightarrow \forall \lambda x(B))$
Redundancy[15]	$\vdash \forall \lambda x(Fx) \leftrightarrow \forall F$ (x is not free in F)
Existence[16]	$\vdash Ft_1 \ldots t_n \rightarrow \exists \lambda x(x=t_i)$

---

[13] Stalnaker 2003, p. 161.

[14] Stalnaker 2006, pp. 268–72. He does not assume that logical questions and metaphysical ones are mutually exclusive, for he says 'many have argued (convincingly, I think) that the metaphysical thesis that there are contingent identities is logically incoherent' (Stalnaker 2006, p. 268). The opposition between the logical and the metaphysical deserves the same fate as other dogmas of logical positivism.

[15] Only the left-to-right direction of redundancy figures in the original 1994 axiomatization, supplemented by two extra axiom schemas: the universal instantiation principle $\vdash \forall \lambda x(\forall F \rightarrow Fx)$ and the permutation principle $\vdash \forall \lambda x(\forall \lambda y(A)) \rightarrow \forall \lambda y(\forall \lambda x(A))$. Stalnaker informs me (personal communication) that the change in the 2003 version was just to improve the economy of the axiomatization: universal instantiation becomes derivable once the biconditional Redundancy principle is available and permutation (which Fine (1983) had shown to be independent of Kripke's 1963 axiomatization of free quantified modal logic without open formulas) is derivable in Stalnaker's system with the help of his principles about identity.

[16] Stalnaker (2003, p. 151) defines the 'existence' predicate E as $\exists \lambda y(x=y)$. Since the latter is an open sentence, not a predicate, he intends $\lambda x(\exists \lambda y(x=y))$. But Stalnaker notes (personal communication) that it is essential for the Existence schema to be stated as it is, rather than with Et so defined as the consequent, since otherwise $Es \leftrightarrow \exists \lambda x(x=s)$ will be underivable. One can prove this by considering a deviant semantics on which all predications and universal quantifications count as true (adding the symmetry principle in the next footnote does not help).

Identity[17] $\qquad$ $\vdash s{=}t_i \rightarrow (Ft_1 \ldots t_i \ldots t_n \rightarrow Ft_1 \ldots s \ldots t_n)$

Universal Generalization $\quad$ If $\vdash A \rightarrow B$ then $\vdash A \rightarrow \forall\lambda x(B^x\!/_t)$

$\qquad\qquad\qquad\qquad\quad$ (t does not occur in A)

The axiom schema Existence is Stalnaker's version of the being constraint. One can check that on his orthodox semantics every axiom schema is valid and every rule of inference (modus ponens, Necessitation, and Universal Generalization) preserves validity. Thus the axiomatization is sound on the orthodox semantics.

To obtain Stalnaker's axioms and rules for the first order non-modal language, delete the K schema and Necessitation. To obtain his axioms and rules for the propositional modal language, delete instead Abstraction, Quantification, Redundancy, Existence, Identity, and Universal Generalization. Since his semantics imposes no special constraints on the accessibility relation R, no axiom schemas such as T, B, or 4 are added: for these purposes his underlying propositional modal logic is the weakest normal one, K, rather than S5.

EI (the essentiality of identity) is derivable in Stalnaker's axiomatization. BF and CBF are of course underivable, since they are invalid on his orthodox semantics, for which the axiomatization is sound. However, although NEI (the necessary essentiality of identity), ND (the necessity of distinctness), and QCBF (qualified CBF) are all valid on the orthodox semantics, they are all underivable in the axiomatization. He proves their underivability by providing unorthodox semantic theories on which the axioms are valid, and the rules of inference preserve validity, but NEI, ND, and QCBF are invalid.

Stalnaker's first unorthodox semantics is a form of counterpart theory. He adds to each model a two-place partial function whose first argument is a member o of the union of the domains of all worlds in the model, whose second argument is a world w, and whose value (if any) is a member of the domain of w, which we may informally conceive as the counterpart of o

---

[17] Obviously, it makes no difference if $x{=}t_i$ in Existence and $s{=}t_i$ in Identity are replaced by $t_i{=}x$ and $t_i{=}s$ respectively. However, if the latter of these replacements is made without the former, then the symmetry principle $s{=}t \rightarrow t{=}s$ is underivable, because a deviant semantics for '=' on which $s{=}t$ is true just if either s and t denote the same thing or s fails to denote validates the new axiomatization without validating symmetry (analogously if the former replacement is made without the latter). The problem arose for an earlier, unpublished version of the system. Delia Graff Fara and Gabriel Uzquiano prompted the correction. Stalnaker supplied the independence argument. I thank all three (personal communications) for this information.

in w. Distinct worlds are constrained to have disjoint domains, so o belongs to the domain of exactly one world, and is constrained to be its own counterpart in that world. The only change in the rules for evaluating singular terms and formulas is that the extension of a variable v at a world w under an assignment $\underline{a}$ is no longer $\underline{a}(v)$ but rather the counterpart (if any) of $\underline{a}(v)$ in w. NEI, ND, and some instances of QCBF are invalid on this semantics.

NEI and ND fail because two members of the domain of one world may have the same counterpart in the domain of another, when all worlds are mutually accessible.

QCBF fails on the semantics because the truth of its antecedent $\Box\forall\lambda x(A)$ at a world w means that for every accessible world $w*$ every member of the domain of $w*$ satisfies A at $w*$, whereas the truth of the consequent $\forall\lambda x(\Box(Ex \rightarrow A))$ at w means that every member of the domain of w with a counterpart in an accessible world $w*$ satisfies A at $w*$, which does not follow from the fact that its counterpart satisfies A at $w*$. For example, setting $A = \forall\lambda y(\Box Ey) \rightarrow \Box Ex$ ('If everything has necessary being, so has x') yields this instance of QCBF:

(8) $\Box\forall\lambda x(\forall\lambda y(\Box Ey) \rightarrow \Box Ex) \rightarrow \forall\lambda x(\Box(Ex \rightarrow (\forall\lambda y(\Box Ey) \rightarrow \Box Ex)))$

The antecedent of (8) is a theorem and so valid on the counterpart-theoretic semantics, for we can derive $\forall\lambda x(\forall\lambda y(\Box Ey) \rightarrow \Box Ex)$ from Abstraction by purely quantificational reasoning and then apply Necessitation. Thus to invalidate QCBF on the counterpart-theoretic semantics we need only invalidate the consequent (9) of (8):

(9) $\forall\lambda x(\Box(Ex \rightarrow (\forall\lambda y(\Box Ey) \rightarrow \Box Ex)))$

This says that everything is such that necessarily if it is something and everything is necessarily something then it is necessarily something, which sounds harmless enough and is valid on the orthodox semantics. But we can invalidate (9) in a counterpart-theoretic model with just three worlds, w_0, w_1, and w_2, all mutually accessible, with domains $\{0\}$, $\{1\}$, and $\{2\}$ respectively. The counterpart relation is reflexive and symmetric but non-transitive: 0 and 1 are mutual counterparts, as are 1 and 2, but 0 and 2 are not counterparts of each other. Then (9) is false at w_0, because 0 does not satisfy $Ex \rightarrow (\forall\lambda y(\Box Ey) \rightarrow \Box Ex)$ at w_1, for 0 satisfies Ex at w_1 since it has a counterpart there, and $\forall\lambda y(\Box Ey)$ is true at w_1 since 1 has a counterpart at each world, but 0 does not satisfy $\Box Ex$ at w_1 since it has no counterpart at w_2.

If one adds QCBF as an axiom schema, one can derive NEI but ND remains underivable. Stalnaker establishes the latter result by providing a second form of unorthodox semantics on which variables behave rigidly but '=' is interpreted as indiscernibility rather than identity. His original axioms and QCBF are valid on this semantics, and the rules preserve validity, but ND is invalid: discernibles could have been indiscernible.

4.4 The significance of Stalnaker's results

What philosophical import does Stalnaker attribute to his independence results? Concerning QCBF (and NEI) he writes:

> The variant [counterpart] semantics brings to the surface an assumption about the relation between the modal properties of an individual in different possible worlds—an assumption implicit in the standard semantics that is not grounded in the nonmodal logic of predication, or in the modal logic of propositions, or in their combination.[18]

Concerning ND, he says:

> The combination of identity theory with modality provides the resources to distinguish identity from a weaker relation [indiscernibility] that cannot be distinguished from it in a nonmodal context. Perhaps this shows that there is in some sense something modal about the concept of identity.[19]

Are these claims justified?

Let us first ask what methodology is implicit in Stalnaker's form of argument. In schematic terms, he considers a language L1 with an axiom system A1 that is sound and complete for a semantics S1 (all and only sentences valid on S1 are derivable in A1), and a language L2 with an axiom system A2 that is sound and complete for a semantics S2. He combines L1 and L2 into a joint language L1+L2, A1 and A2 into a joint axiom system A1+A2, and S1 and S2 into a joint semantics S1+S2 for L1+L2. He then treats A1+A2 as exhausting what the logics of L1 and L2 tell us, when combined, about the logic of L1+L2. But what do 'combine', 'joint', and '+' mean here?

---

[18] Stalnaker 2003, p. 153.
[19] Stalnaker 2003, p. 157.

A growing branch of logic studies different ways of combining logical systems. No one way is right for all cases. Rather, it depends on how one wants to interpret the combined system, which may in turn depend on a subtle interplay of mathematical elegance and intended applications. Consider some of the relevant complexities.[20]

First, it is not always clear what it would be to combine two languages. For example, what is English + Japanese? In the particular case at issue, another way of combining the first-order non-modal language with the propositional modal language would have permitted the application of modal operators only to closed formulas; in Quinean terminology, such a language would have a lower grade of modal involvement.[21] However, let us simply take Stalnaker's way of combining the two languages as given. It is standard enough, and philosophically attractive for its expressive power.

Second, it is not always clear what it would be to combine two semantic theories for different languages. For example, in his orthodox combined semantics, Stalnaker makes the assignment of values to variables absolute, not world-relative, on the plausible grounds that 'open sentences are devices for the formation of complex predicates that express properties of individuals, and not properties of some kind of intension'.[22] But, as observed in section 2.4, one can also give first-order modal languages a semantics in which the assignment of values to variables is world-relative, so that the variables have individual concepts as their intensions. Thus the form of the semantics for the two original languages underdetermines the form of the semantics for the combined language. For the time being, let us simply take Stalnaker's orthodox semantics for the first-order modal language as also given.

Third, it is not always clear what it would be to combine two axiomatic systems for different languages. We have to decide what counts as an instance in one language of an axiom schema or rule of inference originally formulated for another language. More than one extrapolation is generally feasible, since we may but need not permit the distinctive vocabulary of one language to occur in instances of an axiom schema or rule inherited from the axiomatic system for the other language. In the present case, Stalnaker permits such instantiations; the combined system would otherwise be

---

[20] Blackburn and de Rijke 1997 discuss the reasons for combining logics in various ways. In their words, the process involved in choosing the appropriate mode of combination for a given application 'is as much an art as a science' (p. 17). They treat the case of quantified modal logic at pp. 18–22.

[21] See Quine 1953.

[22] Stalnaker 2003, p. 150.

extremely weak. Given his axiomatizations of the two original systems, his way of combining them is natural enough.

There is a more urgent question. Distinguish *logics* (consequence relations, or sets of theorems) from their *axiomatizations* (sets of axioms and inference rules). Many different axiomatizations can generate the same logic. Which axiomatization we choose for a given logic may be just a matter of technical convenience. But then why should we assume that Stalnaker's combined axiomatization generates exactly the logic for the combined language to which one is committed by accepting both his logics for the original languages, even granted that the latter are sound and complete for the original semantic theories for their respective languages? A different pair of axiomatizations of the original logics, when combined in Stalnaker's way, might generate a different logic for the combined language. That logic might not even be sound for the orthodox semantics. Since his methodology involves judging the semantics by the logic, not just the logic by the semantics, such a result might cast as much doubt on his orthodox semantics as on his combined logic.

Here is an example. Replace the earlier axiom schema Identity with this axiom schema, a familiar form of Leibniz's Law:

Identity* $\vdash s=t \rightarrow (A \rightarrow A^s_t)$

Every instance of Identity is an instance of Identity*. Conversely, although instances of Identity* in which A is not a predication are not instances of Identity, in the non-modal language every instance of Identity* is derivable in the original axiomatization. Thus the new axiomatization generates the same logic as Stalnaker's original one in the non-modal language. That logic is sound and complete for the given semantics. Nevertheless, combining (in Stalnaker's way) this new axiomatization of first-order non-modal logic with Stalnaker's axiomatization of propositional modal logic generates a first-order modal logic that is unsound for the orthodox semantics, and strictly stronger than the logic generated by Stalnaker's combined axiomatization. Here is an instance of Identity* that is invalid on the orthodox semantics, where s and t are distinct constants:

(10) $s=t \rightarrow (\Diamond(s=s \ \& \ \neg s=t) \rightarrow \Diamond(s=s \ \& \ \neg s=s))$

The reason is that Stalnaker classifies individual constants as descriptive terms and does not require them to be rigid designators. The orthodox semantics allows them a flexibility it does not allow individual variables (in this respect the epithet 'orthodox' may be misleading). Thus s and t may designate the same individual at one world but distinct individuals at another world accessible from the first. But nothing in the semantics of the two original languages mandates this differential treatment of individual variables and individual constants. On another reasonable way of extrapolating the semantics to the first-order modal language, individual constants as well as individual variables are rigid and Identity* is valid.

Although that particular example depends on Stalnaker's questionable treatment of individual constants, the general point does not. A less controversial example uses an extensionality principle for predicates:

Coextensiveness $\vdash \forall \lambda x(Fx \leftrightarrow Gx) \rightarrow (A \rightarrow A^F/_G)$

For simplicity, F and G here are one-place atomic predicates; $A^F/_G$ is the result of substituting F for G in A. All instances of Coextensiveness in the non-modal language are valid on the standard semantics, but the same schema has clearly invalid instances in the modal language, such as:

(11) $\vdash \forall \lambda x(Fx \leftrightarrow Gx) \rightarrow (\neg \Box \forall \lambda x(Fx \leftrightarrow Gx) \rightarrow \neg \Box \forall \lambda x(Fx \leftrightarrow Fx))$

For F and G may be accidentally coextensive.

The general point is this. The mere soundness and completeness of an axiomatic system for the semantics of a language does not entitle one to extrapolate its axiom schemas and inference rules in the natural way to an extended language as what the logic of the former language has to offer the logic of the latter. Different axiomatizations of the same logic for the former may extrapolate in natural but logically non-equivalent ways to the extended language. Stalnaker makes a similar point about the previous example: 'The validity of the general schema [Identity*], unlike the validity of the identity axioms [Identity], depends on the expressive limitations of the extensional theory'.[23] If one intends to extrapolate a sound and complete axiomatization to an extended language, one must choose axiom schemas and inference rules whose appropriateness does not depend on the expressive limitations of the restricted language. Doing that is no straightforward matter, since proving soundness and completeness for the restricted language is not enough. One needs an informative conception of how the restricted language may legitimately be extended, in both syntax and semantics.

---

[23] Stalnaker 2003, p. 148.

In the present case, of course, Stalnaker has carefully chosen his axioms and inference rules for the original languages so that they remain sound for the orthodox semantics when extrapolated to the combined language. But analogous issues arise about completeness. For one might give a sound and complete axiomatization for the semantics of a restricted language that is unnecessarily weak when extrapolated to more expressive languages.

Here is an example. Stalnaker works with the propositional modal logic K. Like most of the familiar systems of propositional modal logic (including S5), K is decidable. Thus, instead of using Stalnaker's axiom schemas of Propositional Logic and the K schema and rules of Modus Ponens and Necessitation, one can in principle axiomatize K simply by taking all its theorems as axioms, with no other axioms or inference rules. Call that axiom family 'Cheap K'. Since one can mechanically determine whether any given formula is an instance of Cheap K by using any decision procedure for K, that still counts as a formal axiomatic system. Analogously, Stalnaker's axiom family of Propositional Logic in effect axiomatizes non-modal propositional logic simply by taking all its theorems as axioms. Cheap K by itself constitutes a sound and complete axiomatization of K on its usual semantics. Now combine Cheap K in Stalnaker's way with his axiomatization of the logic of his first-order non-modal language (Propositional Logic, Abstraction, Quantification, Redundancy, Existence, Identity, Modus Ponens, and Universal Generalization) into an axiomatic system for the first-order modal language. That system is manifestly inadequate. The instances of Cheap K are just substitution instances in the first-order modal language of theorems of K. There is no rule of Necessitation. One cannot even derive (12):[24]

(12) $\square \forall \lambda x (Fx \rightarrow Fx)$

---

[24] Proof: Consider a deviant semantics in which a model divides its worlds into sensible worlds, at which $\forall$ is interpreted as usual to mean *all*, and silly worlds, at which $\forall$ is interpreted to mean *not all*. The semantics is exactly like Stalnaker's orthodox semantics in all other respects, except that validity is defined as truth at all sensible worlds in all models. On the deviant semantics, all instances of Cheap K are true at every world, sensible or silly, because their truth does not depend on the specific interpretation of $\forall$; a fortiori, Cheap K is valid. Since all instances of Propositional Logic are also instances of Cheap K, Propositional Logic is valid too. Similarly, Modus Ponens preserves validity, because at every world it preserves truth. Abstraction, Quantification, Redundancy, Existence, and Identity are valid because all their instances are true at any sensible world, since their truth at such a world depends only on the interpretation there of the non-modal vocabulary outside the scope of modal operators, which is non-deviant. Similarly, Universal Generalization preserves validity. Thus the envisaged axiomatic system is sound for the deviant semantics. The formula $\forall \lambda x (Fx \rightarrow Fx)$ is derivable in the usual way, and so is sound. It is true at all sensible worlds and false at all silly ones. But since silly worlds may be accessible from sensible ones, (12) itself is false at some sensible worlds in some models, and so is invalid on the deviant semantics. Thus (12) is underivable in the envisaged axiomatic system.

But one could hardly conclude that the underivability of (12) brings to the surface 'an assumption implicit in the standard semantics that is not grounded in the nonmodal logic of predication, or in the modal logic of propositions, or in their combination' in any serious sense. Rather, its underivability is a mere artefact of the specific way in which the propositional modal logic was axiomatized.

The question now naturally arises: are Stalnaker's underivability results similarly artefacts of the specific ways in which he axiomatized the logics of the propositional modal language and the first-order non-modal language? If so, they lack the philosophical significance he claims for them.

4.5 Abstraction and the qualified converse Barcan formula

Let us start with QCBF. The first point to notice is that in Stalnaker's axiomatic system we can derive a schema very close to QCBF:[25]

QCBF* $\quad \Box\forall\lambda x(A) \to \forall\lambda x(\Box(Ex \to \lambda x(A)x))$

From QCBF*, we could easily prove QCBF if we had schema (13):

(13) $\quad \forall\lambda x(\Box(\lambda x(A)x \to A))$

Although (13) is valid on Stalnaker's orthodox semantics, it is unprovable in his axiomatic system, and invalid on his counterpart semantics. In particular, we cannot derive (13) from his axiom schema of Abstraction, because the latter does not allow us to slip a modal operator between the outer and inner occurrences of the λ operator. In a context such as (13), Stalnaker's axiom schemas and inference rules, including Abstraction, provide only very limited constraints on the relation between expressions of the form $\lambda x(A)t$ and A. They do not tell us whether, if you had been such that A held, A would have held.

---

[25] Proof: Where F is a one-place atomic predicate and t an individual constant, $\forall F \to (Et \to Ft)$ is valid on Stalnaker's semantics for the first-order non-modal language, and therefore provable in his complete axiomatization of its logic. Substituting $\lambda x(A)$ for F throughout the proof therefore yields a proof of $\forall\lambda x(A) \to (Et \to \lambda x(A)t)$ in his axiomatic system for first-order modal logic (we can choose t and any other individual constants in the proof so that they do not occur in A, in order to avoid problems with Universal Generalization). Applying Necessitation and the K schema, we obtain $\Box\forall\lambda x(A) \to \Box(Et \to \lambda x(A)t)$, from which Universal Generalization yields QCBF*.

This limitation on Stalnaker's axiomatic system is an artefact of his version of Abstraction. What is needed is a rule to cash out predications of the form $\lambda x(A)t$ however deeply they are embedded. Given a contingentist view such as his on which a true predication requires something for the predicate to apply to, this rule naturally suggests itself:

Free Abstraction   If C results from replacing some or all occurrences of $\lambda y(A)x$ in B by Ex & $A^x/_y$, and $\vdash B$, then $\vdash C$.

The rule is called 'Free Abstraction' because it includes the 'existence' qualification Ex typical of free logic. Stalnaker's own Abstraction schema becomes redundant in the presence of Free Abstraction and his other axiom schemas and inference rules.[26] Thus we lose no theorems by dropping Abstraction and employing Free Abstraction instead.

Since we may put a single variable in place of x and y, Free Abstraction has the special case in which $\lambda x(A)x$ is replaced by Ex & A. Thus from QCBF*, Free Abstraction yields (14):

(14) $\Box \forall \lambda x(A) \rightarrow \forall \lambda x(\Box(Ex \rightarrow (Ex \ \& \ A)))$

From (14) we easily obtain QCBF by dropping a conjunct. Thus by substituting Free Abstraction for Abstraction in Stalnaker's axiomatic system, we obtain a stronger one in which QCBF is derivable.

We must check that Free Abstraction preserves validity on Stalnaker's orthodox semantics for the first-order modal logic. Informally, the point is that abstracting on an open formula with respect to a variable and then applying the resultant predicate to that variable makes no difference when the value of the variable is in the relevant domain but produces falsity otherwise (since that value is excluded from the extension of the predicate), on Stalnaker's orthodox semantics. More formally, we need only show that in any model, $V_a(\lambda y(A)x)(w) = V_a(Ex \ \& \ A^x/_y)(w)$ for any assignment a and world w, for then the compositional nature of the semantics ensures that the sentences B and C in the rule always have the same intension. First, suppose

---

[26] Proof: By Propositional Logic, Universal Generalization, and Modus Ponens we obtain the theorem $\forall \lambda x(\lambda y(A)x \leftrightarrow \lambda y(A)x)$, whence Free Abstraction yields $\forall \lambda x(\lambda y(A)x \leftrightarrow (Ex \ \& \ A^x/_y))$. We need only eliminate the conjunct Ex. Let T be any closed truth-functional tautology. Reasoning as before, we obtain $\forall \lambda y(T)$, and thence $\forall \lambda x(\lambda y(T)x)$, from which Free Abstraction yields $\forall \lambda x(Ex \ \& \ T)$. Combining these results with Propositional Logic, Universal Generalization, Quantification, and Modus Ponens yields Stalnaker's Abstraction schema.

that $V_a(\lambda y(A)x)(w) = 1$. Then $\underline{a}(x) \in V_a(\lambda y(A))(w) \subseteq D(w)$, so $V_a(Ex)(w) = 1$; hence, by the validity of Stalnaker's own Abstraction scheme, $V_a(A^x/_y)(w) = V_a(\lambda y(A)x)(w) = 1$. Thus $V_a(Ex \;\&\; A^x/_y)(w) = 1$. Conversely, if $V_a(Ex \;\&\; A^x/_y)(w) = 1$, then $V_a(Ex)(w) = 1$ and $V_a(A^x/_y)(w) = 1$; but by the former $a(x) \in D(w)$, so by the validity of Abstraction again, $V_a(\lambda y(A)x)(w) = V_a(A^x/_y)(w) = 1$. In every case, therefore, $V_a(\lambda y(A)x)(w) = V_a(Ex \;\&\; A^x/_y)(w)$, as required. By dropping the world variable w throughout the argument, we can also show that Free Abstraction preserves validity on Stalnaker's semantics for the first-order non-modal language.

In the modal case, the equivalence of $\lambda y(A)x$ and $Ex \;\&\; A^x/_y$ on Stalnaker's semantics does not generalize to $\lambda y(A)t$ and $Et \;\&\; A^t/_y$ when t is an individual constant, since $A^t/_y$ may be the result of substituting a non-rigid term t for the rigid variable y within the scope of a modal operator in A. That is why both Stalnaker's original Abstraction schema and Free Abstraction concern only abstraction for variables.

In the first-order non-modal logic, Free Abstraction makes no difference. For his semantics, Stalnaker's original axiomatization is sound and complete; the new axiomatization is sound, as we have seen, and extends Stalnaker's, so it is also complete; thus the two axiomatizations are equivalent. In the first-order modal logic, the new axiomatization is still sound, but properly extends Stalnaker's by yielding QCBF. As Stalnaker notes, NEI is derivable given QCBF. NEI is therefore another theorem of the axiomatization with Free Abstraction in place of Abstraction. Thus the underivability of QCBF and NEI is no deep fact about the relation between the logic of quantification and the logic of modality. It merely reflects Stalnaker's unforced choice amongst ways of formulating the logic of quantification with a λ operator that are equivalent in a non-modal setting but not in a modal one. As we have already seen, such choices can leave utterly innocuous truths of quantified modal logic unprovable. Thus his result casts no metaphysical doubt on QCBF and NEI. Free Abstraction is both formally correct and informally plausible: 'x is such that ... it ...' is equivalent to 'x is something and ... x ...'. NEI and the universal closures of all instances of QCBF are straightforwardly true.

Stalnaker complains that Free Abstraction seems to him 'contrived and less natural' than Abstraction, because it involves 'the replacement of a complex expression with a complex expression with a different constituent structure', although he does not put much weight on the complaint.[27] In any case, his own principle, Abstraction, is not significantly better off in that respect, since it universally generalizes the equivalence of $\lambda y(A)x$ and $A^x/_y$, which are themselves typically two complex expressions with a different constituent structure. For instance, if A is $\neg Fy$, then the former is $\lambda y(\neg Fy)x$, which is not of the form $\neg B$, while the latter is $\neg Fx$, which is of the form $\neg B$. Apart from that, the extra complexity of the conjunction with Ex in Free Abstraction is matched by the extra complexity of the universal quantification and predicate formation with $\forall \lambda x$ in Abstraction. In both cases the extra complexity is required by the domain constraint, which Stalnaker applies to complex predicates. The difference is that Free Abstraction covers all predications with complex predicates and variables in subject position, while Abstraction only covers some.

Could Stalnaker reply to the preceding critique with the claim that the invalidity of QCBF and NEI on his alternative counterpart semantics shows that Free Abstraction itself is metaphysically contentious? Indeed, the derivability of QCBF and NEI from Free Abstraction and the rest of his system implies that Free Abstraction is invalid on the counterpart semantics. For example, that semantics allows an object o outside the domain of a world w to satisfy $\lambda y(\lozenge Gy)x$ at w (because the counterpart of o in w has a counterpart in a world $w*$ accessible from w that belongs to the extension of G in w) even though o does not satisfy $\lozenge Gx$ at w (because no counterpart of o in any world belongs to the extension of G in that world). However, for Stalnaker to object to Free Abstraction on that basis would be to argue in a circle. For his original reason for taking the counterpart semantics seriously was precisely that it validated all the principles of first-order non-modal logic and of propositional modal logic. But now that turns out to be so only on an arbitrary view of the principles of first-order non-modal logic with an unjustified preference for Abstraction over Free Abstraction. For any theorem of first-order non-modal logic, one can rig up an unintended formal semantics on which it is invalid, and a metaphysical fairy tale to add colour to the semantics. Such a methodology is a recipe for shallowness and confusion. But it was not Stalnaker's methodology. His original argument laudably relied on the constraints of first-order non-modal logic and propositional modal logic; it failed only because it made unjustified claims about the limits of those constraints. That is no reason to throw the constraints away altogether, as the direct appeal to the counterpart semantics would do.[28]

In response, Stalnaker proposes a different and looser view of the dialectical situation.[29] On this view, the significance of the more or less orthodox proof theory and semantics of his first-order non-modal logic and propositional modal logic is in helping rebut the charge that he is merely changing the subject by changing the meaning of the apparatus of quantification, predication, and identity, or of the modal operators. The counterpart semantics is not confined to a purely instrumental role. Rather, it is supposed to have some independent attraction as nicely fitting a coherent metaphysical framework, although he does not say what that framework is.

We may agree that Stalnaker's counterpart semantics does not *totally* change the meanings of the relevant expressions, but what matters is whether it leaves them totally unchanged. Even a slight change of meaning can invalidate a logical law. In the present case, the problem is that Stalnaker's proof theory insufficiently constrains the relation between $\lambda x(A)x$ and A when they occur separated by a modal operator from another occurrence of λx needed to bind their free occurrences of x. Thanks to the strategic role of complex predicates in his proof theory, this omission has further knock-on effects. The counterpart semantics subtly exploits the lacuna to invalidate some theorems that are valid on the originally intended orthodox semantics, in effect by tweaking the meaning of $\lambda x(A)$ in modal contexts. So far this is just a minor technical anomaly, not a well-motivated piece of alternative logic, semantics, or metaphysics.

Of course, counterpart semantics in its own right still finds some defenders, who are willing to put up with its ugly complications for the sake of the freedom it delivers from constraints to which they object on metaphysical grounds. But we have already seen that the contentiousness amongst metaphysicians of a principle is quite compatible with its being a valid law of logic. Stalnaker's original argument promised, perhaps unintentionally, to do something more interesting: to introduce an objective procedure for determining how far logic constrains modal metaphysics.

---

[28] The objection was first sketched in Williamson 1996b, and elaborated in Williamson 2006.
[29] Stalnaker 2006, p. 271.

The trouble is that the putatively objective procedure is oversensitive to differences between axiomatizations of the same logic. Metaphysicians who start from the idea that counterpart theory must be logically coherent and then tailor their logic to suit are not even attempting to do the more interesting thing.[30]

4.6 Variables and constants in Stalnaker's system

Free Abstraction is not the only means by which one can argue for the missing theorems QCBF and NEI within something like Stalnaker's approach. In particular, suppose that we are granted the stronger identity principle Identity* from section 4.4, the unrestricted version of Leibniz's Law. Of course, Stalnaker regards Identity* as invalid in modal contexts, because he allows non-rigid individual constants. However, that decision has no obvious bearing on the logical status of QCBF. Individual constants occur neither in the schema itself nor in the instance of it that Stalnaker shows to be invalid on the counterpart semantics.[31] One could instead declare some or all individual constants rigid without undermining the rationale for other aspects of Stalnaker's combined system. Indeed, since he axiomatizes first-order logic using only closed formulas, individual constants are pressed into playing

---

[30] Lewis (1968, pp. 45–6) and some other counterpart theorists (I exclude Stalnaker) claim that they are not really rejecting classical logic (for example, the classical logic of identity) because sentences of quantified modal logic do not really have the semantic structure they superficially appear to have, but rather that given by their counterpart-theoretic translations. However, when quantified modal logic is interpreted by quantified modal sentences of a natural language, those claims about semantic structure must be held accountable to the standard methods of linguistics for assessing claims about the semantics of natural languages. By those standards, it is very doubtful that the counterpart-theoretic translations preserve meaning or semantic structure. If counterpart theorists drop the claims about semantic structure and protest that it is just a theory about the metaphysics underlying sentences of quantified modal logic, then they cannot reconcile their deviant quantified modal logic with classical logic in the sort of way Lewis originally attempted. After all, the truth conditions of a sentence, in particular a quantified modal one, are determined compositionally in accordance with its semantic structure. Even if, metaphysically, modal matters supervene on matters at some much deeper and more natural level, the generalizations of classical logic are not restricted to the subvenient base; they are completely unrestricted, and so apply just as much to the supervening level. For example, the classical laws of identity generalize over absolutely all objects, not just over metaphysically fundamental entities (perhaps the classical logical constants are more natural than naturalness itself). Unclarity on the relation between semantics and metaphysics has made counterpart theory look more defensible than it really is. For some more specific points along related lines see Fara and Williamson 2005.

[31] Stalnaker 2003, p. 153.

a double role, as both descriptive terms and the analogues of free variables ('arbitrary names') in proofs.[32] In effect, the rule of Universal Generalization exploits them in the latter capacity. By contrast, their non-rigidity is justified only by their descriptive content. For since Stalnaker's orthodox semantics treats variables as rigid, the role of closed terms in doing the work of free variables in the corresponding proof theory for quantification would better be served by rigid designators. To mark the difference between the two contrasting tasks for individual constants in Stalnaker's systems, we could divide the constants into two categories: arbitrary names and descriptive terms, where the semantics requires the former but not the latter to be rigid. Identity* would then be valid for arbitrary names but not for descriptive terms.

As already noted, Identity* has only valid instances on Stalnaker's semantics for first-order non-modal logic, so it is in any case unclear with what right he rejects Identity* as a constraint on the semantics for first-order modal logic, given his methodology elsewhere in his discussion. Indeed, as he notes, if singular terms were required to be rigid, with individuals rather than individual concepts as their values, we could replace both Abstraction and Free Abstraction by a much simpler abstraction principle for singular terms:

Abstraction* $\vdash Et \rightarrow (\lambda x(A)t \leftrightarrow A^t_x)$

In response, Stalnaker justifies not requiring individual constants to be rigid by appealing 'to the generality and naturalness of the generalization of extensions to intensions', and adds that it would be 'an artificial limitation of expressive power' to require them to be rigid.[33] However, at best that comment justifies having the category of descriptive terms, whose values are individual concepts. It does not justify omitting the extra category of arbitrary names, whose values are individuals. Since Stalnaker has individual variables whose values relative to assignments are individuals, he is in no position to forbid individual constants whose non-relative values are individuals too. Like Identity*, Abstraction* is valid for such arbitrary names, although not for descriptive terms.

---

[32] Stalnaker 2003, p. 147.
[33] Stalnaker 2006, p. 172. I have corrected what appear to be misprints in the statement of the principle.

In an extension of Stalnaker's axiomatization by Identity* for arbitrary names, we can prove QCBF.[34] As before, one can then derive NEI as a corollary. All that blocks these alternative derivations of QCBF and NEI is the absence of a category of rigid individual constants, in addition to or instead of a category of descriptive terms.[35] That decision on Stalnaker's part is in no way justified, let alone compelled, by first-order non-modal logic or the analogy between intensions and extensions. This reinforces the conclusion that the underivability of QCBF and NEI in Stalnaker's system is an artefact of inessential technical details, and poses no threat to their logical or metaphysical status.

4.7 Abstraction and the necessity of distinctness

We turn to the case of ND, the necessity of distinctness. As Stalnaker notes, it is underivable even when QCBF is added to his axiomatization. More generally, it is underivable when the Free Abstraction rule replaces his Abstraction schema. For Free Abstraction preserves validity on Stalnaker's other unorthodox semantics, on which '=' is reinterpreted to mean indiscernibility but everything else is standard, while ND becomes invalid (see section 4.3). ND would remain underivable even if we were to add the schema Identity* to the axiomatization, because it remains invalid even when we validate Identity* by requiring

---

[34] Proof: For any formula A in which the only free variable is x, and distinct arbitrary names s and t, we have the theorem:

$$\neg A^t/_x \to (A^t/_x \to \neg s{=}t)$$

Then Universal Generalization gives:

$$\neg A^t/_x \to \forall \lambda x(A \to \neg s{=}x)$$

Hence by Quantification:

$$\neg A^t/_x \to (\forall \lambda x(A) \to \forall \lambda x(\neg s{=}x))$$

But in Stalnaker's system we can already prove:

$$Es \to \neg \forall \lambda x(\neg s{=}x)$$

Propositional reasoning from the last two formulas yields:

$$\forall \lambda x(A) \to (Es \to A^t/_x)$$

Hence Necessitation and the K schema give:

$$\Box \forall \lambda x(A) \to \Box(Es \to A^t/_x)$$

But from this Universal Generalization yields QCBF.

[35] To make the logic as free as possible, one could still permit the rigid individual constants to be world-independently empty.

individual constants to be rigid on that unorthodox semantics. Is ND a principle that really cannot be settled by the combination of first-order non-modal logic with identity and propositional modal logic?

Stalnaker himself notes a reason for qualifying his claim that ND cannot be so settled.[36] The unorthodox semantics equates the extension of '=' at a world with the set of ordered pairs of members of the domain of that world that are mutually indiscernible, in the sense that they are in the extension of exactly the same one-place predicates (open or closed, simple or complex, but not containing '=' itself) at that world. Stalnaker's counter-model to ND on the indiscernibility semantics requires two individuals o_1 and o_2 in the domain of a world w that are discernible in w but indiscernible in some world w^* accessible from w. This can happen only if w is not accessible from w^*, for otherwise the discernibility of o_1 and o_2 in w makes them discernible in w^* too by modal predicates: for instance, o_1 but not o_2 is in the extension of $\lambda x(\Box(x=x \rightarrow x=y))$ at w^* on an assignment that maps the variable y to o_1. Thus the counter-model depends on an underlying propositional modal logic that permits non-symmetric accessibility relations. Stalnaker opts for the weakest normal propositional modal logic K, which imposes no constraints whatever on accessibility (since it can be non-reflexive, necessity does not even entail truth in K). If we assume the logic of metaphysical modality to be S5, and confine ourselves to frames for S5, so that accessibility is always an equivalence relation and therefore symmetric, we cannot construct such a counter-model. The same holds of weaker propositional modal logics with the B axiom $p \rightarrow \Box\Diamond p$, which corresponds to the symmetry of accessibility. Indeed, not even symmetry is required. What we in effect noted is that if two objects are indiscernible in a world, they are indiscernible in any world accessible from it, which corresponds to the validity of the theorem EI (the essentiality of identity) of Stalnaker's system. Thus the indiscernibility semantics permits no counter-models to ND based on any frame in which whenever w^* is accessible from w, one can get back from w^* to w in finitely many steps of accessibility, so that any two objects indiscernible in w^* are also indiscernible in w: thus the objects cannot be discernible in w but indiscernible in w^*.[37]

Syntactically, we can derive ND once we strengthen Stalnaker's axiomatization by Free Abstraction on the first-order non-modal side and by the B

[36] Stalnaker 2003, p. 156.

[37] See Chellas and Segerberg 1994 and Williamson 1994 for discussion of modal logics in which whenever $A \rightarrow \Box A$ is a theorem, so is $\neg A \rightarrow \Box\neg A$ (let A be an identity statement).

axiom on the propositional modal side.[38] Thus the underivability of ND in Stalnaker's axiomatization depends on the separate weaknesses of his abstraction principle and his propositional modal logic.

On closer examination, not even the weakness of the propositional modal logic for the modal operator □ in ND is crucial. Suppose that we believe metaphysical necessity to be constrained in ways that undermine principles such as B, or at least that we are not sure that it is not so constrained. Nevertheless, we may still be able to make sense of a stronger, unrestricted form of necessity, which we may think of as *absolute necessity*. Indeed, Stalnaker's semantic framework automatically provides an interpretation for such an operator ■ as ranging over all worlds in the model:

$$V_a(■A)(w) = 1 \text{ if for all } w* \in W, V_a(A)(w*) = 1; \text{ otherwise } V_a(■A)(w) = 0.$$

The dual operator ◆ is treated as a metalinguistic abbreviation of ¬■¬ in the usual way. We may think of □ and ◊ as restrictions of ■ and ◆ respectively by constraints of some kind. Then ■ and ◆ obey the laws of S5 even if □ and ◊ do not. In the resultant bimodal logic of the two sorts of modality, we can derive ND for □ using the extra strength of the logic for ■.[39] Let us see how such a derivation works.

We have a standard set of S5 principles for ■ and ◆:

K $\qquad\qquad$ $\vdash ■(A \rightarrow B) \rightarrow (■A \rightarrow ■B)$

T $\qquad\qquad$ $\vdash ■A \rightarrow A$

E $\qquad\qquad$ $\vdash ◆A \rightarrow ■◆A$

Necessitation $\qquad$ If $\vdash A$ then $\vdash ■A$

We also add a schema linking the two modalities:

---

[38] Proof: As already noted, Free Abstraction yields NEI. From NEI it is routine to derive:

$\forall \lambda x(\forall \lambda y(◊x{=}y \rightarrow ◊□(Ex \rightarrow x{=}y)))$

But from B we can also derive:

$\forall \lambda x(\forall \lambda y(◊□(Ex \rightarrow x{=}y) \rightarrow (Ex \rightarrow x{=}y)))$

From these two we have:

$\forall \lambda x(\forall \lambda y(◊x{=}y \rightarrow (Ex \rightarrow x{=}y)))$

But as in n. 26 we also have $\forall \lambda x(Ex)$, so we can now easily obtain ND by contraposition. The main idea of the proof is from Prior 1955, pp. 206–7.

[39] Stalnaker rejects the idea that metaphysical necessity is a restriction of some more general form of necessity such as 'conceptual necessity' (2003, pp. 202–3). However, the derivation is then still of interest if we reinterpret ■ and ◆ as the metaphysical modalities and □ and ◊ as restrictions of them, for instance to nomological modalities.

Bridge $\vdash \blacksquare A \to \Box A$

The Bridge schema is valid because if A is true in all worlds in the model, a fortiori it is true in all worlds in the model accessible from a given one. In the presence of Necessitation for $\blacksquare$ and the Bridge schema, Necessitation for $\Box$ is obviously redundant and can be dropped from the axiomatization, although we still need the K schema for $\Box$ in addition to that for $\blacksquare$.

Of course, the Bridge schema is essentially a bimodal principle: we cannot hope to derive it from the separate logics of $\blacksquare$ and $\Box$.[40] But it is not clear that Stalnaker can or does object to that. For, analogously, he does not attempt to derive his non-modal logic of quantification with identity from separate non-modal logics of quantification without identity and identity without quantification: his axiom schema of Existence involves both identity and quantification.

ND is provable in the system that results from replacing Stalnaker's Abstraction principle by Free Abstraction in his combined axiomatization and adding the S5 principles for $\blacksquare$ and the Bridge schema. We derive the B schema for $\blacksquare$ from the S5 principles and use it in the way already sketched to derive ND for $\blacksquare$:

ND($\blacksquare$) $\forall \lambda x (\forall \lambda y (\neg x = y \to \blacksquare \neg x = y))$

From the Bridge schema and Universal Generalization we prove that if the non-identity of two things is $\blacksquare$-necessary it is also $\Box$-necessary. Combining that with ND($\blacksquare$) yields ND for $\Box$, as required. We can generalize the result to strengthened versions of ND with an initial $\Box$ and any iteration of the modal operators. In other words, this schema is derivable in the same system, for any natural numbers j and k:[41]

---

[40] Proof: All the other principles remain valid when we reinterpret $\blacksquare A$ as equivalent to A, but Bridge becomes invalid.

[41] Proof: We first prove the Extended Bridge schema $\blacksquare A \to \Box^k A$ by induction on k. When $k = 0$, it reduces to the T schema for $\blacksquare$. Suppose that the Extended Bridge schema holds for k. By Necessitation and the K schema for $\blacksquare$ we prove $\blacksquare \blacksquare A \to \blacksquare \Box^k A$. Since the 4 schema for $\blacksquare$ is derivable in S5 we therefore have $\blacksquare A \to \blacksquare \Box^k A$. But $\blacksquare \Box^k A \to \Box^{k+1} A$ is an instance of the (unextended) Bridge schema, so we have $\blacksquare A \to \Box^{k+1} A$, which completes the proof of the Extended Bridge schema. Thus we can prove

$\forall \lambda x (\forall \lambda y (\blacksquare \neg x = y \to \Box^k \neg x = y))$

From this we derive $\forall \lambda x (\forall \lambda y (\neg x = y \to \Box^k \neg x = y))$ by ND($\blacksquare$). To complete the argument for ND$^+$, apply Necessitation for $\Box$ j times. Somewhat similar results are established in Williamson 1996a, using an 'actually' operator in place of $\blacksquare$. In response to those results, Stalnaker objected that ND$^+$ remains unprovable (despite being valid on the orthodox semantics) even when the QCBF schema and a complete logic for 'actually' are added to his axiomatization, although ND itself is provable (2003, pp. 159–61). The present result shows that to be a feature specific to the logic of 'actually'. In tense logic, the mutual converseness of the accessibility relations for past and future operators enables each of them to perform a similar role to that of $\blacksquare$ in the proof of ND for the other. For discussion see Karmo 1983 and Humberstone 1983.

$$\text{ND}^+ \qquad \Box^j \forall \lambda x (\forall \lambda y (\neg x = y \rightarrow \Box^k \neg x = y))$$

Many similar results can be proved by the same strategy of using first S5 to establish a property of ■ and then the Bridge schema to transfer the property to □.

According to Stalnaker, 'the necessity (or essentiality) of identity is more central to the logic of identity than the necessity of distinctness'.[42] That may well be so in the sense that natural systems of first-order modal logic with identity require significantly richer resources to prove the necessity of distinctness than to prove the necessity (or essentiality) of identity: more axioms or rules of inference and, in some cases, greater expressive power. But proofs of the necessity of distinctness and strengthenings of it such as ND$^+$ need not employ principles that derive neither from first-order non-modal logic nor from propositional (bi)modal logic. The proofs for □ earlier used only principles taken from first-order non-modal logic (including Free Abstraction) with identity and the bimodal logic of □ and ■. No distinctively modal principles specific to '=' were assumed.[43] Thus Stalnaker's suggestion that there may be 'in some sense something modal about the concept of identity' is not supported when one examines the issue in a wider range of logical settings.

4.8 Abstraction and necessitism

The rule of Free Abstraction preserves validity on Stalnaker's orthodox semantics. It involves the awkward-looking extra conjunct Ex, which requires the value of the variable to be in the domain of the relevant world. What happens if we do without that complication?

By deleting the conjunct Ex from Free Abstraction, we obtain this simpler rule (where $A^x/_y$ is as before):

Simple Abstraction   If C results from replacing some or all occurrences of $\lambda y(A)x$ in B by $A^x/_y$, and ⊢ B, then ⊢ C.

---

[42] Stalnaker 2003, p. 161.

[43] Stalnaker later made the clarification that his remark about the lesser centrality of ND was based on its invalidity in the counterpart semantics rather than in the indiscernibility semantics (2006, p. 272). He regards the latter as changing the meaning of '='. This is consistent with the present arguments concerning ND, in the context of the earlier comments on the counterpart semantics.

On Stalnaker's first-order non-modal semantics, Simple Abstraction preserves validity. It even preserves truth in a given model, in the sense that if C results from replacing some or all occurrences of $\lambda y(A)x$ in B by $A^x/_y$, and B is true in a model, then C is true in that model. Admittedly, in any model $V_a(\lambda y(A)x)$ and $V_a(A^x/_y)$ will differ for some formulas A and assignments a, for Stalnaker treats assignments as partial functions from individual variables to members of the domain.[44] For example, if a assigns no value to the variable x, $V_a(\lambda y(\neg Ey)x) = 0$ (because $V_a(x) \in V_a(\lambda y(\neg Ey))$ only if V_a is defined on x); but $V_a(\neg Ex) = 1$ (because $V_a(Ex) = 0$, since $V_a(x) \in V_a(E)$ likewise only if V_a is defined on x). However, no such difference arises when the variable is assigned a value: for any object o in domain of the model, $V_{a[x/o]}(\lambda y(A)x)$ $= V_{a[x/o]}(A^x/_y)$. Now Stalnaker restricts his logic to closed formulas, and in his language a variable x is bound only by the operator λx, which, applied to a formula A, forms a predicate $\lambda x(A)$ whose extension under an assignment a depends only on the extensions of A under assignments $a[x/o]$ that assign x a value o in the domain of the model. Consequently, if C results from replacing some or all occurrences of $\lambda y(A)x$ in B by $A^x/_y$, then $V_a(B) = V_a(C)$ for all assignments a, including those undefined on x. For example, $V_a(\forall \lambda x(\neg \lambda y(\neg Ey)x)) = V_a(\forall \lambda x(\neg \neg Ex)) = 1$. Thus Simple Abstraction preserves validity in the non-modal system.

The corresponding argument fails for Stalnaker's orthodox semantics for his first-order modal language. For example, $V_a(\forall \lambda x(\Box \neg \lambda y(\neg Ey)x))(w) = 1$ since $V_{a*}(\lambda y(\neg Ey))(w*)$ is empty for any assignment $a*$ and world $w*$; but $V_a(\forall \lambda x(\Box \neg \neg Ex))(w) = 0$ if some member of the domain of w is absent from the domain of some $w*$ accessible from w. In general, although $V_a(\lambda y(A)x)(w) = V_a(A^x/_y)(w)$ whenever $V_a(x)$ belongs to the domain of w, a modal operator may intervene between those formulas and the occurrence of λx that binds free occurrences of x in them, so that the truth values of B and C in Simple Abstraction can be sensitive to differences between $V_a(\lambda y(A)x)(w)$ and $V_a(A^x/_y)(w)$ under assignments a such that $a(x)$ belongs only to the domains of worlds other than w. Obviously, that depends on Stalnaker's decision to relativize domains to worlds. For models in which all worlds have the same domain, the earlier argument for the non-modal case generalizes easily to show that Simple Abstraction preserves truth. One can combine Stalnaker's semantics for the propositional modal language with

---

[44] Stalnaker 2003, p. 158. If the domain is empty, there are no such total functions.

his semantics for the first-order non-modal language without relativizing domains to worlds, just as he himself explicitly refrains from relativizing assignments of values to variables to worlds.

Simple Abstraction gives a smoother account of the effect of λ-abstraction than Free Abstraction does, since the content of $\lambda y(A)x$ is unpacked wholly in terms of the input formula A and the variable x, without the introduction of new elements such as Ex. The smoother account *might* be unsatisfactory if the variable were assigned no value, but since Stalnaker confines the logic to closed formulas, in which the variable x cannot occur unbound by λx, the relevant assignments all assign x a value. The truth condition of the formula A is equivalent to a condition on the object assigned to the variable y, and the truth condition of the formula $A^x/_y$ is equivalent to the corresponding condition on the object assigned to the variable x, irrespective of whether it belongs to the domain of the relevant world. Syntactically, once we have a category of rigid names, we can use an even simpler principle that stands to Abstraction* as Simple Abstraction to Free Abstraction. Here t is any such rigid name:

Abstraction** $\vdash \lambda x(A)t \leftrightarrow A^t/_x$

This is the most natural abstraction principle of all. In such a setting, Abstraction** and Simple Abstraction are interderivable. The formal case for the two principles is strong.[45]

Stalnaker relativizes domains to worlds in order not to validate the characteristic theses of necessitism. Similarly, he rejects Simple Abstraction because its addition to his system makes at least some characteristic necessitist theses derivable. One derivation starts with an instance of Stalnaker's Existence schema for a constant t:

(15) $\lambda y(\neg Ey)t \rightarrow Et$

In other words: if something is such that it is not something, then it is something. From (15), Necessitation followed by Universal Generalization gives:

(16) $\forall \lambda x(\square(\lambda y(\neg Ey)x \rightarrow Ex))$

Applying Simple Abstraction to (16), we have:

(17) $\forall \lambda x(\square(\neg Ex \rightarrow Ex))$

---

[45] Carnap endorses such an unrestricted abstraction principle ('λ-conversion') for the λ-operator in his modal languages (1947, p. 185; 1963b, p. 908).

Since $(\neg A \to A) \to A$ is a truth-functionally tautologous schema, by standard reasoning we can derive NE from (17) in this form:

NE $\forall \lambda x (\Box Ex)$

In other words, everything is such that necessarily it is something. Indeed, by applying Necessitation j times before Universal Generalization and i times afterwards, we have this strengthening of NE:

NE⁺ $\Box^i \forall \lambda x (\Box^j Ex)$

Given NE⁺, Ex & $A^x/_y$ is always equivalent to $A^x/_y$, however many modal and other operators they are embedded within: if C results from replacing some or all occurrences of $A^x/_y$ in B by Ex & $A^x/_y$, then $B \leftrightarrow C$ is derivable from NE⁺ in Stalnaker's system. Hence Free Abstraction and Simple Abstraction are interderivable in the presence of NE⁺. As a corollary, since Stalnaker's Abstraction schema is redundant in the presence of Free Abstraction, it is redundant in the presence of Simple Abstraction too.

Simple Abstraction can also be used to derive the unqualified converse Barcan schema CBF, in λ notation. For, as in section 4.5, we can derive the schema QCBF* in Stalnaker's system, from which by NE we can eliminate the qualification Ex, and finally cash out $\lambda x(A)x$ as A by applying Free Abstraction again to yield CBF.

Thus, with Stalnaker's system as the background logic, Simple Abstraction generates many of the most philosophically controversial consequences of necessitism. However, it does not generate them all, for the Barcan schema BF itself remains underivable. To see this, add to Stalnaker's orthodox semantics the non-decreasing domain condition that whenever $w\mathsf{R}w*$, $\mathrm{D}(w) \subseteq \mathrm{D}(w*)$. For reasons explained in section 3.5, this semantics validates CBF but not BF. For similar reasons, it validates NE⁺. Simple Abstraction preserves validity on this semantics. For suppose that C results from replacing some or all occurrences of $\lambda y(A)x$ in a closed formula B by $A^x/_y$, and that B is true at a world w in a non-decreasing Stalnaker model. Let $C*$ result from replacing the same occurrences of $\lambda y(A)x$ in B by Ex & $A^x/_y$. The proof in section 4.5 that Free Abstraction preserves validity on the orthodox Stalnaker semantics also shows that it preserves truth at any given world in any such model. Thus $C*$ is true at w. By the non-decreasing condition, the conjunct Ex will be true at all worlds on all assignments relevant to the semantic evaluation of C and $C*$ at w, which moves to new worlds only by steps of R. Consequently, the semantic evaluation of C at w will have the same result as that of $C*$, so C is true at w too. Therefore Simple Abstraction preserves validity in non-decreasing orthodox Stalnaker models. Since BF is not valid in such models, it is not derivable from Simple Abstraction.

As with ND, the underivability may simply reflect an expressive weakness of the language. For we can derive BF from Simple Abstraction and Stalnaker's system once we add some natural principles for a modal operator $\square^{-1}$ whose accessibility relation R^{-1} is required always to be the converse of the accessibility relation R for $\square$: $wR^{-1}w*$ if and only if $w*Rw$. Naturally, $\Diamond^{-1}$ is $\neg\square^{-1}\neg$. Thus $\Diamond$ and $\Diamond^{-1}$ are related like past and future operators in tense logic.[46] Their interrelationship automatically validates two axiom schemas for their propositional bimodal logic:

Converse$_1$ $\vdash A \rightarrow \square\Diamond^{-1}A$

Converse$_2$ $\vdash A \rightarrow \square^{-1}\Diamond A$

Of course, the K schema for $\square^{-1}$ is also valid, and Necessitation for $\square^{-1}$ preserves validity. Thus we consider the extension of Stalnaker's system with Converse$_1$, Converse$_2$, and K for $\square^{-1}$ as additional axiom schemas, Necessitation for $\square^{-1}$ as an additional rule and Simple Abstraction in place of his Abstraction schema. We can now derive BF for both $\square$ and $\square^{-1}$ using only principles from the propositional bimodal logic of the two operators and first-order non-modal logic. The proofs do not require any extra assumptions about the interaction of modal operators with quantification, predication, and identity.[47]

---

[46] See again Karmo 1983 and Humberstone 1983.

[47] Proof: First derive CBF for $\square^{-1}$ just as it was derived for $\square$, by Simple Abstraction. To derive BF for $\square$, recall that $\forall F \rightarrow (Et \rightarrow Ft)$ is already derivable in Stalnaker's system. By substituting $\lambda x(\square A)$ for F in the proof and then using Universal Generalization, the proof of $\forall \lambda x(Ex)$, and Simple Abstraction we obtain:

$\forall \lambda x(\forall \lambda x(\square A) \rightarrow \square A)$

Applying Necessitation for $\square^{-1}$ gives:

$\square^{-1}\forall \lambda x(\forall \lambda x(\square A) \rightarrow \square A)$

Since we already have CBF for $\square^{-1}$, this yields:

$\forall \lambda x(\square^{-1}(\forall \lambda x(\square A) \rightarrow \square A))$

By standard manipulations we thence obtain:

$\forall \lambda x(\Diamond^{-1}\forall \lambda x(\square A)) \rightarrow \forall \lambda x(\Diamond^{-1}\square A)$

Removing the outer quantifier in the antecedent by Universal Generalization and the modalities in the consequent by Converse$_2$ (contraposed), we have:

$\Diamond^{-1}\forall \lambda x(\square A) \rightarrow \forall \lambda x(A)$

By Necessitation and K for $\square$ we have:

$\square\Diamond^{-1}\forall \lambda x(\square A) \rightarrow \square\forall \lambda x(A)$

Finally, Converse$_1$ allows us to remove the two outer modalities in the antecedent, thereby obtaining BF for $\square$. BF for $\square^{-1}$ is obtained in exactly parallel fashion.

In the special case in which the accessibility relation for $\Box$ is assumed to be symmetric, $\Box^{-1}$ reduces to $\Box$, Converse$_1$ and Converse$_2$ both reduce to the B schema, and the proof of BF reduces to the usual for monomodal systems with CBF and B. In particular, we can derive BF from Stalnaker's system extended by Simple Abstraction and the principles of propositional S5 in the original language without the additional operators. But if one prefers not to rely on those stronger principles of propositional modal logic, one can achieve the same effect by working in the extended language.

Either way, the point is that, absent artificial obstacles, Simple Abstraction (or equivalently, Abstraction**) generates the full range of necessitist commitments. With Stalnaker's system as the background logic, the contingentist cannot afford the simplest, most natural account of λ-abstraction in quantified modal logic.

Contingentists are in a tricky position. If they insist that it is possible to fall under a predicate and yet be nothing, they face the charge that they are unserious about their own contingentism, because they are tacitly restricting the quantifier 'nothing' (section 4.1). If they agree that falling under a predicate entails being something, they slide into necessitism unless they distinguish not falling under a predicate from falling under a negative predicate, which is best done by means of something like the λ operator. If they introduce the λ operator, they still slide into necessitism unless they complicate its logic in awkward ways. Although none of this amounts to a refutation of contingentism, it is evidence that the view goes against the logical grain.

4.9 Stalnaker's criterion of representational significance

Stalnaker's overall reasoning involves a complex interplay of considerations from logic, semantics, and metaphysics. For example, he treats his orthodox semantics and the counterpart-theoretic semantics as reflecting rival metaphysical pictures, between which the central core of quantified modal logic should be neutral. But we saw in section 3.6 that for a contingentist there is no intended inhabited model structure in the usual ungerrymandered sense, because any inhabited model structure that validates exactly the metaphysically universal formulas validates BF. That point applies as much to Stalnaker's models as to anyone else's. What, therefore, is the intended metaphysical import of his formal semantics?

Stalnaker has addressed such issues in detail. He defends a nuanced view on which some but not all aspects of a model have representational significance. He separates the two sorts of aspect by means of an equivalence relation on models. Two models are equivalent if and only if they have the same representational significance. A feature of a model has representational significance if and only if it is invariant across all equivalent models. Analogously, a statement of temperature in degrees Fahrenheit has representational significance, and an equivalent statement in degrees centigrade has the same representational significance, even though the reference to a particular number in the former but not the latter has no representational significance. Much of Stalnaker's discussion focuses on the status of the worlds themselves. What matters more for present purposes is the status of their domains. Here is what he says about it, in relation to an orthodox model for first-order modal logic:

> Any permutation of the 'possible individuals' that preserved identity and difference, as well as the qualitative character of the individuals, and that mapped all *actual* individuals onto themselves would be an equivalent representation—a representation of the same facts, including the modal facts. The domains of other possible worlds (or those members of the domains that are not actually existing individuals) represent the generic possibility of there being individuals of a certain kind, though if individuals of the kinds that might exist did exist, they would be individuals with modal properties, and whatever concrete individuality that actual individuals have.[48]

By the 'possible individuals' here Stalnaker means the members of the union of the domains of all the worlds in the model M. A permutation of them is

---

[48] Stalnaker 2010, p. 24. Confusingly, when he specifies the 'orthodox model' whose representationally significant aspects are to be isolated, what he describes is not a model in the standard sense of modal logic but an inhabited model structure, with a set of worlds, a designated actual world, and a domain for each world, but no constituent to interpret the names and non-logical atomic predicates of the first-order modal language he describes (2010, p. 23). However, the mention of 'the qualitative character of the individuals' in the quoted passage presumably adverts to such an interpretation, since the actual characteristics of something that is being used in the model to represent a non-actual individual are representationally insignificant (otherwise only a golden mountain would represent a merely possible golden mountain). We may therefore assume that the model includes an interpretation of the non-logical vocabulary.

a function that maps each member of the union to a member of the union and is both one-one (distinct members are mapped to distinct members) and onto (every member has some member mapped onto it). Any such permutation σ induces a mapping from M to a model M^σ with the same set of worlds and the same actual world. For example, an individual o is in the domain $D(w)$ of a world w in M if and only if $\sigma(o)$ is in the domain $D^\sigma(w)$ of w in M^σ. The interpretations of the names and non-logical atomic predicates in M^σ are the corresponding modifications of their interpretations in M. For example, o is in the extension of a one-place atomic predicate F at w in M if and only if $\sigma(o)$ is in the extension of F at w in M^σ. Such a mapping automatically preserves the descriptions of all individuals, including identity, difference, and qualitative character, in the sense that any formula A of the language is true at a world w on an assignment $\underline{a}$ in M if and only if A is true at w on the assignment $\underline{a}^\sigma$ in M^σ, where for each variable v, $\underline{a}^\sigma(v) = \sigma(\underline{a}(v))$. Stalnaker also requires σ to fix actuality, in the sense that whenever o belongs to the domain $D(w_@)$ of the actual world $w_@$ of M, $\sigma(o) = o$; consequently, $o \in D(w_@)$ if and only if $\sigma(o) \in D(w_@)$. In the quoted passage, he claims that if σ fixes actuality, M and M^σ are representationally equivalent.

The requirement on σ to fix actuality serves no purpose unless sometimes M and M^σ are not representationally equivalent when σ does not fix actuality. But even if σ does not fix actuality, exactly the same closed sentences are true at any given world w in M as in M^σ. Why care about open formulas, since they lack assignment-independent significance? Stalnaker's idea is presumably this. Each member of $D(w_@)$ represents a particular individual, itself. Consider an open formula A with just one free variable, x. On the proposed view, if A is true in M at $w_@$ on an assignment $\underline{a}$ such that $\underline{a}(x) \in D(w_@)$, M thereby represents the individual $\underline{a}(x)$ as actually having the corresponding property. Although A is also true in M^σ at $w_@$ on $\underline{a}^\sigma$, M^σ thereby represents the individual $\underline{a}^\sigma(x)$ as actually having that property, which is a distinct state of affairs if $\underline{a}^\sigma(x)$ is a distinct individual from $\underline{a}(x)$. That is a representationally significant difference. It cannot arise if σ fixes actuality, for then $\underline{a}^\sigma(x) = \sigma(\underline{a}(x)) = \underline{a}(x)$, since $\underline{a}(x) \in D(w_@)$. By contrast, an individual in the domain of some world but not in $D(w_@)$ represents no particular individual, not even itself. It represents a non-actual individual, but not any particular non-actual individual, just as a picture may represent a dragon without representing any particular dragon (there is no dragon that it represents, because there are no dragons). Thus even if A is true in M at a world w on an assignment $\underline{a}$ such that $\underline{a}(x) \in D(w_@)$, M does not represent the individual $\underline{a}(x)$ as having the corresponding property (possibly, or at w). At best it represents a non-actual individual, but not any particular non-actual individual, as having the property (possibly, or at w). Equally, although A is also true in M^σ at w on $\underline{a}^\sigma$, M^σ does not represent the individual $\underline{a}^\sigma(x)$ as having the property (possibly, or at w), for $\underline{a}^\sigma(x) \notin D(w_@)$. At best M^σ represents a non-actual individual, but not any particular non-actual individual, as having the property (possibly, or at w), which is the same state of affairs as before, even if $\underline{a}^\sigma(x)$ is in fact distinct from $\underline{a}(x)$. That is a representationally insignificant difference. It can arise even if σ fixes actuality. The idea generalizes to open formulas with more than one free variable.

Now consider a model M that invalidates unnecessitated BF. Thus the domain $D(w)$ of some world w in M is not a subset of the domain $D(w_@)$ of the actual world $w_@$ of M. Some individual o in $D(w)$ is not in $D(w_@)$. Independently of M, however, o is an actual individual, just like anything else. Stalnaker denies that there are non-actual individuals; o is an actual individual that represents a non-actual individual (but not any particular non-actual individual). One difference between M and some other models is that o belongs to the domain of the actual world in the latter but not in M. For opponents of BF, including Stalnaker, this difference should count as representationally insignificant, otherwise M would represent o as non-actual (equivalently, represent actuality as not containing o), and therefore represent falsely, since o is actual. Therefore, by Stalnaker's criterion of representational significance as applied to M, o should belong to the domain $D^\sigma(w_@)$ of the actual world in a model M^σ for some actuality-fixing permutation σ. But that is impossible, for if $o \in D^\sigma(w_@)$ then $o = \sigma(i)$ for some $i \in D(w_@)$; but $\sigma(i) = i$ since σ is actuality-fixing for M, so $o = i$, so $o \in D(w_@)$, contrary to hypothesis. Alternatively, we can apply the criterion of representational significance to a model N the domain $D(w_@)$ of whose actual world $w_@$ contains o: the domain $D^\sigma(w_@)$ of the actual world of N^σ contains o if and only if $o = \sigma(i)$ for some $i \in D(w_@)$; but if σ is actuality-fixing for N then o meets the latter condition since $o = \sigma(o)$ and $o \in D(w_@)$, so $o \in D^\sigma(w_@)$. Either way, whether o belongs to the domain of the actual world in a model is invariant under actuality-fixing permutations. Thus Stalnaker's criterion makes the difference between models whose actual world contains o and the rest representationally significant. To sharpen the point: on any assignment $\underline{a}$ such that $\underline{a}(x)$ is o, the formula $\exists y\ x=y$ is false in any model representationally equivalent to M, and true in any model representationally equivalent to N, by the criterion. It therefore commits Stalnaker to the conclusion that M misrepresents actuality as not containing o, and more generally that any counter-model to BF represents falsely.[49]

If Stalnaker is to maintain his opposition to BF, he must modify his criterion of representational significance. One idea is to drop the actuality-fixing condition. Without it, one can simply use a permutation σ that swaps o with an arbitrarily chosen member $o*$ of $D(w_@)$ and leaves every other possible individual fixed; since $o = \sigma(o*) \in D^\sigma(w_@)$, o belongs to the domain of the actual world in M^σ.[50] Thus the difference between models whose actual world contains o and the rest ceases to be representationally significant.

Dropping the actuality-fixing condition is quite contrary to the spirit of Stalnaker's original proposal, for it abolishes the asymmetry in representational significance on which he insists between the actual individuals and the merely possible individuals of a model. Indeed, it deprives the model of all singular representational content. Any two individuals in it are representationally alike, in the sense that it is representationally equivalent to another model in which they are interchanged. That seems to reduce the model to representing purely qualitative information.

Of course, a sentence Fa & $\neg Fb$ may be actually true in a model M in which the constant a actually denotes an individual i while the constant b actually denotes a distinct individual j. Then Fa & $\neg Fb$ will be actually true in all models isomorphic to M, including all permutations of M. But, by the new criterion, they include representationally equivalent models in which

---

[49] Although actuality-fixing permutations fix the set of worlds, the actual world, and the total set of possible individuals, the argument easily generalizes to the much wider class of actuality-fixing isomorphisms of models. An isomorphism from a centred model <W, R, w, D,V> to a centred model <W*, R*, w*, D*,V*> is a pair of functions <ρ, σ>, where ρ is a bijection from W onto W*, R* = {<$\rho(u)$, $\rho(v)$>: <u, v> $\in$ R}, w* = $\rho(w)$, σ is a bijection from $\cup_{u \in W} D(u)$ onto $\cup_{u \in W*} D*(u)$, for $u \in$ W D*($\rho(u)$) = {$\sigma(o)$: $o \in D(u)$}, and the relation between V and V* is constrained analogously to that between D and D*. The isomorphism is actuality-fixing if and only if $w = w$* and $\sigma(o) = o$ for all $o \in$ D(w) (so D*(w) = D(w)). An actuality-fixing permutation is an actuality-fixing isomorphism <ρ, σ> for which $\rho(u) = u$ for all $u \in$ W (so W* = W and R* = R) and $\cup_{u \in W}$ D*(u) = $\cup_{u \in W}$ D(u). A natural and much more general criterion in a similar spirit to Stalnaker's original one is that centred models are representationally equivalent if and only if there is an actuality-fixing isomorphism between them. This new criterion is not exactly a generalization of the old one, for there may be an actuality-fixing isomorphism but no actuality-fixing permutation between <W, R, w, D,V> and <W, R, w, D*,V*>, if the isomorphism needs to permute the members of W (other than w) non-trivially. That is a disadvantage of the isomorphism criterion only if the identity of the worlds in a model has representational significance. In any case, both criteria are vulnerable to the argument in the text about BF.

[50] The proposal assumes that D($w_@$) is not empty, but opponents and proponents of BF can agree on other grounds that a model on which actually (if contingently) there is nothing is a misrepresentation.

a actually denotes *j* while *b* actually denotes *i*. Moreover, if BF fails in M, the models representationally equivalent to M include some in which *i* is non-actual. Although the truth at the actual world of a closed sentence is a representationally significant feature of a model, and the sentence may contain constants, the model represents nothing specific to the particular individuals it has the constants denote.

The variation in reference is not confined to names. Suppose that in M exactly *k* individuals are in the actual extension X of *F*, and exactly *k** individuals in M are not in X. Let Y be any set of exactly *k* individuals in M such that exactly *k** individuals in M are not in Y. Then some permutation σ of the individuals in M maps X onto Y. In the permuted model M^σ the actual extension of *F* is Y. By the new criterion, M^σ is representationally equivalent to M. Thus the actual extension of *F* varies wildly across representationally equivalent models. Only gross structural features such as the cardinality of its actual extension remain invariant. No quality in any natural sense remains invariant. Thus *F* represents no quality in particular.

What looks like the most clearly representational aspect of a model, the relation of closed non-logical atomic expressions to their intensions, turns out to be representationally insignificant, according to the new criterion. Roughly speaking, the model tells us which sentences are true, but not what they mean. It does not even provide a qualitative description. The actual truth of *Fa* & ¬*Fb* represents the information that the actual denotation of *a* belongs to the actual extension of *F* while the actual denotation of *b* does not, but the only non-metalinguistic information one can extract from that is that the domain of the actual world has at least two members.

Thus dropping the actuality-fixing condition leaves the representational significance of a model drastically etiolated. Restoring the condition reinstates the argument for BF. Contingentists have failed to propose any alternative well-motivated, non-gerrymandered criterion that would assign models a rich actuality-involving representational significance without validating the argument for BF.

Of course, we can endow a model with a rich actuality-involving representational significance from outside, for instance by explaining independently of the model how to read the non-logical atomic expressions of the language. But that is to relegate the model to a largely instrumental role. It merely determines which sentences are represented as true; what they mean is determined elsewhere. By contrast, Stalnaker has a more realist view of the model-theoretic semantics. It is supposed to do much of the interpretative work itself. For example, he takes the difference between the orthodox and counterpart model theories to explain the metaphysical difference underlying their disagreement over the evaluation of various formulas. Without a clear criterion for distinguishing representational from non-representational differences between models, such an explanation makes limited sense. In particular, therefore, Stalnaker's formal semantics provides no solid basis for his version of contingentism, articulated by means of the λ operator. It shows various theses to be independent of his system, but for determining which theses are metaphysically universal it is of much less help than one might have hoped.

An option that Stalnaker does not consider is to insert markers for representational significance into the models themselves. For example, we can use the symbol + to mark representational significance and the symbol − to mark its absence. For these purposes, we may restrict attention to models with the following features: the domain of each world contains only ordered pairs of the forms <+, o> and <−, o>; the domain of the actual world contains only pairs of the form <+, o>; if the domain of any world contains <+, o> or <−, o> then the domain of the actual world contains <+, o>. Informally, the identity of o is representationally significant in <+, o> but not in <−, o>. More precisely, for such models we may take <+, o> to represent (not itself but) o, but <−, o> just to represent a merely possible individual (not o). The actual being of London does not prevent <−, London> from representing a non-actual being; the presence of <+, London> in the domain of the actual world still represents London as actual. Thus for purposes of representational significance, isomorphisms must be constant on pairs <+, o> but may permute pairs <−, o>. From a purely model-theoretic perspective, of course, these complications are pointless. They are inert in the definition of truth at a world in a model. Contingentists' need for such artificial and ad hoc extra structure to capture representational significance is one more manifestation of the mismatch between contingentist metaphysics and the standard model theory of quantified modal logic.

5

From First-Order to Higher-Order Modal Logic

5.1 Methodological preliminaries

The semantics of quantified modal logic has made enormous technical progress. Unfortunately, as we saw in preceding chapters, those advances have contributed much less than one might have hoped to resolving the basic philosophical dispute between contingentism and necessitism. They have at least clarified the inferential interrelations of various principles, and provided elegant, tractable ways of modelling the opposing views. But mainstream contingentists must treat key features of the models, especially those needed for counter-models to unnecessitated Barcan formulas, in a somewhat instrumentalist spirit (sections 3.6 and 4.9). On pain of inconsistency, they cannot treat their structure as perspicuously representing that of modal reality. More precisely, although they can insist that a model structure correctly represents many aspects of modal reality, they cannot allow that it validates all and only the metaphysically universal formulas of first-order modal logic. By contrast, necessitists can afford a somewhat more realist attitude to the model theory, but of course even they cannot assume such an attitude in arguing with contingentists.

In recent metaphysics, the talk is usually of possible worlds, rather than of points in models, but the underlying problem is the same. That is hardly surprising, since the possible worlds are treated like points in an intended model, although rarely with the precision of formal semantics. Both the semantic and the metaphysical theories seemingly enable us to discuss modal questions without using modal operators, by replacing them with quantifiers over worlds. Since our logical hold is much firmer on quantifiers than on modal operators, that looks like progress. But when the modal question is how there could have been an F, even though absolutely nothing could have been an F, the attempt to address it in purely extensional language with unrestricted quantifiers leads contingentism to disaster, whatever obfuscation is employed to conceal the inconsistency. Of course, contingentists may consistently insist that a model with increasing domains represents it as possible that something is an F yet for no object o represents it as possible that o is an F. But in so insisting they still use modal operators.

We should resign the deceptive hope of formulating serious arguments for contingentism or necessitism in terms free of modal operators. How then can we make progress? If the quest were for an argument that would silence a committed opponent, both sides could give up right now. The model theory shows both positions to be technically workable. As usual in philosophy, determined defenders of a position will say whatever they have to, however implausible, in order to brazen it out against any objection. A more reasonable benchmark is accumulating evidence about the theoretical advantages and disadvantages of contingentism and necessitism, until those who have not already invested too much on one side or the other are in a position to see which is the better view.

Part of the difficulty is that what are at stake are putative laws of logic, such as BF and CBF, but not ones on which we can easily bring to bear well-established bodies of deductive reasoning, most notably in mathematics, whose core vocabulary lacks metaphysically interpreted modal operators. Nevertheless, we can hope to put the principles at stake in a wider theoretical setting, in which more of their consequences become visible. We saw in Chapter 4 how accidental expressive limitations of a language can distort the assessment of logical principles. Higher-order modal logic widens our theoretical horizons in another and more extensive way. We already had recourse to it in section 3.6: to formulate the standard of metaphysical universality for a formula of first-order modal logic we replaced its non-logical atomic predicate letters by predicate variables, interpreted over properties and relations, and universally quantified the result. As a special case, atomic sentences were replaced by universally quantified 0-place predicate variables, interpreted over propositions. Indeed, we invoked the second-order standard of metaphysical universality to test formal systems because reliance on a model-theoretic standard of validity begs the philosophical questions. This chapter and the next trace more extensive and intricate connections between those questions and principles of second-order modal logic, to determine whether contingentism or necessitism better enables us to develop an adequate system of higher-order modal logic.

A secondary hope is to encourage metaphysicians and other philosophers to make more use of the resources of second-order modal logic. Second-order non-modal logic and first-order modal logic are both, separately, major topics of philosophical discussion. Although both have been extensively criticized by Quine and others, fewer and fewer philosophers find their strictures compelling.[1] Each sort of logic is frequently employed as a framework for articulating philosophical theses and investigating their logical interrelations. Resistance to Quine's case for granting exclusive logical privileges to first-order non-modal logic in respect of modal logic is likely to be positively correlated with resistance to it in respect of second-order logic. Thus one might expect some combination of the two sorts of logic to constitute a natural and more comprehensive background logic for many discussions in metaphysics and other branches of philosophy. It is therefore somewhat surprising to find philosophical discussion and application of second-order modal logic largely absent, despite some pioneering contributions.

Two contrary explanations initially suggest themselves. One is that second-order modal logic is too hard: multiplying together the complexities of second-order logic and of modal logic produces an intractable level of technical complexity. The other explanation is that second-order modal logic is too easy: its difficulties are just those of second-order logic and of modal logic separately, combining which provokes no special further problems of philosophical interest. These putative explanations are less opposed than they first appear, since mere complications may be boring and shallow. Nevertheless, separately and even together, the explanations are not fully satisfying. For the technical complexities of second-order modal logic are no worse than those of many other branches of logic and mathematics (set theory, for instance) to which philosophers standardly appeal. Some of the relevant results are proved in a few lines. Nor are the complexities of second-order modal logic philosophically unrewarding. As we shall see, the interaction of second-order quantifiers with modal operators raises deep issues in logical metaphysics that cannot be factorized into the issues raised by the former and those raised by the latter.

---

[1] The *locus classicus* is Quine 1970.

Such fruitful interaction was already seen in first-order modal logic. Barcan formulas and their converses raise basic metaphysical issues that arise neither in first-order non-modal logic nor in propositional modal logic. In second-order modal logic there are both first-order and second-order Barcan formulas. Perhaps surprisingly, the issues about second-order Barcan formulas and their converses are *not* merely higher-order analogues of the issues about first-order Barcan formulas and their converses. Nevertheless, reflection on the second-order formulas and related second-order principles casts new light on the controversy between contingentists and necessitists over the first-order principles.

Historically, the earliest formal systems of modern logic, such as those of Frege and of Russell and Whitehead, were higher-order. Their first-order fragments were identified only later as of special significance.[2] Similarly, higher-order systems of modal logic go back about as far as first-order ones. We should not assume without argument that first-order modal logic deserves priority.

This chapter focuses on the development and interpretation of formal systems of higher-order modal logic. The next chapter applies them to the dispute between contingentism and necessitism.

5.2 Lewis and Langford: propositional quantification in modal logic

Higher-order modal logic has a significant history, but always on the margins of the mainstream development of modal logic. From a technical perspective, even first-order modal logic has been much less central than unquantified propositional modal logic. However, the addition to the latter of propositional quantifiers is almost as old as modern modal logic itself.

In *Symbolic Logic* (1932), C.I. Lewis and C.H. Langford brought to salience the distinction between material implication and strict implication: in present notation, between $A \rightarrow B$ and $\Box(A \rightarrow B)$. They presented five formal systems for strict implication, S1–S5. But they were not satisfied with making the distinction explicit in their informal explanations of the formalism. They wanted it to be explicit in the formal systems themselves. The problem was that although both the material and strict equivalence of

---

[2] See Eklund 1996 and references therein for further discussion.

the two implications are underivable for many formulas in S1–S5, they are always irrefutable. Thus, while not every instance of (1) is a theorem, no instance of (2) is a theorem:

(1) $\Box((A \to B) \leftrightarrow \Box(A \to B))$

(2) $\neg\Box((A \to B) \leftrightarrow \Box(A \to B))$

The problem arises for every subsystem of S5, the strongest Lewis system and the strongest plausible propositional logic of metaphysical modality. For, to argue in contemporary terms, S5 has a model with just one world, accessible from itself, in which strict implication therefore collapses into material implication; since any instance of (1) is true in that model, no instance of (2) is true, so no instance of (2) is a theorem of S5 or its subsystems. But S5 also has models with many worlds, each accessible from each, in which strict implication therefore does not collapse into material implication; since many instances of (1) are false in such models, they are not theorems of S5 and its subsystems.

Lewis and Langford solve the problem by introducing propositional quantifiers and laying down what they call the 'Existence Postulate', that some proposition is both consistent with and independent of another:[3]

(3) $\exists X \exists Y (\neg\Box(X \to Y) \,\&\, \neg\Box(X \to \neg Y))$

By truth-functional logic, either X materially implies Y or X materially implies $\neg Y$, so in a suitable background logic we can easily derive (4) from (3):

(4) $\exists X \exists Y ((X \to Y) \,\&\, \neg\Box(X \to Y))$

In contemporary terms, (3) corresponds to the constraint on Kripke model structures that at least two worlds must be accessible from the actual world (one to verify X and Y, one to verify X and falsify Y). But merely imposing that constraint on the model theory of the original language does not secure the effect of (3), for it makes no difference to the model-theoretic validity of any unquantified formula A: if A is falsified in some model based on a model structure for S5 ruled out by the constraint, it is also falsified in some model on a model structure for S5 not ruled out by the constraint in which the two worlds accessible from the actual world are indiscernible from each other. The extra expressive power of the propositional quantifiers is essential.

---

[3] Lewis and Langford 1932, p. 179.

We can understand what Lewis and Langford are doing in terms of the notion of metaphysical universality introduced in section 3.3. Recall that a formula of propositional modal logic is metaphysically universal if and only if its universal generalization is simply true. For example, where P and Q are atomic sentences, (6) is the universal generalization of (5), so (5) is metaphysically universal if and only if (6) is true:

(5) $\Box(P \to Q) \vee \Box(P \to \neg Q)$

(6) $\forall X \, \forall Y \, (\Box(X \to Y) \vee \Box(X \to \neg Y))$

By introducing propositional quantifiers, Lewis and Langford enable us to speak of metaphysical universality in the object-language. Of course, we do not gain much by saying that a formula *is* metaphysically universal, for if so we can already help ourselves to any instance of it in the unquantified language. A more significant gain is the ability to *deny* in the object-language that a formula is metaphysically universal. For example, since we can treat $\forall X$ in (6) as the dual $\neg \exists X \, \neg$ of $\exists X$ in (3), the latter is a contradictory of (6). Thus Lewis and Langford's Existence Postulate is tantamount to the denial that (5) is metaphysically universal. As already noted, that denial has no working substitute in the unquantified language.[4]

A simpler instance of the same pattern is this:

(7) $\Box P \vee \Box \neg P$

(8) $\forall X \, (\Box X \vee \Box \neg X)$

Since (8) is the universal generalization of (7), (7) is metaphysically universal if and only if (8) is true. Obviously (8) is false because some propositions are contingent, so (7) is not metaphysically universal. Yet every iterated necessitation of (7) can be consistently added to S5, and indeed to any consistent normal modal system (without quantifiers).[5] We can deny the metaphysical universality of (7) explicitly in the language with propositional quantifiers by asserting the negation of (8), which is equivalent to Lewis and Langford's Existence Postulate (3).

---

[4] See Lewis and Langford 1932, pp. 180–1, for closely related discussion. Whether their understanding of propositional quantification exactly fits the account of metaphysical universality is unclear; p. 182 n. 10, raises more questions than it answers.

[5] This is a corollary of a theorem in Makinson 1971; similarly for (1) and (5). Although S1–S3 are non-normal, the result applies to them because they are subsystems of S5.

Kripke later formulated a modal system with propositional quantifiers that extends S5 by an axiom schema that strengthens the Existence Postulate. He showed that the universal generalization of any non-theorem of S5 is inconsistent in the system.[6] In effect, the system asserts the metaphysical universality of any theorem of S5 and denies the metaphysical universality of any non-theorem of S5. That is related to the argument in section 3.3 that the system of all metaphysically universal formulas is no stronger than S5. Although Robert Bull described Kripke's extra axiom as 'a rather perverse postulate', his remark may reflect the difference between metaphysical and mathematical perspectives on modal logic.[7]

In Kripke models for propositional modal logic, propositional quantifiers have a natural interpretation as ranging over all subsets of the set of worlds, or equivalently over total functions from worlds to truth values. Thus propositional quantification is the intensional analogue of quantification over truth values. Since the interpretation does not require changing the models, it makes the modal logic of propositional quantification a natural extension of propositional modal logic.[8]

A distinctive consequence of the standard possible worlds semantics for propositional quantification is to validate the claim that necessarily some true proposition strictly implies all true propositions, for the singleton of the world of evaluation is always such a strongest truth:

At $\qquad \Box \exists X \, (X \mathbin{\&} \forall Y \, (Y \to \Box(X \to Y)))$

If the modal operators range over all worlds in a model (thereby validating S5), we can informally read At as saying that for every world there is a proposition true in it and nowhere else. To articulate the idea further, let 'Atom(X)' abbreviate this formula:

$\qquad \Diamond X \mathbin{\&} \forall Y \, (\Box(X \to Y) \lor \Box(X \to \neg Y))$

In other words, X is a possibility that strictly implies or excludes every proposition. The standard possible worlds semantics also validates the claims that necessarily there is an atomic truth and that every possibility is strictly implied by an atomic proposition:

---

[6] Kripke 1959a, pp. 12–13.
[7] Bull 1969, p. 257 n. 1.
[8] Seminal work in this tradition includes Fine 1970 and Kaplan 1970; see also Gallin 1975, pp. 79–89.

At$_1$ $\Box \exists X\, (\text{Atom}(X)\ \&\ X)$

At$_2$ $\forall X\, (\Diamond X \rightarrow \exists Y\, (\text{Atom}(Y)\ \&\ \Box(Y \rightarrow X)))$

Indeed, At, At$_1$, and At$_2$ are mutually interderivable in a reasonable background logic.[9]

We can be more explicit about the correspondence between these notions and atoms in the Boolean algebra of propositions used to define metaphysical universality in sections 3.3 and 3.6. We extend the definition of 'faithful interpretation' to propositional quantifiers in the obvious way, by requiring that for such an interpretation I on an assignment a of values to variables, $I_a(\forall V A) = \Pi\{I_{a[V/p]}(A) : p \text{ is a proposition}\}$. We need some assumption about the propositional function L that interprets $\Box$, otherwise the modal formulas may not capture the relevant algebraic properties and relations. For example, if L maps each proposition to itself, then a faithful interpretation treats $\Box$ and $\Diamond$ as redundant and so interprets Atom(X) as equivalent to X itself. In order to capture genuine atomicity in the algebra, we therefore assume that $Lp = 0$ whenever $p \neq 1$. Let I be a faithful interpretation and a an assignment. By standard Boolean reasoning, $I_a(X) \leq I_a(Y)$ if and only if $I_a(X \rightarrow Y) = 1$. Hence $I_a(\Box(X \rightarrow Y)) = 1$ if $I_a(X) \leq I_a(Y)$; $I_a(\Box(X \rightarrow Y)) = 0$ otherwise. Similarly, $I_a(\Diamond X) = 1$ if $I_a(X) \neq 0$; $I_a(\Diamond X) = 0$ otherwise. One can then routinely show that if $I_a(X)$ is an atom in the algebra then $I_a(\text{Atom}(X)) = 1$; otherwise $I_a(\text{Atom}(X)) = 0$. Thus the formula says what it is supposed to say. Of course, $I_a(\text{At}) = I_a(\text{At}_1) = I_a(\text{At}_2) = 1$ because the algebra is atomic by hypothesis.

One may have philosophical qualms about the standard possible worlds interpretation of propositional quantifiers. It uses first-order quantification into name position on individual variables for sets in the metalanguage to interpret quantification into sentence position in the object-language. That mismatch suggests that the interpretation may not be perfectly faithful to the underlying intention. Nevertheless, despite such qualms, we may provisionally regard the semantics as at least a useful first approximation to a legitimate understanding of the propositional quantifiers. The final section of this chapter returns to the issue.

Just as section 3.3 used propositional quantification into sentence position to define metaphysical universality for propositional modal logic, so section 3.6

---

[9] See Gallin 1975, pp. 84–6.

used second-order quantification into predicate position to define meta-physical universality for first-order modal logic. Many of the same points apply, in particular the essential role of such quantification in denials of metaphysical universality. We now turn to that case.

5.3 Second-order modal logic in Barcan and Carnap: identity, individual concepts, and semantic uniformity

Propositional quantifiers aside, the history of second-order modal logic goes back at least to 1947. In that year, Ruth Barcan (Marcus) published 'The identity of individuals in a strict functional calculus of second order', in which she gave the first proof of, in effect, the necessity of identity. Starting from the two systems of first-order modal logic, based on the Lewis systems S2 and S4, in her first 1946 paper, she adds the apparatus for second-order quantification, including an abstraction operator binding individual varia-bles (in present notation, λ), subject to an unrestricted abstraction principle. She goes second-order to define identity rather than treating it as primitive. Indeed, she defines two 'identity' signs, one strict and one material. In present notation, with abstraction on an ordered sequence of variables, she defines strict identity (I) as $\lambda x, y(\forall X \ \Box(Xx \rightarrow Xy))$ and material identity (I_m) as $\lambda x, y(\forall X \ (Xx \rightarrow Xy))$.[10] Since BF and CBF are theorems, strict identity is provably equivalent to the necessitation of material identity. It is trivial in her systems that an individual is strictly identical with itself. Thus if i is materially identical with j, since i is such that i is strictly identical with it, so is j, so i is strictly identical with j. Since the converse is also provable by the T principle, material identity is equivalent to strict identity, and therefore to its own necessitation.[11] That is a form of the necessity of identity.

As in her 1946 papers, Barcan's presentation is entirely proof-theoretic, with no discussion of formal or informal semantics. Although she sometimes

---

[10] The one-way arrows do not make I and I_m non-symmetric: for the converses we can put $\lambda z(\neg Xz)$ for X. Note also that the use of the λ operator permits a contingentist to accept the being constraint for strict and material identity. By contrast, if Ixy and $I_m xy$ simply abbreviate $\forall X \ \Box(Xx \rightarrow Xy)$ and $\forall X \ (Xx \rightarrow Xy)$ respectively, then Ixx and $I_m xx$ abbreviate $\forall X \ \Box(Xx \rightarrow Xx)$ and $\forall X \ (Xx \rightarrow Xx)$, which hold independently of $\exists y \ x=y$.

[11] In the system based on S2 only material equivalence is provable; in the system based on S4 strict equivalence is provable (Barcan 1947).

comments that a formula is underivable, she rarely states her grounds for doing so, although in one case she appeals to an eight-valued matrix in a purely instrumental capacity.[12] By contrast, in *Meaning and Necessity*, Carnap's brief sketch of a second-order extension of his modal language is entirely semantic, with no discussion of proof theory.[13] He proposes taking as values of the second-order variables properties of individuals, in the sense of functions from individuals (or individual constants) to sets of state-descriptions. We can regard the function as mapping each individual to the set of worlds in which it has the property at issue. That is equivalent to treating the value of a second-order variable as an intension in the usual sense for a predicate of individuals.

Unfortunately, there was a catch, as John Myhill later pointed out.[14] For Carnap, an individual variable under an assignment has an intension, an individual concept, as well as an extension, an individual. The truth value of a formula in which the variable occurs free may depend on its intension, not just its extension. For example, (in a state-description, on an assignment) $\Box x=y$ is true if and only if the variables x and y have the same intension; sameness of extension is insufficient. However, Carnap's account makes the intension of a predicate variable X *extensional* in the sense that the truth value of Xx is sensitive only to the extension of x, not to its intension (although Xx may have the opposite truth value in another state-description).[15] Thus he has restricted the values of predicate variables with no corresponding restriction on the semantics of open formulas. The result is widespread failure of standard rules for the second-order quantifiers, such as universal instantiation. Consider (9):

$$(9) \qquad \forall X \, \forall x \, \forall y \, (x=y \rightarrow (Xx \leftrightarrow Xy))$$

This is L-true (true in every state-description) on Carnap's semantics, for if $x=y$ is true then x and y have the same extension, so Xx and Xy have the same truth value because the intension of X is extensional, so $Xx \leftrightarrow Xy$ is true. However, if we instantiate X with the predicate $\lambda z(\Box x=z)$ and cash out the λ terms by Carnap's unrestricted λ-conversion rule, the result is (10):

---

[12] Barcan 1946b, p. 117.

[13] Carnap 1947, pp. 181–2; see also Carnap 1947, pp. 198–202.

[14] Myhill 1963, pp. 300–1.

[15] The distinction goes back to Russell and Whitehead's distinction between extensional and intensional functions, although they use a doxastic rather than a modal context to illustrate intensionality (Whitehead and Russell 1910, p. 196).

(10) $\forall x \, \forall y \, (x=y \rightarrow (\Box x=x \leftrightarrow \Box x=y))$

This is L-false, not L-true, on Carnap's semantics, for in every state-description some distinct individual concepts coincide in extension. Thus second-order universal instantiation fails.

Carnap accepted this criticism and conceded that his 1947 proposal about the values of the second-order variables needed revision.[16] In 1963 he presented a new and more general account of the semantics of higher-order modal languages within a framework of type theory, which he compares to that of Russell and Whitehead in *Principia Mathematica*. He describes two languages; one permits only extensional intensions ('non-modal intensions' or 'extensional properties'), the other permits non-extensional intensions ('modal intensions' or 'non-extensional properties') too. In the latter, the truth value of Xx may depend on the intension of x, not just on its extension.[17]

Carnap applied his new semantic analysis to Barcan's proof of the equivalence of material and strict identity (the necessity of identity). He claims that 'the result should be quite obvious', because what she had defined as I_m was not really material identity, as she intended; rather, it was already strict identity (I). His argument is that since the quantifier in the definiens $\lambda x, y (\forall X \, (Xx \rightarrow Xy))$ for I_m ranges over non-extensional as well as extensional intensions, it requires more than coincidence in extension between x and y.[18] Carnap is right about this much: one cannot prove Barcan's result without instantiating the quantifier with a predicate defined in terms of modal operators or the like. We can instantiate X with $\lambda z(Ixz)$, but I abbreviates $\lambda x, y (\forall X \, \Box(Xx \rightarrow Xy))$. However, in treating such instantiations as making I_m non-extensional, Carnap imposed his own semantics on Barcan's system. Although he could legitimately complain that she provided no alternative semantics, he was not entitled to assume that his was the only one possible. An alternative was already becoming clear as his discussion appeared: assign individuals (not individual concepts) as the values of the first-order variables and extensional intensions as the values of the second-order variables. Such an interpretation makes sense of Barcan's proof as showing that genuine material identity, an (extensional) relation between individuals, entails its own necessitation, however unwelcome such a result

---

[16] Carnap 1963b, p. 909. For his unrestricted λ-conversion rule see Carnap 1947, p. 185: 'Any lambda-operator can be eliminated in S_2 by conversion'.

[17] Carnap 1963a, pp. 890–3.

[18] Carnap 1963a, pp. 893–4.

may be to a logical positivist—since it threatens the supposed connection between necessity and analyticity or logical truth.

In response to Myhill's criticisms, Carnap defended his use of individual concepts in semantics:

> It seems to me that assigning intensions to *all* expressions of the hierarchy of types leads to a greater uniformity of the semantical method, especially for language systems which admit compound individual expressions. In systems of this kind we cannot regard individuals as values of the variables.[19]

The 'compound individual expressions' include definite descriptions, treated as complex singular terms. To put Carnap's point in Kripkean terminology: if we place non-rigid definite descriptions in the same semantic category as first-order variables, we should allow the latter to be non-rigid too. We saw in section 4.6 the awkwardness into which Stalnaker was led by violating that principle. More generally, if one grants a semantic freedom to constants while forbidding it to variables of the same category, one can expect failures of standard quantifier rules such as universal instantiation. The asymmetry is hard to justify. However, one can respect Carnap's principle without allowing first-order variables to be non-rigid, by not assigning them the same type as non-rigid definite descriptions. For example, following Russell, one might treat descriptions as quantifiers. We could even have a type of expressions whose values are individual concepts, if we like, and still have another type of expressions whose values are individuals.

The quoted passage also makes a more general appeal to a principle of semantic uniformity. One might try for such uniformity by equating the intensions of expressions of any given category with functions from worlds (or, more generally, indices) to extensions of the type usually associated with that category.[20] Call them *natural extensions*. Since the natural extension of a first-order variable or constant is an individual, its intension will then be an individual concept. Similarly, since the natural extension of a one-place predicate variable or constant is a set of individuals, its intension will be a function from worlds (or indices) to sets of individuals. But that is an extensional intension: exactly the mismatch Myhill pointed out. A more sophisticated approach is needed.

---

[19] Carnap 1963b, p. 910.
[20] An index may include components other than a world, such as a time.

For purposes of semantic uniformity, a better starting point is the constraint of compositionality. A systematic semantics should assign contents (of some sort) on the principle that the content of a complex expression is determined by the contents of its constituents. For definiteness, we may follow David Lewis by considering an unambiguous language with a categorial grammar and a type-theoretic semantics.[21] Every expression belongs to a unique grammatical category. There are some basic categories, say those of sentences (S) and singular terms (N). For any categories $C, C_1, \ldots, C_n$ there is the category $C/C_1 \ldots C_n$ of expressions that apply to expressions of categories $C_1, \ldots, C_n$ respectively to yield an expression of category C. Every non-basic category is derived from basic categories in a unique way by steps of that sort. For example, a two-place first-level predicate is of category S/NN; it applies to a pair of singular terms to yield a sentence. The semantics assigns every expression of category C a unique content of type t(C). Any entity of type t(C) is an appropriate content for an expression of category C. By compositionality, the content of an expression of category C is determined by the contents of expressions of categories $C/C_1 \ldots C_n$, $C_1, \ldots, C_n$. Thus an entity of type t(C) is determined by entities of types $t(C/C_1 \ldots C_n), t(C_1), \ldots, t(C_n)$. We can therefore regard something of type $t(C/C_1 \ldots C_n)$ as a function from things of types $t(C_1), \ldots, t(C_n)$ to something of type t(C), an idea with roots in Frege's philosophy of language. Lewis gives exactly that rule for what he calls the 'intensions' of expressions of derived categories. He contrasts such intensions with 'Carnapian intensions', functions from indices to natural extensions. For derived categories, Lewis says, 'it is best to foresake extensions and Carnapian intensions in the interest of generality'.[22]

The functional account of types for derived categories says nothing directly about types for basic categories, since the latter are not of the form $C/C_1 \ldots C_n$. In particular, it does not say whether those types contain natural extensions. However, since the functional rule introduces no worlds or indices into things of type $t(C/C_1 \ldots C_n)$ unless they were already present in entities of at least one of the types $t(C_1), \ldots, t(C_n), t(C)$, worlds or indices will figure in the contents of some expressions only if they figure in the contents of some basic expressions. Thus the functional rule indirectly constrains the type of

---

[21] Lewis 1970.

[22] Lewis 1970, p. 197. He describes Carnapian intensions at p. 194 and gives the general rule for appropriate intensions for a derived category at p. 198.

a basic category. Propositional modal logic offers an example. The operator $\Box$ is of category S/S. If the content of a sentence were its natural extension, its truth value, then the content of $\Box$ would be a truth function, which it is not, since $\Box A$ is true for some true sentences A and false for others. By contrast, if the content of a sentence is its Carnapian intension, then $\Box$ can have an appropriate content, a function from Carnapian intensions for sentences to Carnapian intensions for sentences: it maps the function that maps every world to truth to itself, and maps every other function from worlds to truth values to the function that maps every world to falsity.[23] But that content is no Carnapian intension, since it is no function from worlds or indices, even though we could artificially repack the same information into such a function, one that maps each world w to the function that maps the function that maps every world to truth to truth, and maps every other function from worlds to truth values to falsity.[24]

Does semantic uniformity require that if the type for *some* basic category is of Carnapian intensions, then the type for *every* basic category is of Carnapian intensions too? If so, we have an argument that the contents of singular terms (basic category N) are individual concepts, if the contents of sentences (basic category S) are Carnapian intensions. Lewis indeed equates the intensions of expressions of category N with their Carnapian intensions, functions from indices to individuals, but he denies that his account of intensions for derived categories depends on his account of intensions for basic categories.[25]

The appeal to semantic uniformity is in any case shaky, for at least two reasons. First, if basic categories are very few (N, S, perhaps no others), the generalization that the type for every basic category is of Carnapian intensions gains us little in theoretical simplicity, elegance, and explanatory power. Second, even the supposed asymmetry in treatment of categories N and S assumes an ultra-realist interpretation of the possible worlds semantics. Pre-theoretically, while it is quite natural to equate the content of a singular term with an individual, it is rather artificial to equate the content of a sentence with a function from worlds or indices to truth values. We might

---

[23] One will need a more complex account if one does not want the modal operators to range over all worlds (thereby validating S5).

[24] For simplicity, the distinction between indices and worlds is ignored in this discussion of $\Box$.

[25] Lewis 1970, pp. 194 and 200. Semantically, a function from indices to individuals plays the role of an individual concept, but the terminology is slightly awkward, since a Lewisian index contains various features of a linguistic context, in addition to a world and a time (pp. 194–6, 226–31).

regard such a function as a convenient *ersatz* content, good enough for the model theory of a modal language, just as in other contexts a mere truth value is a convenient *ersatz* content, good enough for the model theory of a non-modal language. Perhaps not even a Carnapian intension is a good enough *ersatz* content once propositional attitude ascriptions are added to the language. As already seen, contingentists in particular must avoid an ultra-realist interpretation of possible worlds semantics.[26] Outside the artifice of such semantics, the contents of sentences may be propositions. It is not clear that they really are functions from worlds or indices. Perhaps they are more like Russellian structures of the objects, properties, and relations they are about, or Fregean structures of modes of presentation.[27]

To reinforce the point, consider the semantics of a predicate such as 'is square'. It is of category S/N; it applies to a singular term to yield a sentence. By the compositional rule, its content is a function from things of type t(N) to things of type t(S). On the envisaged view of types for basic categories, things of type t(N) are individuals and things of type t(S) are functions from indices to truth values. Thus the content of 'is square' is a function from individuals to functions from indices to truth values. It maps each individual o to the function that maps each index w to truth if o is square at w and to falsity otherwise. Thus it encodes exactly the same information as the function that maps w to the function that maps o to truth if o is square at w and to falsity otherwise, and as the function that maps w to the sets of o such that o is square at w, the standard possible worlds semantics for that predicate. But no contingentist and not every necessitist will take this semantics in an ultra-realist spirit. For a contingentist, there could have been squares that are actually nothing. No actual function has such a square as an argument; no actual set has such a square as a member. There is no such thing to be an argument or a member. The intension of 'is square' cannot really contain all squares there would have been in counterfactual circumstances. In Stalnaker's terms, not every aspect of the semantics is representationally significant.

We might try explaining what we are up to in the semantics like this. Really, 'is square' refers directly to squareness, the property of being square.

---

[26] As explained in section 1.4, a modal realist such as Lewis counts as a necessitist, not as a contingentist.

[27] David Kaplan proposes such an attitude to possible worlds semantics at pp. 724–5 of his 1975. He criticizes Kripke's discussion of rigid designation as distorted by over-reliance on the possible worlds picture (Kaplan 1989a, p. 493 n. 17), and complains that possible worlds semantics collapses the distinction between direct reference and other forms of obstinately rigid designation (Kaplan 1989b, p. 579).

For the model-theoretic semantics, what matters is which things would have had that property in which circumstances. Mathematically, it is easier to pretend that we have encoded what matters in a set-theoretic construct, such as a function, so that we can bypass modal metaphysics. But our sense of which aspects of the semantics are merely pretence comes from our knowledge of the intended reference. To assign 'is square' different extensions with respect to different worlds and times is in no deep way to treat it as a non-rigid designator; it is merely to acknowledge the non-semantic fact that different things would have been square in different circumstances. In particular, actual squareness is not the set of actually square things. On this view, incidentally, the legitimacy of non-extensional second-level predicates is beyond question: two properties may differ in their own higher-level properties yet coincide in extension. For example, even if whatever has a heart has a kidney and vice versa, having a heart may entail having a heart even though having a kidney does not entail having a heart. Thus the formal semantic asymmetry between a rigid treatment of names and first-order variables and a non-rigid treatment of sentences and predicates is an artefact, reflecting only the set-theoretic encoding of the relevant modal information in the semantic values of sentences and predicates.[28]

Ultimately, that may not be the best way of formulating the idea, since it reduces the semantic difference between names and predicates almost to vanishing point. One might come closer to the intended semantics by using the predicate 'is square' in the metalanguage, not a noun phrase such as 'squareness' or 'the property of being square'. Nevertheless, enough is clear to show, pace Carnap, that treating the contents of singular terms as individuals and the contents of predicates and sentences as Carnapian intensions is consistent with semantic uniformity at the intended level.

The work of Kripke and others in the 1960s made quantifying over individuals the default for the ground level of quantification. It is pre-theoretically more natural and theoretically simpler than quantifying over individual concepts. Since the latter are built up out of individuals as set-theoretic functions, why not start by talking about the individuals themselves? We saw in section 2.4 the difficulties into which quantifying over all individual concepts led Carnap.

[28] Soames 2002, pp. 259–62, rejects a similar view of rigidity for predicates on the grounds that it trivializes the distinction between rigid and non-rigid predicates. That may make it unsuitable for his purposes; it does not do so for ours.

Post Carnap, quantifying over *all* individual concepts gradually became marginal.[29] An apparently more promising approach is to quantify over *some* individual concepts. The picture might be that an individual concept belongs to the domain if and only if its values at different worlds add up to one substance, just as in tense logic an individual concept might belong to the domain if and only if its values at different times are the time slices of one genuine substance. With a model theory on which every set of individual concepts is the domain of lowest level quantification of some model, one can avoid at least some of the technical difficulties that Carnap faced. For example, (11) is no longer valid whenever A is an extensional context for x:

(11) $\Box \exists x A \rightarrow \exists x \Box A$

For although the truth of the antecedent still guarantees that some individual concept satisfies $\Box A$ as a value of x, that concept need not belong to the domain of quantification. Thus 'Necessarily something numbers the planets but nothing necessarily numbers the planets' is no longer treated as inconsistent (on the reading that contradicts an instance of (11)). Furthermore, the restricted interpretation escapes problem of unaxiomatizability. Yet the theory can still subsume as special cases both quantification over all individual concepts and, in effect, quantification over all individuals (qua rigid individual concepts). One can then assess the effect of various conditions on the domain.[30] Such a theory may appear to have the benefits of greater generality. It undoubtedly has instrumental value for investigating many comparatively weak systems of quantified modal logic.

In several ways, the new interpretation does not fit Carnap's case for assigning individual concepts to first-level variables. The general approach of making a non-contingent distinction between those individual concepts privileged to be values of variables and the rest looks metaphysical rather than logical. More specifically, recall Carnap's desideratum of treating definite descriptions and first-level variables as singular terms in a semantically

---

[29] See however the work of Aldo Bressan (1972), strongly advocated by Nuel Belnap (1972). Bressan was influenced by Carnap and motivated by problems in the foundations of physics. See also Parks 1976. For related but even more complex accounts of quantification in modal contexts see, for example, Lambert and van Fraassen 1970 and Scott 1970.

[30] This is what Garson calls the 'intensional interpretation' (2006, pp. 288–93), as opposed to the 'conceptual interpretation' on which the domain must contain all individual concepts (2006, pp. 286–8). For conditions on the domain corresponding to various logical principles see Garson 2006, pp. 293–4. The idea of using a privileged set of individual concepts to represent substances goes back at least to Thomason 1969.

uniform way. For instance, 'the number of planets' is a proper definite description; since exactly one number numbers the planets, there is such a number as the number of planets.[31] However, the intension of that definite description may not be in the domain of individual concepts for purposes of quantification. Indeed, it had better not be if 'Nothing necessarily numbers the planets' is to come out true (on the $\neg \exists x \, \Box A$ reading). Thus a denotation good enough to make the definite description a non-empty singular term is not good enough to serve as a value of a bound variable.

The mismatch between definite descriptions and quantified variables has repercussions in the logic. Read the constant n as 'the number of the planets' and '=' as coincidence of individual concepts at the world of evaluation. Then the envisaged account verifies (12):

(12) $\exists x \, x=n \, \& \, \forall x \, \neg \Box x=n$

But despite the non-emptiness condition in the first conjunct, we cannot apply the rule of universal instantiation to instantiate the second conjunct with n, because (13) is true:

(13) $\Box n=n$

Necessarily, the number of the planets is the number of the planets. For Carnap, the situation is even worse, since he has an unrestricted rule of λ-conversion. Thus (12) and the negation of (13) are equivalent to (14) and (15) respectively:

(14) $\exists x \, x=n \, \& \, \forall x \, \lambda y(\neg \Box y=n)x$

(15) $\lambda y(\neg \Box y=n)n$

Thus the non-modal argument form of free universal instantiation with premises $\exists x \, x=n$ and $\forall x \, Fx$ and conclusion Fn is ruled invalid (put $\lambda y(\neg \Box y=n)$ for F). Similarly, the non-modal argument form of free existential generalization with premises $\exists x \, x=n$ and Fn and conclusion $\exists x \, Fx$ is ruled invalid (put $\lambda y(\Box y=n)$ for F). Both argument forms are valid in all standard versions of free logic. Of course, they remain valid on the new interpretation if one assumes F to be extensional, but Carnap rejected that assumption on grounds of semantic uniformity. Although even more restricted forms of the universal

---

[31] If you have anti-platonist scruples about numbers, try 'the object that is the moon if the coin came up heads and the sun otherwise' instead.

instantiation and existential generalization rules are still available with an auxiliary premise such as $\exists x \; \Box x = n$, the strength of the latter and its modal character merely emphasize how drastically the logic has been curtailed.

Of course, the weaker a logic, the wider the range of theoretical questions on which some will commend it for its neutrality. But weakness is not much more of a virtue in logic than it is anywhere else. Although the parties to a logical dispute sometimes need a logical theory neutral on the question at issue as a shared framework for their dialectic, we have already seen that such ad hoc applications of logic constitute no proper standard of validity. No logical law is neutral in every dialectical context. In a dispute between classical and relativistic physics, a weak physical theory neutral between them may be useful as a shared framework for discussion, but if everyone constrained their physical theories to serve such dialectical purposes physics would grind to a halt. In that respect, logic is less different from the natural sciences than many imagine. If some philosophers persuade themselves that $\exists x \; x = n$ and $\forall x \; Fx$ may be true while Fn is false, it does not follow that arguing from $\exists x \; x = n$ and $\forall x \; Fx$ to Fn really is invalid. Although not all laws of physics are laws of logic, that has nothing to do with whether the former are more controversial than the latter. Rather, the difference is that some terms, such as *mass* and *energy*, are held constant in laws of physics but generalized out in laws of logic, while no term is held constant in laws of logic but generalized out in laws of physics. In that non-dialectical sense, logic is more general than physics. This generality of logic in no way requires us to interpret first-level quantification in modal logic in terms of selected individual concepts rather than individuals.

The semantic and logical case for replacing quantification over individuals by quantification over individual concepts is feeble. Is there a metaphysical case, however little it would have pleased Carnap? The central problem for any such case is this. Individual concepts are functions from worlds or indices to individuals. Presumably, therefore, individuals are prior to individual concepts in the metaphysical order, in the sense that the latter are constituted out of the former, not vice versa. The natural explanatory order is to start talking about individuals and then explain in those terms what individual concepts are.[32] Thus it is metaphysically perverse for one's bottom

---

[32] Garson 2006, pp. 292–3, claims that the selected individual concepts are more real than the individuals that constitute them, and correspond better to ordinary things. His view seems to require an at least partly instrumentalist account of the semantics, which he does not supply.

level domain of quantification to contain only individual concepts, not the individuals out of which they are constituted.

Someone might object that metaphysical commitments cannot be read so easily off a semantic theory. But that objection hardly helps when, as now, we are considering an attempted metaphysical motivation for the semantics.

There is a difference between designing one's preferred theoretical language and describing an already present natural or theoretical language. One has good reason not to theorize in a metaphysically perverse and therefore unperspicuous language, and so good reason to prefer a theoretical language whose bottom level domain of quantification does not contain only individual concepts. But one has no reason of that sort not to describe English or another theoretician's formal language as metaphysically perverse.

For example, David Lewis and other modal realists deny that natural languages and even the formal languages of quantified modal logic present modal metaphysics perspicuously. It would not be self-defeating for them to interpret the first-level quantifiers of such languages over individual concepts. Indeed, Lewis's counterpart theory works in a related way.[33] On his view, the individuals we normally talk about are worldbound: each is part of only one world. My statement 'I could have been thinner' is true because I have a thinner counterpart in some other world, someone sufficiently like me in that world, in relevant respects and compared to its other inhabitants. Lewis translates sentences in a first-order modal language into sentences in the first-order non-modal language of counterpart theory. The latter are supposed to present the same truth conditions as the former in a metaphysically more perspicuous way. One can simulate a version of counterpart theory by quantifying over those individual concepts whose values at any pair of worlds are counterparts of each other. If everything is its only counterpart in its own world and has at least one counterpart in every world and the counterpart relation is reflexive, symmetric, and transitive, it follows that an individual $o*$ in a world $w*$ is a counterpart of an individual o in a world w if and only if some individual concept in the domain maps w

---

[33] Garson 2006, pp. 291–2, treats quantification over a domain of selected individual concepts as a framework for counterpart theory and, in tense logic, for a theory of substances as spatiotemporal worms made up of time slices.

to o and $w*$ to $o*$.[34] However, those assumptions are too strong for most counterpart theorists. In his original presentation of counterpart theory, Lewis denied that it would be plausible to postulate that the counterpart relation is symmetric, or that it is transitive, or that everything has it to something in every world.[35] He later retracted even the postulate that everything is its only counterpart in its own world.[36] Despite the analogies, quantification over individual concepts lacks the flexibility that counterpart theory requires. One could restore some flexibility by allowing partial individual concepts, with no value for some worlds. But even that provides no natural way to simulate a non-symmetric counterpart relation, or one holding between two things in the same world.

As the case of counterpart theory suggests, quantification over individual concepts is marginal to metaphysics as well as to logic and semantics. Richard Montague expressed a view much closer to that which now predominates when he criticized earlier work for 'the drawback of not allowing unrestricted quantification over ordinary individuals' and added 'Without such quantification . . . I do not believe that one can treat ordinary language in a natural way or meet adequately Quine's objections to quantification into indirect contexts'.[37] As he pointed out, in higher-order logic based on quantification over individuals we can still achieve the effect of quantifying over individual concepts by quantifying on a one-place second-order variable and explicitly restricting it with the condition that necessarily it applies to exactly one individual.[38] Individual concepts will play no further role in this book.

Despite its compelling simplicity, the Kripkean account of individual variables in modal logic has always found opponents, although their motivation has gradually changed. The desire for a uniform semantic treatment of individual variables, proper names, and definite descriptions was slowly displaced

---

[34] Proof: Suppose that $o*$ in $w*$ is a counterpart of o in w. By the axiom of choice, some individual concept maps w to o, $w*$ to $o*$, and every other world to a counterpart of o in that world, for by hypothesis if $w = w*$ then $o = o*$ and every world contains a counterpart of o. Then the values of the individual concept at any pair of worlds are counterparts of each other, because they are counterparts of o and therefore of each other, for by hypothesis the counterpart relation is reflexive, symmetric, and transitive. Thus the individual concept qualifies for membership of the domain. The converse is trivial, by definition of the domain.

[35] Lewis 1968, pp. 28–9. For non-transitivity see also Lewis 1986, pp. 219, 245–6.

[36] Lewis 1986, p. 232.

[37] Montague 1970a, pp. 145–6.

[38] Montague 1970a, p. 132.

in that role by a quest for the metaphysical groundwork of individuation. As we saw, the semantic and metaphysical objections pull in contrary directions. Nevertheless, without the earlier history of semantic controversy, it might later have looked much less natural to complicate the general modal and temporal semantics of quantification to fit specific metaphysical theories about the nature of specific kinds of individual, rather than treating any incompatibility as a problem for the latter. David Lewis's brilliantly literal-minded interpretation of possible worlds semantics still gives counterpart theory more influence and prestige in metaphysics than other comparably messy forms of deviant logic enjoy, even though most philosophers are officially committed to rejecting modal realism. But if the decision is made on grounds of simplicity, strength, and naturalness in logic and semantics, compatibly with what we know, then the Kripkean account wins with ease.

5.4 Montague's intensional logic

Montague developed his system IL of higher-order intensional logic through his work on the semantics of natural languages. His methodology is to construct formal languages so flexible that large fragments of natural languages can be translated into them. Having stipulated a semantics for the formal language, he has thereby provided such a semantics for the natural language fragment too. His semantics is model-theoretic: the aim is to characterize formal structural and logical features of meaning, not to single out an intended model. A model has a set of indices or points of reference. Montague conceives an index as a sequence of relevant features of a context of use: a possible world and a time if the language contains modal and tense operators respectively, but also an agent and a place if it contains indexical terms like 'I' and 'here', and so on. For present purposes, we may harmlessly simplify by equating indices with worlds, since only the latter are relevant to modal logic.[39]

Montague also uses his intensional apparatus to handle intentional constructions in natural languages. Once one has associated the sentence 'There are

---

[39] See Montague 1970a, pp. 121–2. From a contemporary perspective, Montague's indices misleadingly conflate distinct roles: a circumstance of evaluation (to be varied by intensional operators in the course of compositional semantic evaluation) and a context of utterance (to assign a reference to an indexical expression, typically not varied in the course of semantic evaluation). The two roles are formally separated in two-dimensional intensional logic. See Kaplan 1989a, pp. 500–10.

talking horses' with a function from worlds to truth values, it is natural to treat that function as the proposition that there are talking horses and analyse 'John believes that there are talking horses' as ascribing a relation of belief between John and the proposition. This aspect of Montague's semantics has been criticized on the grounds that such functions are too coarse-grained to serve as the objects of belief. For any two logically equivalent sentences determine the same function from possible worlds to truth values, so his account implies that whoever believes that $P \to P$ believes that $((Q \to R) \to Q) \to Q$, an implausible result. Fortunately, for present purposes it does not matter. This book is about metaphysical modality, not intentionality. We may therefore ignore whatever complications of Montague's semantics are needed to handle the latter.[40] The logic of metaphysical modality can make do with coarse-grained propositions.

Montague made his intensional language higher-order to accommodate a general semantic theory for natural languages, a 'universal grammar'. Consider, for example, the adjective 'possible' on the ordinary attributive reading discussed in section 1.3, so we may paraphrase 'Everyone is a possible murderer' as 'Everyone could have been a murderer'. Thus 'possible' combines with a common noun phrase to form a more complex common noun phrase. A general compositional semantics for an intensional language assigns each of its semantically significant terms an intension and an extension (relative to a model, in a model-theoretic semantics). 'Possible' is a semantically significant term of English; one can learn what it means. Thus a general compositional semantics for English as an intensional language will assign 'possible' an intension and an extension. They must determine the intension and extension of 'possible F' from the intension and extension of 'F'. The mere extension of 'F' does not determine even the extension of 'possible F'. For instance, 'round square' and 'murderer of Queen Victoria' have the same extension, which maps everything to falsity; that is also the extension of 'possible round square', whereas the extension of 'possible murderer of Queen Victoria' maps many people to truth. Thus both the intension and extension of 'possible' determine the intension and extension of 'possible F' from the intension of 'F'. In effect, the extension of 'possible' is a function from common noun phrase intensions to common noun phrase extensions;

---

[40] Montague tries to defuse the objection by invoking another notion of belief, whose objects are linguistic entities (1970a, p. 139). Muskens 2007 proposes a modification of Montague's system to handle hyperintensionality.

the intension of 'possible' is the corresponding function from common noun phrase intensions to common noun phrase intensions. But the extension of a common noun phrase is a function from individuals to truth values; its intension is a function from worlds to such extensions. Thus the extension of 'possible' is a function m that maps each function f from worlds to functions from individuals to truth values to a function $m(f)$ from individuals to truth values. In particular, for each individual i, $m(f)(i)$ is truth if $f(w)(i)$ is truth for at least one world w; otherwise $m(f)(i)$ is falsity. Correspondingly, the intension of 'possible' is the function that maps each world to m. The intension is constant because we read 'possible' as unrestricted; some restricted readings yield a non-constant intension. Less formally, the intension of 'possible' is the function that maps each property p of individuals to the property of possibly having p. The point is that becoming explicit about the intensional semantics of attributive adjectives forces us to generalize over intensions of a type appropriate to common noun phrases, because we define a function over all such intensions.[41] We thereby enable ourselves to quantify into common noun phrase position: the universal generalization of a sentence A with respect to a variable in that position is true if A is true under the assignment of each appropriate intension to that variable, and false otherwise. In his intensional semantics, Montague formally provides for quantification over each type in his hierarchy. Since he wrote, the semantics of natural languages in the tradition he initiated has been one main application of higher-order modal logic.

Montague's semantics for IL uses a type-theoretic framework with the set of possible individuals and the set of truth values as its two basic types. For any pair of types there is the derived type of functions from one to the other.[42] Of course, were all types so constructed, the logic would be purely extensional. Sentence operators would denote truth functions, because sentences denote truth values, and so on for other categories. To inject intensionality, Montague introduces a set I of worlds (indices). Although I is not itself a type, he has for each type t a type t^I of functions from I to t. In his terminology, if t is the type of possible *denotations* for some category of term, t^I is the type of possible *senses* for that category. The language of

---

[41] Montague gives the intentional example 'alleged murderer' (1970b, pp. 237–43). His treatment of adjectives followed work by Hans Kamp and Terence Parsons.

[42] For IL see Montague 1970b (he calls it 'intensional logic'). Both Gallin 1975 and Muskens 2007 use IL as the starting point of their accounts of higher-order modal logic.

IL has an operator $^\wedge$ that takes a term α of any category to a term $^\wedge\alpha$ whose denotation is the sense of α; thus if α denotes something of type t, $^\wedge\alpha$ denotes something of type t^I. This is reminiscent of Fregean semantics for indirect contexts, such as those supposedly created by belief ascriptions: the denotation of a term in an indirect context is its sense in a direct context. Montague therefore calls his interpretations 'Fregean'.[43]

The language has a sign $\equiv$ for extensional identity. For any terms α and β of the same category, the sentence $\alpha \equiv \beta$ is true at a world if α and β have the same denotation there, and otherwise is false. For a sentence A, tautology T, and world w, the following are all equivalent: $^\wedge A \equiv {}^\wedge T$ is true at w; $^\wedge A$ and $^\wedge T$ have the same denotation at w; A and T have the same sense; A and T have the same truth value at every world. Thus $^\wedge A \equiv {}^\wedge T$ is true at every world if A is; otherwise it is false at every world. Montague therefore equates $\Box A$ with such a sentence. Since the definition does not restrict the range of worlds, it validates the modal system S5; a more complicated account would be needed to generate a weaker modal logic. For simplicity, we focus on such unrestricted accounts.

Montague handles quantification over all members of any type by λ-abstraction. Let t_α be the type for a term α. Then $t_{\lambda v(\alpha)}$ is the type of functions from t_v to t_α. On an assignment $\underline{a}$ of values to variables, $\lambda v(\alpha)$ denotes at w the function that maps each $d \in t_v$ to the denotation at w of α on the assignment $\underline{a}[v/d]$. Thus $\lambda v(A) \equiv \lambda v(T)$ is true at w on a if and only if A is true at w on $a[v/d]$ for every $d \in t_v$. Montague therefore equates $\forall v\, A$ with such a sentence. The usual truth functors are introduced by similar means.

Unfortunately, despite its expressive power, IL is not perspicuously organized as a higher-order modal logic. The problem is a higher-order version of the asymmetry in treatment between variables and constants for which Myhill criticized Carnap. The recursive semantics for IL defines the denotation of each term of the language in a model relative to a world and an assignment of values to variables. The model maps each non-logical atomic constant to a function from worlds to denotations of the appropriate type. That function can map distinct worlds to distinct denotations. However, an assignment simply assigns each variable a denotation of an appropriate type, which it

[43] Montague 1970b, pp. 228–9. Church's work on the logic of sense and denotation (1951) played a significant role in mediating between Fregean and intensional semantics; Montague describes it as appearing to be the 'first serious and detailed attempt to construct' an intensional logic (1970a, p. 145). Church 1973 later interpreted a revised version of the logic in terms of possible worlds.

denotes at every world on that assignment. Thus variables, unlike constants, are rigid in extension. In Fregean terms, variables with the same denotation also have the same sense. For example, since a sentence denotes a truth value, on a given assignment a sentence variable is either true at all worlds or false at all worlds.

The repercussions for IL as a higher-order modal logic are startling. The semantics validates (16), making it true at every world in every model:

(16) $\forall X\, (\Box X \leftrightarrow X)$

This is a step back from Lewis and Langford in 1932. Of course, the modal collapse is not quite as catastrophic as it looks, for Montague's semantics invalidates the move from (16) to (17), where A is a non-logical atomic sentence constant:

(17) $\Box A \leftrightarrow A$

Since A varies in truth value across worlds in some models, (17) is invalid. But this failure of universal instantiation is itself problematic, for A is semantically beyond reproach, unlike the examples that motivate free logic. A similar mismatch affects quantification into predicate position. Montague's semantics validates (18) but not (19), where Y is a one-place second-order variable and F a one-place non-logical atomic predicate constant:

(18) $\forall Y\, \forall x\, (\Box Yx \leftrightarrow Yx)$

(19) $\forall x\, (\Box Fx \leftrightarrow Fx)$

If we try to derive (17) from (16), we can reach (20):

(20) $\lambda X(\Box X)A \leftrightarrow A$

This is valid because $\lambda X(\Box X)$ merely denotes the identity truth function that maps truth to truth and falsity to falsity. But that just reveals a problematic failure of λ-conversion: since (17) is invalid, so is (21):

(21) $\lambda X(\Box X)A \leftrightarrow \Box A$

This instance of λ-conversion fails whenever A is contingently true; it requires no semantic pathology in A. These troubles for Montague's semantics arise at a far more elementary level than the dispute between contingentism and necessitism.[44]

---

[44]   For related criticisms of IL see Muskens 2007, pp. 629–31, 634.

We can still express in IL what we wanted (16) to mean, by quantifying over sentence senses rather than sentence denotations. However, variables for sentence senses do not occupy sentence position, since quantifying into sentence position is quantifying over sentence denotations. Thus the procedure is cumbersome and, in any case, the asymmetry between variables and constants is inadequately motivated. If a constant of a given category can behave in a given way, a variable of the same category should be able to behave in that way too on a suitable assignment.

5.5 The system ML_p of higher-order modal logic

Montague inspired a semantics for higher-modal logic more natural than his own. It is ML_p, developed in detail by his student Daniel Gallin after Montague's murder in 1971. Although IL and ML_p are expressively equivalent, ML_p achieves the same effect as IL by logically and philosophically more perspicuous means.[45] ML_p is based on a type-theoretic hierarchy of individuals and relations, rather than individuals, truth values, and functions. The only underived type is the type e of individuals. For any types $t_1, \ldots, t_n$, there is the derived type $<t_1, \ldots, t_n>$ of relations between things of types $t_1, \ldots, t_n$; such a relation is treated as a function that maps each world to a set of n-tuples of members of $t_1, \ldots, t_n$ respectively, the extension of that relation at that world. There are no other types. Since we equate properties with one-place relations, for any type t, $<t>$ is the type of properties of things of type t.[46] Similarly, since we equate propositions with zero-place relations, $<>$ is the type of propositions. Since $<>$ is the only 0-tuple, the empty set, we can equate truth with its singleton and falsity with the empty set.

Possible worlds enter the hierarchy only as the inputs to relations. One could preserve the overall structure of the hierarchy of individuals and relations while regarding the identification of the latter with functions from

---

[45] See Gallin 1975, pp. 67–78 for exposition of ML_p and pp. 98–105 for comparison with IL. Unlike ML_p, the system in Bressan 1972 is based on individual concepts rather than individuals.

[46] Montague uses 'predicate' or 'relation-in-intension' where 'relation' is used here, and 'relation' for the extension of a predicate at a world, but 'property' in the same way as here (1970a, pp. 122–3). The present terminology has been preferred because philosophers tend to read 'relation' on a par with 'property', and 'predicate' as metalinguistic. He suggests there that the 'idea of construing propositions, properties, and relations-in-intension as functions' from worlds to extensions first occurs in Kripke 1963, although it is at best implicit there.

possible worlds as a mere convenient fiction. In any case, starting the hierarchy with individuals rather than individual concepts involves no troublesome asymmetry between derived and underived types. It is normal for the inductive clause of a definition to have elements not in the base clause.

The language of ML_P has for each type t a countable infinity of non-logical constants and a countable infinity of variables. A variable or constant of type t is a non-logical *symbol* of type t. The only typed logical symbol is '$=$', which is of type $<e, e>$. Formulas are of type $<>$. An atomic formula is any sequence of the form $Ss_1 \ldots s_n$ where $S, s_1, \ldots, s_n$ are symbols of types $<t_1, \ldots, t_n>, t_1, \ldots, t_n$ respectively, although conventionally we write $s_1 = s_2$ rather than $= s_1 s_2$. If A and B are formulas, so are $\neg A$, $A \& B$, and $\Box A$, as is $\forall v A$ for any variable v of any type. Nothing else has a type. Other logical expressions are defined as metalinguistic abbreviations in the usual way.

ML_P has a natural model-theoretic semantics. A *standard inhabited frame* is simply an ordered pair $<W, D>$ of sets W and D. We define the domain dom(t) of each type t in the frame by treating D as the domain of individuals and W as the set of worlds. More formally, where P(X) is the power set of the set X and X^Y is the set of functions from Y to X:

$$\text{dom}(e) = D$$

$$\text{dom}(<t_1, \ldots, t_n>) = (P(\text{dom}(t_1) \times \ldots \times \text{dom}(t_n)))^W$$

A *standard model* based on $<W, D>$ is a triple $<W, D, V>$ where V is a function mapping each non-logical constant c of any type t to $V(c) \in \text{dom}(t)$ (since the language contains individual constants, this means that no model is based on the frame if D is empty). Given a frame, an *assignment* is a function $\underline{a}$ mapping each variable v of any type t to $\underline{a}(v) \in \text{dom}(t)$. Relative to each standard model M = $<W, D, V>$ and assignment $\underline{a}$, each typed expression α has an intension $\text{in}_{M,\underline{a}}(\alpha)$ of the appropriate type, according to these rules, where $w \in W$, v is a variable of type t and $S, s_1, \ldots, s_n$ are symbols of types $<t_1, \ldots, t_n>, t_1, \ldots, t_n$ respectively:

$$\text{in}_{M,\underline{a}}(v) = \underline{a}(v)$$

$$\text{in}_{M,\underline{a}}(c) = V(c)$$

$$\text{in}_{M,\underline{a}}(=)(w) = \{<d, d>: d \in D\}$$

$$\text{in}_{M,\underline{a}}(Ss_1 \ldots s_n)(w) = \{<>: <\text{in}_{M,\underline{a}}(s_1), \ldots, \text{in}_{M,\underline{a}}(s_n)> \in \text{in}_{M,\underline{a}}(S)(w)\}$$

$$in_{M,a}(\neg A)(w) = \{<>\} - in_{M,a}(A)(w)^{47}$$

$$in_{M,a}(A \& B)(w) = in_{M,a}(A)(w) \cap in_{M,a}(B)(w)$$

$$in_{M,a}(\Box A)(w) = \cap_{w^* \in W}\, in_{M,a}(A)(w^*)$$

$$in_{M,a}(\forall v\, A)(w) = \cap_{d \in dom(t)}\, in_{M,a[v/d]}(A)(w)$$

The semantics has been put in this slightly unfamiliar form to show how it works at a single level of content, treated as intensions. However, since in a model M a formula A is true at a world w on an assignment $\underline{a}$ (M, w, $\underline{a} \vDash A$) if and only if $<> \in in_{M,a}(A)(w)$, we can recast the clauses for the intensions of formulas in more familiar truth-conditional form:

M, w, $\underline{a} \vDash Ss_1 \ldots s_n$ if and only if $<in_{M,a}(s_1), \ldots, in_{M,a}(s_n)> \in in_{M,a}(S)(w)$

M, w, $\underline{a} \vDash s_1 = s_2$ if and only if $in_{M,a}(s_1) = in_{M,a}(s_2)$

M, w, $\underline{a} \vDash \neg A$ if and only if not M, w, $\underline{a} \vDash A$

M, w, $\underline{a} \vDash A \& B$ if and only if M, w, $\underline{a} \vDash A$ and M, w, $\underline{a} \vDash B$

M, w, $\underline{a} \vDash \Box A$ if and only if for all $w^* \in W$, M, w^*, $\underline{a} \vDash A$

M, w, $\underline{a} \vDash \forall v\, A$ if and only if for all $d \in dom(t)$, M, w, $\underline{a}[v/d] \vDash A$

An attractive feature of this semantics is that the permissible contents for a non–logical constant of any type are exactly the permissible values for a variable of that type. There is no asymmetry in treatment between constants and variables such as distorted the systems of Carnap, Montague, and Stalnaker. Thus instantiating a universal generalization with a constant of appropriate type becomes unproblematic.

A formula A is valid in a standard model M if and only if M, w, $\underline{a} \vDash A$ for every $w \in W$ and assignment $\underline{a}$. A is *standardly valid* if and only if A is valid in every standard model; a schema is standardly valid if and only if every instance of it is. A is a *standard logical consequence* of a set Γ of formulas if and only if for every standard model M = <W, D, V>, $w \in W$ and assignment $\underline{a}$, if M, w, $\underline{a} \vDash B$ for every $B \in \Gamma$ then M, w, $\underline{a} \vDash A$. Thus A is standardly valid if and only if A is a standard logical consequence of the empty set. We can also define model structures and centred models by designating a member $w_@$ of W as the actual world of M, so that A is true in M if and only if it is true at $w_@$ (on all assignments).

---

[47] $X - Y = \{x \in X: x \notin Y\}$.

The second-order non-modal fragment of ML_p excludes $\Box$ and symbols of types other than e and $<e, \ldots, e>$. For such formulas the modal dimension of a model is inert, so the standardly valid second-order non-modal formulas of ML_p are just the formulas valid on the standard semantics for second-order non-modal logic. As is well known, the latter are not recursively enumerable. Consequently, the standardly valid formulas of ML_p are not recursively enumerable either. Thus no formal axiomatic system is sound and complete for the standard semantics of ML_p. However, as Leon Henkin first showed in the non-modal case, there is a sound and complete axiomatic system for higher-order logic with respect to a wider class of models.[48] The trick is to drop the requirement that the domain of a higher type must contain every set of the relevant kind.

Gallin constructs a Henkin-style generalized semantics for ML_p. The definitions of the intension of a term and the truth of a formula at a world in a model are just as before. The only change is in the recursive clause of the definition of the domain of a type: instead of requiring $\mathrm{dom}(<t_1, \ldots, t_n>)$ to be $(P(\mathrm{dom}(t_1) \times \ldots \times \mathrm{dom}(t_n)))^W$, the new clause merely requires the former to be a non-empty subset of the latter. Since the function dom is no longer uniquely determined by W and the domain D of individuals, dom is made a constituent of the frame in its own right. A *general frame* is such a pair $<W, \mathrm{dom}>$. Similarly, a *general model* is a triple $<W, \mathrm{dom}, V>$. As before, V maps each constant c of type t to $V(c) \in \mathrm{dom}(t)$ and an assignment $\underline{a}$ maps each variable v of type t to $\underline{a}(v) \in \mathrm{dom}(t)$, so the symmetry between constants and variables of the same type is maintained. Validity is defined for general models just like validity for standard models. A formula A is a *g-logical consequence* of a set Γ of formulas if and only if for every general model $M = <W, \mathrm{dom}, V>$, $w \in W$ and assignment $\underline{a}$, if $M, w, \underline{a} \vDash B$ for every $B \in \Gamma$ then $M, w, \underline{a} \vDash A$. A is *g-valid* if and only A is a g-logical consequence of the empty set. We may also regard standard models as those general models $<W, \mathrm{dom}, V>$ in which $\mathrm{dom}(<t_1, \ldots, t_n>)$ is always $(P(\mathrm{dom}(t_1) \times \ldots \times \mathrm{dom}(t_n)))^W$, for purposes of comparison.[49]

It is convenient to extend the use of the symbol '=' to types other than e by stipulating that if S and $S*$ are symbols of type $<t_1, \ldots, t_n>$, and $v_1, \ldots, v_n$

---

[48] See Henkin 1950 and Shapiro 1991, pp. 73–6.

[49] Gallin so defines standard models. This clarifies the relation between general and standard models but obscures the simplicity of the determinants of a standard model. The difference has no repercussions for logical consequence.

are chosen distinct variables of types $t_1, \ldots, t_n$ respectively, then $S=S*$ is this formula:

$$\Box\forall v_1 \ldots \forall v_n \, (Sv_1 \ldots v_n \leftrightarrow S*v_1 \ldots v_n)$$

Hence whenever s and $s*$ are symbols of the same type (derived or under-ived), s and $s*$ have the same intension in a model M on an assignment $\underline{a}$ if and only if in M $s=s*$ is true at $w \in W$ on $\underline{a}$. Thus sameness of intension is expressible for every type.

Gallin provides an axiomatic system and establishes its soundness and completeness for g-logical consequence.[50] Provability ($\vdash$) is inductively defined by these axiom schemas and rules of inference, where $A^s{}_v$ is the result of substituting in A for a variable v of any type any symbol s of that type:

AS1   If A is a truth-functional tautology, $\vdash A$

AS2   If v is not free in A, $\vdash \forall v \, (A \rightarrow B) \rightarrow (A \rightarrow \forall v \, B)$

AS3   If the symbol s is of the same type as v and free for v in A, $\vdash \forall v A \rightarrow A^s{}_v$

AS4   If x is a variable of type e, $\vdash x=x$

AS5   If x and y are variables of type e, $\vdash x=y \rightarrow \Box x=y$

AS6   If s and $s*$ are symbols of the same type as the variable v and free for v in A, $\vdash s=s* \rightarrow (A^s{}_v \rightarrow A^{s*}{}_v)$

AS7 $\vdash \Box A \rightarrow A$

AS8 $\vdash \Box(A \rightarrow B) \rightarrow (\Box A \rightarrow \Box B)$

AS9 $\vdash \neg\Box A \rightarrow \Box\neg\Box A$

RS1   If $\vdash A \rightarrow B$ and $\vdash A$ then $\vdash B$

RS2   If $\vdash A$ then $\vdash \forall v A$

RS3   If $\vdash A$ then $\vdash \Box A$

For any set $\Gamma \cup \{A\}$ of formulas, let $\Gamma \vdash A$ mean that $\vdash (B_1 \& \ldots \& B_n) \rightarrow A$ for some $B_1, \ldots, B_n$ in Γ. Gallin's soundness and completeness theorem says that $\Gamma \vdash A$ if and only if A is a g-logical consequence of Γ.

---

[50] Earlier soundness and completeness results for second-order modal logic include those in Bayart 1958, p. 159 and Cocchiarella 1969c.

Despite the formal tractability of g-logical consequence, general models are more complex and less natural than standard models. Why have arbitrary restrictions on the permissible intensions of the appropriate type for a predicate? Consider Montague's motivating application, the semantics of natural language. The example in section 5.4 was the attributive adjective 'possible'. For present purposes we can parse it as of type <<e>, <e>>, so its content is a two-place relation between properties of individuals. The idea is that a property p has the relation to a property q if and only if q is the property of possibly having p. Restricting the type <e> restricts the cases over which that relation is defined. But it is doubtful that the meaning of 'possible' involves any such restriction. The common noun phrase 'possible F' is meaningful for arbitrarily complex and unnatural common noun phrases 'F'. Given the gerrymandered definition of 'grue', we can understand the phrase 'possible grue emerald'. Similarly, given the reference of 'that condition', we can understand the phrase 'possible satisfier of that condition'. Of course, some conditions may be too complex for us to grasp, but that is a limitation of our performance, not of the meaning of 'possible'. Although we can include any given set of more or less gerrymandered intensions in a general model, the point is that the actual meaning of 'possible' is *already* defined over all intensions of type <e>, and so is not fully expressed in a model that lacks some of them. In this respect, standard models look better suited to natural language semantics.

In this book, the central application of higher-order modal logic is not to natural language semantics, but to logic and metaphysics. Is a restriction to natural properties and relations motivated metaphysically rather than semantically? Some properties and relations may well be more natural than others, but that is not the issue here. Metaphysically universal generalizations of logic are the structural core of metaphysics. We need the best logic we can get. Logic restricted to natural properties and relations is pathetically weak. Imagine such a restricted version of Leibniz's Law for identity: it says that identicals have all their natural properties in common. Someone claims to be Nicolas Sarkozy. We point out that Sarkozy speaks French and he does not. He agrees, but objects that since we have not shown speaking French to be a *natural* property, we have not refuted the identity. Metaphysics based on weak logic wastes its time taking crank theories seriously. It needs a strong logic with laws of unrestricted generality. For example, a better version of Leibniz's Law says that identicals have *all* their properties (however unnatural) in common.[51]

If all natural properties and relations satisfied strong structural generalizations, expressible as laws of higher-order modal logic not satisfied by all unnatural properties and relations, that might be some reason to formulate higher-modal logic with correspondingly restricted quantifiers. But the extensive literature on natural properties and relations has produced no such strong characteristic logic of natural universals. Rather, some of the most informative principles of higher-order modal logic depend on the absence of any naturalness restriction.

The most obvious example of a logical principle of higher-order logic that depends on unnatural properties and relations is the comprehension schema:

Comp $\exists V \Box \forall v_1 \ldots \forall v_n (V v_1 \ldots v_n \leftrightarrow A)$

Here $V, v_1, \ldots, v_n$ are variables of types $\langle t_1, \ldots, t_n \rangle, t_1, \ldots, t_n$ respectively; A is any formula in which V does not occur free. Comp can be necessitated by RS3 and universally generalized by RS2. Whatever condition A defines on $v_1, \ldots, v_n$ (with other free variables in A treated as parameters), however unnatural, by Comp there is a corresponding property or relation.

We need a principle like Comp to rationalize arguments like #:

\#   Alice doesn't smoke cigars but she could have done.

         So, Alice doesn't do something she could have done.

Presumably, # is valid on a suitable reading. To a first approximation, its premise has the form $\neg S(a)$ & $\Diamond S(a)$, where $S(a)$ is 'Alice smokes cigars'. Its conclusion has the corresponding form $\exists X (\neg Xa$ & $\Diamond Xa)$. The general principle underlying such transitions is something like Comp. The relevant instance is $\exists X \Box \forall x (Xx \leftrightarrow S(x))$.

Comp is impredicative, in the sense that it permits the formula A to contain higher-order quantifiers in its turn. For example:

\#\#   It can be fun to be everything bad.

         So, there is something it can be fun to be.

---

[51] In the terminology of Lewis 1983b, a sparse theory of universals such as that defended by Armstrong 1978 is no good for present purposes.

Presumably, ## is valid on a suitable reading. The relevant instance of Comp is of the impredicative form $\exists X \,\Box\forall x\, (Xx \leftrightarrow \forall Y\,(BY \to Yx))$, where B is a second-order predicate ('bad to be'). With the λ operator, we might formalize the premise of ## as $\Diamond F\lambda x(\forall Y\,(BY \to Yx))$ and the conclusion as $\exists X \,\Diamond FX$, where F is a second-order predicate ('fun to be').[52]

Comp is standardly valid. In a standard model $M = \langle W, D, V\rangle$ on an assignment a, the verifying value of V is the function that takes each $w \in W$ to:

$$\{\langle d_1, \ldots, d_n\rangle \in \mathrm{dom}(t_1) \times \ldots \times \mathrm{dom}(t_n) : M, w, a[v_1/d_1] \ldots [v_n/d_n] \vDash A\}$$

If we add a suitable λ-operator to the language, subject to unrestricted λ-conversion, (22) is valid:

(22) $\Box\forall v_1 \ldots \forall v_n\, (\lambda v_1 \ldots v_n(A)v_1 \ldots v_n \leftrightarrow A)$

Then Comp standardly follows from (22) by $\exists$-generalization on $\lambda v_1 \ldots v_n(A)$. By contrast, in some general models, $\mathrm{dom}(\langle t_1, \ldots, t_n\rangle)$ omits the intension of $\lambda v_1 \ldots v_n(A)$ needed as a value of V to verify an instance of Comp, so Comp is not g-valid.

A metaphysically significant consequence of Comp is the equivalence of identity and indiscernibility. For Comp has this instance, where the variables x and y are of type e while X is of type $\langle e\rangle$:

(23) $\exists X \,\Box\forall x\, (Xx \leftrightarrow x=y)$

As a g-logical consequence of the necessitation of the universal generalization on y of (23), we can derive this form of the identity of indiscernibles:

Idind $\Box\forall x\, \forall y\, (x=y \leftrightarrow \forall X\,(Xx \leftrightarrow Xy))$

Of course, the second-order quantifier is not restricted to 'purely qualitative' attributes, or to those predicatively definable without reference to identity.

Idind is standardly valid. It is not g-valid, because it fails in general models with many individuals but only properties and relations that apply everywhere or nowhere.

---

[52] A metaphysical example of impredicativity in higher-order modal logic is Cocchiarella's implementation of Prior's contingentist proposal to reverse the apparently natural order of definition and explain 'exists' in terms of 'has an existence-entailing attribute' rather than vice versa. He takes as primitive a second-order quantifier restricted to 'existence-entailing attributes'. Trivially, 'existence' counts as an 'existence-entailing attribute', and so is quantified over in its own definition. Of course, the informal picture is that whatever has 'existence' does so because it has a predicatively definable 'existence-entailing attribute' too, such as sphericality, but predicative definability concerns modes of presentation of attributes and is too fine-grained to be captured in the logic itself. See Prior 1967, pp. 161–2, and Cocchiarella 1968, 1969a, and 1969b.

We could add Comp as an extra principle to Gallin's axiomatic system presented earlier, and restrict the general models to those in which it is valid. Of course, the resulting logic would still have a recursively enumerable set of theorems, and so be weaker than the standard logic. Even a general model that validates Comp may have highly restricted intensions for most types, because many intensions correspond to no formula of the language, relative to any values of its parameters.

In principle, one could retain Comp while restricting the higher-order quantifiers to properties and relations that are in some sense thinkable or expressible. However, if there are unthinkable or inexpressible properties or relations, that itself is a point of metaphysical significance, which we should be able to articulate. Thus for the purposes of metaphysics, and of logic as its structural core, we should impose no such restriction on our higher-order quantifiers. If we take the possible worlds framework seriously, every intension in the hierarchy corresponds to a proposition, property, or relation in the relevantly indiscriminate sense. For example, if I is an intension of type <e>, then the corresponding property of individuals is something like the property of being such that for some world w, w obtains and one belongs to $I(w)$; likewise for other derived types.[53] Thus standard models are more appropriate than general ones for logical metaphysics.

In a sense, of course, g-logical consequence is more general than standard logical consequence, because it is defined over a wider class of models. But that is the wrong kind of generality for logical metaphysics. Non-standard models differ from standard models in more than the interpretation of non-logical constants. They also differ in their frames <W, dom>, since the standard models are exactly those for which the domain function dom is plenitudinous. Thus non-standard models also differ from standard ones in respects relevant to the evaluation of claims about purely logical structure, in the sense of claims expressed by formulas without non-logical constants. But logical structure is what the logical core of our metaphysics is supposed to characterize. Let A be a standardly valid but not g-valid formula, and $\forall A$ its universal generalization, which contains no non-logical constants. Then $\forall A$ is also standardly valid but not g-valid. Of course, its negation is not g-valid either, for otherwise it would be standardly valid too. Thus g-logic

---

[53] Strictly speaking, the extension of an intension of type <e> is a set of one-tuples of individuals rather than a set of individuals. Following common practice, this book occasionally slurs over the difference for simplicity of exposition where it does not matter.

fails to decide some questions about purely logical structure that standard logic decides, whereas standard logic decides every question about purely logical structure that g-logic decides. Hence g-logic is less informative than standard logic about purely logical structure. A metaphysical theory based on g-logic rather than standard logic is neutral on many of the very questions it is supposed to answer. Moreover, to the extent to which we take models for ML_p seriously, the standard ones are more faithful than the non-standard ones to our intended interpretation. Standard logic remains more promising than general logic.

Admittedly, some standard models differ from others in their frames too, and so in matters of purely logical structure. Not even standard logical consequence is ideally informative. In the long run, logical metaphysics may hope for a still stronger consequence relation, perhaps defined by a single intended frame centred on a designated world. For the time being, absent a sufficiently informative characterization of an intended frame, we may make do with standard logical consequence.

We can put the point in terms of metaphysical universality, the standard for assessing logico-metaphysical theories sketched in sections 3.3 and 3.6. A formula of (modal) logic is metaphysically universal if and only if its universal generalization with respect to all its non-logical constants is true. ML_p, with its perfect match between the interpretations of non-logical constants and of quantifiable variables, is nicely adapted to express this standard, because it contains the universal generalizations of all its own formulas. The generality appropriate to logical metaphysics is that of just such a universal generalization in the object-language.[54] It is not the generality of a generalization in the metalanguage over all model structures, general or standard. It is, at least to a first approximation, the generality of a generalization in the object-language within a single intended standard model structure. The move from general to standard logical consequence is a step in that direction.

5.6 Necessitist and contingentist versions of ML_p

The prima facie reasons in section 5.5 for preferring standard models depend on taking the semantics more or less at face value. As usual, such arguments

---

[54] The treatment of logical laws as universal generalizations in a higher-order object-language is reminiscent of Frege's conception of logic. For a recent account see Goldfarb 2010.

are much less compelling if the model theory is viewed instrumentally, as a mere convenient device for characterizing a consequence relation. Indeed, for dialectical purposes, when we need a background logic that is neutral on some philosophically contentious point, we will sometimes resort to general models. But on a more realist view of the semantics, the case for standard consequence over general consequence is strong.

As already seen, contingentists cannot be fully realist about possible worlds semantics for first-order modal logic. That applies equally to higher-order modal logic when it extends first-order modal logic, as ML$_\text{p}$ does. In any of Gallin's models, standard or general, a quantifier on a variable of type e ranges over a constant domain dom(e) of 'possible entities or individuals'.[55] In this attitude, Gallin follows Montague. Although Montague allows each possible world its own domain, his basic first-order quantifiers are not restricted to the domain of the world of evaluation, but range over the union of the domains of all worlds. As he explains, 'quantification is over *possible* (and not merely *actual*) individuals'. He exemplifies the desirability of such quantifiers for the case of tense logic in the semantics of natural languages with the sentence 'There was a man whom no one remembers'. The point of the world-relative domains is to interpret an atomic 'existence' predicate E, treated as a logical constant. To express quantification over actual individuals, one restricts the basic possibilist quantifier with E.[56] This treatment is fundamentally necessitist and permanentist, since the quantifiers that behave in an apparently contingentist and temporaryist way are analysed as mere restrictions of quantifiers that behave in a necessitist way: although it is contingent and temporary what 'exists', in the sense of E, it is neither contingent nor temporary what there is, in the sense of the unrestricted quantifier.

The necessitist and permanentist orientation of Montague's semantics is deepened by his refusal to impose the domain constraint for the variable domains. He gives 'is remembered by someone' as an example of a one-place predicate whose extension at a time can contain individuals that belong only to the domains of other times, and 'thinks of' as an example of a two-place predicate whose extension at a world can contain pairs of individuals the second of which belongs only to the domains of other worlds.[57]

---

[55] Gallin 1975, p. 10. Although he uses the phrase in describing the semantics of IL, it is meant to carry over to the semantics of ML$_\text{p}$ too.

[56] See Montague 1970a, pp. 125–6 (also 131–2).

[57] Montague 1970a, p. 124.

The necessitism and permanentism of Montague's remarks are manifest in the object-language, for they motivate features of the semantics on which the validity of some formulas depends. Since the domain of fundamental first-order quantification is constant, full BF, full CBF, and NNE are validated. More generally, if X and Y are variables of any type t, any instance of the following forms is both standardly valid and g-valid in ML_P; in every case the validity is closed under necessitation and universal generalization:

BF_t $\Diamond \exists X A \rightarrow \exists X \Diamond A$

CBF_t $\exists X \Diamond A \rightarrow \Diamond \exists X A$

NNE_t $\Box \forall X \Box \exists Y \, X{=}Y$

Of course, when t is e and the quantifiers are restricted by the 'existence' predicate E, the analogous schemas all have invalid instances.

Similarly, all instances of the first-order being constraint with unrestricted quantifiers are valid in ML_P, but restricting the quantifiers in them with E yields invalid formulas (for first-order formulas, standard validity and g-validity coincide). Thus while (24) and (25) are trivially valid in ML_P, (26) and (27) are invalid:

(24) $\Box \forall x \, \Box (Fx \rightarrow \exists z \, x{=}z)$

(25) $\Box \forall x \, \Box \forall y \, \Box (Rxy \rightarrow (\exists z \, x{=}z \,\&\, \exists z \, y{=}z))$

(26) $\Box \forall x \, (Ex \rightarrow \Box (Fx \rightarrow \exists z \, (Ez \,\&\, x{=}z)))$

(27) $\Box \forall x \, (Ex \rightarrow \Box \forall y \, (Ey \rightarrow \Box (Rxy \rightarrow (\exists z \, (Ez \,\&\, x{=}z) \,\&\, \exists z \, (Ez \,\&\, y{=}z)))))$

For (26) and (27) are equivalent in ML_P to the invalid (28) and (29) respectively:

(28) $\Box \forall x \, \Box (Fx \rightarrow Ex)$

(29) $\Box \forall x \, \Box \forall y \, \Box (Rxy \rightarrow (Ex \,\&\, Ey))$

The status of the members of the united domain of quantification as possibilia is manifested by the validity in ML_P of (30) but not of (31):

(30) $\Box \forall x \, \Diamond Ex$

(31) $\Box \forall x \, Ex$

Not surprisingly, Montague does not explain E further than that Ex can be read as 'x exists' or 'x is actual'.[58]

On such a necessitist and permanentist approach, the treatment of metaphysical universality for first-order modal logic and its connection to validity on an intended model structure in section 3.7 extends smoothly to ML_p. We form the universal generalization of a formula of ML_p as usual, by uniformly substituting distinct new variables of the appropriate type for distinct non-logical constants throughout and prefixing the result with universal quantifiers on all its variables (in accordance with given well-orderings of the individual constants, atomic predicates, and variables). Satisfyingly, the universal generalization of a formula of ML_p is itself a formula of ML_p; by contrast, the universal generalization of a first-order modal formula is typically higher-order. A formula is metaphysically universal if and only if its universal generalization is true (on its intended interpretation).

As in the first-order case, the unrestricted reading of the quantifiers does not properly fit the set-theoretic framework of model theory. We follow section 3.7 in first developing the account of metaphysical universality under the pretence that the intended interpretation of the first-order quantifiers is over a given constant set-sized domain D. We postpone lifting this pretence to section 5.7, which treats philosophical problems of interpretation in more depth.

Since we are working with standard models, we can use almost the same intended inhabited model structure as in section 3.7. However, in this section we have been following Gallin in omitting the accessibility relation from the structure because we always assume it to be universal over the set of worlds. We can drop that assumption, use exactly the intended inhabited model structure of section 3.7, subject to the same qualifications about the number of propositions and of objects, and routinely extend the necessitist argument there that the logic of the model structure is sound and complete for metaphysical universality to the corresponding claim for all formulas of ML_p. Thus a formula of ML_p is valid on the intended inhabited model structure if and only if it is metaphysically universal. Alternatively, we can omit the accessibility relation from the structure, on the assumption that it is universal, but then the argument for soundness

---

[58] Montague 1970a, p. 121.

and completeness requires the corresponding S5-like assumption about the necessitation operator L on the Boolean algebra of propositions, that $Lp = 0$ whenever $p \neq 1$.

If we fully interpret all constants of the language, thereby mapping each atomic formula to a unique proposition on each assignment, we have determined a unique faithful interpretation I, where each formula A of the object-language is true (on its intended interpretation) if and only if the proposition $I(A)$ is true. Again as before, we can argue that $I(A)$ is true if and only if A is true in a model M_I on the intended model structure. Since M_I corresponds in a precise sense to the intended faithful interpretation I, it deserves to count as the intended model. Thus we also have an appropriate equivalence for all formulas of ML_P between truth in the intended model and simple truth.

How easily can the Montague-Gallin semantics be tweaked to generate a logic acceptable to contingentists? We focus here on issues of formal structure, leaving to a later chapter the examples from natural language that Montague used to justify his treatment. At the level of individuals, we can stipulatively restrict the basic quantifiers to world-relative domains. How can we carry the semantic construction on to higher types?

One idea is to use a generalized domain constraint to carry the quantifier restriction up. On this view, the extension of an n-place predicate of individuals at a world is a set of n-tuples of members of its domain; likewise for the value of a corresponding n-place predicate variable. What this justifies is a global constraint on intensions, not a world-relative one. Contingentists, doing possible worlds semantics in a semi-instrumentalist spirit, do not restrict the extension of 'eat' at a counterfactual world w in a model to members of the domain of the actual world of the model, since on their view there could have been eaters who are actually nothing. At most, they restrict the extension of 'eat' at w to members of the domain of w, because eating entails being something. Thus the relevant restriction is to those n-place intensions that map every world to a set of n-tuples of members of its domain. Which intensions obey that universally quantified constraint is constant across worlds. Consequently, BF_t, CBF_t, and NNE_t still hold for quantification into predicate position and over all higher types. This makes the supposed failure of the analogous schemas for type e look worryingly anomalous. In the next chapter, we discuss whether contingentist metaphysics can remove or explain away the apparent anomaly. From a formal perspective, the proposed semantic framework is unattractively ad hoc.[59]

A more uniform approach generalizes the contingentist treatment of domains for type e by making the domains of all types world-relative, fixed by the model itself separately for each world-type pair. This invalidates BF_t, CBF_t, and NNE_t for any type t. It perforce uses a version of general models, with a further dimension of complexity. The onus is then on the contingentist's metaphysics to generalize 'existence' or 'actuality' to all higher types. Not only does the approach forfeit the advantages of standard models: as it stands, it fails even to validate the comprehension schema Comp. Of course, by brute force of stipulation one can restrict the semantics to models that validate Comp, but that too is unattractively ad hoc.

From a structural perspective, therefore, necessitism has a clear advantage over contingentism in possible worlds semantics for higher-order modal logic. It gives a much simpler and more elegant picture. Naturally, that does not stop contingentists from arguing that the structural benefits of necessitism are outweighed by its metaphysical costs. Those metaphysical questions are postponed to the next chapter.

5.7 The challenge of interpreting higher-order quantification

We saw in section 3.6 that set-theoretic model theory is not fully faithful to the unrestricted reading of first-order quantification, since no set-sized domain contains absolutely everything. This problem becomes even more acute for the model theory of higher-order logic, modal or non-modal. The simplest case is quantification into one-place predicate position in a non-modal setting, interpreted in the model theory as quantification over all subsets of the domain of individuals. By Cantor's theorem, the domain has more subsets than members, so the second-order quantifiers are interpreted as ranging over more things than the first-order quantifiers range over. This rubs in the failure of the model theory to interpret the first-order quantifiers as genuinely unrestricted: the term 'individual' acts as a restricting device. But the set-theoretic apparatus also undermines the idea that the

[59] Parsons 1983, p. 336, defines a standard model for second-order modal logic to have a fixed domain for the second-order variables even if not for the first-order variables.

second-order quantifiers are doing anything genuinely new, semantically. For although they bind variables in a new syntactic position in the object-language, they are interpreted by ordinary first-order quantifiers over sets in the metalanguage. This provides telling support for Quine's charge that higher-order quantification is just first-order quantification over sets in disguise. The problem generalizes to higher types, and to possible worlds model theory for higher-order modal logic. In particular, it applies to Montague's semantics for IL and Gallin's semantics for ML_p. The sets at issue are merely more complex as one moves to higher types and introduces functions from possible worlds, since functions are equated with sets of ordered pairs.

We postponed the problem in section 5.6, when discussing metaphysical universality, by pretending that the intended interpretation of the first-order quantifiers is over a given constant set-sized domain D. We must now lift the pretence.

A natural proposal on behalf of higher-order quantification is that the set-theoretic semantics is just a mathematically convenient approximation to what is really meant. A more faithful semantics should be formulated in a higher-order metalanguage, with unrestricted first-order quantifiers and higher-order quantifiers irreducible to first-order quantifiers over sets. For the non-modal case, such semantic theories have already been developed, in a tradition initiated by George Boolos.[60] Formally, intensionalizing them by appropriate relativizations to a dimension of possible worlds is a comparatively routine exercise, since that dimension can be treated like an extra argument place for each symbol.

Let us consider the case of ML_p in more detail. Although we can no longer rely on the semantic explanation of its types in set-theoretic terms, we can still use the types to classify the symbols of ML_p. A symbol of type e is a singular term. A symbol of type $\langle t_1, \ldots, t_n \rangle$ applies to symbols of types $t_1, \ldots, t_n$ respectively to form a sentence. For the metalanguage types are understood similarly, but we add a second basic type w, for explicit world variables. This difference in types between the object-language and the metalanguage registers the difference in how they express modality (modal operators in the former, world-talk in the latter), irrespective of whether the

---

[60] See Boolos 1985, Rayo and Uzquiano 1999, Rayo and Williamson 2003, McGee 2003, Rayo 2006, Linnebo and Rayo 2012.

metalanguage is first-order or higher-order. For any natural number n, whenever the metalanguage has types $t_1, \ldots, t_n$ it also has a type $\langle t_1, \ldots, t_n \rangle$. Each type t of ML_P corresponds to a type τt of the metalanguage by the rule that τe is e and $\tau \langle t_1, \ldots, t_n \rangle$ is $\langle \tau t_1, \ldots, \tau t_n, w \rangle$. The *finite types* of the metalanguage are those that belong to the smallest set that contains e, w, and, whenever it contains $t_1, \ldots, t_n$, also $\langle t_1, \ldots, t_n \rangle$. But we add a cumulative infinite limit type λ to the metalanguage: the expressions of type λ are exactly those of any finite type. Thus expressions of type λ also belong to some more specific type, but expressions of type $\langle \lambda \rangle$ do not. For present purposes we need go only slightly beyond λ. For explicitness, we indicate the relevant type of each variable of the metalanguage, and put quotation corners around any object-language expression mentioned in the metalanguage (such quotation names are of type e). We can conveniently extend the identity sign in the metalanguage to all finite types by using $x^\lambda = y^\lambda$ to abbreviate $\forall z^{\langle \lambda \rangle} (z^{\langle \lambda \rangle}(x^\lambda) \leftrightarrow z^{\langle \lambda \rangle}(y^\lambda))$.

In the critical case, we interpret ML_P unrestrictedly. This simplifies the metatheory, since we avoid complications with domains. To simplify further, we replace talk of models and assignments with a single expression ASSIGN, a higher-order analogue of the predicate 'is a model-assignment pair'. The only relevant difference between variable and constant symbols in ML_P is thus that quantification is well-formed for the former but not for the latter. ASSIGN is of type $\langle\langle e, \lambda \rangle\rangle$; it forms a sentence from an expression of type $\langle e, \lambda \rangle$, which in turn forms a sentence from an expression of type e and one of type λ; we need the infinite type to interpret all symbols of the object-language simultaneously and appropriately. If we permit ourselves an infinitary metalanguage, we can regard $\mathrm{ASSIGN}(\underline{a}^{\langle e, \lambda \rangle})$ as the conjunction of the denumerably many conditions of this form for all types t and symbol s of type t in ML_P:

$$\exists x^{\tau t} \forall y^{\tau t} (\underline{a}^{\langle e, \lambda \rangle}(\ulcorner s \urcorner^e, y^{\tau t}) \leftrightarrow x^{\tau t} = y^{\tau t})$$

This is a higher-order analogue of the first-order claim that a model-assignment pair gives a symbol a unique value of the appropriate type. We also need a higher-order analogue of the predicate for being a variant of a given assignment with respect to a given variable: VARIANT, of type $\langle\langle e, \lambda \rangle, \langle e, \lambda \rangle, e \rangle$. For any symbol s, $\mathrm{VARIANT}(\underline{a}^{\langle e, \lambda \rangle}, \underline{b}^{\langle e, \lambda \rangle}, \ulcorner s \urcorner^e)$ is the infinite conjunction of $\mathrm{ASSIGN}(\underline{b}^{\langle e, \lambda \rangle})$ and conditions of this form for variables y of each specific subtype of λ:

$$\forall x^e \, (x^e \neq \ulcorner s_1 \urcorner^e \rightarrow \forall y^\lambda \, (\underline{a}^{<e,\lambda>}(x^e, y^\lambda) \leftrightarrow \underline{b}^{<e,\lambda>}(x^e, y^\lambda)))$$

We do not bother to restrict ASSIGN and VARIANT further to exclude 'junk' applications that play no role in the semantics.

We can now formulate a higher-order theory of truth at a world for ML_P. For symbols $S, s_1, \ldots, s_n$ of ML_P of types $<t_1, \ldots, t_n>, t_1, \ldots, t_n$ respectively:

$$TRUE(\ulcorner Ss_1 \ldots s_n \urcorner^e, \underline{a}^{<e,\lambda>}, w^w) \leftrightarrow \forall X^{<\pi t_1, \ldots, \pi t_n, w>} \, \forall x_1^{\pi t_1} \ldots \forall x_n^{\pi t_n}$$
$$((\underline{a}^{<e,\lambda>}(\ulcorner S \urcorner^e, X^{<\pi t_1, \ldots, \pi t_n, w>}) \,\&\, \underline{a}^{<e,\lambda>}(\ulcorner s_1 \urcorner^e, x_1^{\pi t_1}) \,\&\ldots\&\, \underline{a}^{<e,\lambda>}(\ulcorner s_n \urcorner^e, x_n^{\pi t_n}))$$
$$\rightarrow X^{<\pi t_1, \ldots, \pi t_n, w>}(x_1^{\pi t_1}, \ldots, x_n^{\pi t_n}, w^w))$$

For symbols s_1 and s_2 of ML_P of type e:

$$TRUE(\ulcorner s_1{=}s_2 \urcorner^e, \underline{a}^{<e,\lambda>}, w^w) \leftrightarrow$$
$$\forall x^e \, \forall y^e \, ((\underline{a}^{<e,\lambda>}(\ulcorner s_1 \urcorner^e, x^e) \,\&\, \underline{a}^{<e,\lambda>}(\ulcorner s_2 \urcorner^e, y^e)) \rightarrow x^e = y^e)$$

Here are the equally unsurprising inductive equivalences:

$$TRUE(\ulcorner \neg A \urcorner^e, \underline{a}^{<e,\lambda>}, w^w) \leftrightarrow \neg TRUE(\ulcorner A \urcorner^e, \underline{a}^{<e,\lambda>}, w^w)$$

$$TRUE(\ulcorner A \,\&\, B \urcorner^e, \underline{a}^{<e,\lambda>}, w^w) \leftrightarrow (TRUE(\ulcorner A \urcorner^e, \underline{a}^{<e,\lambda>}, w^w) \,\&\, TRUE(\ulcorner B \urcorner^e,$$
$$\underline{a}^{<e,\lambda>}, w^w))$$

$$TRUE(\ulcorner \Box A \urcorner^e, \underline{a}^{<e,\lambda>}, w^w) \leftrightarrow \forall w_*^w \, TRUE(\ulcorner A \urcorner^e, \underline{a}^{<e,\lambda>}, w_*^w)$$

$$TRUE(\ulcorner \forall v \, A \urcorner^e, \underline{a}^{<e,\lambda>}, w^w) \leftrightarrow \forall \underline{b}^{<e,\lambda>}(VARIANT(\underline{a}^{<e,\lambda>}, \underline{b}^{<e,\lambda>}, \ulcorner v \urcorner^e) \rightarrow$$
$$TRUE(\ulcorner A \urcorner^e, \underline{b}^{<e,\lambda>}, w^w))$$

Many variations on this theme are feasible. One can introduce variable domains for some or all types to appease the contingentist, and an accessibility relation for the opponent of S5.[61]

With such techniques the necessitist can adapt the account in section 5.5 of the intended model structure for ML_P to the demands of genuinely unrestricted quantification, dropping the supposed set domain D and the corresponding restrictions of the quantifiers, both those of type e and those of higher types. The equivalence between metaphysical universality and validity on an intended model structure for formulas of ML_P, and the argument for

---

[61] See Rayo 2006 and Linnebo and Rayo 2012 for more details of similar constructions without a modal dimension.

it, are reformulated in the higher-order metalanguage. Once all constants of ML_p are fully interpreted, the corresponding equivalence between simple truth and truth in an intended model, and the argument for it, are reformulated in the metalanguage extended by (translations of) the non-logical constants of ML_p.

We can still use the original set-theoretic semantics as an unintended interpretation, with arbitrary sets D and W for the domains of types e and w and a set of inaccessible cardinality for the domain of type λ, to prove the consistency of the higher-order metatheory, relative to set theory with inaccessibles. That proves its consistency not just alone but also with any set of formulas of the infinitely higher-order metalanguage that are all true together in some such set-theoretic model. Formally, the construction does not collapse.

The main problem is philosophical, not technical. Informally, how are we to understand the higher-order quantifiers? Giving them a formal semantics in a still higher-order metalanguage does not answer that question, for how are we to understand its higher-order quantifiers in the metalanguage?

The obvious informal approach is by paraphrasing the higher-order quantifiers of the formal object-language in a natural language. But trying to do so reveals the seriousness of the problem. For example, in discussing argument # in section 5.5, we treated $\exists X\, (\neg Xa\ \&\ \lozenge Xa)$ as the formalization of the English sentence 'Alice doesn't do something she could have done'. But 'something' occupies the position of a first-order quantifier, in this case over action types such as smoking cigars. The position being quantified into is that of a noun phrase, the object of the verb 'do', not that of a predicate. The sentence is similar in form to 'Alice doesn't like someone she could have liked', in which the quantifier is manifestly first-order. Even in argument ##, 'something' quantifies into the position of the phrase 'everything bad', which is not a predicate either, for it lacks a verb. Similarly, the philosophical discussion of higher-order quantifiers in earlier sections treated them as ranging over properties and relations. But 'property' and 'relation' are ordinary nouns. Quantifiers such as 'some property' and 'every relation' are simply restricted first-order quantifiers over entities of a special kind.

The same difficulty faces Frege's account of higher-order quantification as quantification over concepts. 'Concept' is an ordinary noun. To say 'No concept is an object' is self-defeating, for in doing so one quantifies into name position and so over objects, on Frege's view: hence his struggles with the concept *horse* that is not a concept. What he really needs is a higher-level predicate that stands to first-level predicates as the first-level predicate 'is an object' stands to names.[62] For the same reason, the attempt to contrast objects and concepts as saturated and unsaturated respectively betrays the point of the enterprise, for since 'unsaturated' is the negation of 'saturated' the two adjectives belong to the same grammatical category: but whereas 'is saturated' is a first-level predicate, we need a higher-level predicate in place of 'is unsaturated' to do the required work. Frege himself had some conception of the difficulty, as his uneasy discussion of the concept *horse* shows. He knew that his explanations required at least a pinch of salt, but greatly underestimated the extent of the problem. He fell into inconsistency by postulating Basic Law V in an attempt to undo the mathematically inconvenient consequences of the distinction between first-level and second-level expressions.[63]

It is quite within the spirit of Frege's philosophy to say that one can state matters perspicuously only by reference to a formal language such as his *Begriffsschrift*. However, although friends of higher-order quantification may insist that the Procrustean assimilation of all quantification to first-order quantification is just a misleading feature of natural languages, their insistence carries limited weight if they cannot tell us how to understand the higher-order quantifiers without reducing them to restricted first-order quantifiers.

The most salient idea for a reading of at least some higher-order natural language that does not treat them as first-order is Boolos's: read them as *plural quantifiers*.[64] The next section examines that idea in a modal setting.

---

[62] See Frege 1892. According to Michael Dummett's memory of Frege's Nachlass (Dummett 1981, pp. 212–13), Frege later took the line proposed for him in the text. Wright 1998 objects that the move does not resolve the problem because a metalinguistic expression such as 'the referent of "is a horse"' still occupies name position. However, the proposed line naturally goes with corresponding ascents in order in a quasi-homophonic metalanguage, which also turn out to be crucial in avoiding metalinguistic versions of Russell's paradox.

[63] Dummett 1991, p. 217, blames the paradox on Frege's use of second-order quantification. Boolos 1993 replies.

[64] Boolos 1984, 1985. George Boolos first introduced me to the plural interpretation of second-order logic when he presented the 1984 paper, then in press, at Trinity College Dublin; I asked him about the principle $Xx \rightarrow \Box Xx$.

5.8 Plural quantification in modal logic

A classic example of plural quantification is due to Peter Geach and David Kaplan: the sentence 'Some critics admire only one another'. It cannot be formalized in first-order logic with identity and the one-place predicate C ('is a critic') and the two-place predicate A ('admires') as the only non-logical constants.[65] Using 'xx' as a plural variable and $\prec$ for 'is one of'(to stand between a singular and a plural term), we can formalize it thus:

(32) $\exists xx\, \forall x\, (x \prec xx \rightarrow (Cx \,\&\, \forall y\, (Axy \rightarrow (\neg x{=}y \,\&\, y{\prec}xx))))$

The corresponding formalization in second-order logic is this:

(32*) $\exists X\, (\exists x\, Xx \,\&\, \forall x\, (Xx \rightarrow (Cx \,\&\, \forall y\, (Axy \rightarrow (\neg x{=}y \,\&\, Xy)))))$

Such examples suggest a more general equivalence between enriching first-order non-modal logic with monadic second-order predicate variables and enriching it with plural variables and the predicate $\prec$. We can roughly convey the idea by speaking of the values of monadic predicate variables as properties and the values of plural variables as pluralities, even though both ways of speaking illicitly reduce the corresponding forms of quantification to ordinary first-order quantification, restricted to properties and pluralities respectively. Something is a member of a plurality if and only if it has the property of being a member of that plurality. Conversely, something has a property if and only if it is a member of the plurality of things that have that property—with the irritating exception of a property that nothing has, which we can take care of by ad hoc means.[66] In extensional languages, that coextensiveness is what matters. More precisely, given a closed formula A of the monadic second-order non-modal language, we can construct an equivalent closed formula $\varphi(A)$ of the plural non-modal language; conversely, given a closed formula B of the plural non-modal language, we can construct an equivalent closed formula $\psi(B)$ of the monadic second-order non-modal

---

[65] See Boolos 1984, p. 57, for David Kaplan's proof. Boolos provides many other examples (1984, pp. 57–62), although I do not share his scruples as to whether the Geach-Kaplan sentence is really acceptable English. What matters most for present purposes is its evident intelligibility on the relevant reading.

[66] The usual assumption is made that 'some Fs' entails 'at least one F' but not 'at least two Fs'. The account can easily be adjusted to the alternatives, on which it has both entailments or neither.

language.[67] The equivalences are expressible as logically true biconditionals in a combination of the two extended languages. Since we can under-stand the formal plural language by translation into English or another natural language, the equivalences give us some grasp of monadic second-order quantification too. Arguably, that grasp does not depend on reduc-ing it to first-order singular quantification over sets, events, or anything else, for attempts to reduce the plural to the singular founder on versions of Russell's paradox.[68]

Plural quantification is a salutary reminder not to assume that natural languages are first-order. It may also suffice for some of the most prominent applications of higher-order logic, namely, to the formalization of mathe-matical theories. For example, second-order arithmetic uniquely characterizes the structure of the natural numbers, because all its models are isomorphic to each other: more precisely, if a model of second-order arithmetic is standard in the sense of second-order logic, it is standard in the sense of arithmetic. Thus second-order logic is strong enough to serve as a background logic for arithmetic. By contrast, any first-order theory of arithmetic with stand-ard models (in the sense of arithmetic) also has non-standard models (in that sense). The difference is that any standard model of second-order logic interprets the second-order axiom of mathematical induction as a gener-alization over all the uncountably many subsets of the domain, while the

---

[67] Proof: Let the logical constants of the monadic second-order language be $\neg$, &, $\exists$, and = (between singular terms). For any two second-order variables X and Y, let xx_X and xx_Y be distinct plural vari-ables. We define a family φ_S of auxiliary functions for each set S of second-order variables (to track those being treated as vacuous) inductively on the construction of a formula A of the monadic second-order language. If A is atomic and contains no second-order variable, $\varphi_S(A)$ is A. If A is atomic and contains a second-order variable, it is of the form Vt; if $V \in S$, $\varphi_S(Vt)$ is $\neg t{=}t$; if $V \notin S$, $\varphi_S(Vt)$ is $t{\prec}xx_V$. Of course $\varphi_S(\neg A)$ is $\neg\varphi_S(A)$ and $\varphi_S(A\ \&\ A^*)$ is $\varphi_S(A)\ \&\ \varphi_S(A^*)$. For first-order v, $\varphi_S(\exists v\ A)$ is $\exists v\ \varphi_S(A)$. If V is second-order, $\varphi_S(\exists V\ A)$ is $\varphi_{S\cup\{V\}}(A)\vee\exists xx_V\ \varphi_{S-\{V\}}(A)$. Finally, let $\varphi(A)$ be $\varphi_{\{\}}(A)$. (Compare the scheme for translating a monadic second-order language into English at pp. 67–8 of Boolos 1984.) Conversely, let the logical constants of the plural language be $\neg$, &, $\exists$, $\prec$ (between a singular term and a plural variable), and = (between singular terms). For any two plural variables xx and yy, let X_{xx} and X_{yy} be distinct monadic second-order variables. We define ψ inductively on the construction of a formula B of the plural language. If B is atomic and contains no plural variable, $\psi(B)$ is B. If B is atomic and contains a plural variable, it is of the form $t{\prec}vv$; $\psi(t{\prec}vv)$ is $X_{vv}t$. Of course $\psi(\neg B)$ is $\neg\psi(B)$ and $\psi(B\ \&\ B^*)$ is $\psi(B)\ \&\ \psi(B^*)$. For singular v, $\psi(\exists v\ B)$ is $\exists v\ \psi(B)$. For plural vv, $\psi(\exists vv\ B)$ is $\exists X_{vv}\ (\exists x\ X_{vv}x\ \&\ \psi(B))$.

[68] See, for example, Oliver and Smiley 2001, Rayo 2002, Yi 2005 and 2006, and McKay 2006, pp. 19–54. For some scepticism see Resnik 1988, Parsons 1990, Hazen 1993, and Linnebo 2003. Linguists unwor-ried by Russell's paradox routinely apply a framework of sets, events, wholes, or the like in first-order terms in the metalanguage to the semantics of plurals; the question is whether there is any systematic obstacle to recasting such semantic theories in higher-order terms.

first-order induction schema is interpreted as a generalization only over the countably many subsets expressible by a formula with values assigned to its free variables (given that the domain and language are countable). For those purposes, a plural reinterpretation of the second-order quantifiers is adequate, since for any non-empty subset of the domain there are its members. For similar reasons, treating the axiom of comprehension or replacement in set theory as a first-order schema misses its intended generality, but treating it as a second-order axiom over standard models of second-order logic secures the intended effect, and a plural reinterpretation is adequate for those purposes too.[69]

Nothing to be said here impugns the intelligibility of plural quantification, its irreducibility to singular quantification, or its utility in mathematical applications. But whether it serves all the purposes of higher-order modal logic is another question.

Plural quantification is not quantification into predicate position, for a plural noun is not itself a predicate: it lacks a verb.[70] Thus plural quantification is not the intended reading even of monadic second-order quantification. That might not matter much, if it did better than our intentions. But the difference has further repercussions, as will become clear. An immediate one is this: we cannot assume that if the symbols s and S are of types $<e>$ and $<<e>>$ respectively, then reinterpreting s in plural terms makes no difference to the truth value of Ss; it is not even obvious that some compensating adjustment in the interpretation of S will always restore the original truth value of the sentence.

Another obvious difficulty for a plural reading of higher-order logic is that it makes no immediate sense of n-adic second-order quantification for $n > 1$. Monadic second-order logic is weaker than full second-order logic.[71] We use n-adic second-order quantification in defining metaphysical universality for a first-order language with n-adic predicate constants. The obvious fix is to interpret it as plural quantification over ordered n-tuples, which can themselves be defined in terms of ordered pairs.[72] Introducing pairs is harmless for most purposes, even though they commit us to infinitely many

[69] See Shapiro 1991, pp. 97–133, for the technical background.

[70] See Simons 1997 and Higginbotham 1998 for related points.

[71] See Gurevich 1985 on (non-modal) monadic second-order logic; the obverse of the loss in strength is a gain in tractability (for instance, in decidability properties).

[72] See Rayo and Yablo 2001, pp. 75–7, for discussion, and Burgess, Hazen, and Lewis 1991 for mereological alternatives.

individuals if we are independently committed to at least two individuals.[73] They also enable impossibilia to be constructed out of possibilia, in a sense to be explained (see section 7.3).[74]

A harder challenge for a plural reading of higher-order logic is to generalize to nth-order quantification for $n > 2$. Talk of pluralities of pluralities hardly helps, for the word 'plurality' involves exactly the problematic reduction of the plural to the singular that the friend of plurals is trying to do without. Nevertheless, some expressions in natural languages appear to contain superplurals, expressions that somehow stand to plurals as plurals stand to singulars. A putative instance is 'these people and those people', as in 'These people and those people play against each other' and 'These people, those people, and these other people play against each other'.[75] Such sentences should entail something of the form $\exists xxx\ Pxxx$ (where P abbreviates 'play against each other'), the superplural analogue of third-order quantification. The more general challenge is to extend the argument to nth-order quantification for all n.[76]

Even if these challenges can be met, the plural approach has a serious limitation in a modal setting. It forces grave restrictions on the comprehension principle Comp. The naive plural analogue of Comp in the monadic second-order case is this:

$$\text{Comp*} \prec \qquad \exists xx\ \Box \forall x\ (x \prec xx \leftrightarrow A)$$

Here the variable xx is not free in A (likewise for the other comprehension principles to be considered). We understand the instances of Comp*$\prec$ and any other $\prec$ principle to include the results of prefixing it with any number of universal singular and plural quantifiers and necessity operators in any order.

Comp*$\prec$ is immediately objectionable, for we can substitute a contradiction for A and deduce that there are some things of which it is impossible

---

[73] We prove the claim, without assuming set theory, from the standard principle that ordered pairs are identical just if they have the same first member and the same second member. For suppose that $x \neq y$. Let $z_0 = \langle x, y \rangle$ and $z_{i+1} = \langle z_i, z_i \rangle$ for all i. Thus $z_{i+1} = z_{j+1}$ only if $z_i = z_j$. Therefore, by induction, if $0 < i < j$ and $z_i = z_j$ then $z_0 = z_{j-i}$. Thus $\langle x, y \rangle = z_{j-i} = \langle z_{j-i-1}, z_{j-i-1} \rangle$, so $x = z_{j-i-1} = y$, a contradiction. Hence $z_i \neq z_j$ whenever $i \neq j$. (The principle yields no expansion if we start with only one individual.)

[74] Contrary to the suggestion at p. 152 of McKay 2006, the semantics of higher-order logic does not require the individuals to be closed under the formation of ordered pairs. The semantic theory displayed in section 5.6 assumes such closure for types but not for individuals.

[75] The example is from Linnebo and Nicolas 2008. For previous suggestions see Landman 1989, Rosen and Dorr 2002, and Oliver and Smiley 2005.

[76] Rayo 2006 argues that the challenge can in principle be met.

for anything to be one, contradicting the standard principle that for any things, something is one of them:

E≺ $\qquad \forall xx \, \exists x \, x \prec xx$

To accommodate E≺, we weaken Comp*≺ thus:

Comp**≺ $\qquad \exists x \, A \rightarrow \exists xx \, \Box \forall x \, (x \prec xx \leftrightarrow A)$

But even Comp**≺ makes trouble. For plurals satisfy a principle of extensionality. If every one of these is one of those and every one of those is one of these, then these just are those, and being one of these just is being one of those, so nothing could have been one of these without being one of those or vice versa. In symbols:[77]

NI≺ $\qquad \forall xx \, \forall yy \, (\forall x \, (x \prec xx \leftrightarrow x \prec yy) \rightarrow \Box \forall x \, (x \prec xx \leftrightarrow x \prec yy))$

This is the plural analogue of the necessity of identity. Given NI≺, Comp**≺ causes almost total modal collapse. For let F be any monadic predicate. Two instances of Comp**≺ on the plural reading are these:

(33) $\qquad \exists x \, Fx \rightarrow \exists xx \, \Box \forall x \, (x \prec xx \leftrightarrow Fx)$

(34) $\qquad \exists x \, x{=}x \rightarrow \exists yy \, \Box \forall x \, (x \prec yy \leftrightarrow x{=}x)$

Given NI≺, (33) and (34) yield (35):[78]

(35) $\qquad \forall x \, Fx \rightarrow \Box \forall x \, Fx$

This is absurd on many interpretations of F. Since I own no dog, everything is not my dog, but since I could have owned a dog, it is not necessary that everything is not my dog. But NI≺ is compelling, so even Comp**≺ must be rejected. Thus, in higher-order modal logic, the price of the plural reading is a drastically restricted comprehension principle.

---

[77] See also Williamson 2003a, p. 457. The aim of a logic of plurals is to codify the principles that hold on a given reading of them, not those that hold on all readings speakers can come up with in a natural language. The claim is that the principles in the text hold on the usual and most natural reading of plurals. See Hewitt 2012 for a different view.

[78] Proof: We may assume $\exists x \, x{=}x$, so $\forall x \, Fx$ yields $\exists x \, Fx$. Thus from (33), (34), and the antecedent of (35) we derive $\exists xx \, \exists yy \, \Box \forall x \, ((x \prec xx \leftrightarrow Fx) \,\&\, x \prec yy)$ by the reflexivity of identity. Since $(A \leftrightarrow B) \,\&\, C$ truth-functionally entails $(A \leftrightarrow C) \leftrightarrow B$, we can thence derive $\exists xx \, \exists yy \, \Box \forall x \, ((x \prec xx \leftrightarrow x \prec yy) \leftrightarrow Fx)$, and so $\exists xx \, \exists yy \, \Box(\forall x \, (x \prec xx \leftrightarrow x \prec yy) \leftrightarrow \forall x \, Fx)$. From this we use NI≺ and the T axiom to derive (35), dropping the redundant plural quantifiers.

246 FROM FIRST-ORDER TO HIGHER-ORDER MODAL LOGIC

Someone might object to NI≺ thus: it is contingent that all and only cordates are renates, so if these are the cordates and those are the renates, these are contingently those. But that objection rests on a scope fallacy over the plural definite descriptions 'the cordates' and 'the renates', analogous to the fallacy involved in the objection to the necessity of identity itself that since it is contingent that the tallest cordate is the tallest renate, if this is the tallest cordate and that is the tallest renate, this is contingently that, which concerns the singular definite descriptions 'the tallest cordate' and 'the tallest renate'. For ease of comparison, we rehearse the diagnosis of the fallacy in the singular case. On the readings on which at least one of 'the tallest cordate' and 'the tallest renate' takes narrow scope with respect to the modal operator 'it is contingent that', it is indeed contingent that the tallest cordate is the tallest renate, but it does not follow that something (this) is contingently something (that). By contrast, on the reading on which both 'the tallest cordate' and 'the tallest renate' take wide scope with respect to 'it is contingent that', the argument is valid but the premise false: it is not contingent that the tallest cordate is the tallest renate.[79] In the plural case the diagnosis is similar. On the readings on which at least one of 'the cordates' and 'the renates' takes narrow scope with respect to 'it is contingent that', it is indeed contingent that the cordates are the renates, but it does not follow that some things (these) are contingently some things (those). By contrast, on the reading on which both 'the cordates' and 'the renates' take wide scope with respect to 'it is contingent that', the argument is valid but the premise false: it is not contingent that the cordates are the renates.

Through further reflection on NI≺, we can clarify the modal logic of plurals. For simplicity, we first work through the argument assuming necessitism and S5 (as in ML_p), and later assess what difference revising those assumptions would make to our conclusions.

We can rearrange NI≺ into equivalent form:

(36) $\forall xx \, \forall yy \, ((\forall x \, (x \prec xx \rightarrow x \prec yy) \, \& \, \forall x \, (x \prec yy \rightarrow x \prec xx)) \rightarrow$
$(\Box \forall x \, (x \prec xx \rightarrow x \prec yy) \, \& \, \Box \forall x \, (x \prec yy \rightarrow x \prec xx)))$

---

[79] For contingentists who accept the being constraint, the identity is contingent for the different reason that the thing in question could have been nothing. They accept the necessity of identity only as restricted to possible circumstances in which the thing is something. The point is then that, under the wide scope reading of the descriptions, the identity is not contingent with respect to those circumstances.

In brief, a right-to-left inclusion and a left-to-right inclusion imply a necessary right-to-left inclusion and a necessary left-to-right inclusion. But the left-to-right inclusion gives no support to the necessary right-to-left inclusion, and the right-to-left inclusion gives no support to the necessary left-to-right inclusion. Given that every one of these is one of those, in excluding the possibility that something could have been one of these yet not one of those it does not help to point out that every one of those is one of these. Hence the right-to-left inclusion should imply the necessary right-to-left inclusion, and (equivalently) the left-to-right inclusion should imply the necessary left-to-right inclusion. Thus NI$\prec$ stands or falls with the inferentially stronger principle NS$\prec$:

NS$\prec$ $\forall xx\, \forall yy\, (\forall x\, (x\prec xx \rightarrow x\prec yy) \rightarrow \Box\forall x\, (x\prec xx \rightarrow x\prec yy))$

If these are (at least) some of those, then necessarily these are (at least) some of those. We rely on NS$\prec$ in what follows.

Next, we assume the plural analogue of singletons for sets. There are some things of which necessarily this is the only one:

Single$\prec$ $\forall x\, \exists xx\, \Box\forall y\, (y\prec xx \leftrightarrow x=y)$

For short: necessarily this is the only one of this(pl). In necessitist S5, NS$\prec$ and Single$\prec$ entail the principle that if something is one of some things, it is necessarily one of them:[80]

N$\prec$ $\forall x\, \forall xx\, (x\prec xx \rightarrow \Box x\prec xx)$

If this is one of these, then by Single$\prec$ this(pl) are some of these, so by NS$\prec$ necessarily this(pl) are some of those, so by Single$\prec$ again necessarily this is one of these. For a necessitist, N$\prec$ is the analogue of the widely accepted principle that set membership is rigid: a member of a set could not have failed to be a member of that set.[81]

Since we are assuming necessitist S5, from N$\prec$ we can derive the parallel principle that if something is not one of some things, it is necessarily not one of them:

---

[80] Proof: Omitting initial universal quantifiers, NS$\prec$ and Single$\prec$ yield this:
$\exists xx\, (\Box\forall y\, (y\prec xx \leftrightarrow x=y)\ \&\ \forall yy\, (\forall y\, (y\prec xx \rightarrow y\prec yy) \rightarrow \Box\forall y\, (y\prec xx \rightarrow y\prec yy)))$. From that we derive $\exists xx\, \forall yy\, (\forall y\, (x=y \rightarrow y\prec yy) \rightarrow \Box\forall y\, (x=y \rightarrow y\prec yy))$. Routine simplifications then yield N$\prec$.

[81] Versions of the rigidity of set membership are defended by Fine 1981b, pp. 179–80, Parsons 1983, pp. 286, 299–300, Forbes 1985, p. 109, and Bricker 1989, p. 387. Unlike Fine and Forbes, Bricker refuses to qualify the principle for possible worlds not containing the member or set. Parsons explains his position on that issue at p. 300.

N¬≺ $\forall x\,\forall xx\,(\neg x{\prec}xx \to \Box\neg x{\prec}xx)$

The reasoning is like that from the necessity of identity to the necessity of distinctness.[82] With more expressive power, we can dispense with the appeal to S5 for $\Box$ in ways similar to those discussed in section 4.7 with regard to deriving the necessity of distinctness from the necessity of identity.

Together, N≺ and N¬≺ present a clear and simple picture; ≺ is not contingent:[83]

NC≺ $\forall x\,\forall xx\,(\Box x{\prec}xx \lor \Box\neg x{\prec}xx)$

We can also argue in reverse, deriving NI≺, NS≺, N≺, and N¬≺ from NC≺ in the framework of necessitist S5.

We still need a comprehension principle for plurals that does not collapse modal distinctions. For that, we defang Comp**≺ by omitting the necessity operator (although we can still necessitate the whole conditional):

Comp≺ $\exists x\,A \to \exists xx\,\forall x\,(x{\prec}xx \leftrightarrow A)$

This is harmless. It is just a standard non-modal comprehension principle for plurals (although modal operators are allowed in A). But combining it with NC≺ turns it into a strong modal comprehension principle:

Comp⁺≺ $\exists x\,A \to \exists xx\,\forall x\,((A \to \Box x{\prec}xx)\ \&\ (\neg A \to \Box\neg x{\prec}xx))$

Conversely, from Comp⁺≺ we can derive Comp≺ and, less trivially, Single≺ (put $x{=}y$ for A and use the necessity of identity and distinctness). Combining Comp⁺≺ and NI≺, we can also derive NC≺, and thence NS≺, N≺, and N¬≺. Thus Comp⁺≺ and NI≺ form a strong modal theory of plurals in the setting of necessitist S5.

Modulo its restriction to non-vacuous formulas A, Comp⁺≺ is equivalent to the monadic second-order special case of a second comprehension principle that Gallin formulates for ML$_P$. He calls it 'extensional comprehension':[84]

EC $\Box\exists V\,(Rn(V)\ \&\ \forall v_1 \ldots \forall v_n\,(Vv_1 \ldots v_n \leftrightarrow A))$

---

[82] In necessitist S5, we have both singular and plural versions of BF and CBF, and so can validly omit initial universal quantifiers in reasoning. Necessitating N≺ and reasoning in K yields $\Diamond x{\prec}xx \to \Diamond\Box x{\prec}xx$. Since S5 contains the B principle, that gives $\Diamond\Box x{\prec}xx \to x{\prec}xx$, from which contraposition gives $\neg x{\prec}xx \to \Box\neg x{\prec}xx$.

[83] In the terminology of Montague 1970a, pp. 122, 132, ≺ is a relation; see also Gallin 1975, p. 77.

[84] See Gallin 1975, pp. 77–8.

Here $Rn(V)$ abbreviates $\forall v_1 \ldots \forall v_n \, (\Box V v_1 \ldots v_n \vee \Box \neg V v_1 \ldots v_n), v_1, \ldots, v_n$ are of types $t_1, \ldots, t_n$ respectively, and V is a variable of type $\langle t_1, \ldots, t_n \rangle$ not free in A. EC is standardly valid, because we can secure $Rn(V)$ by rigidifying the extension of $\lambda v_1, \ldots, v_n(A)$ at the world of evaluation. But Gallin shows that, proof-theoretically, EC is surprisingly strong. EC does not follow g-logically from Comp; not even its monadic second-order case does.[85] Indeed, EC is g-logically equivalent given Comp to the axiom At of atomic propositions in section 5.2. However, the proof essentially depends on coding the complete state of the world in a third-order intension; At does not follow g-logically given Comp from the monadic second-order case of EC.[86] Nor therefore does the plural comprehension principle Comp$^+$≺ establish atomic propositions.

If a necessitist's core modal theory of plurals consists of NI≺ and Comp$^+$≺, how much of it can a contingentist accept? The overall picture should not change radically, for the logical differences between contingentism and necessitism disappear when we restrict the modal operators or the first-order quantifiers or both to a limited range over which being is uncontroversially non-contingent: the grosser logical issues arise even within such a limited range. For instance, the absurdity of (35) remains demonstrable within that range. Nevertheless, subtler disagreements emerge once the restriction is lifted.

In some cases the contingentist accepts the same principle as the necessitist but draws fewer consequences from it. For example, both sides accept E≺ and its necessitation:

(37) $\Box \forall xx \, \exists x \, x{≺}xx$

The necessitist then applies the plural form of CBF to derive (37) from (38):

(38) $\forall xx \, \Box \exists x \, x{≺}xx$

By contrast, (38) looks quite implausible to the contingentist: if these are Tom, Dick, and Harry, why should it be necessary that something is one of them, if it is contingent that anything is Tom, Dick, or Harry? Indeed, given Single≺, which is innocent even from a contingentist perspective, (38) yields the necessity of being: everything is necessarily something.[87] Thus

---

[85] See Gallin 1975, pp. 112–15, corollary 15.3 and theorem 15.4 (for n = 1) respectively. The restriction to the non-vacuous case makes no difference to the result because the vacuous case is a g-logical consequence of Comp.

[86] See Gallin 1975, pp. 87–9, theorem 11.5, and p. 116, theorem 15.5, respectively.

[87] For $\exists xx \, \Box \forall y \, (y{≺}xx \leftrightarrow x{=}y)$ and $\forall xx \, \Box \exists y \, y{≺}xx$ entail $\Box \exists y \, x{=}y$.

the contingentist rejects (38), and with it the plural form of CBF. 'Varying domains' for singular quantifiers require 'varying domains' for plural quantifiers too.

Here is a trickier issue for the contingentist. Tom, Dick, and Harry are in the actual circumstances. Tom and Dick, but not Harry, are in some possible circumstances C. Let these be Tom and Dick, and those be Tom, Dick, and Harry. Thus in the actual circumstances every one of these is one of those. Therefore, by NS≺, every one of these is one of those in C too. Since Tom is one of these in C, Tom is one of those in C. But are those in C, since Harry is actually one of those and is not in C? If those are in C, then both NS≺ and NI≺ have false necessitations. For by contingentist lights in C every one of those is one of these and vice versa, so, applying NS≺ or NI≺ to C, in the actual circumstances every one of those is one of these too, which is false because Harry is actually one of those but not one of these. Thus, for a contingentist who wants to retain NS≺ as a necessary principle, in C Tom is one of those, even though there are not those for Tom to be one of. Thus a form of the plural being constraint fails.

On the envisaged contingentist view, the formula $\forall x\,(x{\prec}xx \leftrightarrow x{\prec}yy)$ does not properly capture a plural analogue of identity, since these and those satisfy it in C even though Harry could have been one of those without being one of these. To define a proper analogue, the contingentist would have to enlarge the scope of the quantification somehow to take in Harry: in effect, to simulate necessitist quantification and read it back into NI≺ and NS≺. Chapter 7 assesses the prospects for doing so.[88] On these assumptions, the universal quantifiers in Comp≺ and Comp⁺≺ presumably require similar modifications, otherwise they lack the requisite generality. For present purposes this option is not very interesting, since it is largely an attempt to talk like a necessitist while thinking like a contingentist.[89]

---

[88] In the notation of Chapter 7, the relevant formula is $\uparrow\Box\forall x\downarrow(x{\prec}xx \leftrightarrow x{\prec}yy)$.

[89] The formalization in Bricker 1989, p. 389, of the plural de re reading of 'Every F might be G' as (in present notation) $\exists xx\,(\forall y\,(y{\prec}xx \leftrightarrow Fy)$ & $\Diamond{<}\forall x{>}\,(x{\prec}xx \rightarrow Gx))$ (where the angle brackets indicate an 'outer', 'possibilist' reading of the quantifier) depends on the assumption that $x{\prec}xx$ can be true even at a world in which there are not all the objects assigned to the variable xx. For otherwise, even if the possibilist quantifier sweeps up all those objects, $x{\prec}xx \rightarrow Gx$ will be vacuously true for each of them at that world even if Gx is false, and the formalization may receive a truth value that does not fit the intended reading of the original sentence. This is analogous to Bricker's assumption that something may belong to a set even at a world that does not contain that set (1989, p. 387). It is unclear what right the contingentist has to the assumption on which Bricker's formalization depends, if the outer quantifiers are eliminated in favour of modal operators and inner quantifiers, as he contemplates (1989, p. 394).

A more full-blooded contingentist response is to accept both singular and plural being constraints and revise NS$\prec$ by conditioning the consequent:

NS$_C\prec$ $\qquad \forall xx\, \forall yy\, (\forall x\, (x\prec xx \to x\prec yy) \to \Box(\exists x\, x\prec yy \to$
$\qquad\qquad \forall x\, (x\prec xx \to x\prec yy)))$

The idea is that if there are these and those and every one of the former is one of the latter, then if one of those had not been (like Harry in C), those would not have been, so nothing would have been one of those (by the plural being constraint), and the condition $\exists x\, x\prec yy$ fails. Of course, NS$_C\prec$ requires no condition $\exists x\, x\prec xx$, since its falsity entails the vacuous truth of $\forall x\, (x\prec xx \to x\prec yy)$.

For this full-blooded contingentist, NI$\prec$ holds unrevised, for if there are these and those and every one of these is one of those and vice versa, then if one of these had not been, nothing would have been one of these or those, so they are vacuously coextensive. As usual, the contingentist will necessitate NI$\prec$ but not apply plural CBF.

On the same view, N$\prec$ requires modification, for although Harry is one of those, he would not have been if there had not been those. The natural, minimal revision is this:

N$_C\prec$ $\qquad \forall x\, \forall xx\, (x\prec xx \to \Box(\exists y\, y\prec xx \to x\prec xx))$

For if there had not been those, nothing would have been one of those. N$_C\prec$ is analogous to a contingentist rigidity principle for set membership. By contrast, the contingentist will accept N$\neg\prec$ unrevised, since $\neg x\prec xx$ is vacuously true in circumstances without the things at issue.

Since the non-modal comprehension principle Comp$\prec$ is neutral between necessitism and contingentism, we may combine it with N$_C\prec$ and N$\neg\prec$. The result is this contingentist modification of Comp$^+\prec$:

Comp$^+_C\prec$ $\qquad \exists x\, A \to \exists xx\, \forall x\, ((A \to \Box(\exists y\, y\prec xx \to x\prec xx))\, \&$
$\qquad\qquad (\neg A \to \Box\neg x\prec xx))$

Although contingentists can accept Comp$^+_C\prec$ in the setting of a contingentist S5 system with NI$\prec$, it does not fully capture their view of comprehension for plural modal logic. Let these verify Comp$^+_C\prec$ as values of the variable xx when A is 'x is Tom or Dick'. It does not follow that there are still these in counterfactual circumstances in which there is Tom and there is Dick, for the conditional $\exists y\, y\prec xx \to x\prec xx$ may be vacuously true. In crude terms,

Comp$^+$$_C$$\prec$ lets the postulated pluralities be too modally fragile. Instead of $\exists y\ y\prec xx$ as antecedent, a universal generalization is needed over everything that *actually* satisfies A, to the effect that it is still something in the counterfactual circumstances. But that sort of backward-looking generalization is inexpressible in standard quantified modal logic. Extra model operators are needed. Chapter 7 discusses their significance. For now, we simply observe that although contingentist plural modal logic can be developed, it lacks the neatness of its necessitist analogue.[90]

Although semantics in set-theoretic terms is not the intended interpretation of plural quantifiers, it does provide consistency proofs for plural modal logic. To that end, the necessitist can take the values of plural variables as nonempty subsets of the constant domain D, the plural quantifiers as ranging over all such values, and $\prec$ as a logical constant for set membership. The most pertinent semantic clauses are these:

M, w, $\underline{a}$ $\vDash$ $v\prec vv$ if and only if $\underline{a}(v) \in \underline{a}(vv)$

M, w, $\underline{a}$ $\vDash$ $\forall vv\, A$ if and only if whenever $d \subseteq$ D and
$$d \neq \{\}, \text{M}, w, \underline{a}[vv/d] \vDash A$$

The world parameter w does not appear on the right-hand side of either clause: the plural structure is perfectly rigid. Any such necessitist model validates Comp$\prec$, Comp$^+$$\prec$, E$\prec$, N$\prec$, N$\neg\prec$, NC$\prec$, NI$\prec$, NS$\prec$, and Single$\prec$, however necessitated and universally generalized, and a fortiori their contingentist weakenings. The robust contingentist restricts the semantic clauses to the domain of w:

M, w, $\underline{a}$ $\vDash$ $v\prec vv$ if and only if $\underline{a}(v) \in \underline{a}(vv) \subseteq$ D(w)

M, w, $\underline{a}$ $\vDash$ $\forall vv\, A$ if and only if whenever $d \subseteq$ D(w) and
$$d \neq \{\}, \text{M}, w, \underline{a}[vv/d] \vDash A$$

Within the relevant domains, the plural structure is rigid. Any such contingentist model validates Comp$\prec$, Comp$^+$$_C$$\prec$, E$\prec$, N$_C$$\prec$, N$\neg\prec$, NI$\prec$, NS$_C$$\prec$, and

___

[90] Rumfitt 2005, pp. 113–17, defends a principle (M) apparently similar to N$_C$$\prec$: (in present notation): $x\prec xx \rightarrow \Box(\text{E}^2xx \rightarrow x\prec xx)$, where E^2xx is defined as equivalent to $\forall y\ (y\prec xx \rightarrow \text{E}y)$ and may be read 'xx exist'; Ey may be read 'y exists'. However, Rumfitt countenances a definition on which Ey is equivalent to $\exists z\ y=z$, which would make the condition E^2xx trivial and redundant and so (M) equivalent to N$\prec$. Since Rumfitt is no necessitist, his intention might better be captured in the notation of Chapter 7 by defining E^2xx as $\uparrow\Box\forall y\ (y\prec xx \rightarrow \downarrow\text{E}y)$. For detailed discussion of contingentist comprehension principles related to Comp$^+$$_C$$\prec$ see Uzquiano 2011.

Single≺, as well as singular and plural being constraints, however necessitated and universally generalized. At the very least, neither necessitist nor contingentist plural modal logic collapses.

Whether the plural modal logic is contingentist or necessitist, it cannot formalize arguments like # and ## in section 5.5. 'Alice doesn't do something she could have done' is not equivalent to 'Alice isn't one of some things she could have been one of', and 'There is something it can be fun to be' is not equivalent to 'There are some things it can be fun to be one of', for the plural versions are rigid, unlike the originals. There are no things such that being one of them is necessarily equivalent to smoking cigars; nor are there things such that being one of them is necessarily equivalent to being everything bad. Plurals are thoroughly extensional.

For purposes of formalizing pure mathematics, the extensionality of plurals is at worst harmless, at best a virtue. Each theorem has an adequate formalization without explicit modal operators. Although we may implicitly necessitate it for application to merely possible circumstances, that is no obstacle to extensionality, since we still reason with its unnecessitated form under the counterfactual supposition.

On a modal-structural interpretation of mathematics, every theorem makes an implicitly modal claim: in very rough first-order terms, mathematics is the science of all possible structures. A mathematical theorem is typically interpreted as the necessitation of a closed second-order universal generalization, but that is the same *de dicto* pattern as before of modal operators prefixed to non-modal formulas.[91] On the plural interpretation of the second-order quantifiers, one needs only the necessitation of the non-modal comprehension principle Comp≺, not a distinctively *de re* comprehension principle such as the necessitist Comp$^+$≺ or the contingentist Comp^+_C≺. Of course, in applying mathematics to reach a conclusion of the form $\forall y \ \Box A$, one may need *de re* instances of necessitated and then universally generalized Comp≺, such as (39):

$$(39) \qquad \forall y \ \Box(\exists x \ Rxy \rightarrow \exists xx \ \forall x \ (x≺xx \leftrightarrow Rxy))$$

Nevertheless, one is still relying on Comp≺, not on a stronger comprehension principle like Comp$^+$≺ or Comp^+_C≺ with distinctive commitments to the plural analogue of modal persistence conditions.

---

[91] See Hellman 1989, pp. 30–1, 72–3. His system is second-order rather than plural, but the same point applies.

By contrast, a modal interpretation of quantifiers in mathematics introduces the modal operators locally in a formula rather than globally. The idea
may be that the 'indefinite extensibility' of mathematical generality concerns
potentiality rather than actuality. Such a reading of mathematical language
has more distinctively *de re* commitments. For instance, if the first-order
and second-order quantifiers in the true formula (40) are implicitly modal,
its explicitly modal form is (41):

(40) $\forall x \exists X \forall y \, (Xy \leftrightarrow x=y)$

(41) $\Box\forall x \Diamond\exists X \Box\forall y \, (Xy \leftrightarrow x=y)$

The truth of (41) depends on the second-order analogue of modal persistence conditions. In rough first-order terms, if necessarily any given property
could have had any given extension, (41) would be false. Both the necessitist and the contingentist plural modal logics sketched earlier yield the plural
analogue of (41), by Single≺; Comp≺ is not enough, however much it is
necessitated and universally generalized. In general, the plural reading is
adequate for the main mathematical applications of second-order modal
logic. The primarily extensional structure of mathematics makes that hardly
surprising.[92]
   For many non-mathematical purposes, however, a plural reading of
second-order logic is inadequate, as we saw for arguments like # and ##.
In Chapter 6, some such cases prove of special significance for metaphysics.

5.9 Non-plural interpretations of higher-order modal logic

Even if English lacks quantification of the predicate itself, it has quantification of the complement of the copula. We can amplify 'Ben could have been
something he is not' with 'namely, boring' or 'namely, a butcher'. If Ben

---

[92] See Linnebo 2010 for the mathematical application of plural modal logic and Parsons 1983,
pp. 298–341, for the closely related case of modal set theory. For some such applications S5 is unsuitable as an underlying propositional modal logic, since an indefinitely modally growing hierarchy
needs a transitive but non-symmetric accessibility relation, as for S4; see Parsons 1983, p. 317. Linnebo
2010 works with S4.2 (which extends S4 by the axiom schema $\Diamond\Box A \rightarrow \Box\Diamond A$), but his construction
works for any modal logic between S4.2 and Triv (whose characteristic axiom is $\Box A \leftrightarrow A$), including S5.

could have been boring but is not boring, or could have been a butcher but is not a butcher, then Ben could have been something he is not. Although the predicate contains 'is' as well as 'boring' or 'a butcher', the range of permissible variation in the complement of the copula is great enough to make the result equivalent to quantification of the predicate. For whatever the predicate 'VPs', 'S VPs' is equivalent to 'S is such that it VPs', from which 'S is something' follows. Although we can ask 'What is S?', the degree of nominalization involved seems slight. Thus plural quantification is not the only plausible candidate for higher-order quantification in natural language. The examples also show that quantification of the complement of the copula, unlike plural quantification, is not in general rigid.[93]

A deflationary response is that such quantification is merely substitutional: 'Ben could have been something he is not' is true if and only if some sentence of the form 'Ben could have been F and Ben is not F' is true. Arbitrarily complex substitutions for 'F' are permitted. In a formal language with quantification into predicate position, we may need a λ operator to form complex predicates, given the distinction between predicates and open formulas (see section 4.1). To avoid circularity, we may forbid impredicative substitutions for 'F' that contain such a quantifier. Less restrictively, we may construct a hierarchy of substitutional quantifiers in which the substitution instances for a substitutional quantifier at a given level contain substitutional quantifiers only from lower levels. To increase the range of substitution instances, we may permit substitutions for 'F' that contain free individual variables. Thus the truth of 'Ben could have been within a mile of x and Ben is not within a mile of x' for some value of the variable x suffices for the truth of 'Ben could have been something he is not', even if no closed term of the language denotes such a value. Substitutional quantifiers are definable for any grammatical position in the language.

The familiar trouble with substitutional quantification is that it is too sensitive to the expressive power of the language. When we add new words undefinable in the old language, we add new substitution instances and change the truth values of some substitutionally quantified sentences. The

[93] For an account of second-order quantification in which the copula plays a crucial role see Wiggins 1984. A recent account of second-order quantification in terms of common nouns is Besson 2009; see also Gupta 1980. Frege 1979, p. 62, downplays the copula as a mere grammatical device (also Dummett 1981, p. 214); Wright 1998, pp. 250–1 argues that doing so conflicts with Frege's account of incomplete expressions.

use of free individual variables in substitution instances does not solve the problem, for it is equivalent to adding proper names for all individuals, which does not eliminate the oversensitivity. For example, a standard first-order language for arithmetic already has numerals for all natural numbers; since it has only countably many formulas with one free variable, it can define only countably many of the uncountably many subsets of the set of natural numbers. Thus one can always increase the expressive power of the language by adding a new primitive monadic predicate whose extension is a previously undefinable subset. Similarly, one can always increase the expressive power of a first-order language for set theory by adding new primitive predicates. The same goes for non-mathematical cases.

The worry is not that substitutional quantification is in any way ill defined. If the language without substitutional quantifiers has a well-defined truth-conditional semantics, so has the language with substitutional quantifiers.[94] The point is rather that the substitutional semantics is not faithful to the intended meaning of quantifying the complement of the copula. I ask 'Could Ben have been something he is not?' Someone may answer the question by introducing a new expression 'F' with a previously inexpressible meaning into the language, getting us to understand it in the usual way, by means of examples, and then explaining why 'Ben could have been F and Ben is not F' is true. That does not merely answer the question I can ask in the new language by saying 'Could Ben have been something he is not?' It answers the question I asked in the same words in the old language. The conclusion 'Ben could have been something he is not' was already expressible; only the premise 'Ben could have been F and Ben is not F' was previously inexpressible. The intended meaning of quantifying the complement of the copula is not bound by the expressive limitations of the language in the way the substitutional account postulates.

A substitutionalist might grudgingly respond to the objection by including merely future or possible substitution instances for 'F' in future or counterfactual extensions of English. Of course, what counts for the truth of the quantified sentence in a context of utterance C is the truth of a substitution instance A in C, not in different circumstances in which the language would contain A, otherwise some quantified metalinguistic sentences receive the wrong truth value. This proposal can be developed in contrasting directions.

---

[94] See Kripke 1976.

One way requires the serious possibility of a community using the counter-factual extension as its language, and so meeting the cognitive preconditions for accessing the meanings at issue. But any such constraint risks imposing unintended restrictions on the quantifiers, just as we do not always intend to restrict our first-order quantifiers to objects each of which can be separately designated by a thinker.[95] Another way treats the extensions of English simply as abstract languages, irrespective of whether they could really be spoken, and comes much closer to adequacy.[96] It is also much less distinc-tively substitutionalist. When we try to explain in general terms what counts as an abstract language, and so what counts as a possible semantics for an expression of a given type, such as a monadic predicate, we find ourselves employing higher-order quantifiers of the very sorts at issue, and the substi-tutional aspect of the account becomes an idle wheel. However the proposal is developed, it also risks a form of Russell's paradox if it makes unrestricted higher-order quantification equivalent to first-order quantification over possible extensions of a language, interpreted expressions or the like, although the details depend on those of the proposed account.[97]

Substitutional and even quasi-substitutional accounts of higher-order quantification are ultimately inadequate first rough gestures in the right direction. In an attempt to do better, we may start with a naive explanation, in first-order terms, and then filter out the inaccuracies. Suppose that a lan-guage has expressions of a particular semantic category. Those expressions have semantic values of a particular type. When competent speakers of the language encounter a new atomic expression of that category, they are already prepared for it to have a semantic value of that type. Their prepared-ness facilitates their learning which particular semantic value it has. Thus their linguistic competence already provides the groundwork for under-standing quantifiers that bind variables of the given category: they range over every semantic value of the given type, whether or not any expression of the original language has or could have that value. Even if such quanti-fiers are not added to the language, we need them for a metalanguage capable of expressing a Tarskian theory of logical consequence for it, if we treat at

---

[95] See also Williamson 2007, pp. 16–17 on quantifying over the unthinkable.

[96] See Davies 1981, pp. 114–19 (expanding on an idea in Evans 1977), for a detailed truth-theoretic account of first-order quantification in such abstract semi-substitutional terms, and pp. 136–42 for its extension to quantification into predicate position (even in a modal setting).

[97] Compare the heuristic account of higher-order quantification in terms of first-order quantification over structured Fregean thoughts in Wright 2007.

least one atomic expression of the given category as a non-logical constant, since we must generalize over all semantic values of the appropriate type for that expression.

That explanation involves first-order quantification over semantic values; 'value' is an ordinary noun. One lesson of Russell's paradox is that even unrestricted first-order quantification is not fully adequate for the semantics of predicates.[98] Thus the preceding explanation is inaccurate. We can formulate an accurate explanation only after we have introduced quantifiers of the sort in question. Is that a vicious circularity? It is quite general in semantics. First we understand expressions of a given semantic category, then we reflect on their meaning. If introducing higher-order quantifiers of a given sort constitutes a genuine advance in expressive power, we cannot expect to explain them before introducing them. What we can hope to do is to account for them in retrospect, by using them to rewrite the inaccurate first-order explanation in more accurate higher-order terms, to explain how our understanding of those quantifiers is rooted in our understanding of closed expressions of the same category as the quantified variables.[99]

Sceptics may still fear an illusion of understanding. But how can one check that an expression is meaningful before one understands it? Of course, if one recognizes that other people already understand it, then one can deduce that it is meaningful, but that is not the kind of foundational reassurance the sceptic seeks, and in any case is unavailable when expressions of a new semantic category are introduced for the very first time. Talk, like life as a whole, is an inherently risky business. We must go ahead as best we can, pulling back when things go wrong rather than waiting for a guarantee in advance that they cannot go wrong. In that spirit, we may continue to use a formal language such as ML_p with higher-order quantifiers without attempting to reduce them to first-order terms. The semantics of the language, and in particular of those quantifiers, would be given in still higher-order terms, and so on. We will also use the unintended set-theoretic model theory,

---

[98] See Williamson 2003a, pp. 425–6, for the details of the argument as applied to a Tarskian theory of logical consequence. If the account of higher-order quantification in Bostock 1998 is taken at face value it is vulnerable to such a paradox, since it uses first-order quantification over interpretations, but it may more charitably be read along the lines in the text. The account in Rayo and Yablo 2001 uses 'somehow', which in English is uncomfortably close to a first-order quantifier over ways, but it too may be read along lines similar to those proposed.

[99] In avoiding any slide down the orders, Prior 1971, pp. 34–9, becomes rather cryptic, but his account is similar in spirit to the proposed account.

standard or generalized, both as an expository device to be taken with a grain of salt and as a formal check on the consistency of our constructions (relative to set theory).

Reassuringly, the practice of using a higher-order language does not collapse. The most salient aspect of that practice is the inferential one. The higher-order quantifiers do not prove equivalent to first-order devices. But this should not tempt us to try explaining them in purely inferential terms, for example by formulating suitable introduction and elimination rules. Not only is inferentialism a dubious approach in general, it faces a special obstacle in the incompleteness of higher-order logic.[100] Since arithmetic can be coded in any of the higher-order systems at issue, Gödel's incompleteness theorems apply. A simpler point is that the relevant proof systems are compact, in the sense that whatever is provable from a set of premises Γ is provable from some finite subset of Γ. Although humans can describe and investigate non-compact consequence relations, the inferential moves we can make in practice are all compact. But higher-order logical consequence is not compact: although we can describe and investigate it, we cannot fully embody it in our practice. For example, let $\exists_n F$ be a standard first-order formalization of 'There are at least n planets', Γ the set of $\exists_n F$ for all natural numbers n, and $\exists_\infty F$ a standard second-order formalization of 'There are infinitely many planets'. Then $\exists_\infty F$ is a logical consequence of Γ, but not of any finite subset of Γ. To deny that $\exists_\infty F$ is a logical consequence of Γ is in effect to deny that 'infinitely many' can be formalized in higher-order logic, and thereby to deprive the latter of much of its mathematical and logical value.[101] Thus the rules on which the inferentialist account is based are not both sound and complete for higher-order logic. The argument applies just as much in the modal as in the non-modal case.

Despite the incompleteness of higher-order logic, the meanings of the higher-order quantifiers may still somehow supervene metaphysically on our use of them, non-semantically described: but the former cannot be read off the latter from the outside. Rather, one must take the plunge, participate in the practice oneself, and, all being well, thereby understand them from

---

[100] For a critique of some inferentialist assumptions see Williamson 2007, pp. 73–133 and 281–5.

[101] Wright 2007 addresses a specific challenge to an inferentialist account of higher-order logic from Gödel incompleteness, but not that from non-compactness. He appears to be working with a conception of higher-order logical consequence restricted in ways that tend to undermine his intended application of it to his neo-logicist project in the philosophy of mathematics.

the inside. That is no special feature of the higher-order quantifiers; it is the normal case with understanding.

A popular question to press on higher-order logic is whether the extra it adds to our commitments is in *ontology* or in *ideology*. Does it commit us to new things, or just to new ways of thinking about the old things?

The question has strong Quinean presuppositions of which those who ask it do not always seem aware.[102] Why should the only alternative to ontology be ideology? By definition, ontology concerns what there is. Claims of the form 'There is a G' are naturally paraphrased by first-order sentences of the form $\exists x\ Gx$. The quantification in 'There is a G' is not into predicate position, even if 'G' is replaced by 'property', 'relation', or 'concept'. Ontology is part of metaphysics. The content of the ontological commitment is true if there is a G and false otherwise. Its truth value depends on how the mostly non-linguistic world is, as characterized in first-order terms. By contrast, ideology is defined as a semantic matter: what ideas can a language express? An ideological commitment is not a truth or falsehood about the mostly non-linguistic world. Even with respect to non-metalinguistic sentences, it concerns meaningfulness rather than truth. If higher-order quantifiers are neither reducible to first-order terms nor metalinguistic, then a higher-order commitment of the form $\exists X\ \Phi X$ is typically neither ontological nor ideological. Thus the dichotomy between ontology and ideology insinuates the presupposition that metaphysical questions are first-order. Although Quineans endorse that assumption, it is deeply contentious, not to be sneaked in without argument through the use of familiar terminology. Attempts to use the dichotomy without its Quinean presuppositions confuse the authors as much as their readers.

One effect of the dichotomy between ontology and ideology on debates about higher-order quantification has been to convey the misleading impression that if such quantification lacks ontological commitment then it is somehow metaphysically lightweight, just a convenient manner of speaking. Its friends may present that as a virtue, while its critics accuse them of smuggling in something heavyweight. But not all metaphysical commitment is ontological commitment. The irreducibly higher-order metaphysical claim $\exists X\ \Phi X$ may run just as great an epistemic risk of falsification by non-linguistic reality as the first-order metaphysical claim $\exists x\ Gx$. Higher-order quantification

---

[102] The terminology of the contrast goes back to Quine 1951.

sometimes enables us to avoid extra ontological commitment, but it typically does so at the cost of extra higher-order metaphysical commitment. The reasons for going higher-order are quite different: for example, the demands of a good response to Russell's paradox. The Quinean overemphasis on ontological commitment has distorted metaphysics. Ontological commitments matter for the same sorts of reasons as other theoretical commitments do: they have a risk of being false (and a compensating chance of being true), and sometimes they increase the complexity of a theory. They should be subsumed under that general heading, not singled out for special treatment.[103]

It may be objected that quantification imports no extra commitment, for if the unquantified sentence *Fa* logically entails ∃x *Fx* then we are already committed to ∃x *Fx* in accepting *Fa*, and likewise if *Fa* logically entails ∃X *Xa* then we are already committed to ∃X *Xa* in accepting *Fa*.[104] But that objection misconstrues the dialectical context. Of course we are in some sense committed to every genuine logical consequence of what we accept. But saying so is of little help when we are trying to determine which logic is correct. For that purpose we must treat competing logics as competing theories. Even if a higher-order logic is in fact correct, it still embodies distinctive theorems in a distinctive language, whose theoretical costs and benefits can be weighed and compared with those of its rivals, such as first-order set theories.

As with theory choice in other disciplines, the proper emphasis in logic is not on minimizing commitments, but on maximizing strong, simple generalizations consistently with what we know. The next chapter applies such a methodology to the choice between necessitist and contingentist theories in higher-order modal logic.

---

[103] Of course, Carnap and some other philosophers with positivist tendencies deny that ontological questions have true or false answers. See Chalmers, Manley, and Wasserman 2009 for recent essays on such matters (its title and subtitle jointly manifest the conflation of metaphysics with ontology about which I am complaining). See also Rosen 2002a, Hirsch 2011, and Sider 2011.

[104] See Wright 2007.

6

Intensional Comprehension Principles and Metaphysics

6.1 Comprehension and higher-order necessitism

Higher-order modal logic is not only of interest in its own right. It also provides a wider setting in which to assess principles of first-order modal logic, by drawing out more of their consequences. In particular, it illuminates the contrast between contingentism and necessitism. In this chapter, we will see how contingentism is caught between conflicting theoretical pressures in the higher-order case. On one hand, considerations of systematicity in higher-order logic—in particular, adequate comprehension principles—favour what can be loosely described as the necessary being of haecceistic properties whose possible application is connected to a unique individual. On the other hand, further considerations of systematicity in general metaphysics favour a connection in modal status between haecceistic properties and individuals, so that if some individuals have contingent being, some haecceistic properties have contingent being too. By contrast, necessitism avoids this tension.

Of course, when comparing contingentism and necessitism, we can uncritically assume no form of possible worlds semantics for higher-order modal logic, which we have already seen to be radically misleading from a contingentist perspective (sections 3.6 and 4.9). Rather, we should assess principles of higher-order modal logic in the object-language by theoretical virtues such as strength, simplicity, and compatibility with what we already know.

A good example is the comprehension principle Comp from section 5.5. For present purposes we may conveniently focus on the special case Comp_M where the higher-order variable is monadic (whence the subscript 'M') and second-order:

$$\text{Comp}_M \qquad \exists X \,\Box\forall x \,(Xx \leftrightarrow A)$$

Here x is an individual variable that may occur free in the formula A and X is a monadic first-level predicate variable that does not occur free in A. Any result of prefixing an instance of Comp_M with any number of necessity operators and universal quantifiers of any type (binding parameters in A) in any order also counts as an instance of Comp_M. For heuristic purposes we may bracket the warnings about nominalization in sections 5.7 and 5.9 and roughly paraphrase Comp_M as saying that there is a property having which is strictly equivalent to being such-and-such, where the open formula A says of the value of the variable x that it is such-and-such. It is the property of being such-and-such. In some logics we can derive Comp_M by $\exists$-generalization from the elementary λ-conversion principle $\Box\forall x\,(\lambda x(A)x \leftrightarrow A)$, as noted in section 5.5, and we can regard the property as the referent of the predicate $\lambda x(A)$. In any case, Comp_M is an attractive comprehension principle as it stands.

We saw that the standard possible worlds model theory for ML_p validates all instances of Comp_M. Although that will not convince contingentists or even all necessitists that Comp_M is metaphysically universal, it does at least show the schema to be integral to one consistent and formally elegant picture of modal reality. Independently of the formal semantics, we also saw that something like Comp_M is the rationale for pre-theoretically compelling arguments by second-order generalization, such as # and ## in section 5.5. The latter consideration carries as much weight for contingentists as for necessitists.

As previously explained, and still in nominalizing shorthand, Comp_M requires an abundant theory of properties, on which open sentences like 'x is not red' and 'x is red or green' define properties, for we can put $\neg Rx$ or $Rx \lor Gx$ for A. In this sense, sharing a property does not imply similarity. Whatever the virtues of a sparse theory of natural properties for other purposes, we saw it to be unsuitable for a good theory of higher-order logic, modal or non-modal. Without a reasonably strong comprehension principle, higher-order logic is impotent, because we cannot instantiate its higher-order universal generalizations when we need to. We therefore adopt Comp_M as a working hypothesis.

Comp_M implies a second-order analogue of the necessitist principle NNE for properties: necessarily every property is necessarily something. To see this, we must first formalize the second-order principle. For a first-order variable x, the open sentence 'x is something' is formalized as $\exists y\, x{=}y$. Thus to formalize 'X is something' for a second-order variable X we need the analogue for predicates of the identity predicate for individual terms. For reasons explained in sections 5.3 and 5.5, the natural candidate is necessary coextensiveness. Hence the analogue of $x=y$ is $\Box\forall x\,(Xx \leftrightarrow Yx)$, so the analogue of $\exists y\,x=y$ is $\exists Y\,\Box\forall x\,(Xx \leftrightarrow Yx)$, and the analogue of NNE is this:

$$\text{NNE}_{\text{M}} \qquad \Box\forall X\,\Box\exists Y\,\Box\forall x\,(Xx \leftrightarrow Yx)$$

But if we instantiate Comp_{M} with Yx for A and the prefix $\Box\forall Y\,\Box$, the result is $\Box\forall Y\,\Box\exists X\,\Box\forall x\,(Xx \leftrightarrow Yx)$, which is trivially equivalent to NNE_{M}. In a rough nominalizing paraphrase, Comp_{M} entails that properties have non-contingent being.

A similar point holds for any higher type: the general comprehension principle Comp entails the corresponding analogue of NNE for that type. Of course, Comp does not entail NNE itself, since it is not a comprehension principle for individuals. As noted in section 5.5, NNE fails in some formal models of Comp.

Deriving the analogues of NNE takes much less than the full strength of Comp. Only predicative instances are needed, in which the schematic letter A is replaced by a formula with no higher-order quantifiers, indeed no quantifiers at all.

The significance of the result depends on the analogy between identity and necessary coextensiveness, which in turn requires the latter to obey the following intersubstitutability principle, analogous to Leibniz's Law: $\Box\forall x\,(Px \leftrightarrow Qx)$ entails $B \to B*$ whenever B and $B*$ differ only in one's having an unbound occurrence of P where the other has an unbound occurrence of Q, and likewise for other types. That entailment is not automatic, for at least three reasons.

First, if the background propositional modal logic lacks the S4 principle $\Box A \to \Box\Box A$, then $\Box\forall x\,(Fx \leftrightarrow Gx)$ will not entail $\Box\Box\forall x\,(Fx \leftrightarrow Gx)$. Since $\Box\forall x\,(Fx \leftrightarrow Gx)$ does entail the trivial logical truth $\Box\Box\forall x\,(Fx \leftrightarrow Fx)$, it does not guarantee the intersubstitutability of F and G.

Second, even if the background propositional modal logic is S5, the intersubstitutability principle may still fail in the absence of the being constraint:

$$(1) \qquad \Box\forall x\,\Box(Gx \to \exists y\,x=y)$$

We can show this formally by considering a Kripke model with varying domains in which the accessibility relation holds universally, without treating the model as the intended interpretation. At each world w, let the extension of F be the domain of w and the extension of G be the union of the domains of all worlds. Thus F and G coincide in extension over the domain of each world, so $\Box\forall x\ (Fx \leftrightarrow Gx)$ is true throughout the model. But throughout the model (1) is false while the result of putting F for G in (1) is true. Thus the intersubstitutability principle fails in the model.

Third, even if the background propositional modal logic is S5 and all instances of the being constraint hold, the intersubstitutability principle may still fail if the logic is hyperintensional, because $\Box\forall x\ (Fx \leftrightarrow Gx)$ does not entail $\Phi F \to \Phi G$ for some atomic second-level predicate Φ.

These difficulties make less difference to the overall upshot than one might expect, for if they force a revision of $\mathrm{NNE_M}$, they also force a matching revision of $\mathrm{Comp_M}$. For example, if the S4 principle fails, a closer analogue of $x{=}y$ than $\Box\forall x\ (Fx \leftrightarrow Gx)$ is $\Box^\omega\forall x\ (Fx \leftrightarrow Gx)$, where $\Box^\omega$ is equivalent to the infinite conjunction of the n-fold iteration of $\Box$ for all natural numbers n. The latter formula, unlike the former, automatically guarantees the coextensiveness of F and G in any possible, or possibly possible, or ... , circumstance. $\mathrm{NNE_M}$ must then be revised accordingly. But by the same token we must substitute $\Box^\omega$ for $\Box$ in $\mathrm{Comp_M}$ to achieve its intended effect, which is to postulate a property having which is equivalent to satisfying the predicate $\lambda x(A)$. Similarly, if the being constraint fails, a closer analogue of $x{=}y$ than $\Box\forall x\ (Fx \leftrightarrow Gx)$ is $\Box\forall x\ \Box(Fx \leftrightarrow Gx)$ since it extends the equivalence of F and G to merely possible beings (loosely speaking); again, $\mathrm{NNE_M}$ must be revised accordingly. But by the same token we must change $\mathrm{Comp_M}$ to $\exists X\ \Box\forall x\ \Box(Xx \leftrightarrow A)$ to achieve its intended effect. If both principles fail, we can use $\Box^\omega\forall x\ \Box^\omega(Fx \leftrightarrow Gx)$ as the analogue of $x{=}y$, and revise $\mathrm{NNE_M}$ and $\mathrm{Comp_M}$ accordingly. In each case the revised version of $\mathrm{Comp_M}$ entails the revised version of $\mathrm{NNE_M}$. For what it is worth, one can also check that $\mathrm{Comp_M}$ is valid on the correspondingly revised version of the standard semantics for $\mathrm{ML_P}$ in section 5.5. In the relevant settings, the considerations that favour the revised versions of $\mathrm{Comp_M}$ closely resemble those that favoured $\mathrm{Comp_M}$ itself.

If the logic is hyperintensional, the appropriate analogue of $x{=}y$ may be the third-order generalization $\forall\Phi\ (\Phi F \leftrightarrow \Phi G)$. Correspondingly, we strengthen $\mathrm{Comp_M}$ enough to deliver $\exists X\ \forall\Phi\ (\Phi X \leftrightarrow \Phi\lambda x(A))$.[1] The argument from

---

[1] We need a decent third-order comprehension principle for $\forall\Phi\ (\Phi F \leftrightarrow \Phi G)$ to imply intersubstitutability. Let A be any formula in which X and Y are free for Z and Φ is not free. Let $A^X/_Z$ be the result of substituting X for all free occurrences of Z in A. Suppose that the third-order comprehension principle delivers $\forall X\ \forall Y\ \exists\Phi\forall Z\ (\Phi Z \leftrightarrow A)$. By routine quantificational logic we derive $\forall X\ \forall Y\ \exists\Phi\ ((\Phi X \leftrightarrow A^X/_Z)\ \&\ (\Phi Y \leftrightarrow A^Y/_Z))$, and so $\forall X\ \forall Y\ (\forall\Phi\ (\Phi X \leftrightarrow \Phi Y) \to (A^X/_Z \leftrightarrow A^Y/_Z))$. Similarly, using $\mathrm{Comp_M}$ (but not its modal strength) as well, we can derive $\forall\Phi\ (\Phi F \leftrightarrow \Phi G) \to (A^F/_Z \leftrightarrow A^G/_Z)$. Semantically, $\forall\Phi\ (\Phi F \leftrightarrow \Phi G)$ has its intended effect only if the third-order domain is sufficiently full.

such a comprehension principle to the revised version of NNE_M still goes through if $\Phi\lambda x(Yx)$ and ΦY are equivalent, as they will be if the hyperintensionality is not too extreme. In any case, the sorts of intentional and metalinguistic construction that motivate hyperintensional higher-order logics are far from the concerns of this book and may be omitted from the formal language. Hyperintensionality arises at the level of thought and linguistic meaning, and should be explained at that level, not at the level of anything like a general theory of properties and relations. For present purposes, a coarser-grained intensional standard of individuation is more plausible, and certainly much simpler.

Stepping back from these details, we can formulate the general connection between comprehension and the second-order analogue of necessitism more abstractly. Suppose that we have an analogue of identity for predicates, which provides suitable principles of reflexivity and intersubstitutability. When A and B are formulas we can express it by writing $A \equiv_x B$ rather than explicitly relating $\lambda x(A)$ and $\lambda x(B)$. In place of $Comp_M$ we have:

$Comp_M{}^*$ $\exists X (Xx \equiv_x A)$

As before, any prefix of necessity operators and universal quantifiers of any type in any order is allowed. If we have the λ-conversion principle $\lambda x(A) \equiv_x A$, we may regard $Comp_M{}^*$ as derived from it by $\exists$-generalization. In place of NNE_M we have:

$NNE_M{}^*$ $\Box\forall X \Box\exists Y (Xx \equiv_x Yx)$

If we instantiate $Comp_M{}^*$ with Yx for A and the prefix $\Box\forall Y \Box$, the result is $\Box\forall Y \Box\exists X (Xx \equiv_x Yx)$, which is trivially equivalent to $NNE_M{}^*$ by a permutation of the variables X and Y and the equivalence of $Xx \equiv_x Yx$ to $Yx \equiv_x Xx$, which follows from intersubstitutability. Thus the connection between comprehension and the second-order analogue of necessitism is robust; it does not depend on minor details of the analogue of identity. The argument generalizes easily to any higher type.

Having seen how to extend the arguments to other logical settings, we may stick for definiteness to the simplest. In the rest of this chapter we assume that the logic is based on S5 and is intensional rather than hyperintensional. For present purposes we also assume the being constraint, although later in the chapter we consider the effects of lifting it. Thus $\Box\forall x (Fx \leftrightarrow Gx)$ entails $B \rightarrow B^*$ whenever B and B^* differ only in substitutions of F for

G or vice versa, as specified earlier. The original Comp_M holds, and NNE_M follows as a corollary.

The power of S5 enables us to derive second-order analogues of the full Barcan schema BF and its full converse CBF from NNE_M:

BF_M $\quad \Diamond \exists X A \rightarrow \exists X \Diamond A$

CBF_M $\quad \exists X \Diamond A \rightarrow \Diamond \exists X A$

The argument is simply the second-order analogue of the argument in section 2.2 from NNE to full BF and full CBF themselves, since necessary coextensiveness behaves in all the relevant ways like identity in this setting. As usual, all this generalizes to higher types.

We have seen that the natural comprehension principle for higher-order modal logic entails the analogues of necessitism at all orders beyond the first. Contingentists have two strategies in response. They may accept that comprehension principle and argue that the difference between first-order and higher-order quantification is deep enough to justify postulating the asymmetry in logic. Alternatively, they may reject that comprehension principle and seek another that does not entail the higher-order analogues of necessitism. The next section explores the former strategy; sections 6.3 and 6.4 explore the latter.

6.2 Individuals and their haecceities

Suppose that the contingentist accepts the comprehension principle Comp, and in particular Comp_M. We can thence derive some connections between the first-order and second-order quantifiers. For putting $x=y$ for A and adding the prefix $\Box \forall y \; \Box$ gives this instance of Comp_M:

(2) $\quad \Box \forall y \; \Box \exists X \; \Box \forall x \; (Xx \leftrightarrow x=y)$

This says that necessarily for each thing o necessarily there is the property of being o: having the property is necessary and sufficient for being identical with o.

In several respects, (2) is a very modest application of Comp_M. If we treat '=' as an atomic predicate, (2) is a predicative instance of Comp_M, because its right-hand side contains no higher-order quantifiers, indeed, no quantifiers at all, just as in the derivation of NNE_M. Of course, as discussed in sections 5.3 and 5.5, we can define identity in terms of second-order quantification, by $\lambda x, y (\forall X\ (Xx \leftrightarrow Xy))$, in which case (2) becomes an impredicative principle: but such a definition achieves only minor economies, and identity is as good a candidate as one could wish to be taken as primitive. Anyway, for present purposes we found no good reason to fear impredicativity. Moreover, since any set serves simultaneously as both the first-order and the second-order domain in some formal model of (2), it runs no risk of a Russell-like paradox.

Let us informally write 'X is a haecceity of y' for $\Box \forall x\ (Xx \leftrightarrow x=y)$ and 'X is a haecceity' for $\Diamond \exists y\ \Box \forall x\ (Xx \leftrightarrow x=y)$.[2] Then (2) says that necessarily everything necessarily has a haecceity. The haecceity is unique, in the strong sense that necessarily for every haecceity of y necessarily every haecceity of y is necessarily coextensive with it. For in S5 nothing of the form $\Box A$ is contingent, so it is not contingent whether something is a haecceity of y; but if both X and Y are haecceities of y then they are necessarily coextensive with each other, as each is necessarily coextensive with being y and necessary coextensiveness is an equivalence relation. Since necessary coextensiveness is the analogue of identity in the present setting, that suffices for uniqueness. Furthermore, a haecceity determines a unique individual, in the strong sense that necessarily if X is a haecceity of something y then necessarily X is also a haecceity of something z only if y and z are identical. For, necessarily, whatever X is a haecceity of has X, and X is a haecceity of z too only if whatever has X is identical with z.

Clearly, in some sense there is a one-one correspondence between individuals and their haecceities. It is tempting to go further, and say that there is a one-one correspondence between *possible* individuals and their haecceities. However, such talk is radically misleading. Contingentists and necessitists should agree that there are no merely possible individuals, where 'x is a merely possible individual' is equivalent to 'x is not something but could have been something' on the unrestricted reading of the quantifier. Trivially, everything is actually something (see section 1.6). For necessitists, there is no contingency in what individuals or haecceities there are, so the actual one-one correspondence between individuals and their haecceities covers

---

[2] In settings in which necessary coextensiveness ($\Box \forall x\ (Xx \leftrightarrow Yx)$) is not the proper analogue of identity, 'X is a haecceity of y' must be redefined to accord with the proper analogue, in ways discussed in section 6.1.

all possibilities. For most contingentists, there could have been individuals other than every actual one. In this section, we have supposed that the contingentist accepts $Comp_M$, and therefore NNE_M. Given those principles, there actually are properties that could have been the haecceities of individuals other than every actual one. Thus not every haecceity is the haecceity of something; some haecceities merely could have been the haecceity of something.

Haecceities as just characterized resemble the individual essences on which Alvin Plantinga bases his contingentist account of quantified modal logic.[3] For Plantinga, a property X is an essence if and only if possibly something cannot be something without having X, and necessarily nothing else has X. A second-order version of Plantinga's theory would entail (2). Moreover, he holds, essences have necessary being: my essence would be uninstantiated but still something were I nothing. That is why he uses essences as surrogates for 'possible individuals' to make possible worlds semantics metaphysically respectable: there are no merely possible individuals, but there are merely possibly instantiated essences. Thus (2) and NNE_M generate a theory of haecceities very similar to Plantinga's theory of individual essences. However, this also means that, given $Comp_M$, contingentism is subject to objections analogous to those made to Plantinga's contingentist theory.[4]

The initial challenge is this. Informally write 'X tracks y' for 'X is a haecceity of y and X cannot be a haecceity of anything other than y', with 'X is a haecceity of y' defined as previously. Then, given the background logic, my haecceity necessarily tracks me. Even if I had never been, by $Comp_M$ there would still have been a property tracking me (and only me). But how can it lock onto me in my absence? In those circumstances, what makes me rather than something else its target?

One suggestion is that my haecceity tracks me by somehow being built out of me and the identity relation. But then how could there still be such a property when there is no such thing as me for it to be built out of? Anyway, such constituent structure is highly problematic for coarse-grained properties, since radically different structures may be logically equivalent, and thereby yield the same coarse-grained property. We may rule out explanations of tracking that appeal to any supposed constituent structure of properties.

---

[3] See Plantinga 1974, pp. 70–87, for the general strategy, and Jager 1982 for its detailed implementation. For some recent discussion see Bennett 2006 and Woodward 2011.

[4] See Fine 1985 and Menzel 1990, pp. 363–7; for some replies to criticisms see Plantinga 1983 and 1985.

A parallel challenge can be raised in terms of anti-haecceities, defined like haecceities except with $\neg x=y$ in place of $x=y$ and established by a corresponding application of Comp_M. My anti-haecceity is the property of not being me. Using parallel definitions, it follows that necessarily I have an anti-haecceity that anti-tracks me, because necessarily it is an anti-haecceity of me and cannot be an anti-haecceity of anything else. How can my anti-haecceity lock onto me in my absence? In those circumstances, what makes me rather than something else its target?

The challenges are especially pressing on those contingentists who accuse necessitists of making the modal float unacceptably free of the non-modal (see sections 1.3 and, in more detail, 8.2). For the danger is that the tracking by haecceities and the anti-tracking by anti-haecceities violate just such a contingentist constraint. If contingentists fall back on the retort that their view is no *more* counter-intuitive than necessitism, they presumably expect the decision between the two views to be made on general theoretical grounds, such as simplicity and strength. But that too is dangerous ground for contingentists, since NNE, the defining principle of necessitism, gives a far simpler and stronger theory than its negation does. Let us therefore investigate how well contingentism can meet the challenges.

We can put the underlying problem in more general terms. By NNE_M, properties have necessary being. Nevertheless, as haecceities and anti-haecceities illustrate, by Comp_M they must also be capable of tracking or anti-tracking a particular individual even when, by contingentist lights, there is no such individual to be tracked or anti-tracked. Does any plausible metaphysics of properties combine these features?

Sometimes, of course, one individual is essentially uniquely related to others that by contingentist lights could all have been something even if it had been nothing.[5] This knife could not have been made without being made of this handle and this blade, and nothing else could have been made of them in exactly the same way, but those constituents could have been made without this knife ever being made of them. Since this knife can be essentially uniquely characterized in terms of the two constituents, surely their being suffices for the being of its haecceity and anti-haecceity, whether or not this knife is something. Thus contingentists can easily deny the universal generalization that the non-being of something entails the non-being

---

[5] 'Related' here is being used loosely, not subject to the being constraint that whatever is related is something.

of its haecceity or anti-haecceity. However, examples like the knife and its constituents do not solve their problem, for by their lights the handle and the blade are contingent beings too. Thus the necessitist simply asks: how could there be the haecceity or anti-haecceity of this knife if there were not even this handle and this blade?

To solve the problem by the relational strategy, the contingentist requires this for each individual i: necessarily, there are some individuals to which i is essentially uniquely related. What are such individuals supposed to be? Are they ineluctable simples of which everything else is composed, or ideas in the mind of God? For the constituents that physics can discern of a macroscopic material object are unpromising candidates for necessary being, individually and even collectively, by contingentist standards: they could all have been nothing together. There is no good independent evidence for the hypothesis that what tokens of ultimate particles there are is non-contingent. Not only does the relational strategy involve grandiose metaphysical or even physical commitments of one sort or another, they are huge concessions to necessitism. Moreover, they tend to undermine the motivation for the contingentist residue. The natural starting point for the contingentist's rejection of the necessitist's contingently non-concrete objects is that they are mere postulates of abstract metaphysical speculation, with no basis in common sense or natural science. The relational strategy for saving haecceities and anti-haecceities involves just such speculation, and leads to postulating significantly more complicated metaphysical structure beyond the reach of common sense or natural science than necessitism itself requires.

Alternatively, if contingentists reject the relational strategy, they may envisage properties as purely qualitative in some sense. But then the nature of individuals must permit them to be tracked and anti-tracked, and more generally *locked onto*, by purely qualitative properties. For example, suppose that exactly the same qualitative possibilities are open to Tweedledum and Tweedledee. If contingently there were no Tweedledum, no Tweedledee, and no other individuals relevantly related to them, there would still be their haecceities, one tracking only Tweedledum, the other tracking only Tweedledee. But in those counterfactual circumstances how could a purely qualitative property lock onto one of them to the exclusion of the other? By hypothesis, a purely qualitative characterization would fit both or neither. Thus the purely qualitative conception of properties may well require a highly contentious form of the identity of indiscernibles for individuals, on which qualitative identity entails numerical identity. That is a far less plausible claim than the trivial form of the identity of indiscernibles that permits non-qualitative properties such as identity with y. We have no serious evidence against the metaphysical possibility of a symmetrical universe in which every individual can be reflected (rotated, translated) onto its qualitative double.[6]

The problem for the purely qualitative conception of properties is not just that it leads to an implausible form of the identity of indiscernibles. The latter in turn leads to a conception of individuals themselves as purely qualitative in nature. But they must not be purely qualitative in the way in which properties are supposed to be purely qualitative, for the latter way was supposed to explain why properties are necessarily something, and the contingentist denies that individuals are necessarily something. Thus kinds of pure qualitativeness seem to multiply.

The contingentist might conceive an individual as a bundle of purely qualitative properties, held together by a primitive purely qualitative higher-order compresence relation and individuated by the properties in the bundle, where both the properties and the relation have necessary being but are only contingently instantiated: were the compresence relation not instantiated, there would be no individual.[7] The theory becomes still more elaborate once fitted out with an account of the persistence of individuals across times and possibilities, since an individual typically has many of its purely qualitative properties, such as shape and size, temporarily and contingently. Alternatively, if the theory denies identity through change and through contingency, not only is that yet another implausible consequence, which requires still more theoretical complexity to save the appearances, it also fits badly with the underlying motivation for contingentism, by treating a vast range of apparent contingency as an illusion. Thus the purely qualitative conception drags the contingentist into proliferating complications of metaphysical theory with no independent plausibility. They are not what most philosophers who signed on to contingentism bargained for.

---

[6] See Hawthorne 2003, pp. 106–8, for an overview of various forms of the identity of indiscernibles. Those who resist natural counterexamples to the strong form in the text often do so by offering alternative hypotheses consistent with the principle that save the appearances: but absent any independent reason to accept the principle, the alternative hypotheses, even if possible, are no evidence for the impossibility of the original hypothesis, which is the counterexample.

[7] The compresence relation may be multigrade, in the sense that it may hold between different numbers of properties.

Nor is the notion of the purely qualitative altogether clear. Which properties count as purely qualitative? We may even count relational properties as purely qualitative when they are definable without reference to specific individuals: for example, being inside a hollow sphere, as opposed to being inside *this* hollow sphere. Thus purely qualitative properties may be extrinsic and relational. Such properties still seem to satisfy NNE_M. They are also preserved under any symmetries of the universe. The picture is that purely qualitative properties correspond to predicates of the form $\lambda v(A)$, where A contains no individual constants and no free individual variables except v, but may contain quantifiers of any order. Although $Comp_M$ also has instances such as (2) in which A contains individual constants or individual variables as parameters, the corresponding 'impure' predicate $\lambda v(A)$ may be supposed to pick out a property that could in principle also be picked out by a 'pure' predicate $\lambda v(B)$, where the formula B satisfies the restrictions. Unfortunately, the syntactic criterion is of limited help, since the reference of a syntactically atomic predicate such as 'Hellenic' may nevertheless be fixed in relation to particular people or places. The notion of a predicate that does not semantically 'involve' any particular individual is itself far from clear. Here the coarse-grained individuation of properties by necessary coextensiveness exacerbates the problem, as already noted, because it undermines the idea that properties have constituent structure analogous to that of predicates, for necessarily coextensive predicates may have utterly dissimilar constituent structures. Thus a property's involving an individual cannot be explained as the individual's being a constituent of the property.[8]

Given the unclarity in the notion of the purely qualitative, the argument that the purely qualitative conception of properties yields an implausible metaphysics of individuals can only be provisional. But the onus is on a proponent of that conception to supply the requisite clarification, preferably in a way that avoids the bad metaphysical consequences. As yet there is no sign of that happening, and the argument stands.

By appealing to the purely qualitative conception or the previous relational strategy, contingentists talked their way into worse trouble. They do better to adopt a more minimalist approach, denying that they must provide any metaphysically deeper account of how properties and relations are individuated than one in terms of their modal application conditions, on which

---

[8] For some sceptical discussion of the distinction between qualitative and non-qualitative properties in a modal setting see Stalnaker 2012, pp. 52–70.

necessary coextensiveness is analogous to identity. Such a minimalist contingentist endorses $Comp_M$, and with a similar attitude its generalization Comp to all higher types, while insisting that we need no more explanation of how my haecceity singles me out in my absence than that it is the property that, necessarily, applies to something if it is me and not otherwise.

One danger for minimalist contingentism is that the minimalism leaves the contingentism looking suspiciously ad hoc, its combination with Comp a messy hybrid. As seen in section 6.1, Comp implies necessitism at every order except the first. The onus is on the metaphysician who postulates such logical differences between orders to justify the asymmetry in treatment. Minimalism deprives the contingentist of the resources needed to provide a satisfying justification.

The problem can also be put in more metaphysical terms. According to the minimalist contingentist, if your parents had never met, there would not have been you, a merely possible person, but there would still have been your haecceity. The latter claim depends on a minimalist standard of being for properties, on which they can be even in circumstances in which they leave no trace. The former claim, that there would not have been you, depends on a non-minimalist standard of being for individuals, on which they can be only in circumstances on which they leave some trace. Of course, this talk of leaving a trace is metaphorical, but it is the minimalist contingentist who needs to cash out the metaphor. The default preference is for a uniform metaphysics, on which being is contingent at all orders or none. Given the minimalist comprehension principle $Comp_M$ or Comp, second-order being is not contingent. Therefore the default preference favours a metaphysics on which being is not contingent at any order including the first, in other words, full-blooded necessitism.

The minimalist contingentist may reply that there is a compelling metaphysical difference between the first-order quantifiers and their higher-order analogues, because the former range over (although perhaps not exclusively over) sparse flesh-and-blood 'thick' particulars, whose being requires causal activity and spatiotemporal location, while the latter range only over plenitudinous bloodless 'thin' universals, whose being requires only a well-defined application condition. But even if we grant that metaphysical difference for the sake of argument, it does not justify the asymmetry in the treatment of the quantifiers, because it does not really explain the non-contingency of higher-order being. Take my haecceity for example: of course there is *actually* a well-defined application condition, but to draw from that premise the conclusion that there *would have been* that well-defined application condition even if there had not been me is to assume the second-order version of CBF, one of the very principles to be explained. The condition is defined by the assignment of me as value to the parameter y in the predicate $\lambda x(x=y)$. Without me, there is nothing to assign, so no such assignment. Indeed, 'well-defined application condition' is barely more than a notational variant of 'property', in the relevant plenitudinous sense. To put it the other way round: conceiving the second-order quantifiers as ranging over legitimate semantic values for predicates automatically validates second-order CBF only if conceiving the first-order quantifiers as ranging over legitimate semantic values for names automatically validates first-order CBF.

Could the minimalist contingentist claim instead that higher-order quantifiers, unlike first-order ones, are somehow not really in the scope of modal operators prefixed to them? For example, in a formula of the form $\Box\exists X A$, rather than $\Box$ operating on the result of $\exists X$ operating on A, $\Box$ and $\exists X$ might somehow operate 'simultaneously' on A. That is to postulate a grammatical difference between first-order and higher-order quantifiers that in no way follows from any metaphysical difference in what they range over. One could just as easily postulate a reading of the first-order quantifiers on which they are 'scoped out', not really in the scope of the modal operators prefixed to them. Such a reading would trivially validate NNE. Presumably that would not be a decisive argument for necessitism, because it would not decide in favour of NNE on a reading of the first-order quantifiers that is *not* 'scoped out'. Similarly, why should the scoped out reading of NNE_M settle the issue in favour of NNE_M on a reading of the second-order quantifiers that is *not* scoped out? There is such a reading, for the metaphysical differences imply nothing about the purely semantic question of scope. In any case, the grammar of a formal language of higher-order modal logic such as ML_p is clear: higher-order quantifiers do occur in the scope of modal operators.[9]

The safest line for the minimalist contingentist may be even more minimalist: to lay down Comp as a comprehension principle attractive simply

---

[9] For related issues see the discussion of analogues of branching quantifiers in section 7.7. A related but different contingentist strategy is to simulate the second-order quantifier in $Comp_M$ by a combination of modal operators and quantifiers of another type (substitutional quantifiers, plural quantifiers, or individual quantifiers in an infinitary language). Some problems for such an approach are explained in sections 7.5–7.8. The present chapter concerns contingentist theories that do not attempt reductions of quantification into predicate position to something else.

for its general theoretical virtues, and derive the non-contingency of higher-order being as a corollary, but uphold the contingency of first-order being as common sense. Such an ultra-minimalist contingentist abjures any attempt to explain or justify the asymmetry on deeper metaphysical grounds, as likely just to lead to trouble. Since some formal models validate the combination of Comp with (first-order) contingentism, it is internally consistent.

Nevertheless, ultra-minimalist contingentism is unsatisfying. The issue is not whether totally committed ultra-minimalist contingentists can hang on to their position at all costs. As usual in philosophy, they can. The question is whether ultra-minimalist contingentism is the best option available to enquirers who are not already committed. In particular, how well does it compare to necessitism on the evidence so far?

Both necessitism and ultra-minimalist contingentism are consistent with what we already know from common sense and science. Initially, necessitism may have seemed a weirder view than contingentism, by making the modal properties of contingently non-concrete things in some sense float free of their non-modal properties (sections 1.3 and 8.2). But the ultra-minimalist version of contingentism forfeits any such advantage over necessitism, by making the modal behaviour of the corresponding uninstantiated haecceities float similarly free of their non-modal behaviour. Of course, if the distinction between modal and non-modal properties collapses, then the supposed initial advantage for contingentism was an illusion anyway. In either case, contingentism cannot rely on the populist rhetoric of weirdness. Rather, both theories have to be motivated theoretically. They need to be compared on the usual dimensions for theory choice in science. In general, necessitism does better than contingentism on the theoretical virtue of strength. Of course, if we define comparative strength for theories by stipulating that T is stronger than T* if and only if T entails T* and T* does not entail T, then neither necessitism nor contingentism is stronger than the other, since neither entails the other. But that definition is inappropriate for the dimension of strength in scientific theory choice, since we typically have to choose between mutually inconsistent but individually consistent theories, none of which entails any of the others. Rather, our interest is in a less formal sense of strength as *informativeness*, where a universal generalization such as a proposed scientific law typically counts as stronger because more informative than its negation. In that sense, necessitism, a necessitated universal generalization, is stronger than contingentism, its negation. In particular, it is stronger than ultra-minimalist contingentism, for the ultra-minimalism adds only the strong comprehension principle Comp, which it shares with necessitism. Furthermore, necessitism surpasses ultra-minimalist contingentism in simplicity, symmetry, and elegance. For necessitism makes being necessary at all orders, while ultra-minimalist contingentism makes it contingent at the first order but necessary at all higher orders, without even attempting to rationalize the asymmetry. When they are compared by the normal standards of theory choice in science, necessitism trumps ultra-minimalist contingentism.

Full-blooded contingentists may also object to all forms of minimalist contingentism that they are not contingentist enough, because they deny the contingency of being at higher orders. Since Comp requires that denial, full-blooded contingentists may therefore reject Comp, and seek an alternative comprehension principle that lacks its higher-order necessitist consequences. Since they are independently committed to not taking possible worlds semantics at face value, the validity of Comp in the most natural forms of such semantics will not impress them. The next two sections examine different sorts of alternative comprehension principle for contingentist higher-order modal logic.

6.3 Non-modal comprehension

One natural way for a contingentist to weaken the strong modal comprehension principle Comp is to omit its modal element, specifically the modal operator between the two quantifiers. In the case of $Comp_M$, the result is this:

$Comp_M^-$ $\exists X \forall x\, (Xx \leftrightarrow A)$

As before, x is an individual variable that may occur free in the formula A and X is a monadic first-level predicate variable that does not occur free in A. Any result of prefixing an instance of $Comp_M^-$ with necessity operators and universal quantifiers of any type in any order also counts as an instance of $Comp_M^-$.

To see the point of the weakening, consider the instance of $Comp_M^-$ with the same prefix and the same substitution for A as (2), the haecceity-yielding instance of $Comp_M$:

(2⁻) $\Box \forall y\, \Box \exists X \forall x\, (Xx \leftrightarrow x=y)$

This does not imply any modal locking onto individuals. When I am the value of the variable y, it requires only that in each possible circumstance, if I am something then there is a property that I alone have (but perhaps in other possible circumstances other individuals have it, or I lack it even though I am something), and if I am nothing then there is a property that nothing has (but perhaps in other possible circumstances something has it). Thus (2⁻) lacks the consequences of (2) that made trouble for contingentism. The constraint on the extension of X is modally local rather than global.

As the absence of visible modal operators makes clear, Comp_M^- is in some fundamental way a non-modal principle. Of course, we can necessitate its instances, as in (2⁻), and we can also substitute formulas with modal operators for A, but in those respects Comp_M^- is no different from a principle of non-modal propositional logic such as the law of non-contradiction $\neg(A\ \&\ \neg A)$. Indeed, if we add the condition $\exists x\, A$, Comp_M^- holds even on a plural reading of the second-order quantifier, despite the vast difference explained in section 5.8 between the plural and intensional readings.

Of course, to check the consequences of Comp_M^- properly we must consider the totality of its instances, which requires a more formal approach. We can use variants on the Henkin-style general models of section 5.5 in a purely instrumental capacity to show the formal consistency of Comp_M^- with various claims. In all the models to come, every world is accessible from every world, so S5 is valid. Since S5 is the strongest reasonable propositional modal logic for metaphysical modality, if a formula cannot be derived from Comp_M^- with S5 as the underlying propositional modal logic, it cannot be derived from Comp_M^- with any reasonable underlying propositional modal logic for metaphysical modality. For every world w, $\text{dom}(w)$ is the domain of individuals in w and $\text{DOM}(w)$ the domain of properties in w. We can ignore higher types and polyadic relations since extending the models to them is a routine exercise. As usual, $\text{DOM}(w)$ is a set of intensions, total functions from worlds to sets of individuals. In all the models to come, for any worlds w and $w*$, if $I \in \text{DOM}(w)$ then $I(w*) \subseteq \text{dom}(w*)$, which restricts the second-order quantifiers to intensions that satisfy the being constraint (as in (1)). If a formula cannot be derived from Comp_M^- with the being constraint, it cannot be derived from Comp_M^- without the being constraint.

We can use such models to prove that Comp_M^- is consistent with $\neg\text{NNE}\ \&\ \neg\text{NNE}_M$, so that it allows the first-order contingentist to be a second-order contingentist too.[10] A similar argument shows that Comp⁻, the generalization of $\text{Comp}_M{}^-$ to all higher types, is consistent with the family of negations of the analogues of NNE for all types. Thus $\text{Comp}_M{}^-$ permits a thoroughgoing contingentism over all types. We can use the same sort of model to show that $\text{Comp}_M{}^-$ is also consistent with the negation of (2), so that it does not require haecceities.[11] We can also tweak the models to show that not even the combination of $\text{Comp}_M{}^-$ with the analogues of NNE for all types requires haecceities.[12]

Such results show that $\text{Comp}_M{}^-$ is weak enough for the contingentist's purposes. However, it may be too weak. For example, it does not under-write pre-theoretically valid arguments by second-order generalization like # and ## in section 5.5. To be more precise, consider (3), where T is an atomic two-place predicate constant:

$$(3) \qquad (Taa \,\&\, \Diamond\neg Taa) \rightarrow \exists X \,(Xa \,\&\, \Diamond\neg Xa)$$

A typical instance of (3) can be roughly paraphrased as a banal truth such as 'If Alice contingently talks to herself, there is something that Alice contingently does'. One can derive (3) from Comp_M and the being constraint (to tie up loose ends about non-being) in any reasonable second-order modal

---

[10] Proof: Write $w, \underline{a} \vDash A$ to mean that the formula A is true at the world w on the assignment $\underline{a}$ of values to variables, leaving the model parameter tacit. Consider any set W with at least two members and a variable domain function dom on W that assigns non-empty domains to at least two worlds. We work only with intensions that are non-empty in at most one world. More precisely, for each $w \in$ W, DOM(w) contains just those intensions I such that I(w) ⊆ dom(w) and I($w*$) = {} for every $w* \in$ W other than w. Then every instance of $\text{Comp}_M{}^-$ is true throughout the model, since for every formula A, $w \in$ W, and assignment $\underline{a}$, there is an intension I ∈ DOM(w) such that I(w) = {$d \in$ dom(w): $w, \underline{a}[x/d] \vDash A$}, so $w, \underline{a}[X/I] \vDash \forall x\,(Xx \leftrightarrow A)$, so $w, \underline{a} \vDash \exists X \forall x\,(Xx \leftrightarrow A)$. But NNE$_M$ is false throughout the model. For let w and $w*$ be distinct members of W such that dom(w) ≠ {}, and I ∈ DOM(w) be such that I(w) = dom(w). For if J ∈ DOM($w*$) then J(w) = {}, so I and J are not coextensive at w. Now if $\underline{a}$ is an assignment and $d \in$ dom(w), then $w, \underline{a}[X/I][Y/J][x/d] \vDash Xx$ but not $w, \underline{a}[X/I][Y/J][x/d] \vDash Yx$. Since dom($w$) ≠ {}, not $w, \underline{a}[X/I][Y/J] \vDash \forall x\,(Xx \leftrightarrow Yx)$, so not $w*, \underline{a}[X/I][Y/J] \vDash \Box\forall x\,(Xx \leftrightarrow Yx)$; since J was an arbitrary member of DOM($w*$), not $w*, \underline{a}[X/I] \vDash \exists Y \Box\forall x\,(Xx \leftrightarrow Yx)$, so not $w, \underline{a}[X/I] \vDash \Box\exists Y \Box\forall x\,(Xx \leftrightarrow Yx)$, so not $w, \underline{a} \vDash \forall X \Box \exists Y \Box\forall x\,(Xx \leftrightarrow Yx)$, so for $w** \in$ W $w** \vDash \neg$NNE$_M$; $w** \vDash \neg$NNE because dom is variable. Therefore $\neg$NNE & $\neg$NNE$_M$ holds throughout the model.

[11] Proof: We simply require two worlds w and $w*$ with overlapping individual domains, for if $d \in$ dom(w)∩dom($w*$) then (2) requires the second-order domain of every world to contain an intension I such that I(w) = I($w*$) = {d}; but the models are so constructed that the second-order domains contain only intensions that yield non-empty extensions in at most one world. If each individual in the model belongs to the first-order domains of at least two worlds, no individual has a haecceity in the model.

[12] Proof: Make the first-order domain constant and let the constant second-order domain contain all and only intensions that yield non-empty extensions in at most one world.

logic.[13] But (3) does not follow from Comp_M^- and the being constraint in general models, even with the help of NNE and its higher-order analogues.[14]

Another example of the weakness of Comp_M^- is the underivability from it of (4):

(4) $(\forall x\,(Rxx \leftrightarrow Sxx)\ \&\ \neg\Box\forall x\,(Rxx \leftrightarrow Sxx)) \rightarrow$
$$\exists X\,\exists Y\,(\forall x\,(Xx \leftrightarrow Yx)\ \&\ \neg\Box\forall x\,(Xx \leftrightarrow Yx))$$

For instance, if it is contingent that all and only those who scratch themselves scratch themselves at least once but less than a trillion times, then there are contingently coextensive properties, the property of scratching oneself and the property of scratching oneself at least once but less than a trillion times. General models of the same sort as for (3) show that even with the help of the being constraint, or indeed NNE and all its higher-order analogues (or the negations of NNE and its analogues), Comp_M^- does not yield (4). By contrast, (4) is a routine consequence of Comp_M.

The rationale for both (3) and (4) comes from a conception of the values of the second-order variables as properties for which coextensiveness does not imply identity, although necessary coextensiveness does: a non-extensional but intensional view. By contrast, (3) and (4) are not plausible on an extensional view, for example Boolos's plural interpretation of second-order logic (with suitable provision for the vacuous case). No individuals are such that necessarily they are all and only those who scratch themselves, or all and only those who scratch themselves at least once but less than a trillion times (see section 5.8). But one might expect the two conceptions to agree on (5):

---

[13] Proof: An instance of Comp_M is $\exists X\,\Box\forall x\,(Xx \leftrightarrow Txx)$, from which one derives $\exists X\,\Box(\exists x\,a{=}x \rightarrow (Xa \leftrightarrow Taa))$ in free quantified modal logic. But two instances of the being constraint are $\Box(Xa \rightarrow \exists x\,a{=}x)$ and $\Box(Taa \rightarrow \exists x\,a{=}x)$, from which $\Box(\neg\exists x\,a{=}x \rightarrow (Xa \leftrightarrow Taa))$ follows in any normal propositional modal logic. By uncontentious moves in second-order S5 we then have $\exists X\,\Box(Xa \leftrightarrow Taa)$, hence $\exists X\,((Taa\ \&\ \Diamond\neg Taa) \leftrightarrow (Xa\ \&\ \Diamond\neg Xa))$, hence (3). If one rejects the being constraint, one will revise Comp_M as explained in section 6.1, and the argument for (3) should still go through. The reason for using Taa rather than Fa is that in Gallin's general models constants must be assigned values in the domain for variables of the same type (see section 5.5).

[14] Proof: Let M be a general model with at least two worlds and constant domains, where the second-order domain for one-place predicates is the set of all *constant* functions from worlds to subsets of the first-order domain, but the second-order domain for two-place predicates is the set of *all* functions from worlds to subsets of the Cartesian product of the first-order domain with itself. All instances of Comp_M^-, the being constraint, and NNE and its higher-order analogues are true throughout M. The consequent of (3) is false throughout M, because only a non-constant intension will verify it as the value of X. But we can assign a non-constant intension to T with a non-constant diagonal and so arrange for the antecedent of (3) to be true at some world in M, so that (3) is false at that world. With minor variations we can make the counter-model contingentist at the first order, or all orders, instead.

(5) $\forall Y \, \forall Z \, \exists X \, \Box \forall x \, (Xx \leftrightarrow (Yx \, \& \, Zx))$

To put it crudely, just as any two extensions have an intersection, any two intensions have a conjunction. But Comp_M^- does not even entail (5). More generally, let % express one of the sixteen binary truth functions. Then one can show that Comp_M^- entails (6) only in the trivial case when % expresses either the left projection, $A \% B$ being always equivalent to A, or the right projection, $A \% B$ being always equivalent to B:[15]

(6) $\forall Y \, \forall Z \, \exists X \, \Box \forall x \, (Xx \leftrightarrow (Yx \, \% \, Zx))$

Thus Comp_M^- does not yield the most elementary non-trivial closure principles for which one would hope in a systematic theory of abundant properties. For example, it does not require properties to be closed under negation or disjunction, in the sense of (6). Without such Boolean combinations of properties, second-order logic is crippled.

Contingentists could simply add instances of (6) to Comp_M^- in formulating their theory of higher-order modal logic. But such ad hoc moves carry little weight in science. You cannot free ride on the predictive successes of a rival theory just by adding its predictions to your own, even when it is consistent with them. The lack of theoretical integration makes cobbled-together theories

---

[15] Proof: Start with any (constant) first-order domain D with at least two members. P(D) is the power set of D. As the set of worlds W use the set of all permutations of P(D). For $X \subseteq D$ let I_X be the intension such that $I_X(\pi) = \pi(X)$ for all $\pi \in W$. Let the (constant) monadic second-order domain be $\{I_X : X \subseteq D\}$. Let $\pi*$ be the inverse of π. For $\pi \in W$ and $X \subseteq D$, $I_{\pi*(X)}(\pi) = \pi(\pi*(X)) = X$; thus at any world each subset of the first-order domain is the extension of some intension in the second-order domain, so Comp_M^- is true throughout the model. With harmless ambiguity we use '%' for the symbol of the object-language, the truth function it expresses and the operation the latter induces on the subsets of D (thus & induces intersection). We show that (6) is true throughout the model only if the truth function % is one of the two projections. Suppose that there are subsets Y and Z of D such that Y%Z ≠ Y and Y%Z ≠ Z. Let $X \subseteq D$. Since P(D) has at least four members, there is a permutation π of P(D) such that $\pi(Y) = Y$, $\pi(Z) = Z$, but $\pi(X) \neq Y\%Z$. Consequently, $\pi(X) \neq \pi(Y)\%\pi(Z)$, so $I_X(\pi) \neq I_Y(\pi)\% \, I_Z(\pi)$, so (6) is false throughout the model. Hence (6) is true throughout the model only if for all Y, $Z \subseteq D$ either Y%Z = Y or Y%Z = Z. Then D%D = D, so the truth function % yields a truth when applied to a pair of truths. Similarly, $\{\}\%\{\} = \{\}$, so the truth function % yields a falsehood when applied to a pair of falsehoods. This leaves only four possibilities for the truth function %: it is either conjunction, disjunction, or one of the two projections. But it is not conjunction, for if d and e are two members of D then $\{d\} \cap \{e\} = \{\}$. Similarly, it is not disjunction, for $\{d\} \cup \{e\} = \{d, e\}$. Therefore the truth function % is one of the two projections. Since NNE and its second-order analogue hold in the model, the result holds even if they are added to the background logic. The model can easily be extended to verify all higher-order analogues of NNE. We can also extend it to falsify NNE, for example by adding a world with an empty individual domain. Since we can arrange for Comp_M^- to be preserved under these extensions, its consistency with $\neg$(6) when % is not a projection is robust to reasonable variations in the background logic.

like that far less explanatorily powerful than their well-integrated rivals, such as necessitism with Comp.

We can see the weakness of Comp_M^- from another perspective by viewing abundant properties as *conditions*. One may enquire into the necessary or sufficient conditions for life to evolve on a planet, or for someone to have the right to vote under a given constitution. Let A be 'life evolves on planet x', 'x has the right to vote under this constitution', or whatever. There is no guarantee that our language in its current form has the expressive resources to articulate all such conditions, for instance for life. In the simplest case, asking about necessary conditions for A is asking about $\lambda X(\Box\forall x\ (A \rightarrow Xx))$; asking about sufficient conditions is asking about $\lambda X(\Box\forall x\ (Xx \rightarrow A))$. A (partial) answer to the question may be, for example, 'A necessary condition for having the right to vote under this constitution is being at least 18 years old' (the conditions for having the right to vote under a given constitution need not cut nature at its joints; they may be outrageously gerrymandered). Let B be 'x is at least 18 years old'. The form of the answer is $\Box\forall x\ (A \rightarrow B)$. That answers the original question about necessary conditions, $\lambda X(\Box\forall x\ (A \rightarrow Xx))$, only if (7) holds, to connect the question to the answer:

(7) $\exists X\ \Box\forall x\ (Xx \leftrightarrow B)$

But (7) is an instance of Comp_M, not of Comp_M^-. A similar point applies even to enquiry into conditions that are not metaphysically necessary or sufficient, but only physically or normally or probably or other things being equal so, for those still involve a modal correlation of some sort between the relevant A and B. In general, (7) is still needed to get the same modal correlation between A and Xx. Thus Comp_M^- is too weak adequately to underpin the role of second-order logic in serving theoretical enquiry.

6.4 Non-singular comprehension

If contingentists are to formulate a comprehension principle weaker than Comp_M but strong enough for the purposes of theoretical enquiry, they need an alternative approach. A natural starting point is the idea that first-order contingency induces corresponding higher-order contingency: what properties there are depends on what individuals there are, because some properties ontologically depend on individuals in the way my haecceity ontologically depends on me. Without the individual, there is no property.

The simplest version of this approach has a slightly Aristotelian flavour. The proposal is roughly that an open formula defines a property just if it is satisfied. That yields the following monadic ('M') contingentist ('C') comprehension principle:

$Comp_{MC0}$ $\exists x\, A \leftrightarrow \exists X\, \Box \forall x\, (Xx \leftrightarrow A)$

The same provisos apply as to $Comp_M$. The results of prefixing instances of $Comp_{MC0}$ with necessity operators and universal quantifiers of any type in any order also count as instances of $Comp_{MC0}$.

On this view properties are not closed under such Boolean operations as negation and conjunction. According to $Comp_{MC0}$, there is a property of being self-identical, but no property of being self-distinct; likewise, there is a property of being rough and a property of being smooth, but no property of being both rough and smooth.

In any case, $Comp_{MC0}$ does not solve the problem of anti-haecceities, for it has this instance:

(8) $\Box \forall y\, \Box(\exists x\, \neg x{=}y \leftrightarrow \exists X\, \Box \forall x\, (Xx \leftrightarrow \neg x{=}y))$

Thus the only circumstances in which there is no anti-haecceity of me are those in which there is only me (but not even my proper parts). Even if such circumstances are possible, which is unlikely, they make little difference. For the problem as posed in section 6.2 arises just as much for more easily possible circumstances in which there are many things, none of them suitably related to me by contingentist standards. How can my anti-haecceity be in those circumstances? More plausibly for the contingentist, the being of my anti-haecceity depends on my being, not on that of something else. A comprehension principle suited to that more plausible view will make the being of the property at issue depend on the being of the things denoted by the parameters and non-logical constants in the defining formula.

That argument warrants no blanket ban on all instances of the comprehension schema with parameters or non-logical constants. Indeed, such instances are essential for second-order logic to serve some of its central logical and mathematical roles. For example, to capture the full intent of the principle of mathematical induction one must use a second-order formulation:

MI $\forall X\, ((X0\, \&\, \forall n\, (Xn \rightarrow Xsn)) \rightarrow \forall n\, Xn)$

284 INTENSIONAL COMPREHENSION PRINCIPLES AND METAPHYSICS

Here the quantifier $\forall n$ is restricted to the natural numbers, 0 stands for zero, and s for the successor function. If zero has a property, and the successor of any natural number that has it has it too, then every natural number has the property. In mathematics, we need MI to generate consequences like (9), where a is an individual constant:

(9) $(Ra0 \mathbin{\&} \forall n\,(Ran \to Rasn)) \to \forall n\,Ran$

But (9) follows from MI by universal instantiation only if (10) holds:

(10) $\exists X\,\forall n\,(Xn \leftrightarrow Ran)$

If our comprehension principle forbids the formula A to contain parameters or non-logical constants (such as a), we cannot expect it to yield (10) (an instance of Comp_M^-), let alone (11) (an instance of Comp_M):[16]

(11) $\exists X\,\square\forall n\,(Xn \leftrightarrow Ran)$

The envisaged contingentist proposal is instead to condition the relevant instance of Comp_M on the being of anything specified in the formula A. For example, in the haecceity principle (2), A is just $x=y$, in which the only parameter or non-logical constant is the variable y (x is not a parameter because it is bound by the universal quantifier in Comp_M itself). Thus the relevant being condition is just $\exists x\,x=y$, and the conditioned version of (2), with the same prefix as before, is (12):

(12) $\square\forall y\,\square(\exists x\,x=y \to \exists X\,\square\forall x\,(Xx \leftrightarrow x=y))$

Unlike (2), (12) does not imply that there is my haecceity even if there is not me. Thus it avoids the feature that made (2) problematic in a contingentist setting. The same goes for the corresponding principle for anti-haecceities: since the defining formula $\neg x=y$ contains the same non-logical constants and parameters as $x=y$, the qualifying condition $\exists x\,x=y$ is the same:

(13) $\square\forall y\,\square(\exists x\,x=y \to \exists X\,\square\forall x\,(Xx \leftrightarrow \neg x=y))$

The general form of the new contingentist comprehension principle is this:

Comp_{MC} $E_A \to \exists X\,\square\forall x\,(Xx \leftrightarrow A)$

---

[16] For ease of exposition, the difference between the restricted quantifier $\forall n$ and the unrestricted quantifier $\forall x$ in Comp_M and Comp_M^- is ignored. Taking account of it does not materially change the argument.

Here E_A is the analogue of the condition $\exists x\ x{=}y$ in (12) and (13), depending on the structure of the formula A. The same provisos apply as to Comp_M. The results of prefixing instances of Comp_{MC} with necessity operators and universal quantifiers of any type in any order also count as instances of Comp_{MC}, as in (12) and (13).

Comp_{MC} has only a one-way conditional as its main connective, rather than the biconditional in Comp_{MC0}, because the defining formula A may contain redundant parameters or non-logical constants. For example, if A is the logical truth $x{=}a \to x{=}a$, then E_A is $\exists x\ x{=}a$, but the left–hand side of the principle $\exists X\ \Box\forall x\ (Xx \leftrightarrow (x{=}a \to x{=}a))$ holds simply because there is the necessarily universal property of self-identity, whatever the truth value of $\exists x\ x{=}a$.

Care is needed in defining the being condition E_A. We might try equating it with the conjunction of $\exists x\ t{=}x$ for each individual constant or parameter t in A (if A contains no such terms, E_A is a tautology). However, that definition does not fit the underlying motivation, on which contingencies of first-order being produce contingencies of higher-order being, so that we must also take account of higher-order constants or parameters in A. Indeed, if E_A were so limited to first-order terms, we could still derive un-conditional NNE_M from Comp_{MC} as in section 6.1, for the relevant formula A is simply Yx, which lacks individual constants and parameters; thus the commitment to the non-contingency of second-order being would remain. To avoid it, E_A must also have conjuncts analogous to $\exists x\ t{=}x$ for each higher-order non-logical constant or parameter in A too, of the form de-scribed in 6.1. When A is Yx, the one such expression is the second-order parameter Y; so E_{Yx} is $\exists X\ \Box\forall x\ (Yx \leftrightarrow Xx)$. Thus the correct instantiation of Comp_{MC} for Yx in place of A is logically trivial:

(14) $\quad \Box\forall Y\ \Box(\exists X\ \Box\forall x\ (Yx \leftrightarrow Xx) \to \exists X\ \Box\forall x\ (Xx \leftrightarrow Yx))$

With the proper definition of E_A, Comp_{MC} is a comprehension principle for second-order free modal logic.[17]

The non-modal comprehension principle Comp_M^- in the previous sec-tion is not derivable from Comp_{MC}, since the latter holds vacuously when the being condition E_A fails. However, advocates of Comp_{MC} may have to

[17] For a well-developed contingentist theory of coarse-grained propositions, properties, and relations whose being may be contingent on that of individuals see Fine 1977b and 1980. A recent discussion of second-order free logic is Besson 2009.

posit $Comp_M^-$ as well, for routine mathematical reasons. For example, consider the higher-order completeness property of an ordering relation, that any property with an upper bound has a least upper bound. To be an upper bound of a property is to be at least as great (in the sense of the ordering) as everything that has the property. To be a least upper bound of the property is to be an upper bound of the property that every upper bound of the property is at least as great as. We say 'any property' rather than 'any set' to avoid an unwanted restriction to set size. Formally, let $\leq$ define any quasi-reflexive anti-symmetric transitive relation; it need not be over numbers; it does not matter whether $u{\leq}v$ stands for an atomic formula or a complex one.[18] Then $\leq$ has this completeness property if and only if (15) holds:

(15) $\forall X \, (\exists y \, \forall x \, (Xx \rightarrow x{\leq}y) \rightarrow$
            $\exists y \, (\forall x \, (Xx \rightarrow x{\leq}y) \, \& \, \forall z \, (\forall x \, (Xx \rightarrow x{\leq}z) \rightarrow y{\leq}z)))$

For instance, the non-negative real numbers have this completeness property with respect to their usual ordering, while the non-negative rational numbers do not. But the assumption (15) serves its intended mathematical purpose only if it can be properly *applied*. More specifically, from (15) we must be able to derive any instance of (16), by plugging in the formula A in place of Xx (where A may contain x but not y or z free):

(16) $\exists y \, \forall x \, (A \rightarrow x{\leq}y) \rightarrow$
            $\exists y \, (\forall x \, (A \rightarrow x{\leq}y) \, \& \, \forall z \, (\forall x \, (A \rightarrow x{\leq}z) \rightarrow y{\leq}z))$

But in general to derive (16) from (15) we need something like $Comp_M^-$, to provide a property over which the second-order quantifier ranges co-extensive with A. Indeed, we need something like the full modal closure of $Comp_M^-$ so that we can derive (16) from (15) in modal contexts for all parameters. We could have reached the same conclusion by considering many other ways of applying second-order mathematics.

The combination of the two comprehension principles $Comp_{MC}$ and $Comp_M^-$ is ungainly, although a contingentist might argue that $Comp_M^-$ as well as $Comp_{MC}$ is motivated by a view on which whatever individuals there are can be used to define properties ontologically dependent on them. In particular, $Comp_M^-$ is motivated by the option of defining X by a finite or infinite disjunction of the form $\lambda x(x = a_0 \vee x = a_1 \vee x = a_2 \vee \ldots)$, where

---

[18] The relation $\leq$ is quasi-reflexive if and only if $x \leq x$ and $y \leq y$ whenever $x \leq y$; it is anti-symmetric if and only if $x = y$ whenever $x \leq y$ and $y \leq x$.

the individuals $a_0, a_1, a_2, \ldots$ all have being. Since Comp_M cannot be derived from Comp_M^- and Comp_{MC} together (see Appendix 6.7), combining the two comprehension principles does not collapse the restrictive contingentist strategy.

However, the argument for Comp_M^- has a modal analogue. For consider this higher-order modal completeness property of $\leq$: any possible property that can have a modal upper bound can have a modal least upper bound. The term 'modal upper bound' is defined simply by prefixing every universal quantifier with a necessity operator and the other quantifiers and the ordering symbol itself with a possibility operator. Formally:

$$(17) \qquad \Box\forall X \; (\Diamond\exists y \; \Box\forall x \; (Xx \to \Diamond x{\leq}y) \to$$
$$\Diamond\exists y \; (\Box\forall x \; (Xx \to \Diamond x{\leq}y) \; \& \; \Box\forall z \; (\Box\forall x \; (Xx \to \Diamond x{\leq}z) \to \Diamond y{\leq}z)))$$

As before, it does not matter for mathematical purposes whether $\leq$ is an atomic predicate; we can regard $x{\leq}y$, $x{\leq}z$, and $y{\leq}z$ as simply abbreviating appropriate formulas in which the relevant variables occur free. Now the assumption (17) serves its intended purpose only if it can be properly *applied*. More specifically, from (17) we must be able to derive any instance of (18), by plugging in the formula A in place of Xx (where A may contain x but not y or z free):

$$(18) \qquad \Diamond\exists y \; \Box\forall x \; (A \to \Diamond x{\leq}y) \to$$
$$\Diamond\exists y \; (\Box\forall x \; (A \to \Diamond x{\leq}y) \; \& \; \Box\forall z \; (\Box\forall x \; (A \to \Diamond x{\leq}z) \to \Diamond y{\leq}z))$$

But in general to derive (18) from (17) we need something like Comp_M, to provide a property over which the second-order quantifier ranges necessarily coextensive with A. Indeed, we need something like the full modal closure of Comp_M to derive (18) from (17) in modal contexts for all parameters. We could have reached the same conclusion by considering many other ways of applying second-order modal mathematics. But what guarantee has the contingentist that there even could be a property necessarily coextensive with A? For example, the parameters in A may not be all compossible; informally, it may be impossible for all the relevant objects to be together.[19]

Not even the combination of Comp_M^- and Comp_{MC} permits the derivation of (18) from (17); see Appendix 6.7 for a proof. Thus even when the

---

[19] For more on the problem of incompossibles see section 7.5. For the failure of contingentist attempts to simulate second-order quantifiers with infinite sequences of modalized first-order quantifiers see section 7.7.

resources of the two main contingentist strategies for restricting the comprehension principle are combined, the result is still too weak for reasonable logical and mathematical purposes.

We saw in section 6.2 that the prospects are poor for reconciling contingentism with the strong comprehension principle $Comp_M$ for second-order modal logic. In sections 6.3 and 6.4, we have seen that replacing $Comp_M$ with weaker comprehension principles prevents second-order logic from adequately serving the logical and mathematical purposes for which we need it. By contrast, $Comp_M$ fits nicely with necessitism. Thus, on present evidence, necessitism is much better placed than contingentism to integrate with the sort of comprehension principle that second-order modal logic needs if it is to serve as a framework for general systematic enquiry.

6.5 From properties to propositions

The case for necessitism in sections 6.1–6.4 is abductive. Necessitist theories of higher-order modal logic do better than contingentist ones, by the normal standards for comparing scientific theories. By those standards, a contingentist reply that merely attacks $Comp_M$ and specifies no alternative comprehension principle, at least almost equally clear and workable, is feeble, since it does not make contingentism a serious rival theory. Still, we can organize some aspects of the case for necessitism into deductive arguments. Doing so highlights some links between the considerations in sections 6.1–6.4 and arguments already formulated in earlier debates on modal metaphysics. However, it also brings out the advantages of an abductive methodology over a deductive one in clarifying the relative strengths and weaknesses of contingentism and necessitism.

A simple deductive argument for necessitism in terms of haecceities has two premises:

P1 $\Box\forall y\ \Box\exists X\ \Box\forall x\ (Xx \leftrightarrow x{=}y)$

P2 $\Box\forall y\ \Box(\exists X\ \Box\forall x\ (Xx \leftrightarrow x{=}y) \rightarrow \exists x\ x{=}y)$

By P1, necessarily everything necessarily has a haecceity. By P2, having a haecceity strictly implies being something. Therefore, by elementary first-order modal reasoning, necessarily everything is necessarily something, the central thesis of necessitism:

NNE $\Box\forall y\ \Box\exists x\ x{=}y$

NNE follows from P1 and P2 because any instance of the argument schema from $\Box\forall y\ \Box A$ and $\Box\forall y\ \Box(A \to B)$ to $\Box\forall y\ \Box B$ is valid. Of course, the main work is in supporting the premises. P1 is an instance of Comp_M; the most directly relevant considerations are the comparisons between it and weaker comprehension principles in sections 6.3 and 6.4. The less formal meta-physical considerations in 6.2 about properties that track particulars give some support to P2. But, despite its plausibility as a principle, we also saw in 6.2 that the idea of tracking one particular by means of others, such as its constituents, provides a prima facie objection to P2 in its full generality. We cannot adequately compare contingentist and necessitist theories without investigating their relative systematic power more extensively than in the scope of a single deductive argument. We did just that in the previous sections.

A parallel argument has the individual's anti-haecceity in place of its haecceity; simply insert a negation sign before $x{=}y$ in P1 and at the first occurrence in P2.

On the usual assimilation of propositions to 0-place properties, similar arguments for NNE have propositions instead of 1-place properties. Here are two premises:

P1a $\Box\forall y\ \Box\exists P\ \Box(P \leftrightarrow \exists x\ x{=}y)$

P2a $\Box\forall y\ \Box(\exists P\ \Box(P \leftrightarrow \exists x\ x{=}y) \to \exists x\ x{=}y)$

The argument from P1a and P2a to NNE is another instance of the valid schema from $\Box\forall y\ \Box A$ and $\Box\forall y\ \Box(A \to B)$ to $\Box\forall y\ \Box B$. In crudely reifying paraphrase: by P1a necessarily everything necessarily has the proposition that it is something; by P2a having the proposition that one is something strictly implies being something; therefore, necessarily everything is necessarily something.

A parallel argument puts the proposition that the individual is nothing in place of the proposition that it is something; simply insert a negation sign before $\exists x\ x{=}y$ in P1a and at the first occurrence (but not the second) in P2a.

P1a is simply an instance of the analogue of $Comp_M$ for sentences rather than monadic predicates:

$$Comp_P \qquad \exists P \, \Box(P \leftrightarrow A)$$

Here P is a sentence variable not free in A; any result of prefixing an instance of $Comp_P$ with necessity operators and universal quantifiers of any type in any order is also an instance of $Comp_M$. The support for $Comp_P$ is broadly similar to that for $Comp_M$. Indeed, they are both simply special cases of Comp, the powerful general comprehension principle for higher-order modal logic.

The support for P2a obviously does *not* come from the general schema $\exists P \, \Box(P \leftrightarrow A) \rightarrow A$, for that is in effect the absurd principle that every proposition is true. Rather, what support P2a are less formal metaphysical considerations similar to those that support P2. In articulating them, we must be clear about what sort of propositions we are assuming.[20] On a Russellian view of propositions as structured complexes of the objects, properties, and relations they are about, it is presumably necessary that the proposition that I am something is something only if I am something, for I am an essential constituent of the proposition that I am something. Even on a neo-Fregean view of propositions as thoughts, cognitive values of sentences, or modes of presentation of truth values, the link to me may be essential to the proposition that I am something, if the mode of presentation is object-dependent. If so, by a being constraint the proposition is something only if I am something. Perhaps one can argue for necessitism in such Russellian or neo-Fregean terms. But neither view is quite relevant here, for both Russellians and neo-Fregeans individuate propositions in too fine-grained a way for present purposes. They agree that there are distinct but necessarily equivalent propositions: for example, expressed by sentences with radically different structures that are logically equivalent, yet not obviously so. But P2a implies that if any proposition is necessary and sufficient for me to be something, then I am something; it does not specify that the proposition is that I am something. For both Russellians and neo-Fregeans, a proposition may be necessary and sufficient for me to be something

---

[20] Once again, talk of postulating propositions does no justice to the difference between quantifying into sentence position (as P1a and P2a do) and quantifying into name position. The text employs the first-order manner of speaking for its familiarity and simplicity; the literally relevant points can be made more laboriously with quantification into sentence position.

without being the proposition that I am something. Thus even if I am an essential constituent of the proposition that I am something or it is otherwise essentially linked to me, and by P1a necessarily some proposition is necessary and sufficient for me to be something, it might not be the proposition that I am something, so we are not yet in a position to conclude that necessarily I am something. Furthermore, the case in sections 6.1–6.4 for Comp, and more specifically $Comp_M$, was premised on a coarse-grained approach to higher-order individuation that makes necessary equivalence the higher-order version of identity. The possible worlds semantics in section 5.5 has the same outcome. In particular, it makes necessarily equivalent propositions identical. The coarse-grained approach is incompatible with Russellianism, and even more obviously with neo-Fregeanism. Thus an attempt to argue for necessitism from premises like P1a and P2a in a Russellian or neo-Fregean framework would need to justify the comprehension principle underlying P1a along rather different lines from those sketched earlier.

The salient coarse-grained account of propositions is Stalnaker's, which treats them as sets of possible worlds. It is a convenient way of thinking, but we have seen good reason for contingentists not to take possible worlds semantics at face value (section 3.6), and Stalnaker's criterion for isolating their representationally significant aspects gives results that are incorrect by the standard of his own contingentism (section 4.9). Contingentists may instead treat necessarily equivalent propositions as the same without treating them as the same set of worlds. For both contingentists and necessitists, conceiving propositions as the 0-place analogue of 1-place properties and many-place relations is a helpful alternative to the Russellian and neo-Fregean conceptions, for it is much less tempting to regard properties and relations as Russellian structured complexes or neo-Fregean modes of presentation. The simplest natural standard of individuation for properties and relations is necessary equivalence.

Of course, none of this means that the Russellian and neo-Fregean accounts are illegitimate or useless, for example in handling ascriptions of intentional states. There may be both coarse-grained propositions and fine-grained propositions. It is just that the fine-grained ones involve complications unnecessary for the interpretation of higher-order modal logic as a background logic for general metaphysics.

With these clarifications, P1a is simply an instance of the preferred comprehension principle Comp. The case for P2a is less straightforward. Why cannot there be a (false) proposition necessary and sufficient for me to be something when I am nothing? The response is as in section 6.2: no well-developed metaphysical theory explains how a proposition can always modally lock onto an individual when there is no such individual to lock onto, just as no such theory explains how a property (such as a haecceity or anti-haecceity) can always modally lock onto an individual when there is no such individual to lock onto. However, the modal locking onto is less exclusive for positive and negative attributions of being than it was for haecceities and anti-haecceities. The latter are locked onto uniquely, since on logical grounds the haecceity (or anti-haecceity) of one thing could not have been the haecceity (or anti-haecceity) of another. By contrast, the coarse-grained proposition that this is something (or that this is nothing) may also be the coarse-grained proposition that that is something (or that that is nothing), where this and that are distinct. For example, if it is necessary and sufficient for the singleton set {Socrates} to be something that Socrates is something, then the coarse-grained proposition that {Socrates} is something just is the coarse-grained proposition that Socrates is something, even though Socrates is not his singleton. Thus in modally locking onto Socrates the proposition also modally locks onto {Socrates}. Modal locking is less exclusive even for apparently singular propositions than for haecceities and anti-haecceities. That is a good reason to put the argument for necessitism primarily in terms of haecceities or anti-haecceities rather than propositions.

Nevertheless, the difference in exclusiveness may not blunt the argument with propositions too much. For the contingentist is still challenged to provide a well-developed metaphysical theory that explains how a proposition can always lock onto a particular individual (in the less exclusive modal sense just sketched) even when there is no such individual to lock onto. In section 6.2 we assessed ways in which contingentists might try to meet the corresponding challenge for properties. Although some moves were available to them, the prospects for turning them into an effective comprehensive strategy for defending contingentism were poor. In that respect, the difference between coarse-grained properties and coarse-grained propositions is not crucial. More specifically, one of the most urgent parts of the challenge in section 6.2 was to explain how haecceities could discriminate modally between qualitatively identical particulars in the absence of any relevant particulars. In many such cases, whether one particular is something is not equivalent to whether the other is. The problem was raised for Tweedledum and Tweedledee, not for Socrates and {Socrates}. Tweedledum may be something even though Tweedledee is nothing, and vice versa, so the coarse-grained proposition that Tweedledum is something and the coarse-grained proposition that Tweedledee is something are distinct, as are their negations. Hence the failure of coarse-grained propositions to be fully exclusive to given individuals does not occur where the contingentist needs it. Thus the anti-contingentist considerations still carry weight when developed in terms of propositions rather than properties.

The tension between contingentism and the 'Aristotelian' comprehension principle Comp_{MC0} in section 6.4 can be regimented as a similar argument. The analogue of P1 is the left-to-right direction of (8), the relevant instance of Comp_{MC0}:

P1b $\qquad \Box\forall y\, \Box(\exists x\, \neg x=y \to \exists X\, \Box\forall x\, (Xx \leftrightarrow \neg x=y))$

Correspondingly, we use the analogue of P2 for anti-haecceities:

P2b $\qquad \Box\forall y\, \Box(\exists X\, \Box\forall x\, (Xx \leftrightarrow \neg x=y) \to \exists x\, x=y)$

In effect, the considerations in section 6.2 that favour P2 also favour P2b. To complete the deductive argument for NNE, we need not assume the un-conditional antecedent $\exists x\, \neg x=y$ of P1b; the conditional $\neg\exists x\, x=y \to \exists x\, \neg x=y$ will do instead. It merely posits that there is something, identical with y or not. For since the argument schema from $\neg A \to B$, $B \to C$, and $C \to A$ to A is valid in truth-functional logic (by the transitivity of $\to$ and reductio ad absurdum), the corresponding schema from $\Box\forall y\, \Box(\neg A \to B)$, $\Box\forall y\, \Box(B \to C)$, and $\Box\forall y\, \Box(C \to A)$ to $\Box\forall y\, \Box A$ is valid in quantified modal logic. The required conditional is an instance of a theorem schema of standard first-order logic, $\neg\exists x\, D \to \exists x\, \neg D$:

P3b $\qquad \Box\forall y\, \Box(\neg\exists x\, x=y \to \exists x\, \neg x=y)$

NNE follows from P1b, P2b, and P3b by uncontroversial principles of quantified modal logic. Analogously to previous cases, however, objections can be made to P2b, despite its attraction: in the end, contingentism and necessitism can be adequately compared only with an abductive methodology.

Some contingentists may object to P3b that since it entails $\Box\exists x\, x=x$, it illegitimately excludes the counterfactual possibility of there being abso-lutely nothing. That commitment corresponds to the minimal ontological commitment of standard first-order non-modal logic, the theorem $\exists x\ x=x$. Such contingentists can avoid any such commitment by weakening P3b thus:

P3b* $\Box \forall y\ \Box(\exists x\ x=x \to (\neg \exists x\ x=y \to \exists x\ \neg x=y))$

P3b* is uncontroversial, since $\exists x\ x=x \to (\neg \exists x\ x=y \to \exists x\ \neg x=y)$ is a theorem even of non-modal free logic. However, weakening P3b to P3b* scarcely helps contingentists avoid the argument, for P1b, P2b, and P3b* still entail a qualified form of NNE by uncontroversial modal reasoning:

NNE* $\Box \forall y\ \Box(\exists x\ x=x \to \exists x\ x=y)$

In other words, necessarily everything is necessarily something, except when there is absolutely nothing, which concedes almost (but not quite) everything to necessitism. Most contingentists hold, for example, that London could have been nothing even while there was something else.

The analogous modification of the argument from P1a and P2a to NNE is much simpler. The analogue of Comp$_{MC0}$ for quantification into sentence position is really a comprehension principle for facts rather than propositions:

Comp$_{PC0}$ $A \leftrightarrow \exists P\ \Box(P \leftrightarrow A)$

However, the argument requires only the left-to-right direction of Comp$_{PC0}$, which has no factive consequences. The relevant case is this:

P1c $\Box \forall y\ \Box(\neg \exists x\ x=y \to \exists P\ \Box(P \leftrightarrow \neg \exists x\ x=y))$

Correspondingly, we use P2c in place of P2a:

P2c $\Box \forall y\ \Box(\exists P\ \Box(P \leftrightarrow \neg \exists x\ x=y) \to \exists x\ x=y)$

The pros and cons for P2c are similar to those for P2a earlier. P1c and P2c yield NNE by straightforward modal reasoning. Roughly: if you were nothing, there would be the proposition that you were nothing; but if there were that proposition, you would be something; therefore, you could not be nothing.

The paraphrase was rough because it reifies propositions, quantifying into singular noun phrase position ('the proposition that you were nothing') where P1c and P2c quantify into sentence position (P). But we can also formulate a less peremptory version of the argument in a framework that really does reify propositions.[21] We add to the language an operator π that applies to a formula A to give a singular term $\pi(A)$ denoting the proposition that A expresses (on a given assignment).[22] The English equivalent is 'the proposition that . . .'. We also add a truth predicate T, applicable to propositions rather than sentences. We can derive the analogue of P1c from these two premises:

Pod $\Box\forall y\ \Box(\neg\exists x\ x=y \rightarrow T\pi(\neg\exists x\ x=y))$

P1d $\Box\forall y\ \Box(T\pi(\neg\exists x\ x=y) \rightarrow \exists x\ x=\pi(\neg\exists x\ x=y))$

By Pod, if you were nothing, the proposition that you were nothing would be true. Pod follows from an instance of the minimalist schema $T\pi(A) \leftrightarrow A$ for propositional truth, to which necessity operators and universal quantifiers may be prefixed in any order.[23] Necessarily, the proposition that snow is white is true if and only if snow is white. By P1d, if the proposition that you were nothing were true, that proposition would be something. P1d is an instance of the being principle for truth, $Tt \rightarrow \exists x\ x=t$, to which necessity operators and universal quantifiers may again be prefixed in any order, where t is any singular term. Necessarily, a proposition would be true only if there were something to be true. The analogue of P2c is the third premise:

P2d $\Box\forall y\ \Box(\exists x\ x=\pi(\neg\exists x\ x=y) \rightarrow \exists x\ x=y)$

By P2d, if the proposition that you were nothing were something, you would be something. The pros and cons for P2d are similar to those already discussed for P2a and P2c. By standard quantified modal logic, Pod, P1d, and P2d entail NNE.

The argument looks more familiar when we instantiate the variable y with a proper name and write it out in English:

Poe   Necessarily, if Socrates is nothing then the proposition that Socrates is nothing is true.

[21] Technically, since coarse-grained propositions can be modelled as subsets of the domain of worlds, independently of the domain of individuals, they can be included in the latter domain consistently with Cantor's theorem, unlike coarse-grained n-place properties for $n \geq 1$. That by itself does not resolve apparent paradoxes about the number of metaphysically possible worlds; for discussion see Kaplan 1994 and section 3.7.

[22] Stalnaker 2010, p. 27, uses such notation.

[23] In his defence of the unnecessitated minimalist principle for propositional truth, Paul Horwich, 1998, p. 21, suggests that the necessitated version may be derivable from the assumption that the unnecessitated version is explanatorily fundamental.

P1e   Necessarily, if the proposition that Socrates is nothing is true then the proposition that Socrates is nothing is something.

P2e   Necessarily, if the proposition that Socrates is nothing is something then Socrates is something.

NEe   Necessarily, Socrates is something.

Versions of this argument with 'exists' in place of 'is something' have been much debated in the literature, often in contraposed form, so that they are in effect treated as reducing the conjunction of the premises Poe, P1e, and P2e to absurdity.[24] The use of 'is something' in place of 'exists' clarifies what is really at stake, and the discussion of necessitism shows that the conclusion NEe is not really absurd. The corresponding argument from P1c and P2c with quantification into sentence position indicates that neither the postulation of such objects as propositions nor the use of a truth predicate is crucial. The earlier arguments with quantification into predicate rather than sentence position should help discourage any idea that the point turns on what truth bearers can be thought or said. Rather, the appropriate setting in which to evaluate such arguments is the general appraisal of comprehension principles for intensional logic, with respect to both their logical power and their metaphysical systematicity.

6.6 Truth in a world and truth of a world

There is a difference between what we can truly think or say in our actual circumstances about some merely possible circumstances and what could be truly thought or said in those counterfactual circumstances, if they obtained. We can validly reason from the counterfactual hypothesis that thought never occurs, even though trivially if thought never occurred, no one would ever entertain that or any other hypothesis. For non-minimalist contingentists, there is contingency not just in such cognitive access to propositions, but in what propositions there are: in particular, the proposition that Socrates is nothing may be as contingent a being as Socrates himself. On this view,

---

[24] For Prior's version see his 1967, pp. 149–51, and Fine 1977a, pp. 149–50. For Plantinga's version see his 1983 and 1985, pp. 341–9, and for criticism Fine 1985. For a version closer to the present one see Williamson 2002a, and for criticism Rumfitt 2003, Efird 2010, and Stalnaker 2010.

although *we* can truly apply the proposition to a world in which Socrates is nothing, there would be no such proposition if that world obtained. The proposition is true *of* the world but not *in* the world. Arguments like those in section 6.5 are often accused of violating such a distinction.[25]

Of course, the arguments in section 6.5 do not mention possible worlds, nor are they committed to analysing modality in such terms. Nevertheless, the spirit of the distinction between truth in a world and truth of a world is relevant to them. For the contingentist may deny Poe, which conditionally predicates truth of the proposition that Socrates is nothing within the scope of the necessity operator ('truth in a world'), while explaining away its plausibility by arguing that the proposition somehow correctly characterizes the possibility at issue from our actual standpoint ('truth of a world').

Stalnaker propounds a developed version of the strategy.[26] He starts with a primitive entailment relation between propositions (E) and a primitive monadic property of propositional truth (T). A proposition is necessary if and only if every proposition entails it; it is possible if and only if it does not entail every proposition. A proposition q is a contradictory of a proposition p if and only if no possible proposition both entails p and entails q, and only a necessary proposition is both entailed by p and entailed by q. Every proposition has exactly one contradictory. To exclude a proposition is to entail its contradictory. A world is a possible proposition that entails or excludes every proposition. Every possible proposition is entailed by at least one world. The actual world is the unique world that entails every true proposition. A proposition p is true *of* a world w if and only if w entails p (Ewp); p is true *in* w if and only if w entails the proposition that p is true ($Ew\pi(Tp)$).[27] Since Socrates could have been nothing, the proposition that Socrates is nothing is possible, and so is true of at least one possible world w ($Ew\pi(\neg \exists x\, s=x)$). But, on Stalnaker's view of propositions, we may assume that w also

[25] Fine uses the terminology of 'inner' and 'outer' truth in his critique of Plantinga (1985, p. 163) and in his detailed technical account of the distinction (1980). See also King 2007, p. 81.

[26] See Stalnaker 2010. The details of the exposition here are consistent with the letter of his account and follow from its spirit.

[27] The terminology of 'truth in a world' and 'truth of a world' suggests a subtler distinction than Stalnaker is making, since on his view 'truth of a world' has no clear connection with truth. However, that point still leaves his objection to be addressed. The spatial associations of the phrases 'truth *in* a world' and '*inner* truth' are also misleading, since they suggest a picture of a world as a proper part of reality, an inside that has an outside, contrary to the agreed unrestricted reading of the quantifiers in modal contexts.

entails that the proposition that Socrates is nothing is itself nothing, and therefore is not true, so w does not entail that the proposition that Socrates is nothing is true $(\neg Ew\pi(T\pi(\neg\exists x\ s{=}x)))$. Thus the proposition that Socrates is nothing is true of w but not true in w. By the transitivity of entailment, that Socrates is nothing does not entail that the proposition that Socrates is nothing is true $(\neg E\pi(\neg\exists x\ s{=}x)\pi(T\pi(\neg\exists x\ s{=}x)))$. Consequently, Stalnaker denies premise Poe (and Pod). In modal terms, he accepts the minimalist schema $T\pi(A) \leftrightarrow A$ but rejects its necessitation $\Box(T\pi(A) \leftrightarrow A)$.

One must be cautious in applying Stalnaker's framework, for it does not satisfy all the expected logical relations. In particular, entailment is not necessary truth-preservation: Epq is not generally equivalent to $\Box(Tp \rightarrow Tq)$. The putative equivalence fails in both directions. For example, if the proposition that Socrates is nothing cannot be true because it is something only if he is, then its truth strictly but vacuously implies the truth of any proposition whatsoever; but since the proposition that Socrates is nothing is possible by Stalnaker's contingentism, it does not entail every proposition. Thus the truth of one proposition may strictly imply the truth of another even though the former proposition does not entail the latter. Conversely, suppose that (by contingentist standards) Solomon is essentially a child of David. Therefore, by those standards, the proposition that David never has children entails the proposition that Solomon is nothing, but in some worlds the proposition that David never has children is something and true; in those worlds, Solomon is nothing, so the proposition that Solomon is nothing is itself nothing, and so not true. Thus one proposition may entail another even though the former can be true while the latter is not true.[28] But contingentists might learn to live with such apparent anomalies.

How is Stalnaker's strategy to be applied to the other arguments for NNE in section 6.5, from P1 and P2, from P1a and P2a, from P1b, P2b and P3b or P3b*, and from P1c and P2c? They employ no truth predicate, so the generalization is not mechanical. However, since Stalnaker extends the contingency of being from ordinary concrete individuals to propositions, the spirit of his approach seems to permit a further extension to higher-order quantifiers. Thus in each case the contingentist denies the relevant instance of a comprehension principle: P1, P1a, P1b, and P1c. This corresponds to

---

[28] Given quantification into sentence position, we might still characterize E modally as
$\lambda p,q(\exists P\,\exists Q\ (p = \pi(P)\ \&\ q = \pi(Q)\ \&\ \Box(P \rightarrow Q)))$.

Stalnaker's implicit rejection of the first-order comprehension schema for propositions:

Comp$_1$ $\exists x \, \Box(Tx \leftrightarrow A)$

For Stalnaker, even unprefixed Comp$_1$ fails when A is read as 'Socrates is nothing': no proposition is true in all and only the worlds in which Socrates is nothing. By contrast, the other premises of the arguments seem largely correct on his account. P2, P2a, P2b, and P2c are all similar in spirit to the being constraint, which he is at least provisionally willing to grant.[29] P3b* (but not P3b) and P4b correspond to theorems of his quantified modal logic. Thus in each case only the instance of the comprehension principle remains for him to deny.

Unfortunately, although Stalnaker is committed to rejecting the strong comprehension principles at issue, he proposes no alternative. That is not very surprising, since he addresses a form of the argument for NNE that does not emphasize its dependence on a comprehension principle. But once the connection is clear, we must ask whether his strategy is compatible with comprehension principles strong enough for purposes of a systematic modal theory. In sections 6.3 and 6.4 we saw how unsatisfactory in that respect are the natural weakenings of Comp; similar points apply to their analogues for Comp$_1$. Those weakenings are just the ones his strategy suggests. Thus generalizing his account threatens to cripple higher-order modal logic as a framework for systematic theorizing.

Although the phrases 'truth in a world' and 'truth of a world' (or $Ew\pi(Tp)$ and Ewp) are not synonymous, that semantic distinction does not compensate for an inadequate comprehension principle or prevent the phrases from being materially or even logically equivalent. Nor does it somehow help the rival, minimalist contingentist strategy in section 6.2. Quite the opposite: by emphasizing the distinction between actual and counterfactual higher-order resources, it makes more urgent the demand that minimalism refuses to meet: to explain the alleged asymmetry between first-order and higher-order being in point of contingency. Indeed, an integral part of Stalnaker's account is the treatment of the contingency of propositions as a natural corollary of the contingency of ordinary concrete individuals, which is analogous to the treatment of higher-order contingency as a natural corollary of first-order contingency.

---

[29] See Stalnaker 2010, p. 25.

The problems just raised for Stalnaker's strategy do not depend on accidental features of its execution. From a contingentist starting point, his argument goes with the grain of the distinction between truth in a world and truth of a world. It may suffice to block the arguments of section 6.5, if they are taken in isolation as purporting to establish necessitism on self-evident premises. But they are better treated as formal synopses of the extended comparison in earlier sections of the strengths and weaknesses of various comprehension principles for higher-order modal logic. For those purposes, distinguishing truth in a world from truth of a world does not constitute an adequate case for preferring a weak comprehension principle to a strong one.[30]

---

[30] King 2007, pp. 82–95, develops a different account of truth at a world, with structured pro-positions, to make room for actualism. Unfortunately for King, it still validates crucial instances of unnecessitated BF. Let P be any property, and E the trivial property of being something. We argue from King's recursive definition of truth at a world for propositions (p. 83), as extended and refined for quantified propositions (pp. 218–22). Let [. . .,P] and [. . .,E] be the corresponding propositional frames (analogues of the open formulas 'x has P' and 'x has E'). Suppose that [POSSIBLY,[[SOME . . . [. . .,E]],[. . .,P]]] (the proposition that possibly something has P) is true at the actual world $w_@$. Then [[SOME . . . [. . .,E]],[. . .,P]] is true at some world $w*$ accessible to $w_@$. So [o,E] and [o,P] are true at $w*$ for at least one thing o. Hence [POSSIBLY,[o,P]] is true at $w_@$. Moreover, by King's actualism, o is actually something, so [o,E] is also true at $w_@$. Therefore [[SOME . . . [. . .,E]],[POSSIBLY,[. . .,P]]] (the proposition that something possibly has P) is true at $w_@$, as required. Since P can be a property such as being a child of Wittgenstein, this is just the sort of consequence that King's account was supposed to avoid. A similar problem arises for the would-be actualist account of modal thinking in Peacocke 1999, pp. 119–202, with admissible assignments instead of worlds. The actualist nature of the admissible assignments validates unnecessitated BF (Williamson 2002b, pp. 650–1; Rosen 2002b is also relevant), which Peacocke had described as 'intuitively invalid' (1999, p. 153). In response, Pea-cocke claims that an actualist can accept BF on a reductionist account of possibilia (2002a, 2002b), although the details are unclear. In any case, his account is threatened by a cruder form of modal collapse. He writes 'for there to exist a possible object that is φ is for it to be consistent with the Principles of Possibility and non-modal truths that there is an admissible assignment under which the open sentence or concept x is φ is true' (2002a, p. 493). In his example, even if nothing is a quantity of the chemical element N, it is still possible for there to be a quantity of N because 'It is consistent with the Principles of Possibility and non-modal truths that there is an admissible assign-ment under which the open sentence or concept x is a quantity of N is true'. However, one non-modal truth is that (absolutely) nothing is a quantity of N. How is it consistent with the Principles of Possibility and that non-modal truth that there is an admissible assignment under which x is a quantity of N is true? If the Principles permit $\lambda x(x$ is a quantity of N$)$ to be assigned a property other than be-ing a quantity of N, or to be assigned that property while making the open sentence x is a quantity of N true, that would have unfortunate knock-on effects and run counter to Peacocke's treatment in other cases. For example, he says that it is inconsistent with the Principles of Possibility and the non-modal truth that Hesperus is Phosphorus that there is an admissible assignment under which x is identical with Hesperus and distinct from Phosphorus is true (2002b, p. 675). Moreover, on Peacocke's view, if o is not a quantity of N, the fundamental kind K of o is presumably inconsistent with being a quantity of N, so if x is a quantity of N were assigned truth when x was assigned o, x is a K would have to be assigned falsity, contrary to one of Peacocke's constitutive Principles of Possibility (1999, p. 145, and 2002a, p. 493). For relevant discussion see Sullivan 1998, Williamson 2002b, pp. 652–4, and Peacocke 1998 and 2002b, pp. 666–8.

6.7 Appendix

This appendix proves a result used in section 6.4, that $Comp_M^-$ and $Comp_{MC}$ do not enable us to derive the instance (18) of the modalized least upper bound principle (17) from (17) itself. Since (18) is straightforwardly derivable from (17) and the unrestricted comprehension principle $Comp_M$, the result also shows that $Comp_M$ cannot be derived from $Comp_{MC}$ and $Comp_M^-$ together.

For convenience, we reproduce the principles at issue:

$Comp_M$ $\exists X \Box \forall x \, (Xx \leftrightarrow A)$

$Comp_M^-$ $\exists X \, \forall x \, (Xx \leftrightarrow A)$

$Comp_{MC}$ $E_A \rightarrow \exists X \Box \forall x \, (Xx \leftrightarrow A)$

(17) $\Box \forall X(\Diamond \exists y \, \Box \forall x \, (Xx \rightarrow \Diamond x {\leq} y) \rightarrow$
         $\Diamond \exists y \, (\Box \forall x \, (Xx \rightarrow \Diamond x {\leq} y) \, \& \, \Box \forall z \, (\Box \forall x \, (Xx \rightarrow \Diamond x {\leq} z) \rightarrow \Diamond y {\leq} z)))$

(18) $\Diamond \exists y \, \Box \forall x \, (A \rightarrow \Diamond x {\leq} y) \rightarrow$
         $\Diamond \exists y \, (\Box \forall x \, (A \rightarrow \Diamond x {\leq} y) \, \& \, \Box \forall z \, (\Box \forall x \, (A \rightarrow \Diamond x {\leq} z) \rightarrow \Diamond y {\leq} z))$

Here x but not y, z, or X may occur free in A. Any result of prefixing an instance of $Comp_M$, $Comp_M^-$, or $Comp_{MC}$ with necessity operators and universal quantifiers in any order also counts as an instance of that schema. The formula E_A is a conjunction with at least $\exists x \, x{=}v$ as a conjunct for each individual variable v free in A. Formulas of the form $u {\leq} v$ may have a complex definition.

Predictably, we construct a general model in which $Comp_M^-$, $Comp_{MC}$, and (17) hold but (18) fails. We start with any infinite set X. Let S be the set of infinite subsets of X whose complement in X is also infinite. The set of worlds W will be $\{{<}i, d{>} : i \in d \in S\}$. For the first-order domain function, let $dom({<}i, d{>}) = \{\{\}, \{i\}, d\}$. Thus the outer domain $D = \cup_{w \in W} dom(w)$ contains the empty set, the singletons of all members of X, and all infinite subsets of X with an infinite complement in X. The plan is to order these sets by the subset relation. Since the upper bounds in D of any two singletons are the infinite sets in D that include both, and from any such upper bound one can obtain another by removing a suitable element, the two singletons have no least upper bound in D. The idea is to restrict the second-order domain to exclude such counterexamples to (17), although they remain counterexamples to an appropriate instance of (18), while still satisfying $Comp_M^-$ and $Comp_{MC}$.

The only non-logical constant in the language is a binary predicate R. Its intension is $V(R)(w) = \{<d, e> \in \text{dom}(w)^2: d \subseteq e\}$. Thus R defines the subset relation restricted by the domain function; the restriction is imposed out of respect for the being constraint. To make the defined term $\leq$ express the unrestricted subset relation over D, we proceed as follows. First we define singleton(y) as $\lozenge \exists x \, \exists z \, (Rxy \, \& \, \neg x{=}y \, \& \, Ryz \, \& \, \neg y{=}z)$, which has the intended effect given the structure of dom. Then we let $x{\leq}y$ abbreviate this formula:

$$\forall z \, Rxz \lor \Box \forall z \, (\text{singleton}(z) \rightarrow (\lozenge Rzx \rightarrow \lozenge Rzy))$$

To see that this has the right effect, let d and e be members of D, $\underline{a}$ an assignment of values to variables such that $\underline{a}(x) = d$ and $\underline{a}(y) = e$, and $w \in$ W. Then $w, \underline{a} \vDash x{\leq}y$ if and only if condition # holds: either d is a subset of every member of dom(w) or for every $i \in$ X, if $\{i\}$ is composible with d and $i \in d$ then $\{i\}$ is composible with e and $i \in e$ (members of D are composible just if the domain of some world contains both). We check that # implies that $d \subseteq e$. If the first disjunct of # holds, then d is $\{\}$, the least member of the domain of any given world, so $d \subseteq e$. Suppose that the second disjunct of # holds, and let $i \in d$. Then either $d = \{i\}$ or d is infinite. In both cases $\{i\}$ is composible with d, so $i \in e$ by the second disjunct of #. Thus again $d \subseteq e$. Conversely, we check that if $d \subseteq e$ then # holds. Suppose that $d \subseteq e$. If d is empty then the first disjunct of # holds. If d is a singleton then the only singleton composible with d is d itself, and e is either d or infinite; in both cases d is composible with e, so the second disjunct of # holds. If d is infinite then every singleton composible with d is composible with e, and again the second disjunct of # holds. Hence if $d \subseteq e$ then # holds. Thus $\leq$ expresses the unrestricted subset relation.

We must define suitable domains for monadic second-order quantification. Let INT be the set of monadic intensions; for I $\in$ INT and $w \in$ W, I(w) $\subseteq$ dom(w). To define the second-order domain function we need some auxiliary notions. Let perm(X) be the set of permutations of X. Each $\pi \in$ perm(X) induces a permutation of entities built out of X in the natural way; thus for $d \subseteq$ X, $\pi(d) = \{\pi(i): i \in d\}$; for $i \in d$, $\pi(<i, d>) = <\pi(i), \pi(d)>$; for I $\in$ INT and $w \in$ W, $\pi(I)(\pi(w)) = \pi(I(w))$; for an assignment $\underline{a}$ of values to variables, $\pi(\underline{a})(v) = \pi(\underline{a}(v))$. Clearly, the induced mapping π acts as a permutation on W and on INT. For any of the entities s on which the induced mappings are defined let fix(s) = $\{\pi \in$ perm(X): $\pi(s) = s\}$. Note (i): if $d \in$ dom(w)

and $\pi \in \text{fix}(w)$ then $\pi \in \text{fix}(d)$ (by the definitions of dom and fix). For the second order domain function DOM, let $\text{DOM}(w) = \{I \in \text{INT}: \text{fix}(w) \subseteq \text{fix}(I)\}$; informally, the individuals in w fix the properties in w. Note (ii): for $\pi \in \text{perm}(X)$ the whole model is a fixed point of the induced π; in particular, $\pi(V(R)) = V(R)$.

Having constructed the model, we verify that it has the required features.

(I) The model validates Comp_M^-. Proof: Let $w \in W$ and $s \subseteq \text{dom}(w)$. Choose $I \in \text{INT}$ such that $I(w) = s$ and $I(w*) = \{\}$ if $w* \neq w$. We show that $I \in \text{DOM}(w)$. Let $\pi \in \text{fix}(w)$. Then $\pi(I)(w) = \pi(I)(\pi(\pi^{-1}(w))) = \pi(I(\pi^{-1}(w))) = \pi(I(w)) = \pi(s) = s = I(w)$ by note (i). Similarly, if $w* \neq w$, then $\pi(I)(w*) = \pi(I(\pi^{-1}(w*))) = \pi(\{\}) = \{\} = I(w*)$. Hence $\pi(I) = I$, so $\pi \in \text{fix}(I)$; since π was arbitrary, $\text{fix}(w) \subseteq \text{fix}(I)$, so $I \in \text{DOM}(w)$. Thus Comp_M^- holds.

(II) The model validates Comp_{MC}. Proof: Let A be a formula in which the second-order variable X is not free, $\underline{a}$ be an assignment, and $w \in W$. Suppose that $w, \underline{a} \vDash E_A$. Thus for any first-order variable v free in A, $\underline{a}(v) \in \text{dom}(w)$, and for any second-order variable V free in A, $\underline{a}(V) \in \text{DOM}(w)$. We must show that for some $I \in \text{DOM}(w)$, for every $w* \in W$ and $d \in \text{dom}(w*)$: $d \in I(w*)$ if and only if $w*, \underline{a}[X/I][x/d] \vDash A$, or equivalently if and only if $w*, \underline{a}[x/d] \vDash A$ (since X is not free in A). Choose $I \in \text{INT}$ such that for all $w* \in W, I(w*) = \{d \in \text{dom}(w*): w*, \underline{a}[x/d] \vDash A\}$. We show that $I \in \text{DOM}(w)$. Let $\pi \in \text{fix}(w)$. We must show that $\pi(I) = I$. Let $w* \in W$. Suppose that $d \in \pi(I)(w*)$. Then $\pi^{-1}(d) \in I(\pi^{-1}(w*))$, so $\pi^{-1}(d) \in \text{dom}(\pi^{-1}(w*))$ and $\pi^{-1}(w*), \underline{a}[x/\pi^{-1}(d)] \vDash A$. From the former, $d \in \text{dom}(w*)$ by note (ii). From the latter, $\pi(\pi^{-1}(w*)), \pi(\underline{a}[x/\pi^{-1}(d)]) \vDash A$ by (ii), so $w*, \pi(\underline{a}[x/\pi^{-1}(d)]) \vDash A$. For any first-order variable v, if v is free in A and $v \neq x$ then $\underline{a}[x/\pi^{-1}(d)](v) = \underline{a}(v) \in \text{dom}(w)$ so $\pi(\underline{a}[x/\pi^{-1}(d)])(v) = \pi(\underline{a}(v)) = \underline{a}(v)$ by (i); $\pi(\underline{a}[x/\pi^{-1}(d)])(x) = \pi(\underline{a}[x/\pi^{-1}(d)](x)) = \pi(\pi^{-1}(d)) = d$; if v is not free in A the assignment to v makes no difference to the evaluation of A. For any second-order variable V, if V is free in A then $\underline{a}(V) \in \text{DOM}(w)$ so $\pi \in \text{fix}(\underline{a}(V))$ so $\pi(\underline{a}[x/\pi^{-1}(d)])(V) = \pi(\underline{a}(V)) = \underline{a}(V)$; if V is not free in A the assignment to V makes no difference to the evaluation of A. Consequently, $w*, \underline{a}[x/d] \vDash A$, so $d \in I(w*)$. Thus $\pi(I)(w*) \subseteq I(w*)$. Since $\pi^{-1} \in \text{fix}(w)$ too, $\pi^{-1}(I)(\pi^{-1}(w*)) \subseteq I(\pi^{-1}(w*))$ by a parallel argument, so $I(w*) = \pi(\pi^{-1}(I)(\pi^{-1}(w*))) \subseteq \pi(I(\pi^{-1}(w*))) = \pi(I)(w*)$, so $\pi(I)(w*) = I(w*)$. Hence $\pi(I) = I$. Thus $\text{fix}(w) \subseteq \text{fix}(I)$, so $I \in \text{DOM}(w)$. Thus Comp_{MC} holds.

(III) The model validates (17). Proof: For $I \in INT$ let $sum(I) = \bigcup_{w \in W} I(w)$, and $\bigcup sum(I) = \bigcup_{w \in W} \{i: i \in j$ for some $j \in I(w)\}$. Let $E = \{sum(I): I \in \bigcup_{w \in W} DOM(w)\}$. In the model, (17) holds if and only if every set in E with an upper bound in D has a least upper bound in D in the sense of $\subseteq$. We prove this as follows. Let $\langle i, d \rangle \in W$ (so $i \in d$) and $I \in DOM(\langle i, d \rangle)$. We first establish two lemmas.

Lemma (a): Suppose that for some $j \in \bigcup sum(I)$, $j \in d - \{i\}$. Suppose further that $k \in d - \{i\}$. Then for some $\pi \in perm(X)$, $\pi(i) = i$, $\pi(j) = k$ and $\pi(d) = d$. Since $\pi \in fix(\langle i, d \rangle)$ and $I \in DOM(\langle i, d \rangle)$, $\pi \in fix(I)$, so $\pi(I) = I$, so $\pi(\bigcup sum(I)) = \bigcup sum(I)$. But then $k = \pi(j) \in \pi(\bigcup sum(I)) = \bigcup sum(I)$. Thus $d - \{i\} \subseteq \bigcup sum(I)$.

Lemma (b): Suppose that for some $j \in \bigcup sum(I)$, $j \in X - d$. Suppose further that $k \in X - d$. Arguing as for (a), one shows that $X - d \subseteq \bigcup sum(I)$.

Using lemmas (a) and (b), we consider four cases.

Case 1: Both $(\bigcup sum(I)) \cap d - \{i\}$ and $(\bigcup sum(I)) \cap (X - d)$ are non-empty. Then by (a) and (b), $X - \{i\} \subseteq \bigcup sum(I)$. Since the complement of $(X - \{i\})$ in X is finite, $\bigcup sum(I) \subseteq e$ for no $e \in D$, so $sum(I)$ has no upper bound in D.

Case 2: $(\bigcup sum(I)) \cap d - \{i\}$ is non-empty but $(\bigcup sum(I)) \cap (X - d)$ is empty. Then by (a), $(d - \{i\}) \subseteq \bigcup sum(I) \subseteq d$, so $\bigcup sum(I)$ is an infinite subset of X with an infinite complement, so $\bigcup sum(I) \in D$, so $\bigcup sum(I)$ is the least upper bound of $sum(I)$ in D.

Case 3: $(\bigcup sum(I)) \cap (d - \{i\})$ is empty but $(\bigcup sum(I)) \cap (X - d)$ is non-empty. Then by (b), $(X - d) \subseteq \bigcup sum(I) \subseteq (X - d) \cup \{i\}$, so $\bigcup sum(I)$ is again an infinite subset of X with an infinite complement in X, so $\bigcup sum(I) \in D$, so $\bigcup sum(I)$ is the least upper bound of $sum(I)$ in D.

Case 4: Both $(\bigcup sum(I)) \cap (d - \{i\})$ and $(\bigcup sum(I)) \cap (X - d)$ are empty. Then $\bigcup sum(I) \subseteq \{i\}$, so either $\bigcup sum(I) = \{\}$ and $\{\}$ is the least upper bound of $sum(I)$ in D or $\bigcup sum(I) = \{i\}$ and $\{i\}$ is the least upper bound of $sum(I)$ in D.

Thus the model validates (17).

(IV) The model does *not* validate (18). Proof: Let A be the formula $x = u \vee x = v$, j and k distinct members of X, and a an assignment such that $a(u) = \{j\}$ and $a(v) = \{k\}$. Thus $w, a \vDash$ (18) just in case if $\{\{j\}, \{k\}\}$ has an upper bound in D, it has a least upper bound in D. The upper bounds of $\{\{j\}, \{k\}\}$ in D are exactly the infinite subsets of X that contain j and k and have an infinite complement in X. Since there is no least such subset, $\{\{j\}, \{k\}\}$ has upper bounds in D but no least upper bound in D.

7

Mappings between Contingentist and Necessitist Discourse

7.1 Communication between contingentists and necessitists

Imagine a contingentist and a necessitist engaged in conversation. They intend to speak strictly and literally. The necessitist says 'There is a possible child of Wittgenstein' ($\exists x \lozenge CWx$). The contingentist does not believe him. She denies that there are contingently non-concrete things to be the merely possible people the necessitist postulates. Nevertheless, the contingentist does not completely dismiss the necessitist's claim. She finds a kernel of truth in it. For she agrees with this much: Wittgenstein could have had a child ($\lozenge \exists x\ CWx$). She might therefore regard the second sentence as the cash value of the first in the necessitist's mouth. Does this idea generalize to all necessitist talk?

Now the contingentist says 'No human could have been something non-human' ($\neg \exists x\ (Hx\ \&\ \lozenge \exists y\ (x=y\ \&\ \neg Hy)))$. The necessitist does not believe her. He holds that a human could have been something non-concrete, and therefore non-human (since humans are creatures of flesh and blood). Nevertheless, the necessitist does not completely dismiss the contingentist's claim. He finds a kernel of truth in it. For he agrees with this much: no human could have been something concrete but non-human ($\neg \exists x\ (Hx\ \&\ \lozenge \exists y\ (x=y\ \&\ COy\ \&\ \neg Hy)))$ (see section 1.2). He might therefore regard the second sentence as the cash value of the first in the contingentist's mouth. Does this idea generalize to all contingentist talk?

These questions recall the obscure disputes between actualism and possibilism, and between presentism and eternalism, for systematic mappings from the talk of one side to the talk of the other figured in them significantly. Kit

Fine showed how to define for each formula A in a first-order modal language for actualists a corresponding formula $(A)^{pos}$ in a first-order modal language for possibilists, and for each formula B in the possibilist language a corresponding formula $(B)^{act}$ in the actualist language.[1] To postpone technical details: the main business of $(A)^{pos}$ is to replace the actualist's quantifiers in A with possibilist quantifiers restricted by a predicate 'exists', while the main business of $(B)^{act}$ is to replace the possibilist's quantifiers in B with actualist quantifiers prefixed by modal operators. Informally, the idea is that the possibilist interprets the actualist's talk of 'what there is' as talk only of what has an additional property, 'existence', while the actualist interprets the possibilist's talk of 'what there is' as talk of what there could be. The actualist accepts A just when the possibilist accepts $(A)^{pos}$, and the possibilist accepts B just when the actualist accepts $(B)^{act}$. The mappings also preserve most aspects of logical form. In standard possible world semantics, where possibilist quantifiers range over the whole outer domain and actualist ones just over the inner domain of the world of evaluation, for actualist formulas A and possibilist formulas B the mixed formulas $A \leftrightarrow (A)^{pos}$ and $B \leftrightarrow (B)^{act}$ are true at every world in every model. Consequently, the mappings are mutually inverse, up to logical equivalence: both the actualist formula $A \leftrightarrow ((A)^{pos})^{act}$ and the possibilist formula $B \leftrightarrow ((B)^{act})^{pos}$ are true at every world in every model.

Such mappings were described as 'translations'.[2] A translation is supposed to preserve meaning, mapping synonyms to synonyms. The implication is that the apparent disagreement between actualism and possibilism is merely verbal, at least for matters expressible in first-order modal language. For suppose that the actualist accepts A just when the possibilist accepts $(A)^{pos}$, the possibilist accepts B just when the actualist accepts $(B)^{act}$, and the actualist accepts a sentence D whose orthographic negation $\neg D$ the possibilist accepts. By hypothesis, the possibilist accepts $(D)^{pos}$. So if the mapping $(\ )^{pos}$ is a translation, the possibilist already accepts something synonymous with the actualist's D. Hence what the possibilist, if consistent, means by $\neg D$ does not contradict what the actualist means by D. Again, by hypothesis, the actualist accepts $(\neg D)^{act}$. So if the mapping $(\ )^{act}$ is a translation, the actualist already

---

[1] See especially Fine 1977a.

[2] See Fine 1977a, pp. 118–19; Forbes 1985, p. 243; Pollock 1985, pp. 130–2; Correia 2007. The word 'translation' also has a technical use in mathematical logic, on which translations need not even preserve truth value; that use is not employed in this book.

accepts something synonymous with the possibilist's $\neg D$. Hence what the actualist, if consistent, means by D does not contradict what the possibilist means by $\neg D$. Thus the apparent first-order modal dispute between the actualist and the possibilist is an illusion.

One might argue that at least one mapping fails to preserve fine-grained meaning, on the grounds that $((A)^{\text{pos}})^{\text{act}}$ typically has more semantic complexity than A, and so is not synonymous with A, while $((B)^{\text{act}})^{\text{pos}}$ typically has more semantic complexity than B, and so is not synonymous with B. This allows either mapping to preserve fine-grained meaning, if the other does not. Analysis cannot go in both directions at once. But even if we stop calling the mappings translations, we can still base a similar argument on the weaker assumption that they preserve logical rather than semantic features. More precisely, suppose that for all actualist formulas A and possibilist formulas B the formulas $A \leftrightarrow (A)^{\text{pos}}$ and $B \leftrightarrow (B)^{\text{act}}$ are true at every world in every model. As before, the actualist accepts A just when the possibilist accepts $(A)^{\text{pos}}$, and the possibilist accepts B just when the actualist accepts $(B)^{\text{act}}$. Suppose that everything the actualist accepts is true at a world w in a model M. Let the possibilist accept B. Hence, by hypothesis, the actualist accepts $(B)^{\text{act}}$, so it is true at w in M. Also by hypothesis, $B \leftrightarrow (B)^{\text{act}}$ is true at w in M. Therefore B is true at w in M. Thus everything the possibilist accepts is true at w in M. Hence the possibilist's theory follows model-theoretically from the actualist's theory. Conversely, by a similar argument, the actualist's theory follows model-theoretically from the possibilist's theory. Thus the two theories are model-theoretically equivalent. Once again, actualism and possibilism are far too close for comfort.

The actualist and the possibilist may still disagree at a finer-grained level, about whose language is more fundamental.[3] The actualist says that the sentence A in their mouth is already fully analysed, while the sentence $\neg A$ in the possibilist's mouth needs a deeper analysis as $(\neg A)^{\text{act}}$. The latter replies that, on the contrary, it is the sentence $\neg A$ in their mouth that is already fully analysed, while the sentence A in the actualist's mouth needs a deeper analysis as $(A)^{\text{pos}}$. They may disagree about whose quantifiers are more natural or

---

[3] Kit Fine informs me (personal communication) that he no longer requires the mappings to provide synonyms or even logical equivalents: a ground that is sufficient but not necessary for the original may do for his purposes. Forbes later questioned and now rejects the claim that the mappings preserve meaning (1989, p. 34; 2008, p. 283). For a vigorous defence of the view that the actualist can understand possibilist claims and still disagree with them in the absence of any such translation see Plantinga 1985, pp. 330–1.

basic. Still, the inexpressibility of the dispute in more robust and tractable terms would be a disappointing outcome. For presumably the ordering in terms of relative naturalness or basicness is supposed to be of metaphysical interest because it is not determined just by the psychology of speakers, but rather by non-linguistic features of reality as a whole. If so, the dispute would be more perspicuous if each side could formulate its view of the disputed features in less extrinsic terms.

Rather than trying to make sense of the confused dispute between actualism and possibilism, we can more profitably replace it with enquiry into clearer issues in roughly the same territory. Perhaps the deepest of those is the dispute between contingentism and necessitism. Chapter 6 made a start on resolving that dispute, by tracing how necessitism is better suited than contingentism to higher-order modal logic. Nevertheless, the mappings $(\ )^{act}$ and $(\ )^{pos}$ suggest strategies for contingentists and necessitists to use in communicating fruitfully with each other despite their metaphysical differences. For example, just as $(A)^{pos}$ substitutes for the actualist's quantifiers in A possibilist quantifiers restricted by a predicate 'exists', the necessitist might substitute for quantifiers in the contingentist's mouth quantifiers restricted by a predicate for what the contingentist takes there to be. Conversely, just as $(B)^{act}$ substitutes for the possibilist's quantifiers in B actualist quantifiers prefixed by modal operators, the contingentist might substitute for quantifiers in the necessitist's mouth quantifiers prefixed by the same modal operators.

But what exactly is the point of such substitutions? As Chapter 1 explained, contingentists and necessitists speak a common language. For purposes of the debate, they have agreed to use the unrestricted interpretation of the quantifiers, and the metaphysical interpretation of the modal operators. They mean the same by any given formula. What they differ over is which formulas are true. In particular, although they mean the same by NNE ($\Box\forall x\ \Box\exists y\ x=y$), necessitists assert NNE while contingentists deny NNE. The disagreement between them is genuine, not merely verbal. For either of them to reinterpret the other's words is not to move from misunderstanding to understanding: it is to move in the opposite direction.

Nor should we forget the people who are committed to neither side. One can easily understand NNE in its intended sense, and ask oneself whether it is true, without forming an opinion either way. If one subsequently comes to accept or reject it, one does not thereby change the meaning of the formula. Indeed, the whole community might be undecided, or positively agnostic, especially on such an abstruse theoretical question. As in all other branches of science, enquiry in logic can be conducted by those who want to find the truth, knowing they have not yet done so.

We can imagine a philosopher claiming 'The language is indeterminate between two interpretations, one on which NNE is true and one on which it is false, until the community decides in favour of NNE or against it'. But we can also imagine a philosopher making the analogous claim for any other scientific hypothesis in place of NNE. There is no reason to take most such claims seriously. Is it any different for NNE? We have no idea how to verify or falsify NNE by observation or experiment, but why should that be the key test? It is not what matters in mathematical enquiry, for instance. It sounds like a relic of a verificationist theory of meaning. Indeed, Chapter 6 showed how we might decide for or against NNE by standards of theory choice similar to those in other branches of science.

We should in any case decline the challenge to demonstrate from a neutral starting point that our language has a unique intended interpretation. For a sceptic can always doubt whether the language of the attempted demonstration itself has a unique intended interpretation. If it has not, the attempted demonstration is equivocal, and presumably worth little. An infinite regress of futile attempts at demonstration looms.

A more productive attitude is to treat the shared language of enquiry as clear enough to be getting on with, while always being ready to clarify it further as and when the need arises. In that spirit, we will continue to assume that necessitists and contingents mean the same by NNE, and disagree over its truth value. The assumption is pre-theoretically plausible, no serious reason has emerged to doubt it, and technical results later in this chapter will confirm that necessitism and contingentism are not structurally related to each other in the manner of notational variants.

No translations are needed between the language of necessitists and the language of contingentists, because they are the same language, with the same semantics. Nevertheless, each side may feel that the best way to extract some useful value from sentences as used by the other is to transform them somehow, in order to eliminate their unwanted theoretical commitments. If we meet a Viking who tells us that Thor is angry, we may disbelieve him but still learn that thunder is on the way. Similarly, necessitists and contingentists may be able to learn from each other, even when each side's speech is imbued with theoretical commitments the other side rejects. Each side needs to do something analogous to transforming 'Thor is angry' into 'Thunder is on the way'.

How is such a process to be understood? In precisely what relation is the original sentence supposed to stand to its transform? The answers are by no means obvious. Some transformations are ad hoc, as when a mother maps her son's grumpy comments on various topics to 'He's hungry'. But in the present case something more general seems to be involved, since the expectation of finding useful value by eliminating theoretical commitments is prior to the particular utterances of the other side. Nor is the expectation confined to assertions: each side may hope to find such value in the other's questions too. Thus a more systematic approach is needed, both in specifying each side's mappings from the other's sentences to its own and in explaining what conditions those mappings are supposed to meet. This chapter develops one way of understanding what is going on, and studies its consequences. Perhaps there are other ways too, but if so it is unclear what they are, and an adequate treatment of even one way is hard enough.

The present approach casts mappings similar to $(\ )^{act}$ and $(\ )^{pos}$ in a subtler role than that of translations. To appreciate what it is, suppose that some sentences of the common language are *neutral*, in the sense that they do not raise any issues at stake between necessitism and contingentism. For example, the sentence 'Wittgenstein was born in 1889' and its negation might count as neutral, and 'Wittgenstein is necessarily something' and its negation as non-neutral. Necessitists and contingentists can agree over neutral sentences. Of course, a particular necessitist and a particular contingentist may happen to disagree about the date of Wittgenstein's birth, just as two necessitists or two contingentists may disagree with each other about it. But such incidental disputes are as it were a private matter between them. They are not ramifications of the dispute between necessitism and contingentism as such.

Suppose that a mapping $(\ )^{nec}$ can be defined such that for every sentence A of the common language, $(A)^{nec}$ is a neutral sentence of the common language equivalent to A for the necessitist: $(A)^{nec} \leftrightarrow A$ is a theorem of the necessitist theory. In a particular case, the necessitist accepts D while the contingentist rejects D. Since the necessitist accepts the biconditional $(D)^{nec} \leftrightarrow D$, the necessitist also accepts $(D)^{nec}$. But $(D)^{nec}$ is neutral, so the contingentist can accept $(D)^{nec}$ too, incidental slips aside. Thus the contingentist can treat $(D)^{nec}$ as the kernel of truth in what they regard as the necessitist's mistaken assertion of D. Of course, the contingentist rejects the biconditional

$(D)^{\mathrm{nec}} \leftrightarrow D$, since they accept its left-hand side and reject its right-hand side, but they know that the necessitist accepts the biconditional, and that is the point.

Similarly, suppose that a mapping ( )^{con} can be defined such that for every sentence A of the common language, $(A)^{\mathrm{con}}$ is a neutral sentence of the common language equivalent to A for the contingentist: $(A)^{\mathrm{con}} \leftrightarrow A$ is a theorem of the contingentist theory. In the earlier case, the contingentist accepts $\neg D$ while the necessitist rejects $\neg D$. Since the contingentist accepts the biconditional $(\neg D)^{\mathrm{con}} \leftrightarrow \neg D$, they also accept $(\neg D)^{\mathrm{con}}$. But $(\neg D)^{\mathrm{con}}$ is neutral, so the necessitist can accept $(\neg D)^{\mathrm{con}}$ too, incidental slips aside. Thus the necessitist can treat $(\neg D)^{\mathrm{con}}$ as the kernel of truth in what they regard as the contingentist's mistaken assertion of $\neg D$. Of course, the necessitist rejects the biconditional $(\neg D)^{\mathrm{con}} \leftrightarrow \neg D$, since they accept its left-hand side and reject its right-hand side, but they know that the contingentist accepts the biconditional, and that is the point.

Since they are in dispute between the necessitist and the contingentist, neither D nor $\neg D$ is trivial. Since $(D)^{\mathrm{nec}}$ and $(\neg D)^{\mathrm{con}}$ are not in dispute, we lack that guarantee of their non-triviality. If D and $\neg D$ merely articulate each side's opposition to the other, $(D)^{\mathrm{nec}}$ and $(\neg D)^{\mathrm{con}}$ may indeed be trivial. In other cases, however, they may express useful information ('Thunder is on the way').

It would be a fundamental error to suppose that $(D)^{\mathrm{nec}}$ is what the necessitist 'really means' by the disputed sentence D, or what the contingentist believes the necessitist to really mean by it. It would be an equally fundamental error to suppose that $(\neg D)^{\mathrm{con}}$ is what the contingentist really means by the disputed sentence $\neg D$, or what the necessitist believes the contingentist to really mean by it. For it is common knowledge that the non-neutral sentence D lacks the semantic features that make the sentence $(D)^{\mathrm{nec}}$ neutral, and that the non-neutral sentence $\neg D$ lacks the semantic features that make $(\neg D)^{\mathrm{con}}$ neutral. Thus it is common knowledge that neither mapping preserves meaning. As already emphasized, the disputed sentences already have clear shared meanings, well understood by all parties. Neither side is entitled to patronize the other by treating them as linguistically incompetent, unable to express their own views accurately in their own language. Each side knows what it is doing when it speaks. In particular, when necessitists assert NNE to contingentists, who respond by denying it, both the assertion and the denial should be taken at face value. Necessitists are asserting NNE itself, not irrelevantly asserting the neutral (NNE)^{nec},

312 MAPPINGS BETWEEN CONTINGENTIST AND NECESSITIST DISCOURSE

whose truth is not in dispute. For, by hypothesis, necessitists accept $(NNE)^{nec} \leftrightarrow NNE$; since they also accept NNE, they accept $(NNE)^{nec}$; since it is neutral and necessitists accept it, contingentists do so too. Similarly, contingentists are denying NNE itself, not irrelevantly denying the neutral $(NNE)^{con}$, whose falsity is not in dispute. For, by hypothesis, contingentists accept $(NNE)^{con} \leftrightarrow NNE$; since they reject NNE, they reject $(NNE)^{con}$; since it is neutral and contingentists reject it, necessitists do so too.

What each mapping achieves is to factorize the consequences of an arbitrary sentence on the given metaphysical theory into consequences of the theory itself and neutral consequences. Conversely, the two sorts of consequence together entail the original claim. For example, given the necessitist theory, a sentence A entails the neutral sentence $(A)^{nec}$. Trivially, given the theory, A also entails the biconditional $(A)^{nec} \leftrightarrow A$ since the theory alone entails it. Together, $(A)^{nec}$ and $(A)^{nec} \leftrightarrow A$ entail A. Similarly, given the contingentist theory, A entails the neutral sentence $(A)^{con}$. Trivially, given the theory, A also entails the biconditional $(A)^{con} \leftrightarrow A$ since the theory alone entails it. Together, $(A)^{con}$ and $(A)^{con} \leftrightarrow A$ entail A. Starting from the same assignment of truth values to all neutral sentences, the two metaphysical theories extend it to mutually incompatible assignments of truth values to all non-neutral sentences.

Think of sentences as goods, and neutral sentences as coins in a common currency. Then $(A)^{nec}$ represents the cash value of A to the necessitist, for whom they are equivalent. Similarly, $(A)^{con}$ represents the cash value of A to the contingentist, for whom they are equivalent. Thus the mapping $(\ )^{nec}$ enables contingentists and agnostics to work out what necessitists will pay for goods. The mapping $(\ )^{con}$ enables necessitists and agnostics to work out what contingentists will pay. Although the two sides differ sharply in how much they value various non-cash goods, their knowledge of each other enables them to engage in profitable trade. They communicate.

Instead of treating necessitists as hopelessly mistaken, contingentists can use the mapping $(\ )^{nec}$ to credit them with genuine cognitive achievements, modulo one pervasive metaphysical mistake, to see them as tracking genuine distinctions which they misdescribe through relying on false theoretical assumptions. Conversely, necessitists can use the mapping $(\ )^{con}$ to take the corresponding view of contingentists.

So far, however, we have been proceeding on the mere supposition that there are such mappings as $(\ )^{nec}$ and $(\ )^{con}$. Those mappings were themselves characterized in terms of an as yet vague and undefined notion of neutrality. It is time to start filling in the details. The next two sections explain how the project can be successfully carried out for a first-order modal language under some assumptions about the type of necessitism and contingentism at issue. From section 7.5 onwards, the chapter explores systematic obstacles to carrying out the project once sets or plurals are introduced. More specifically, it will turn out that necessitists can still eliminate unwanted theoretical commitments from questions contingentists ask, but contingentists can no longer eliminate unwanted theoretical commitments from questions necessitists ask. If the latter are raising genuine questions, as they certainly appear to be, then contingentists are forbidden by their theoretical commitments from engaging adequately with those questions.

7.2 Mapping contingentist talk to neutral talk

The most obvious candidate definition of neutrality is that a sentence is neutral just if it concerns only concrete objects and their properties and relations, 'the realm of the concrete'. That is still not sufficiently precise, but in any case it faces a more urgent problem. If some mapping meets the constraints on $(\ )^{nec}$, then every sentence is equivalent to a neutral one on the necessitist theory. If some mapping meets the constraints on $(\ )^{con}$, then every sentence is equivalent to a neutral one on the contingentist theory. Given the proposed definition of neutrality, it follows that there is such a mapping as $(\ )^{nec}$ only if the necessist theory makes every sentence equivalent to one about the concrete, and there is such a mapping as $(\ )^{con}$ only if the contingentist theory makes every sentence equivalent to one about the concrete. Why should either the necessitist or the contingentist theory have that consequence, unless it is close to some form of nominalism on which everything is concrete? But the dispute between necessitism and contingentism is orthogonal to the dispute between nominalism and platonism. Both necessitism and contingentism seem to be consistent with a rich theory of abstract objects, such as numbers and sets, on which not all claims about them are equivalent to claims about the realm of the concrete. We want a broader notion of neutrality, to avoid saddling necessitism or contingentism with reductive ontological projects irrelevant to their main concern. A good place to look is in the contingentist's positive view.

Why do contingentists reject the necessitist postulation of contingently non-concrete objects, such as merely possible people? As just noted, the reason is often not any objection to the non-concrete as such. It may rather be an objection to the *contingently* non-concrete. Contingentists may regard the line between the concrete and the non-concrete as neither contingent nor changing. Alternatively, they may have a more developed positive conception on which necessarily everything is *grounded* in the concrete, in some sense in which the necessitist's contingently non-concrete objects do not count as so grounded. Being concrete trivially entails being grounded in the concrete, but being grounded in the concrete does not entail being concrete. An abstract object may be grounded in the concrete without itself being concrete. For example, the contingentist may hold that no set is concrete, but that a set is grounded in the concrete if and only if all its members are. Thus even the empty set is grounded in the concrete, vacuously. Indeed, all pure sets are, on the standard conception of sets.[4] Numbers and other abstract objects may count as similarly grounded in the concrete, perhaps through one or more stages of logicist abstraction.

For present purposes, we can leave many details of the envisaged contingentist metaphysics vague or unsettled. What matters for now is that it involves a putatively necessary condition on being, symbolized thus:

$$\text{CON}_C \qquad \Box \forall x \ Cx$$

We might read Cx as 'x is not contingently non-concrete', or as 'x is grounded in the concrete', or in some other way as filling in the contingentist constraint on being CON_C. As a schematic reading, to cover all those options, we use 'x is chunky'. Thus the envisaged contingentists hold that necessarily everything is chunky (a claim vaguely reminiscent of actualism), and reject the necessitist's contingently non-concrete objects because they are not chunky. We assume that they have explained the predicate C clearly enough to enable necessitists and agnostics to grasp what chunkiness is, and to agree that the necessitist's contingently non-concrete objects are not chunky. But necessitists reject CON_C, and typically deny that everything is chunky.

---

[4] Proof: Let s_0 be a pure set not grounded in the concrete. By hypothesis, some $s_1 \in s_0$ is also not grounded in the concrete. Since any member of a pure set is itself a pure set, we can iterate the argument ad infinitum. But that yields an infinite descending chain of membership, which contradicts the Axiom of Foundation.

Even contingentists whose original unreflective rejection of necessitism was not premised on CON_C may welcome it as offering a theoretical *explanation* for the alleged falsity of necessitism. Obviously, the bare defining thesis of contingentism, $\neg NNE$, entails no necessitated universal generalization as informative as CON_C. But adding the strong, simple necessitated universal generalization CON_C to $\neg NNE$ yields a theory with far more abductive power. Moreover, it has the theoretical virtue of providing a bold unitary answer to Quine's ontological question 'What is there?': 'The chunky'. Call the conjunction of $\neg NNE$ with CON_C on an appropriate reading of C *chunky-style* contingentism.

Of course, CON_C is not the only way of theoretically extending contingentism. For example, someone might argue against NNE on the basis of liberalism about possibility, claiming that there are no necessary connections between disjoint concrete objects, so any of them could have been without the others. What the latter contingentist diagnoses as the fault in necessitism is not its postulation of non-chunky objects but its restriction on possibility.

The arguments of this chapter (but not of previous ones) apply specifically to chunky-style contingentism. It provides a natural proposal as to which sentences to count as neutral: those purely about the realm of the chunky. For contingents of other sorts, it is unclear what notion of neutrality there is of the kind described in section 7.1, and unclear in the absence of such a notion what the constraints are supposed to be on any transformation that one side applies to the other's sentences. Although the abstract structural nature of the arguments later in the chapter provides some grounds for hope that they will generalize to other forms of contingentism and necessitism, the task can be tackled adequately only once those other forms have been articulated explicitly and precisely. The challenge to proponents of other forms of contingentism is to show rigorously how their favoured form overcomes the limitations of chunky-style contingentism explained in this chapter.

In the context of chunky-style contingentism, we can equate neutrality with being purely about the chunky realm. But when is a sentence purely about the chunky realm? To make the question more tractable, we provisionally assume the sentence to be in a first-order modal language with identity, whose non-logical vocabulary includes the monadic predicate C for chunkiness, as in CON_C. Later sections will consider extensions of the language. The simplest procedure is this. We recursively define the result of inserting all the required restrictions to the chunky into an arbitrary formula. A formula is *overtly neutral* just if it is the result of inserting all the required restrictions into some formula. However, overtly neutral formulas will be equivalent in an uncontentious background logic to formulas that are not overtly neutral. Since it is convenient to count the latter formulas as neutral too, we define a (simply) *neutral* formula as one equivalent to an overtly neutral formula in the background logic. By convenient coincidence, it turns out that we may identify the result of inserting all the required restrictions into A with $(A)^{con}$, so the mapping $(\,)^{con}$ will play a double role.

The most obvious requirement on an overtly neutral formula is for all its quantifiers to be restricted to chunky objects. Consequently, the recursive clause for the primitive first-order quantifier $\exists$ is that $(\exists v\, A)^{con}$ is $\exists v\, (Cv\ \&\ (A)^{con})$. Thus C plays the same restricting role as the predicate for 'exists' in the mapping $(\,)^{act}$ from actualist discourse to possibilist discourse in the previous section. However, the predicate C itself should not be read as 'exists', for that reading does not yield suitably neutral formulas: when 'exists' is taken in the purely logical sense as equivalent to the unrestricted 'is something', then the restriction makes no difference, because $\exists x\, (\exists y\ x{=}y\ \&\ (A)^{con})$ is uncontentiously equivalent to $\exists x\, (A)^{con}$. Similarly, that reading of C reduces CON_C to the uncontentious logical truth $\Box\forall x\, \exists y\ x{=}y$. To make CON_C capture a distinctively contingentist claim, read C as 'is chunky', not as 'exists'.

In some contexts, a non-logical reading of 'exists' restricts it to chunky objects. Although that restriction makes no intensional difference according to chunky-style contingentists, because necessarily everything satisfies it by CON_C, they should still agree that it makes a cognitive one, because necessitists deny the equivalence of the restricted and unrestricted formulas. For example, while necessitists reject CON_C as stating the distinctively chunky-style contingentist claim that necessarily everything is chunky, they accept the corresponding restricted formula (1) as stating only the trivial logical truth that necessarily everything chunky is chunky:

(1) $\Box\forall x\, (Cx \rightarrow Cx)$

However, restricting the quantifiers in a formula by C does not quite suffice to make it overtly neutral. For consider (2):

(2) $\exists x\, (Cx\ \&\ \Diamond(x{=}x\ \&\ \neg Cx))$

It says that something chunky could have been self-identical without being chunky. The only quantifier in (2) is restricted by C. Nevertheless, (2) is contested. Necessitists will typically accept (2), for example on the grounds that although there could have failed to be any such chunky thing as Socrates, in that case Socrates would still have been something (although not a man) and therefore self-identical. By contrast, chunky-style contingentists who accept the being constraint for identity will reject (2), on the grounds that self-identity strictly implies being something and so by CON_C being chunky. Thus (2) should not count as neutral, let alone as overtly neutral. The problem is that since $x=x$ occurs in (2) separated from Cx by $\Diamond$, evaluating (2) involves evaluating $x=x$ at counterfactual circumstances where Cx is false: the possibility operator can take us outside the realm of the chunky. The natural solution is to define $(Fv_1 \ldots v_n)^{con}$ as $Fv_1 \ldots v_n$ & Cv_1 & $\ldots$ & Cv_n for each atomic formula $Fv_1 \ldots v_n.$[5] Thus (2) is not overtly neutral, because it contains the atomic formula $x=x$ not conjoined with Cx. In an overtly neutral sentence, the only atomic formulas we need evaluate are predications of chunkiness and of anything else under the assumption that all the individuals in question are chunky.

Despite the restrictions, even the conjunction $Fv_1 \ldots v_n$ & Cv_1 & $\ldots$ & Cv_n can be non-neutral in the ordinary sense between contingentism and necessitism on some interpretations of F. In the simplest case, $n = 0$ and F is just a sentence letter, an atomic formula without individual variables, so $(F)^{con}$ is just F itself. But we can informally interpret a sentence letter as expressing a metaphysically contentious claim such as NNE or CON_C. Then contingentists and necessitists would disagree over $(F)^{con}$. Similarly, if we informally interpret the monadic atomic predicate F as expressing the property of being possibly both self-identical and non-chunky, making Fx informally equivalent to $\Diamond(x=x$ & $\neg Cx)$, then the apparently innocuous formula $(\exists x\, Fx)^{con}$, which is $\exists x\, (Cx$ & $(Fx$ & $Cx))$, becomes informally equivalent to the non-neutral (2).[6] In such cases, the meaning of the atomic formula takes us outside the realm of the chunky from circumstances in which all the denoted objects are chunky. Obviously, no formal condition on sentences can isolate such cases, any more than a formal condition can

---

[5] This treatment of non-logical predicates is comparable to the notion of a restricted formula in Fine 1981a, p. 296.

[6] The mapping ( )^{con} typically produces formulas with such redundant conjuncts of the form Cv. It is possible but unnecessary to avoid them by complicating the definition of the mapping.

guarantee that the predicate C expresses chunkiness. Rather, we must informally stipulate that the atomic predicates and sentence letters of the language are to be understood in ways that enable contingentists and necessitists to agree on their application to chunky objects.[7] This stipulation does not make the extra conjuncts in the definition of $(A)^{con}$ redundant when A is atomic, for without it (2) would still count as overtly neutral.

The mapping $(\ )^{con}$ preserves modal operators in an overtly neutral formula, because the dispute between contingentism and necessitism does not concern possibility or necessity per se, but rather what there would be in various possible circumstances. The mapping also preserves truth functors. Thus we have a recursive definition of $(\ )^{con}$. The base clause is that $(Fv_1 \ldots v_n)^{con}$ is $Fv_1 \ldots v_n$ & Cv_1 & $\ldots$ & Cv_n for each atomic formula $Fv_1 \ldots v_n$, as already explained. For the recursive clauses, $(\neg A)^{con}$ is $\neg(A)^{con}$; $(A \ \& \ B)^{con}$ is $(A)^{con}$ & $(B)^{con}$. $(OA)^{con}$ is $O(A)^{con}$ for each primitive modal operator O in the language; $(\exists v \, A)^{con}$ is $\exists v \, (Cv \ \& \ (A)^{con})$.

As already explained, a formula is overtly neutral just if it is $(A)^{con}$ for some formula A. Trivially, therefore, $(\ )^{con}$ maps every formula of the language to an overtly neutral one. Since a formula is neutral just if it is equivalent to an overtly neutral formula, A is neutral just if $A \leftrightarrow (B)^{con}$ is a theorem of the background logic for some formula B. Trivially, every overtly neutral formula is neutral. An example of a neutral but not overtly neutral formula is $\exists x \, \exists y \, (Cx \ \& \ x=y)$: it is logically equivalent to $\exists x \, (Cx \ \& \ (Cx \ \& \ Cx))$, which is in turn $(\exists x \, Cx)^{con}$. In consequence of the recursive clauses for $(\ )^{con}$, whenever A and B are neutral formulas, so are $\neg A, A \ \& \ B, \Box A, \Diamond A, \exists v \, (Cv \ \& \ A)$, and $\forall v \, (Cv \rightarrow A)$.

We may expect chunky-style contingentism to make every formula equivalent to a neutral one. For since $(A)^{con}$ simply results from inserting various restrictions to the chunky in A, while the chunky-style contingentist claim CON_C says that necessarily everything satisfies those restrictions, we may expect A to be equivalent to the overtly neutral $(A)^{con}$ given CON_C. To check this properly, we must specify the background logic.

For purposes of comparison, we will use the same background logic as for the discussion of necessitism in the next section. This logic constitutes common ground between contingentism and necessitism; it need not be the full logic of either side. We can specify it model-theoretically, without

---

[7] For C and '=', the agreement is a known fact, not a stipulation.

committing anyone to assigning the model theory a more than purely instrumental role. We use a slight variant of Kripke semantics with variable domains. Specifically, a model is an ordered triple $<W, D, V>$, where W is a non-empty set, the domain function D maps each $w \in W$ to a set $D(w)$ (which may be empty), and V maps each non-logical n-place atomic predicate F to a function $V(F)$ that maps each $w \in W$ to a set $V(F)(w) \subseteq D(w)^n$. For simplicity, there is no accessibility relation; the modal operators are treated as quantifiers over all of W, so the principles of $S5$ are automatically validated. They are not at stake in the dispute between contingentism and necessitism.

The most disputable feature of the model theory in its present role is its imposition of the being constraint. Since $V(F)(w) \subseteq D(w)^n$, a non-logical atomic predicate applies to an n-tuple of individuals at a world only if they all belong to its domain, and the corresponding formulas of the object-language are theorems of the logic. The rationale for this constraint was explained in section 4.1. Nevertheless, one might wonder why the model theory is committed on this point, rather than letting some models violate the being constraint while others satisfy it.

As far as the model theory goes, the status of the identity predicate as a logical constant makes a non-committal stance awkward, although technically feasible, to maintain. Normally, a model makes special provision only for the non-logical predicate constants; V assigns them intensions. By contrast, a general policy is supposed to determine the intension of '=' in a model as a function of its components W and D. Only two policies are reasonable. Either in every model the formula $u=v$ is true at a world w on an assignment $\underline{a}$ if and only if $\underline{a}$ assigns the same object to the variables u and v, or in every model $u=v$ is true at a world w on an assignment $\underline{a}$ if and only if $\underline{a}$ assigns the same object to u and v and, in addition, that object belongs to $D(w)$. The first policy clearly violates the being constraint for '=', so imposing the constraint on all non-logical predicate constants would be ad hoc. The second policy clearly respects the being constraint for '='; since the case against the constraint is strongest for formulas of the form $u=u$; not imposing it on all non-logical predicates would be ad hoc. Either way, one is committed for or against the being constraint.

That argument is not decisive, for we may permit an ad hoc treatment of identity in the model theory when the latter is serving a purely instrumental function. A different point is closer to the concerns of this chapter. Suppose that the background logic, while in other respects as already described, does not impose the being constraint (3) on a non-logical monadic predicate F (the case of polyadic predicates is similar):

(3) $\Box\forall x\ \Box(Fx \rightarrow \exists y\ x{=}y)$

Then the formula (4) is not equivalent to any neutral formula given CON_C:[8]

(4) $\exists x\ \Diamond Fx$

Informally, the reason is this. The truth value of a neutral formula depends only on what happens in the realm of the chunky. CON_C extends that realm to all individuals wherever they are something. But without the being constraint for F, the truth value of (4) is sensitive to what individuals do when they are nothing and non-chunky, in particular to whether they satisfy F.

A drastic response to the problem is to strengthen CON_C to (5):

(5) $\Box\forall x\ \Box Cx$

Even without the being constraint, every formula is equivalent to a neutral formula given (5), because it ensures that necessarily everything satisfies the restriction to the chunky even in circumstances where it is nothing. But that does not help, because the chunky-style contingentist rejects (5), as does virtually everyone else. If the Inn had not been a river or any other geographical feature, it would not have been chunky. Indeed, the special case of the being constraint for chunkiness is overwhelmingly plausible:

(6) $\Box\forall x\ \Box(Cx \rightarrow \exists y\ x{=}y)$

The nature of chunkiness excludes the possibility of being simultaneously chunky and nothing. But together, (5) and (6) entail NNE. Thus any contingentist who accepts (6) rejects (5), on pain of inconsistency.

---

[8] Proof: Define two models $M = \langle W, D, V\rangle$ and $M^* = \langle W, D, V^*\rangle$, where $W = \{0, 1\}$; $D(0) = \{0\}$; $D(1) = \{1\}$; $V(C)(0) = V^*(C)(0) = \{0\}$; $V(C)(1) = V^*(C)(1) = \{1\}$; $V(F)(0) = \{1\}$; $V(F)(1) = \{0\}$; $V^*(F)(0) = V^*(F)(1) = \{\}$; for any other atomic predicate G, $V(G)(0) = V^*(G)(0)$ and $V(G)(1) = V^*(G)(1)$. By induction on the complexity of A, we prove that $(A)^{con}$ is true at $w \in W$ on an assignment a in M if and only if $(A)^{con}$ is true at w on a in M^*. The only interesting case is when A is Fv, so $(A)^{con}$ is Fv & Cv; then $V(F)(0) \cap V(C)(0) = \{1\} \cap \{0\} = \{\} = \{\} \cap \{0\} = V^*(F)(0) \cap V^*(C)(0)$ and $V(F)(1) \cap V(C)(1) = \{0\} \cap \{1\} = \{\} = \{\} \cap \{1\} = V^*(F)(1) \cap V^*(C)(1)$. The rest of the induction is routine, because M and M^* differ only in the intension of F. Now suppose that CON_C entails $(4) \leftrightarrow (A)^{con}$ for some formula A. Hence the truth value of (4) at $w \in W$ on an assignment a in the model M is the truth value of $(A)^{con}$ at w on a in M (because CON_C is true throughout M), which is the truth value of $(A)^{con}$ at w on a in M^* (by what has just been shown), which is the truth value of (4) at w on a in M^* (because CON_C is true throughout M^*). But (4) is true throughout M and false throughout M^*. Therefore (4) is not equivalent to any neutral formula given CON_C.

For chunky-style contingentists, it is necessary that the realm of the chunky exhausts what there is, although contingent what that realm contains. To take a predicate as primitive and yet apply it outside the realm of the chunky violates the spirit of their view. We may therefore assume that the chunky-style contingentist holds that every primitive predicate entails chunkiness in all its terms. For a two-place predicate R, for example:

(7) $\quad \Box\forall x \,\Box\forall y \,\Box(Rxy \rightarrow (Cx \,\&\, Cy))$

But (7) combined with (6), the being constraint for C, yields the being constraint for R:

(8) $\quad \Box\forall x \,\Box\forall y \,\Box(Rxy \rightarrow (\exists z \; x{=}z \,\&\, \exists z \; y{=}z))$

A corresponding argument applies to any n-place atomic predicate for any $n \geq 0$. Thus endorsing the being constraint for all atomic predicates is quite in the spirit of chunky-style contingentism. Since necessitism trivializes the being constraint, we may legitimately treat the constraint as not at stake in the chunky-style dispute between contingentism and necessitism, and therefore build it into the background logic, as we have done.[9]

In this background logic with the being constraints, CON_C entails $(A)^{\mathrm{con}} \leftrightarrow A$ for every formula A of the first-order modal language, so every formula is equivalent to a neutral one (proposition 1.8; all such references are to propositions formally stated in appendix 7.9). Moreover, the choice of $(A)^{\mathrm{con}}$ is unique up to logical equivalence, in the sense that any neutral formula equivalent given CON_C to A is logically equivalent to $(A)^{\mathrm{con}}$ independently of CON_C (proposition 1.10). In particular, if A itself is neutral, it is logically equivalent to $(A)^{\mathrm{con}}$ independently of CON_C. Nothing weaker than CON_C suffices to derive all the biconditionals $(A)^{\mathrm{con}} \leftrightarrow A$, for CON_C follows from $(\mathrm{CON}_C)^{\mathrm{con}} \leftrightarrow \mathrm{CON}_C$ (proposition 1.6), and so from any theory from which all such biconditionals follow. Indeed, $(\mathrm{CON}_C)^{\mathrm{con}}$ is just a trivial logical truth.

The chunky-style contingentist claim CON_C is independent of neutral formulas in the sense that its addition to a set of neutral formulas always constitutes a conservative extension: a neutral formula follows from the set together with CON_C only if it already followed from the set without CON_C (proposition 1.9). Any chunky-style contingentist theory T entails CON_C

---

[9] For detailed discussion of closely related issues see Fine 1981a.

and so can be factorized into CON_C and the set of its neutral consequences: the consequences of T are exactly the consequences of the combination of CON_C and the neutral consequences of T (proposition 1.12). The logical relations between chunky-style contingentist theories simply mirror the logical relations between their neutral parts (proposition 1.11). Once one has chosen CON_C and which neutral formulas to accept, nothing else remains to be decided.

The bare contingentist claim $\neg$NNE plays no distinctive technical role in this analysis. The key is the chunky-style contingentist claim CON_C. Formally, CON_C is consistent with the necessitist claim NNE in the background logic, since both are true in constant domain models in which C applies to everything at every world. However, (NNE)^{con} is this formula:

(9) $\Box \forall x \, (Cx \rightarrow \Box \exists y \, (Cy \,\&\, (x{=}y \,\&\, Cx \,\&\, Cy)))$

In the background logic with the being constraint for C, the formula $\exists y \, (Cy \,\&\, (x{=}y \,\&\, Cx \,\&\, Cy))$ simplifies to Cx, so (9) is equivalent to (10):

(10) $\Box \forall x \, (Cx \rightarrow \Box Cx)$

This excludes the possibility of contingent chunkiness. But chunky-style contingentists, necessitists, and most others can agree that many counter-examples to (5) are also counterexamples to (10); the river Inn is contingently chunky. Thus chunky-style contingentists reject NNE because their claim CON_C makes NNE equivalent to the more or less uncontroversially false neutral claim (10). Of course, the biconditional (NNE)$^{con} \leftrightarrow$ NNE itself is controversial. Although chunky-style contingentists accept it, necessitists typically reject it, because they accept NNE and typically reject (NNE)^{con}.

We have thus carried out the programme of section 7.1 for chunky-style contingentism in first-order modal logic. Agreeing with chunky-style contingentists over all neutral formulas, necessitists and agnostics can thence work out the latter's attitude to any non-neutral formula given their acceptance of CON_C, and thereby extract a neutral cash equivalent of any formula in such a contingentist's mouth.

The next task is to carry out the corresponding task for necessitism. We aim to define both an appropriate form of necessitism, corresponding to chunky-style contingentism, and a mapping ( )^{nec} for which every formula A is equivalent to the neutral formula $(A)^{nec}$ given that form of necessitism, to enable contingentists and agnostics to extract a neutral cash equivalent of any formula in such a necessitist's mouth.

Naturally, we will use the same definition of neutrality as before, even though it involves $(\ )^{\text{con}}$. That mapping played two separate roles in this section: to define neutrality and to map each formula to a neutral equivalent given chunky-style contingentism. For necessitism, only the analogue of the second task requires a new mapping.

7.3 Mapping necessitist talk to neutral talk

A typical necessitist claim is that there is something that could have been a golden mountain:

(11) $\exists x \, \Diamond Gx$

The necessitist also accepts the equivalence of (11) with (12), by BF and CBF:

(12) $\Diamond \exists x \, Gx$

Since being a golden mountain uncontentiously requires being chunky, the necessitist accepts the strict equivalence of (12) and (13):

(13) $\Diamond \exists x \, (Cx \ \& \ Gx)$

Thus the characteristic necessitist claim (11) is strictly equivalent in necessitist eyes to the neutral formula (13). The point obviously extends to other chunkiness-entailing predicates in place of G. Can we use it to find neutral equivalents in necessitist eyes of all formulas in the first-order modal language?

Difficulties appear as soon as we try generalizing the example to cases where a formula restricts the quantifier:

(14) $\exists x \, (\neg Cx \ \& \ \Diamond Gx)$

Obviously, (14) is not in general equivalent to the neutral (15) in necessitist eyes:

(15) $\Diamond \exists x \, (Cx \ \& \ \neg Cx \ \& \ Gx)$

For (15) is blatantly inconsistent, while necessitists typically accept (14) on the present interpretation: there is something non-chunky that could have been a golden mountain. In this case, they may regard (14) as strictly equivalent to the neutral (16):

(16) $\lozenge \exists x \, (Cx \, \& \, Gx)$

But many necessitists will accept (16) and reject (14) on other interpretations of G. For example, if they accept numbers as chunky, when G stands for numberhood they will accept (16) because they accept $\exists x \, (Cx \, \& \, Gx)$, but reject (14) because anything non-chunky is no number and so no possible number. In general, we need more resources to define a neutral formula $(\exists x \, A)^{nec}$ equivalent to $\exists x \, A$ given necessitism.

In moving the possibility operator in (14) to prefix the quantifier in (15), we went wrong by interfering with the evaluation of $\neg Cx$, making it characterize the possibility in (15) rather than actuality as in (14). More generally, the idea was to construct a neutral equivalent for necessitists of an unrestricted quantifier in terms of what could be chunky. Thus in defining $(\exists x \, A)^{nec}$, we restrict the quantifier by C and compensate modally by prefixing $\lozenge$, but then in $\lozenge \exists x \, (Cx \, \& \, (A)^{nec})$ the conjunct $(A)^{nec}$ corresponding to A in the original formula has fallen into the scope of $\lozenge$, contrary to what we intended.

A quick fix is to use a rigidifying 'actually' operator @ to return the evaluation of the inner formula to the actual world. Thus one would define $(\exists x \, A)^{nec}$ as $\lozenge \exists x \, (Cx \, \& \, @(A)^{nec})$. For example, if (following $(\,)^{con}$) $(Cx)^{nec}$ is equivalent to Cx, $(Gx)^{nec}$ to $Cx \, \& \, Gx$, and $(\,)^{nec}$ preserves truth functors and modal operators, then $(14)^{nec}$ would be equivalent to the neutral (17):

(17) $\lozenge \exists x \, (Cx \, \& \, @(\neg Cx \, \& \, \lozenge(Cx \, \& \, Gx)))$

There could have been something chunky that is actually a non-chunky, possible chunky golden mountain. Necessitists can accept at least the material equivalence of (14) and (17).

However, the 'actually' operator does not deliver what we need when the quantifier occurs in the scope of a modal operator in the original sentence. For example, the necessitist accepts the uncontentious claim that there could have been no tigers (not even non-chunky ones):

(18) $\lozenge \neg \exists x \, Tx$

The proposed definition of $(18)^{nec}$ yields the neutral (19):

(19) $\lozenge \neg \lozenge \exists x \, (Cx \, \& \, @(Tx \, \& \, Cx))$

Since S5 makes the initial occurrence of $\lozenge$ in (19) redundant, (19) in effect falsely denies the possibility of something chunky that is actually a chunky tiger. Since there actually are tigers, which are of course chunky, that possibility is actual. Thus (18) is not equivalent to (19) for necessitists. The trouble with @ is that it undoes the effect not just of the modal operator it was introduced to counteract but of all other modal operators in whose scope it occurs. We need a different modal device to undo the effect just of the target modal operator.

A standard solution to the analogous problem for mappings of possibilist talk to actualist talk is to use a pair of modal operators, $\uparrow$ and $\downarrow$, where an occurrence of $\downarrow$ exempts its scope from the modal effect of operators between it and the previous occurrence of $\uparrow$.[10] The same technique is applicable here (Appendix 7.9 has technical details). Such operators seem to make sense. We may charitably assume that they are intelligible even to non-necessitists. We therefore redefine $(\exists x\,A)^{nec}$ as $\uparrow\lozenge\exists x\,(Cx\ \&\ \downarrow(A)^{nec})$. For example, $(18)^{nec}$ becomes (20):

$$(20)\qquad \lozenge\neg\uparrow\lozenge\exists x\,(Cx\ \&\ \downarrow(Tx\ \&\ Cx))$$

Kit Fine compares $\uparrow$ and $\downarrow$ to 'once' and 'then' in tense logic. Using 'then' modally rather than temporally, we might even put (20) into English as 'It could have been impossible for there to be something chunky that would then have been a chunky tiger', which is true on the relevant reading. For necessitists, (18) and (20) on their present interpretations are strictly equivalent.

Even with these refinements to $(\ )^{nec}$, the putative necessitist equivalence of $(A)^{nec}$ and A depends on significant assumptions about the necessitist's views. Consider the hypothesis that something could not be chunky:

$$(21)\qquad \exists x\,\neg\lozenge Cx$$

As now defined, $(21)^{nec}$ is trivially equivalent to (22):

$$(22)\qquad \uparrow\lozenge\exists x\,(Cx\ \&\ \downarrow\neg\lozenge Cx)$$

But in an S5 setting $Cx\ \&\ \downarrow\neg\lozenge Cx$ is equivalent to $Cx\ \&\ \neg\lozenge Cx$, for $\neg\lozenge Cx$ is not contingent. Since $Cx\ \&\ \neg\lozenge Cx$ is inconsistent, so is (22). Thus $(21)^{nec}$

---

[10] See Fine 1977a, pp. 143–4, Forbes 1989, pp. 27–9, and also Bricker 1989, pp. 384–5. Fine credits earlier work by Frank Vlach on tense logic from 1970; see Vlach 1973.

is equivalent to (21) only on a necessitist theory inconsistent with (21). We therefore need a necessitist analogue of CON_C strong enough to entail (23):

(23) $\forall x \, \Diamond Cx$

We must envisage a necessitist who asserts that everything is possibly chunky. Indeed, in necessitist S5, (23) entails the apparently stronger (24):

(24) $\Box \forall x \, \Diamond Cx$

For in S5 (23) entails $\forall x \, \Box \Diamond Cx$, which entails (24) by BF. Thus we must envisage a necessitist who asserts that necessarily everything is possibly chunky. We can regard (23) as corresponding to a picture of necessitist ontology as the minimal rounding out of the chunky-style contingentist ontology to make NNE true.

Section 7.5 raises an objection to (23) on necessitist grounds. Nevertheless, we may work with (23) for the time being; without it, the contingentist's task of eliminating unwanted theoretical equivalents from necessitist talk becomes even harder.

A further condition for the necessitist equivalence of $(A)^{nec}$ and A emerges when we reflect on atomic formulas. For a non-logical n-place atomic predicate F, the natural way to make $Fv_1 \ldots v_n$ overtly neutral is by conjoining it with a restriction to the neutral, $Cv_1 \, \& \ldots \& \, Cv_n$. Thus $(Fv_1 \ldots v_n)^{nec}$ is the same as $(Fv_1 \ldots v_n)^{con}$. But that yields equivalences only if F cannot apply to non-chunky things. To be precise, consider the open formula (25):

(25) $Fx_1 \ldots x_n \rightarrow (Cx_1 \, \& \ldots \& \, Cx_n)$

Since $(\ )^{nec}$ preserves truth functors and adds every atomic conjunct in the consequent as a conjunct to the antecedent, $(25)^{nec}$ is a truth-functional tautology. By the recursive structure of $(\ )^{nec}$, $(26)^{nec}$ is also a logical truth:

(26) $\Box \forall x_1 \ldots \forall x_n \, (Fx_1 \ldots x_n \rightarrow (Cx_1 \, \& \ldots \& \, Cx_n))$

Thus a theory entails the equivalence $(26)^{nec} \leftrightarrow (26)$ only if it entails (26). Of course, CON_C entails (26). Necessitists normally reject CON_C and so must obtain (26) by other means, if at all. Some may simply reject (26), and apply primitive non-logical predicates to non-chunky things. However, it is in the spirit of the preferred form of necessitism explained in Chapter 1 to characterize non-chunky things mainly in modal or temporal terms, through the properties they would or could have if they were chunky, or did have when they were chunky, or will have when they are chunky. Such necessitists may be happy to confine their primitive non-logical predicates to those meeting the constraint (26). Indeed, in necessitist S5, (26) entails the apparently stronger (27):

(27) $\Box \forall x_1 \ldots \Box \forall x_n \, \Box(Fx_1 \ldots x_n \to (Cx_1 \& \ldots \& Cx_n))$

For, by the S4 axiom, (26) entails $\Box''(26)$, which entails (27) by CBF and the background quantified modal logic. Thus we envisage a necessitist who asserts (27) for every primitive non-logical predicate in the language.

However, we cannot apply the same treatment to the primitive logical constant '='. For if we do, $(v_1=v_2)^{nec}$ is $v_1=v_2 \& Cv_1 \& Cv_2$, which is not equivalent to $v_1=v_2$ for necessitists, since even non-chunky objects are self-identical. We can make the point in terms of closed formulas too. A theorem of the background logic says that necessarily everything is self-identical:

(28) $\Box \forall x \; x=x$

By a treatment of '=' like that for primitive non-logical predicate constants, $(28)^{nec}$ is trivially equivalent to (29):

(29) $\Box \uparrow \Box \forall x \, (Cx \to \downarrow(x=x \& Cx))$

But (29) says in effect that necessarily whatever could be chunky is chunky. We are envisaging a necessitist who also claims that necessarily everything could be chunky, as in (24). Together, the two claims entail that necessarily everything is chunky, the chunky-style contingentist claim CON_C, which cannot reasonably be combined with NNE. Thus the necessitist should reject (29), and with it the equivalence of (28) and (29). We must therefore find a different neutral formula to be $(v_1=v_2)^{nec}$. The natural candidate is $\Diamond(v_1=v_2 \& Cv_1 \& Cv_2)$. For necessitism makes identity a non-contingent relation, in the sense that it is either necessary or impossible for it to hold between given things. More specifically, since individual variables are treated as rigid in the background logic, $v_1=v_2$ entails $\Box(\exists x \, x=v_2 \to v_1=v_2)$ (where x is a variable distinct from v_1 and v_2) and $\neg v_1=v_2$ entails $(\exists x \, x=v_1 \& \exists x \, x=v_2) \to \Box \neg v_1=v_2$. NNE makes those being conditions redundant. Consequently, since $\Diamond(v_1=v_2 \& Cv_1 \& Cv_2)$ entails $\Diamond v_1=v_2$, it also entails $v_1=v_2$ given NNE. Conversely, given NNE, $v_1=v_2$ entails $\Box v_1=v_2$; since we also have $\Diamond Cv_1$ by the chunky-style necessitist (24), we can derive $\Diamond(v_1=v_2 \& Cv_1)$ by propositional modal logic, and thence, by the indiscernibility of identicals in those possible circumstances, $\Diamond(v_1=v_2 \ \& \ Cv_1 \ \& \ Cv_2)$. Thus the desired necessitist equivalence of $(v_1=v_2)^{nec}$ to $v_1=v_2$ holds on the new definition, which we therefore adopt.[11]

Some other relations might be handled in the same way as identity. Set membership is an example. For a non-chunky object is presumably a member of its singleton set, so $v_1 \in v_2$ is not generally equivalent to $v_1 \in v_2 \ \& \ Cv_1 \ \& \ Cv_2$. But necessitism arguably makes membership a non-contingent relation. More specifically, necessitists and contingentists should agree that $v_1 \in v_2$ entails $\Box(\exists x \ x=v_2 \to v_1 \in v_2)$ and that $\neg v_1 \in v_2$ entails $(\exists x \ x=v_1 \ \& \ \exists x \ x=v_2) \to \Box \neg v_1 \in v_2$, because these principles help articulate the sense in which the identity and being of sets depend on the identity and being of their members. NNE makes those being conditions redundant. Consequently, since $\Diamond(v_1 \in v_2 \ \& \ Cv_1 \ \& \ Cv_2)$ entails $\Diamond v_1 \in v_2$, it also entails $v_1 \in v_2$ given NNE. Conversely, given NNE, $v_1 \in v_2$ entails $\Box v_1 \in v_2$; since we also have $\Diamond Cv_2$ by the necessitist (24), we can derive $\Diamond(v_1 \in v_2 \ \& \ Cv_2)$ by propositional modal logic and thence $\Diamond(v_1 \in v_2 \ \& \ Cv_1 \ \& \ Cv_2)$ by the principle mentioned in section 7.2 that a set is chunky just if all its members are. Since the equivalence of $v_1 \in v_2$ and $\Diamond(v_1 \in v_2 \ \& \ Cv_1 \ \& \ Cv_2)$ follows from necessitist principles, we could adopt the latter as a definition of $(v_1 \in v_2)^{nec}$. For simplicity, however, we omit such a predicate from the language. Modal set theory raises specific problems, to be considered in section 7.5.[12]

Like $(\ )^{con}$, $(\ )^{nec}$ preserves all truth functors and modal operators. Thus $(\neg A)^{nec}$ is $\neg(A)^{nec}$, $(A \ \& \ B)^{nec}$ is $(A)^{nec} \ \& \ (B)^{nec}$, and $(OA)^{nec}$ is $O(A)^{nec}$ for each primitive modal operator O in the language. These clauses and the earlier stipulations for atomic formulas and quantifiers recursively define

---

[11] The argument generalizes to a deduction of $x=y \leftrightarrow \Diamond(x=y \ \& \ Fx \ \& \ Fy)$ from $\Diamond Fx$ in the bare necessitist framework, for any one-place predicate F. Thus if Rxy expresses a criterion of identity for F things, in the sense that $Fx \ \& \ Fy$ strictly implies $x=y \leftrightarrow Rxy$ (so $\Diamond(x=y \ \& \ Fx \ \& \ Fy)$ is equivalent to $\Diamond(Rxy \ \& \ Fx \ \& \ Fy)$), then $\Diamond(Rxy \ \& \ Fx \ \& \ Fy)$ expresses a criterion of identity for possible F things, in the sense that $\Diamond Fx \ \& \ \Diamond Fy$ strictly implies $x=y \leftrightarrow \Diamond(Rxy \ \& \ Fx \ \& \ Fy)$. For example, given a criterion of identity for persons, the necessitist can automatically generate a modal criterion of identity for possible persons. The complaint that this does not explain how a bloodless and fleshless merely possible person could have been a flesh and blood person does not properly concern the identity relation, since it targets $\Diamond Fx$ rather than $x=y$. None of this is to concede the poorly motivated general demand for criteria of identity as metaphysical or epistemological groundings of identity claims in claims of some other kind. A coincidence between identity and another relation for things of a given kind casts light on that kind, not on identity, which is already well understood. For more discussion see Williamson 1990a, pp. 148–53.

[12] For similar issues about identity and membership in relation to mappings from possibilist talk to actualist talk, see Fine 1977a, pp. 132–5, and 1981a, and Forbes 1989, pp. 45–77.

$(\ )^{\text{nec}}$. One can easily check that $(A)^{\text{nec}}$ is overtly neutral, and therefore neutral, for every formula A of the language (proposition 1.15).

We want an appropriate necessitist postulate to entail the biconditional $(A)^{\text{nec}} \leftrightarrow A$ for every formula A of the language. As already seen, such a postulate must entail (23) (everything is possibly chunky) and (26) for every non-logical atomic predicate F (necessarily only chunky things figure in its extension). The postulate will be the necessitist counterpart of the contingentist auxiliary postulate CON_C. However, whereas the contingentist auxiliary did not need to entail the defining claim $\neg\text{NNE}$ of contingentism, the necessitist auxiliary must entail the defining claim NNE of necessitism. For $(\text{NNE})^{\text{nec}}$ is this formula:

$$(30) \qquad \Box{\uparrow}\Box\forall x\,(Cx \to {\downarrow}\Box{\uparrow}\Diamond\exists y\,(Cy\ \&\ {\downarrow}\Diamond(x{=}y\ \&\ Cx\ \&\ Cy)))$$

But this is a theorem of the background logic. In S5, both occurrences of ${\downarrow}$ are redundant, because they prefix non-contingent modal formulas, so both occurrences of ${\uparrow}$ are also redundant, as are the modal operators that prefix them, so (30) is true simply because necessarily everything chunky is self-identical. Thus, in the background logic, the necessitist auxiliary entails $(\text{NNE})^{\text{nec}} \leftrightarrow \text{NNE}$ only if it also entails NNE.

Let NEC_C be the conjunction of NNE, (23), and (26) for every non-logical atomic predicate F.[13] We may call this auxiliary necessitist postulate *chunky-style necessitism*. It is hardly surprising that the strong necessitated universal generalization NNE plays a more positive role in chunky-style necessitism than its correspondingly weak negation plays in chunky-style contingentism. In the background logic, NEC_C entails the biconditional $(A)^{\text{nec}} \leftrightarrow A$ for every formula A of the language (proposition 1.21). Thus, like chunky-style contingentism, chunky-style necessitism makes every formula equivalent to a neutral one. Naturally, the necessitist neutral equivalent of a given formula will often be uncontentiously non-equivalent to its contingentist neutral equivalent. For instance, as just noted, $(\text{NNE})^{\text{nec}}$ is an uncontroversial theorem of the background logic, while, as seen in section 7.2, $(\text{NNE})^{\text{con}}$ is implausible from both contingentist and necessitist perspectives.

The choice of $(A)^{\text{nec}}$ is unique up to logical equivalence, in the sense that any neutral formula equivalent to A given NEC_C is logically equivalent to

---

[13] If there are infinitely many non-logical atomic predicates in the language, we must define NEC_C as a theory with infinitely many axioms rather than as a conjunction. Doing so makes only a minor difference to the technical development.

$(A)^{\text{nec}}$ independently of NEC_C (proposition 1.23).[14] In particular, if A itself is neutral, it is logically equivalent to $(A)^{\text{nec}}$ independently of NEC_C. Nothing weaker than NEC_C suffices to derive all the biconditionals $(A)^{\text{nec}} \leftrightarrow A$, for NEC_C follows from $(\text{NEC}_C)^{\text{nec}} \leftrightarrow \text{NEC}_C$ (proposition 1.19), and so from any theory from which all those biconditionals follow. Indeed, $(\text{NEC}_C)^{\text{nec}}$ is just an uncontentious theorem of the background logic.

The chunky-style necessitist postulate NEC_C is independent of neutral formulas, just as CON_C is, because its addition to a set of neutral formulas always constitutes a conservative extension: a neutral formula follows from the set together with NEC_C only if it already followed from the set without NEC_C (proposition 1.22). Any theory T that is chunky-style necessitist in the sense of entailing NEC_C can be factorized into NEC_C and the set of its neutral consequences: the consequences of T are exactly the consequences of the combination of NEC_C and the neutral consequences of T (proposition 1.25). The logical relations between chunky-style necessitist theories simply mirror the logical relations between their neutral parts (proposition 1.24). Once one has chosen NEC_C and which neutral formulas to accept, nothing else remains to be decided.

Chunky-style contingentism and chunky-style necessitism constitute alternative ways to extend an agreed evaluation of neutral formulas to evaluations of all non-neutral formulas too. We can be more specific about the relation between their respective auxiliary postulates CON_C and NEC_C in the background logic. We saw in section 7.2 that CON_C is consistent with NNE. We can now make the stronger point that CON_C is consistent with NEC_C, because both are true in all models with constant domains all of whose members are in the extension of C at every world. We also saw that CON_C entails the equivalence of NNE with the neutral formula (10), which says that necessarily everything chunky is necessarily chunky. That claim is quite implausible; every material object is arguably a counterexample from both contingentist and necessitist perspectives, albeit in slightly different

---

[14] The uniqueness of the neutral equivalent would fail if neutrality only required the restrictions on the quantifiers, not those on atomic formulas. For example, both $\Box\forall x\,(Cx \to x{=}x)$ and $\Box\forall x\,(Cx \to \Box x{=}x)$ would count as neutral; they are equivalent to each other given NEC_C but not without it (since self-identity entails being something in the background logic). The uniqueness of neutral equivalents would also fail if the background logic did not include the being constraint, even on the tighter definition of neutrality in the text. For example, both $\forall x\,(Cx \to Cx)$ and $\forall x\,(Cx \to \Box(Cx \to \exists y\,(Cy\,\&\,x{=}y)))$ are neutral; they would be equivalent to each other given NEC_C but not without it, if $Cx \to \exists y\,x{=}y$ were invalid. If uniqueness fails, one cannot properly measure what a formula is worth to the necessitist in the common currency of neutral formulas.

ways. Thus (10) also follows from CON_C and NEC_C together, since NNE is a conjunct of the latter. We may assume that chunky-style contingentists and chunky-style necessitists agree in accepting the neutral formula $\neg$(10). Together, CON_C, NEC_C, and $\neg$(10) form an inconsistent triad, any two members of which are mutually consistent. The formula (10) plays a special role here. It is no mere random implausible neutral consequence of the conjunction CON_C & NEC_C. Rather, it is the strongest neutral consequence of that conjunction: a neutral formula follows from CON_C & NEC_C just if it follows from (10) (proposition 1.28).

Given the compelling neutral assumption $\neg$(10), CON_C and NEC_C constitute incompatible ways of extending agreed evaluations of neutral sentences to evaluations of all non-neutral sentences. Some philosophers may be tempted to conceive this situation in neo-positivist terms, treating the non-neutral sentences as 'metaphysical' and CON_C and NEC_C as rival linguistic conventions for using those sentences rather than as hypotheses, true or false. Such a view is more obscure than the sort of metaphysics it attempts to displace. All the basic vocabulary of the non-neutral sentences is already present in neutral sentences too. If a realist attitude is appropriate to the semantics of neutral sentences, it is unclear what room is left for a non-realist attitude to the semantics of non-neutral sentences. As already emphasized, contingentists, necessitists, and agnostics use the same language with the same meanings but different beliefs. Results later in the chapter further undermine the idea of contingentism and necessitism as just incompatible conventions.

A different idea, still with a non-realist slant, is that the contingentist and the necessitist can each regard the other's discourse as a convenient fiction. For the contingentist, the necessitist's fiction is, in part, that necessarily everything is necessarily something. For the necessitist, the contingentist's fiction is, in part, that necessarily everything is chunky. On this view, each party regards the other's story as, for some purposes, a helpfully vivid way of picturing modal information. Such fictionalism provides no serious alternative to the mappings ( )^{con} and ( )^{nec}. Those mappings enable each side to extract useful information from many of the other's claims. When the contingentist says A, the necessitist fictionalist may indeed conclude 'A is true in the contingentist fiction', which says something about contingentism, but—in frequent contrast with $(A)^{\mathrm{con}}$—not yet anything useful about the subject matter of A. Similarly, when the necessitist says B, the contingentist fictionalist may conclude 'B is true in the necessitist fiction', which says something about necessitism, but—in frequent contrast with $(B)^{nec}$—not yet anything useful about the subject matter of B. After all, the idea that we can learn from fiction is trivialized by the explanation that what we learn from it are facts such as that in the novel Anna Karenina kills herself, not least because we learn just as much of that sort from bad fiction as from good. The mappings avoid such trivialization.[15]

Rather than claiming to provide an alternative to the mappings, a fictionalist may try to exploit them, by treating CON_C as the contingentist's fiction and NEC_C as the necessitist's. The fictionalist would still have to explain why, if the non-neutral sentence B is true in the necessitist's fiction, as is the non-neutral biconditional $(B)^{nec} \leftrightarrow B$, the neutral sentence $(B)^{nec}$ is true *simpliciter*, not just true in the necessitist's fiction; likewise for the contingentist's fiction. Perhaps both fictions are supposed to incorporate all true neutral sentences. But there is no evidence that either the contingentist or the necessitist treats either CON_C or NEC_C as a fiction rather than a theory. The useful work here is being done by the mappings, not by the talk of fiction. Fictionalism is equally unhelpful for understanding the results later in the chapter.

7.4 Modalism and anti-modalism

From section 7.5 onwards, we will explore some obstacles to extending the method of neutral equivalents to a wider setting. Before doing so, however, we pause to consider some pertinent issues about the role of possible worlds

---

[15] A similar problem tells against the proposal to treat the subjunctive conditional 'If necessitism obtained, A' as what the contingentist can extract from the necessitist's plain 'A', and 'If contingentism obtained, B' as what the necessitist can extract from the contingentist's plain 'B'. Of course, the contingentist and the necessitist regard the obtaining of necessitism and contingentism respectively as impossible; the proposal assumes that the impossibility of the antecedent does not trivially imply the truth of the subjunctive conditional. Granted that assumption, 'If necessitism obtained' presumably functions in the contingentist's mouth very like 'In the necessitist fiction', and 'If contingentism obtained' in the necessitist's mouth very like 'In the contingentist fiction'. The predictable difficulty is that so far contingentists have been given no way to derive useful information about the subject matter of A from what they take to be the counterpossible conditional 'If necessitism obtained, A', and necessitists have been given no way to derive useful information about the subject matter of B from what they take to be the counterpossible conditional 'If contingentism obtained, B'. The mappings $(\ )^{con}$ and $(\ )^{nec}$ are needed to fill the gap. In any case, counterpossible subjunctive conditionals arguably are trivially true; see Williamson 2007, pp. 171–5.

semantics in that method. They are closely related to issues about its role in the dispute between actualism and possibilism.

Much of the debate between actualists and possibilists revolved around the legitimacy or illegitimacy of quantification over possible worlds. Such quantification was seen as far more problematic for actualists than for possibilists, since it was unclear that the former could acknowledge non-actual worlds, especially those supposed to contain non-actual individuals. In response, actualists tried to show how they could simulate possibilist discourse, and thereby gain the advantages of quantification over worlds without the unwanted theoretical commitments. Actualists' use of less standard modal operators such as $\uparrow$ and $\downarrow$ was one focus of controversy. They were suspected of being, not the innocent scope-indicating devices they were presented as, but a Trojan horse for quantification over possible worlds. They look like devices of cross-reference; what is the cross-reference to if not worlds?[16]

The actualism–possibilism debate overlapped and interacted in complex ways with a debate between modalism and anti-modalism. According to a modalist such as Prior, quantification over worlds can be reductively explained in terms of modal operators.[17] According to anti-modalists such as David Lewis, it is the reverse: modal operators can be reductively explained in terms of quantification over worlds. If a modal operator is itself a quantifier over worlds, or a device of cross-reference between variables for worlds, it cannot be used in a modalist explanation of quantification over worlds. Of course, worlds constitute only one sort of basis amongst many to which a philosopher might attempt to reduce metaphysical modality. For example, some have tried to reduce necessity and possibility to matters of linguistic convention or logical consequence.[18] However, for the clarificatory purposes of this brief section, we may treat reduction to quantification over worlds as the relevant form of anti-modalism.

Our concern here is the dispute between contingentism and necessitism, which does not map straightforwardly onto either the dispute between actualism and possibilism (whatever they are) or that between modalism and

---

[16] For an exchange on this issue see Melia 1992 and Forbes 1992.

[17] A reductive explanation need not be eliminativist. Given a reductive explanation of water to H_2O, there is water because there is H_2O. Thus the modalist may allow that there are possible worlds, and use modal operators to explain what those worlds are.

[18] A recent example is Sider 2011.

anti-modalism. The present use of possible worlds model theory to characterize the background logic is rather unproblematic, since that role is algebraic and instrumental. However, the need for the additional operators $\uparrow$ and $\downarrow$ in neutral formulas such as $(\exists x\, A)^{\text{nec}}$ raises the question whether the contingentist can understand them without using quantifiers over possible worlds as constituents of the intended interpretations of the formulas, rather than in a merely instrumental role. More generally, how does the dispute between contingentism and necessitism interact with that between modalism and anti-modalism?

By itself, necessitism is consistent with modalism, with anti-modalism, and with the conjunction of the negation of modalism and the negation of anti-modalism. The necessary being of objects entails nothing about the relative explanatory priority of modal operators and quantification over worlds.

Contingentism is inconsistent with central forms of anti-modalism. For reasons explained in sections 3.6 and 4.9, contingentists cannot take possible worlds semantics at face value. They can use a model theory such as Kripke's to characterize a system of quantified modal logic, as here, and in various other instrumentalist ways, but to stop there is to abandon anti-modalism, since one cannot reductively explain modal operators in terms of a framework to which one takes a merely instrumentalist attitude. A contingentist anti-modalist explanation of a formula of quantified modal logic such as ¬NNE cannot help itself to either modal operators or full quantification over the inhabitants of counterfactual worlds. It is quite unclear how what remains could provide an adequate explanation.

The tension between contingentism and anti-modalism makes a first-order language with quantification over worlds but no modal operators a hopelessly misleading medium for the debate between contingentism and necessitism. One cannot fairly capture what is at stake in NNE by asking whether all worlds have the same domain. It is far safer to pose the issues in the pre-theoretically well-understood language of quantified modal logic, without prejudging whether it is ultimately reducible to a language that lacks modal operators.

That contingentism excludes anti-modalism does not immediately imply that it requires modalism. Perhaps there is no reductive explanation in either direction. However, since contingentists cannot take possible worlds semantics at face value as the intended interpretation of the language, they are under pressure to explain it in other terms, and the obvious candidates for those other terms are modal operators. Thus we may expect contingentists to be modalists, once they realize what is at stake.

If contingentists are not anti-modalists, whether or not they are modalists, they are not obliged to explain their claimed failures of unnecessitated BF in terms of possible worlds semantics or any other semantic framework that eschews modal operators in the metalanguage. They may prefer a more homophonic style of semantics, in which a semantic theory for a modal object-language is formulated in a modal metalanguage.[19]

Does some independent argument for anti-modalism make trouble for contingentists? The arguments against contingentism in Chapter 6 and later sections of this chapter do not depend on anti-modalism. They use possible worlds model theory only in an instrumentalist spirit. Although one may well find the extant arguments for anti-modalism quite unconvincing, it is unnecessary to debate their merits here. For the sake of argument, it is dialectically appropriate to assume that contingentists can understand modal operators, including $\uparrow$ and $\downarrow$, without incurring anti-modalist commitments to which they are not entitled. If the assumption is false, there is a short-cut to the conclusion which this chapter reaches by a longer route: contingentists cannot always eliminate unwanted theoretical commitments from necessitist discourse when they want to.

Section 8.4 will revisit the relation of possible worlds to the intended interpretation of modal language, and reach a cautiously modalist conclusion.

7.5 The problem of incompossibles

The chunky-style necessitism of section 7.3 faces a problem. When combined with plausible modal assumptions about sets, it yields dubious consequences about non-sets. This section explains the problem and discusses what to do about it.

Here is a quick version of the argument; it will be made rigorous later. Any two things belong to some set. For example, o and $o*$ have a pair set $\{o, o*\}$. By the chunky-style necessitist principle (23) that anything could be chunky, $\{o, o*\}$ could be chunky. In section 7.2, we applied the notion of

---

[19] See Davies 1978, Gupta 1978 and 1980, Peacocke 1978, and Rumfitt 2001.

chunkiness to sets by the rule that a set is chunky just if all its members are
chunky. Thus if $\{o, o*\}$ were chunky, so would be o and $o*$. Hence o and $o*$
could be both chunky. Of course, (23) already entails that o could be chunky
and $o*$ could be chunky; what is new is that those two possibilities could be
realized together. This is the result:

$$(31) \qquad \forall x\, \forall y\, \Diamond(Cx \;\&\; Cy)$$

We can easily extend the argument to derive the possible co-chunkiness of
any number of things, but (31) is already disturbing enough. Suppose that o
is an ordinary concrete object, and that $o*$ could have been an ordinary
concrete object. For o and $o*$, being chunky just amounts to being concrete.
Therefore, by (31), o and $o*$ could have been concrete together. But what
prevents the preconditions for o to be concrete from clashing with the preconditions for $o*$ to be concrete?

We cannot regard (31) as merely an aspect of the necessitist convention
or fiction, for under necessitist assumptions it has problematic consequences
within the realm of the chunky, such as this neutral formula:

$$(32) \qquad \Box \forall x\, (Cx \rightarrow \Box \forall y\, (Cy \rightarrow \Diamond(Cx \;\&\; Cy)))$$

Contingentists have no corresponding reason to accept (31) or (32). They
can allow the incompossibility of the being of o with the being of $o*$, in
which case it is impossible for there to be such a set as $\{o, o*\}$, given the
being constraint on membership. For contingentists, incompossibility may
take the most radical form, at the level of being. They typically deny the
analogue of (32) in which 'has being' replaces C. For necessitists, incompossibility in that radical form is anyway ruled out, since being is not contingent. They must assert the analogue of (32) with 'has being' in place of C.
The problem is that they should be able to allow incompossibility in a less
radical form, the proposition that not every two possibly chunky things are
possibly chunky together, but (31) excludes even that. Necessitists should be
able to deny (31).[20]

---

[20] The problem that sets of incompossible possibles are not even possible is raised in Fine 1977b, p. 141;
Fine 1981b, p. 183; Salmon 1987, p. 48. Salmon raises a parallel problem for singular Russellian propositions about such individuals (1987, p. 48), as does Peacocke 1978, pp. 481–2, for the sequences of such
individuals required by a naive Tarskian truth theory for a first-order modal language; see also Stalnaker 2012, pp. 142–3. For the relevance of incompossible possibles to the theory of rigid designation
see Williamson 1988.

To emphasize the problem, consider two plausible counterexamples to (31) and (32):

(i) A human h could grow from a sperm s and an egg e. A human $h*$ could grow from the sperm s and an egg $e*$ distinct from e. But there could not be both a human h and a human $h*$. For given the essentiality to humans of their origins (conditional on their being chunky), there could be a human h only by growing from s and e, and there could be a human $h*$ only by growing from s and $e*$. Given the nature of the entities, h cannot grow from s and e while $h*$ grows from s and $e*$. Thus there could not be both a human h and a human $h*$. For h and $h*$, to be chunky is to be human. Therefore, it is impossible for h and $h*$ to be chunky together. Although the chunkiness of h and the chunkiness of $h*$ are separately possible, they are not compossible.[21]

(ii) Let fww be the concrete, unrepeatable token event of the First World War, in all its terrible detail. Instead of fww, a concrete, unrepeatable token event gep of a golden era of world peace from 1914 to 1918 could just about have happened, if Princip had missed at Sarajevo. For possible concrete, unrepeatable token events such as fww and gep, to be chunky is to happen. But fww and gep could not have both happened. For fww could not have happened without a major war in Europe in 1914–1918, while gep could not have happened with a major war there then. If an event similar to fww had happened somewhere else or at another time, it would not have been fww, and if an event similar to gep had happened somewhere else or at another time, it would not have been gep. Therefore, it is impossible for fww and gep to be chunky together. Although the chunkiness of fww and the chunkiness of gep are separately possible, they are not compossible.[22]

Neither (i) nor (ii) is an uncontentious counterexample to (31) or (32). Each example depends on background metaphysical assumptions that have been questioned. Anti-essentialists may deny (i), and those who regard events as abstract objects may deny (ii). Nevertheless, each of (i) and (ii) is independently plausible, and their disjunction—which suffices for the problem of incompossibility—is even more plausible. Those assumptions are even plausible given the bare necessitist doctrine. They become problematic only when combined with the chunky-style necessitism of section 7.3 and its extension to

---

[21] See Salmon 1987, pp. 47–8, for this example and Kripke 1980 for the essentiality of origins.

[22] One obtains a suitable metaphysics of events for this example by adding a modal dimension to the account in Davidson 1970, although doing so might not have been congenial to Davidson himself.

set theory. For the necessitist to deny that there is at least one case relevantly like (i) and (ii) as just described would be to give a very vulnerable hostage to fortune. The necessitist has good reason to avoid (31) and (32).[23]

We must first check the informal argument for (31) from chunky-style necessitism, to identify its tacit premises in the modal theory of sets. The first premise is that any two things (or one) belong to some set:

(33) $\forall x \, \forall y \, \exists z \, (x \in z \, \& \, y \in z)$

This is an elementary principle of standard non-modal set theories. On some views, there are proper classes, too large to be sets or belong to them; they would violate (33) when taken as values of the variables x and y. However, the applications of (33) relevant to (i) and (ii) concern possible humans and possible events, not proper classes. The cases are too different for putative violations of (33) by proper classes to constitute a very useful precedent for violations of it by possible humans or possible events.

The second premise is the inheritance principle that sets are chunky just when all their members are:

(34) $\Box \forall z \, (Sz \rightarrow (Cz \leftrightarrow \forall x \, (x \in z \rightarrow Cx)))$

Here the predicate S stands for sethood. Since only sets have members in the relevant sense, we can extract the useful corollary that members of chunky things are themselves chunky. We are working within a necessitist theory, so we can also push the necessity operator inside the universal quantifiers by CBF:

(35) $\forall x \, \forall z \, \Box (x \in z \rightarrow (Cz \rightarrow Cx))$

Without (35), the connection between chunkiness and neutrality would be undermined. For how can the being of a set be ontologically neutral between contingentism and necessitism if the being of one of its members is not neutral between them?

The chunky-style necessitist theory NEC_C tells us that the set (z) in (33) could be chunky, but we cannot yet combine that with (35) to conclude that the individuals (x and y) would then be chunky too, because that depends

---

[23] For their proponents, truthmakers provide many more examples of incomposables, since any potential truthmaker for a contingent proposition p is incompatible with any potential truthmaker for another contingent proposition q incompatible with p. However, for reasons discussed in section 8.3, necessitists must reject truthmaker theory, so such examples are not pertinent here.

on their still being members of the original set in those possible circumst-ances. To fill the gap, we need the principle of membership rigidity, that membership is a non-contingent relation, already mentioned in section 7.3:

$$(36) \qquad \forall x \, \forall z \, (\Box x \in z \lor \Box \neg x \in z)$$

Membership rigidity is the analogue for sets of the rigidity principle NC$\prec$ for plurals endorsed in section 5.8. It is an independently compelling principle in the modal metaphysics of sets; it helps articulate the nature of sets as individuated simply by their members. Since we are working within a necessitist theory, we have no need to qualify the disjunct $\Box x \in z$ in (36) to permit exceptions when the putative member or set lacks being.[24]

We can now complete the argument. By (35) and (36), if one thing be-longs to another, the latter cannot be chunky unless the former is:

$$(37) \qquad \forall x \, \forall z \, (x \in z \rightarrow \Box(Cz \rightarrow Cx))$$

Thus the non-modal postulation of a pair set gives something whose chunkiness strictly implies that of both members. More precisely, (33) and (37) entail (38):

$$(38) \qquad \forall x \, \forall y \, \exists z \, \Box(Cz \rightarrow (Cx \, \& \, Cy))$$

By the chunky-style necessitist claim (23) that anything can be chunky, we can conclude that any two things can be chunky together. More precisely, (23) and (38) entail (31), as required.[25]

The argument points to a weakness in the motivation for (23). The idea was that we can minimally round out a contingentist ontology of chunky things to meet the necessitist constraint NNE just by postulating the non-chunky being of those things whenever they are not chunky, thereby pos-tulating only possibly chunky things.[26] But that neglects the role of other

---

[24] The rigidity of set membership is defended by Fine 1981b, pp. 179–80, Parsons 1983, pp. 286 and 299–300, Forbes 1985, p. 109, and Bricker 1989, p. 387. Unlike Fine and Forbes, Bricker and Parsons refuse to qualify the principle for possible worlds that do not contain the member or set.

[25] The argument does not assume that only chunky things can stand in the membership relation. It does not preclude the treatment of $\in$ contemplated in section 7.3, like that of '=' rather than that of an ordinary non-logical atomic predicate for which the relevant instance of (26) (which would here be $\Box \forall x \, \forall z \, (x \in z \rightarrow (Cx \, \& \, Cz)))$ is a conjunct of NEC$_C$.

[26] There is no suggestion that the postulated objects are in any way created by the mental act of postu-lating them, or by its possibility. In most cases at least, the postulates are more plausibly conceived as true or false conjectures as to what there is independently of the act or possibility of postulation. Indeed, for the necessitist, if there are the postulated objects, they would have been even had there been no thinking thing to postulate them.

ontological closure principles that postulate new objects from ones already given. Set-theoretic principles such as (33) do exactly that. If those ontological principles are sufficiently general, they constrain the new ontology, and may force us to postulate new objects characterized in relation to the contingently non-chunky objects postulated in the first round.[27] The objects postulated only in the second round will not be even possibly chunky, for the necessitist agrees with the contingentist over the realm of the chunky, in particular over its possible extent. The pair set of two possibly chunky but not possibly co-chunky objects is just such an object. It is postulated in the second round, when principles of closure under set-theoretic operations are applied to the results of the initial round of necessitist postulation.

One way of responding to the objection is by modifying the chunky-style postulate NEC_C, for example by restricting the claim of possible chunkiness in the problematic conjunct (23) to non-sets. However, not only does such a restriction look suspiciously ad hoc: the underlying problem does not depend on an ontology of sets. We can raise it in plural terms instead. Rather than singular quantifiers over sets of individuals, we use plural quantifiers over the individuals themselves. We have already noted the extensive similarities between the modal metaphysics of sets and that of plurals, as sketched in section 5.8. Plural variables conveniently mark out the problem area for discussion. Those who prefer a set-theoretic framework should be able to transpose the discussion in section 7.6 back into their favoured terms.

7.6 Extending the framework to plurals

Sections 7.2 and 7.3 constructed mappings between necessitist and contingentist discourse for a first-order modal language. The challenge is to extend that programme to a second-order modal language. One legitimate way of interpreting a second-order language is by means of plurals, as Boolos showed. Chapter 6 explained some disadvantages of a contingentist approach to second-order modal logic on an intensional interpretation of the second-order variables. By comparison, the prospects for a contingentist

---

[27] There may be no need of a third round of postulation, if, as is plausible, the application of set-theoretic and other closure principles to postulates acceptable to necessitists generates only postulates equally acceptable to necessitists.

approach to plural modal logic seemed less bleak in section 5.8. In what
follows, we use the notation of second-order modal logic, as in Chapter 6,
but on a plural interpretation, which gives contingentists their best chance.
Moreover, plurals hold out some hope of finessing the problem raised in
section 7.5 about sets whose members are incompossibly chunky. Thus we
will consider the project of constructing mappings between necessitist and
contingentist discourse for a modal language with plural quantification.

To keep the analogy with set theory conveniently tight, we allow the
analogue of the empty set. As usual this slightly complicates the explanation
of the second-order quantifiers in terms of plurals, in the manner of
section 5.8, making the use of second-order rather than plural notation
less misleading.

On a plural interpretation, quantification with n-place second-order
variables for $n > 1$ is usually simulated by quantification with 1-place second-
order variables, interpreted plurally over ordered n-tuples. For present
purposes, however, that device is problematic, because the ordered pair
$<o, o*>$ raises the same problem as the unordered pair set $\{o, o*\}$ did in the
previous section, when o and $o*$ can be chunky separately but not together.
It is therefore better to add n-place second-order variables directly to the
object-language even for $n > 1$. Although they are hard to read plurally in
English, formally they can be handled by straightforward analogy with
1-place variables. Informally, the plan just for this chapter is to consider relations in extension rather than relations in intension. Many of the following
points apply even to a second-order modal language with only 1-place
variables, but it is most interesting and technically most natural to work
with the full power of second-order logic.[28]

Many extensions of the language can easily be envisaged. For example,
we could add higher-order atomic predicate constants with argument places
for second-order variables. For simplicity, however, we confine the language
to those expressive resources most directly relevant to the differences between contingentism and necessitism to be explored in this chapter.

We must extend the background logic in section 7.2 to the second-order
language. This logic is common ground between contingentists and necessitists. It was characterized by a possible worlds model theory in a set-theoretic
framework, employed in a purely instrumentalist spirit. We use the same

[28] See Shapiro 1991, pp. 221–6, for the limitations of monadic second-order logic.

models as before, triples $<W, D, V>$, where D is the domain function, not mandatorily constant. At a world of evaluation $w \in W$, quantification with a first-order variable is restricted to members of $D(w)$. Similarly, quantification with a second-order n-place variable is restricted to subsets of $D(w)^n$, sets of ordered n-tuples of members of $D(w)$. For reasons already explained, this is not the philosophically intended interpretation of the language, but a technically tractable way of characterizing a consequence relation. As explained in section 5.8, the plural reading is rigid, unlike the intensional reading in Chapter 6, so we assign a world-independent extension to a second-order variable. Thus the values of all variables in the language are world-independent. The quantifiers slightly modify this world-independence by imposing a restriction to the domain of the world of evaluation, representing what there could be together. Just as $\exists v\, A$ is true at a world w on an assignment a if and only if, for some $s \in D(w)$, A is true at w on the assignment $a[v/s]$, so $\exists V\, A$ is true at w on a if and only if, for some $S \subseteq D(w)^n$, A is true at w on $a[V/S]$.[29]

On this extensional semantics, quantification with a second-order 1-place variable behaves formally like quantification over sets. Informally, assigning sets as values of the second-order variables is unfaithful to their intended plural interpretation. On the latter, for instance, the 1-place variable X might be assigned all and only sets, even though there is no set of all sets. A perfectly faithful interpretation would employ plural quantifiers in the metalanguage to interpret the plural quantifiers of the object-language.[30] The arguments to come could be adapted to such a plural metalanguage. For familiarity and technical ease, however, a set-theoretic metalanguage does better in the merely instrumental role.[31]

We must also specify a semantic clause for atomic formulas. The simplest truth condition is that $Vv_1 \ldots v_n$ is true at w on a just if $<a(v_1), \ldots, a(v_n)> \in a(V)$. However, that condition violates the first-order being constraint for

---

[29] Note that $\bigcup_{w \in W} P(D(w)^n) \subseteq P(\bigcup_{w \in W} D(w)^n) \subseteq P((\bigcup_{w \in W} D(w))^n)$, where P is the power set operation. Any member of one of the latter not in $\bigcup_{w \in W} P(D(w)^n)$ is not quantified over as a value of a second-order variable at any world. It contains n-tuples whose components are not all co-present at any world. For the contingentist, they are mere artefacts of the model, impossible combinations. For the necessitist, a model represents a genuine possibility only if its domain function D is constant, in which case the inclusions are identities.

[30] See Boolos 1985, Bricker 1989, p. 389, and Rayo and Uzquiano 1999.

[31] Shapiro 1991, pp. 141–7, discusses principles that imply that the restriction to set-sized domains makes no difference to which formulas are valid in (non-modal) second-order logic. The arguments of this chapter are robust with respect to such issues.

second-order variables, since it does not require that $\underline{a}(v_i) \in D(w)$ for $1 \leq i \leq n$. Thus (39) would not be valid:

(39) $\Box \forall V \Box \forall x_1 \ldots \Box \forall x_n \Box (V x_1 \ldots x_n \rightarrow (\exists y\ x_1{=}y\ \&\ \ldots\ \&\ \exists y\ x_n{=}y))$

By contrast, in section 7.2, we required the intension function V in a model $<W, D, V>$ to respect the first-order being constraint for each non-logical n-place atomic predicate F: $V(F)(w) \subseteq D(w)^n$ for every $w \in W$. Since $F v_1 \ldots v_n$ is true at w on $\underline{a}$ just if $<\underline{a}(v_1), \ldots, \underline{a}(v_n)> \in V(F)(w)$, $F v_1 \ldots v_n$ is true at w on $\underline{a}$ only if $\underline{a}(v_i) \in D(w)$ for $1 \leq i \leq n$. Thus (40), the analogue for F of (39), is valid:

(40) $\Box \forall x_1 \ldots \Box \forall x_n \Box (F x_1 \ldots x_n \rightarrow (\exists y\ x_1{=}y\ \&\ \ldots\ \&\ \exists y\ x_n{=}y))$

We applied the same policy to identity: $v_1{=}v_2$ is true at w on $\underline{a}$ only if $\underline{a}(v_i) \in D(w)$ for $1 \leq i \leq 2$. There is no principled reason for treating V differently in this respect. Indeed, its interpretation on a given assignment determines a legitimate interpretation for F too, so the validity of (40) requires that of (39). Informally, when $n = 1$, we can put the point in plural terms: this could not have been one of those if there had been no such thing as this. Thus we require the truth of $V v_1 \ldots v_n$ at w on $\underline{a}$ to imply that $\underline{a}(v_i) \in D(w)$ for $1 \leq i \leq n$.

That first-order being constraint (39) for V is not enough. In plural terms, this could not have been one of those if there had been no such things as those. More generally, we require the truth of $V v_1 \ldots v_n$ at w on $\underline{a}$ to imply that $\underline{a}(V) \subseteq D(w)^n$. The latter constraint implies the former, for the truth of $V v_1 \ldots v_n$ at w on $\underline{a}$ in any case implies that $<\underline{a}(v_1), \ldots, \underline{a}(v_n)> \in \underline{a}(V)$, so if $\underline{a}(V) \subseteq D(w)^n$ then $\underline{a}(v_i) \in D(w)$ for $1 \leq i \leq n$. The new constraint is strictly stronger than the old, for even if $<a(v_1), \ldots, \underline{a}(v_n)> \in \underline{a}(V)$ and $\underline{a}(v_i) \in D(w)$ for $1 \leq i \leq n$, $\underline{a}(V)$ may contain another n-tuple that is not in $D(w)^n$. Since the formula $\exists X \Box \forall x_1 \ldots \forall x_n (V x_1 \ldots x_n \leftrightarrow X x_1 \ldots x_n)$ is true at a world w on an assignment $\underline{a}$ just if $\underline{a}(V) \subseteq D(w)^n$, given the new constraint, the constraint validates this formula in the object-language:[32]

---

[32] We assume X to be a distinct variable from V. Proof of the claim about truth conditions: Trivially, $\Box \forall v_1 \ldots \forall v_n (V v_1 \ldots v_n \leftrightarrow X v_1 \ldots v_n)$ is true at w on $\underline{a}[X/\underline{a}(V)]$. Thus if $a(V) \subseteq D(w)^n$, then $\exists X \Box \forall v_1 \ldots \forall v_n (V v_1 \ldots v_n \leftrightarrow X v_1 \ldots v_n)$ is true at w on a. Conversely, suppose that $\exists X \Box \forall v_1 \ldots \forall v_n (V v_1 \ldots v_n \leftrightarrow X v_1 \ldots v_n)$ is true at w on $\underline{a}$. Thus for some $S \subseteq D(w)^n$, $\Box \forall v_1 \ldots \forall v_n (V v_1 \ldots v_n \leftrightarrow X v_1 \ldots v_n)$ is true at w on $\underline{a}[X/S]$. Since $\underline{a}$ is an assignment, $\underline{a}(V) \subseteq D(w*)^n$ for some world $w*$. Thus $\forall v_1 \ldots \forall v_n (V v_1 \ldots v_n \rightarrow X v_1 \ldots v_n)$ is true at $w*$ on $\underline{a}[X/S]$, so $\underline{a}(V) = \underline{a}[X/S](V) \subseteq S$. Since $S \subseteq D(w)^n$, $\underline{a}(V) \subseteq D(w)^n$.

(41) $\Box \forall V \Box \forall x_1 \ldots \Box \forall x_n \Box (Vx_1 \ldots x_n \rightarrow$
$$\exists X \Box \forall x_1 \ldots \forall x_n \, (Vx_1 \ldots x_n \leftrightarrow Xx_1 \ldots x_n))$$

By contrast, in the case of an atomic predicate, although $V(F)(w) \subseteq D(w)^n$ by definition of a model, the analogue of (41) is invalid:

(42) $\Box \forall x_1 \ldots \Box \forall x_n \Box (Fx_1 \ldots x_n \rightarrow$
$$\exists X \Box \forall x_1 \ldots \forall x_n \, (Fx_1 \ldots x_n \leftrightarrow Xx_1 \ldots x_n))$$

The reason for the asymmetry is that for present purposes we are interpreting second-order variables extensionally but predicate constants still intensionally. Non-extensional predicates cannot be expected to satisfy (42), as presently interpreted. For example, if you are sitting, it does not follow that some things are necessarily such that they and only they are sitting. By contrast, (41) is correct on its presently intended informal reading. Necessarily, if this had been one of those then some things would have been those, so necessarily those. To repeat: in the model theory, we stipulate that $Vv_1 \ldots v_n$ is true at w on $\underline{a}$ just if $<\underline{a}(v_1), \ldots, \underline{a}(v_n)> \in \underline{a}(V) \subseteq D(w)^n$. That corresponds to the robust contingentist semantics for plurals in section 5.8. For necessitists, the constraint is harmless, for in a constant domain model nothing outside $D(w)$ is quantified over at any world. Thus the constraint is common ground.

The next step is to extend the definitions of neutrality and the mapping ( )^{con} to the second-order language. Just as a set is chunky if and only if all its members are chunky, so some things are collectively chunky if and only if each of them is individually chunky. Consequently, it is pointless to introduce a primitive plural analogue of 'chunky' to be applied collectively rather than distributively. Some things are collectively grounded in the concrete if and only if each of them is grounded in the concrete. More generally, some things collectively meet the chunky-style contingentist standard for being some things if and only if each of them meets the chunky-style contingentist standard for being something. In the model theory, this corresponds to the condition $\underline{a}(V) \subseteq V(C)(w)^n$ on the n-place variable V. In extending the mapping ( )^{con}, we can achieve the effect of this restriction by using the non-modal formula $\forall x_1 \ldots \forall x_n \, (Vx_1 \ldots x_n \rightarrow (Cx_1 \, \& \ldots \& \, Cx_n))$, which we abbreviate as $V{\le}C$. For second-order quantifiers, we define $(\exists V A)^{con}$ as $\exists V \, (V{\le}C \, \& \, (A)^{con})$. Similarly, for atomic formulas, we define $(Vv_1 \ldots v_n)^{con}$ as $Vv_1 \ldots v_n \, \& \, V{\le}C$. These restrictions have exactly the intended effect of a restriction to the collectively and individually chunky.[33] Since the new clauses in the definition of $(\ )^{con}$ are faithful to the intended conception of neutrality, as before a formula A is neutral just if it is logically equivalent to $(B)^{con}$ for some formula B. Trivially, $(A)^{con}$ itself is always neutral.

The results about the mapping $(\ )^{con}$ for the first-order language (propositions 1.1–1.12) also extend smoothly to the second-order case (propositions 2.1–2.9). Each formula A of the second-order language is equivalent to the neutral formula $(A)^{con}$ given the chunky-style auxiliary assumption CON_C. Thus one can calculate in a neutral currency the cash value to contingentists of any sentence they utter.

The difficulty is in the corresponding process for necessitism. The challenge is to define for each formula A of the second-order language a neutral formula $(A)^{nec}$ equivalent to A given a chunky-style necessitist theory such as NEC_C. The crucial case is the clause for formulas of the form $\exists V A$. Since $(\exists v\, A)^{nec}$ was $\uparrow\Diamond\exists v\ (Cv\ \&\ \downarrow(A)^{nec})$, at first sight the obvious proposal is to define $(\exists V A)^{nec}$ as $\uparrow\Diamond\exists V\ (V{\leq}C\ \&\ \downarrow(A)^{nec})$. In effect, the necessitist's talk of pluralities is reduced to talk of possibilities of pluralities of chunky things. But that naive idea fails. Consider (43):

(43) $\forall x\ \forall y\ \exists X\ (Xx\ \&\ Xy)$

This is the plural analogue of the Pairing Axiom in set theory, and is at least as obvious. A typical instance is that there are some things of which London is one and Paris is one. If we define $(43)^{nec}$ on the envisaged lines, it implies that any two things could be two of some chunky things. That simply revives the problem of incompossible chunkiness in section 7.5. The possible human h could be chunky, and the possible human $h*$ could be chunky, but they could not be chunky together, and so could not be two of some chunky

---

[33] The matter is slightly more complicated than it sounds, because $V{\leq}C$ is vacuously true at any world w for which not $\underline{a}(V) \subseteq D(w)^n$, so not $\underline{a}(V) \subseteq V(C)(w)^n$ (for $V(C)(w)^n \subseteq D(w)^n$ by the first-order being constraint for C). We must therefore check that the definitions have the intended effect. Quantified formulas: Suppose that $\exists V\ (V{\leq}C\ \&\ (A)^{con})$ is true at w on $\underline{a}$. Then for some $S \subseteq D(w)^n$, $V{\leq}C\ \&\ (A)^{con}$ is true at w on $\underline{a}[V/S]$. Let $\underline{b}$ be any assignment differing from $\underline{a}[V/S]$ at most on $v_1, \dots, v_n$. Then $\underline{b}(V) = S \subseteq D(w)^n$, so $Vv_1 \dots v_n$ is true at w on $\underline{b}$ if and only if $< \underline{b}(v_1), \dots, \underline{b}(v_n)> \in \underline{b}(V)$. Hence, since $V{\leq}C$ is true at w on $\underline{a}[V/S]$, $S \subseteq V(C)(w)^n$. Thus $(A)^{con}$ is true at w on $\underline{a}[V/S]$ for some $S \subseteq V(C)(w)^n \subseteq D(w)^n$. Conversely, it is straightforward to show that if $(A)^{con}$ is true at w on $\underline{a}[V/S]$ for some $S \subseteq V(C)(w)^n \subseteq D(w)^n$ then $\exists V\ (V{\leq}C\ \&\ (A)^{con})$ is true at w on $\underline{a}$. Thus $\exists V\ (V{\leq}C\ \&\ (A)^{con})$ has just the recursive truth condition we want for $(\exists V A)^{con}$. Atomic formulas: Suppose that $Vv_1 \dots v_n\ \&\ V{\leq}C$ is true at w on $\underline{a}$. Since $Vv_1 \dots v_n$ is true at w on $\underline{a}$, $\underline{a}(V) \subseteq D(w)^n$, so since $V{\leq}C$ is true at w on $\underline{a}$, $\underline{a}(V) \subseteq V(C)(w)^n$. Thus, by the truth of $Vv_1 \dots v_n$ again, $<\underline{a}(v_1), \dots, \underline{a}(v_n)> \in \underline{a}(V) \subseteq V(C)(w)^n \subseteq D(w)^n$. The converse is straightforward. Thus $Vv_1 \dots v_n\ \&\ V{\leq}C$ has just the truth condition we want for $(Vv_1 \dots v_n)^{con}$.

things. Since chunky-style necessitists have as such no reason to exclude such examples, they will normally reject the equivalence of (43) and (43)^{nec}, so defined. For the same reason, they will not extend their theory NEC_C by the plural analogue $\forall X \, \Diamond X {\leq} C$ of its singular conjunct (23), $\forall x \, \Diamond Cx$, since the plural claim is presumably false on their view.

Of course, for all these considerations show, there may be some other definition of a mapping ( )^{nec} for which $(A)^{\text{nec}}$ is always a neutral equivalent of A, given NEC_C. After all, (43) is valid in the background logic, and so equivalent to any trivial neutral logical truth. But we can show that there is no such redefinition of ( )^{nec}, because some formulas of the second-order modal language have no neutral equivalent given NEC_C. Strictly speaking, the phenomenon already arises with atomic formulas, since even Xx is not equivalent under NEC_C to any neutral formula.[34] Philosophically, this is not yet very significant, since an open formula (understood as such) is unsuitable for independent use in a speech act. But some closed formulas are also not equivalent under NEC_C to any neutral formula.

One case involves the ancestral of a relation, which is definable in the plural language, but not generally in neutral terms. Given NEC_C, the formalization of 'a has the ancestral of the possibly-R relation to b' has no neutral equivalent.[35] Even though R itself is necessarily restricted to chunky things, possibly-R may not be. For example, let R be 'interbreed'. If two

---

[34] See Williamson 2010, p. 744 for a proof. The problem does not arise for atomic formulas with predicate constants, because under NEC_C they hold only among chunky things. By contrast, necessitists cannot add $Xx \to Cx$ to NEC_C, otherwise $\Box \forall X \, \forall x \, (Xx \to Cx)$ becomes derivable: since they already have $\Box \forall x \, \exists X \, Xx$, they then obtain $\Box \forall x \, Cx$, which they reject.

[35] A suitable formula is $\forall X \, (\forall x \, \forall y \, (\Diamond Rxy \to (Xx \to Xy)) \to (Xa \to Xb))$, which we may abbreviate as $A(a,b)$. Strictly speaking, since the formal language lacks individual constants, a and b are free variables in the formalization, although we can treat them as names relative to a given assignment. Suppose that $\text{NEC}_C \vDash A(a,b) \leftrightarrow B(a,b)$ for some neutral formula $B(a,b)$. Then $\text{NEC}_C \vDash \forall a \, \forall b \, (A(a,b) \leftrightarrow B(a,b))$ since a and b are not free in NEC_C. Let D be $\exists X \, (\exists x \, Xx \, \& \, \exists x \, \neg Xx \, \& \, \forall x \, \forall y \, (\Diamond Rxy \to (Xx \to Xy)))$. Then $\vDash D \leftrightarrow \exists a \, \exists b \, \neg A(a,b)$, so $\text{NEC}_C \vDash D \leftrightarrow \exists a \, \exists b \, \neg B(a,b)$, so $\text{NEC}_C \vDash D \leftrightarrow \uparrow \Diamond \exists a \, (Ca \, \& \, \Diamond \exists b \, (Cb \, \& \, \downarrow \neg B(a,b)))$. But the right-hand side of this biconditional is a neutral formula, contrary to theorem 2.15 in Williamson 2010, p. 743, which says that D has no neutral equivalent given NEC_C (there called Aux[Nec]). Thus $A(a,b)$ has no neutral equivalent given NEC_C. Moreover, let E be $\exists X \, (\exists x \, (\Diamond Fx \, \& \, Xx) \, \& \, \exists x \, (\Diamond Fx \, \& \, \neg Xx) \, \& \, \forall x \, \forall y \, (\Diamond Rxy \to (Xx \to Xy)))$, where F is atomic. Suppose that $\text{NEC}_C \vDash E \leftrightarrow G$ for some neutral formula G. Let σ be the operation of uniformly substituting C for F. Thus $\sigma \text{NEC}_C \vDash \sigma E \leftrightarrow \sigma G$. Since F occurs in NEC_C only in the conjunct $\Box \forall z \, (Fz \to Cz)$, and $\sigma \Box \forall z \, (Fz \to Cz)$ is the logical truth $\Box \forall z \, (Cz \to Cz)$, NEC_C entails σNEC_C, so $\text{NEC}_C \vDash \sigma E \leftrightarrow \sigma G$. But $\sigma \text{NEC}_C \vDash \sigma E \leftrightarrow D$ since $\text{NEC}_C \vDash \Diamond Cx$, so $\text{NEC}_C \vDash D \leftrightarrow \sigma G$, which again contradicts 2.15 since σG is neutral too. Thus E too has no neutral equivalent given NEC_C, which suffices for the illustrative examples on pp. 706–7 of Williamson 2010. Note that the proof of corollary 2.16 (concerning a formula like E except for lacking the first two occurrences of $\Diamond$) at p. 743 is incorrect, since the result of substituting $z{=}z$ for Fz in the conjunct of NEC_C for F does not follow from NEC_C.

things interbreed, both are chunky. But, for a necessitist, if they merely *can* interbreed, it merely follows that they *can* both be chunky (together); it does not follow that both *are* chunky. Moreover, neither 'interbreed' nor 'can interbreed' is transitive. If *a* and *b* can interbreed, and *b* and *c* can interbreed, it does not follow that *a* and *c* can be both chunky (together), let alone interbreed: the possibility that *a* is chunky and the possibility that *c* is chunky may be mutually exclusive; likewise for the endpoints of longer chains of possible interbreeding links. Thus, given simply that *a* has the ancestral of the possibly interbreeding relation to *c*, so there are individuals $a_0, a_1, \ldots, a_n$ such that $a = a_0$, $a_n = c$, and a_i and a_{i+1} can interbreed for $0 \leq i < n$, no particular finite limit follows to how many sets of compossibly chunky individuals are needed to complete the chain from *a* to *c*. These informal considerations adumbrate the formal proof that, given NEC_C, the corresponding formula has no neutral equivalent in the language. Even if some informative bio-metaphysical theory combined with NEC_C entails the metaphysically necessary equivalence of '*a* has the ancestral of possible interbreeding to *c*' to a neutral formula, that is a non-logical matter, since it depends on the interpretation of R ('interbreeds' is no logical constant).

Of course, contingentists can use exactly the same formula as necessitists, with exactly the same meaning, to define the ancestral of possible interbreeding. The difference is that for chunky-style contingentists *a* has the ancestral of possible interbreeding to *c* only if *a* is linked to *c* by a finite chain of chunky individuals, each two adjacent members of which can interbreed, whereas for chunky-style necessitists the chain may have non-chunky (although possibly chunky) links. The difference is asymmetric because the necessitist can calculate in neutral terms the cash value of the contingentist's claims about the ancestral of possible interbreeding, whereas many of the necessitist's claims about the relation have no such neutral cash value.

Here is an even simpler example. The quantifier 'infinitely many' is definable in the second-order language, using a two-place second-order variable. Given NEC_C, the formalization of 'There are infinitely many possible *F*s' ('Infinitely many things are possible *F*s') has no neutral equivalent.[36] For example, substitute 'star' for *F*. Although a star is chunky, for necessitists a possible star need not be. An infinity of possible stars does not logically entail a possible infinity of stars, since for all logic says it may be metaphysically

---

[36] This was proved by Peter Fritz; see Fritz forthcoming for closely related results about any generalized quantifier that is not first-order definable.

impossible for infinitely many of them to be stars together. Even if some informative cosmo-metaphysical theory entails the metaphysical possibility of infinitely many stars together, that is a non-logical matter, since it depends on the interpretation of F ('star' is no logical constant).

As before, contingentists can use exactly the same formula as necessitists, with exactly the same meaning, to define the quantifier 'infinitely many'. The difference is that for chunky-style contingentists there are infinitely many possible stars (infinitely many things are possible stars) only if infinitely many *chunky* things are possible stars, whereas for chunky-style necessitists merely possible stars need not be chunky. The difference is asymmetric because the necessitist can calculate in neutral terms the cash value of the contingentist's claims about an infinity of possible stars, whereas many of the necessitist's claims about it have no such neutral cash value.

Can the contingentist just deny that the relevant formulas raise any intelligible question in necessitist discourse beyond those they raise in contingentist discourse? That hard line lacks plausibility.

Imagine necessitists dividing pairs of chunky individuals a, c into two lists, one of those where a has the ancestral of possible interbreeding to c (according to them) and one of the rest. Contingentists accuse them of wrongly putting some pairs on the first list. In each case of disagreement, the two parties agree that there is no chain from a to c, adjacent members of which can interbreed, all of whose links involve only chunky objects. The contingentists immediately conclude that a does not have the ancestral of possible interbreeding to c. By contrast, in view of various biological possibilities, the necessitists hold that there is a chain from a to c, adjacent members of which can interbreed, some of whose links involve non-chunky objects. Both parties realize that their dispute is fundamentally in metaphysics, not biology. The contingentists should be able to acknowledge that the necessitists are marking a genuine biological distinction, even though by contingentist lights they are mischaracterizing it as the distinction between those pairs where a has the ancestral of possible interbreeding to c and the rest. The contingentists may want to keep the necessitists' biology while dumping their metaphysics. The trouble is that they cannot separate the former from the latter, because the necessitists' biology depends on formulations with no neutral equivalent.

Similarly, imagine necessitists dividing natural kinds that necessarily have only chunky members into two lists, one of those with infinitely many possible members (according to them) and one of the rest. Contingentists accuse them of wrongly putting some kinds on the first list. In each case of disagreement, the two parties agree that the kind has only finitely many chunky possible members (that is, only finitely many chunky things are possible members). The contingentists immediately conclude that the kind has only finitely many possible members (that is, only finitely many things are possible members). By contrast, in view of various natural scientific possibilities, the necessitists hold that it has infinitely many non-chunky possible members. Both parties realize that their dispute is fundamentally in metaphysics, not natural science. The contingentists should be able to acknowledge that the necessitists are marking a genuine distinction, even though by contingentist lights they are mischaracterizing it as the distinction between those kinds with infinitely many possible members and the rest. As before, the contingentists may want to keep the necessitists' natural science while dumping their metaphysics. The trouble is again that they cannot separate the former from the latter, because the necessitists' natural science depends on formulations with no neutral equivalent.

We can sharpen the implausibility of attributing an illusion of understanding to necessitists. Say that a has a 0-length R-chain to b just if $a = b$, and that for each natural number n, a has an $(n + 1)$-length R-chain to b just if for some z, a has an n-length R-chain to z and z has R to b. Thus a has the ancestral of R to b just if for some natural number n, a has an n-length R-chain to b. For each natural number n, 'a has an n-length R-chain to b' has a formalization $R^n ab$ in first-order logic. Similarly, 'a has an n-length possibly-R-chain to b' has a formalization $(\lozenge R)^n ab$ in the first-order fragment of the present modal logic, and therefore has a neutral equivalent $((\lozenge R)^n ab)^{nec}$ given NEC_C by the main result of section 7.3. Thus, from a contingentist perspective, when necessitists use the sentence 'a has an n-length possibly-R-chain to b' it is fruitful to treat them as getting at the further proposition literally expressed by $((\lozenge R)^n ab)^{nec}$ (on a given assignment of values to a and b), since it is one on which all sides can agree, rather than the proposition literally expressed by the necessitists' original non-neutral formulation. But 'a has the ancestral of possibly-R to b' is equivalent to the infinite disjunction of the instances of 'a has an n-length possibly-R-chain to b' for all natural numbers n. Thus, from a contingentist perspective, when necessitists use the sentence 'a has the ancestral of possibly-R to b' it should be fruitful to treat them as getting at the infinite disjunction of the further propositions expressed by the neutral sentences, as one on which all sides can agree, rather than the proposition literally expressed by the non-neutral formulation. Unfortunately, no neutral sentence literally expresses that infinite disjunction.

Similarly, for each natural number n, 'There are at least n Fs' has a formalization $\exists_{\geq n}F$ in first-order logic, so 'There are at least n possible Fs' has a formalization $\exists_{\geq n}\Diamond F$ in the first-order fragment of the present modal logic, and therefore has a neutral equivalent $(\exists_{\geq n}\Diamond F)^{nec}$ given NEC_C. Thus, from a contingentist perspective, when necessitists use the sentence 'There are at least n possible Fs' it is fruitful to treat them as getting at the further proposition literally expressed by $(\exists_{\geq n}\Diamond F)^{nec}$, since it is one on which all sides can agree, rather than the proposition literally expressed by the necessitists' original non-neutral formulation. But 'There are infinitely many possible Fs' is equivalent to the infinite conjunction of the instances of 'There are at least n possible Fs' for all natural numbers n. Thus, from a contingentist perspective, when necessitists use the sentence 'There are infinitely many possible Fs' it should be fruitful to treat them as getting at the infinite conjunction of the further propositions expressed by the neutral sentences, as one on which all sides can agree, rather than the proposition literally expressed by the non-neutral formulation. Unfortunately, no neutral sentence literally expresses that infinite conjunction.

In both cases, it is very hard to avoid the impression that if contingentists dismiss necessitists' way of using such formulas without neutral equivalents as simply vitiated by their metaphysical assumptions, they are missing something. A more promising reaction is to expand the language, for example by adding infinite conjunctions and disjunctions, to include neutral equivalents of the formulas at issue within necessitist discourse. Section 7.7 will examine that approach. Before that, we briefly consider an alternative strategy.

The aim is to define for each sentence of the language a neutral equivalent given the auxiliary chunky-style necessitist theory. So far we have taken that theory to be NEC_C. But if we strengthen the necessitist theory, more sentences will become equivalent within it, and we may be able to find neutral equivalents without expanding the language.

One such strengthening is loosely based on Plantinga's interpretation of quantified modal logic in terms of quantification over essences, here treated in first-order terms. Introduce a non-logical two-place atomic predicate constant E. Read Exy as 'x is an essence of y'. NEC_C already entails that the essence-of relation holds only between chunky things, because it has the relevant instance of (26) as a conjunct:

(44) $\Box\forall x\,\forall y\,(Exy \rightarrow (Cx\,\&\,Cy))$

In addition, postulate that everything has a possible essence, that possible essences are necessarily chunky, and that no two things share a possible essence. More formally, expand NEC_C to ESS_C by adding these axioms:

(45) $\forall y\,\exists x\,\Diamond Exy$

(46) $\forall x\,\forall y\,(\Diamond Exy \rightarrow \Box Cx)$

(47) $\forall x\,\forall y\,\forall z\,((\Diamond Exy\,\&\,\Diamond Exz) \rightarrow y{=}z)$

Given ESS_C, plural quantification over any individuals can be simulated in neutral terms by plural quantification over the corresponding essences. Consider, for example, 'a has the ancestral of possibly-R to b', formalized thus:

(48) $\forall X\,(\forall x\,\forall y\,(\Diamond Rxy \rightarrow (Xx \rightarrow Xy)) \rightarrow (Xa \rightarrow Xb))$

Given ESS_C (including the analogue of (44) for R), (48) is equivalent to (49):

(49) $\forall X\,(X{\leq}C \rightarrow (\forall x\,(\Box Cx \rightarrow \forall y\,(\Box Cy \rightarrow$
$(\Diamond\exists u\,(Cu\,\&\,Exu\,\&\,\exists v\,(Cv\,\&\,Eyv\,\&\,Ruv)) \rightarrow$
$(Xx \rightarrow Xy)))) \rightarrow \forall x\,(\Box Cx \rightarrow \forall y\,(\Box Cy \rightarrow$
$((\Diamond(Exa\,\&\,Ca)\,\&\,\Diamond(Eyb\,\&\,Cb)) \rightarrow (Xx \rightarrow Xy))))))$

By a routine check, (49) is equivalent to the overtly neutral formula (49)^{con} in the background logic. Clearly the technique can be generalized to other sentences.[37]

The proposal faces objections similar to those pressed in section 6.2 against a different implementation of Plantinga's strategy. The shift from second-order haecceities to first-order chunky essences does not make the view metaphysically more plausible. How a necessarily chunky essence modally tracks the corresponding contingently chunky individual remains a mystery.

There is also a special objection to the present use of the strategy: it does not fit the dialectical context. For Plantinga is a contingentist. He invokes essences to make sense of quantified modal logic within a contingentist

[37] Some complications still arise, since not even ESS_C gives the open formula Xx a neutral equivalent.

setting. But the present challenge is to find neutral equivalents for plurally quantified sentences given a *necessitist* theory. The Plantinga-style postulates (45)–(47) had to be added to the necessitist auxiliary NEC_C, not to the contingentist auxiliary CON_C. Thus the question is not whether contingentists have good reason to postulate (45)–(47), but whether necessitists have. Perhaps a few necessitists will like (45)–(47). But they are not needed to solve any problem for necessitists, for they have no special difficulty in making sense of quantified modal logic. Consider chunky-style necessitists who see no reason to postulate (45)–(47). They too use sentences of such forms as '*a* has the ancestral of possibly-*R* to *b*' and 'There are infinitely many possible *F*s', and contingentists still face the challenge of seeing what they are getting at. Postulating necessarily chunky essences on their own behalf does not help them meet that challenge when necessitists reject those postulates. It merely exacerbates the problem. For disagreement over necessarily chunky essences manifests a difference between the two sides in the realm of the chunky itself. Thus not even the realm of the chunky constitutes neutral ground between them any more.

The point generalizes. It is not specific to Plantinga's strategy. Adding extra postulates to NEC_C so as to provide neutral equivalents for more sentences given the auxiliary theory does not enable contingentists to see what necessitists are getting at in their use of those sentences if the latter reject the new postulates. A different approach is needed. We therefore turn to the idea of expanding the language, already suggested by the earlier examples.

7.7 Infinitary languages

We saw that sentences of some problematic forms will have neutral equivalents given the auxiliary necessitist theory if the language is expanded to permit infinite conjunctions and disjunctions. Can those examples be generalized? The challenge is to specify for each formula A of the infinitary language with plural variables and quantifiers a neutral formula $(A)^{nec}$ equivalent to A given the auxiliary necessitist theory NEC_C.

The natural strategy is to adapt Kit Fine's standard proposal for recursively 'translating' second-order possibilist discourse into actualist terms.[38]

---

[38] See Fine 1977a, pp. 146–8; 1977b, pp. 161–2; 2003, pp. 173–4.

One replaces the second-order quantifier with an infinite string of first-order quantifiers, each of which is then modified by modal operators as in the standard 'translation' of first-order possibilist discourse into actualist discourse. In the present setting, we follow the mapping $(\;)^{nec}$ on first-order formulas instead. That strategy leads to something like the following definition:[39]

$$(\exists V A)^{nec} \text{ is } \uparrow \lozenge \exists x_0 \, (Cx_0 \;\&\; \lozenge \exists x_1 \, (Cx_1 \;\&\; \lozenge \exists x_2 \, (Cx_2 \;\&\; \ldots \downarrow (A)^{nec}) \ldots)$$

Similarly, to define $(Vv)^{nec}$, we first replace Vv by an infinite disjunction $v=x_0 \vee v=x_1 \vee v=x_2 \vee \ldots$, for new variables $x_0, x_1, x_2, \ldots$, and then replace each disjunct $v=x_i$ by $(v=x_i)^{nec}$, which is $\lozenge(v=x_i \;\&\; Cv \;\&\; Cx_i)$. Simplifying the result yields this logically equivalent definition:

$$(Vv)^{nec} \text{ is } \lozenge(Cv \;\&\; (v=x_0 \vee v=x_1 \vee v=x_2 \vee \ldots))$$

The definitions can be generalized to n-place second-order variables for any natural number n.[40,41] A reassuring feature is that in finite models suitably long but finite initial segments of the quantifier strings and disjunctions give the required effect, and another quantifier or disjunct of the relevant sort is logically redundant. Thus the definitions seem to be the natural projection into the infinite of a successful strategy in the finite case.

Nevertheless, as an attempt to explain in neutral terms what necessitists are getting at in their use of straightforward plural constructions, the appeal to an infinitary language is initially surprising. One expects finitary languages such as the necessitist uses to precede infinitary ones in the order of human understanding. However, a finitary language might gesture towards a reality more perspicuously represented in infinitary terms. Instead, we will consider two more specific problems for the proposal.

The first is this. We expect a single formula, even one infinitely long, to form some sort of unity. If so, the variables in it should form a set: if they can be united into a formula, they can be united into a set. Let its

---

[39] Intermediate occurrences of $\uparrow$ and $\downarrow$ have been dropped because they are redundant. The variables x_i must be selected to avoid clashes in $(A)^{nec}$.

[40] In the definition of $(\exists V A)^{nec}$, replace the string of variables $x_0, x_1, x_2, \ldots$ by the doubly indexed string $x_{0,1}, x_{0,2}, \ldots, x_{0,n}, x_{1,1}, x_{1,2}, \ldots, x_{1,n}, x_{2,1}, x_{2,2}, x_{2,3} \ldots$. For the definition of $(Vv_1 \ldots v_n)^{nec}$, replace $Vv_1 \ldots v_n$ by $(v_1=x_{0,1} \;\&\; v_2=x_{0,2} \;\&\; \ldots \& v_n=x_{0,n}) \vee (v_1=x_{1,1} \;\&\; v_2=x_{1,2} \;\&\; \ldots \& v_n=x_{1,n}) \vee (v_1=x_{2,1} \;\&\; v_2=x_{2,2} \;\&\; \ldots \& v_n=x_{2,n}) \vee \ldots$, then replace each atom $v_i=x_{j,i}$ by $\lozenge(Cv_i \;\&\; v_i=x_{j,i})$.

[41] The definitions in the text treat V as non-empty, for they make $(\forall V \exists y_1 \ldots \exists y_n \, Vy_1 \ldots y_n)^{nec}$ a valid formula. To allow for the empty case, replace $(A)^{nec}$ in the definition of $(\exists V A)^{nec}$ by $(A*)^{nec} \vee (A)^{nec}$, where $A*$ results from replacing each atomic formula in which V occurs free in A with a contradiction.

cardinality be κ. When we simulate the necessitist's plural quantification with an infinite sequence of modally qualified quantifiers as before, two quantifiers with the same variable would involve redundancy, so in effect we use at most κ quantifiers. The result therefore simulates a plural quantifier restricted to pluralities of cardinality at most κ, a reading of 'some things, of which there are at most κ', not the unrestricted 'some things'. For instance, if the formula has only countably many variables, we are in effect quantifying only over countable pluralities. We have lifted the restriction to finite pluralities implicit in the corresponding construction for a finitary language, but without removing cardinality bounds altogether. Yet no such bound is implicit in the plural quantifier as used unrestrictedly by necessitists. They can truly say 'There are some things of which every set is one', quantifying over all sets whatsoever, singularly with 'every set' and plurally with 'there are some things'. But there are more than κ sets, since by Cantor's theorem a set with κ members (such as the set of variables in the formula) has more than κ subsets. Thus the simulation in the infinitary first-order language is not equivalent to the plural original. Similarly, claims of the form 'There are more Fs than Gs' involve no absolute bounds on how many Fs or Gs there are.[42]

If the whole infinitary language contains only set-many variables, then the cardinality of that set is an upper bound on the size of the pluralities over which the strategy enables one to simulate quantification. But even if the language contains more than set-many variables, each sentence is still set-sized and therefore imposes its own upper bound on the size of the pluralities over which it simulates quantification. It is not just that the language prevents one from simulating quantification over larger than set-sized pluralities by these means. In notionally performing a speech act in the language, one must choose a particular sentence to perform it with. Whatever sentence one chooses, one is choosing a particular set-sized cardinal κ and a restriction to simulating quantification to pluralities of size at most κ, even if one could have chosen a larger set-sized cardinal κ^+ instead. One is

---

[42] Fine (2003, p. 169) raises a similar problem for proxy reductions of possibilia, but does not discuss its implications for his own non-proxy reduction. He informs me (personal communication) that he may have been presupposing a view of 'indefinitely extensible' quantification over set domains. The additional resources in Fine 2005b may also be relevant. Such a view contrasts with the absolutist conception of unrestricted quantification assumed in this book. For present purposes (which differ from Fine's), it also fails to provide any particular neutral infinitary formula equivalent to the target plurally quantified sentence given the auxiliary necessitist theory.

forced to choose an inadequate sentence, even though one has some discretion over the degree of inadequacy.

Resorting to a sentence schema with infinitely many instances, indeed more than set-many, does not help. A crowd of inadequate candidates is no substitute for an adequate candidate. In committing to a schema, one commits to each of its instances. But when the assertion to be simulated takes the original form $\exists VA$, the problem is that each candidate simulating sentence is too strong, because it introduces a restriction on the size of the verifying plurality not present in the original. Combining one over-strong claim with infinitely many others that are also over-strong to various degrees merely yields a schema that is as over-strong as any of them. Nor does obscure talk of indefinite extensibility address the specific problems raised in any useful way.

At this point a defender of the strategy might resort to postulating sentences without a set-like unity. By hypothesis, such a sentence can contain too many variables to form a set. This proposal raises in a peculiarly intense form the concern about the order of explanation. Contingentists cannot make legitimate cognitive use of necessitist discourse by their own standards just through knowing that the sentences necessitists utter have neutral equivalents according to the background necessitist theory. Contingentists also need to know what those neutral equivalents are, and understand them, if they are to use them as cash values of the necessitist utterances. But contingentists are human; how can they understand a sentence as large in the number of its constituents as the set-theoretic universe? If they take quite simple, ordinary necessitist plural discourse seriously enough to embark on the attempt, but in doing so are forced to try to think in a language whose possibility is a wild speculation, and whose sentences would in any case be scarcely accessible to us, that suggests that their metaphysical commitments are blocking their access to better modes of cognition available to necessitists. If so, that is further abductive evidence against contingentism.

An alternative strategy for contingentists is to gain expressive power by simulating the necessitist's use of the plural quantifier in neutral terms with an infinite string of modally qualified *plural* quantifiers restricted to chunky objects. That suggests replacing the earlier definitions of $(\exists VA)^{\mathrm{nec}}$ and $(Vv)^{\mathrm{nec}}$ by something along these lines:

$$(\exists VA)^{\mathrm{nec}} \text{ is } \uparrow \lozenge \exists X_0\,(X_0 {\leq} C\,\&\,\lozenge \exists X_1\,(X_1 {\leq} C\,\&\,\lozenge \exists X_2\,(X_2 {\leq} C\,\&\,\ldots \downarrow (A)^{\mathrm{nec}})\ldots)$$

$$(Vv)^{\mathrm{nec}} \text{ is } \lozenge((X_0 v\,\&\,X_0 {\leq} C) \vee (X_1 v\,\&\,X_1 {\leq} C) \vee (X_2 v\,\&\,X_2 {\leq} C) \vee \ldots)$$

From a necessitist perspective, the redefined $(\exists V\, A)^{nec}$ has the effect of quantifying over pluralities consisting of the union of κ pluralities of things that can be chunky together, if κ is the number of second-order variables in the quantifier string. This will raise the upper bound on the size of the pluralities quantification over which is being simulated (the unions) above κ if more than κ things can be chunky together. Even so, however, the result will not generally be equivalent to the original given NEC_C or any other natural auxiliary necessitist theory. For example, necessitists have no obvious reason to assume that of any collection of more than κ possibly chunky things, at least two can be chunky together. But a plurality of more than κ things no two of which can be chunky together is not the union of any κ pluralities of things that can be chunky together.

Necessitists had a clear although not decisive reason to accept the postulate of NEC_C that everything is possibly chunky: if the fundamental error in a contingentist ontology of chunky objects is that it omits the category of the contingently non-chunky, then one can hope to get from chunky-style contingentism to chunky-style necessitism by adding that category in order to obtain NNE; the result will be an ontology of possibly chunky objects. Chunky-style necessitists have no corresponding reason to accept that every plurality is the union of κ pluralities of things that can be chunky together. What there are for unrestricted plural quantifiers to range over simply depends on what there is for unrestricted singular quantifiers to range over. There is no room for independent determination of the former. In particular, since there was no limitation of size on the singular quantifiers, there was no limitation of size on the plural quantifiers. Thus necessitists will not generally be willing to expand their auxiliary theory with the postulates needed to obtain the equivalences $(A)^{nec} \leftrightarrow A$. Not even infinite strings of modally qualified plural quantifiers will give contingentists the desired neutral cash value of necessitist discourse.

The second problem for the proposed use of infinitary languages is independent of the first. It arises even if we ignore uncountable pluralities and uncountable quantifier strings. We can simply focus on sequences of countably many occurrences of quantifiers and modal operators, ordered as an ω-sequence like the natural numbers. We may further assume that the quantifiers occur uniformly, either all $\exists$ or all $\forall$, as in the proposed definitions of $(\exists V\, A)^{nec}$ and the corresponding dual definitions of $(\forall V\, A)^{nec}$. The difficulty is in explaining what an infinite prefix like

$\lozenge \exists x_0 \ (Cx_0 \ \& \ \lozenge \exists x_1 \ (Cx_1 \ \& \ \lozenge \exists x_2 \ (Cx_2 \ \& \ \ldots$

could mean to a contingentist. A parallel difficulty arises for an analogous infinite sequence with plural quantifiers; it need not be discussed separately.

The difficulty is not common to all infinitary devices for constructing sentences. The truth conditions of infinite conjunctions and disjunctions are clear enough. An infinite conjunction is true if and only if every conjunct is true; an infinite disjunction is true if and only if some disjunct is true. But no such easy explanation is available for the proposed infinitely deep string of quantifiers and modal operators, each with the next in its scope. Not every ω-sequence of meaningful operators itself constitutes a meaningful operator. The simplest example is negation. Let $\neg\neg \ldots$ be an ω-sequence of negations. Prefixing $\neg$ to such a sequence still gives an ω-sequence of negations. Thus for any sentence A, $\neg(\neg\neg \ldots A)$ is $\neg\neg\neg \ldots A$, which is just $\neg\neg \ldots A$, so $\neg\neg \ldots A$ is its own negation. But nothing in the meaning of a standard negation operator $\neg$ provides for such a non-bivalent case. Although the language assigns a meaning to $\neg\neg \ldots \neg A$ for each finite sequence $\neg\neg \ldots \neg$, it assigns no meaning to $\neg\neg \ldots A$ for the infinite sequence. Similarly, for a positive or negative integer x, let sx and px be $x + 1$ and $x - 1$ respectively. Although every finitary expression of the form $f_0 \ldots f_n x$ has a well-defined meaning, where each f_i is either s or p, an infinitary expression such as $spsps \ldots x$ has none. To take an example of an ω-sequence of alternating modal operators and quantifiers, just as the proposed sequence is, it is quite unclear what meaning to assign to 'There cannot be someone S_0 such that there cannot be someone S_1 such that there cannot be someone S_2 such that . . . such that $S_0, S_1, S_2, \ldots$ are all friends of each other'. There is no natural default way to construct an appropriate meaning for such infinitary expressions that will work except when something special goes wrong. The onus is on contingentists to explain what they intend the infinite sequence of modal operators and restricted quantifiers to mean.[43]

Sometimes a bracketing of such an infinite expression gives it a natural meaning, although the meaning may vary with the bracketing. For example, $(\neg\neg)(\neg\neg) \ldots A$ is naturally understood as equivalent to A (given classical logic), but $\neg(\neg\neg)(\neg\neg) \ldots A$ to $\neg A$. Similarly, since s and p are mutual inverses,

---

[43] See Leitgeb and Hieke 2004 for an account of the syntax of languages that permit infinite self-embeddings, with some proposals about semantics. However, their theory does not (and is not claimed to) solve the present problem.

$(sp)(sp) \ldots x$ is naturally understood as equivalent to x, but $s(ps)(ps) \ldots x$ to sx. In proposing their infinitary expressions, contingentists may legitimately indicate a preferred bracketing, to facilitate interpretation. In effect, they have already done so, since each quantifier is to be understood together with its preceding modal operator. But that yields no cancelling out of the sort that works for $\neg\neg$, sp, or ps.

Nevertheless, the present case might be thought to have relevantly special features. Let O_i be the operator that takes the coarse-grained truth conditions of A to the coarse-grained truth conditions of $\Diamond \exists x_i\, (Cx_i\ \&\ A)$. Thus our concern is the sequence $O_0 O_1 O_2 \ldots$. The O_i operators all commute with each other (in an S5 setting), in the sense that $O_i O_j$ is always the same function as $O_j O_i$, and they are all idempotent, in the sense that $O_i O_i$ is always the same function as O_i. Those two formal constraints together might be hoped to fix $O_0 O_1 O_2 \ldots$ uniquely in some natural way, because O_0, O_1, $O_2, \ldots$ behave like operators that act independently of each other, each having a one-off effect on its own dimension, so that the effect of $O_0 O_1 O_2 \ldots$ is just to combine all those one-off effects. But the two formal constraints together have no such consequence. To see this, consider any total ordering, however unnatural, of (coarse-grained) truth conditions; it is a transitive, anti-symmetric, connected relation. The global axiom of choice implies that there are such orderings. Let $q_0, q_1, q_2, \ldots$ be any ω-sequence of truth conditions. For each i, let O_i be the operator such that for any truth condition p, $O_i(p)$ is the maximum of p and q_i in the sense of the ordering. These operators obey both formal constraints. They all commute with each other, because $O_i(O_j(p))$ and $O_j(O_i(p))$ are both always the maximum of p, q_i, and q_j. They are all idempotent, because $O_i(O_i(p))$ and $O_i(p)$ are both always the maximum of p and q_i. If p and $q_0, q_1, q_2, \ldots$ have a least upper bound, then it is the natural value for $O_0 O_1 O_2 \ldots (p)$. But if they have no least upper bound, then in this setting there is no natural value for $O_0 O_1 O_2 \ldots (p)$. For many total orderings of an infinite set, many infinite subsets have no least upper bound. Thus the two formal constraints together do not generally fix a unique value for $O_0 O_1 O_2 \ldots$ in any natural way.

Let us consider the case of quantifiers in more detail. For a non-modal language, the semantics of a first-order quantifier $\exists$ can easily be extended to the case in which it binds infinitely many variables $x_0, x_1, x_2, \ldots$. Just as $\exists x A$ is true on an assignment $\underline{a}$ if and only if A is true on some assignment $\underline{a}*$ that differs from $\underline{a}$ at most in the value of the variable x, so $\exists x_0, x_1, x_2, \ldots A$

is true on an assignment $\underline{a}$ if and only if A is true on some assignment $\underline{a}*$ that differs from $\underline{a}$ at most in the values of the variables $x_0, x_1, x_2, \ldots$. This explanation works equally well whether the sequence of variables is finite or infinite in length. It serves to assign a natural meaning to the string $\exists x_0 \, \exists x_1 \, \exists x_2, \ldots A$ when the sequence of variables is infinite if it is equated semantically with $\exists x_0, x_1, x_2, \ldots A$.

For a modal language with a simple possible worlds semantics that involves no accessibility relation between worlds, such an explanation can be extended to a sentence of the form $\uparrow \lozenge \exists x_0 \, (Cx_0 \, \& \, \lozenge \exists x_1 \, (Cx_1 \, \& \, \lozenge \exists x_2 \, (Cx_2 \, \& \, \ldots \downarrow A) \ldots))$. It is true at a world w on an assignment $\underline{a}$ just if A is true at w on an assignment $\underline{a}*$ that differs from $\underline{a}$ at most in the values of the variables $x_0, x_1, x_2, \ldots$, where for each i $\underline{a}*(x_i)$ belongs to the extension of C at some world (assumed to be a subset of the domain of that world); otherwise the formula is true at no world on $\underline{a}$. A necessitist sympathetic to possible worlds semantics may accept such an explanation. But it should not satisfy a *contingentist*. For it is framed in a non-modal metalanguage that treats the domains of all worlds as laid out together, available for their members to be simultaneously quantified over. We saw in previous chapters that although contingentists can use possible worlds model theory as a technical device for various purposes, they cannot use it to give the intended truth conditions of quantified modal sentences without subverting their own theory. The infinitary formula is genuinely neutral only if its truth conditions can be explained compatibly with contingentism.

Another strategy for interpreting the infinitely deep embedding is to treat the sentences at issue as involving infinitely branching modalized quantification, in which no modalized quantifier is in the scope of any other. Thus we are to treat the structure of the sentence as something like $\uparrow \{ \lozenge \exists x_i \, (Cx_i \, \&)_{i \in I} \downarrow A \}$, where $\{ \lozenge \exists x_i \, (Cx_i \, \&)_{i \in I}$ is treated as an unordered set of sentence operators (the indices merely distinguish variables). The problem is that a finite or infinite set of unordered sentence operators rarely has a natural meaning as an operator in its own right. What, for example, does the set $\{ \Box, \lozenge \}$ mean? If we interpret $\{ \Box, \lozenge \} A$ like $\Box \lozenge A$ or $\Box A \lor \lozenge A$, it is equivalent in S5 to $\lozenge A$. If we interpret $\{ \Box, \lozenge \} A$ like $\lozenge \Box A$ or $\Box A \, \& \, \lozenge A$, it is equivalent in S5 to $\Box A$. Neither way of interpreting it seems better than the other. An example closer to the one at issue is the set $\{ \lozenge \exists x_i \, (Dx_i \, \&) \}_{i \in \{1,2\}}$. To interpret $\{ \lozenge \exists x_i \, (Dx_i \, \&) \}_{i \in \{1,2\}} \, Rx_1 x_2$, we must decide whether it requires $Rx_1 x_2$ to be composible with Dx_2, as in $\lozenge \exists x_1 \, (Dx_1 \, \& \, \lozenge \exists x_2 \, (Dx_2 \, \& \, Rx_1 x_2))$, or with Dx_1, as in $\lozenge\exists x_2 \, (Dx_2 \, \& \, \lozenge\exists x_1 \, (Dx_1 \, \& \, Rx_1x_2))$, or with both, or with neither: none of those four options is logically equivalent to any of the others. This particular difficulty is avoided in the case of $\uparrow\{\lozenge\exists x_i \, (Cx_i \, \&\}_{i\in I} \downarrow A)$ only because the $\downarrow$ operator returns one to the original world of evaluation (as a necessitist might say). Very special conditions are required for an unordered family of sentence operators to constitute a further sentence operator.

By using the method of Skolem functions, Henkin provided a way of interpreting some branching structures of quantifiers. His interpretation can be applied to partial orderings of restricted quantifiers of $\exists$ and $\forall$ forms, even when the partial ordering is infinite but orders no quantifier ahead of any other, as in our case. Barwise gave a semantics for further sorts of branching generalized quantifiers in natural languages.[44] However, the only apparent way of extending the available semantic treatments of branching quantifiers to modalized examples such as $\uparrow\{\lozenge\exists x_i \, (Cx_i \, \&\}_{i\in I} \downarrow A)$ is by treating the modal operators as quantifiers, just as in possible worlds semantics, which contingentists cannot use to give intended truth conditions. Thus the branching quantifiers approach does not solve the problem of interpretation for contingentists. They still have not explained the intended truth conditions of their infinitary formulas consistently with their own metaphysics.

Whence are contingentists to take the terms in which they explain the intended truth conditions, if not from their finitary quantified modal language? But that takes us round in a circle, for the problem was that on the very point at issue contingentists had found reason to regard their finitary language as expressively inadequate, while the sentences of the infinitary language are still waiting to be assigned meanings. In view of these problems, the presumption must be that if contingentists take themselves already to understand the infinitary formulas, they think so because, unwittingly, they look at them from the necessitist perspective of possible worlds semantics. They presuppose necessitism in explaining what they want the infinitary formulas to mean.

A more inferentialist strategy for contingentism avoids such cheating. We can try regarding (50), supposed to contain an ω-sequence of operators, as the inferential limit of the finitary formulas (51_n) as n goes to infinity:

(50) $\quad \uparrow\lozenge\exists x_0 \, (Cx_0 \, \& \, \lozenge\exists x_1 \, (Cx_1 \, \& \, \lozenge\exists x_2 \, (Cx_2 \, \& \, \dots \downarrow A) \dots)$

(51_n) $\quad \uparrow\lozenge\exists x_0 \, (Cx_0 \, \& \, \lozenge\exists x_1 \, (Cx_1 \, \& \, \dots \lozenge\exists x_n \, (Cx_n \, \& \, \downarrow A) \dots)$

---

[44] See Henkin 1961, Barwise 1978, and Peters and Westerståhl 2006, pp. 66–72, 363–4.

To assess what sort of inferentialist explanation is available to a chunky-style contingentist, consider entailment within the contingentist auxiliary theory CON_C. Then (51_m) entails (51_n) whenever $m \leq n$ (CON_C makes the additional conjuncts Cx_i redundant). Thus the sequence (51_1), (51_2), (51_3), ... is monotonically decreasing in logical strength (for some formulas A it may bottom out in a fixed point). Just as the limit of a monotonically decreasing sequence of real numbers bounded below is their greatest lower bound, so the inferential limit of the propositions expressed by (51_1), (51_2), (51_3), ... should be the inferentially strongest proposition that each of them is as strong as. That proposition is their disjunction, for each of them entails it (by disjunction introduction) and anything they each entail their disjunction entails too (by disjunction elimination). As already noted, infinite conjunctions and disjunctions are not problematic in the way that infinite strings of modalized quantifiers are.

Unfortunately for contingentists, however, the inferentialist account generates the wrong proposition. In effect, it simulates quantification only over finite pluralities. The underlying problem arises even in non-modal cases. Reading Nx as 'x is a natural number' and Sxy as 'x's successor is y', (52) says that there are some natural numbers closed under successor:

$$(52) \qquad \exists X \, (\exists x \, Xx \, \& \, \forall x \, (Xx \to Nx) \, \& \, \forall x \, \forall y \, (Sxy \to (Xx \to Xy)))$$

On this reading, (52) is true: all the natural numbers constitute a verifying plurality. Now replace the plural quantifier in (52) with an infinite string of singular quantifiers and treat the result as the inferential limit as n goes to infinity of the results of replacing the infinite string with a finite string of n singular quantifiers. Just as before, the limit proposition is the disjunction of the propositions expressed by the corresponding finite formulas. That disjunction is false. Each disjunct is false, for the nth disjunct implies that there are some natural numbers, at most n of them, closed under successor, which is false. Thus the inferentialist account yields the wrong truth value. In effect, it presupposes that all pluralities are finite. Essentially the same problem sinks the inferentialist account of (50) as the limit of (51_n) as n goes to infinity.[45]

It would be pointless for contingentists simply to stipulate that (50) is to mean the disjunction of (51_n) over all finite n. For the point of formulas of

---

[45] For more details see Williamson 2010, pp. 719–20.

the form of (50) was to capture in neutral terms the chunky-style necessitist use of plural quantification. Given the auxiliary chunky-style necessitist theory, the plurally quantified formula that (50) was introduced to simulate is not generally equivalent to the disjunction of (51_n) over all finite n. Thus (50) cannot do the work chunky-style contingentists introduced it to do, if it is equivalent to the disjunction of (51_n) over finite n. So the envisaged inferentialist strategy fails.

Does some alternative inferentialist account of (50) avoid treating it as the limit of a sequence of the finitary formulas? Such an account might use an infinitary consequence relation. But how would it distinguish the intended meaning of (50) from all other meanings, or even from all other logically inequivalent meanings? Merely accepting the rule that (51_n) entails (50) for each finite n, while rejecting the rule that (50) entails whatever (51_n) entails for each finite n, does not uniquely characterize an inferential role for (50). It does not even differentiate (50) from a tautology, or from the disjunction of (51_n) for all finite n and another sentence logically independent of them all. Appealing to inferentialism is mere whistling in the dark.[46]

A clearer strategy is to abandon the use of infinite strings of operators and use instead the far less problematic devices of standard infinitary logic: quantifiers binding arbitrarily large sets of variables; conjunctions or disjunctions with arbitrarily large sets of conjuncts or disjuncts. After all, we saw how countable conjunctions or disjunctions can handle the examples in section 7.6. However, despite this initial success, the new strategy does not go very far.

Many standard mathematical notions expressible in non-modal finitary second-order logic are not expressible in infinitary first-order logic with arbitrarily large set-sized formulas. For example, 'There are at least as many

---

[46] Further evidence that infinite strings of operators can create illusions of understanding comes from the deviant set-theoretic Axiom of Determinacy (AD), which postulates a winning strategy for one player for any two-person ω-length game of perfect information in which players take it in turns to choose integers, the first player winning if the resultant sequence of integers is in a given set S and the second player winning otherwise. AD is inconsistent with the Axiom of Choice. But it appears to be representable as an infinitary disjunctive schema:

$$\exists x_0 \, \forall y_0 \, \exists x_1 \, \forall y_1 \, \exists x_2 \, \forall y_2 \ldots A \vee \forall x_0 \, \exists y_0 \, \forall x_1 \, \exists y_1 \, \forall x_2 \, \exists y_2 \ldots \neg A$$

Here the quantifiers range over integers and A means that the ω-sequence $x_0, y_0, x_1, y_1, x_2, y_2, \ldots$ belongs to S. By the standard de Morgan equivalences of $\exists v \, \neg A$ to $\neg \forall v \, A$ and $\forall v \, \neg A$ to $\neg \exists v \, A$, the right-hand disjunct looks as though it should be equivalent to the negation of the left-hand disjunct, in which case AD would follow by the law of excluded middle. Set theorists rarely treat this as a serious argument for AD.

Fs as Gs' and 'There are exactly as many Fs as Gs' are expressible in the former but not the latter.[47] Given any formula of second-order non-modal logic with no equivalent in infinitary first-order logic, one can construct a sentence of second-order modal logic with no neutral equivalent under NEC_C in infinitary second-order modal logic, simply by prefixing each occurrence of a non-logical atomic predicate constant with ◊. Thus sentences such as (53) and (54) have no neutral equivalent, given the auxiliary chunky-style necessitist theory:

(53)   There are at least as many possible planets as possible stars.

(54)   There are exactly as many possible planets as possible stars.

By contrast, sentences such as (55) have neutral equivalents on the auxiliary theory, since they can be formalized in finitary first-order modal logic:

(55)   There are at least a trillion possible planets and at least a trillion possible stars.

If contingentists claim that necessitists use sentences like (55) to mark genuine distinctions, but do not so use sentences like (53) and (54), they risk discrediting their contingentism: the cases are too similar.

Peter Fritz has also shown that some generalized quantifiers expressible in standard infinitary non-modal first-order logic also yield sentences of second-order modal logic with no neutral equivalent under NEC_C in infinitary second-order modal logic, even with generalized quantifiers. One such quantifier is 'uncountably many things'.[48] Formalizations of sentences such as (56) have no neutral equivalent in infinitary second-order modal logic given the auxiliary necessitist theory:

(56)   There are uncountably many possible stars.

---

[47] These results are easy corollaries of a downward Löwenheim-Skolem theorem for infinitary first-order logic (Dickmann 1985, p. 339, theorem 3.1.1). Dickmann lists the following more sophisticated examples of mathematically significant classes that can be characterized in a finitary second-order language but not in an infinitary first-order language: topological spaces; compact spaces; discrete spaces; T_i spaces ($i = 0, \ldots, 5$); regular, completely regular, normal, completely normal spaces; metrizable spaces; Stone spaces, extremally disconnected spaces; complete uniform spaces; topological groups, rings, and modules; complete partial and linear orderings; complete lattices and complete distributive lattices; complete Boolean algebras and complete atomic Boolean algebras; completely distributive Boolean algebras (1985, p. 323). See also Shapiro 1991, p. 242.

[48] See Fritz forthcoming.

By contrast, formalizations of sentences such as (57) have neutral equivalents under NEC_C in infinitary first-order modal logic, since they are equivalent to infinite conjunctions of first-order modal formulas:

(57)   There are infinitely many possible stars.

Again, if contingentists claim that necessitists use sentences like (57) to mark genuine distinctions, but do not so use sentences like (56), they risk discrediting their contingentism.

These examples show that the problems for contingentism start well before we have gone all the way to a second-order language. They already arise in a first-order modal language with second-order definable generalized quantifiers, as in (53), (54), and (56). Many other variations can be played on the same themes. For example, the results still hold when propositional quantifiers are added to the language.[49]

In short, the necessitist can draw more distinctions than the contingentist can. Every distinction the contingentist can draw can be drawn in neutral terms, so the necessitist can draw it too. The converse fails. The necessitist can draw distinctions the contingentist cannot, because they cannot be drawn in neutral terms. That would not matter if those extra distinctions were bogus. But the contingentist cannot plausibly dismiss them like that, because they are too intimately related to distinctions the latter is committed to regarding as genuine. Thus necessitism provides a clearer view than contingentism of modal reality.

We must be circumspect, because the robustness of such arguments should be tested by extending them to a variety of logical settings. We might extend the formal language, or the auxiliary necessitist theory, or both. We must also remember that the results primarily concern chunky-style necessitism and chunky-style contingentism, which are not the only versions of necessitism and contingentism. On present indications, however, the results are technically robust. Moreover, a contingentist of any sort is challenged to account for a necessitist's use of sentences such as (53), (54), and (56). If their versions of those doctrines are not both chunky-style, that only exacerbates the difficulty of finding variants of those sentences acceptable to the contingentist, for the chunky-style versions were designed specifically to facilitate the construction of such variants. Nor does replacing chunky-style

---

[49] See Fritz forthcoming.

contingentism by another version of the doctrine mitigate the implausibility of dismissing the necessitist's use of the sentences at issue as merely erroneous, not getting at any truth at all. On present evidence, therefore, the asymmetry in powers of discrimination between necessitism and contingentism is serious, and favours necessitism. Contingentism is not so much parsimonious as impoverished.

7.8 Further applications

The form of argument used in this chapter can be applied to issues raised elsewhere in the book. For example, contingentists sometimes respond to problems like those in Chapter 6 for a contingentist theory of abundant properties by invoking infinite strings of modalized first-order quantifiers, as in (50), in order to simulate quantification over intensions. They permit the latter to vary in extension across worlds by co-indexing sentence-letters W_i (think 'world i obtains') with modal operators $\Diamond_i$ (think 'there is a possible world i') to simulate quantification over worlds. For instance, (58) is simulated as (59):

(58) $\exists X \, \Box \forall x \, (Xx \leftrightarrow Fx)$

(59) $\uparrow \Diamond_0 \exists x_0 \, \Diamond_1 \exists x_1 \, \Diamond_2 \exists x_2 \ldots \downarrow \Box \forall x \, (((W_0 \ \& \ x{=}x_0) \vee (W_1 \ \& \ x{=}x_1) \vee (W_2 \ \& \ x{=}x_2) \vee \ldots) \leftrightarrow Fx)$

As noted in section 7.4, it is hardly obvious that contingentists can help themselves to anything as close to quantification over worlds as the devices of modal cross-reference in (59). But that point need not be pressed, since we saw in section 7.7 that an infinite string of modalized quantifiers like that in (59) is not a legitimate resource for contingentism. Thus the attempted simulation fails.

Alternatively, contingentists may try to simulate quantification over intensions otherwise by embedding first-order quantifiers over interpreted predicates within modal operators, and generalizing about what those predicates would be true of. The hope is to transcend thereby the expressive limitations of the predicates available in any specific possible circumstance. Haecceities and anti-haecceities correspond to predicates of the forms $\lambda x(x{=}a)$ and $\lambda x(\neg x{=}a)$, where a is an individual constant. Even if there are such predicates for a given individual only in possible circumstances in which there is that individual, the contingentist can still generalize modally about haecceities and anti-haecceities, using the devices of modal cross-reference. Since the contingentist has no good reason to exclude the possibility of an individual metaphysically incapable of being named, predicates with free variables as parameters, such as $\lambda x(x=y)$ and $\lambda x(\neg x=y)$, may also be permitted. To simulate quantification over intensions adequately, the contingentist must simulate quantification over the disjunctions of the haecceities of many individuals, even if the individuals are not compossible. Such disjunctions correspond to predicates like $\lambda x(x=y \lor x=z)$ with many parameters. But simulating quantification over infinite such disjunctions without unwarranted presuppositions of compossibility again involves an infinite string of modalized quantifiers, and the proposal fails for the same reason as before.

Another application of the argument of section 7.7 is to contingentist attempts to state the intended truth conditions of sentences of a first-order modal language with an unrestricted reading of the quantifiers. We saw in section 3.6 that contingentists cannot do that by specifying an intended possible worlds model, on pain of validating the Barcan formula. But they can still hope to formulate a quasi-homophonic theory of truth (not truth-in-a-model) for the quantified modal object-language in a quantified modal metalanguage. Doing so might even have the additional advantage of being more faithful to the intended meanings of the object-language expressions.

In formulating a truth theory, the standard procedure is first to define the truth of a formula relative to an assignment of values to variables, and then to define absolute truth as truth relative to all such assignments. But such assignments are problematic for the contingentist. For example, many contingentists accept (60), which says that two-way incompossibility can occur:

(60) $\Diamond \exists x \, \Diamond \exists y \, \neg \Diamond (\exists z \; x=z \; \& \; \exists z \; y=z)$

On a conventional truth theory, the truth of (60) on its intended interpretation requires at least the possibility of an assignment to the variables x and y on which $\neg \Diamond (\exists z \; x=z \; \& \; \exists z \; y=z)$ is true on its intended interpretation, so that the value of x is incompossible with the value of y. But then the assignment itself is impossible, for its being involves the being of the values it assigns to both variables. The natural move for the contingentist at this point is to simulate quantification over assignments with strings of modalized quantifiers over individual values for the variables. Since an assignment assigns values to all the infinitely many variables in the language, these strings will be infinitely long, and therefore unavailable to contingentists for the same reason as before.

Contingentists may stave off disaster by simulating assignments to only finitely many variables at a time, for each formula of the language contains only finitely many variables. However, for purposes of semantic theorizing, they will need to simulate the *general* notion of truth under such an assignment. Thus they will need some analogue of the open formula 'A is true on a', where the free variables A and a range over formulas and finite assignments. They will simulate the variable a with a set of individual variables of the metalanguage. Since a may be assigned an assignment defined on n variables of the object-language, the simulating set must contain at least n variables. But there is no finite upper bound on n, so the simulating set must contain infinitely many variables. Thus the analogue of 'A is true on a' will contain infinitely many free variables. That requires the use of infinite conjunctions in the metalanguage.[50] Although not objectionable in itself, that makes the contingentist's problem recur in the metametalanguage. For the relevant infinite conjunctions in the metalanguage contain infinitely many variables. Therefore, once we formulate a theory in a metametalanguage of the intended truth conditions of formulas of the metalanguage, we must simulate assignments to infinitely many variables at a time. Since that requires an infinitely long string of modalized quantifiers in the metametalanguage, which makes sense only from the perspective of necessitism, the contingentist has merely delayed the problem by one step of semantic ascent. Thus, on present evidence, contingentism is subject to a dangerous form of semantic instability: if one starts from contingentism, a few stages of semantic reflection on one's developing theory take one to a standpoint incompatible with contingentism.

The asymmetries between necessitism and contingentism in sections 7.6–7.7 also reinforce the point that the dispute between them is in no interesting sense merely verbal or notational.[51] That should be obvious anyway, since the contingentist denies what the necessitist affirms in a common language, both parties holding themselves responsible to public meanings rather than stipulating idiosyncratic alternatives. Nevertheless, in case of

---

[50] See Peacocke 1978, pp. 480–9. His motivation for so formulating his modal truth theory is technical; he does not object to infinite strings of modalized quantifiers as such.
[51] Compare Hirsch 2011.

lingering scepticism, let A be any closed sentence with no neutral equivalent given the auxiliary necessitist theory NEC_C. Suppose that a formula B is offered as, in the contingentist's mouth, substantially equivalent (in whatever sense is relevant to matters of merely notational variance) to A in the necessitist's mouth. As already seen, B will have a neutral equivalent $(B)^{con}$ given CON_C. Thus $(B)^{con}$ in the contingentist's mouth is substantially equivalent to B in the contingentist's mouth. Moreover, since it is neutral, $(B)^{con}$ in the necessitist's mouth is substantially equivalent to $(B)^{con}$ in the contingentist's mouth. Therefore, by the transitivity of substantial equivalence, $(B)^{con}$ in the necessitist's mouth is substantially equivalent to A in the necessitist's mouth.[52] Consequently, $(B)^{con}$ is equivalent to A given the necessitist's theory NEC_C. But that contradicts the supposition that A has no neutral equivalent given NEC_C. Therefore, by reductio ad absurdum, A in the necessitist's mouth is not substantially equivalent in the relevant sense to any formula in the contingentist's mouth. Thus the necessitist theory NEC_C and the contingentist theory CON_C are no mere notational variants of each other.

One can argue along very similar lines that possibilism and actualism are no mere notational variants of each other, contrary to what is often claimed. Although the content of the two doctrines is much less clear than in the case of necessitism and contingentism, the obscurity of both possibilism and actualism does not make them substantially equivalent to each other in the relevant sense.

Analogous arguments can also be given in the case of time, favouring permanentism over temporaryism. Indeed, in the more obscure dispute between eternalism and presentism, examples involving generalized quantifiers similar to those in section 7.7 have already been used. For instance, David Lewis challenges presentists to analyse in their terms sentences such as 'There have been infinitely many kings named John' (compare 'There are infinitely many possible stars'), in order to cast doubt on the truth of presentism.[53] Ted Sider challenges sceptics who claim that the dispute between presentism and eternalism is merely verbal to analyse in presentist terms sentences of the form 'Half the objects from all of time that are Ks are Ls' (compare 'There are at least as many possible planets as possible stars').[54]

---

[52] Approximate substantial equivalence need not be transitive, but exact substantial equivalence must be, which is what matters for present purposes.

[53] Lewis 2004, pp. 6–7.

[54] Sider 2006, pp. 91–2.

Peter Fritz notes that in both cases his proof techniques, developed for the modal applications, can be used to establish that there is no equivalence of the required kind.[55]

Whether such results refute presentism depends on what is meant by that obscure term. Primarily, they favour permanentism (the analogue of necessitism) over temporaryism (the analogue of contingentism). Once permanentism is granted, they may not damage a view with some flavour of 'presentism' on which the present time is metaphysically but not specifically ontologically privileged over past and future times: for example, A-theoretic permanentism.[56] If the present time is the only one that obtains, it does not follow that there are temporary objects. Similarly, the arguments in this chapter primarily favour necessitism over contingentism. Once necessitism is granted, they may not damage a view with some flavour of 'actualism' on which the actual world is metaphysically but not specifically ontologically privileged over other possible worlds: for example, modalist necessitism. If the actual world is the only one that obtains, it does not follow that there are contingent objects. Section 8.4 takes up related issues.

7.9 Appendix

This appendix gives more details of the technical background to Chapter 7.

We start with the first-order modal language $L1_\square$. It has countably many individual variables, a finite number of atomic non-logical predicate constants each with a fixed finite number of argument places, including the 1-place predicate constant C, the atomic 2-place logical predicate identity constant = (in practice, it is always clear whether it is being used as a symbol of the object-language or the metalanguage), the usual truth functors ($\neg$, &, $\vee$, $\rightarrow$, $\leftrightarrow$), modal operators ($\Diamond$, $\square$, $\uparrow$, $\downarrow$) and first-order quantifiers ($\exists$, $\forall$). Of those operators, $\neg$, &, $\Diamond$, $\uparrow$, $\downarrow$, and $\exists$ are treated as primitive, the others as metalinguistic abbreviations in the usual way. Only slight adjustments in what follows are needed for a language with infinitely many non-logical atomic predicates.

In this appendix, a model is a triple $<W, D, V>$ where W is a non-empty set, D is a function mapping each $w \in W$ to a set $D(w)$, and V is a function

---

[55] Fritz forthcoming.
[56] See section 5.9 for more on the distinction between metaphysics and ontology.

mapping each non-logical n-place predicate constant F to a function $V(F)$ mapping each $w \in W$ to $V(F)(w) \subseteq D(w)^n$. We allow $\cup_{w \subseteq W} D(w)$ to be empty (so $\lozenge \exists x\ x{=}x$ is invalid). In that case there are no assignments of values in $\cup_{w \in W} D(w)$ to variables (since we require assignments to be total), so we allow values outside $\cup_{w \in W} D(w)$ to be assigned.[57]

To accommodate the modal operators $\uparrow$ and $\downarrow$, the model theory relativizes the evaluation of a formula in a model at a world on an assignment to a finite sequence of worlds; the sequence parameter acts as a sort of memory. Consider a model $M = <W, D, V>$. Let $W^{<\omega}$ be the set of finite sequences of members of W, $< >$ the empty sequence, and $s^{\wedge}w$ the result of appending $w \in W$ to the sequence s. For a set S, diag(S) is $\{<o, o>: o \in S\}$. $M, w, s, \underline{a} \vDash A$ iff the formula A is true in the model M at $w \in W$ relative to $s \in W^{<\omega}$ on the assignment $\underline{a}$. We define this relation recursively. Here F is any non-logical n-place atomic predicate constant; $v, v_1, \ldots, v_n$ are any individual variables; $\underline{a}[v/o]$ is the assignment like $\underline{a}$ except that it assigns o to v; $w \in W$; $s \in W^{<\omega}$.

$M, w, s, \underline{a} \vDash Fv_1 \ldots v_n$ iff $<\underline{a}(v_1), \ldots, \underline{a}(v_n)> \in V(F)(w)$

$M, w, s, \underline{a} \vDash v_1{=}v_2$ iff $<\underline{a}(v_1), \underline{a}(v_2)> \in$ diag($D(w)$)

$M, w, s, \underline{a} \vDash \neg A$ iff not $M, w, s, \underline{a} \vDash A$

$M, w, s, \underline{a} \vDash A \,\&\, B$ iff $M, w, s, \underline{a} \vDash A$ and $M, w, s, \underline{a} \vDash B$

$M, w, s, \underline{a} \vDash \exists v\, A$ iff for some $o \in D(w)$: $M, w, s, \underline{a}[v/o] \vDash A$

$M, w, s, \underline{a} \vDash \lozenge A$ iff for some $w* \in W$: $M, w*, s, \underline{a} \vDash A$

$M, w, s, \underline{a} \vDash \uparrow A$ iff $M, w, s^{\wedge}w, \underline{a} \vDash A$

$M, w, s^{\wedge}x, \underline{a} \vDash \downarrow A$ iff $M, x, s, \underline{a} \vDash A$

$M, w, < >, \underline{a} \vDash \downarrow A$ iff $M, w, < >, \underline{a} \vDash A$

As an example, we check that the formula $\uparrow \lozenge \exists x \downarrow A$ has the intended effect of quantification over the outer domain $\cup_{w \in W} D(w)$: $M, w, s, \underline{a} \vDash \uparrow \lozenge \exists x \downarrow A$ iff $M, w, s^{\wedge}w, \underline{a} \vDash \lozenge \exists x \downarrow A$ iff for some $w* \in W$: $M, w*, s^{\wedge}w, \underline{a} \vDash \exists x \downarrow A$ iff for some $w* \in W$ and $o \in D(w*)$: $M, w*, s^{\wedge}w, \underline{a}[x/o] \vDash \downarrow A$ iff for some $w* \in W$ and $o \in D(w*)$: $M, w, s, \underline{a}[x/o] \vDash A$ iff for some $o \in \cup_{w* \in W} D(w*)$: $M, w, s, \underline{a}[x/o] \vDash A$, as required. Note that the world parameters have been

---

[57] See Williamson 1999b for discussion of the corresponding problem for non-modal logic.

restored to their original values (w and s) by the end of the computation. The alternative semantics for $\uparrow$ and $\downarrow$ which uses just two world parameters[58] is insufficiently general because it lacks this feature: the clause for $\uparrow$ 'forgets' the original value of one parameter, which therefore cannot be recovered later in the evaluation. The use of finite sequences of worlds solves the problem by enhancing memory power.[59]

For a set of formulas S: M, w, s, $\underline{a} \vDash$ S iff M, w, $\underline{a} \vDash A$ for every $A \in$ S. If S and T are single formulas or sets of such, S $\vDash$ T iff M, w, s, $\underline{a} \vDash$ T whenever M, w, s, $\underline{a} \vDash$ S; $\vDash$ S iff $\{\} \vDash$ S.

We recursively define the mapping $(\ )^{\mathrm{con}}$ for $\mathrm{L\textsc{i}}_\square$, where F is any n-place atomic predicate (logical or non-logical):

$$(Fv_1 \ldots v_n)^{\mathrm{con}} = Fv_1 \ldots v_n \ \& \ Cv_1 \ \& \ldots \& \ Cv_n$$

$$(\neg A)^{\mathrm{con}} = \neg(A)^{\mathrm{con}}$$

$$(A \ \& \ B)^{\mathrm{con}} = (A)^{\mathrm{con}} \ \& \ (B)^{\mathrm{con}}$$

$$(\Diamond A)^{\mathrm{con}} = \Diamond(A)^{\mathrm{con}}$$

$$(\uparrow A)^{\mathrm{con}} = \uparrow(A)^{\mathrm{con}}$$

$$(\downarrow A)^{\mathrm{con}} = \downarrow(A)^{\mathrm{con}}$$

$$(\exists v\, A)^{\mathrm{con}} = \exists v\, (Cv \ \& \ (A)^{\mathrm{con}})$$

A formula A is *neutral* iff for some B, $\vDash A \leftrightarrow (B)^{\mathrm{con}}$. Trivially, $(A)^{\mathrm{con}}$ is always neutral. A set of formulas is neutral iff all its members are.

Notation: M = <W, D, V> is any model, $w \in$ W, $s \in$ W$^{<\omega}$ and $\underline{a}$ is any assignment. M^{con} is the model <W, D^C, V^C> where D$^C(w) = V(C)(w)$ and V$^C(F)(w) = V(F)(w) \cap V(C)(w)^n$. CON$_C$ is $\square\forall x\, Cx$. Neutral(S) = \{A: A is neutral and S $\vDash$ A\}.

For brevity we state the following results without proof.[60]

I.I. $(A \in \mathrm{L\textsc{i}}_\square)$ M, w, s, $\underline{a} \vDash (A)^{\mathrm{con}}$ iff M^{con}, w, s, $\underline{a} \vDash A$

I.2. $(A, B \in \mathrm{L\textsc{i}}_\square)$ If $\vDash A \leftrightarrow B$ then $\vDash (A)^{\mathrm{con}} \leftrightarrow (B)^{\mathrm{con}}$

I.3. $(A \in \mathrm{L\textsc{i}}_\square)$ $\vDash ((A)^{\mathrm{con}})^{\mathrm{con}} \leftrightarrow (A)^{\mathrm{con}}$

---

[58] See Forbes 1989, pp. 28–9.
[59] With minor differences the technique goes back to Vlach 1973 and Hodes 1984 (see also Correia 2007).
[60] Proofs of all the results are in Williamson 2010, pp. 729–48 (with trivial differences of presentation).

1.4. $(A \in Li_\square)$ If A is neutral, $\vDash (A)^{con} \leftrightarrow A$

1.5. $M^{con}, w, s, \underline{a} \vDash CON_C$

1.6. $(CON_C)^{con} \leftrightarrow CON_C \vDash CON_C$

1.7.   If $M, w, s, \underline{a} \vDash CON_C$ then $M^{con} = M$

1.8. $(A \in Li_\square)$ $CON_C \vDash (A)^{con} \leftrightarrow A$

1.9. $(A \in Li_\square, S \subseteq Li_\square)$ If A and S are neutral, then $S, CON_C \vDash A$ only if $S \vDash A$

1.10. $(A,B \in Li_\square)$ If B is neutral and $CON_C \vDash A \leftrightarrow B$ then $\vDash (A)^{con} \leftrightarrow B$

1.11. $(S,T \subseteq Li_\square)$ If $S \vDash CON_C$ and $T \vDash CON_C$ then $S \vDash T$ iff $Neutral(S) \vDash Neutral(T)$

1.12. $(T \subseteq Li_\square)$ If $T \vDash CON_C$ then $T \dashv\vDash Neutral(T), CON_C$

Next we define the mapping ( )^{nec} for $Li_\square$, where F is any n-place non-logical atomic predicate:

$(Fv_1 \ldots v_n)^{nec} = Fv_1 \ldots v_n \ \& \ Cv_1 \ \& \ldots \& \ Cv_n$

$(v_1 = v_2)^{nec} = \Diamond(v_1 = v_2 \ \& \ Cv_1 \ \& \ Cv_2)$

$(\neg A)^{nec} = \neg(A)^{nec}$

$(A \ \& \ B)^{nec} = (A)^{nec} \ \& \ (B)^{nec}$

$(\Diamond A)^{nec} = \Diamond(A)^{nec}$

$(\uparrow A)^{nec} = \uparrow(A)^{nec}$

$(\downarrow A)^{nec} = \downarrow(A)^{nec}$

$(\exists v \, A)^{nec} = \uparrow \Diamond \exists v \, (Cv \ \& \ \downarrow(A)^{nec})$

More notation: For $M = \langle W, D, V \rangle$, M^{nec} is the model $\langle W, D^N, V^C \rangle$, where V^C is as before and $D^N(w) = \cup_{w^* \in W} V(C)(w^*)$. If $z_1, \ldots, z_n$ are the first n distinct variables and F any non-logical n-place predicate, $F \leq C$ is $\forall z_1 \ldots \forall z_n (Fz_1 \ldots z_n \to (Cz_1 \ \& \ldots \& \ Cz_n))$. NEC_C is the conjunction of $\square \forall x \, \square \exists y \, x = y$, $\forall x \, \Diamond Cx$ and $\square F \leq C$ for all such predicates F.

The results about $(\ )^{\text{nec}}$ correspond to those about $(\ )^{\text{con}}$.

1.13. $(A \in \text{L}1_\square)$ $M, w, s, \underline{a} \vDash (A)^{\text{nec}}$ iff $M^{\text{nec}}, w, s, \underline{a} \vDash A$

1.14. $(A, B \in \text{L}1_\square)$ If $\vDash A \leftrightarrow B$ then $\vDash (A)^{\text{nec}} \leftrightarrow (B)^{\text{nec}}$

1.15. $(A \in \text{L}1_\square)$ $(A)^{\text{nec}}$ is neutral

1.16. $(A \in \text{L}1_\square)$ $\vDash ((A)^{\text{con}})^{\text{nec}} \leftrightarrow (A)^{\text{con}}$

1.17. $(A \in \text{L}1_\square)$ If A is neutral, $(A)^{\text{nec}} \leftrightarrow A$

1.18. $M^{\text{nec}}, w, s, \underline{a} \vDash \text{NEC}_C$

1.19. $(\text{NEC}_C)^{\text{nec}} \leftrightarrow \text{NEC}_C \vDash \text{NEC}_C$

1.20.   If $M, w, s, \underline{a} \vDash \text{NEC}_C$ then $M^{\text{nec}} = M$

1.21. $(A \in \text{L}1_\square)$ $\text{NEC}_C \vDash (A)^{\text{nec}} \leftrightarrow A$

1.22. $(A \in \text{L}1_\square, S \subseteq \text{L}1_\square)$ If A and S are neutral, then $S, \text{NEC}_C \vDash A$ only if $S \vDash A$

1.23. $(A, B \in \text{L}1_\square)$ If B is neutral and $\text{NEC}_C \vDash A \leftrightarrow B$ then $\vDash (A)^{\text{nec}} \leftrightarrow B$

1.24. $(S, T \subseteq \text{L}1_\square)$ If $S \vDash \text{NEC}_C$ and $T \vDash \text{NEC}_C$ then $S \vDash T$ iff Neutral(S) $\vDash$ Neutral(T).

1.25. $(T \subseteq \text{L}1_\square)$ If $T \vDash \text{NEC}_C$ then $T \dashv \vDash$ Neutral(T), NEC_C

1.26. $\vDash (\text{CON}_C)^{\text{nec}} \leftrightarrow \square \forall x\ (Cx \rightarrow \square Cx)$

1.27. $\vDash (\text{NEC}_C)^{\text{con}} \leftrightarrow \square \forall x\ (Cx \rightarrow \square Cx)$

1.28. $(A \in \text{L}1_\square)$ If A is neutral, NEC_C & $\text{CON}_C \vDash A$ iff $\square \forall x\ (Cx \rightarrow \square Cx) \vDash A$

Now we extend $\text{L}1_\square$ to a second-order modal language $\text{L}2_\square$ by adding for each natural number n a countable infinity of n-place second-order variables, bindable by $\exists$ (no confusion with first-order quantification results). The models are as before. An assignment is any total function from variables. The new semantic clauses are these:

$M, w, s, \underline{a} \vDash V v_1 \ldots v_n$ iff $\langle \underline{a}(v_1), \ldots, \underline{a}(v_n) \rangle \in \underline{a}(V) \subseteq D(w)^n$

$M, w, s, \underline{a} \vDash \exists V A$ iff for some $S \subseteq D(w)^n$: $M, w, s, \underline{a}[V/S] \vDash A$

For example, we check the invalidity of second-order BF and CBF. Let $M = <W, D, V>$ where $W = \{w_1, w_2\}$, $D(w_1) = \{0\}$, and $D(w_2) = \{0, 1\}$. Thus:

$$M, w_1, s, \underline{a} \vDash \Diamond \exists X \, \exists x \, \exists y \, (Xx \,\&\, Xy \,\&\, \neg x{=}y)$$

For $M, w_2, s, \underline{a} \vDash \exists X \, \exists x \, \exists y \, (Xx \,\&\, Xy \,\&\, \neg x{=}y)$. But we do not have:

$$M, w_1, s, \underline{a} \vDash \exists X \, \Diamond \exists x \, \exists y \, (Xx \,\&\, Xy \,\&\, \neg x{=}y)$$

For at w_1 the second-order quantifier is restricted to subsets of $\{0\}$. Conversely, we have:

$$M, w_2, s, \underline{a} \vDash \exists X \, \Diamond \exists x \, (\Diamond Xx \,\&\, \neg Xx)$$

For $M, w_1, s, \underline{a}[X/\{0, 1\}][x/0] \vDash \Diamond Xx \,\&\, \neg Xx$. But we do not have:

$$M, w_2, s, \underline{a} \vDash \Diamond \exists X \, \exists x \, (\Diamond Xx \,\&\, \neg Xx)$$

For if $M, w, s, \underline{a} \vDash \neg Xx$, $\underline{a}(x) \in D(w)$, and $\underline{a}(X) \subseteq D(w)$, then $\underline{a}(x) \notin \underline{a}(X)$ so not $M, w, s, \underline{a} \vDash \Diamond Xx$.

We extend the definition of $(A)^{\mathrm{con}}$ to $L2_\square$ by these clauses, where $V{\leq}C$ is $\forall x_1 \ldots \forall x_n \, (V x_1 \ldots x_n \rightarrow (C x_1 \,\&\, \ldots \,\&\, C x_n))$:

$$(V v_1 \ldots v_n)^{\mathrm{con}} = V v_1 \ldots v_n \,\&\, V{\leq}C$$

$$(\exists V A)^{\mathrm{con}} = \exists V \, (V{\leq}C \,\&\, (A)^{\mathrm{con}})$$

In the context of $L2_\square$, A is neutral iff $\vDash A \leftrightarrow (B)^{\mathrm{con}}$ for some formula B of $L2_\square$.

The results 1.1–1.12 about $(\ )^{\mathrm{con}}$ for $L1_\square$ all extend smoothly to $L2_\square$, including the key result that every formula A is equivalent given CON_C to a neutral formula. But no mapping $(\ )^{\mathrm{nec}}$ maps each formula A of $L2_\square$ to a formula of $L2_\square$ equivalent to A given NEC_C. For example, this formula can be shown not to be equivalent to any neutral formula of $L2_\square$ given NEC_C: $\exists X \, (\exists x \, Xx \,\&\, \exists x \, \neg Xx \,\&\, \forall x \forall y \, (\Diamond Rxy \rightarrow (Xx \rightarrow Xy)))$.

The negative result generalizes to infinitary languages. Let $L2$ be the non-modal fragment of $L2_\square$, excluding the predicate constant C, and $L1_{\infty\infty}$ be an infinitary first-order non-modal language with the same predicate constants as $L2$ and an unlimited supply of variables; it is closed under $\neg, \exists$ binding any set of first-order variables and $\wedge$ over any set of formulas (Dickmann 1985). $L2_{\infty\infty\square}$ is an infinitary second-order modal language with the resources of $L1_{\infty\infty}$ and an unlimited supply of second-order variables, the predicate constant C, $\exists$ binding any set of second-order variables, and the operators $\square$, $\uparrow$, and $\downarrow$. The model theory for the infinitary languages is standard (see section 5.7 for some relevant discussion). In particular, the models for $L1_{\infty\infty}$ and $L2_{\infty\infty\square}$ are just those for the corresponding finitary non-modal and modal languages respectively.

We extend the mapping $(\ )^{\mathrm{con}}$ to $L2_{\infty\infty\square}$ in the obvious way:

$$(\wedge_{i\in I} A_i)^{\mathrm{con}} = \wedge_{i\in I} (A_i)^{\mathrm{con}}$$

$$(\exists\{v_i\}_{i\in I}\, A)^{\mathrm{con}} = \exists\{v_i\}_{i\in I} ((\wedge_{i\in I} Cv_i)\ \&\ (A)^{\mathrm{con}})$$

$$(\exists\{V_i\}_{i\in I}\, A)^{\mathrm{con}} = \exists\{V_i\}_{i\in I} ((\wedge_{i\in I} V_i {\le} C)\ \&\ (A)^{\mathrm{con}})$$

As usual, $A \in L2_{\infty\infty\square}$ is neutral iff for some $B \in L2_{\infty\infty\square}$, $\vDash A \leftrightarrow (B)^{\mathrm{con}}$.

For any formula A of L2, let $A^{\lozenge}$ be the result of prefixing $\lozenge$ to each non-logical predicate constant in A. Then we can show that for any closed formula A of L2, $A^{\lozenge}$ is equivalent to a neutral formula of $L2_{\infty\infty\square}$ given NEC_C only if A is logically equivalent to a formula of $L1_{\infty\infty}$. But many closed formulas A of L2 are logically equivalent to no formula of $L1_{\infty\infty}$.[61] Therefore the corresponding formulas $A^{\lozenge}$ of $L2_{\infty\infty\square}$ are not equivalent given NEC_C to any neutral formula of $L2_{\infty\infty\square}$.[62]

---

[61] See Dickmann 1985, p. 323.

[62] For some relevant general negative results and a flexible proof technique see Fritz forthcoming.

8

Consequences of Necessitism

8.1 The necessary framework of objects

Chapters 6 and 7 focused on the disadvantages of contingentism as a logical metaphysics, by comparison with necessitism. This chapter develops a necessitist alternative more fully. This section employs a formal language to describe more systematically and precisely the necessary and permanent ontological framework for metaphysics that necessitism and permanentism provide. Section 8.2 isolates a sense in which necessitists should view modal properties as irreducible to non-modal ones, and evaluates such a commitment. Section 8.3 explains why necessitism entails that there are no truthmakers on a hard-line conception of the latter, and why that consequence is unworrying. Section 8.4 discusses theories that deny contingency and change in more radical ways than necessitism and permanentism do, and finds the semantic arguments for such theories much less compelling than some take them to be.

A passage from Wittgenstein's *Tractatus*, already quoted in section 1.1, adumbrates the necessitist and permanentist outlook: 'Objects are what is unalterable and subsistent; their configuration is what is changing and unstable' (2.0271). To clarify this conception, we can describe a formal language for speaking purely about this necessary and permanent framework of objects. Every formula of the language will be, if true, a necessary and permanent truth; if false, a necessary and permanent falsehood. We saw in section 3.7 that necessitists (unlike contingentists) can straightforwardly use quantification over possible worlds to give the intended truth conditions of their sentences in compositional terms. For similar reasons, permanentists (unlike temporaryists) can straightforwardly use quantification over times to do likewise. Adopting a necessitist and permanentist perspective, we may therefore quantify over both possible worlds and times to describe the semantics of the language more conveniently.

We do not speak of models, because the language has no non-logical semantic features to vary over models. Our concern is simply to give the intended truth conditions of formulas. When we speak of possible worlds in the metalanguage, we mean genuinely metaphysically possible worlds, along the necessitist lines explained in section 3.7, rather than members of an arbitrary set W as a constituent of a model. Similarly, when we speak of times in the metalanguage, we mean genuine past, present, and future times, rather than members of an arbitrary set T as a constituent of a model.

The language has countably many singular variables $x, y, z, \ldots$ and countably many plural variables $xx, yy, zz, \ldots$. An assignment assigns exactly one object to each singular variable and some objects to each plural variable; for convenience, we may slightly diverge from English and allow the vacuous case where an assignment assigns no objects to a plural variable.[1] Assignments are not relative to worlds or times. The language has no constant singular or plural terms.

Formulas are evaluated on an assignment relative to both a possible world and a time, but only to register their constancy on both dimensions. A formula is *rigid* just if, for every assignment a, it is either true on a relative to every world and time or false (so not true) on a relative to every world and time. Thus every formula of the language will be rigid.

There are two primitive predicates, $=$ and $\prec$, both treated as logical constants. An atomic formula is either of the form $u=v$, where u and v are singular variables, or of the form $u \prec vv$, where u is a singular variable and vv is a plural variable. A formula $u=v$ is true on an assignment a at a world w at a time t if and only if the object a assigns u is identical with the object a assigns v. As discussed in section 1.7, on a necessitist and permanentist view identity is a necessary and permanent matter, so w and t need not be mentioned on the right-hand side of the biconditional. A formula $u \prec vv$ is true on a at w at t if and only if the object a assigns u is one of the objects a assigns vv. As discussed in section 5.8, on a necessitist and permanentist view,

---

[1] Strictly, the talk of 'assignments' should be rephrased in plural terms, as in Rayo and Uzquiano 1999, to permit unrestricted plural quantification without a Russell-type paradox. See also sections 3.7 and 5.7.

being one of is a necessary and permanent matter too, so again *w* and *t* need not be mentioned on the right-hand side of the biconditional. Thus every atomic formula is rigid.

To build complex formulas, we use the primitive operators ¬, &, ◊, and **S**, and the primitive quantifier ∃. Other standard operators are introduced by the usual metalinguistic abbreviations. The semantic clauses are also the usual ones. Let *A* and *B* be any formulas, *a* any assignment, *w* any world, and *t* any time.

For the truth functors, *A* & *B* is true on *a* at *w* at *t* if and only *A* is true on *a* at *w* at *t* and *B* is true on *a* at *w* at *t*; ¬*A* is true on *a* at *w* at *t* if and only if *A* is not true on *a* at *w* at *t*. Evidently, these biconditionals transmit rigidity from right to left: if the truth values of *A* and *B* are independent of *w* and *t* for given *a*, so are the truth values of *A* & *B* and ¬*A*.

For the modal operator, ◊*A* is true on *a* at *w* at *t* if and only if *A* is true on *a* at some possible world at *t*. This clause too transmits rigidity from right to left. Indeed, it would make ◊*A* rigid at least with respect to the modal dimension even if *A* were not, for '*w*' does not occur on the right-hand side. Proponents of a propositional modal logic weaker than S5 for metaphysical modality would lose the latter feature by qualifying 'some possible world' with 'accessible from *w*'. For them, ◊*A* could be modally non-rigid if *A* were modally non-rigid.[2] However, if *A* is modally rigid, then even the clause with 'accessible from *w*' added makes ◊*A* modally rigid too.[3]

For the temporal operator, **S***A* is true on *a* at *w* at *t* if and only if *A* is true on *a* at *w* at some time. As before, this clause transmits rigidity from right to left. It would also make **S***A* rigid at least with respect to the temporal dimension even if *A* were not, for '*t*' does not occur on the right-hand side. It does not share that feature with operators such as **P** ('in the past') and **F** ('in the future'); **P***A* and **F***A* could be temporally non-rigid if *A* were temporally non-rigid. However, if *A* is rigid, then even **P***A* and **F***A* are rigid,

---

[2] Formally, the same situation might arise even for proponents of S5 if they allow accessibility to be an equivalence relation with more than one equivalence class; but such a view lacks obvious motivation.

[3] Formally, if *A* is rigid, ◊*A* will be rigid too provided that either every world or no world has access to no world. The condition obtains because metaphysical necessity entails truth (L*p* ≤ *p* for every proposition *p* in the sense of the Boolean algebra in Chapter 3), so accessibility is reflexive (and the T axiom is metaphysically universal).

provided that time has no first or last moment respectively. For simplicity, we omit **P** and **F** from the language.[4]

For the quantifier, $\exists v\, A$ is true on $\underline{a}$ at w at t if and only if A is true on some assignment that differs from $\underline{a}$ at most in what it assigns to v at w at t; likewise for plural variables. Yet again, the clause transmits rigidity from right to left. It would not do so if varying domains were associated with world-time pairs, 'some assignment' were restricted to assignments assigning the variable at issue a value (or, in the plural case, values) in the domain associated with the pair $<w, t>$, and some but not all world-time pairs were associated with the empty domain. Under those circumstances, although a truth-functional tautology A is rigid, because true on every assignment at every world at every time, $\exists v\, A$ is non-rigid, because false on $\underline{a}$ at w at t if the domain associated with $<w, t>$ is empty, but true otherwise. Of course, permanentist necessitists reject any such restriction of the quantifier in the metalanguage for contexts such as this in which the unrestricted reading of the quantifier in the object-language is intended.

Thus every formula of the language, open or closed, is rigid. Consequently, all instances in the language of the schemas $\Box A \leftrightarrow A$, $\mathbf{S}A \leftrightarrow A$, and $\Box \mathbf{S}A \vee \Box \mathbf{S}\neg A$ are true on every assignment at every possible world at every time. Hence all such instances are absolutely true, that is, true on every assignment at the actual world at the present time. Since the language contains no non-logical constants for present purposes, every absolutely true formula is metaphysically universal in the sense of Chapters 3 and 5, and of course conversely. The absolutely true formulas are closed under the rules of modus ponens, necessitation and permanentization (its analogue for

[4] For simplicity, the temporal operators have been interpreted as quantifiers over a constant set of times (here 'times' covers past, present, and future moments, whether or not past and future moments count as moments *simpliciter*). However, it may be plausibly argued that it is contingent what times there are (compatibly with necessitism; perhaps a time could have been a merely possible time): for example, there could have been more times than there actually are. If so, we obtain a purer temporal operator by restricting the quantifier to what are times in the world of evaluation. This creates various complications: if there could have been no time then $\mathbf{S}\forall x\, x{=}x$ is a contingent truth, and so non-rigid. Since our primary interest here is in the modal dimension, we avoid such issues by stipulating that $\mathbf{S}$ ranges over a constant domain comprising merely possible times as well as actual ones, without prejudice to the legitimacy and interest of the alternative interpretation. An unrestricted treatment of the temporal dimension fits this book's overall approach. Some appropriate stipulation for evaluating atomic formulas at w at t where t is not a time in w must also be made. Since the natural clauses for the modal operators quantify over all possible worlds, not just those in which the given value of the parameter t is a time, such a stipulation is anyway needed.

$\ulcorner\mathbf{S}\urcorner$, 'always'), and uniform substitution. They constitute a skeletal plural modal logic that is also a piece of basic metaphysics.

We can envisage many extensions of the language all formulas of which are rigid too. The features some or all of which we could so add include: variables for superplurals of higher types, obligatorily constant in extension across worlds and times; uses of $\exists$ binding arbitrarily large sets of variables of a given type; generalized quantifiers; conjunctions and disjunctions of arbitrarily large sets of formulas; further modal and temporal operators, including multidimensional ones such as $\uparrow$ and $\downarrow$. They introduce no non-logical constants and only mildly enhance the metaphysical picture.

With or without such additions, the language has the expressive power to describe a necessary and permanent structure of objects, taken separately and together, that constitutes a space for the play of contingency and change. To describe the general scope for such contingency and change, we must reintroduce predicate variables permitted to vary in extension across worlds and times, reverting to a more expressively powerful language such as ML_P in section 5.5. To describe specific contingencies and changes, we must reintroduce corresponding predicate constants and constant singular and plural terms. For the rest of this chapter we employ languages with such non-rigid formulas.

8.2 Supervenience in question

When necessitists postulate contingently non-concrete objects, they are often suspected of allowing the modal to float illicitly free of the non-modal.[5] For example, a non-concrete merely possible child of Wittgenstein has the modal property of being a possible child of Wittgenstein, with no apparent grounding in its non-modal properties. Before ruling on the relation of the modal to the non-modal, we must be more precise about what exactly is at issue. A promising way to do so is by formulating the alleged phenomenon as a failure of supervenience, a modal difference with no corresponding non-modal difference. For example, a merely possible child of Wittgenstein differs modally from a merely possible child of Russell, because only the former has the modal property of being a possible child of Wittgenstein (on

---

[5] For simplicity we may ignore the temporal dimension for the present; although permanentism raises formally analogous issues, many will find them less pressing (but see Sider 2001, pp. 35–42).

the relevant form of essentialism about origins); is there any corresponding non-modal difference between them? This section explores such questions of supervenience within a necessitist framework.

The distinction between 'modal' and 'non-modal' properties and relations is much less clear than is often assumed. For instance, is identity a modal relation? The formula $x=y$ contains no modal operator, but is strictly equivalent to the modal formula $\Box x=y$. We cannot classify identity as a non-modal relation but necessary identity as a modal one, for on the coarse-grained conception of properties and relations appropriate to the concerns of this book, the necessary equivalence of identity and necessary identity makes them the same relation. Nor can we classify identity as 'implicitly' a modal relation just because $x=y$ entails a modal formula, for *every* formula entails some modal formulas: most simply, Fx entails $\Diamond Fx$. That 'x is square' entails 'x is possibly square' does not make squareness a modal property. Whether a predicate defines a modal property or relation depends only on its intension: given only an intension, how do we classify it as modal or as non-modal?

At the syntactic level, some relevant distinctions are easily made, at least for a given formal language. Consider a first-order modal language whose only primitive operators are $\Diamond$, $\neg$, $\&$, $\exists$, and λ. A formula is *purely non-modal* just if it has no occurrences of $\Diamond$. It is *fully modalized* just if it has atomic formulas only in the scope of modal operators. Thus any atomic formula is purely non-modal and not fully modalized; any formula of the form $\Diamond A$ is fully modalized and not purely non-modal; $\neg A$ is purely non-modal just if A is purely non-modal, and fully modalized just if A is fully modalized; $A \& B$ is purely non-modal just if both A and B are purely non-modal, and fully modalized just if both A and B are fully modalized; $\exists v\, A$ is purely non-modal just if A is purely non-modal, and fully modalized just if A is fully modalized. No formula is both purely non-modal and fully modalized. A formula is *hybrid* just if it is neither purely non-modal nor fully modalized. With the λ-operator, we make corresponding distinctions amongst predicates. The difficulty is in determining how best to project these distinctions onto the corresponding intensions, even granted a unique intended model for the language. For formulas classified differently may be intensionally equivalent. For example, if the atomic formula A has the necessary intension, then the purely non-modal formula A, the fully modalized formula $\Diamond A$, and the hybrid formula $\Diamond A \rightarrow A$ all determine the same intension;

likewise for any purely non-modal tautology in place of A. How, and on what basis, do we classify that intension?

In necessitist S5 (although typically not in weaker modal systems), every fully modalized formula is rigid: on a given assignment its intension returns the same truth value at every world. This suggests the proposal that an intension is modal just if it is constant across worlds. But that criterion does not generalize properly to more expressive languages. For example, although sentences with counterfactual conditionals or operators for physical or practical possibility are modal in the philosophically relevant sense, many of them express contingencies: 'If you had turned round, you would have seen her'; 'You could easily have reached the jam'. Moreover, if we count all non-constant intensions as non-modal and put them in the supervenience base, we trivialize the supervenience of the modal on the non-modal, for every constant intension is a truth function of two non-constant intensions.[6]

At the level of intensions, no appropriate formal criterion for selecting a supervenience base of 'non-modal' intensions suggests itself. This is no problem for necessitists. If the relevant cut between the modal and the non-modal cannot be made, the sort of objection to necessitism at issue in this section does not get off the ground. For the sake of argument, however, suppose that contingentists have somehow or other isolated a class of 'categorical', non-modal properties and relations to form a suitable supervenience base, and have introduced enough predicate constants into the language (infinitely many, no doubt) to express them all and nothing else. For example, they might regard the supervenience base as comprising the perfectly natural properties and relations. Given an intended model of the language, we can now make sense of questions about whether the modal supervenes on the non-modal. The proposed supervenience base in effect consists of the intensions of the purely non-modal formulas and predicates. We can focus on the putative supervenience of fully modalized formulas and predicates on them, since the original objection was raised in such terms. For example, there is the purely non-modal formula Rxy, read 'x is a child of y', and the fully modalized formula $\Diamond Rxy$. Since our present concern is with the consequences of necessitism, we assume that the model validates necessitist S5.

---

[6] Proof: Work with intensions of a given type; apply truth functors to them in the natural way. We may assume that there are non-constant (i.e. contingent) intensions. Let i be a constant intension, and j a non-constant intension. Then $i \leftrightarrow j$ is also non-constant, for if it were constant so would be $i \leftrightarrow (i \leftrightarrow j)$, which it is not, since $i \leftrightarrow (i \leftrightarrow j) = j$. But $(i \leftrightarrow j) \leftrightarrow j = i$.

Here is a simple-minded initial attempt to state the required superveni-ence thesis. Let F be any n-place predicate (which may be complex and contain free variables as parameters), $o_1, \ldots, o_n, o_1{}^*, \ldots, o_n{}^*$ any individuals, and w and w^* any possible worlds. Call $<o_1, \ldots, o_n, w>$ *F-similar* to $<o_1{}^*, \ldots, o_n{}^*, w^*>$ if and only if for every assignment $\underline{a}$, $<o_1, \ldots, o_n>$ satisfies F at w on $\underline{a}$ just if $<o_1{}^*, \ldots, o_n{}^*>$ satisfies F at w^* on $\underline{a}$. Call $<o_1, \ldots, o_n, w>$ *non-modally similar* to $<o_1{}^*, \ldots, o_n{}^*, w^*>$ if and only if they are F-similar for every purely non-modal predicate F. An n-place predicate F *supervenes on the non-modal* if and only if for all individuals $o_1, \ldots, o_n, o_1{}^*, \ldots, o_n{}^*$ and worlds w and w^*, if $<o_1, \ldots, o_n, w>$ is non-modally similar to $<o_1{}^*, \ldots, o_n{}^*, w^*>$ then $<o_1, \ldots, o_n, w>$ is F-similar to $<o_1{}^*, \ldots, o_n{}^*, w^*>$.

For $n = 0$, supervenience on the non-modal is trivial. In this special case non-modal similarity amounts to a relation between worlds: w is non-modally similar to w^* just if the same purely non-modal formulas are true at w and w^* on each fixed assignment. Any fully modalized formula is rigid in necessitist S5, so the same fully modalized formulas are true at all worlds on each fixed assignment. All worlds are the same in all modal respects. Thus variation in truth value between worlds comes only from atomic formulas outside the scope of modal operators. Consequently, if two worlds are non-modally similar, they are A-similar for every formula A of the language.[7] Thus every formula supervenes on the non-modal.

If the language contains an atomic predicate for identity, the result ex-tends to all predicates. For suppose that $<o_1, \ldots, o_n, w>$ is non-modally similar to $<o_1{}^*, \ldots, o_n{}^*, w^*>$. Let A be the purely non-modal formula $x_1 = y_1 \,\&\, \ldots \,\&\, x_n = y_n$ (where $y_1, \ldots, y_n$ are n variables distinct from $x_1, \ldots, x_n$), and $\underline{a}$ an assignment such that $\underline{a}(y_i)$ is o_i for $1 \leq i \leq n$. Thus $<o_1, \ldots, o_n>$ satisfies $\lambda x_1 \ldots x_n(A)$ at w on $\underline{a}$. Hence $<o_1{}^*, \ldots, o_n{}^*>$ satisfies $\lambda x_1 \ldots x_n(A)$ at w^* on $\underline{a}$, so $\underline{a}(y_i)$ is $o_i{}^*$ for $1 \leq i \leq n$. Thus $o_i{}^*$ is o_i for $1 \leq i \leq n$. Let F be any fully modalized formula. By rigidity, $<o_1, \ldots, o_n>$ satisfies F at all worlds or none, on a fixed assignment. Thus $<o_1, \ldots, o_n>$ satisfies F at w just if $<o_1{}^*, \ldots, o_n{}^*>$, which is $<o_1, \ldots, o_n>$, satisfies F at w^* on that assignment. Therefore every fully modalized predicate supervenes on the non-modal. As before, the result generalizes to all predicates of the language.

To understand what is going on, let o_1 be a merely possible child of Wittgenstein and o_2 a merely possible child of Russell; o_2 is not a possible

---

[7] As usual, 0-place predicates are identified with formulas.

child of Wittgenstein. Read Cxa as 'x is a child of Wittgenstein'. Thus o_1 satisfies $\lambda x(\lozenge Cxa)$ at any world and o_2 satisfies it at no world, whatever the assignment. If o_1 and o_2 satisfy the same purely non-modal predicates at the actual world, $\lambda x(\lozenge Cxa)$ fails to supervene on the non-modal. But o_1 and o_2 differ in their purely non-modal predicates at any world, because o_1, unlike o_2, satisfies $\lambda x(x=y)$ on an assignment $\underline{a}$ for which $\underline{a}(y)$ is o_1. Thus the case is no counterexample to the supervenience of the modal on the non-modal in the sense just defined. The difference in identity between o_1 and o_2 counts as a non-modal difference.

The argument makes two significant assumptions, in addition to necessitism: that S5 is the correct background propositional modal logic, and that identity is a non-modal relation. The assumption of necessitism is uncontroversial in this dialectical context, for the question is what it entails. Both the additional assumptions can be questioned. However, doing so is an unpromising way for contingentists to press the supervenience objection. They are trying to show necessitism to have wild consequences. If necessitists can avoid those consequences simply by endorsing S5 and the non-modal nature of identity, both mainstream positions, then it is the contingentist objection that depends on wild assumptions. For S5 is the simplest, most natural, and standard propositional modal logic for metaphysical modality, and by itself has no distinctively necessitist consequences. Similarly, it would be eccentric to treat identity as importing a modal element into elementary logic or mathematics. The equivalence of being identical to being necessarily identical (and to being possibly identical) no more makes identity modal than its equivalence to being always identical (and to being sometimes identical) makes identity temporal.[8]

A more promising line for contingentists is to acquiesce in necessitists' acceptance of S5 and the non-modal nature of identity, but to define a more discriminating sort of supervenience incompatible with the necessitist view. The idea is that the necessitist must deny the supervenience of *general* (or

---

[8] In response to the classification of the property of being the river Inn as non-modal in Williamson 1998, Winfried Löffler writes: 'Then the following seems conceivable: An object x may be the river Inn in world$_1$, and a possible river in world$_2$, but it does not follow that it is the possible Inn in world$_2$. And it seems to be possible that x is a river in world$_2$, but e.g., the Mississippi' (1998, p. 277). He adds that this is not excluded by the necessity of identity and distinctness. Löffler may have misunderstood what I mean by calling a property 'non-modal'. A non-modal property can have modal consequences (being square entails being possibly square). Names are rigid designators; 'Inn' and 'Mississippi' name distinct rivers; the Inn is necessarily a possible river and necessarily distinct from the Mississippi ($i{\neq}m \rightarrow \Box i{\neq}m$), although not necessarily a river.

qualitative) modal properties on *general* non-modal properties, where properties such as being identical with o_1 do not count as general. We suppose
that contingentists have somehow or other isolated a class of general 'categorical', non-modal properties and relations to form a suitable supervenience base, and have introduced enough predicate constants into the language
(infinitely many, no doubt) to express them all and nothing else. At the
syntactic level, the general predicates are those that contain no individual
constants or free variables, which act as individual parameters. Thus $\lambda x(x{=}y)$
is not a general predicate, although $\lambda xy(x{=}y)$ and $\lambda x(x{=}x)$ are. Call $<o_1, \ldots,$
$o_n, w>$ *non-modally similar* to $<o_1{*}, \ldots, o_n{*}, w{*}>$ *in general respects* if and only
if they are F-similar for every general purely non-modal predicate F. An
n-place predicate F *supervenes on the general non-modal* if and only if for all
individuals $o_1, \ldots, o_n, o_1{*}, \ldots, o_n{*}$ and worlds w and $w{*}$, if $<o_1, \ldots, o_n, w>$
is non-modally similar to $<o_1{*}, \ldots, o_n{*}, w{*}>$ in general respects then
$<o_1, \ldots, o_n, w>$ is F-similar to $<o_1{*}, \ldots, o_n{*}, w{*}>$.

For $n = 0$, the situation hardly changes: all general formulas trivially supervene on the general non-modal. In this special case, non-modal similarity in
general respects amounts to a relation that holds between worlds just if the
same general purely non-modal formulas (closed formulas without individual constants or modal operators) are true at them. As before, the same
fully modalized formulas (general and non-general) are true at all worlds on
each fixed assignment. Thus variation in truth value between worlds comes
only from atomic formulas outside the scope of modal operators. Consequently, every general formula supervenes on the general non-modal.

For $n > 0$, the situation is now very different. General modal predicates
may fail to supervene on the general non-modal, even in the setting of
necessitist S5, with identity treated as non-modal (and general). Here is a toy
example. There are just two possible worlds, w and $w{*}$, two individuals, o and
$o{*}$, and one non-logical predicate constant, the one-place F. The extension
of F at w is empty; its extension at $w{*}$ contains only o. Informally, regard
both individuals as concrete in $w{*}$ but not in w. If we take w in isolation
from $w{*}$, it is perfectly symmetrical between o and $o{*}$. Thus o and $o{*}$ satisfy
the same general purely non-modal predicates at w.[9] Formally, $<o, w>$ is

---

[9] Technically, the permutation that interchanges o and $o{*}$ is an automorphism of the non-modal model
corresponding to w. Although the pair $<o, o{*}>$, unlike $<o, o>$, fails to satisfy the general two-place
predicate '$=$', this produces no difference between o and $o{*}$ at the level of one-place predicates. In
Quinean terms, o and $o{*}$ are weakly but neither moderately nor strongly discriminable in this non-
modal model (Quine 1976).

non-modally similar to $<o*, w>$ in general respects. However, since $\lozenge Fx$ is true at w if o is assigned to x but not if $o*$ is, $<o, w>$ is not $\lambda x(\lozenge Fx)$-similar to $<o*, w>$. Thus the general fully modalized predicate $\lambda x(\lozenge Fx)$ does not supervene on the general non-modal in this model.[10] Of course, the real issue is whether such failures of supervenience occur in the intended model, but from a necessitist perspective there is no obvious obstacle. Let o be a merely possible mountain, $o*$ a merely possible river, M express the property of being a mountain, and $w_@$ be the actual world. Then perhaps $<o, w_@>$ is non-modally similar to $<o*, w_@>$ in general respects, but o satisfies $\lambda x(\lozenge Mx)$ while $o*$ does not, so the general modal does not supervene on the general non-modal in the intended model.

The examples show that necessitism may undermine even a weaker form of the supervenience of the modal on the non-modal. An n-place predicate F *weakly supervenes on the general non-modal* if and only if for all individuals $o_1, \ldots, o_n, o_1*, \ldots, o_n*$ and worlds w, if $<o_1, \ldots, o_n, w>$ is non-modally similar to $<o_1*, \ldots, o_n*, w>$ in general respects then $<o_1, \ldots, o_n, w>$ is F-similar to $<o_1*, \ldots, o_n*, w>$. Weak supervenience ignores cross-world differences between individuals.[11] The examples a moment ago of failures of (strong) supervenience also exemplify failures of weak supervenience.

Is the non-supervenience of the general modal on the general non-modal a bad outcome? Pre-theoretically, most of us do not expect the general temporal to supervene on the general non-temporal.[12] That two objects should have differed qualitatively in the past without differing qualitatively in the present is hardly surprising. Two pebbles qualitatively distinct at one time may become qualitatively identical through a process of erosion. For a permanentist, the differences between a long-vanished ant and a long-vanished bee may have left no trace in the present. In this respect, why should there be an asymmetry between the modal and the temporal? Although the analogy must break down at some point, it should at least discourage us from assuming without argument that the general modal supervenes on the general non-modal.

---

[10] Of course, the non-general one-place predicate $\lambda x(x=y)$ (not to be confused with the general two-place predicate $\lambda xy(x=y)$) does not supervene on the general non-modal either, since it is satisfied by o but not $o*$ when y is assigned o, but that is expected. Such failures of the *non*-general to supervene on the general non-modal are inevitable, unless the non-modal similarity of individuals in general respects entails their identity, in which case the qualification 'general' makes no difference to the supervenience base and supervenience is trivialized as before.

[11] See Kim 1984 and McLaughlin 1995 for more discussion.

[12] Perhaps Sider (2001, pp. 35–7) is an exception.

Most contemporary philosophers are more inclined to identify reality with the actual world than with the present time. However, if modal differences were unreal, they could hardly be required to supervene on non-modal differences. For necessitists and contingentists alike, there are real modal differences. But they might be deemed reducible to non-modal differences, and necessitism condemned for blocking the reduction. Still, such objections are unimpressive without far more detail about the nature and justification of the reductionist project, and far more evidence of its feasibility. In particular, why should it require general modal properties to supervene on *general* non-modal properties, rather than on the totality of non-modal properties, including non-general ones?

The reductionist idea may be that the mere distinctness of o and $o*$ does not explain why o is a possible mountain and $o*$ is not, rather than vice versa. If so, the requirement is (in principle) to explain the modal in terms of the non-modal.[13] That demand is not obviously legitimate. If we start with a purely non-modal explanans, how do we reach the modal explanandum without assuming some general principles relating the modal to the non-modal? But such principles are themselves not purely non-modal. Perhaps contingentists will permit the explanans to include reductive equations of modally specified properties and relations with non-modally specified properties and relations, as well as purely non-modal hypotheses. But then they must also justify the assumption that the reductive equation may not pair a modal specification in purely general terms with a non-modal specification not in purely general terms, for otherwise the supervenience of the general modal on the general non-modal will still not be forthcoming.

Before trying to take the discussion much further, we should recall that we are working with a largely schematic distinction between modal and non-modal properties and relations, as opposed to a syntactic distinction amongst formulas and predicates. No criterion is on the table for determining whether to include something (such as the property of strength, or of weakness) specified without overtly modal terms (such as 'can' and 'must') in the putative non-modal supervenience base. The terms 'strong' and 'weak' are not *overtly* modal, but they may still be *covertly* modal, for instance by being implicitly dispositional. Thus a property specifiable in not overtly

---

[13] The requirement is only 'in principle' because in practice we may be unable to single out in thought the relevant contingently non-concrete particulars, let alone know much about them. In such cases we can supply only schematic explanations.

modal terms may still be modal. Perhaps any property specifiable in overtly non-modal terms is non-modal, but how are we to judge whether a not overtly modal atomic predicate is overtly non-modal? To say that the non-modal concerns what *is* rather than what *can* or *must* be hardly helps: how to decide whether, for instance, strength and weakness are a matter of what is or of what can or must be is just the original problem. Nor is logical or strict equivalence to an overtly modal predicate a reliable guide to the modal nature of the property or relation expressed, as already seen in the case of identity: $\lambda xy(x=y)$, $\lambda x(Fx \rightarrow Fx)$, and $\lambda x(Fx \,\&\, \neg Fx)$ (where F is non-modal in whatever sense is relevant) are logically equivalent to $\lambda xy(\Box x=y)$, $\lambda x(\Box(Fx \rightarrow Fx))$, and $\lambda x(\Box(Fx \,\&\, \neg Fx))$ respectively, but in none of these cases is the underlying property or relation genuinely modal.[14] The distinction between modal and non-modal properties and relations is in poor shape.

Reductionists can give bite to their programme by listing the elements of their non-modal base in informative detail.[15] But then it is clear that they are engaging in speculative metaphysics rather than merely articulating pre-theoretically compelling common sense, for how do they know when the list is long enough? Although speculative metaphysics is a legitimate enter-prise, contingentists cannot safely take for granted the soundness of such a speculative reductionist programme in trying to refute necessitism. They may prefer reductionist contingentism to anti-reductionist necessitism, but that does not show the latter to violate anything like a pre-theoretic constraint.

Alternatively, reductionists may refuse to list the elements of their non-modal base in informative detail, preferring to characterize them more abstractly, for example in terms of a postulated category of fundamental or perfectly natural properties and relations. That too is legitimate speculation, but far too shaky to serve as a premise in a dialectically effective 'refutation' of necessitism.

A more modest strategy for contingentists is to try to transfer the burden of explanation onto their opponents. Necessitists claim that there are two merely possibly concrete things, o and $o*$, such that o is a possible star and $o*$ is not. Without relying on any general distinction between modal and non-modal properties, contingentists can still challenge them to say in

---

[14] What matters is that necessitists accept the equivalences, even if contingentists do not, for we are assessing the consequences of necessitism for supervenience.

[15] Compare the discussion of Humean Supervenience in Lewis 1994.

virtue of what o is a possible star and $o*$ is not, rather than vice versa. But if necessitists respond in overtly modal terms, what principled complaint can such contingentists make?

Some necessitists may bluntly insist that they are under no obligation to explain why o is a possible star and $o*$ is not, rather than vice versa, in more basic terms. But suppose, alternatively, that what it is to be a star can be explained: it is to be an ⎯S⎯. Therefore it is necessary that something is a star if and only if it is an ⎯S⎯, and necessitists can use that strict equivalence for their explanatory purposes. Thus they can explain why o is a possible star and $o*$ is not, rather than vice versa, by starting from the explanans that o is a possible ⎯S⎯ and $o*$ is not. Any explanation of a difference between o and $o*$ must somewhere assume another difference between o and $o*$. Sooner or later the regress of explanations comes to an end. Why cannot that end come with the difference between being a possible ⎯S⎯ and not being one? If the metaphysical distinction between the modal and the non-modal makes sense, we can put the idea thus: things have irreducibly modal natures. The complaint against this form of necessitism is not that it does not explain modally specified phenomena, but that it does not explain them in non-modal terms. That complaint is unlikely to worry such necessitists.

Other necessitists may be reluctant to pack so much into the natures of particulars. For them, another option is available. It is a form of anti-essentialism, on which the same general possibilities are open to all particulars. Thus every possible river is a possible mountain and vice versa, although of course *this* river could not have been *that* mountain, or vice versa. Such a necessitist may expand the earlier toy model by adding a third world $w**$ at which the extension of the predicate F contains only $o*$, so that $o*$ as well as o satisfies the general fully modalized predicate $\lambda x(\lozenge Fx)$. Indeed, the structure of the whole model is preserved by permuting both the individuals o and $o*$ and the worlds $w*$ and $w**$. In the expanded model, o and $o*$ satisfy the same general fully modalized predicates at any world, and the general modal supervenes on the general non-modal. Any model can be expanded similarly to one in which all individuals satisfy the same general fully modalized predicates and supervenience holds.[16] Like contingentism, necessitism

---

[16] More precisely, the result is that any model can be expanded by adding worlds to one in which for $n \geq 0$, the sequences $\langle o_1, \ldots, o_n \rangle$ and $\langle o_1*, \ldots, o_n* \rangle$ satisfy the same general fully modalized n-place predicates at any world provided that $o_i = o_j$ just if $o_i* = o_j*$ for $1 \leq i, j \leq n$. Obviously the result does not extend to non-general predicates, since o satisfies $\lambda x(x=y)$ on an assignment $\underline{a}$ and $o*$ does not if $o \neq o*$ and $\underline{a}(y) = o$. A related metaphysical view is the minimalist essentialism for which Mackie 2006 argues.

leaves open a wide range of options as to how much essentialism one accepts. To choose between them would exceed the scope of this book.

As for contingentists' use of reductionist premises about modality in arguing against necessitism, the proper methodology is this. First, let them achieve some explanatory success in carrying through their reductionist programme within their contingentist framework. Then, if they can do that, we shall be in a position to judge how far that explanatory success depends on the contingentist framework. If it cannot be reproduced within necessitism, that really will add weight on the contingentist side of the scales. But, so far, programmes for reducing the modal to the non-modal have had only the slightest explanatory success within a contingentist framework. Currently, by far the best developed reductionist programme for modality is David Lewis's modal realism, which is an eccentric form of necessitism (see section 1.4).

Some contingentists identify possibility with consistency given (true) axioms and (truth-preserving) rules of some special sort.[17] Thus, if no theorem of the system says that you are something, then your non-being is possible, and your being contingent. But such theories currently show little promise of unifying our account of which truths are necessary, which contingent, and so lack the explanatory value of successful reductions in science. From an anti-reductionist perspective, what unifies the system is that the axioms are supposed to be all necessary and the rules all necessity-preserving, but that unification is unavailable to the reductionist, on pain of conceding the game.[18]

Combining contingentism, reductionism, and essentialism, someone may claim that Shakira is necessarily a human, if anything, because part of what it is to be Shakira is to be a human; by contrast, Shakira is only contingently a singer, if anything, because for Shakira to be a singer, if anything, is no part of what it is to be any given things. The phrase 'what it is to be' here is supposed to be non-modal, but to stand in an explanatory relation to the modal because it concerns essential natures.[19] One may doubt the explanatory value of such claims: perhaps, as with virtus dormitiva, it is quite low but still non-zero. However, its explanatory value, if any, differs little from that of a corresponding necessitist account: Shakira is necessarily a human, if

---

[17] Sider 2011, pp. 266–91, gives such an account of modality; he calls it 'Humean'.

[18] 'The core idea of the Humean account … is that necessary truths are truths of certain more or less arbitrarily selected kinds' (Sider 2011, p. 271).

[19] See Fine 1994 for such a non-modal account of essence, which of course has roots in Aristotle (see his *Metaphysics*, book Z, 1029–31).

concrete, because part of what it is to be Shakira is to be a human, if concrete; by contrast, Shakira is only contingently a singer, if concrete, because for Shakira to be a singer, if concrete, is no part of what it is to be any given things. The necessitist simply replaces the contingentist's 'if anything' by 'if concrete' and adds the qualification to what it is to be Shakira. Those are just the modifications one would expect in switching from a contingentist framework to a necessitist one. They do not affect the underlying strategy of explaining modal matters in terms of essential natures. This result, one may conjecture, is typical of contingentist reductionist programmes for modality: their explanatory success, if any, depends on contingentism, if at all, only in superficial ways.

On current evidence, contingentism is no better placed than necessitism to explain modally specified phenomena in non-modal terms.

8.3 No truthmakers

The truthmaker principle says that every truth is made true by some thing. The latter may be called a 'fact', a 'state of affairs', a 'trope': generically, a 'truthmaker'. The principle can make large differences in metaphysics, contracting the class of truths or expanding the class of things.[20] But it is inconsistent with necessitism, on elementary assumptions. This section clarifies some aspects of the truthmaker principle, expounds its inconsistency with necessitism, and explains why it is badly motivated; its loss should not be regretted.

David Armstrong tries to voice a compelling pre-theoretical idea behind the truthmaker principle in what he describes as 'perhaps the fundamental argument' of his book *A World of States of Affairs*.[21] Given a truth (in this case, that *a* is *F*), he asks:

> Must there not be something about the world that makes it to be the case, that serves as an ontological background, for this truth? (Making to be the case here, of course, is not causal making to be the case.)

---

[20] For sympathetic expositions of the truthmaker principle see Mulligan, Simons, and Smith 1984, Fox 1987, and Armstrong 2004. Fine 1982b supplies technical background on relevant modal issues. Two recent collections of essays, some critical, on truthmaking and its historical background are Beebee and Dodd 2005 and Lowe and Rami 2009.

[21] The quotations are from p. 115 of Armstrong 1997.

Armstrong's question expects the answer 'Yes'.

What is this non-causal sense of 'make to be the case' or 'make true'?[22] For Armstrong, x makes p true only if the being of x is strictly sufficient for the truth of p:

> In the useful if theoretically misleading terminology of possible worlds, if a certain truthmaker makes a certain truth true, then there is no alternative world where that truthmaker exists but the truth is a false proposition.[23]

What about the converse? If the being of x is strictly sufficient for the truth of p, does it follow that x makes p true? If so, anything whatsoever would make the proposition that circles are circles true, since that proposition is a necessary truth, for the truth of which the being of anything whatsoever is trivially strictly sufficient. Moreover, if p strictly implies q, then whatever makes p true would also make q true. Thus whatever makes you human would also make you a mammal. Many truthmaker theorists prefer a finer-grained conception of making true.[24]

For present purposes we need not fix a sufficient condition for making true; Armstrong's necessary condition will suffice. For given that his condition is indeed necessary for making true, the truthmaker principle that every truth is made true by something entails the weaker principle that for every truth p something meets Armstrong's necessary condition for making p true. More explicitly, the weaker principle says that (necessarily) every truth is necessitated by the being of something, so each proposition strictly implies the being of something whose being strictly implies that proposition. In first-order modal logic we can formalize this as a schema open to necessitation:

TM $A \rightarrow \exists x\, \Box(\exists y\, x{=}y \rightarrow A)$

Since the intended notion of sufficiency in the truthmaker principle is metaphysically necessary implication, we can give $\Box$ in TM its usual

---

[22] Like many other theorists of truthmaking, Armstrong often moves freely between formulations like 'x makes the proposition that a is F true' that involve explicit truth ascriptions and those that do not, like 'x makes a F'. For simplicity we do likewise in this initial exposition, although the difference between the formulations will later emerge as significant.

[23] Armstrong is not using 'existence' for some restricted form of being (see Armstrong 1997, pp. 79, 173, and 250 for his objections to such a view).

[24] Compare the criticisms of modal accounts of essence as too coarse-grained in Fine 1994. The two issues are closely related, since on such a view, already mentioned in section 8.2, the essence of x is what (non-causally) makes x what it is. Fine accepts that if x is essentially F then the being of x is strictly sufficient for x to be F (it necessitates that x is F), but he denies the converse.

metaphysically modal reading. A in TM can be any formula in which the variable x does not occur free. In the usual way, the result of prefixing an instance of TM with universal quantifiers and necessity operators in any order also counts as an instance of TM (the schemas introduced in this section should be understood this way too). The phrase 'truthmaker principle' itself will be reserved not for TM but for the informal principle enunciated by Armstrong and explained as entailing TM. Since necessitism is inconsistent with TM, given uncontentious assumptions, it is also inconsistent with the truthmaker principle.

The inconsistency can be made plain in terms of a Kripkean model theory with variable domains where all worlds are mutually accessible. TM requires the formula A to be true at a world only if its domain contains an individual o such that A is true at every world whose domain contains o. Thus the domain of every world contains o only if A is true at every world. Hence if all instances of TM are true in a model with a constant domain, every formula of the language is either true at every world or false at every world (on a fixed assignment). The combination of TM and necessitism is incompatible with contingency.

The argument can be reformulated without reference to possible worlds or model theory. We work directly in any necessitist normal modal logic. The condition $\exists y\ x{=}y$ in TM is redundant by the necessity of being or the converse Barcan formula. Thus TM entails $A \rightarrow \exists x\ \Box A$, in which $\exists x$ is vacuous because x is not free in A. Hence TM entails the disastrous schema $A \rightarrow \Box A$. The truthmaker principle drags us from the non-contingency of being to the non-contingency of truth. Contrapositively, given that the language contains contingent truths, TM is inconsistent with necessitism.

As that version of the argument makes clear, even the weaker principle of unnecessitated TM (TM minus its necessitations) is inconsistent with necessitism.[25] TM was preferred to unnecessitated TM on the assumption that the truthmaker principle is intended as the claim that metaphysically there *cannot* be a truth without a truthmaker, not just that (perhaps contingently) there is none. That fits the status proponents apparently accord the truthmaker principle of a metaphysical axiom. One difference between TM and unnecessitated TM is that, in a contingentist setting, TM is a rich source of the kind of ontological incompossibility discussed in section 7.5, while

---

[25] See Fox 1987, p. 189, for an unnecessitated formulation otherwise like TM.

unnecessitated TM is not. This can be seen most easily by considering a Kripke model with variable domains in which TM holds. Let A_1 and A_2 be incompatible contingent formulas: A_1 is true at a world w_1 and A_2 is true at a world w_2, but at no world are both A_1 and A_2 true. By TM, the domain of w_1 contains a member o_1 that belongs to the domains of only those worlds at which A_1 is true, and the domain of w_2 contains a member o_2 that belongs to the domains of only those worlds at which A_2 is true. Thus the domain of no world contains both o_1 and o_2, so they are ontologically incompossible. The argument can obviously be extended to any set, however large, of mutually incompatible contingent formulas; it delivers an equally large set of mutually ontologically incompossible possible individuals. Of course, contingentists cannot take that way of stating the result at face value for metaphysical purposes, since they have no intended Kripke model, but at least for arbitrarily large finite sets of mutually incompatible contingent formulas the upshot is expressible by a formula of first-order logic such as (1) (in the two formula case):[26]

(1) $\lozenge \exists x \, \lozenge \exists y \, \neg \lozenge (\exists z \, x{=}z \,\&\, \exists z \, y{=}z)$

By contrast, unnecessitated TM has no such consequences, because it only guarantees actual truthmakers for actual truths; all such truthmakers are automatically compossible. In some Kripke models of unnecessitated TM, there are many mutually incompatible contingent formulas but the domain of each world is a subset of the domain of the actual world, so no ontological incompossibility holds. Such models also show that unnecessitated TM is compatible with the unnecessitated Barcan formula in S5.[27]

Properly to assess the contrast between necessitism and contingentism with respect to TM, we must check that TM has no comparably trivializing effect in a contingentist setting. We can do so by constructing a wide range of variable domain Kripke models that validate TM. We want to avoid the suspicion that the consequences of TM have been artificially restricted by accidental expressive limitations of the language, so that the truth of all its instances in the model still permits some propositions corresponding to no formula A in TM to lack truthmakers. We therefore do more, by constructing a wide range of inhabited frames with variable domains on which TM

---

[26] For the problem for contingentists of generalizing such formulas to the infinite case see section 7.7.
[27] By giving up the symmetry of accessibility, we can build models of S4 and unnecessitated TM in which even the necessitated Barcan formula (but not its converse) holds.

is valid: every instance of TM is true at every world on any assignment in any model based on the frame. As usual, we assume that all worlds are mutually accessible; thus the frame validates S5.[28] A necessary and sufficient condition for it to validate TM is this: the domain of each world has a member that belongs to the domain of no other world. The condition is obviously sufficient for TM to be valid on the frame. It is necessary because for each world w there is a model in which a given atomic formula A is true at w and no other world; that instance of TM holds in the model only if the domain of w has a member that belongs to the domain of no other world. Such a 'truthmaker' is sufficient for every truth at that world. However, we will construct inhabited frames that also have more selective 'truthmakers'.

Start with an arbitrary set W as the set of worlds and an arbitrary function dom from members of W to sets; in simple cases, we can regard dom(w) as the set of ordinary individuals in w. We expand dom to a domain function dom$^+$ by adding 'truthmakers'. For model-theoretic purposes, we use the sets of worlds that contain a given world w as the truthmakers at w. Assume that dom(w) never contains a set of worlds (if necessary, replace the original model by an isomorphic copy with that feature). Formally:

$$\mathrm{dom}^+(w) = \mathrm{dom}(w) \cup \{X \subseteq W : w \in X\}$$

Although sets of worlds are not plausible candidates for genuine truthmakers, they serve present purposes, since we are not trying to construct an intended model (which contingentists cannot have anyway), but just to establish formal consistency results by model-theoretic means. Any model based on

---

[28] Although we have been assuming an S5 framework, Armstrong's combinatorial metaphysics may require him to reject the B schema $A \to \Box\Diamond A$, which is derivable in S5 and corresponds to the symmetry of the accessibility relation, and take S4 as his background modal logic instead (Lewis 1999, p. 202). But without the B schema TM may lack the intended modal force of the truthmaker principle. Consider a model where W = $\{w, w*\}$, w has access to both worlds but $w*$ has access only to itself, dom(w) = $\{o, o*\}$ and dom($w*$) = $\{o*\}$. Then TM holds at both worlds, because o verifies $A \to \exists x \Box(\exists y\ x=y \to A)$ at w (since o belongs to the domain of no other world) and $o*$ verifies it at $w*$ (where $\Box$ is redundant since no other world is accessible, so it is equivalent to $A \to \exists x\ (\exists y\ x=y \to A)$), which is equivalent to $A \to \exists x\ x=x$ by non-modal reasoning). Nevertheless, if the atomic formula P is false at w but true at $w*$, the supposed truthmaker $o*$ for P in $w*$ is in the domain of w too, even though P is false there, while o makes nothing true in $w*$ because it is outside the domain of $w*$. Accessibility in this model is reflexive and transitive, so the theorems of S4 all hold, but it is not symmetric, and the instance $\neg P \to \Box\Diamond\neg P$ of the B schema is false at w. To put the point independently of possible worlds and model theory, if a contingentist's background modal logic is S4 rather than S5, the principle $\Box(A \to \exists x\ @(\exists y\ x=y \to A))$, where @ is the 'actually' operator, is not derivable from TM. Similar problems occur if accessibility is non-transitive. They do not affect the argument for the inconsistency of the truthmaker principle with necessitism, since TM remains a necessary condition for the truthmaker principle to hold.

W and dom$^+$ automatically validates TM. Indeed, it validates an even stronger principle:

TM$^+$ $A \rightarrow \exists x \,\Box(\exists y \; x=y \leftrightarrow A)$

Let X be the set of worlds at which A is true on a given assignment $\underline{a}$; then X is a 'truthmaker' for A in the model, because $\Box(\exists y \; x=y \leftrightarrow A)$ is true at any world on the assignment $\underline{a}[x/X]$ (since x does not occur in A); thus if A is true at a world w on $\underline{a}$ then X $\in$ dom$^+$(w), so $\exists x \,\Box(\exists y \; x=y \leftrightarrow A)$ is true at w on $\underline{a}$. Consequently, every instance of TM$^+$, and so every instance of TM, is true at every world on every assignment in the model. This construction shows that in a contingentist setting TM and TM$^+$ are consistent with arbitrarily many ordinary individuals, arbitrarily many worlds, and arbitrary contingencies of being for 'ordinary' individuals.

We can validate a still stronger principle by starting with an arbitrary set W but making dom(w) empty for each $w \in$ W (read $\exists!$ as 'for exactly one'):

TM$^+$! $A \rightarrow \exists! x \,\Box(\exists y \; x=y \leftrightarrow A)$

For $\Box(\exists y \; x=y \leftrightarrow A)$ is true on the assignment $\underline{a}[x/Y]$ only if Y is the set of worlds at which A is true on $\underline{a}$. However, TM$^+$! is metaphysically quite implausible. For example, when A is a tautology, the corresponding instance of TM$^+$! reduces to the theologically evocative formula $\exists! x \,\Box \exists y \; x=y$: there is exactly one necessary being (the intersection of the domains of all worlds has exactly one member).[29] But that is doubtful even for a contingentist, since it is incompatible with the principle that the singleton set of a necessary being is another necessary being. More generally, any formula of the form $\exists! x \,\Box(\exists y \; x=y \leftrightarrow A)$ is incompatible with the principle that everything has a singleton distinct from it but which has being in the same possible circumstances. Indeed, since we may put $\exists y \; z=y$ for A in TM$^+$! and universally quantify the result with respect to z, TM$^+$! implies that no two things have being in exactly the same possible circumstances.

TM$^+$ is much less cramping than TM$^+$!, since it allows us to choose the function dom to multiply arbitrarily things that are in exactly the same possible circumstances as each other. Nevertheless, many friends of truthmakers

---

[29] The same substitution shows that the analogous strengthening of TM, $A \rightarrow \exists! x \,\Box(\exists y \; x=y \rightarrow A)$ (open to necessitation), entails the Parmenidean thesis $\exists! x \; x=x$ (open to necessitation: necessarily, there is exactly one thing). Horgan and Potrč 2000 defends the more modest thesis that there is exactly one concrete thing.

will find even TM⁺ too strong. For example, they may want a truthmaker for a disjunction to be a truthmaker for one of the disjuncts too, but its being will be necessary and sufficient both for the truth of the disjunction and for the truth of the disjunct only in the degenerate case in which the disjunction implies that disjunct. Thus they do not in general accept that the being of a given truthmaker for x is necessary as well as sufficient for the truth of x. They see no reason to accept TM⁺. Only TM, not TM⁺ and still less TM⁺!, is reasonably treated as a corollary of the truthmaker principle.

One might try to liberalize TM by letting several things collectively make A true. But that may make no difference, if the set of them or their sum turns out individually to make A true too.[30] Even if the plural analogue of TM does not collapse into the original principle, it remains incompatible with necessitism, given the contingency of truth, by an obvious generalization of the previous argument.

Many theorists broadly sympathetic to the truthmaker principle are willing to restrict it in the face of recalcitrant examples, such as accidental universal generalizations, to a privileged subclass of truths, perhaps just to those that are atomic in some sense.[31] But not even so draconian a restriction restores consistency with necessitism. For friends of truthmakers assume that they are worth having only if at least some contingent truths have truthmakers. But necessitism entails that no contingent truths have truthmakers.

Another proposed weakening of the truthmaker principle to avoid counterexamples is the claim that 'truth supervenes on being', in John Bigelow's phrase. On the reading relevant here, the idea is that if possible worlds are alike in what has being, they are alike in what is true.[32] We can formalize it with the operators ↑ and ↓ from section 7.9 to achieve the effect of modal cross-reference:

TSB $\quad A \rightarrow \uparrow\Box(\neg A \rightarrow (\exists x \neg\downarrow\exists y\, x{=}y \lor \uparrow\Diamond x \downarrow(\neg\exists y\, x{=}y\, \&\, \downarrow\exists y\, x{=}y)))$

---

[30] See Fox 1987, p. 189.

[31] See Mulligan, Simons, and Smith 1984.

[32] See Bigelow 1988, p. 133. Following David Lewis, it has become customary to interpret the phrase according to the weaker principle at p. 159 of Bigelow 1988, where 'being' covers how things are as well as whether they are, so that 'the slogan means that no two possibilities can differ about what's true unless they also differ in what things there are, or in how they are'; 'how they are' is then expanded as 'which perfectly natural properties and relations they instantiate' (Lewis 1992, pp. 206–7). So interpreted, it is consistent with necessitism. For present purposes, however, the stronger interpretation of the slogan as TSB is more pertinent.

The disjunction means that either the new $\neg A$-world has an inhabitant the old world lacks or vice versa. In terms of inhabited frames where all worlds are mutually accessible, TSB corresponds to this condition: no two worlds have the same domain. The condition is obviously sufficient for TSB to be valid on the frame. It is necessary because for each world w an atomic formula A is true at w and no other world in some model; that instance of TSB holds in the model only if the domain of w differs from the domain of every other world. Clearly this condition follows from the frame condition corresponding to TM, that the domain of each world has a member that belongs to the domain of no other world, but not conversely. Although the supervenience of truth on being is widely held not to capture the idea of truth*making*, it is worth considering as a metaphysical proposal in its own right. But it too is inconsistent with necessitism, given the contingency of truth: if all worlds have the same domain, then the only way for them all to have different domains is for there to be just one world. We can put the argument without reference to worlds. If truth supervenes on being, then the contingency of truth entails the contingency of being; since necessitism contradicts the contingency of being, it is inconsistent with the supervenience of truth on being given the contingency of truth. More formally, by NNE, $\exists y\ x=y$ in TSB is necessary, so both disjuncts of the disjunction in TSB are impossible, so TSB simplifies to $A \rightarrow \Box A$. Thus the necessitist denies that truth supervenes on being in the relevant sense.

Why should the supervenience of truth on being and the truthmaker principle itself seem so compelling to so many philosophers? If a proposition is true, *something* must be different from a world in which it is false. In some sense of those words they express a platitude. But these principles assign them a quite specific sense. For they treat 'something' as an individual quantifier, binding a variable in name position. The truthmaker variable x in TM is the subject of a first-level being predicate defined by identity and a quantifier; likewise in TSB. In effect, TM and TSB connect sentences (A) with variables in name position. But why should 'something' in the platitude be best treated as quantifying into name position?

In sections 5.7 and 5.9 we observed the strong pressure exerted by English and other natural languages to assimilate all quantification to quantification into name position, but found no reason to assume that the pressure reflects the structure of reality itself. Rather, we saw the feasibility of formal languages with quantification into predicate or sentence position, whose intended interpretation can be faithfully given only in a formal metalanguage using quantification into predicate or sentence position again. Why not take the platitude as a fumbling attempt to express a simple truth more accurately articulated with quantification into sentence position?[33]

$$\text{TM}_p \qquad A \rightarrow \exists P \, (P \, \& \, \Box(P \rightarrow A))$$

Here the variable P is not free in A. In the terminology of section 5.9, the commitments that TM_p generates are *metaphysical*, but not *ontological*.

TM_p follows easily from the special case Comp_p from section 6.5 of the strong comprehension principle Comp for higher-order modal logic introduced in section 5.5 and defended at length in Chapter 6:

$$\text{Comp}_p \qquad \exists P \, \Box(P \leftrightarrow A)$$

For $\Box(P \leftrightarrow A)$ entails $A \rightarrow (P \, \& \, \Box(P \rightarrow A))$ by elementary modal logic, so $\exists P \, \Box(P \leftrightarrow A)$ entails $\exists P \, (A \rightarrow (P \, \& \, \Box(P \rightarrow A)))$, which yields TM_p by standard quantifier manipulation. If the instances of Comp_p are logical truths, so are those of TM_p. In some higher-order modal logics we can simply derive Comp_p by generalizing on the first occurrence of A in $\Box(A \leftrightarrow A)$ and necessitating the result. In any case, replacing the formalization TM by TM_p enables us to capture the truistic aspect of the truthmaker principle.

Of course, neither TM nor TM_p is intended to capture the truth*making* aspect of the principle. Does capturing it require a shift back to quantification into name position? We may semi-formally represent that aspect by modifying TM thus:

$$\text{Tmake} \qquad A \rightarrow \exists x \, (A \text{ because } \exists y \, x{=}y)$$

But we may also represent the truth*making* aspect by modifying TM_p thus:

$$\text{Tmake}_p \qquad A \rightarrow \exists P \, (A \text{ because } P)$$

Unlike TM_p, Tmake_p has no obvious claim to logical or universal truth. In particular, deriving it by generalization from $A \rightarrow (A \text{ because } A)$ is

[33] Russell's insistence in 'The Philosophy of Logical Atomism' that one can assert facts (in another word, truthmakers) but cannot name them (1956, pp. 187–9) may be a gesture distorted by natural language at the irreducibility of sentences to names. Since 'fact' is a noun, the question arises why one cannot name the fact that dogs bark 'Mary', by stipulation. In contrast, '"Mary" names dogs bark' is simply ill formed, because 'names' requires a noun phrase, not a sentence, as its grammatical object. '"Mary" names the fact that dogs bark' is well formed but involves just the nominalization at issue.

pointless, since anything of the form 'A because A' is presumably false. How could we exclude an object's brute possession of a property?

The difference in structure between P and $\exists y\ x=y$ may give Tmake a more explanatory look than Tmake$_P$. However, the narrowly circumscribed form of the explanans in Tmake produces its own problem of circularity. If we substitute $\exists y\ a=y$ for A in Tmake, the result is (2):

(2) $\exists y\ a=y \rightarrow \exists x\ (\exists y\ a=y$ because $\exists y\ x=y)$

What value of the variable x verifies the consequent of (2) when the antecedent is true? Suppose that the constant a denotes the individual o. If we propose o as the verifying value, we face an obvious charge of circularity, for we are claiming in effect that o is something because o is something. If we propose anything other than o as the verifying value, we face the hard regressive question: why should the being of each thing be explained by the being of something else?

The truthmaker principle was not intended to make a mystery of the brute being of some things. Rather, the truth*making* aspect of the principle complements its *truth*making aspect, in a dimension not represented in any of the formalizations so far. We have been following much of the literature on truthmakers by riding roughshod over the distinction between, for example, making this be square and making the proposition that this is square be true. Once explanatory priority is at issue, we can no longer ignore the distinction. For the natural view is that (3) is true and (4) false:

(3)   The proposition that this is square is true because this is square.

(4)   This is square because the proposition that this is square is true.

No metaphysically loaded correspondence theory of truth is needed for the plausible point that how things are with a subject matter explains the truth values of propositions about that subject matter, not vice versa. That point often seems to be in the mix when truthmaker theorists try to motivate their view. But it too requires no metaphysically loaded truthmaker principle. In the notation of section 6.5, we can generalize our acceptance of (3) and rejection of (4) by accepting PBT (the explanatory priority of being to truth) and rejecting PTB (the explanatory priority of truth to being):

PBT $T\pi(A)$ because A.

PTB A because $T\pi(A)$.

Doing so in no way favours an ontological truthmaker principle such as (a restricted version of) Tmake over a far more modest principle such as (a restricted version of) $Tmake_p$. Quite the opposite: the cases where PBT supplies a verifying instance of Tmake (those in which A is of the form $T\pi(\exists y\ x{=}y)$) constitute only a narrow subclass of the cases where PBT supplies a verifying instance of $Tmake_p$ (those in which A is of the form $T\pi(B)$). Since considerations of explanatory priority and propositional truth have done nothing to support a truthmaker principle incompatible with necessitism, we return to the comparison between the ontologically loaded TM and the truistic TM_p.[34]

Someone might try to reconcile TM with necessitism by interpreting the explicit quantifiers in TM as restricted, say to concrete things (or to chunky things in the sense of section 7.2).[35] On the restricted principle, each proposition strictly implies the concreteness of something whose concreteness strictly implies that proposition. For example, a necessitist might allow that if this tile is square, something concrete o is such that, necessarily, if (and only if) o is concrete, this tile is square. But such a reinterpretation preserves the letter of TM at the expense of its spirit. For on the truthmaking view at issue, if an object o is a truthmaker for the proposition that this tile is square, then o itself—not its possession of a property unnecessary for its being, such as concreteness—is sufficient for this tile to be square.[36] For if the required sufficient condition is just for a given object to possess a given property that may be unnecessary for its being, we need look no further than the tile itself and its possession of the property of squareness. Thus the proposed reinterpretation of TM not only misses the spirit of the truthmaker principle but undermines its motivation. The incompatibility of TM with necessitism runs deep.

The purely objectual nature of truthmaking helps bring out the difference between TM and TM_p. For reasons already explained, quantification into sentence position as in TM_p is best understood as *sui generis*, neither objectual nor substitutional. Nevertheless, even if someone insists on interpreting

---

[34] For related critiques of truthmaker theory see Schnieder 2006, Horwich 2008, and Fine 2012. Most of the points in this section come from Williamson 1999a.

[35] Extending the restriction to any quantifiers in the sentence substituted for the schematic letter A would be pointless.

[36] In this respect not even Tmake is perfectly faithful to the intended spirit: according to Tmake, not the object itself but that it has the property of being something is what does the explaining. A more faithful rendering might be $A \to \exists x\ (A$ because of $x)$.

402   CONSEQUENCES OF NECESSITISM

$\exists P$ in it as objectual, TM_p still does not collapse into TM. For the relevant object will be a proposition or class of possible worlds, whose being does not entail its truth. There are false propositions, and classes of possible worlds without the actual world. Thus the truth of the consequent of TM_p, $\exists P\ (P\ \&\ \Box(P \to A))$, does not entail the truth of the proper analogue of the consequent of TM, $\exists P\ \Box(\exists Q\ P=Q \to A)$. The proposition that this is square in no sense makes this square.

Some metaphysicians may hope to turn TM_p into a more informative principle by restricting the quantifier $\exists P$ to fundamental truths, in some sense to be explained. The new principle would not follow from the comprehension principle $Comp_p$, but might be good metaphysics in its own right. We will not pursue that option here, because it is neutral between necessitism and contingentism. What are incompatible with necessitism are first-order versions of the truthmaker principle or the supervenience of truth on being such as TM, TM^+, $TM^+!$, TSB, and on plausible assumptions T make.

The impression that some first-order principle in the spirit of TM is an intuitively compelling insight depends on ignorance or neglect of the possibilities for non-nominal quantification. As so often, the metaphysicians who most insist that their concern is with reality, not language, are thereby those most in danger of unwittingly projecting features of language onto all of reality. Even when language plays a purely instrumental role in philosophy, like other scientists we must study how our instruments function and sometimes malfunction, lest our naive use of them lead us into gross errors.

Some proponents of the truthmaker principle may concede that it has no compelling a priori justification, but argue that its explanatory success adequately justifies it a posteriori. The general abductive form of such a justification is consonant with the methodology of this book. What is doubtful in this case is the supposed explanatory success. For example, truthmaker theorists make much of their ability to embarrass antecedently unpopular views in the philosophy of mind such as phenomenalism and behaviourism by demanding truthmakers for the required claims about counterfactual phenomenal states or behaviour.[37] But the effectiveness of their demands, such as it is, derives from the effectiveness of much less ontologically loaded demands to explain why the counterfactuals hold. To insist that the explanans must take the form of a truthmaking entity merely

---

[37] See Armstrong 2004, pp. 1–4.

makes the demand easy to dismiss. In any case, if an entity were required, a phenomenalist or behaviourist with truthmaking inclinations could blithely postulate a fact, state of affairs, or trope with the required modal profile, no more obscure in nature than the facts, states of affairs, or tropes that other friends of truthmakers postulate. If such an entity is explanatorily worthless, that reinforces the point that the real problems for phenomenalism and behaviourism are explanatory; they do not depend on the peculiar ontology of truthmakers. Furthermore, once truthmaker theorists start making exceptions for claims such as 'There is no golden mountain', for which no plausible truthmaker suggests itself, they are in a much weaker position to derive the falsity of phenomenalism or behaviourism from the absence of a suitable truthmaker, and the explanatory track record of the truthmaker principle becomes still feebler.[38] The abductive case for truthmakers in the sense of TM is negligible.[39]

Incompatibility with the truthmaker principle is not a cost of necessitism; it is a benefit. Although the principle may be rejected from a contingentist perspective too, necessitism removes it more cleanly.

8.4 Contingency, change, and difference

If one has gone as far as necessitism, why not go further? The crude version of that thought is: if being is necessary, why not everything else too? In itself, the rhetorical question lacks force. The reasons for postulating the necessity of being do not seem to generalize. A smooth theory of higher-order modal logic requires a rigid framework for the play of contingency, but has no difficulty with the play itself. Although the collapse of all modal distinctions would simplify the theory still further, drastically so, it would also erase most of the phenomena to be explained, which are themselves modal. As for truthmaker principles, we saw in section 8.3 that they induce modal collapse in a necessitist setting but lack the independent support needed for that to count seriously in favour of modal collapse, given necessitism. At this naive level, it is unproblematic to make necessitism the stopping point.

---

[38] The principle that truth supervenes on being, even when interpreted as here in the strong sense of TSB, has more resources than the truthmaker principle for handling universal generalizations.

[39] See Daly 2005 and Liggins 2005 for more discussion of the explanatory role of truthmakers. The abductive case for TSB is not much stronger.

On further thought, the picture is less reassuring. Unlike contingentism, necessitism allows possible worlds semantics to be taken at face value, when we use it to give the intended interpretation of quantified modal logic (see sections 3.6 and 3.7). So far, that is another of necessitism's benefits. But when we reflect on such uses of possible worlds semantics, a danger appears.

Normally, possible worlds semantic theories are formulated in a metalanguage without primitive modal operators.[40] Such metatheories interpret the modal operators of the object-language as quantifiers over worlds. For present purposes, the most relevant aspect of the metalanguage is not its specifically metalinguistic vocabulary, such as a truth predicate and a device for quotation, but its apparatus for stating the typically non-metalinguistic conditions which the metatheory can then identify as the truth conditions of sentences of the object-language. When the latter sentences involve modal operators, quantifiers over worlds are central to that apparatus. For simplicity, we may therefore provisionally ignore the specifically metalinguistic aspect of the metalanguage. Taking it back into account will not substantially change the argument. What is the position of the metatheorist who follows a common line in taking such a metalanguage at face value, as *perspicuous* in the sense that it explicitly articulates the relevant semantic structure of the metatheoretic claims?

Consider a non-metalinguistic modal sentence of English qua object-language, for example 'Contingently, Napoleon died in 1821', formalized as Dna & $\neg\Box Dna$. What corresponds to the two-place predicate D of the object-language is a three-place predicate $D*$ of the metalanguage, where $D*xtw$ formalizes 'x died at time t in world w'.[41] An extra argument place is added for a world parameter. Why is it contingent that Napoleon died in 1821? The question is simply intended to elicit what the contingency consists in, stated in the terms of the metalanguage. What the metatheorist has to tell us is that Napoleon died in 1821 in the actual world but not in every possible world. More formally, the answer in the non-modal metalanguage is the first-order sentence $D*naw_@$ & $\neg\forall w\, D*naw$, where the constant or contextually dedicated variable $w_@$ refers to the actual world and the variable w is restricted to possible worlds. Thus the modal operator $\Box$ is explained by the quantifier $\forall w$ over worlds. Similarly, if we ask the simpler

---

[40] The theory of intended model structures in sections 3.3 and 3.7 is a more complicated case. It is considered later.

[41] For simplicity, years are treated as times rather than as intervals of times.

non-modal question why Napoleon died in 1821, again intended constitutively rather than causally, what the metatheorist has to tell us is that Napoleon died in 1821 in the actual world; more formally, the answer in the non-modal metalanguage is the first-order sentence $D*naw_@$.[42]

For present purposes, what is most striking in such an account is that something contingent, that Napoleon died in 1821, is claimed to consist in something necessary, that $D*naw_@$. For it is necessary, not contingent, that Napoleon died in 1821 *in the actual world*. Although he could have survived 1821 in some other world, he could not have survived 1821 in the actual world in some other world, on the intended rigid reading of 'actual'. For our metatheorist, the term $w_@$ does not abbreviate a definite description such as 'the world that obtains', which might designate the actual world non-rigidly, for then the metalanguage would be non-perspicuous, by concealing relevant semantic structure. Rather, $w_@$ is simply a constant or contextually dedicated variable that designates a particular world rigidly. Thus what appears as contingency in the object-language is treated in the metalanguage as a mere difference between possible worlds. The pertinent relations between the given possible worlds and what happens in them are not themselves contingent.[43]

The constitutive claim '*C* because *N*' is problematic whenever '*C*' expresses something contingent and '*N*' something necessary. Thus it is problematic to claim that it is contingent that Napoleon died in 1821 because $D*naw_@$ & $\neg\forall w\, D*naw$. More simply, it is problematic to claim that

---

[42] We must be careful about the logic of contingency. That it is contingent *whether* Napoleon died in 1821 is not itself contingent. For 'It is contingent whether Napoleon died in 1821' is formalized in the first-order modal language as $\neg\Box\neg Dna$ & $\neg\Box Dna$, which is necessary: $(\neg\Box\neg A$ & $\neg\Box A) \rightarrow \Box(\neg\Box\neg A$ & $\neg\Box A)$ is a theorem schema of propositional S5 (even those who reject S5 in general may accept the particular instance of that schema for Dna in place of A). On the 'whether' reading, whatever is contingent is non-contingently contingent. But 'Contingently, Napoleon died in 1821' is equivalent to 'It is contingent that Napoleon died in 1821', not to 'It is contingent whether Napoleon died in 1821'; like the former and unlike the latter, it entails the non-modal 'Napoleon died in 1821'. If it is contingent *that* Napoleon died in 1821, that itself *is* contingent. For 'It is contingent that Napoleon died in 1821' is formalized in the first-order modal language as Dna & $\neg\Box Dna$, which is provably contingent-if-true: $\neg\Box(A$ & $\neg\Box A)$ is a theorem schema of any extension of the propositional system KT (since $\Box(A$ & $\neg\Box A)$ entails $\Box A$ by the first conjunct and $\neg\Box A$ by the second), and therefore in particular is a theorem schema of S5. Whatever contingently obtains contingently contingently obtains.

[43] The application of counterpart theory even to the worlds themselves would not undermine the argument. A counterparthood relation between a counterfactual world in which Napoleon died in 1822 and the actual world would be inappropriate in this context, because for present purposes the essence of a possible world consists in what is true in it (by contrast, the essence of a time does not plausibly consist in what is true at it). In any case, modal realism is a very deviant form of necessitism from the perspective of this book. See also Sider 2011, p. 248 n. 18.

Napoleon died in 1821 because $D*naw_@$. Granted, $D*naw_@$ is more naturally read as 'Napoleon died in 1821 in the actual world' than as 'Napoleon died in 1821', and it is necessary that Napoleon died in 1821 in the actual world, but that does not alleviate the problem. For $D*naw_@$ is all that is available in the non-modal metalanguage to say what the truth that Napoleon died in 1821 consists in.

Does this mean that the metalanguage, when taken at face value, leaves us only an illusion of contingency? Such metatheorists may protest that they are not *denying* contingency, just explaining what it consists in: differences between possible worlds. Since there really are differences between possible worlds, there really is contingency. This may remind the reader of Berkeley's insistence that he is not denying material objects, just explaining what they consist in: congeries of suitably interrelated sense impressions. Since there really are congeries of suitably interrelated sense impressions, there really are material objects.

The comparison with Berkeley also casts light on the interaction between metaphysical and semantic issues. His semantics for talk about material objects is not a matter of indifference to metaphysics, because it has disturbing consequences for the meaning of much of our metaphysical discourse. Similarly, when taken at face value, possible worlds semantics for modal talk is not a matter of indifference to metaphysics, because it too has disturbing consequences for the meaning of much of our metaphysical discourse.

Our envisaged metatheorist treats the non-modal metalanguage as explanatorily prior to the modal object-language, a more fundamental level of description. Thus, in the constitutive sense, Napoleon died in 1821 because $D*naw_@$; he did so contingently because $D*naw_@$ & $\neg \forall w\, D*naw$. In this way, all contingent truths are constitutively explained by purely necessary ones. If so, contingency is no very radical phenomenon. In that sense, the explanatory priority of possible worlds to possibility excludes *radical contingency*. A truth is radically contingent if and only if it does not consist in necessary truths.

One could try making the metalinguistic description contingent by adding the conjunct '$w_@$ obtains' ($Ow_@$). But that would be an exception to the envisaged metatheorist's principles. If 'It is contingent that x died in 1821' corresponds to $D*xaw_@$ & $\neg \forall w\, D*xaw$, then by parity of treatment 'It is contingent that x obtains' corresponds to $O*xw_@$ & $\neg \forall w\, O*xw$ ('x obtains in $w_@$ but not in every world'), where $O*$ is the result of explicitly relativizing O to a world just as $D*$ is the result of explicitly relativizing D to a world. To make one special atomic predicate an exception to the metatheoretic account of contingency is ad hoc and unprincipled. The interesting, threatening proposal is the uniform one, with thoroughgoing relativization to worlds in the metalanguage.

The same problem arises for metalinguistic truths. For example, it is contingent that the English sentence 'Napoleon died in 1821' expresses a truth. What matters here is not just whether the semantics of English itself is contingent, since even if it is, it will not be contingent enough for that example: English could have had exactly the semantics it actually has, even if 'Napoleon died in 1821' had expressed a falsehood.[44] Truth values are typically contingent even when the semantics is fixed. For simplicity, we continue to focus on non-metalinguistic examples.

Non-radically contingent truths consist in necessary truths. Typically, such an account treats contingency as necessary difference: it compares the results of putting different values in an argument place, usually for worlds. By contrast, something is radically contingent only if, the values of all its parameters held fixed, it could still have been otherwise.[45] However, a non-radically contingent truth might consist in necessary truths in other ways too. Suppose that the account of the modal operators bypasses worlds, and quantifies directly over relevant similarity relations between counterparts instead. If, for theoretical purposes, those similarity relations and the relevant non-modal matters (such as the death of Napoleon) are best described in a metalanguage whose own counterpart relation is only identity, then again contingent truths consist in necessary ones, and radical contingency is still excluded.[46]

A similar issue arises if, as often happens, metatheorists formulate the semantics for a tensed object-language in a tenseless metalanguage, to which they give explanatory priority.[47] Consider, for example, the sentence 'Temporarily, I am sitting', formalized as Si & $\neg ASi$, where $\mathbf{A}$ formalizes 'always'. What corresponds to the one-place predicate S of the object-language is a

---

[44] Of course, no contingency in the semantics of English is relevant to constitutively explaining why Napoleon died in 1821, since his death is not a metalinguistic matter.

[45] See also the account of saturation at Sider 2011, pp. 247–57, and of monadic truth in Cappelen and Hawthorne 2009.

[46] Some materials for such an approach can be found in Dorr 2011.

[47] For present purposes, 'tense' should be understood liberally, as applying to any linguistic device relevantly similar to tense in familiar natural languages.

two-place predicate $S^{\#}$ of the metalanguage, where $S^{\#}xt$ formalizes 'x is sitting at time t' (for simplicity, we here ignore the modal dimension). An extra argument place is added for a time parameter. Why is it temporary that I am sitting? What the metatheorist has to tell us is that I am sitting now but not at every time. More formally, the answer in the untensed metalanguage is the first-order sentence $S^{\#}it_0$ & $\neg\forall t\, S^{\#}it$, where the singular term t_0 refers to now, the present time, the time of the context, and the variable t is restricted to times. Thus the temporal operator **A** is explained by the quantifier $\forall t$ over times. Similarly, if we ask the simpler question why I am sitting, again intended constitutively rather than causally, what the metatheorist has to tell us is that I am sitting now; more formally, the answer in the untensed metalanguage is the first-order sentence $S^{\#}it_0$.

For present purposes, what is most striking here is that something temporary, that I am sitting, is claimed to consist in something permanent, that $S^{\#}it_0$. For it is permanent, not temporary, that I am sitting *now*. Although I was standing an hour ago, I was not standing now an hour ago, on the intended temporally rigid reading of 'now'. For our metatheorist, the term t_0 does not abbreviate a definite description such as 'the present time', which might designate the present time non-rigidly, for then the metalanguage would be non-perspicuous, by concealing relevant semantic structure. Rather, t_0 is simply a constant or contextually dedicated variable that designates a particular time rigidly. Thus what appears as transience in the object-language is treated in the metalanguage as a mere difference between times. The pertinent relations between the given times and what happens at them are not themselves temporary.

Does this mean that the metalanguage leaves us only an illusion of change? Defenders of semantics with quantification over times are likely to object that they are not *denying* change, just explaining what it consists in: differences between times. This too may remind the reader of Berkeley's defence.

Our envisaged metatheorist treats the untensed metalanguage as explanatorily prior to the tensed object-language, a more fundamental level of description. Thus, in the constitutive sense, I am sitting because $S^{\#}it_0$; I am doing so temporarily because $S^{\#}it_0$ & $\neg\forall t\, S^{\#}it$. In this way, all temporary truths are constitutively explained by purely permanent ones. If so, change is no very radical phenomenon. In that sense, the explanatory priority of times to tense excludes *radical change*. A truth is radically transient if and only if it does not consist in permanent truths.

Non-radically transient truths consist in permanent truths. Typically, such an account treats change as permanent difference: it compares the results of putting different values in an argument place, usually for times. By contrast, something is radically transient only if, the values of all its parameters held fixed, it still was or will be otherwise. However, a non-radically transient truth might consist in permanent truths in other ways too. Suppose that the account of the temporal operators bypasses times, and quantifies directly over relevant relations between counterpart temporal slices instead. If, for theoretical purposes, those relations and the relevant synchronic matters (such as my sitting) are best described in a metalanguage whose own temporal counterpart relation is only identity, then again transient truths consist in permanent ones, and radical change is still excluded.[48]

The problem does not arise if the extensional metalanguage is itself treated as unexplanatory, in a more or less instrumentalist spirit, leaving genuine explanation of contingent or transient truths for something closer to a homophonic semantics in an intensional metalanguage. It is harmless to code radically contingent truths by necessary ones, or radically transient truths by permanent ones, if we recognize that truths do not consist in their codes, and that which code works is itself contingent or temporary.

A related attitude is arguably apposite even to an intended possible worlds model structure, as in sections 3.3 and 3.7. Since its worlds correspond one-one with metaphysical possibilities, and its logic is sound and complete for metaphysical universality, its significance is much greater than that of an arbitrary model structure amongst many which collectively encode some information about metaphysical modality. That does not make the intended model structure fully explanatory. It was constructed in terms of a Boolean algebra of propositions with an additional necessitation operator L, a modal device: if p is the proposition that Napoleon died in 1821, Lp is the false proposition that it is necessary that Napoleon died in 1821. If $w^\wedge$ is the conjunction of all (actual) truths, Napoleon died in 1821 if and only if $w^\wedge \leq p$ in the sense of the Boolean algebra; it is necessary that $w^\wedge \leq p$, but contingent that Napoleon died in 1821. There was no suggestion that Napoleon died in 1821 *because* $w^\wedge \leq p$, in the constitutive or any other sense. More plausibly, $w^\wedge \leq p$ if and only if Napoleon died in 1821 because $w^\wedge$ is the conjunction of all truths, where both the explanandum (the biconditional)

---

[48] See again Dorr 2011 for materials for such an approach.

and the explanans (that $w^\wedge$ is the conjunction of all truths) are contingent. It is contingent which atom is the conjunction of all truths. Thus which model structure is intended is contingent too; if the conjunction of all truths had been $w*$ rather than $w^\wedge$, the intended model structure would have been $<W^\wedge, R^\wedge, w*>$ rather than $<W^\wedge, R^\wedge, w^\wedge>$. In the constitutive-explanatory order, the intended model structure was assigned no precedence over the simple contingent propositions from which it was constructed; it was the other way round. To that extent, our attitude to the intended model structure retained an instrumental aspect. We used it for its inferential convenience, not any explanatory priority.

Nevertheless, many semanticists and metaphysicians treat such an extensional metalanguage as an explanatory framework explanatorily prior to any intensional language. That calls into question the reality of radical contingency or radical change.

In reflecting on these issues, we must keep track of at least three languages: we start with a natural language, formalize it in a formal object-language, and give the latter's semantics in a semi-formal metalanguage. Typically, the formal object-language handles modality and tense with modal and temporal operators, while the metalanguage handles them with quantifiers over worlds and times. In this respect the natural language is usually taken to resemble the formal object-language rather than the metalanguage, for otherwise it would be simpler and more direct to formalize the natural language in an object-language with quantifiers over worlds and times rather than modal and temporal operators. However, the assumption has been challenged.[49] Natural languages manage modal and temporal cross-reference in ways so closely analogous to those in which they manage explicitly quantificational cross-reference that the best explanation may seem to be by postulating a single system for quantifying over individuals, worlds, and times, in natural languages and perhaps even in underlying cognitive structures. In sections 7.3 and 8.3 the standard modal operators had to be eked out by $\uparrow$ and $\downarrow$ to achieve the required modal cross-reference. The process may be taken further with indices on modal operators. We can achieve the same effects in natural languages. Such devices look increasingly like notational variants on quantifiers over worlds. Thus argument places for world and time parameters are postulated in predicates. When the tacit

---

[49] See Cresswell 1990, King 2003, Schlenker 2006, and Schaffer 2012.

world and time variables occur free, their values are fixed contextually: by default, a free world variable refers to the world of the context ('the actual world'), and a free time variable refers to the time of the context ('now', 'the present time'). On this view, the standard formal languages of modal and temporal logic are just artefacts of misformalization, with artificially re-stricted expressive power. That strengthens the hand of metatheorists who take as their explanatory starting point a metalanguage with quantifiers and extra argument places for worlds or times. In any case, whether our modal and temporal talk is relativized to worlds and times from the start, or merely gets explained in such terms once we engage in metalinguistic reflection, no room seems to be left for radical contingency or radical change.

Our envisaged metatheorist explains (5), directly or indirectly, as (5Q):

(5)   Contingently $A(w,t)$

(5Q) $A(w,t)$ & $\neg\forall w\, A(w,t)$

Here $A(w,t)$ is the result of regimenting an English sentence to make its implicit variables explicit, including w for a world and t for a time. When $A(w,t)$ occurs unembedded, free occurrences of w are assigned the world of the context by default. Similarly, (6) is explained as (6Q):

(6)   Temporarily $A(w,t)$

(6Q) $A(w,t)$ & $\neg\forall t\, A(w,t)$

When $A(w,t)$ occurs unembedded, free occurrence of t are assigned the time of the context by default.

The notation $A(w,t)$ suggests a formula with just one free world variable and just one free time variable. How can we apply the pattern (5)/(5Q) to a formula with several world variables, or the pattern (6)/(6Q) to one with several time variables? Which of the variables should be quantified? Imagine Wanda ranking worlds according to some criterion. Presumably, (7) is to be explained as something like (7Q), where $RWw_1w_2w_3t$ abbreviates 'In w_3 at t, Wanda ranks w_1 at least as high as w_2':[50]

(7)   Contingently, Wanda ranks w_1 at least as high as w_2.

(7Q) $RWw_1w_2w_3t$ & $\neg\forall w_3\, RWw_1w_2w_3t$

[50] If it helps, read RW as 'world-ranks', a predicate that takes only world terms in the relevant places.

But how does the quantifier in (7Q) introduced by 'contingently' know to bind the world variable w_3 in $RWw_1w_2w_3t$ and not the world variable w_1 or w_2? That is, how does the formal semantics predict that the result of applying the 'contingently' operator to $RWw_1w_2w_3t$ is (7Q) rather than a formula in which w_1 or w_2 is bound instead of w_3? For example, binding w_1 rather than w_3, as in (8Q), corresponds to something like (8):

(8)   Wanda ranks w_1, but not every world, at least as high as w_2.

(8Q) $RWw_1w_2w_3t$ & $\neg\forall w_1\, RWw_1w_2w_3t$

But (7) has no reading equivalent to (8). For (8) and (8Q) are false if in the relevant world at the relevant time Wanda ranks w_2 last, but that cannot falsify (7); her ranking could easily have been different. If we try unselectively quantifying all the world variables, as in (9Q), that corresponds to something like (9):

(9)   Wanda ranks w_1 at least as high as w_2, and does not necessarily rank all worlds equally highly.

(9Q) $RWw_1w_2w_3t$ & $\neg\forall w_1\, \forall w_2\, \forall w_3\, RWw_1w_2w_3t$

But (9) is quite different in meaning from (7). For, unlike (7), (9) is true if Wanda ranks w_1 above w_2, irrespective of whether her ranking could have been different. The only choice of world variables in $RWw_1w_2w_3t$ to bind that does not give clearly unintended consequences is w_3 alone.

Similarly, imagine Tania ranking times according to some criterion. Presumably, (10) is to be explained as something like (10Q), where $RTt_1t_2wt_3$ abbreviates 'In w at t_3, Tania ranks t_1 at least as high as t_2':[51]

(10)   Temporarily, Tania ranks t_1 at least as high as t_2.

(10Q) $RTt_1t_2wt_3$ & $\neg\forall t_3\, RTt_1t_2wt_3$

But how does the quantifier in (10Q) introduced by 'temporarily' know to bind the time variable t_3 in $RTt_1t_2wt_3$ and not the time variable t_1 or t_2? That is, how does the formal semantics predict that the result of applying the 'temporarily' operator to $RTt_1t_2wt_3$ is (10Q) rather than a formula in which t_1 or t_2 is bound instead of t_3? For example, binding t_1 rather than t_3, as in (11Q), corresponds to something like (11):

---

[51] If it helps, read RT as 'time-ranks', a predicate that takes only time terms in the relevant places.

(11)   Tania ranks t_1, but not every time, at least as high as t_2.

(11Q) $RTt_1t_2wt_3$ & $\neg\forall t_1 \, RTt_1t_2wt_3$

But (10) has no reading equivalent to (11). For (11) and (11Q) are false if in the relevant world at the relevant time Tania ranks t_2 last, but that cannot falsify (10); her ranking (we may assume) will soon be different. If we try unselectively quantifying all the world variables, as in (12Q), that corresponds to something like (12):

(12)   Tania ranks t_1 at least as high as t_2, and does not always rank all times equally highly.

(12Q) $RTt_1t_2wt_3$ & $\neg\forall t_1 \, \forall t_2 \, \forall t_3 \, RTt_1t_2wt_3$

But (12) is quite different in meaning from (10). For, unlike (10), (12) is true if Tania ranks t_1 above t_2, irrespective of whether her ranking was or ever will be different. The only choice of time variables in $RTt_1t_2wt_3$ to bind that does not give clearly unintended consequences is t_3 alone.

In some sense, not all differences between worlds are instances of contingency, and not all differences between times are instances of change. Of course, if in a world w_3 at a time t the possible world w_1 has a property p while the possible world w_2 lacks p, then *something* is contingent: it is contingent whether a world obtains that has p in w_3 at t. But that is not the putative contingency at issue when we ask whether w_1's having p is contingent. Similarly, if in a world w at a time t_3 the time t_1 has a property q while the time t_2 lacks q, then *something* changes: it is a temporary matter whether a time is present that has q in w at t_3. But that is not the putative change at issue when we ask whether t_1's having q is temporary.[52]

With our understanding of English, we can see at once which variable to quantify in modelling 'contingently' or 'temporarily'. But if a semantic theory is supposed to explain modal and temporal constructions in terms of variables for worlds and times, treated symmetrically with variables for individuals, then it requires some general mechanism for selecting the appropriate variable. The difficulty is that from the standpoint of the meta-language without modal or temporal operators, all the world variables in

---

[52] For purposes of argument, we can count Cambridge changes as genuine changes, and analogously extrinsic contingencies as genuine contingencies. Compare Humberstone 1996b, p. 209, on merely Cambridge contingencies.

RW$w_1w_2w_3t$ look equally good, as do all the time variables in RT$t_1t_2wt_3$. The problem tends to go unnoticed, because discussion concentrates on examples in which world and time parameters are postulated only as tacit extra arguments of predicates. But natural languages also enable us to talk quite explicitly about possibilities and times, as in this very paragraph. There is no formal obstacle to atomic predicates with arbitrarily many world parameters and arbitrarily many time parameters.[53]

Might the treatment of modality and tense in natural language depend on a linguistic universal, that all atomic predicates of a human natural language have at most one distinguished argument place for a world variable, and at most one distinguished argument place for a time variable, however many other argument places they also have? Modal and temporal constructions could then be explained as quantifying the variables in the former and latter distinguished places respectively.[54] Explicit argument places for worlds, such as the variables w_1 and w_2 occupy in (7), and explicit argument places for times, such as t_1 and t_2 occupy in (10), would normally count as undistinguished. The linguistic universal would be logically unmotivated, since first-order languages flouting it are easy to construct. The distinguished argument place might be marked for modality or tense somewhat as the place of 'Edinburgh' in 'Edinburgh is north of London' but not in 'London is south of Edinburgh' is linguistically marked as the subject position, even though the two sentences are equivalent. As the Chomskyan tradition has emphasized, linguistic universals indicate more about the distinctively human capacity for language when they are logically unmotivated.

However, the hypothesis that our modal and temporal thinking relies on linguistically marked argument places for worlds and times underestimates its robustness. No such special apparatus is needed to raise questions of contingency and transience:

---

[53] Schlenker concedes 'It might be that there is an element of asymmetry between individuals on the one hand and times and worlds on the other in that atomic predicates may take several individual arguments but do not generally take several time or world arguments', while noting 'One could for instance argue that *after* is a binary predicate of moments' (2006, p. 510). In his illustrative formal semantics, 'atomic predicates take a single world and a single time argument, but may take n individual arguments for n≥0' (p. 531); although he suggests that 'this is largely for reasons of technical convenience' (p. 510), the need for such a restriction seems to go deeper.

[54] Non-contingent atomic predicates might also be permitted to lack a distinguished argument place for a world variable, and atemporal ones to lack a distinguished argument place for a time variable. The identity predicate is an obvious candidate in both cases. This would result in harmlessly vacuous quantification.

(13)   Is it necessary or contingent that $E = mc^2$?

(14)   Is it permanent or temporary that $E = mc^2$?

(15)   Are the principles of special relativity necessary or contingent?

(16)   Are the principles of special relativity permanent or temporary?

These are intelligible, non-trivial questions. Many reasonable people will answer 'Permanent' to (14) and (16), 'Contingent' to (13) and (15); other reasonable people will disagree, in both cases on a variety of grounds. In (13) and (14), the content at issue is given by the equation '$E = mc^2$', to be understood by the rules not of English but of mathematical notation as applied to physics. That notation was not set up with an argument place for a world variable. In (15) and (16), the contents are specified less directly by the plural definite description 'the principles of special relativity'. No assumption is made as to what language or notation the principles are expressed in. A fortiori, they are not assumed to be expressed with anything like an argument place for a world variable.

If we understand physical laws as universal generalizations over all times (or all spacetime points), that does not quite explain the non-triviality of (14) or (16), since the required variable for a time (or spacetime point) is already bound. However, we might make non-trivial sense of (14) and (16) by somehow replacing the universal quantifier over times (or spacetime points) by a λ-operator and then asking whether all times (or spacetime points) satisfy the resultant condition. But that does not explain the non-triviality of (13) or (15). Articulating the mathematics behind '$E = mc^2$' or 'the principles of special relativity' reveals no universal quantification over worlds.

In any case, an implied time variable or quantifier over times is hard to take seriously for mathematical laws, such as principles of set theory:

(17)   Is it necessary or contingent that $\forall x\, \forall y\, \exists z\, (x \in z\ \&\ y \in z)$?

(18)   Is it permanent or temporary that $\forall x\, \forall y\, \exists z\, (x \in z\ \&\ y \in z)$?

(19)   Are the principles of pure set theory necessary or contingent?

(20)   Are the principles of pure set theory permanent or temporary?

These too are intelligible, non-trivial questions, most clearly for the modal questions (17) and (19), but plausibly for the temporal questions (18) and

(20) too.[55] Although most people may answer 'Necessary' to (17) and (19), and 'Permanent' to (18) and (20), the answers 'Contingent' and 'Temporary' are neither meaningless nor blatantly inconsistent, and might be based on interesting (if mistaken) grounds. In (17) and (18), the content at issue is given by the formula $\forall x\, \forall y\, \exists z\, (x \in z\ \&\ y \in z)$, to be understood by the rules not of English but of an explicit first-order non-modal language, with no argument places for world or time variables. In (19) and (20), the contents are specified less directly by the phrase 'the principles of set theory'. No special assumption is made as to what language or notation the principles are expressed in.[56] A fortiori, they are not assumed to be expressed with anything like an argument place for a world or time variable. Indeed, we could even raise such questions about the mathematical or physical theories of extraterrestrial beings with a cognitive apparatus quite different from our own.

Nor is it plausible that we can understand mathematical and logical formulas only by translating them into a natural language. One great advantage of such formulas is that, above a low level of complexity, they are much easier to understand for those who have mastered the relevant notation than are the cumbersome natural language sentences by which they might be laboriously and roughly paraphrased. For example, strings of four or five quantifiers are far clearer in logical notation than in natural language. Although the formal notation is usually introduced with an initial explanation in natural language, that does not mean that a translation is on offer, still less that we must use it to understand the formal language. For example, the casual remarks with which the technical notion of a set and the symbol $\in$ are normally introduced fall notoriously short of what the pupil is to grasp. Again, it would be bizarre to suggest that we can only understand two-dimensional matrix notation in mathematics by translating it into a one-dimensional description in a natural language; we do far better moving in the opposite direction. For many purposes, one must learn to think in mathematical notation.

We can raise similar questions at a general level about what extraterrestrials or non-human animals believe, without even knowing exactly what they

---

[55]   It is much less clear what is intended by the question 'Are the principles of pure set theory ubiquitous or not?'.

[56]   If the phrase 'the principles of pure set theory' in practice has several non-equivalent readings, that is an inessential feature of the example.

believe. Is all of what they believe necessary, or is some of it contingent? Is all of it permanent, or is some of it temporary? At least for non-human animals, it is far more plausible that some or all of what they believe is contingent than that all of it is necessary. We can make such assessments without attempting to express their beliefs in a human natural language, because we can appeal to the general consideration that what non-human animals mainly need to form beliefs about are contingent features of their environment.

Indeed, the form of the proposed semantics for natural languages itself undermines any claimed limitation of human understanding to symbolism satisfying the supposed requirement of privileged argument places for worlds and times. For given the postulated expressive resources, one can simply define predicates violating the supposed requirement. For example, if the three-place predicate R has one distinguished argument place for worlds and one distinguished argument place for times, the predicate $\lambda x(\exists w\,\exists t\,Rxwt)$ has no argument* places for worlds or times, while $\lambda x,w,w^*,t,t^*(Rxwt\,\&\,Rxw^*t^*)$ has two for worlds and two for times.

Of course, questions such as (13)–(20) can all be paraphrased with explicit quantification over worlds or times. For example, in the mathematical case we have questions like these:

(21)   Is it the case that $\forall w$ in w: $\forall x\,\forall y\,\exists z\,(x\in z\,\&\,y\in z)$?

(22)   Is it the case that $\forall t$ at t: $\forall x\,\forall y\,\exists z\,(x\in z\,\&\,y\in z)$?

(23)   Is it the case that for every principle p of pure set theory $\forall w$ in w: p holds?

(24)   Is it the case that for every principle p of pure set theory $\forall t$ at t: p holds?

Parallel formulations are available in the physical case too. The crucial point is the role of the phrase 'in w' in (21) and (23) and 'at t' in (22) and (24). Applied to a sentence A, 'in w' forms the sentence 'in w: A' and 'at t' forms the sentence 'at t: A'. In (21) and (22), A is $\forall x\,\forall y\,\exists z\,(x\in z\,\&\,y\in z)$, from which the variables w and t are absent. But that does not make 'in w' or 'at t' redundant. A philosopher of mathematics so inclined can still non-absurdly (if mistakenly) argue that in the actual world $\forall x\,\forall y\,\exists z\,(x\in z\,\&\,y\in z)$ but in some counterfactual world not $\forall x\,\forall y\,\exists z\,(x\in z\,\&\,y\in z)$, or vice versa, or perhaps that now $\forall x\,\forall y\,\exists z\,(x\in z\,\&\,y\in z)$ but at some past time not

$\forall x\ \forall y\ \exists z\ (x \in z\ \&\ y \in z)$, or vice versa. The natural explanation is that 'in w' is a modal operator, 'in w: A' being equivalent to $\square(w$ obtains $\rightarrow A)$, and that 'at t' is a temporal operator, 'at t: A' being equivalent to $\mathbf{A}(t$ is present $\rightarrow A)$.

For (23) and (24), someone might argue that the English verb 'holds' itself introduces tacit world and time variables, so we can replace 'in w: p holds' in (23) and 'at t: p holds' in (24) by something like 'holds(p, w, t)'. But that does not save the semantic reduction of modal and tense operators to quantifiers and variables for worlds and times. For within the underlying metatheoretic framework, worlds and times are not logically privileged; a principle's holding relative to a world and a time is formally analogous to its holding relative to a cat and a dog. If the principle happens to be a relation between cats and dogs, then it holds relative to a cat and a dog just in case the cat has the relation to the dog. If the principle happens to be a relation between worlds and times, then it holds relative to a world and a time ('holds(p, w, t)') just in case the world has the relation to the time. If worlds and times are not logically privileged, there is no more reason to regard a theorem of pure set theory in a standard formal language as expressing a relation between worlds and times than there is to regard it as expressing a relation between cats and dogs. To make non-trivial sense of 'holds(p, w, t)', we must interpret it as something like 'in w: at t: p holds'. Since '$\forall w$ in w:' is not redundant in (23), and '$\forall t$ at t:' is not redundant in (24), we are back with the modal operator 'in w' and the temporal operator 'at t'.[57]

A parallel argument rules out the attempt to make non-trivial sense of (21) and (22) as asking about the worlds and times relative to which the proposition that $\forall x\ \forall y\ \exists z\ (x \in z\ \&\ y \in z)$ holds.

The conjecture that humans can understand mathematical formulas with no overt world or time variable only by covertly adding one at some level

---

[57] The basic logic of operators of the forms 'in w' and 'at t' is rather straightforward. They commute with all truth functors. For example, 'in w $\neg A$' is equivalent to '$\neg$(in $w A$)' and 'in w $(A\ \&\ B)$' to '(in $w A$) & (in $w B$)'. Applying one after another is redundant, in the sense that 'in w (in $w* A$)' is equivalent to 'in $w* A$' and 'at t (at $t* A$)' to 'at $t* A$', although 'in w (at $t A$)' and 'at t (in $w A$)' are mutually equivalent (but on the last equivalence see also n. 4). For a necessitist, by analogy with BF and CBF, 'in w' also commutes with both individual quantifiers, in the sense that 'in $w \exists x A$' is equivalent to '$\exists x$ in $w A$' and 'in $w \forall x A$' to '$\forall x$ in $w A$' (the two equivalences are equivalent to each other since negation also commutes with 'in w', by the duality of the quantifiers). Similarly, 'at t' commutes with both individual quantifiers for a permanentist. Such operators were originally formalized by Arthur Prior in tense logic; see Prior 1968, pp. 117–38, Bull 1970, and Blackburn 2007. They have since been extensively studied in both modal and tense logic in the field now known as *hybrid logic*; for a survey see Areces and ten Cate 2007.

of cognitive processing does not save opponents of the operator readings of 'in w' and 'at t'. For the only available way of 'adding' such a parameter with an appropriate interpretation is precisely by applying the operator at issue to the formula. For example, in doing the semantics of an extended language for set theory with modal and temporal operators, we may add argument places for world and time variables to the membership predicate, in order not to make membership necessary and permanent for purely semantic reasons, as opposed to metaphysical ones. Thus $x \in_{wt} y$ is read '$x \in y$ at t in w'. But here too 'in w' is a modal operator and 'at t' a temporal one. Far from making explicit argument places already implicit in the ordinary set-theoretic use of $\in$, we have applied modal and temporal operators to encode the relevant modal and temporal phenomena artificially in a single four-place predicate.

Our capacity to apply the apparatus of quantification in natural language to possible worlds or less specific possibilities constitutes no good evidence against the view that natural language phrases such as 'it is contingent that' and 'in that possible world' function as genuine modal operators. Rather, it is only to be expected on that view. Starting with a modal operator for necessity or possibility, as is well known, one can then develop conceptions of possible worlds and possibilities.[58] Although contingentism makes some aspects of the construction problematic, as seen in section 3.6, one can carry it through by thinking in effect in necessitist terms, as discussed in sections 3.3, 3.7, and 5.6. Without theoretical reflection on modality, speakers of a natural language may exploit such forms of thought in their ordinary modal thinking. Those more or less sophisticated levels of modal thought do not make the more basic one redundant, even for explanatory purposes.

For all the preceding arguments show, the English words 'necessarily' and 'possibly' themselves may correspond to the complex operators '$\forall w$ in w:' and '$\exists w$ in w:', rather than to the simpler operators $\Box$ and $\Diamond$. Since the complex operators still contain the modal operator 'in w', they pose no threat to radical contingency. A similar point goes for temporal operators. The view of modal and temporal operators in natural language as quantifiers over worlds and times respectively may be almost correct, neglecting only the crucial role of the modal operator 'in w' and the temporal operator 'at t'. Alternatively, natural languages may employ the simpler operators, and

---

[58] Fine 1977a is a classic treatment.

exploit their equivalence to the complex quantified ones less directly. There is no need to resolve that issue here. What matters for radical contingency and radical change is the nature of relativization to worlds and times, not whether we quantify over them.

On some theories of the semantics of natural languages, the fundamental form of tacit quantification is over situations, states, or events, rather than worlds and times.[59,60] The earlier arguments generalize to such an approach, for there are no tacit variables for situations, states, or events in many mathematical formulas and other truth bearers from outside human natural languages to which we can meaningfully and non-trivially apply modal and temporal qualifiers such as 'contingently' and 'temporarily'. For example, if we apply situation semantics to set theory, although we can meaningfully write 'in s, $x \in y$', where s is a situation variable, 'in s' functions there as a quasi-modal operator similar to 'in w'.[61] It does not make explicit an invisible third argument place for a situation variable that was present in '$\in$' all along.

Here is an analogy for the role of relativization to worlds, times, or situations. We start by judging actions as *fair* or *unfair*. Later, as we observe more or less systematic differences between individuals or societies in such judgements, we acquire the conception of different *standards* by which they may be made. We add a parameter for a standard: an action may be fair 'by my standard', unfair 'by yours'. We sometimes quantify explicitly over standards: the action is fair 'by some standards'. Now some theorist proposes that the dyadic standard-relative notion 'x is fair by standard s' is explanatorily more basic than the monadic notion 'x is fair'. The most naive way of explaining

---

[59] See Schlenker 2006, pp. 523–6, for the application of such a view to the present issues.

[60] Of course, quantification over situations or events simulates modal operators only if the situations include all possible situations, or the events all possible events, rather than just actual ones. The semantics must not regard as concrete the situations or events supposedly corresponding to counterfactual possibilities, if it is to avoid discrediting itself by falling into something like David Lewis's modal realism. If in some such abstract situation or event you committed murder or there are talking donkeys, it does not follow that you committed murder or there are talking donkeys. Thus the semantic theory will need the capacity to restrict quantifiers over abstract situations or events to those that actually occur. See Kratzer 1989, pp. 612–15, on the metaphysics of situations. Davidson's original application of quantification over events to the semantics of adverbs involved a conception of events as actually occurring concrete particulars (Davidson 1967, 1970), and would require reformulation if counterfactual events were included.

[61] The logic of the operator 'in s' will be slightly different from that of 'in w', since situations, unlike worlds, are conceived as typically partial: thus '$\neg$(in s A)' will not entail 'in s $\neg A$'. There are also delicate questions about the interaction of 'in s' and quantifiers when s is partial; their commutativity for total situations (worlds) is not affected.

the monadic notion in terms of the dyadic one is simply indexical: 'x is fair' amounts to 'x is fair by our standard'. But such relativism is obviously wrong, since we know that our standards may be incorrect: for all we know, something is fair by our standards, but not fair, or vice versa. The theorist might try to fine-tune that proposal by talking in the usual way about what our standards would be after more experience, reflection, and so on. That way is a degenerating research programme of ever more complex proposals that either remain vulnerable to some form of the original objection or rely on notions such as the 'improvement' of a standard, which help themselves to something like the idea of a *correct* standard, which one may approximate better or worse. Cutting to the chase, the theorist may propose that 'x is fair' amounts to 'x is fair by the correct standard'. Unlike the relativist proposals, this one at least gets the extension of 'fair' right.[62] But of course it does so trivially, because the correct standard is just the standard s such that, necessarily, an action is fair if and only if it is fair by s. Thus the monadic notion of fairness has been smuggled back into the notion of the correct standard. It has not been reduced to the dyadic notion. The monadic notion remains explanatorily prior. In 'x is fair by standard s', the operator 'by standard s' is applied to 'x is fair'; it does not make explicit a parameter that was implicit in 'x is fair' all along.

Naturally, in making judgements of monadic fairness and unfairness, we employed correct or incorrect standards all along, but to conclude that those standards were parameters in the contents of our judgements is merely confused. When we judge 'x is fair by standard s' we employ a further meta-standard, which may differ from s—we can be wrong about whether something is fair by a given standard—but that does not mean that we are really judging 'x is fair by standard s by standard $s*$', on pain of an infinite regress.

For some notational purposes, such as formalization in an extensional language, it may be convenient to take a dyadic predicate F for 'x is fair by standard s' and a constant c for 'the correct standard of fairness' as basic vocabulary, and define a monadic predicate for 'x is fair' in terms of them, as $\lambda x(Fxc)$. But that should not blind one to the underlying explanatory order. When we judge 'x is fair', we are not judging something of the form 'x is fair by standard s', not even 'x is fair by the correct standard'. Similarly, when

---

[62] Non-realists about fairness will have to find another example. The logical points should in any case be clear.

we judge 'x obtains', we are not judging something of the form 'x obtains in world w', not even 'x obtains in the actual world'. Just as the correct standard of fairness is the one by which things are fair if and only if they are in fact fair, so the actual world is the one in which things obtain if and only if they do in fact obtain. We can still formulate formal semantic theories with quantification over worlds and times; doing so is often very convenient, since it is easier to work in an extensional metalanguage. But that should not persuade us that contingencies really are just differences between worlds, for in the crucial respects the world-relative notions are not explanatorily basic. Similar logical points apply in the case of times, and of situations.

On the modalist view just defended, contingency *is* radical contingency. We can assert that there is contingency, using the term in the radical sense, with a simple formula such as (25):[63]

(25) $\exists P\,(\Diamond P\ \&\ \Diamond\neg P)$

Of course, if the anti-modalist explanation of modality in terms of worlds rejected earlier were right, (25) would not concern radical contingency; but anti-modalism is wrong.[64] Similarly, material objects are radically material: being a material object excludes being a construction out of ideas in the mind. We can assert that there are material objects in the radical sense with the simple sentence 'There are material objects'. Of course, if Berkeley were right, that sentence would not concern radically material objects; but he is wrong. The formula (25) expresses the intended controversial claim; that it does so is another controversial claim. Both claims are true.

It is hardly surprising that the semantic study of natural languages lacks the power to show up radical contingency and radical change as illusions. Whether they are real does not depend on how human linguistic or cognitive apparatus happens to have evolved. We have seen no good reason to doubt the natural view that most of what matters most to us is, to a frightening extent, radically contingent and radically transient. But we *have* found reason to locate the reckless play of contingency and transience within a logical space whose structure is necessary and permanent.

---

[63] There is a formal analogy between the claim that there is radical contingency, as formalized in (25) and the claim that there is vagueness in reality, as formalized in Williamson 2003b, p. 701, which deserves to be explored. The analogy does not imply that the two claims stand or fall together.

[64] I find the analogous argument for radical change plausible but slightly less compelling, because I find temporal questions of the forms of (18) and (20) less clearly non-trivial than the corresponding modal questions of the forms of (17) and (19).

Methodological Afterword

The study of modal logic takes many legitimate forms. It is pursued within both mathematics and computer science, for example. It is also pursued within philosophy. In this book it has taken the form of a metaphysical enquiry. We fixed interpretations of the modal operators, as expressing metaphysical possibility and necessity, and of the quantifiers, as unrestricted, in accord with the ambitions of metaphysics. Modal logic in this form aims to discover which generalizations in such terms are true. The true generalizations constitute a quantified modal logic, but we do not know ahead of enquiry which one. At least in this area of philosophical logic, our task is not to justify principles that already play a fundamental role in our thinking. Rather, it is in a scientific spirit to build and test theories that codify putatively true generalizations of the sort at issue, to find out which are true. Those theories are not about our language or thought, or any other actual or possible creatures' language or thought, except incidentally, since they are about everything whatsoever. Like mathematics, the enterprise is part of science but not specifically of natural science. Although nothing in theory precludes the application of results from any branch of natural science to the present enquiry, we have seen little evidence that they would be of much help in practice. It would hardly be relevant to carry out special experiments or make special measurements. A combination of logico-mathematical reasoning with elementary modal knowledge in particular cases turns out to be far more useful.

In some looser ways, the methodology of this book is akin to that of a natural science. Both are abductive. Very general theories are formulated in a formal notation that facilitates complex rigorous deductions of their consequences. The theories are judged partly on their strength, simplicity, and elegance, partly on the fit between their consequences and what is independently known. The fit has at least two dimensions. Theories should not entail anything we are in a position to falsify, since then they are false. Equally, the more they entail of what we are in a position to verify independently, the better. 'Entail' here means by the standards of the theory in question, rather than by the correct standards, since we are trying to find out what the latter are: logic here is no mere background framework but the very thing at issue.

Some metaphysicians claim that criteria such as simplicity and elegance are applicable only to theories about absolutely fundamental matters, and so should not be applied to theories of metaphysical modality in the absence of good evidence that it is absolutely fundamental. That claim embodies a serious methodological error, whatever exactly is meant by 'absolutely fundamental'. Abductive criteria such as simplicity and elegance are used in theory comparison throughout the special sciences. Indeed, they are methodologically required, for without them the special sciences would become hopelessly bogged down in a proliferation of ad hoc, gerrymandered high-level theories. Even if the special sciences are in some sense reducible in principle to fundamental science, methodologically the application of abductive criteria in fundamental science is no substitute for their direct application in the special sciences, because in practice theories in the special sciences (such as biology and psychology) are typically and appropriately purpose-built and compared in their own right, not derived as mere corollaries of theories in fundamental science, even though consistency with the latter may be a significant constraint. The putative reductions depend on putative bridge laws connecting properties and relations in the special sciences to properties and relations in fundamental science; those bridge laws may easily be too complex and uncertain for the putative derivations to be feasible. Moreover, the constraints run both ways. True theories in fundamental science must be consistent with what we know at higher levels. We should reject a theory of fundamental physics if it entails that there are no living beings. Similar methodological considerations govern philosophy too. Even if a special branch of philosophy is in some sense reducible in principle to fundamental metaphysics, methodologically the application of abductive criteria in fundamental metaphysics is often no substitute for their direct application in the special branch, because in practice theories in the special branch are typically and appropriately purpose-built and compared in their own right, not derived as mere corollaries of theories in fundamental metaphysics, even though consistency with the latter may be a significant constraint. The putative reductions depend on putative bridge laws connecting properties and relations in the special branch to properties and relations in fundamental metaphysics; those bridge laws may easily be too complex and uncertain for the putative derivations to be feasible. Moreover, the constraints run both ways. True theories in fundamental metaphysics must be consistent with what we know at higher levels. We should reject a theory of fundamental metaphysics if it entails that there are no living beings. Good methodology permits the application of abductive criteria of elegance and simplicity to theories of metaphysical modality even if we have not resolved the obscure question whether it is absolutely fundamental.

The abductive method involves independent testing of a theory's consequences. What independently testable consequences can a modal logic have? We must begin the enquiry with some minimal capacity to assess simple modal claims correctly in particular cases, just as we need some minimal capacity to assess simple claims about the physical world correctly in particular cases before we can start doing scientific physics. For example, we can assess some simple instances of a proposed axiom schema for modal logic, under the metaphysical interpretation, by assessing the particular ascriptions of metaphysical possibility or necessity that form its constituents; their truth values may be reasonably uncontroversial. The extreme generality of logical principles makes it quite hard for unsound modal logics of reasonable strength to avoid obviously false consequences, such as a collapse of the distinction between necessity and possibility. Thus a reasonably strong modal logic with no obviously false theorems already deserves to be taken very seriously.

Can the method be described as inference to the best explanation of the modal data? Of course, a modal logic is at too high a level of generality to explain specific modal matters, such as why it is possible for you to be married but not possible for you to be a married bachelor. However, a logical law can still articulate and generalize a pattern in the data. For example, we find no case in which a material conditional is necessary, and so is its antecedent, but its consequent is not. The corresponding axiom schema, known as K, is a principle of every normal modal logic. In a modest way, it explains the pattern in the modal data by bringing it under a universal law. The explanation is appropriately non-causal because the explanandum is uncaused; it would hold no matter what causes were at work. For present purposes, however, it is unnecessary to insist on the specifically explanatory nature of the enterprise. What matters is the search for universal laws to order, unify, and generalize what we already know. The argument is not simply inductive, because it is vital for a particular modal principle, such as K, to be integrated into a total modal logic, such as S5, with the required theoretical virtues. In this context, Peirce's term 'abduction' may be more suggestive than 'inference to the best explanation'.

As in natural science, the abductive method does not require us to be infallible about the data. We may easily misjudge particular modal claims, just as we may easily make errors of observation and measurement. We must be careful not to dismiss a true theory on the basis of false 'data'. Every science has its own ways of checking data. When a proposed law of modal logic is rejected (on its metaphysical interpretation), the grounds are typically putative counterexamples consisting of simple modal claims, available for everyone to assess. Moreover, the community is not usually satisfied with a single example, but checks whether it instantiates a general recipe for producing more falsifications of the proposed law, in case the original example had misleading incidental features. That is reminiscent of the need for experiments to be repeatable. Naturally, not even these controls guarantee that the community will never accept false 'data', and consequently reject a true theory. But in the long run such misjudgements tend to generate a proliferation of anomalies, spreading outwards from the original error. Once a good explanation is offered of how such a mistake could be made, and more advantages in other respects of the rejected theory over its competitors are brought to attention, the community eventually revises its view.

Sciences typically begin in confusion. At first, there are no established standards. All claims to expertise are contested by rivals. The most elementary principles of one theory are contradicted by those of another. Nevertheless, gradually some order emerges. In a mature science, despite a few troublemaking dissenters, there are established standards, acknowledged experts, and accepted elementary principles. Above all, much more is known about both the subject matter and how to investigate it. With this knowledge, proposed new data and theories can be scrutinized more reliably than before. As a mathematical discipline, modal logic has been in that mature state for more than half a century. Much of that expertise is applicable, and sometimes applied, to modal logic even when pursued as metaphysics. For example, by any non-sceptical standard the theorems of the normal propositional modal logic KT are known to hold for metaphysical modality, and can even be shown to include all formulas valid on that interpretation in a standard propositional modal language with no iteration of modal operators. These results can then be used to help test candidate laws in the more contested field of quantified modal logic, by drawing out their consequences. Once the technical aspects of the situation are well understood, the remaining philosophical questions take a clearer form, and become correspondingly more tractable, although still very hard.

An incidental benefit of these methodological reflections is that they provide an answer to some traditional aspersions on metaphysics. To put the doubts plainly, just what features, visible from outside, differentiate it from a pseudo-science, with pseudo-experts and pseudo-knowledge? In the case of modal logic as metaphysics, such features have been grouped under two heads. First, there is the role of formalization and formal proof. The latter comprises both proof in a formal system for the formal object-language and proof by normal mathematical standards in a natural language as a metalanguage for the formal language. That first general feature is as easy to recognize as the role of mathematics in physics. It enables us to discriminate by uncontroversial technical means the theorems from the non-theorems of a proposed modal logic. Second, there is the role of pre-theoretic modal knowledge, accessible to almost any reasonable, intelligent person. That second general feature enables us to subject some theorems of the proposed logic on the metaphysical interpretation to independent test. Together, the two features differentiate modal logic as metaphysics from any pseudo-science.

Of course, a sceptic who doubts that there is modal knowledge will not be impressed by the second feature, just as a sceptic who doubts that there is logical or mathematical knowledge will not be impressed by the first feature, and a sceptic who doubts that there is knowledge of the external world will not be impressed by the pretensions of natural science. But it is not the business of science to answer the determined sceptic. Such a character, always ready to raise the stakes by widening the area in doubt, is beyond the reach of good sense, and must be left to find his own way out of the corner into which he has painted himself. Although even non-sceptics can wonder *how* we gain our elementary pre-theoretical modal knowledge, that is not the concern of this book.[1] Like any other scientific enquiry, metaphysics as

---

[1] See Williamson 2007, pp. 134–78, for a sketch of an account.

modal logic is rooted in our pre-scientific cognitive capacities. In doing science, we exercise much greater intellectual caution than is appropriate in ordinary life, but stop short of taking caution to the limit, on pain of total intellectual paralysis.

To equate the methodology of modal logic as metaphysics with the application of formal methods to pre-theoretic modal knowledge is a massive oversimplification. Even skimming through the contents of this book reveals a far more complex picture. Nevertheless, the presence of those two factors already suffices to show the enterprise to be highly constrained in truth-directed ways. Once a discipline has attained that status, it is in a position to refine its methodology autonomously, by an iterative bootstrapping process characteristic of science. That too has happened through the decades over which modal logic as metaphysics has developed, and can be expected to go further. But, like any other scientific enquiry, modal logic as metaphysics is fruitful only when pursued with the sort of educated instinct that comes through training for and experience of the enquiry, although even they offer no guarantees. Such good sense is irreducible to knowledge of explicit rules, because any explicit rule can be applied unwisely.

Modal logic as metaphysics resembles other branches of metaphysics in depending on the pre-theoretical knowledge and disciplined instincts of its practitioners. However, for modal logic as metaphysics to be pursued by the methodology prevalent in some areas of contemporary metaphysics would be a disaster. For it would involve abandoning its chief advantage: its strongly though not purely formal character. Some metaphysical theories are so informal that it is quite unclear what they entail. Whenever an opponent claims to draw false consequences from them, a proponent has the option of denying that they really follow. Sometimes metaphysicians seem to reserve the right to make up their theory's consequence relation as they go along. That has the advantage of rendering their theory hard to refute, but the disadvantage of undermining its 'predictive' power. When things are deemed to follow from a theory only once they have been independently confirmed, it gains little confirmation from them, because it gave so little reason to expect them rather than their contraries to hold. Even when the need to revise such a theory is acknowledged, the informality of its formulation is conducive to ad hoc fixes, which are harder to make at the level of generality characteristic of logic. Of course, some areas of metaphysics are far more suitable than others for formal methods; they are no panacea. Even when they are applicable, their use in testing philosophical theories typically depends on auxiliary hypotheses, just as when theories are tested in natural science. Such hypotheses rightly give defenders of the theories some wiggle room. Nevertheless, nothing differentiates contemporary metaphysics from a pseudo-science more clearly than its formal methods, where non-trivially applied. They are one of the few things to give us reasonable hope of doing better than our predecessors, who were so far from our inferiors in intellect and good sense.

The opposite disaster would be for modal logic as metaphysics to be pursued by purely formal, mathematical means. Everything that distinguishes its subject matter, the combination of metaphysical possibility and necessity with unrestricted generality, from other interpretations of quantified modal logic would be lost, as incapable of proof. Without some reliance on our initial capacity to distinguish what could have been from what could not, we cannot get started. As for our aim, what we want is not a weak modal logic, neutral on the relevant metaphysical questions. Rather, we want a strong modal logic that answers those metaphysical questions. This book has proposed such a logic: higher-order necessitist S5. To its opponents, the challenge is to show that their favoured alternative does better by the same abductive methodology.

Bibliography

Adams, Robert M. 1974: 'Theories of actuality', *Noûs*, 5, pp. 211–31.

———1981: 'Actualism and thisness', *Synthese*, 49, pp. 3–41.

Addison, John W., Henkin, Leon, and Tarski, Alfred (eds) 1965: *The Theory of Models*. Amsterdam: North Holland.

Agazzi, Evandro (ed.) 1980: *Modern Logic—A Survey: Historical, Philosophical, and Mathematical Aspects of Modern Logic and its Applications*. Dordrecht: Reidel.

Almog, Joseph 1989: 'Logic and the world', *Journal of Philosophical Logic*, 18, pp. 197–220.

———, Perry, John, and Wettstein, Howard (eds) 1989: *Themes from Kaplan*. Oxford: Oxford University Press.

Areces, Carlos, and ten Cate, Balder 2007: 'Hybrid logics', in Blackburn, van Benthem, and Wolter 2007, pp. 821–68.

Arló-Costa, Horacio 2002: 'First order extensions of classical systems of modal logic: the role of the Barcan schemas', *Studia Logica*, 71, pp. 87–118.

Armstrong, David 1978: *A Theory of Universals Volume II: Universals and Scientific Realism*. Cambridge: Cambridge University Press.

———1997: *A World of States of Affairs*. Cambridge: Cambridge University Press.

———2004: *Truth and Truthmakers*. Cambridge: Cambridge University Press.

Bacon, Andrew 2011: 'Quantificational logic and empty names'. Typescript.

Bacon, John 1980: 'Substance and first-order quantification over individual-concepts', *The Journal of Symbolic Logic*, 45, pp. 193–203.

Baker, Alan 2003: 'Quantitative parsimony and explanatory power', *The British Journal for the Philosophy of Science*, 54, pp. 245–59.

Baldwin, J.M. (ed.) 1901: *Dictionary of Philosophy and Psychology*, 3 vols. New York: Macmillan.

Baldwin, Thomas 1996: 'There might be nothing', *Analysis*, 56, pp. 231–8.

Barcan, Ruth C. 1946a: 'A functional calculus of first order based on strict implication', *The Journal of Symbolic Logic*, 11, pp. 1–16.

———1946b: 'The deduction theorem in a functional calculus of first order based on strict implication', *The Journal of Symbolic Logic*, 11, 115–18.

——1947: 'The identity of individuals in a strict functional calculus of second order', *The Journal of Symbolic Logic*, 12, pp. 12–15. [See also Marcus, Ruth Barcan.]

Barwise, Jon 1978: 'On branching quantifiers in English', *Journal of Philosophical Logic*, 8, pp. 47–80.

—— and Solomon Feferman (eds) 1985: *Model-Theoretic Logics*. New York: Springer-Verlag.

Bayart, Arnould 1958: 'La correction de la logique modale de premier et second ordre S5', *Logique et Analyse*, 1, pp. 28–44.

——1959: 'Quasi-adéquation de la logique modale de second ordre S5 et adéquation de la logique modale de premier ordre S5', *Logique et Analyse*, 2, pp. 99–121.

Beall, J.C. (ed.) 2003: *Liars and Heaps: New Essays on Paradox*. Oxford: Clarendon Press.

Beebee, Helen, and Dodd, Julian (eds) 2005: *Truthmakers: The Contemporary Debate*. Oxford: Clarendon Press.

Běhounek, Libor, and Bílková, Marta (eds) 2005: *The Logica Yearbook 2004*. Prague: Filosofia.

Belnap, Nuel 1972: 'Foreword', in Bressan 1972, pp. xiii–xxv.

Bennett, Karen 2005: 'Two axes of actualism', *The Philosophical Review*, 114, pp. 297–326.

——2006: 'Proxy "actualism"', *Philosophical Studies*, 129, pp. 263–94.

Bergmann, Gustav 1960: 'The philosophical significance of modal logic', *Mind*, 69, pp. 466–85.

Bermúdez, José Luis (ed.) 2005: *Thought, Reference, and Experience: Themes from the Philosophy of Gareth Evans*. Oxford: Clarendon Press.

Besson, Corine 2009: 'Externalism, internalism, and logical truth', *The Review of Symbolic Logic*, 2, pp. 1–29.

Bigelow, John 1988: *The Reality of Numbers*. Oxford: Clarendon Press.

Bird, Alexander 2007: *Nature's Metaphysics: Laws and Properties*. Oxford: Clarendon Press.

Blackburn, Patrick 2007: 'Arthur Prior and hybrid logic', *Synthese*, 150, pp. 329–72.

——, and de Rijke, Martin 1997: 'Why combine logics?', *Studia Logica*, 59, pp. 5–27.

——, ——, and Venema, Yde 2001: *Modal Logic*. Cambridge: Cambridge University Press.

——, van Benthem, Johan, and Wolter, Frank (eds) 2007: *Handbook of Modal Logic*. Amsterdam: Elsevier.

Boolos, George 1984: 'To be is to be a value of a variable (or to be some values of some variables)', in his 1998, pp. 54–72. Originally published in *The Journal of Philosophy*, 81, pp. 430–49.

——1985: 'Nominalist platonism', in his 1998, pp. 73–87. Originally published in *The Philosophical Review*, 94, pp. 327–44.

——1993: 'Whence the contradiction?', in his 1998, pp. 220–36. Originally published in *Aristotelian Society*, sup. 67, pp. 213–33.

——1998: *Logic, logic, and logic.* Cambridge, MA: Harvard University Press.

Bostock, David 1998: 'On motivating higher-order logic', in Smiley 1998, pp. 29–43.

Bradley, Ben 2009: *Well-Being and Death.* Oxford: Clarendon Press.

Bressan, Aldo 1972: *A General Interpreted Modal Calculus*, with an introduction by Nuel Belnap. New Haven: Yale University Press.

Bricker, Phillip 1987: 'Reducing possible worlds to language', *Philosophical Studies*, 52, pp. 331–55.

——1989: 'Quantified modal logic and the plural *de re*', *Midwest Studies in Philosophy*, 14, pp. 372–94.

Broome, John 2004: *Weighing Lives.* Oxford: Oxford University Press.

Bull, Robert 1969: 'On modal logic with propositional quantifiers', *The Journal of Symbolic Logic*, 34, pp. 257–63.

——1970: 'An approach to tense logic', *Theoria*, 36, pp. 282–300.

Burgess, John P. 1998: '*Quinus ab omni naevo vindicatus*', in his 2008, pp. 203–35. Originally published in *Canadian Journal of Philosophy*, supplement, 23, pp. 25–65.

——1999: 'Which modal logic is the right one?', in his 2008, pp. 169–84. Originally published in *Notre Dame Journal of Formal Logic*, 40, pp. 81–93.

——2003: 'Which modal models are the right ones (for logical necessity)?', *Theoria* (San Sebastián), 18, pp. 145–58.

——2008: *Mathematics, Models and Modality: Selected Philosophical Essays.* Cambridge: Cambridge University Press.

——, Hazen, Allen, and Lewis, David 1991: 'Appendix on pairing', in Lewis 1991, pp. 121–49.

Burks, Arthur 1951: 'The logic of causal propositions', *Mind*, 60, pp. 363–82.

Callender, Craig (ed.) 2011: *The Oxford Handbook of Philosophy of Time.* Oxford: Oxford University Press.

Campbell, Joseph, O'Rourke, Michael, and Shier, David (eds) 2002: *Meaning and Truth—Investigations in Philosophical Semantics.* New York: Seven Bridges Press.

Cappelen, Herman, and Hawthorne, John 2009: *Relativism and Monadic Truth.* Oxford: Oxford University Press.

Carlson, Erik, and Sliwinski, Rysiek (eds) 2001: *Omnium-gatherum: Philosophical Essays Dedicated to Jan Österberg on the Occasion of his Sixtieth Birthday.* Uppsala: Department of Philosophy, Uppsala University (Uppsala Philosophical Studies 50).

Carnap, Rudolf 1946: 'Modalities and quantification', *The Journal of Symbolic Logic*, 11, pp. 33–64.

——1947: *Meaning and Necessity: A Study in Semantics and Modal Logic*. 2nd edn, with supplements, 1956. Chicago: Chicago University Press.

——1952: 'Meaning postulates', *Philosophical Studies*, 3, pp. 65–73. Reprinted in Carnap 1947, 2nd edn, pp. 222–9.

——1963a: 'My conceptions of the logic of modalities', in Schilpp 1963, pp. 889–900.

——1963b: 'John Myhill on modal logic and semantics', in Schilpp 1963, pp. 908–11.

Cartwright, Richard 1994: 'Speaking of everything', *Noûs*, 28, pp. 1–20.

Chagrov, Alexander, and Zakharyaschev, Michael 1997: *Modal Logic*. Oxford: Clarendon Press.

Chalmers, David J., Manley, David, and Wasserman, Ryan (eds) 2009: *Metametaphysics: New Essays on the Foundations of Ontology*. Oxford: Clarendon Press.

Chellas, Brian, and Segerberg, Krister 1994: 'Modal logics with the MacIntosh rule', *Journal of Philosophical Logic*, 23, pp. 67–86.

Church, Alonzo 1943: Review of Quine 1943, *The Journal of Symbolic Logic*, 8, pp. 45–7.

——1951: 'A formulation of the logic of sense and denotation', in Henle, Kallen and Langer 1951, pp. 3–24.

——1973: 'Outline of a revised formulation of the logic of sense and denotation (part I)', *Noûs*, 7, pp. 24–33.

Cocchiarella, Nino 1968: 'Some remarks on second order logic with existence attributes', *Noûs*, 2, pp. 165–75.

——1969a: 'Existence entailing attributes, modes of copulation and modes of being in second order logic', *Noûs*, 3, pp. 33–48.

——1969b: 'A second order logic of existence', *The Journal of Symbolic Logic*, 34, pp. 57–69.

——1969c: 'A completeness theorem in second order modal logic', *Theoria*, 35, pp. 81–103.

——1975: 'On the primary and secondary semantics of logical necessity', *Journal of Philosophical Logic*, 4, pp. 13–27.

——1986: *Logical Investigations of Predication Theory and the Problem of Universals*. Naples: Bibliopolis.

——, and Freund, Max 2008: *Modal Logic: An Introduction to its Syntax and Semantics*. Oxford: Oxford University Press.

Copeland, Jack 1982: 'A note on the Barcan formula and substitutional quantification', *Logique et Analyse*, 25, pp. 83–6.

——(ed.) 1996: *Logic and Reality: Essays on the Legacy of Arthur Prior*. Oxford: Clarendon Press.

——2002: 'The genesis of possible worlds semantics', *Journal of Philosophical Logic* 31, pp. 99–137.

Correia, Fabrice 2007: 'Modality, quantification, and many Vlach-operators', *Journal of Philosophical Logic*, 36, pp. 473–88.

—— and Schnieder, Benjamin (eds) 2012: *Metaphysical Grounding: Understanding the Structure of Reality*. Cambridge: Cambridge University Press.

Corsi, Giovanna 2003: 'BF, CBF and Lewis semantics', *Logique et Analyse*, 46, pp. 103–22.

Cresswell, Max 1990: *Entities and Indices*. Dordrecht: Kluwer.

——1991: 'In defence of the Barcan formula', *Logique et Analyse* 135/136, pp. 271–82.

——1995: 'Incompleteness and the Barcan formula', *Journal of Philosophical Logic* 24, pp. 379–403.

Crisp, Thomas 2003: 'Presentism', in Loux and Zimmerman 2003, pp. 211–45.

Crossley, John, and Humberstone, Lloyd 1977: 'The logic of "actually"', *Reports on Mathematical Logic*, 8, pp. 11–29.

Daly, Chris 2005: 'So where's the explanation?', in Beebee and Dodd 2005, pp. 85–103.

Davidson, Donald 1967: 'The logical form of action sentences', in his 1980, pp. 105–22. Originally published in Rescher 1967, pp. 81–120.

——1970: 'Events as particulars', in his 1980, pp. 181–7. Originally published in *Noûs*, 4, pp. 25–32.

——1980: *Essays on Actions and Events*. Oxford: Clarendon Press.

Davies, Martin 1978: 'Weak necessity and truth theories', *Journal of Philosophic Logic*, 7, pp. 415–39.

——1981: *Meaning, Quantification, Necessity: Themes in Philosophical Logic*. London: Routledge & Kegan Paul.

——, and Humberstone, Lloyd 1980: 'Two notions of necessity', *Philosophical Studies*, 38, pp. 1–30.

Deasy, Daniel 2013: *Permanents: In Defence of a Permanentist A-Theory*. Oxford: D.Phil. thesis.

Deutsch, Harry 1990: 'Contingency and modal logic', *Philosophical Studies*, 60, pp. 89–102.

——1994: 'Logic for contingent beings', *Journal of Philosophical Research*, 19, pp. 273–329.

Dickmann, M.N. 1985: 'Larger infinitary languages', in Barwise and Feferman 1985, pp. 317–63.

Dorr, Cian 2011: *Counterparts*. Typescript.

Dummett, Michael 1981: *Frege: Philosophy of Language*, 2nd edn. London: Duckworth.

——1983: 'Could there be unicorns?', in Dummett 1993, pp. 328–48. Original version published as 'Könnte es Einhörner geben?', *Conceptus*, 17, pp. 5–10.

——1991: *Frege: Philosophy of Mathematics*. Cambridge, MA: Harvard University Press.

——1993: *The Seas of Language*. Oxford: Clarendon Press.

Efird, David 2010: 'Is Timothy Williamson a necessary existent?', in Hale and Hoffmann 2010, pp. 97–107.

Eklund, Matti 1996: 'On how logic became first-order', *Nordic Journal of Philosophical Logic*, 1, pp. 147–67.

Enayat, Ali, Kalantari, Iraj, and Moniri, Mojtaba (eds) 2006: *Logic in Tehran: Proceedings of the Workshop and Conference on Logic, Algebra and Arithmetic, held October 18–22, 2003* (ASL Lecture Notes in Logic 26). Natick, MA: A.K. Peters.

Epicurus 1997: 'Letter to Menoeceus', in Inwood and Gerson 1997, pp. 28–31.

Etchemendy, John 1990: *On the Concept of Logical Consequence*. Cambridge, MA: Harvard University Press.

Evans, Gareth 1977: 'Pronouns, quantifiers and relative clauses (I)', in Evans 1985, pp. 76–152. Original version published in *The Canadian Journal of Philosophy*, 7, pp. 467–536.

——1985: *Collected Papers*. Oxford: Clarendon Press.

——, and McDowell, John (eds) 1976: *Truth and Meaning*. Oxford: Clarendon Press.

Ewald, William (ed.) 1996: *From Kant to Hilbert: A Source Book in the Foundations of Mathematics*, 2 vols. Oxford: Oxford University Press.

Fara, Michael, and Williamson, Timothy 2005: 'Counterparts and actuality', *Mind*, 114, pp. 1–30.

Field, Hartry 2009: 'What is the normative role of logic?', *Aristotelian Society*, sup. 83, pp. 251–68.

Fine, Kit 1970: 'Propositional quantifiers in modal logic', *Theoria*, 36, pp. 336–46.

——1977a: 'Prior on the construction of possible worlds and instants', in Prior and Fine 1977, pp. 116–68.

——1977b: 'Properties, propositions and sets', *Journal of Philosophical Logic*, 6, pp. 135–91.

——1978: 'Model theory for modal logic—part II: the elimination of *de re* modality', *Journal of Philosophical Logic*, 7, pp. 277–306.

——1980: 'First-order modal theories', *Studia Logica* 39 (1980): 159–202.

——1981a: 'Model theory for modal logic part III: existence and predication', *Journal of Philosophical Logic*, 10, pp. 293–307.

——1981b: 'First-order modal theories I—sets', *Noûs*, 15, pp. 177–205.

——1982a: 'The problem of non-existence I. Internalism', *Topoi*, 1, pp. 97–140.

——1982b: 'First-order modal theories III—facts', *Synthese*, 53, pp. 43–122.

——1983: 'The permutation principle in quantificational logic', *Journal of Philosophical Logic*, 12, pp. 33–7.

——1985: 'Plantinga on the reduction of possibilist discourse', in Tomberlin and van Inwagen 1985, pp. 145–86.

———1994: 'Essence and modality', *Philosophical Perspectives*, 8, pp. 1–16.

———2003: 'The problem of possibilia', in Loux and Zimmerman 2003, pp. 161–79.

———2005a: *Modality and Tense: Philosophical Papers*. Oxford: Clarendon Press.

———2005b: 'Class and membership', *Journal of Philosophy*, 102, pp. 547–72.

———2006: 'Relatively unrestricted quantification', in Rayo and Uzquiano 2006, pp. 20–44.

———2012: 'A guide to ground', in Correia and Schnieder 2012, pp. 37–80.

Føllesdal, Dagfinn 1968/1969: 'Quine on modality', *Synthese*, 19, pp. 147–57.

———2004: *Referential Opacity and Modal Logic*. London: Routledge. Original version submitted as Ph.D. thesis, Harvard University, 1961.

Forbes, Graeme 1985: *The Metaphysics of Modality*. Oxford: Clarendon Press.

———1989: *Languages of Possibility*. Oxford: Blackwell.

———1992: 'Melia on modalism', *Philosophical Studies*, 68, pp. 57–63.

———2008: 'Critical review of Kit Fine, *Modality and Tense*', *Philosophical Review*, 117, pp. 275–87.

Fox, John 1987: 'Truthmaker', *Australasian Journal of Philosophy*, 65, pp. 188–207.

Frauchiger, Michael, and Essler, Wilhelm (eds) forthcoming: *Themes from Barcan Marcus*. Lancaster, New Brunswick: Ontos Verlag.

Frege, Gottlob 1892: 'On concept and object', in Geach and Black 1960, pp. 42–55. Originally published as 'Über Begriff und Gegenstand', *Vierteljahrsschrift für wissenschaftliche Philosophie*, 16, pp. 192–205.

———1979: *Posthumous Writings*, ed. by H. Hermes, F. Kambartel, and F. Kaulbach, trans. by P. Long and R. White. Oxford: Blackwell.

Fritz, Peter forthcoming: 'Modal ontology and generalized quantifiers', *Journal of Philosophical Logic*.

Gabbay, Dov, and Guenthner, Franz (eds) 1984: *Handbook of Philosophical Logic*, vol. 2. Amsterdam: Reidel.

———, ———(eds) 2001: *Handbook of Philosophical Logic*, 2nd edn, vol. 3. Dordrecht: Kluwer.

Gale, Richard (ed.) 2002: *The Blackwell Guide to Metaphysics*. Oxford: Blackwell.

Gallin, Daniel 1975: *Intensional and Higher-Order Modal Logic: With Applications to Montague Semantics*. Amsterdam: North-Holland.

Gallois, André 1998: *Occasions of Identity*. Oxford: Clarendon Press.

Garson, James W. 1984: 'Quantification in modal logic', in Gabbay and Guenthner 1984, pp. 249–307. Revised and updated in Gabbay and Guenthner 2001, pp. 267–324.

———2005: 'Unifying quantified modal logic', *Journal of Philosophical Logic*, 34, pp. 621–49.

———2006: *Modal Logic for Philosophers*. Cambridge: Cambridge University Press.

Gendler, Tamar Szabó, and Hawthorne, John (eds) 2002: *Conceivability and Possibility*. Oxford: Clarendon Press.

Gibbard, Allan 1975: 'Contingent identity', *Journal of Philosophical Logic*, 4, pp. 187–221.

Goldblatt, Robert, and Mares, Edwin 2006: 'A general semantics for quantified modal logic', *Advances in Modal Logic*, 6, pp. 227–46.

Goldfarb, Warren 2010: 'Frege's conception of logic', in Potter and Ricketts 2010, pp. 63–85.

Gómez-Torrente, Mario 1999: 'Logical truth and Tarskian logical truth', *Synthese*, 117, pp. 375–408.

Gray, Jeremy, and Ferreiros, José (eds) 2006: *The Architecture of Modern Mathematics*. Oxford: Oxford University Press.

Gregory, Dominic 2001: 'B is innocent', *Analysis*, 61, pp. 225–9.

Gupta, Anil 1978: 'Modal logic and truth', *Journal of Philosophical Logic*, 7, pp. 441–72.

——1980: *The Logic of Common Nouns*. New Haven: Yale University Press.

Gurevich, Yuri 1985: 'Monadic second-order theories', in Barwise and Feferman 1985, pp. 479–506.

Hale, Bob, and Hoffmann, Aviv (eds) 2010: *Modality: Metaphysics, Logic, and Epistemology*. Oxford: Oxford University Press.

Halldén, Sören 1951: 'On the semantic non-completeness of certain Lewis calculi', *The Journal of Symbolic Logic*, 16, pp. 127–9.

Haller, Rudolf, and Brandl, Johannes (eds) 1990: *Wittgenstein—Towards a Re-Evaluation: Proceedings of the 14th International Wittgenstein-Symposium*, 3 vols. Vienna: Hölder-Pichler-Tempsky.

Hawthorne, John 2003: 'Identity', in Loux and Zimmerman 2003, pp. 99–130.

——2006: *Metaphysical Essays*. Oxford: Clarendon Press.

——, and Uzquiano, Gabriel 2011: 'How many angels can dance on the point of a needle? Transcendental theology meets modal metaphysics', *Mind*, 120, pp. 53-81.

Hayaki, Reina 2005: 'The transience of possibility', *European Journal of Analytic Philosophy*, 1, pp. 25–36.

Hazen, Allen 1986: 'A fallacy in Ramsey', *Mind*, 95, pp. 496–8.

——1993: 'Against pluralism', *Australasian Journal of Philosophy*, 71, pp. 132–44.

Hellman, Geoffrey 1989: *Mathematics without Numbers: Towards a Modal-Structural Interpretation*. Oxford: Clarendon Press.

Henkin, Leon 1950: 'Completeness in the theory of types', *The Journal of Symbolic Logic*, 15, pp. 81–91.

——1961: 'Some remarks on infinitely long formulas', in Henkin and others 1961, pp. 167–83.

——, and others 1961: *Infinitistic Methods: Proceedings of the Symposium on the Foundations of Mathematics*. Oxford: Pergamon Press.

Henle, Paul, Kallen, Horace, and Langer, Susanne (eds) 1951: *Structure, Method, and Meaning: Essays in Honor of Henry M. Shaffer*. New York: Liberal Arts Press.

Hershenov, David 2007: 'A more palatable Epicureanism', *American Philosophical Quarterly*, 44, pp. 170–80.

Hewitt, Simon 2012: 'Modalising plurals', *Journal of Philosophical Logic*, 41, pp. 853–75.

Heylen, Jan 2010: 'Carnap's theory of descriptions and its problems', *Studia Logica*, 94, pp. 355–80.

Higginbotham, James 1998: 'On higher-order logic and natural language', in Smiley 1998, pp. 1–27.

Hintikka, Jaakko 1961: 'Modality and quantification', *Theoria*, 27, pp. 119–28.

—— 1980: 'Standard vs. non-standard logics: higher-order, modal, and first-order logics', in Agazzi 1980, pp. 183–96.

—— and Sandu, Gabriel 1995: 'The fallacies of the New Theory of Reference', *Synthese*, 104, pp. 245–83.

Hirsch, Eli 2011: *Quantifier Variance and Realism: Essays in Metaontology*. Oxford: Oxford University Press.

Hochberg, Herbert 2002: 'From logic to ontology: some problems of predication, negation, and possibility', in Jacquette 2002, pp. 281–92.

Hodes, Harold 1984: 'On modal logics which enrich first-order S5', *Journal of Philosophical Logic*, 13, pp. 423–54.

Horgan, Terry, and Potrč, Matjaž 2000: 'Blobjectivism and indirect correspondence', *Facta Philosophica*, 2, pp. 249–70.

Horwich, Paul 1998: *Truth*, 2nd edn. Oxford: Clarendon Press.

—— 2008: 'Being and truth', *Midwest Studies in Philosophy*, 32, pp. 258–73.

Hughes, George, and Cresswell, Max 1968: *An Introduction to Modal Logic*. London: Methuen.

——, —— 1984: *A Companion to Modal Logic*. London: Methuen.

——, —— 1996: *A New Introduction to Modal Logic*. London: Routledge.

Humberstone, Lloyd 1983: 'Karmo on contingent non-identity', *Australasian Journal of Philosophy*, 61, pp. 188–91.

—— 1996a: 'Homophony, Validity, Modality', in Copeland 1996, pp. 215–36.

—— 1996b: 'Intrinsic/extrinsic', *Synthese*, 108, pp. 205–67.

—— 2005: 'Modality', in Jackson and Smith 2005, pp. 534–614.

—— 2007: 'Modal logic for other-world agnostics: neutrality and Halldén incompleteness', *Journal of Philosophical Logic*, 36, pp. 1–32.

Humphreys, Paul W., and Fetzer, James H. (eds) 1998: *The New Theory of Reference—Kripke, Marcus, and its Origins*. Dordrecht: Kluwer.

Ibn-Sina 1970: *Al-Ibara*, ed. Mahmud al-Khozairi. Cairo: Dar-al-Katib-al-Arabi.

Inwood, Brad, and Gerson, L.P. trans. and eds. 1997: *Hellenistic Philosophy: Introductory Readings*, 2nd edn. Indianapolis: Hackett.

Jackson, Frank, and Smith, Michael (eds) 2005: *The Oxford Handbook of Contemporary Philosophy*. Oxford: Oxford University Press.

Jacquette, Dale (ed.) 2002: *A Companion to Philosophical Logic*. Oxford: Blackwell.

Jager, Thomas 1982: 'An actualist semantics for modal logic', *Notre Dame Journal of Formal Logic*, 23, pp. 335–49.

Kanger, Stig 1957a: *Provability in Logic*. Stockholm: Almqvist & Wiksell.

——1957b: 'The morning star paradox', *Theoria*, 23, pp. 1–11.

——1957c: 'A note on quantification and modalities', *Theoria*, 23, pp. 133–4.

Kaplan, David 1970: 'S5 with quantifiable propositional variables', *The Journal of Symbolic Logic*, 35, p. 355.

——1975: 'How to Russell a Frege-Church', *The Journal of Philosophy*, 72, pp. 716–29.

——1979: 'On the logic of demonstratives', *Journal of Philosophical Logic*, 8, pp. 81–98.

——1989a: 'Demonstratives: an essay on the semantics, logic, metaphysics, and epistemology of demonstratives and other indexicals', in Almog, Perry, and Wettstein 1989, pp. 481–563.

——1989b: 'Afterthoughts', in Almog, Perry, and Wettstein 1989, pp. 565–614.

——1994: 'A problem in possible-worlds semantics', in Sinnott-Armstrong, Raffman, and Asher 1994, pp. 41–52.

Karmo, Toomas 1983: 'Contingent non-identity', *Australasian Journal of Philosophy*, 61, pp. 185–7.

Kim, Jaegwon 1984: 'Concepts of supervenience', *Philosophy and Phenomenological Research*, 65, pp. 257–70.

King, Jeffrey 2003: 'Tense, modality, and semantic values', *Philosophical Perspectives*, 15, pp. 195–245.

——2007: *The Nature and Structure of Content*. Oxford: Oxford University Press.

Kneale, William, and Kneale, Martha 1962: *The Development of Logic*. Oxford: Clarendon Press.

Knuuttila, Simo 1993: *Modalities in Medieval Philosophy*. London: Routledge.

Kracht, Marcus 1999: 'Modal logics that need very large frames', *Notre Dame Journal of Formal Logic*, 40, pp. 141–73.

Kratzer, Angelika 1989: 'An investigation of the lumps of thought', *Linguistics and Philosophy*, 12, pp. 607–53.

Kremer, Michael 1997: 'Martí on descriptions in Carnap's S2', *Journal of Philosophical Logic*, 26, pp. 629–34.

Kripke, Saul 1959a: 'A completeness theorem in modal logic', *The Journal of Symbolic Logic*, 24, pp. 1–14.

——1959b: 'Semantical analysis of modal logic (abstract)', *The Journal of Symbolic Logic*, 24, pp. 323–4.

——1963: 'Semantical considerations on modal logic', in Linsky 1971, pp. 63–72. Originally published in *Acta Philosophica Fennica*, 16, pp. 83–94.

——1965: 'Semantical analysis of modal logic II: non-normal modal propositional calculi, in Addison, Henkin and Tarski 1965, pp. 206–20.

——1971: 'Identity and necessity', in Munitz 1971, pp. 135–64.

——1976: 'Is there a problem about substitutional quantification?', in Evans and McDowell 1976, pp. 325–419.

——1980: *Naming and Necessity*. Oxford: Blackwell.

——1992: 'Individual concepts: their logic, philosophy, and some of their uses', *Proceedings and Addresses of the American Philosophical Association*, 66, pp. 70–3.

——2011: *Philosophical Troubles: Collected Papers, Volume I*. Oxford: Oxford University Press.

Lambert, Karel (ed.) 1969: *The Logical Way of Doing Things*. New Haven: Yale University Press.

——(ed.): 1970: *Philosophical Problems in Logic: Some Recent Developments*. Reidel: Dordrecht.

—— and van Fraassen, Bas 1970: 'Meaning relations, possible objects, and possible worlds', in Lambert 1970, pp. 1–19.

Landman, Fred 1989: 'Groups I', *Linguistics and Philosophy*, 12, pp. 559–605.

Leitgeb, Hannes, and Hieke, Alexander 2004: 'Circular languages', *Journal of Logic, Language and Information*, 13, pp. 341–71.

Lemmon, John 1960: 'Quantified S4 and the Barcan formula' (abstract), *The Journal of Symbolic Logic*, 25, pp. 391–2.

——1966a: 'Algebraic semantics for modal logic I', *The Journal of Symbolic Logic*, 31, pp. 48–65.

——1966b: 'Algebraic semantics for modal logic II', *The Journal of Symbolic Logic*, 31, pp. 191–218.

——1966c: 'A note on Halldén-incompleteness', *Notre Dame Journal of Formal Logic*, 7, pp. 296–300.

Leng, Mary, Paseau, Alexander, and Potter, Michael (eds) 2007: *Mathematical Knowledge*. Oxford: Oxford University Press.

Lewis, Clarence I., and Langford, Cooper H. 1932: *Symbolic Logic*. New York: Dover.

Lewis, David 1968: 'Counterpart theory and quantified modal logic', in Lewis 1983a, pp. 26–46. Original version in *The Journal of Philosophy*, 65, 113–26.

——1970: 'General semantics', in Lewis 1983a, pp. 189–232. Original version in *Synthese*, 22, pp. 18–67.

——1973: *Counterfactuals*. Oxford: Blackwell.

——1983a: *Philosophical Papers*, vol. 1. Oxford: Oxford University Press.

——1983b: 'New work for a theory of universals', *The Australasian Journal of Philosophy*, 61, pp. 343–77.

——1986: *On the Plurality of Worlds*. Oxford: Blackwell.

——1991: *Parts of Classes*. Oxford: Blackwell.

——1992: 'Armstrong on combinatorial possibility', in Lewis 1999, pp. 196–214. Originally published in *Australasian Journal of Philosophy*, 70, pp. 211–24.

——1994: 'Humean Supervenience debugged', *Mind*, 103, pp. 473–90.

——1999: *Papers in Metaphysics and Epistemology*. Cambridge: Cambridge University Press.

——2004: 'Tensed quantifiers', *Oxford Studies in Metaphysics*, 1, pp. 3–14.

Liggins, David 2005: 'Truthmakers and explanation', in Beebee and Dodd 2005, pp. 105–15.

Lindström, Sten 1998: 'An exposition and development of Kanger's early semantics for modal logic', in Humphreys and Fetzer 1998, pp. 203–33.

——2001: 'Quine's interpretation problem and the early development of possible worlds semantics', in Carlson and Sliwinski 2001, pp. 187–213.

Linnebo, Øystein 2003: 'Plural quantification exposed', *Noûs*, 37, pp. 71–92.

——2010: 'Pluralities and sets', *The Journal of Philosophy*, 107, pp. 144–64.

——, and Nicolas, David 2008: 'Superplurals in English', *Analysis*, 68, pp. 186–97.

——, and Rayo, Agustín 2012: 'Hierarchies ontological and ideological'. *Mind*, 121, pp. 269–308.

Linsky, Bernard, and Zalta, Edward 1994: 'In defense of the simplest quantified modal logic', *Philosophical Perspectives*, 8, pp. 431–58.

——, ——1996: 'In defense of the contingently nonconcrete', *Philosophical Studies*, 84, pp. 283–94.

Linsky, Leonard (ed.) 1971: *Reference and Modality*. Oxford: Oxford University Press.

Löffler, Winfried 1998: 'On almost bare possibilia. Reply to Timothy Williamson', *Erkenntnis*, 48, pp. 275–9.

Loptson, Peter 1980: 'Logic and contingent existence', *History and Philosophy of Logic*, 1, 171–85.

Loux, Michael and Zimmerman, Dean (eds) 2003: *The Oxford Handbook of Metaphysics*. Oxford: Oxford University Press.

Lovibond, Sabina, and Williams, S.G. (eds) 1996: *Identity, Truth and Value: Essays for David Wiggins*. Oxford: Blackwell.

Lowe, Jonathan, and Rami, Adolf (eds) 2009: *Truth and Truth-Making*. Stocksfield: Acumen.

Mackie, Penelope 2006: *How Things Might Have Been: Individuals, Kinds, and Essential Properties*. Oxford: Clarendon Press.

Makinson, David 1971: 'Some embedding theorems for modal logic', *Notre Dame Journal of Formal Logic*, 12, pp. 252–4.

Mancosu, Paolo 2006: 'Tarski on models and logical consequence', in Gray and Ferreiros 2006, pp. 209–37.

Marcus, Ruth Barcan 1961: 'Modalities and intensional languages', *Synthese*, 13, pp. 303–22. Reprinted with revisions in Marcus 1993, pp. 3–23.

——1962: 'Interpreting quantification', *Inquiry*, 5, pp. 252–9.

——1967:'Essentialism in modal logic', *Noûs*, 1, pp. 90–6. Reprinted with revisions in Marcus 1993, pp. 45–51.

——1971: 'Essential attribution', *The Journal of Philosophy*, 68, pp. 187–202. Reprinted with revisions in Marcus 1993, pp. 53–70.

——1985/1986:'Possibilia and possible worlds', in Marcus 1993, pp. 189–213. Original version in *Grazer Philosophische Studien*, 25–6, pp. 107–33.

——1993: *Modalities: Philosophical Essays*. Oxford: Oxford University Press. [See also Barcan, Ruth C.]

Markosian, Ned 2004: 'A defense of presentism', *Oxford Studies in Metaphysics*, 1, pp. 47–82.

Martí, Genoveva 1994:'Do modal distinctions collapse in Carnap's system?', *Journal of Philosophical Logic*, 23, pp. 575–93.

——1997: 'Rethinking Quine's argument on the collapse of modal distinctions', *Notre Dame Journal of Formal Logic*, 38, pp. 276–94.

McGee, Vann 1992:'Two problems with Tarski's theory of consequence', *Proceedings of the Aristotelian Society*, 92, pp. 273–92.

——2003:'Universal universal quantification', in Beall 2003, pp. 357–64.

McKay, Thomas 2006: *Plural Predication*. Oxford: Oxford University Press.

McKinsey, John 1941:'A solution of the decision problem for the Lewis systems S2 and S4 with an application to topology', *The Journal of Symbolic Logic*, 6, pp. 117–34.

——1945:'On the syntactical construction of systems of modal logic', *The Journal of Symbolic Logic*, 10, pp. 83–96.

——1948/1949,'A new definition of truth', *Synthese*, 7, pp. 428–33.

——, and Tarski, Alfred 1948:'Some theorems about the sentential calculi of Lewis and Heyting', *The Journal of Symbolic Logic*, 13, pp. 1–15.

McLaughlin, Brian 1995:'Varieties of supervenience', in Savellos and Yalçin 1995, pp. 16–59.

Melia, Joseph 1992:'Against modalism', *Philosophical Studies*, 68, pp. 35–56.

Menzel, Christopher 1990:'Actualism, ontological commitment, and possible world semantics', *Synthese*, 85, 355–89.

——1991:'The true modal logic', *Journal of Philosophical Logic*, 20, pp. 331–74.

Montague, Richard 1960:'Logical necessity, physical necessity, ethics, and quantifiers', in Montague 1974, pp. 71–83. Originally published in *Inquiry*, 4, pp. 259–69.

——1970a: 'Pragmatics and intensional logic', in Montague 1974, pp. 119–47. Originally published in *Synthese*, 22, pp. 68–94.

——1970b:'Universal grammar', in Montague 1974, pp. 222–46. Originally published in *Theoria*, 36, pp. 373–98.

——1974: *Formal Philosophy: Selected Papers of Richard Montague*. Edited with an introduction by Richmond Thomason. New Haven: Yale University Press.

Movahed, Zia 2006: 'Ibn-Sina's anticipation of Buridan and Barcan formulas', in Enayat, Kalantari, and Moniri 2006, pp. 248–55.

Mulligan, Kevin, Simons, Peter, and Smith, Barry 1984: 'Truth-makers', *Philosophy and Phenomenological Research*, 44, pp. 287–321.

Munitz, Milton (ed.) 1971: *Identity and Individuation*. New York: New York University Press.

Muskens, Reinhard 2007: 'Higher order modal logic', in Blackburn, van Benthem, and Wolter 2007, pp. 621–53.

Myhill, John 1958: 'Problems arising in the formalization of intensional logic', *Logique et Analyse*, 1, pp. 74–83.

——1963: 'An alternative to the method of extension and intension', in Schilpp 1963, pp. 299–310.

Nagel, Thomas 1970: 'Death', in Nagel 1979, pp. 1–10. Originally published in *Noûs*, 4, pp. 73–80.

——1979: *Mortal Questions*. Cambridge: Cambridge University Press.

Nolan, Daniel 1997: 'Quantitative parsimony', *The British Journal for the Philosophy of Science*, 48, pp. 329–43.

O'Hear, Anthony (ed.) 2002: *Logic, Thought and Language*. Cambridge: Cambridge University Press.

Oliver, Alex, and Smiley, Timothy 2001: 'Strategies for a logic of plurals', *The Philosophical Quarterly*, 51, pp. 289–306.

——, ——2005: 'Plural descriptions and many-valued functions', *Mind*, 114, pp. 1039–68.

Parfit, Derek 1984: *Reasons and Persons*. Oxford: Oxford University Press.

Parks, Zane 1976: 'Investigations into quantified modal logic—I', *Studia Logica*, 35, pp. 109–25.

Parsons, Charles 1983: *Mathematics in Philosophy: Selected Essays*. Ithaca: Cornell University Press.

——1990: 'The structuralist view of mathematical objects', *Synthese*, 84, pp. 303–46.

Parsons, Terence 1980: *Nonexistent Objects*. New Haven: Yale University Press.

——1994: 'Ruth Barcan Marcus and the Barcan Formula', in Sinnott-Armstrong, Raffman, and Asher 1994, pp. 3–11.

Peacocke, Christopher 1978: 'Necessity and truth theories', *Journal of Philosophical Logic*, 7, pp. 473–500.

——1998: 'The principle-based conception of modality: Sullivan's question addressed', *Mind*, 107, 847–9.

——1999: *Being Known*. Oxford: Oxford University Press.

——2002a: 'Principles for possibilia', *Noûs*, 36, pp. 486–508.

——2002b: 'The principle-based account of modality: elucidations and resources', *Philosophy and Phenomenological Research*, 64, pp. 663–79.

Peirce, Charles Sanders 1901: 'Modality', in Baldwin 2001, vol. 2, pp. 89–93.

Percival, Philip 2011: 'Predicate abstraction, the limits of quantification, and the modality of existence', *Philosophical Studies*, 156, pp. 389–416.

Pérez Otero, Manuel 2010: 'Possible worlds: structure and stuff', *Philosophical Papers*, 39, pp. 209–37.

Peters, Stanley, and Westerståhl, Dag 2006: *Quantifiers in Language and Logic*. Oxford: Clarendon Press.

Plantinga, Alvin 1974: *The Nature of Necessity*. Oxford: Clarendon Press.

——1976: 'Actualism and possible worlds', *Theoria*, 42, pp. 139–60.

——1983: 'On existentialism', *Philosophical Studies*, 44, pp. 1–20.

——1985: 'Replies', in Tomberlin and van Inwagen 1985, pp. 313–96.

Pollock, John 1981: 'A refined theory of counterfactuals', *Journal of Philosophical Logic*, 10, pp. 239–66.

——1985: 'Plantinga on possible worlds', in Tomberlin and van Inwagen 1985, pp. 121–44.

Potter, Michael, and Ricketts, Tom (eds) 2010: *The Cambridge Companion to Frege*. Cambridge: Cambridge University Press.

Priest, Graham 2005: *Towards Non-Being: The Logic and Metaphysics of Intentionality*. Oxford: Clarendon Press.

——2008: *An Introduction to Non-Classical Logic: From If to Is*, 2nd edn. Cambridge: Cambridge University Press.

Prior, Arthur Norman 1955: *Formal Logic*. Oxford: Clarendon Press.

——1956: 'Modality and quantification in S5', *The Journal of Symbolic Logic*, 21, pp. 60–2.

——1957: *Time and Modality*. Oxford: Clarendon Press.

——1967: *Past, Present and Future*. Oxford: Clarendon Press.

——1968: *Papers on Time and Tense*, new edition 2003, ed. by P. Hasle, P. Øhrstrom, T. Braüner, and J. Copeland. Oxford: Oxford University Press. Original edition published in 1968. Oxford: Clarendon Press.

——1971: *Objects of Thought*, ed. by P.T. Geach and A.J.P. Kenny. Oxford: Clarendon Press.

——, and Fine, Kit 1977: *Worlds, Times and Selves*. London: Duckworth.

Putnam, Hilary 1967: 'Time and physical geometry', *The Journal of Philosophy*, 64, pp. 240–7.

Quine, Willard Van Orman 1943: 'Notes on existence and necessity', *The Journal of Philosophy*, 40, pp. 113–27.

——1948/1949: 'On what there is', in Quine 1961, pp. 1–19. Originally published in *Review of Metaphysics*, 2, pp. 21–38.

——1951: 'Ontology and ideology', *Philosophical Studies*, 2, pp. 11–15.

——1953: 'Three grades of modal involvement', in Quine 1966, pp. 156–74. Originally published in Quine and others 1953, pp. 65–81.

——1960: *Word and Object*. Cambridge, MA: MIT Press.

——1961: *From a Logical Point of View*, 2nd edn. New York: Harper & Row.

——1966: *The Ways of Paradox and Other Essays*. New York: Random House.

——1969: *Ontological Relativity and Other Essays*. New York: Columbia University Press.

——1970: *Philosophy of Logic*. Englewood Cliffs: Prentice Hall.

——1976: 'Grades of discriminability', *The Journal of Philosophy*, 73, pp. 113–16.

—— and others 1953: *Proceedings of the XIth International Congress of Philosophy, Brussels 1953*, vol. 14. Amsterdam: North-Holland.

Rami, Adolf 2009: 'Introduction: truth and truth-making', in Lowe and Rami 2009, pp. 1–36.

Ramsey, Frank 1925: 'The foundations of mathematics', in Ramsey 1978, pp. 152–212. Originally published in *Proceedings of the London Mathematical Society*, ser. 2, 25, pp. 338–84.

——1927: 'Facts and propositions', in Ramsey 1978, pp. 40–57. Originally published in *Aristotelian Society*, sup. 7, pp. 153–70.

——1978: *Foundations: Essays in Philosophy, Logic, Mathematics and Economics*, ed. by D.H. Mellor. London: Routledge and Kegan Paul.

Rasiowa, Helena, and Sikorski, Roman 1963: *The Mathematics of Metamathematics*. Warsaw: Pánstwowe Wydawnictwo Naukowe.

Rayo, Agustín 2002: 'Words and objects', *Noûs*, 36, pp. 436–64.

——2006: 'Beyond plurals', in Rayo and Uzquiano 2006, pp. 220–54.

——, and Gabriel Uzquiano 1999: 'Toward a theory of second-order consequence', *Notre Dame Journal of Formal Logic*, 40, pp. 315–25.

——, ——(eds) 2006: *Absolute Generality*. Oxford: Clarendon Press.

——, and Williamson, Timothy 2003: 'A completeness theorem for unrestricted first-order languages', in Beall 2003, pp. 331–56.

——, and Yablo, Stephen 2001: 'Nominalism through de-nominalization', *Noûs*, 35, pp. 74–92.

Reimer, Marga 1997: 'Could there have been unicorns?', *International Journal of Philosophical Studies*, 5, pp. 35–51.

Rescher, Nicholas (ed.) 1967: *The Logic of Decision and Action*. Pittsburgh: University of Pittsburgh Press.

——1968: *Studies in Logical Theory*. Oxford: Blackwell.

Resnik, Michael 1988: 'Second-order logic still wild', *The Journal of Philosophy*, 85, pp. 75–87.

Rosen, Gideon 2002a: 'A study in modal deviance', in Gendler and Hawthorne 2002, pp. 283–307.

——2002b: 'Peacocke on modality', *Philosophy and Phenomenological Research*, 64, pp. 641–8.

———, and Dorr, Cian 2002: 'Composition as fiction', in Gale 2002, pp. 151–74.

Routley, Richard 1980: *Exploring Meinong's Jungle and Beyond: An Investigation of Noneism and The Theory of Items*. Canberra: Australian National University.

Ruben, David-Hillel 1988: 'A puzzle about posthumous predication', *The Philosophical Review*, 97, pp. 211–36.

Rumfitt, Ian 2001: 'Semantic theory and necessary truth', *Synthese*, 126, pp. 283–324.

———2003: 'Contingent existents', *Philosophy* 78, pp. 461–81.

———2005: 'Plural terms: another variety of reference?', in Bermúdez 2005, pp. 84–123.

———2010: 'Logical necessity', in Hale and Hoffmann 2010, pp. 35–64.

Russell, Bertrand 1956: *Logic and Knowledge*, ed. by Robert Marsh. London: Allen and Unwin.

Salmon, Nathan 1982: *Reference and Essence*. Princeton: Princeton University Press.

———1987: 'Existence', in Salmon 2005, pp. 9–49. Originally published in *Philosophical Perspectives*, 1, pp. 49–108.

———1989: 'The logic of what might have been', *Philosophical Review*, 98, pp. 3–34.

———1993: 'This side of paradox', *Philosophical Topics*, 21, pp. 187–97.

———1998: 'Nonexistence', in Salmon 2005, pp. 50–90. Originally published in *Noûs*, 32, pp. 277–319.

———2002: 'Mythical objects', in Salmon 2005, pp. 91–107. Originally published in Campbell, O'Rourke, and Shier 2002, pp. 105–23.

———2005: *Metaphysics, Mathematics, and Meaning*. Oxford: Clarendon Press.

Savellos, Elias, and Yalçin, Ümit (eds) 1995: *Supervenience: New Essays*. Cambridge: Cambridge University Press.

Schaffer, Jonathan 2012: 'Necessitarian propositions', *Synthese*, 189, pp. 119–62.

Schilpp, Paul (ed.) 1963: *The Philosophy of Rudolf Carnap*. La Salle: Open Court.

Schlenker, Philippe 2006: 'Ontological symmetry in language: a brief manifesto', *Mind and Language*, 21, pp. 504–39.

Schnieder, Benjamin 2006: Troubles with truth-making: necessitation and projection', *Erkenntnis*, 64, pp. 61–74.

———2007: 'Mere possibilities: a Bolzanian approach to non-actual objects', *Journal of the History of Philosophy*, 45, pp. 525–50.

Schumm, George 1981: 'Bounded properties in modal logic', *Zeitschrift für Mathematische Logik und Grundlagen der Mathematik*, 27, pp. 197–200.

———1993: 'Why does Halldén-completeness matter?', *Theoria*, 59, pp. 192–206.

Schurz, Gerhard 2005: 'Logic, matter of form, and closure under substitution', in Behounek and Bilkova 2005, pp. 33–46.

Scott, Dana 1970: 'Advice on modal logic', in Lambert 1970, pp. 143–73.

Scroggs, Schiller Joe 1951: 'Extensions of the Lewis system S5', *The Journal of Symbolic Logic*, 16, pp. 112–20.

Segerberg, Krister 1971: *An Essay in Classical Modal Logic*, 3 vols. Uppsala: Filosofiska studier.

Shapiro, Stewart 1987: 'Principles of reflection and second-order logic', *Journal of Philosophical Logic*, 16, pp. 309–33.

——1991: *Foundations Without Foundationalism: A Case for Second-Order Logic*. Oxford: Clarendon Press.

Sider, Theodore 2001: *Four-Dimensionalism: An Ontology of Persistence and Time*. Oxford: Clarendon Press.

——2006: 'Quantifiers and temporal ontology', *Mind*, 115, pp. 75–97.

——2009: 'Williamson's many necessary existents', *Analysis*, 69, pp. 50–8.

——2011: *Writing the Book of the World*. Oxford: Clarendon Press.

Simons, Peter 1997: 'Higher-order quantification and ontological commitment', *Dialectica*, 51, pp. 255–71.

Sinnott-Armstrong, Walter, with Raffman, Diana and Asher, Nicholas (eds) 1994: *Modality, Morality and Belief: Essays in Honor of Ruth Barcan Marcus*. Cambridge: Cambridge University Press.

Smiley, Timothy (ed.) 1998: *Philosophical Logic*. Oxford: Oxford University Press, for the British Academy.

Soames, Scott 2002: *Beyond Rigidity: The Unfinished Semantic Agenda of Naming and Necessity*. Oxford: Oxford University Press.

Solomon, Robert 1976: 'Is there happiness after death?', *Philosophy*, 51, pp. 189–93.

Stalnaker, Robert 1968: 'A theory of conditionals', in Rescher 1968, pp. 98–112.

——1977: 'Complex predicates', *The Monist*, 60, pp. 327–39.

——1984: *Inquiry*. Cambridge, MA: MIT Press.

——1994: 'The interaction of modality with quantification and identity', in Stalnaker 2003, pp. 144–61. Originally published in an earlier form in Sinnott-Armstrong, Raffman, and Asher 1994, pp. 12–28.

——2003: *Ways a World Might Be: Metaphysical and Anti-Metaphysical Essays*. Oxford: Clarendon Press.

——2006: 'Responses', in Thomson and Byrne 2006, pp. 250–95.

——2010: 'Merely possible propositions', in Hale and Hoffmann 2010, pp. 21–34.

——2011: 'The metaphysical conception of analyticity', *Philosophy and Phenomenological Research*, 82, pp. 507–14.

——2012: *Mere Possibilities: Metaphysical Foundations of Modal Semantics*. Princeton: Princeton University Press.

——, and Thomason, Richmond 1968a: 'Modality and reference', *Noûs*, 2, pp. 359–72.

——, ——1968b: 'Abstraction in first order modal logic', *Theoria*, 34, pp. 203–7.

Stephanou, Yannis 2000: 'Necessary beings', *Analysis*, 60, pp. 188–91.

Sullivan, Peter 1998: 'The modal extension principle: a question about Peacocke's approach to modality', *Mind*, 107, pp. 653–60.

Tarski, Alfred 1936: 'On the concept of logical consequence', in Tarski 1983, pp. 409–20. First published as 'O pojciu wynikania logicznego', *Przegląd Filozoficzny*, 39, pp. 58–68.

——1983: *Logic, Semantics, Metamathematics*, 2nd edn. Trans. J.H. Woodger, ed. J. Corcoran. Indianapolis: Hackett.

Taylor, James 2005: 'The myth of posthumous harm', *American Philosophical Quarterly*, 42, pp. 311–22.

Thomason, Richmond 1969: 'Modal logic and metaphysics', in Lambert 1969, pp. 119–46.

——1970: 'Some completeness results for modal predicate calculi', in Lambert 1970, pp. 56–76.

Thomason, Steve 1975: 'Categories of frames for modal logic', *The Journal of Symbolic Logic*, 40, pp. 439–42.

Thomasson, Amy 1999: *Fictional Metaphysics*. Cambridge: Cambridge University Press.

Thomson, Judith, and Byrne, Alex (eds) 2006: *Content and Modality: Themes from the Philosophy of Robert Stalnaker*. New York: Oxford University Press.

Tomberlin, James, and van Inwagen, Peter (eds) 1985: *Alvin Plantinga*. Dordrecht: Reidel.

Uzquiano, Gabriel 2011: 'Plural quantification and modality', *Proceedings of the Aristotelian Society*, 111, pp. 219–50.

van Benthem, Johan 1979: 'Canonical modal logics and ultrafilter extensions', *The Journal of Symbolic Logic*, 44, pp. 1–8.

——2002: 'Modal logic', in Jacquette 2002, pp. 391–409.

van Fraassen, Bas 1966: 'Singular terms, truth-value gaps and free logic', *The Journal of Philosophy*, 63, pp. 481–95.

van Inwagen, Peter. 1977. 'Creatures of fiction', *American Philosophical Quarterly*, 14, pp. 299–308.

Vlach, Frank. 1973. ' "Now" and "then": a formal study in the logic of tense anaphora'. Doctoral dissertation, UCLA.

Whitehead, Alfred North, and Russell, Bertrand 1910: *Principia Mathematica*, volume 1. Cambridge: Merchant Books.

Wiggins, David 1976: 'The de re "must": a note on the logical form of essentialist claims', in Evans and McDowell 1976, pp. 285–312.

——1984: 'The sense and reference of predicates: a running repair to Frege's doctrine and a plea for the copula', *The Philosophical Quarterly*, 34, pp. 126–42.

——1994: 'The Kant–Frege–Russell view of existence: toward the rehabilitation of the second-level view', in Sinnott-Armstrong, Raffman, and Asher 1994, pp. 93–113.

Williamson, Timothy 1987/1988: 'Equivocation and existence', *Proceedings of the Aristotelian Society*, 88, pp. 109–27.

——1988: 'On rigidity and persistence', *Logique et Analyse*, 121/2, pp. 89–91.

——1989: 'Being and being so', *Acta Analytica*, 4, pp. 93–114.

——1990a: *Identity and Discrimination*. Oxford: Blackwell.

——1990b: 'Necessary identity and necessary existence', in Haller and Brandl 1990, vol. 1, pp. 168–75.

——1994: 'Non-genuine MacIntosh logics', *Journal of Philosophical Logic*, 23, pp. 87–101.

——1996a: 'The necessity and determinacy of distinctness', in Lovibond and Williams 1996, pp. 1–17.

——1996b: Review of Sinnott-Armstrong, Raffman, and Asher 1994, *Philosophy*, 71, pp. 167–72.

——1998: 'Bare possibilia', *Erkenntnis*, 48, pp. 257–73.

——1999a: 'Truthmakers and the converse Barcan formula', *Dialectica*, 53, pp. 253–70.

——1999b: 'A note on truth, satisfaction and the empty domain', *Analysis*, 59, pp. 3–8.

——2000a: 'Existence and contingency', *Proceedings of the Aristotelian Society*, 100, pp. 117–39.

——2000b: 'The necessary framework of objects', *Topoi*, 19, pp. 201–8.

——2002a: 'Necessary existents', in O'Hear 2002, pp. 233–51.

——2002b: 'Peacocke on modality', *Philosophy and Phenomenological Research*, 64, pp. 649–54.

——2003a: 'Everything', *Philosophical Perspectives*, 17, pp. 415–65.

——2003b: 'Vagueness in reality', in Loux and Zimmerman 2003, pp. 690–715.

——2006: 'Stalnaker on the interaction of modality with quantification and identity', in Thomson and Byrne 2006, pp. 123–47.

——2007: *The Philosophy of Philosophy*. Oxford: Blackwell.

——2010: 'Necessitism, contingentism, and plural quantification', *Mind*, 119, pp. 657–748.

—— forthcoming: 'Barcan formulas in second-order logic', in Frauchiger and Essler forthcoming.

Wittgenstein, Ludwig 1921: *Tractatus Logico-Philosophicus*, trans. D.F. Pears and B.F. McGuinness. London: Routledge, 1974 (revised edn). Originally published in *Annalen der Naturphilosophie*, 14, pp. 185–262.

Woodward, Richard 2011: 'The things that aren't actually there'. *Philosophical Studies*, 152, pp. 155–66.

Wright, Crispin 1998: 'Why Frege did not deserve his *granum salis*. A note on the paradox of "the concept horse" and the ascription of Bedeutungen to predicates', *Grazer Philosophische Studien*, 55, pp. 239–63.

———2007: 'On quantifying into predicate position: steps towards a (new)tralist perspective', in Leng, Paseau, and Potter 2007, pp. 150–74.

Wroński, Andrzej 1976: 'Remarks on Halldén completeness of modal and intermediate logics', *Bulletin of the Section of Logic*, 5, pp. 126–9.

Yi, Byeong-Uk 2005: 'The logic and meaning of plurals. Part I', *Journal of Philosophical Logic*, 34, pp. 459–506.

———2006: 'The logic and meaning of plurals. Part II', *Journal of Philosophical Logic*, 35, pp. 239–88.

Yourgrau, Palle 1987: 'The dead'. *The Journal of Philosophy*, 84, pp. 84–101.

Zalta, Edward 1988: *Intensional Logic and the Metaphysics of Intentionality*. Cambridge, MA: MIT Press.

Zermelo, Ernst 1930: 'On boundary numbers and domains of sets: new investigations in the foundations of set theory', in Ewald 1996, vol. 2, pp. 1219–33. Originally published as 'Über Grenzzahlen und Mengenbereiche: Neue Untersuchungen über die Grundlagen der Mengenlehre', *Fundamenta Mathematicae*, 16, pp. 29–47.

Zimmerman, Dean 2011: 'Presentism and the space-time manifold', in Callender 2011, pp. 163–246.

Index

see also domains; frames; model structures;
    truth at a world in a model; truth
    everywhere in a model; truth in a
    model
modes of presentation 53, 141, 209, 228,
    290–1
Montague, R. 66, 81, 215–21, 223, 226,
    231–4, 236, 248
Movahed, Z. 45
MU (modal system) 95–102, 105, 107–11,
    114–18
see also metaphysical universality
Mulligan, K. 391, 397
Muskens, R. 217–18, 220
Myhill, J. 67, 204, 206, 219
mythology 131, 137, 152–4

Nagel, T. 29
natural extensions 206–8
natural kinds 8, 44, 90, 348–9
natural laws see laws of nature; modality,
    nomological
natural properties 226–7, 263, 382, 388,
    397
natural quantifiers 307–8
natural relations 226–7, 382, 397
natural science 27, 213, 271, 349, 423,
    426–7, 429
see also laws of nature; science
naturalness 3, 14, 177, 226–7, 263, 307–8,
    382, 388, 397
NC≺ (in plural logic) 248, 252, 339
N_C≺ (in plural logic) 251–2
ND (necessity of distinctness) 162–3,
    165–7, 179–83, 187
ND⁺ (necessary necessity of
    distinctness) 182–3
NE (necessitist principle) 186
NE⁺ (necessitist principle) 186
NEC_C (chunky-style necessitist
    theory) 329–32, 338–40,
    345–7, 349–52, 356, 363–4,
    368, 372–5
necessitation (closure under) 34, 37, 39–44,
    69, 80, 87–9, 96–9, 103, 107–8,
    110–11, 128, 133, 164–5, 171,
    181–2, 187, 232, 298, 379, 392,
    396
necessitism xi–xii, 2–10, 12–22, 24–30, 34,
    36, 38, 43–4, 46, 55, 68, 75, 129,
    132, 136–41, 143, 145–6, 148–9,
    154–6, 158–9, 162, 185–6, 188,

195–8, 209, 220, 231–3, 235, 238,
    246–54, 261–3, 266–8, 270–1,
    274–7, 282, 288–94, 296, 300, 305,
    308–19, 321–42, 344–50, 352–6,
    359–60, 362–5, 367–9, 376–7,
    379–91, 393–5, 397–8, 401–5,
    418–19, 429
chunky-style necessitism 327, 329–31,
    337–40, 345–50, 352, 356,
    362–4
see also NEC_C
higher-order necessitism 264–70,
    273–81, 285
modalist necessitism 369
see also NNE
necessity see modality
necessity of distinctness see distinctness,
    necessity of
necessity of identity see identity,
    necessity of
NEI (necessary essntiality of identity) 162,
    165–7, 174–5, 177, 179, 181
see also identity, necessity of
neighbourhood semantics 127
neutral formulas 310–18, 320–4,
    326–7, 329–32, 334, 336, 338,
    344–56, 359, 362–4, 368–9,
    372–5
see also chunkiness
Nicolas, D. 244
NI≺ (in plural logic) 245–52
NNE (necessary necessity of being) 38,
    41–2, 44, 138, 154, 156, 232,
    234–5, 263–70, 273, 275, 278–81,
    285, 289, 293–5, 298–9, 308–9,
    311–12, 315, 317, 320, 322,
    326–31, 334, 339, 356, 398
NNE_M 264–70, 273, 275, 278–81, 285
NNE_M* 266
NNE_t 232, 234–5
see also necessitism
Nolan, D. 9
nominalism 313
nominalization 255, 263–4, 289, 294–5,
    398–9, 402
nomological modality see modality,
    nomological
non-decreasing frames see frames,
    non-decreasing
non-increasing frames see frames,
    non-increasing
non-modal similarity 383

Printed and bound by CPI Group (UK) Ltd, Croydon, CR0 4YY